STUDIES IN ORIENTAL CULTURE

NUMBER 10 *The Unfolding of Neo-Confucianism*

The
Unfolding
of
Neo-Confucianism

BY WM. THEODORE DE BARY
AND THE CONFERENCE ON
SEVENTEENTH-CENTURY
CHINESE THOUGHT

COLUMBIA UNIVERSITY PRESS   NEW YORK

Library of Congress Cataloging in Publication Data

Conference on Seventeenth-Century Chinese Thought,
  Bellagio, Italy, 1970.
  The unfolding of Neo-Confucianism.

  (Studies in oriental culture, no. 10)
  "This volume is the product of a Conference on Seventeenth-Century Chinese Thought,
held at the Villa Serbelloni in September 1970, under the sponsorship of the Committee on
the Study of Chinese Civilization of the American Council of Learned Societies."
  Includes bibliographical references.
  1. Neo-Confucianism—Congresses. 2. Confucianism—
Relations—Buddhism—Congresses. 3. Buddha and Bud-
dhism—Relations—Confucianism—Congresses.
I. De Bary, William Theodore, 1919-   ed.
II. American Council of Learned Societies Devoted to Humanistic Studies. Committee on
Studies of Chinese Civilization. III. Title. IV. Series.
B127.N4C66 1970   181'.09'512   74-10929
ISBN 0-231-03828-3
ISBN 0-231-03829-1 (pbk.)

This book is dedicated to

T ' A N G   C H U N - I

*in recognition of a lifetime devoted to
Neo-Confucian studies and in appreciation
of the personal qualities of mind and
spirit which he brought to our
collaborative work*

PREFACE

This volume is the product of a conference on seventeenth-century Chinese thought, held at the Villa Serbelloni in September, 1970, under the sponsorship of the Committee on the Study of Chinese Civilization of the American Council of Learned Societies. It represents the second stage in a continuing exploration of neglected areas of premodern Chinese thought, the first stage of which opened up the Ming period and produced *Self and Society in Ming Thought,* 1970.

In attempting to explore and explain the important transition from the Ming to the Ch'ing period, we have been led back to the roots in the past from which the new growth sprang, retracing and indeed rediscovering in some fundamental respects the inner development of Neo-Confucianism. Thus, despite the exploratory nature of our work, our findings have more often been of underlying continuities than of striking discontinuities. Likewise, instead of magnifying foreign contacts and external influences, we have followed the dialogue of Chinese thinkers among themselves and kept close to the mainstream of Chinese thought from which the intellectual leaders of the new age drew so heavily.

In the late Ming that dialogue included a substantial representation of Buddhism. Some readers may wonder why, in a book entitled *The Unfolding of Neo-Confucianism,* there should be three articles dealing with the Buddhist revival in the late Ming. The reason is that Neo-Confucianism as it evolved in the Wang Yang-Ming school gave a strong stimulus to Buddhism in the sixteenth and seventeenth centuries, bringing a revival which both reflected Neo-Confucian tendencies and contributed in return to the reaffirmation of Neo-Confucian values. This is a fascinating period for the study of ecumenism, syncretism, and a universalist humanism in the context of a historical situation which saw great social and political change, intellectual ferment, and religious renewal.

The Conference itself ranged into areas not fully reported on here. Father Albert Chan presented new sidelights on seventeenth-century China through the reactions of Catholic missionaries to China during their first century of activity there, based on researches in long-neglected archives in Europe. Professor Minamoto Ryōen discussed the Neo-Confucian sources of the so-called practical learning (*jitsugaku*) of Japan. It became evident, however, that the full significance of these developments could only be assessed through more extensive and systematic comparative study, which we hope can be achieved through subsequent conferences and publications. In the meantime the more closely interrelated studies presented herein can help to establish a firmer base on which to pursue the extensions of Neo-Confucian thought into a wider world of experience and activity.

The vicissitudes of university life in recent years have complicated and slowed the task of preparing these studies for publication. Were it not for the encouragement and support of many friends, this project would have been delayed almost indefinitely and the final product would have proven even more defective and liable to mistakes than the reader will now find it. Julia Ching, Irene Bloom, Carol Gluck, and Albert Lutley have read the final manuscript and made numerous corrections. Mary Hue, Nancy Hinman, Arlene Jacobs, and Sallie Mitchell have rendered substantial assistance in processing the papers, and Mary Virginia Kahl in the final editing. In this stage especially, the manifold contributions of Mrs. Bloom have been of crucial help. The last push needed to complete my own writing became more pleasure than strain thanks to the warm hospitality of William and Betsy Olson and the officers of the Rockefeller Foundation at the Villa Serbelloni in July, 1972. But above all it is to my wife Fanny Brett de Bary that I owe the most gratitude for sharing in every aspect of the work, from beginning to end.

New York; February, 1974   *Wm. Theodore de Bary*

EXPLANATORY NOTE AND ABBREVIATIONS USED

The style of this book in sinological matters follows that adopted for *Self and Society in Ming Thought* (Columbia University Press, 1970), to which the reader is referred for any explanation needed and for general bibliographical references. In notes to this volume, the Ming book is referred to simply as *Self and Society*.

Abbreviations of Chinese titles are identified at the point of the first appearance except in the cases of the following standard works:

KHCPTS   Kuo-hsüeh chi-pen ts'ung-shu

MJCCTLSY   *Ming-jen chuan-chi tzu-liao so-yin*, National Central Library. Taipei, 1964

MJHA   *Ming-ju hsüeh-an*

MS   *Ming shih*

SPPY   Ssu-pu pei-yao

SPTK   Ssu-pu ts'ung-k'an

TSCC   Ts'ung-shu chi-ch'eng

TT   Tao tsang

W. T. de B.

CONTRIBUTORS

ARAKI KENGO is a graduate of Kyushu University and is now Professor of Chinese Philosophy in its Faculty of Letters, specializing in Sung-Ming thought and Buddhism. His principal works include *Buddhism and Confucianism (Bukkyō to jukyō)* (1963); and *Studies in Ming Thought (Mindai shisō kenkyū)* (1972).

WILLIAM S. ATWELL is completing a doctorate in East Asian Studies at Princeton University with a dissertation on the scholar-official Ch'en Tzu-lung (1608–47). His particular interest is in the social and intellectual history of sixteenth- and seventeenth-century China.

WING-TSIT CHAN is Professor Emeritus of Chinese Philosophy and Culture at Dartmouth College and Anna R. D. Gillespie Professor of Philosophy at Chatham College. Representative of his numerous works on Chinese philosophy are his *Source Book in Chinese Philosophy* (1963), his translation *Instructions for Practical Living and Other Neo-Confucian Writings by Wang Yang-ming* (1963), and his translation of *Chu Hsi's Reflections on Things at Hand* (1967).

already in 1970

CHUNG-YING CHENG is Professor of Philosophy at the University of Hawaii and works in the fields of Chinese philosophy, comparative philosophy, and American logical philosophy. He has published studies in classical Chinese logic, Confucianism, and Neo-Confucianism, including a book, *Tai Chen's Inquiry into Goodness* (1969). He is the founder and editor of the *Journal of Chinese Philosophy* and is currently working on a book dealing with the philosophies of Chu Hsi and Wang Yang-ming.

EDWARD T. CH'IEN is a Ph.D. candidate at Columbia University and is working on a full-scale study of Chiao Hung to be entitled "The Late Ming Neo-Confucian Synthesis in Chiao Hung." He has taught at Sam Houston State University in Texas.

WM. THEODORE DE BARY is Carpentier Professor of Oriental Studies at Columbia University, where he also currently serves as Vice President and Provost. A former President of the Association for Asian Studies, he is the editor and co-author of *Sources of Chinese Tradition, Sources of Japanese Tradition, Sources of Indian Tradition*, and, most recently, *Self and Society in Ming Thought*.

KRISTIN YÜ GREENBLATT is Assistant Professor of Religion at Rutgers, the State University of New Jersey. She was trained in Chinese philosophy and Buddhism at Tunghai University, Taiwan, and at Columbia University, where she received her Ph.D. degree with a dissertation on "The Career of a Buddhist Monk: Yun-chi Chu-hung." Her field of interest is the history of Chinese Buddhism since the T'ang Dynasty.

RICHARD JOHN LYNN is Assistant Professor of Chinese at the University of Massachusetts, Amherst, and has been lecturer in Chinese at the University of Auckland, New Zealand (1970–72). He is currently working on a book-length study of the life and writings of Kuan Yün-shih (1286–1324). His fields of special interest include the literature, literary criticism, and aesthetics of the literati tradition of Yüan, Ming, and Ch'ing times.

IAN MCMORRAN is lecturer in Classical Chinese at Oxford University, where he obtained his doctorate for a thesis entitled "Wang Fu-chih and his Political Thought." He has specialized in Chinese intellectual history, and is currently engaged on research in the late Ming period. A comprehensive study by him of Wang Fu-chih's life and thought is to be published soon.

WILLARD J. PETERSON is Assistant Professor of East Asian Studies at Princeton University, has an M.A. from the School of Oriental and African Studies, University of London, and a Ph.D. from Harvard University. He has published a biography of Ku Yen-wu and other articles.

TANG CHUN-I is Professor of Philosophy and Director of the Institute for Advanced Chinese Studies, New Asia College, Chinese University of Hong Kong. He was educated in China at the Sino-Russian University, Peking University, and the National Central University. He helped to found New Asia College, of which he served as dean from its inception until 1966. The most recent of his many books in Chinese philosophy is *Chung-kuo che-hsüeh yüan-lun* (Studies in the origin and development of Chinese philosophical ideas), of which four volumes have already been published.

WEI-MING TU is Associate Professor of History, University of California at Berkeley. He was educated at Tunghai University and Harvard University (Ph.D., 1968), and has taught at Princeton University. His fields of interest include Confucianism, Chinese intellectual history, and religious philosophies of Asia. Currently he is working on Neo-Confucian humanism.

PEI-YI WU is Associate Professor of Classical and Oriental Languages at Queens College, City University of New York, and Visiting Associate Professor of Chinese at Columbia University. He is currently doing a study on Chinese autobiography in the sixteenth and seventeenth centuries.

CONTENTS

The Unfolding of Neo-Confucianism

Neo-Confucianism has meant many things in recent literature on China. Few of them would have suggested that this body of thought or way of life had a capacity to grow, to develop, to unfold.[1]

One stereotype pictures the Neo-Confucian as a stern patriarchal figure, the embodiment and enforcer of a puritanical morality, rigidly demanding conformity to a traditional pattern of conduct which allowed the individual no freedom or enjoyment in life.

Another typical role for the Neo-Confucian has been as guardian or servant of the established political order, defending the interests of a dynastic system and "feudal" ruling class which fought change in any form.

To modern reformers and revolutionaries in China these are the predominant roles in which Neo-Confucians have been cast. Another view, put forth by Max Weber, has recognized the inapplicability of the term "feudal" to the traditional bureaucratic order in China, and has identified the characteristic role and life style of the mandarin as that of the "gentleman," the model of conventional behavior, of good taste, of rational adjustment to the world. In him reason served not as a force for change and progress, for the rational transformation of the world, but only for rational adjustment to the world as it is, to the status quo.[2]

Though Weber affirms, and almost celebrates, the humanistic and aesthetic qualities of the Confucian gentleman, in the end he sees the Confucianism of the later dynasties (i.e., what we call Neo-Confucianism) as "a relentless canonization of tradition." [3] Moreover, it was a completely secularized tradition, devoid of prophetic zeal and moral dynamism. In contrast to the Puritan ethic in the West, Confucianism according to Weber notably lacked any contrast between "God" or "nature" and "statutory law" or "convention." [4] "There was no leverage for influencing conduct through inner forces freed of tradition and convention." [5]

Nor is this view confined to a social theorist like Weber, who sees China too much perhaps in terms of generalized comparisons and dichotomies suggested by Western experience.[6] The late Joseph Levenson, at the outset of his study, *Confucian China and Its Modern Fate*, asserts that "in pre-modern China respect for precedent was one of the prime Confucian attitudes that pervaded intellectual life." [7] To define this Confucian traditionalism, Levenson speaks of "the conscious will to narrow the vision" as constituting its essence. [8]

The tendency to see Neo-Confucianism primarily as a rigid orthodoxy and ideological tool of an authoritarian system has been further propagated in widely used texts introducing China to the West. For example:

> [The new Confucian orthodoxy] became an ever more effective mechanism for the circulation, through the study of the classics and the examination system, of the Confucian doctrines of loyalty and social responsibility and conformity. . . . After the expulsion of the Mongols and the reestablishment of Chinese control over China under the Ming dynasty (1368–1644), the Sung Neo-Confucianism, because of its very inclusiveness, became a strait-jacket on the Chinese mind. The Ming rulers used it as a tool of government. Chu Hsi's system became a dogma. Mencius became the greatest sage after Confucius. The Four Books and Five Classics became the intellectual fare of all ambitious men, as though Chinese society could find refuge by turning back into its own cultural heritage and could protect itself by staying within an established framework of ideas. . . . In this atmosphere of orthodoxy there was little incentive for the development of scientific method. It was during this Neo-Confucian period . . . that China certainly fell behind the West in technology. [9]

And again—"The Confucian world-view had been stated for all time in the classics and in the lasting, orthodox interpretation of them by the Sung Neo-Confucian scholars of the 12th century." [10]

To question this view is not to stigmatize it as a tissue of modern myths and prejudices, superimposed on a misunderstood past. There are indeed aspects of Neo-Confucianism which correspond to the characterizations above. So far, however, the tendency to view premodern China as static or stagnant, and to identify Confucianism too closely with the rigidities of the dynastic system, has prevented us from looking behind the outward appearances of an "unchanging China" to see its inner life and dynamism. The full story of the development of Neo-Confucianism over the second millennium A.D., seen in a larger historical perspective, may show this phase of Confucian thought and experience to have more relevance to the future of China than anything the comparatively superficial encounter with the West has yet revealed. What is more important, the experience of the Chinese in these centuries may also prove relevant to our future in the West as we increasingly confront problems long familiar to the Chinese.

Weber was certainly right in speaking of Confucianism as the most secularized of the world's religions. Neo-Confucianism, as the creed and code of the educated elite, was committed from the start to service of the state, and the dominance of the bureaucracy in later China strongly conditioned the institutional life and outlook of the Confucian scholar. Nor was Weber mistaken in asserting that the Confucian gentleman was far more adjusted to the world, less work-driven, and more aesthetic in his approach than the Puritan who put himself at the service of a prophetic conscience and economic rationality. But to say that Neo-Confucianism either began or ended there—as a polite obeisance to an authoritarian system—is what must be questioned.

In fulfilling his commitment to humane public service and political leadership in dynasty after dynasty, the Confucian was able to contribute a rational ethos, a standard of service, and a continuity of experience to the government of China such as no other state in human history has enjoyed. Yet in that very attempt he stood exposed, both as keeper of the Chinese social conscience and custodian of its institutions, to the inevitable shortcomings of the system. For him to live by his principles required both idealism and compromise, both firmness and flexibility. His record would never be anything but mixed, since his achievements would never match his aspirations.

The Neo-Confucian record was mixed also in that its aims and activities were variegated and often consciously ambivalent. Thus the two stereotypes presented above each represent a valid concern of the Neo-Confucian "gentleman." Weber pointed to his gentility, his style, his sense of proportion—those qualities which suggest the dominance of the aesthetic sense over an uncompromising moral conscience. And yet the other and more commonly known stereotype of the Neo-Confucian is precisely that of a rigid moralist who takes a stern view both of man's sensual impulses and his desire for material gain, in sharp contrast to Weber's characterization. It is, moreover, a view of Neo-Confucian orthodoxy which has long standing among Chinese critics of the system,[11] and is not attributable merely to the myopia and astigmatism of Western eyes. The Neo-Confucian might appear to be a dilettante or a prude, a connoisseur of beauty or an ascetic moralist, but it was the ensemble of the underlying positive values expressed by these conventional labels which established Neo-Confucianism as the spiritual and cultural basis of East Asian civilization in the thirteenth to nineteenth centuries.

The seventeenth century, which serves as the focus of this book, stands at about the midpoint in this long period of Neo-Confucian dominance and, if our interpretation is correct, this century may also represent a turning point in its development. How to interpret that turning, however, has been disputed. A prevalent view in the earlier decades of the twentieth century saw Neo-Confucianism as having lost all genuine vitality by the seventeenth century. New trends of thought were breaking away from Neo-Confucian dogmas, and an era of intellectual enlightenment was dawning which only the dead hand of the past, supported by the political repression of Manchu conquerors, held back. In these terms, the seventeenth century could be pictured by some as a kind of watershed in the development of Chinese thought, marking the emergence of the Chinese mind from a dark age of introspection and metaphysical escapism—into a new day of robust empiricism, scientific criticism, and materialism. This general view has had many adherents, but its most prominent spokesmen have been Liang Ch'i-ch'ao,[a] Hu Shih,[b] and more recently Hou Wai-lu.[c] [12]

An opposing view, as expressed by T'ang Chun-i,[d] does not dispute the historical facts but seeks to give them a different meaning. For T'ang the change that took place represented a falling-away from the highest levels attained by Chinese thought. He considers the greatest achievements of Neo-Confucianism to have lain in the spiritual realm depreciated by Hu. To him the "super-moral ideas" of the Neo-Confucians, especially in the sixteenth century, "should be taken as expressions of their highest moral experience." [13] The shift in thought from the beginning of the Ch'ing dynasty, in the mid-seventeenth century, he sees as the start of a long decline: "Chinese thought from the end of Ming to recent years has gradually left the spirit of Neo-Confucianism, which paid more attention to the spiritual values of human life, and now pays more attention to social, utilitarian, technical and natural values of human life." [14]

In contrast to both these interpretations, the Weberian view cuts across time and seems to deny that any such development could have significantly altered the static pattern of Confucian thought.

An important Japanese contribution to the discussion, made by the intellectual historian Shimada Kenji, has adapted the Weberian critique to a reinterpretation of the Wang Yang-ming school and its popular manifestations in the late Ming. In his *Chūgoku ni okeru kindai shii no za-*

setsu [e] (The Frustration of Modern Thought in China) Shimada has seen the "innate knowledge" or "good knowing" (*liang-chih*) [f] of Wang Yang-ming [g] as a potent concept and force for rationality in the Weberian sense, freeing the Chinese mind from the accepted doctrines and social conventions of Confucian tradition. The spontaneous exercise of this "innate knowledge" enhanced greatly the autonomy of the individual self, functioning much as Weber saw the Puritan conscience doing in the process of volitional and ethical rationalization in the West. Above all, if free inquiry and the searching criticism of accepted values were characteristic of the modern temper, Shimada believed that the radical humanism of the left wing of the Wang Yang-ming school had gone far, in principle at least, toward undermining the basis of the traditional order in China.[15]

The fact that these new and modernizing tendencies could not survive the repression of the established order or the Manchu conquest does not diminish their importance as a potential historical alternative developed from within Confucianism and largely ignored by Weber or others who have stressed China's immunity to change. In subsequent writings Shimada has extended his analysis and deepened it to show that the roots of this new humanism lay in the thought of Chu Hsi [h] and other Sung philosophers [16] while its influence extended to the modern reformers K'ang Yu-wei [i] and T'an Ssu-t'ung.[j]

ORTHODOXY AND THE NEO-CONFUCIAN MOVEMENT

In the meantime progress has been made in exploring the full scope and variety of Neo-Confucian thought. The Conference on Ming Thought, from which issued the volume of studies entitled *Self and Society in Ming Thought*, has helped to illuminate some of the distinctive developments in this period, their links to Sung thought, and their carryover into the Ch'ing. The clearer delineation of continuity and change in the development of Neo-Confucian thought by scholars such as Ch'ien Mu, and, more recently, Yü Ying-shih, helps us to recognize it as a process of growth rather than as a static pattern. What others have written off as a sterile orthodoxy, a dead weight from the past, an obsolete but immovable fixture of the old order, now emerges as a more dynamic and constructive process. In this new light seventeenth-century thought can be explained as the fruit of sustained growth, rather than be made to appear as an inexplicable and anomalous flash of "enlightenment" that came from nowhere and went nowhere.[17]

First to be recognized is that Neo-Confucianism did not begin life as an orthodoxy, and did not even end as a simple and single dogma. The sense of a need for orthodoxy was present in the beginning of the Confucian revival in the tenth and eleventh centuries, but a fully developed response to that need was a long time in forming and an even longer time in gaining official acceptance in the thirteenth century and after. The initial impulse in the Sung was reformist and revivalist: to reorder society, and reestablish the long-neglected values which had supposedly inspired the ideal order of the early sage-kings. A neoclassical movement, one might call this, but with strong romantic inspiration. It took an enthusiastic idealism to believe that the ancient order could be restored in such changed circumstances, and an uncommon confidence in man to achieve his own redemption in the world after centuries of Buddhist despair and detachment. The will to order things, and the belief in man's unique creative role in accomplishing this task, was central to the Confucian resurgence that produced what we called Neo-Confucianism.

This is not the place to recount the many fields of social and cultural endeavor in which this will to order things found expression in the Sung.[18] The creative and expansive power of the movement must, however, be stressed to anyone still mesmerized by the thought that the "essence of traditionalism" (as Neo-Confucianism represented it) "was the conscious will to narrow the vision." This was rather a liberal and liberating vision of man's creative powers. It depended upon a conscious ordering of human priorities—a process of self-limitation, perhaps, but a deliberate discipline and regulated growth which would lead upward and outward, uniting man to Heaven-and-earth and all things.

The second stage in this growth came with the disillusionment that followed its initial failures in the Northern Sung. Social reformism, and especially the ambitious, determined program of Wang An-shih,[k] had ended in something much less than the promised millennium. Despite their access to power and the benevolent patronage of Sung rulers, the Neo-Confucians had encountered human limitations in the executing of their grand designs. Chu Hsi recognized the setback for what it was: an excess of optimism, a doctrinaire idealism, a lack of practical experience, and an underestimating of the disciplined effort demanded by the magnitude of the task.[19]

Lest disillusionment end in despair, Chu Hsi readjusted and reordered his human priorities. To some eyes his "adjustment to the world" may appear to be a yielding by the Confucian to the requirements of an autocratic system, and his political philosophy might seem no more than a tame and involuted reformism—in effect a graceful withdrawal from the political battle. And it is true that Sung Confucians, relatively secure as members of the leisured and cultured gentry, did not incline to revolutionary solutions. In this case, however, there was neither a passive yielding to autocratic power nor an abandonment of the struggle, but rather a recognition that one had to come to terms with an unpromising historical situation and certain inherent limitations of the human condition. Far from being passive or fatalistic, their response to social needs assumed the character of a religious mission and was embodied in an educational program through which, they believed, the social order could one day be transformed. Even the supposedly quietistic practices adopted for contemplative self-cultivation were designed not to suspend the will or render the mind insensible to suffering, but, on the contrary, to heighten one's moral sensitivity and strengthen one's resolve.[20]

Hence the rational adjustment of the Neo-Confucian was conjoined, rather than juxtaposed, to the task of rational transformation in which Weber and others saw the Confucian as failing. Here again, the Neo-Confucian record will be seen as mixed, with the individual's adjustment varying from quiet accommodation to intransigent opposition or withdrawal. It was "mixed" also in the sense that the Neo-Confucian did not stake everything on politics alone, so that failure in one direction did not preclude success in others.

THE NEO-CONFUCIAN COMMITMENT

Where the reformers of the Northern Sung had manifested an almost messianic zeal in pursuit of the ideal social order set forth in the classical books of rites, the followers of Chu Hsi showed a rare commitment and dedication to a new vision of the human order, based this time on an educational program and way of life that would carry one virtually from cradle to grave. Chu Hsi describes his own "conversion" to the Way of the Sage in terms of a decisive renunciation of Taoism and Buddhism (to which he had been strongly attracted earlier) and a total commitment to the Confucian Way.[21] There was an intensity about it, a total serious-ness, which reminds us of other famous religious conversions; a mobiliz-ing too, of his full energies for a life of sustained activity in behalf of the newfound cause, reminiscent of St. Paul's conversion to Christianity or Kumārajīva's to Mahāyāna Buddhism. The structure of Chu Hsi's *Reflec-tions on Things at Hand (Chin-ssu lu)*,[1] discussed elsewhere in this vol-ume,[22] reflects his belief in the need to commit oneself to a definite goal in life, and many of its later readers in the Ming and Ch'ing had similar conversion experiences.[23]

In these cases commitment represented conscious selection of one path and rejection of others, but one would underestimate the liberating, ac-tivating power of the experience if he were to think of it as "the conscious will to narrow the vision," which "is the essence of traditionalism." In personal terms Chu Hsi and other Neo-Confucians have the experience almost of being reborn and gaining a new life. In terms of tradition they feel called to "advance in the Way" and enlarge it. There is the seeming paradox, then, of restricting one's choice and yet expanding one's vision, of choosing first one kingdom and then finding all else added to it.

For Chu Hsi and the Neo-Confucians that expanded vision of human fulfillment was achievable only through an ordered pattern of education and growth—regulating in almost fanatical detail every aspect of one's per-sonal and social life—food, dress, living arrangements, daily routine, family and community life, and so on.[24] Though usually justified by some scriptural reference, these minute prescriptions derived from no prevailing convention or established norm. Theirs was a "respect for prec-edent" that broke with convention. Indeed to the ordinary mind this passion of the "School of the Way" (*tao hsüeh*) [m] for ritual precision seemed odd and ridiculous. "School of the Way" was originally a derisive title, implying a pretentious manner and obsessive behavior. Chu Hsi's followers, however, chose not to disown the title but to try to live up to its pretensions. It is as if professors and students in a university today had decided to demonstrate their seriousness and dedication by wearing aca-demic cap and gown as daily dress and reviving the trivium and the quadrivium as the basis of their curriculum, so as not to be, in the manner of Sunday Christians, academicians only at Commencement exercises. The fact that some schools still prescribe the cap and gown for the classroom and serious educators have spoken for a return to the seven liberal arts would not lessen the total impression on society at large of there being something arcane in such behavior. To the Neo-Confucian it did not matter. He expected to suffer something for his convictions, and ridicule he could live with. Indeed, his "adjustment to the world" allowed for being at odds with his own generation, and to that extent seeming "maladjusted." He was prepared to appear in the eyes of the conventional man as what one might call a "fool for Confucius," if thereby convention could be reordered and reintegrated into a meaningful way of life.

The unthinking man accepted things as they were. The "noble man" accepted his responsibility consciously to transform himself and the world in accordance with the Heavenly norms that constituted both his conscience and his natural endowment and potentiality. Every action, every experience, made some difference in the development of that potentiality. Nothing could go unexamined or unevaluated; whatever he saw, heard, or touched should be ordered to the fulfillment of his moral character and the genuine expression of a valid life-style—to his "advancement in the Way."

To Chu Hsi and the other Neo-Confucians this was a process of growth and maturation. It might include illumination as part of the process—a sense of things becoming clear and meaningful—but not usually as a single sudden experience to which everything else was subordinated. Character building required an ordered learning sequence. Chu Hsi's contribution historically as an educator, and not solely as a philosopher, lay in his recognition of the need for a definite curriculum with graded texts. If the *Great Learning* provided eight steps (*pa mu*) [n] in the cultivation of the gentleman or noble man according to the classical ideal of higher education, it was essential that there also be a primer for the basic training of the young, formulating in quite specific terms the social and moral discipline prerequisite to more advanced philosophical studies. With the assistance of his colleague Liu Tzu-ch'eng, Chu provided this in the *Lower Education* (*Hsiaoĩhsüeh*),[o] a title suggesting both a hierarchy of learning and Chu Hsi's active interest in its lower as well as its higher reaches.[25]

Another standard text Chu helped compile, the *Reflections on Things at Hand* (*Chin-ssu lu*), bespoke both the modesty and practicality of Chu's approach to education, bringing the ideal of the sages down to earth and within reach of any man desirous of improving himself.[26] It was a concise anthology of quotations dealing with basic self-cultivation, recommended as a simple, practical introduction for those not yet ready for metaphysics. Similarly in the *Outline and Digest of the General Mirror* (*T'ung-chien kang mu*) [P] Chu undertook to condense Ssu-ma Kuang's [q] massive general history, *The General Mirror for Aid in Government* (*Tzu-chih t'ung chien*),[r] so that its lessons emerged with greater clarity when they were freed from the mass of historical detail. Where Ssu-ma Kuang's sense of relevance was scholarly and comprehensive, Chu Hsi's was pedagogical and selective. Along with the Four Books as commented on by Chu, these three—the *Lower Education, Reflections on Things at Hand,* and the *Outline and Digest of the General Mirror*—became basic texts in the well-defined curriculum of the later Chu Hsi school.

In the contents of these works we may observe how Chu Hsi achieved a balance between moral and intellectual training. Respect for knowledge and the lifelong pursuit of learning was a fundamental human obligation, an essential part of man's duty to prepare himself for the service of others. A correlative obligation was to give precedence in study to socially relevant knowledge.

Confucius, however, had said that man should not be a "mere tool." [27] Neo-Confucians often reminded themselves of this, recognizing that man's response to Heaven, his fulfillment of his nature, could not be limited to his social utility. In the midst of social and political engagement there was a need to keep some part of himself not subservient to the demands of state or society. To the Neo-Confucian, the aesthetic and spiritual, or (in Professor T'ang's terms) "supermoral" concerns represent this area of freedom. Much of it was expressed in journals, lyrical poetry, prose-poetry, travel diaries written in a contemplative frame of mind, painting and calligraphy, and the appreciation of art expressed in poetic inscriptions. These, however, were higher concerns. The *Lower Education* (*Hsiao-hsüeh*) and *Reflections on Things at Hand,* consciously focusing on what is basic and primary, allow for, but do not stress, them.

The life of the Neo-Confucian, then, as well as the life of Neo-Confucianism, was many-sided. Neo-Confucian thought and activity progressed through the pursuit of one or another of these interests and concerns, as historical circumstances allowed or encouraged them to grow, but always with some sense of maintaining a proper balance. Tensions existed among them—between scholarship and public service, intellectual inquiry and moral cultivation, activity and contemplation, the practical and the aesthetic—and often the tension developed to the point of strain or cleavage. Modern interpreters of Neo-Confucianism have perhaps seen it in terms of one or another of these polarities and have not recognized them as dynamic unities, or seen that the tension and interaction among them was a source of both vitality and adaptability for the longer term.

Given this versatility and flexibility, it becomes more difficult for us to define the limits of Neo-Confucian philosophy or orthodoxy. The Confucian revival in the Sung was a broad historical process, and the Neo-Confucianism which emerged from it was neither a static philosophy nor a set of fixed doctrines, but a movement which grew precisely through successive efforts to redefine tradition and reformulate orthodoxy.

AMBIVALENT VALUES AND THE VALUE OF AMBIVALENCE

The "School of the Way" is one term applied to Neo-Confucianism which suggests the sense of directive movement or dynamic process. A contrasting term for the dominant Neo-Confucian philosophy has been School of Principle or Reason (*li-hsüeh*) [s] or the philosophy of human nature (*hsing-li-hsüeh*) [t] in which the word *li* expresses the belief in immutable principles or norms governing the process of change and growth. It further conveys the Confucian sense, not merely of the order discoverable in the regularities of things, but also of the indispensable role of man in ordering them and especially in regulating himself. In differentiating things, man made a difference to the universe. Ordering things, he fulfilled the cosmic order.

Understandably this emphasis on order has appeared excessively rationalistic to some and politically repressive to others. But the philosophy of Chu Hsi, or of the Ch'eng-Chu School to which *li-hsüeh* usually refers, also represents a dualism of *li* and *ch'i* [u] (ether, material force) in which the latter term stresses the reality of the physical universe and the physical nature of man. From the standpoint of the early Neo-Confucians as they reacted to the Buddhist view of the world as insubstantial and illusory, the physical reality of things was as much to be reaffirmed as the rational and moral order. From the further vantage point of the seventeenth century, Neo-Confucianism might even be viewed as predominantly the School of Ether (ch'i-hsüeh),ᵛ since the physical aspect of reality came to dominate over the rational in the minds of later thinkers. Thus we could emphasize one or the other aspect of this basic dichotomy, li or ch'i, and thereby underscore the change in thought from one period to another. Better still, we can recognize that the underlying ambivalence of Neo-Confucianism on these points proved to be its greatest strength, allowing contrasting tendencies to fructify, rather than simply to negate one another.

The ambivalence of Neo-Confucianism appears also in the use of the term School or Study of the Mind (hsin-hsüeh) ʷ for another aspect of the movement. Most often this name has been used to assign a basic value to mind or intuition as opposed to principle and its objective study. But virtually all of Neo-Confucian philosophy can be interpreted as a discipline of the mind. Professor Araki's paper for this volume discusses it as such in relation to Buddhism. Moreover it is misleading to think of the Ch'eng-Chu School as wholly rationalist and distrustful of intuition, or to see the Lu-Wang School (commonly called the School of Mind) as denying either the rational order or principle. When the seventeenth-century intellectual historian Huang Tsung-hsi ˣ wrote a preface to his survey of Ming Confucian thought, the Ming-ju hsüeh-an,ʸ he referred to Ming philosophy in general as the "philosophy of principle," though it was mostly concerned with mind and he assuredly meant to include Wang Yangming as a major contributor to the "philosophy of principle." [28]

Neo-Confucianism then may be characterized by its own image of the tree or plant, rooted in certain constant human concerns and activities, branching out conceptually and in new cultural forms, but with no new growth so unbalanced and unsupported that it would fall of its own weight. The basic activities of the Confucian, learning and social action, flowed from man's capacity to know and to act. But learning itself might be related more and less directly to action, and vice versa. Thus, study or learning could be understood by Chu Hsi (using terms from the Mean,

27) in the sense of the pursuit of scholarship or intellectual inquiry (*tao wen hsüeh*) [z] relevant to human needs but sometimes detached from social or political activity; or it could be pursued as moral or spiritual cultivation ("preserving one's moral nature" *tsun te hsing*), [aa] again with the same possibilities in regard to engagement and disengagement. [29] As heir to a considerable corpus of literature, the Neo-Confucian could devote himself to scholarship in the sense of book learning, if only he had the leisure and means to sustain it. As a man concerned for others and sensitive to their needs, however, he could not free himself from the responsibility for leadership that went with education. For this, book learning alone would not suffice. At times, indeed, it seemed irrelevant or distracting.

I have discussed elsewhere the difficulty of maintaining a balance between these two concerns, and the burden felt by Confucians as scholarly literature accumulated in the Ming. [30] In the seventeenth century, with the burden of culture growing, the strain intensified between those who achieved prodigious feats of classical scholarship, and those like Yen Yüan [ab] (as discussed in Professor Tu's paper) for whom the philological and phonological feats of the so-called Han learning constituted a massive exercise in irrelevancy and impracticality. No doubt the Manchu success in giving the country peace and prosperity, together with their lavish patronage of classical scholarship, contributed to a situation in which the Confucian might well succumb to an exclusively scholarly life, or else, if he did not, might vehemently complain about the pendantry of those who did. But there is a steady linking of scholarly study and moral concern antedating this historical development, and we can thus recognize it as a constant and typical Neo-Confucian problem to which different thinkers and schools offered varying answers. What is perhaps most significant, however, is that even the "orthodox" came up with new and unexpected solutions, and as these are disputed different orthodoxies arise.

NEO-CONFUCIAN INTERIORITY

In the school of Chu Hsi the balance between intellectual and moral/spiritual cultivation is more nearly maintained than that between individual cultivation and service to society. I discuss elsewhere the comparative imbalance in favor of individual cultivation, as opposed to political involvement, in Chu Hsi's teaching.[31] For him the new balance is stated in terms of intellectual inquiry and moral/spiritual cultivation, or between the study, the "searching out of principle" (*ch'iung li*) [ac] and "abiding in reverence" (*chü ching*),[ad] which for many generations of scholars summed up the aims of the Ch'eng-Chu school.

Chu Hsi also spoke of devoting "half the day to book-learning (*tu shu*) [ae] and half to quiet-sitting" (*ching-tso*).[af] [32] These two activities then, gave a working definition to the search for principles and the practice of reverence. Principles of course could be found elsewhere than in books, and nothing betrays Chu Hsi's own scholarly proclivities more than the choice of book learning here to represent intellectual inquiry. Even more revealing, however, of Chu Hsi's time and spiritual climate is the choice of quiet-sitting, an adaptation of Buddhist meditation and quite without precedent in earlier Confucianism, as the preferred form of moral/spiritual cultivation.

For half of one's time and effort, or anything approaching that, to be spent in contemplative activity was an innovation of profound significance, far outweighing in practical importance any of the theoretical concepts or terms assimilated from other traditions into Chu Hsi's philosophical structure. First, it signified that Neo-Confucian cultivation would, to a remarkable and unprecedented degree, be self-centered—that is, focused on the individual person and carried on in relative isolation.[33] Second, it portended a deep interiorization of Confucian cultivation and explains why, in spite of the ostensible dualism of *li* and *ch'i* in Chu Hsi's theoretical structure, the search for principle even in the Ch'eng-Chu school led to the convergence of objective and subjective learning in the mind.

It is evident from this how the balance struck between one set of polarities—intellectual and moral cultivation—and the specific cultural definition given it in the Sung, could significantly alter the total balance in the system. Even in a tradition constantly seeking the Mean it was possible to give constant values new meanings, to develop new thrusts and counterthrusts, new relationships and configurations, in an effort once again to achieve a new balance. Controversy arose, for instance, over Chu Hsi's philosophy of human nature, which was seen as attributing evil to man's physical nature. There is little basis for this in Chu's theoretical position, as Fung Yu-lan pointed out in discussing Chu's later critics.[34] What may well have fueled the issue, however, was the practical implication of quiet-sitting as a discipline of the mind over the bodily desires, opposing a pure and quiescent principle to disturbing psychophysical influences on the mind. Together with the religious intensity of its practitioners, this produced a strong puritanical strain in the Ch'eng-Chu school. In this light, however, the preoccupation of Ming Neo-Confucians with the mind, far from making a sharp break with the Ch'eng-Chu school, appears as a natural outgrowth from it.

The dominant tone of the new "orthodoxy" was established by this combination of scholarship and spiritual training, and by the religious zeal with which these Neo-Confucians propagated their well-defined, carefully-articulated, and consciously-shaped way of life. Official recognition, when it came belatedly, only confirmed the prior acceptance and practice of this teaching by much of the scholarly community. In the Ming state, orthodoxy attempted only to use the new teaching in a neatly packaged, simplified, and digestible form—primarily through adoption of the Ch'eng-Chu commentaries on the classics in the civil service examinations. By contrast, Chu Hsi's own recommendations for the content of such examinations (ignored by his state "sponsors") included a wide range of scholarly literature that was far more representative of the breadth of learning (*po hsüeh*) [ag] which his school aimed to encourage.[35] Nor did state orthodoxy promote so assiduously the forms of spirituality integral to the new "faith." The new interiority did not lend itself to bureaucratic routinization. It was in fact more likely to engender autonomous thought and activity than anything of use to the state.

Orthodox Confucian teaching, as distinct from state ideological orthodoxy, was promoted by individual thinkers and teachers who followed the new way of life, or seriously attempted to do so, while accepting by and large Chu Hsi's philosophical system and scholarly work. Most leading thinkers of the Ming were produced by this system, growing out of it even if they eventually outgrew it. From it they received their basic intellectual orientation and spiritual formation. In this sense one may say that the Ch'eng-Chu school, which established itself late in the Sung period, exerted its greatest influence in the Ming, while one may also say that Ming thought had its own characteristic quality, attributable in part to its further exploration and development of the system.

NEO-CONFUCIAN RELIGIOSITY AND RITUAL

An important element in the religious side of the new system was the performance of ritual. This, too, despite its formal character, should be thought of as largely voluntary and so subject to individual variation. It answered more to the need for formal means of self-expression and a deep feeling for ritualized action which unites one to a higher, more enduring order of being. We find evidence of compulsive behavior in this area, but few signs of compulsion. If to ordinary observers the early Neo-Confucians seemed obsessive in their espousal of an archaic ritual as opposed to prevailing convention, in the later tradition there are individuals who manifest an extraordinary, not to say neurotic, fixation over ritual behavior.

One such example in the Ming is Hu Chü-jen [ah] (1434–84), a most indomitable defender of Ch'eng-Chu orthodoxy and eventually enshrined as a Confucian worthy. Hu's fanatic insistence on the performance of every detail in the burial and mourning rites, long since abandoned by most others, not only led to serious impairment of his health, but also subjected him to ridicule and involved him in litigation and a jail sentence.[36] "Orthodoxy" canonized such heroic, and yet, by ordinary standards, extreme or "foolish," asceticism and self-sacrifice.

A similar example is found in Professor Tu's discussion of Yen Yüan in the early Ch'ing,[37] who engaged in intense, meticulous, prolonged, and nearly fatal mourning, taking the place of his absent and missing father, for someone he thought to be his grandmother. The discovery later that she was only a foster parent induced a crisis of faith and eventual abandonment of the Ch'eng-Chu system by Yen Yüan. In this case, despite his repudiation of the philosophy and of what passed for Chu Hsi's *Family Ritual*,[ai] there is no indication that Yen rejected ritual as such. He merely substituted a different (and actually more archaic) set of formal disciplines which he believed more practical. Indeed it is probably significant that among the independent outgrowths of the Ch'eng-Chu system in the Ming, including the teaching of Wang Yang-ming, there is no actual protest against ritual. Contrary to the typical modern view of ritual as "dead," reformers in China most often saw the lapse in or neglect of

Confucian ritual, rather than its obsolescence, as the cause of social decay and moral corruption.

In the spiritual development of Neo-Confucian orthodoxy as it was propagated by scholars and not by the state, the most remarkable formal practice was undoubtedly "quiet-sitting." A fuller description of this practice is given later.[38] What I wish to note here is that the observance of this new practice became almost a criterion of orthodoxy. A reason for this no doubt lay in the inherent difficulty of moral training beyond a rudimentary and mechanical level. Quiet-sitting was a definite spiritual exercise that could be programmed into one's life. It provided a specific discipline and regimen in matters of conscience and spiritual direction not susceptible of detailed external regulation.

The extent to which this practice became established in "orthodox" Ch'eng-Chu schools wherever Neo-Confucianism spread in China, Japan, and Korea is only one indication of its pervasive influence and decisive character. Few important thinkers of the early Ming were untouched by it. To Ch'en Hsien-chang [aj] (1428–1500), though he became increasingly independent of Ch'eng-Chu philosophy, it was a standard practice. Wang Yang-ming, too, was trained in quiet-sitting and once recommended it to his disciples. His decision later to deemphasize it marked a crucial turning point in the development of his own thought and practice. He had doubts about it as too passive and routine a procedure, likely to preempt the wider field of conscientious action in which "good-knowing" should be exercised.[39]

What takes place then is a striking reversal of roles. The more liberal and activist followers of Wang Yang-ming, including Wang Chi,[ak] Wang Ken,[al] and most of the T'ai-chou school,[am] tend to abandon quiet-sitting as too "quietistic" and unrelated to real life. If one considers that this same "left-wing" of the Wang Yang-ming school has been known for its affinity to Ch'an Buddhism, one can appreciate the irony in a "Wild Ch'an" Confucian like Li Chih [an] ridiculing the Neo-Confucians for their posing as sages in the posture of "quiet-sitting." [40] All ridicule aside, however, the characterization was apt and the reversal of roles almost complete. Those considered more traditional or orthodox in both the Chu and Wang schools were, with few exceptions, so identified by their cultivation of quiescence and the faithful practice of quiet-sitting, a guarantee of their moral seriousness, their disciplined life, and their dedication to the achievement of Sagehood, the goal of Neo-Confucian self-cultivation.[41]

THE INNER STRUGGLE OF NEO-CONFUCIANISM

As we have seen, the Neo-Confucian synthesis was not a static one, but contained within itself the vitality to generate new forms, the strength to engage in self-criticism, and the resilience to contain stresses and strains. The new direction which Ming thought took with Ch'en Hsien-chang and Wang Yang-ming emerged from their struggles to attain Sagehood, from the torment they experienced in trying to live up to the canons of the Ch'eng-Chu school. Unable to meet all the demands made upon them, they redefined sagehood so that they could live with it. Professor Araki speaks of Ch'en's "pathetic outcry: 'back to the natural,' " which signified a critical turning point in the development of his thinking. Why "pathetic"? Not, obviously, because he had some theoretical problem to resolve, but because of the intense psychological strain induced by his training in the Ch'eng-Chu school. The same strains and crises appear also in Wang Yang-ming, Wang Ken, Lo Ju-fang,[ao] Kao P'an-lung,[ap] and other Ming thinkers.[42] But even when their resolution of the crises involves a rejection of some Ch'eng-Chu formulation, it is usually in fulfillment of another value within the tradition, such as, in Ch'en's case, its basic naturalism or, in Lo's, the essential goodness of human nature; or in Wang Yang-ming's, to ease the tension between two values, such as knowledge and action.[43]

The case of Lo Ju-fang (1515–88), a leading thinker of the T'ai-chou school and an important influence on the romantic literature of the late Ming, is illustrative of this. It suggests how a new liberal humanism may have emerged almost directly from such austere spiritual exercises and the reaction to them. Lo's early intense effort to achieve enlightenment through quiet-sitting induced a morbid condition from which he was cured by the "medicine" of Yen Chün,[aq] a libertarian follower of Wang Ken who stressed the goodness of human desires rather than the need to curb them.[44]

In the *Ming-ju hsüeh-an* of Huang Tsung-hsi we can observe how early leaders of the Ch'eng-Chu school in the Ming struggled with the attainment of sagehood and how much of their teaching centered on mind control and quiet-sitting.[45] In his paper for the Ming Thought Conference, Professor Wing-tsit Chan pointed to the strong emphasis on the mind in this school during the early Ming, and its comparative inattention to Sung metaphysics.[46] Professor Wilhelm's study of the Sung school in the Ch'ing period likewise stresses the importance of quiet-sitting and mind control.[47] Significantly, the *Reflections on Things at Hand (Chin-ssu lu)* seems to have played a key role in the "conversion" of leading Sung School thinkers in the early Ch'ing, such as Lao Shih [ar] and Ch'eng Tsai-jen.[as] [48] And now Professor Chan's study for this volume of the *Hsing-li ching-i,*[at] the official manual of Ch'eng-Chu orthodoxy in the Ch'ing, brings out its relative stress on the moral and practical side and its deemphasis of metaphysics. In Korea and Japan, too, the Ch'eng-Chu schools largely conformed to this pattern,[49] centering often upon the *Chin-ssu lu* as an inspiration and guide to the attainment of sagehood, and on quiet-sitting, mind-control, and scholarly study as complementary ingredients in its spiritual and cultural discipline.

This, then, represents the essential Ch'eng-Chu tradition or orthodox school among scholars and thinkers, which may be contrasted to the orthodoxy upheld by the state through the official schools and the civil service examinations. I have discussed elsewhere the tensions which existed between this independent Ch'eng-Chu tradition and state-sponsored orthodoxy.[50] Although for many individuals the two were not mutually exclusive, the former tended to emphasize quiet-sitting and study of the *Chin-ssu lu* as a guide to personal cultivation while the latter stressed literary skill—mastering the approved essay form—and the study of Ch'eng-Chu commentaries for use in the examinations.

The question of genuine orthodoxy, however, is significant not only in relation to the routinization or exploitation of Confucianism by the state. It has a bearing, as we have seen, on the role of the Ch'eng-Chu school itself in contributing to new trends of thought which came to be regarded as heterodox. In the past, what has been stressed in these new trends has been their departure from tradition or revolt against authority. Often the discussion has been in hackneyed terms, relying heavily on the conventional currency of "protest" without recognizing the indebtedness of protesters to the past. Here the case of Wu Yü-pi [au] (1392–1469), an early leader of the Ch'eng-Chu school in the Ming, may give us some insight into the problem.

CONFUCIAN AUTHENTICITY AND ORTHODOX
NONCONFORMITY

At the beginning of his survey of Ming Confucian thought, Huang
Tsung-hsi chooses to present Wu Yü-pi first, as if he were in some sense
the fountainhead of Ming thought. Wu was indeed a patriarchal figure.
Both as the teacher of other influential Ming thinkers and because of his
personal character, he stood as a shining example of Confucian virtue to
later generations. But he typifies Ming thought in other less conventional
and more significant ways. Wu was the son of a court offical and destined by virtue of his personal talents and educational opportunities to
take a place in the ranks of the scholar-officials. In the course of his
schooling, however, Wu encountered Chu Hsi's record of the development of the Ch'eng brothers' school, the *I-lo yüan-yüan lu,*[av] a work
which has much in common with the final chapter of the *Chin-ssu lu* for
its biographical accounts of the Sung philosophers, stressing their life-
styles and personal character, rather than the development of their doctrines as such.[51] The deep impression these made on Wu is comparable
to a religious conversion. He resolved to follow their example and strive
to achieve sagehood. This high calling, however, proved for Wu to be incompatible with an official career. Like many others of his generation,
Wu recoiled at serving the usurper Yung-lo, who had martyred the
heroic Fang Hsiao-ju.

It is significant that this renunciation did not simply sacrifice official
position, with its powers and perquisites, in order to pursue a life of
scholarship and philosophical speculation. Wu's interest in the classics
was intensely personal, rather than scholastic. Though he proceeded to
immerse himself in study of the classics and the Sung philosophers, he
did so with a view to self-reformation and not erudition of the sort displayed in the typical commentaries on the classics. Huang Tsung-hsi
relates that Wu secluded himself from the world and pondered the Four
Books, Five Classics, and the discourses of the Sung philosophers for
their direct relevance to his own personal life and self-cultivation.[52] The
Chin-ssu lu, too, was a basic text for him, and for the same reasons.

This inner drive to achieve a kind of sanctity—in Confucian terms characterized by a state of purity (*shun*), integrity (*ch'eng*), and serenity (*tan*) or composure (*ching*) [aw]—was accompanied by symptoms of alienation from ordinary society and the established forms of social intercourse which one does not normally expect to find in a model of traditional virtue or a "pillar" of orthodoxy. Although Wu went through with the marriage arranged for him by his father, on the wedding night he refused to enter the wedding chamber with his bride. In his dress he preferred the simplest of clothing, and the shabbiness of his attire would have embarrassed his father more had not it been so far out of keeping with one of his social standing that few people recognized him as the son of an official.[53] This preference for a life of simplicity and frugality, if not of poverty, stayed with him to the end. His willingness to take students signified that he intended no total disassociation from human society, but his insistence on manual work as an accompaniment to Confucian learning, his laboring in the fields with his students (who had to accept the same demanding régime), and his steadfast adherence to the plainest of dress, gave his life the note of simplicity, purity, and rigor that once had characterized monastic existence under the sterner of the Ch'an masters.

Such austerity and unconventionality are not unfamiliar to us in the roles of the anchorite or the prophet. Christ, in speaking of John the Baptist, reminded his listeners of the radical difference between the true man of God and those who accommodated themselves to power and prevailing opinion. "What did you go out into the desert to see? A reed shaken by the wind? . . . A man clothed in soft garments? Behold those who wear soft garments are in the houses of kings. A prophet? Yes, I tell you and more than a prophet. . . ." (Matthew 11.)

Much of this might apply to Wu Yü-pi as a Confucian purist, but the comparison yields both a resemblance and a difference. The resemblance to the prophet underscores the uncompromising spirit of Neo-Confucianism as a commitment to the ideal of sagehood. It suggests that at the heart of this "orthodoxy" lay a sharp juxtaposition of ideals and actualities and a constant creative tension between the two. From this point of view, instead of simply "adjusting to the world," Neo-Confucianism could generate a radical critique of prevailing mores as falling short of traditional ideals, and the Confucian purist could take his stand also as a nonconformist, unwilling to accommodate himself to the decadent ways of his own time. In this respect Wu Yü-pi stands as another Neo-Confucian exception to Weber's characterization of the Confucian mentality as always seeking "adjustment to the world," "deifying wealth," and as being incapable of the "peculiar confinement and repression of natural impulse which was brought about by strictly volitional and ethical rationalization and ingrained in the Puritan." [54]

A difference, however, lies in the fact that Wu Yü-pi is no anchorite or hermit and shows little of the fire and indignation of the prophet. He does not abandon mankind or threaten doom on a wayward and corrupt generation. Wu's moral authority and lofty character stand as a silent reproach to unworthy Confucians, yet he does not set himself up in judgment on others, but aspires rather to an elevation of spirit which in the end would reconcile him to the world and men. Even feelings of righteous anger which other Neo-Confucians might not think incompatible with an "unperturbed mind," Wu struggles to control. As a purist he seeks to be free, not from contamination by others, but from the Puritan's impulse to find fault with or renounce the world. As a rigorist he demands everything of himself and expects little from other men. [55]

The aim of Wu's self-cultivation was, through quiescence (*ching*), [ax] and especially through quiet-sitting, to achieve reverence (*ching*), [ay] a state of mind he frequently characterized as being at peace with both Heaven and man. He was fond of the expression in the *Mean* which describes the noble man as "not complaining against Heaven or grumbling against men." [56] "In high station he does not treat his subordinates with contempt; in low station he does not curry favor with his superiors. He rectifies himself and seeks nothing of others, so that he has no complaints" (*Mean*, XIV). For Wu, a man should have such steadfast adherence to principle and such control of his own feelings that he could preserve equanimity in the face of all adversity. He should have achieved such a firm stance in life that no misfortune or disgrace could shake him, and his heart should be so free and pure of any resentment that he would never find himself "complaining against Heaven or grumbling against men." [az] [57]

As one committed to the attainment of sagehood, Wu allowed that he had once had some doubts concerning his own capacity to achieve this goal. He remarks in his *Journal* (*Jih-lu*) [ba] that Chu Hsi had spoken of his teacher, Li T'ung, [bb] as one who never lost his temper or showed his anger. Wu sighed in mixed admiration and despair: "By what kind of discipline did he ever achieve this? Even with a life-long effort I could never come to that." He further noted, however, Chu Hsi's comment that Li originally had been a brash and unruly person, and had achieved his later self-control only through hard work. From this Wu became convinced that the capacity for sagehood did not come with birth, nor did the achieving of equanimity depend on contact only with persons one liked and admired, such as sages and worthies. He concluded that "becoming a sage or a worthy is something one can learn. Human nature is basically good and man's character (or disposition, *ch'i-chih*) [bc] can be transformed." [58]

Wu's *Journal* also records his experience of lying sick in bed one night, unable to sleep. His mind was disturbed by household problems; he was full of worries, his thoughts were confused, and his spirits were "unclear." He resolved to exert every effort to improve his moral character and concern himself with nothing else. Thereupon his mind became settled and "his spirits cleared. . . ." [59]

It was through such constant self-examination and effort of will that Wu achieved the strength of character and loftiness of mind which impressed later Confucians like Liu Tsung-chou. [bd] [60] It is true that he made almost no contribution to the development of Neo-Confucian speculative philosophy, [61] but that is not the criterion to be applied here. Wu's spiritual and moral qualities became the hallmark of the Ch'eng-Chu school as an authentic "orthodoxy"—its moral earnestness, its serious attention to personal cultivation, its high standards of conduct, its purism, and indeed its claim to a certain spiritual elevation or transcendence.

ORTHODOXY: DOCTRINE OR WAY OF LIFE?

To some, orthodoxy stood for fixed moral principles, rigidly adhered to through constant self-examination. It was to this that reformers turned back in the neoorthodoxy of the Tung-lin movement at the end of the Ming, as they sought desperately to halt the drift toward moral laxity, social decay, and political corruption. Nevertheless, even for the Tung-lin, there was more to their neoorthodoxy than a simple objective code of traditional morality. Quiet-sitting and the search for spiritual transcendence were also important. In this way spiritual cultivation and mind control became quite as characteristic of the Ch'eng-Chu school in later China and Japan as was the traditional social morality so often identified with orthodoxy.

Thus the orthodox tradition, even more than a set moral code or philosophical system, was a life-style, an attitude of mind, a type of character formation, and a spiritual ideal that eluded precise definition. This was all the more true in a tradition which prized naturalness and spontaneity as much as the Confucians did. One encounters in fact some of the same difficulties in identifying orthodoxy as in Zen tradition, which must allow for an irreducible minimum of individual intuition or personal realization, and thus for adaptation or differentiation. Hence even a spokesman for Ch'eng-Chu orthodoxy such as Hsüeh Hsüan,[be] though a believer in the value of book learning, can speak of the Way of the Sages as a "wordless teaching" attained essentially through personal experience.[62]

As expressed in the arts, especially in poetry and painting, the question of "orthodoxy" is inseparably bound up with disciplined mastery and qualities of personal character and style which it is impossible to define in terms of any formula or doctrine. Chu Hsi, in his youth, studied earlier masters of Chinese poetry and consciously imitated their styles. As he matured and developed his own powers and personality, he allowed himself greater freedom. Orthodox models served, then, not for the imposition of uniformity, but as a training and testing ground for his own self-expression.[63]

Where Neo-Confucian spirituality affords a degree of openness to new experience, and—especially in Ming thought—develops an enlarged, more expansive view of what it means to be human, sectarian labels or traditional affiliations become of secondary importance. In contrast to the virulent anti-Buddhist, anti-Taoist tone of the early Sung revival, Ming Confucians often claim as more fundamentally "human" certain dimensions of spiritual experience which historically or in narrower scholastic terms might have been identified as Buddhist, Taoist, or syncretic. If an idea, attitude, or practice contributes to one's personal cultivation, self-control, literary mastery, physical well-being, social poise, or spiritual freedom, what matter that it is shared with or borrowed from the Buddhists or Taoists (as with quiet-sitting)? If Buddhist disciplines and insights, or Taoist techniques of body- or breath-control, enhance or deepen one's personal integration, need they be spurned as tainted by philosophies incompatible in theory with Confucianism? If the test of truth is personal experience and practical accomplishment, and the basic value of Confucianism is "humanity" as exemplified in personal character, conduct, and cultural refinement, what theoretical or sectarian considerations can weigh very heavily in judging the living achievement?

TRADITION: SELF-CRITICAL AND SELF-RENEWING

Neo-Confucians, insisting on the need for some standard of orthodoxy or fidelity to tradition, endowed the classics with far more authority as the ultimate test of truth than most Ch'an Buddhists would have allowed to the sūtras. And yet even the classics provided no simple, objective standard. The Confucian revival in the Sung, from its inception, had been engaged in reinterpretation of the classics and redefinition of the canon. The assigning of special importance to the so-called Four Books was one result of this process. New significance was found in the early texts as Sung scholars sought to rediscover their meaning in what might be called a "post-Buddhist" age. Why indeed should they be satisfied with the Han and T'ang commentaries? If Confucian tradition, as previously interpreted, seemed pedantic, antiquarian, and unequal to the contemporary challenge, who was to say that earlier commentators had exhausted the matter, that no further word could be pronounced on these subjects?

From the outset, then, Neo-Confucians insisted on orthodoxy and yet at the same time exercised the right to question and reconsider the established standard of orthodoxy on the basis of both new experience and fresh evidence. But if the Sung masters themselves could exercise such critical review and engage in reinterpretation of the classical heritage, was not that example—of putting tradition to the test of reason and experience—more significant as a model for their followers than any of the specific doctrines the Ch'engs and Chu Hsi propounded? While reaffirming the objective importance of orthodox tradition, in their understanding of it were they not putting a higher value on inner reflection and rational judgment than on mechanical adherence to established formulations or accepted views? And by inviting every man to realize the truth that was within him through the attainment of sagehood, did they not also encourage him to put the words of the sages, as found in the classics, to the test of personal experience, investigation, and reformulation? Ni Yüan-lu,[bf] in the seventeenth century, noted the point in the preface to his own commentary on the *Book of Changes:* [64]

> The *Changes* has been a controversial subject among scholars for more than a thousand generations. When all this talent in a thousand generations has been employed to establish a single [*Book of*] *Changes* and yet there is still dispute, how can there be a standard [interpretation of the] *Changes?* And yet it is regarded as a crime to contradict even the casual remarks of the Ch'eng brothers and Chu Hsi! Now I am only following Confucius' interpretation, without daring to inject my own ideas into it. But suppose King Wen and the Duke of Chou should take to chastising rebels; Confucius would have to apologize. However, if we took Confucius [on our side] to question the Ch'engs and Chu, the Ch'engs and Chu would have to bow their heads. Thus it is that the Way may be clarified and made easy to practice.

Thus a critical method and spirit of doubt were from the start implicit in the whole Neo-Confucian enterprise, and did not appear suddenly with the reexamination of canonical texts in the seventeenth and eighteenth centuries. Achievements in this latter phase of Confucian scholarship emerged from intervening centuries in which Neo-Confucians reopened and reformulated in a most fundamental way the central teachings of Confucian self-cultivation. Ni Yüan-lu himself illustrates the point well. Not only was he deeply concerned with reasserting traditional Confucian morality in a corrupt age, but he also set a high example of Confucian dedication to public service as a statesman at the end of the Ming and proved equal to the final test of Confucian virtue—readiness to die for his sovereign when the dynasty collapsed.[65] Yet Ni was also a devout Buddhist. In an age of flourishing syncretism, one might take his Buddhism as a sign of heterodoxy, but would we be justified in considering him less of an orthodox Confucian for this, against the testimony of his own life as an exemplification of Confucian ideals? The same question may be asked with regard to Chin Sheng,[bg] a faithful Buddhist and Ming loyalist who sacrificed his life as the culmination of devoted service to his dynasty and steadfast resistance to the Manchus.[66]

What makes Ni's case all the more revealing is the link he provides to the pragmatic and utilitarian tendency in the seventeenth century.[67] In him we see the new realism emerging from the same power of critical skepticism and openness to new experience which led Ni and other Neo-

Confucians in that age to new forms of religious experience. Chiao Hung,[bh] Li Chih, and Fang I-chih [bi] are other examples illustrating this skeptical rationalism combined with religious syncretism (Taoism and Ch'an), while Hsü Kuang-ch'i's [bj] conversion to Christianity reflects the same openness to new forms of learning and experience in both science and religion.[68]

HYPOCRISY, ECCENTRICITY, AND SAGEHOOD

Confronted by the official orthodoxy and conscious of the disparity between its public professions and actual performance, Neo-Confucians had frequent occasion to doubt the genuineness of that kind of orthodoxy. As students of the *Mean,* moreover, they had had an exacting standard of personal cultivation set for them by the demand to be "watchful over themselves when alone," in the inmost recesses of their hearts and minds.[69] Outward conformity could not hide inward duplicity. Nor could one achieve authentic moral character and true realization of the Way simply by having a due regard for the feelings and opinions of others or by yielding to the social pressures which so strongly reinforced morality in traditional China.

There were similar difficulties with the idea that the classics, or more broadly the classical tradition, could provide objective criteria of orthodoxy in any final sense. Rote learning and a mechanical repetition of canonical prescriptions would produce either a dull and lifeless individual or what Confucius called a "goody-goody" (*hsiang-yüan*).[bk] [70] To both Confucius and Mencius the discovery of a mean between bland conformity and unruly self-assertion was an individual thing, a matter of trial and error, experience and growth. Short of achieving that Mean, it was better to err on the side of excess and spontaneous enthusiasm than on the side of timid conformity.[71]

In the Ming there was much discussion of the point, and sentiment ran strongly in favor of what Julia Ching has called, in connection with Wang Yang-ming, the "mad ardour" (*k'uang*) [bl] of his desire and drive for sagehood.

Yang-ming's entire life was an expression of mad ardour. His was the daring of the magnanimous man, driven by a restless energy, to fulfill limitless ambitious, not for worldly success but for the attainment of absolute values. The quality ap-

peared in him from a very early age, as when he doubted the words of his precep-
tor that the greatest thing to do in life was to "study and pass the examinations,"
and offered his own alternative "to learn how to become a sage." [72]

In Wang Yang-ming, whom we are accustomed to think of as an independent, if not heterodox, figure, such "mad ardour" may not seem
surprising. One takes it, too, almost as a matter of course with radical followers of Yang-ming such as Wang Ken, knights-errant like Yen
Chün [bm] and Ho Hsin-yin,[bn] or unrestrained individualists like Li
Chih.[73] The matter takes on different proportions, however, when we
find Tung-lin reformers, who turned back to Chu Hsi and traditional morality, likewise choosing the wild and impetuous in preference to the hyp-
ocrites, the conventional "thieves of virtue" (te chih tse) [bo] or the goody-
goodies.[74] Among the Tung-lin this was not simple unconventionality,
but a characteristic of the most dedicated followers of the Confucian
Way, the bravest fighters against corruption at court, who took as their
models the unconventional but orthodox Confucians of the early Ming.

Nor is this "mad ardour" to be confused with the eccentricity, whether
studied or unaffected, which by now had become a familiar trait in her-
mits and recluses who thereby showed their contempt for the world and
human society. For Neo-Confucians it signified neither world renunciation nor idiosyncrasy, and stood far from either the self-indulgence of
many Wei-Chin hedonists or the weird habits of Taoist "immortals" like
Chang La-ta [bp] or Chang San-feng.[bq] [75] This was the independence and
uncompromising spirit of men totally dedicated to the service of mankind, and mad, like Wang Yang-ming, only because the depth of their
human concern set them at odds with a complacent society.[76] It was a
sign of their true humanity, their genuineness as individuals, their authenticity as Confucians.

Wu Yü-pi and his followers demonstrate early the centrality of this tendency in Neo-Confucian thought. The pupil of Wu most identified with
so-called Ch'eng-Chu orthodoxy, Hu Chü-jen, followed his master in his
abstention from the civil service examinations, preferring a life of poverty, simplicity, and spiritual rigor which stressed the achieving of a state
of reverence.[77] Ch'en Hsien-chang, after studying under Wu Yü-pi, likewise gave up thoughts of an official career, and secluded himself to practice quiet-sitting and cultivate quiescence. His life-style stressed simplicity, frugality, and the combination of study, "sitting," and farm-

ing—"half-peasant, half-scholar," as he put it in one of his poems—which carries on in the manner of Wu Yü-pi.[78] Ch'en eventually developed his own philosophy, taking issue with certain Ch'eng-Chu formulations, but it emerged from the kind of spiritual orientation and discipline which that school inculcated, and emphasized one "orthodox" practice, quiet-sitting, at the expense of another, book learning. Finally, Wu's pupil Lou Liang,[br] who likewise preferred the simple life, confirmed Wang Yang-ming's vocation to sagehood through study and emulation of the Sung masters. Even before this Wang had been inspired with such a desire to achieve the purity and transcendence of the sage that he, too, turned away from the civil examinations as a path to official service, engaged in an intensive quest for self-fulfillment, and, like Wu, sacrificed the pleasures of the nuptial bed in his search for spiritual guidance.

I have already discussed in *Self and Society in Ming Thought* how the consuming ambition for sagehood underlay the spiritual strivings of prominent Ming thinkers, and in this they were obeying the main impulse of the Neo-Confucian movement, even when that impulse carried them beyond the bounds of accepted formulations.[79] Neither deviant behavior nor spiritual inversion should be considered alone as what set the tone for Ming Neo-Confucians. Wang Yang-ming was conscious of his own spiritual wandering and spoke of having almost succumbed as a young man to different temptations and distractions, including Buddhism and Taoism, but he went on to a life of exceptional activity, social commitment, and heavy responsibilities, showing deep inner resources in the face of extraordinary adversities. And what is true for him is characteristic of the Ming as a whole. For all its seeming "quietism" it is the period most notable for the number and greatness of its Confucian martyrs and its long record of political protest. This most Neo-Confucian of ages, from its inner intensity and tempered will, also produced the most heroic example that could be invoked from the past in protest against contemporary despotism in China—Hai Jui.[bs] [80]

THE WORKING-OUT OF NEO-CONFUCIANISM

Whatever the moral influence of the Ch'eng-Chu school in later China—and this may be debatable—it is important to recognize that, contrary to the general impression, neither organizationally nor numerically was this school a dominant force. The number of Ming and Ch'ing thinkers identifiable with it is comparatively small. Among Ch'ing thinkers, who lamented what they believed to be a strong Ming drift away from "orthodoxy," there was something of an orthodox Sung school revival, but again the dominant intellectual trends ran in other directions, especially toward the so-called Han learning, and there was a continuing rejection of Sung doctrines among leading thinkers. The situation in Tokugawa Japan was roughly comparable, though I shall not enter into the details here.

It is significant, however, that the new trends which came to dominate the intellectual and cultural scene drew upon the Ch'eng-Chu school as a working system, if not upon its specific doctrines. Just as the search of Wu Yü-pi and Hsüeh Hsüan for moral perfection and spiritual peace pointed to the fundamental value of personal experience through interior contemplation and practical action, so did this same emphasis on personal experience, inwardness, and practicality become the common characteristic of late Ming schools which were otherwise quite diverse. In this respect the observations in Wu's journal, his reflections and comments on his daily experiences, are typical of the self-consciousness which becomes such a marked feature of late Ming literature. His frequent relating of his dreams further suggests a deeper awareness of the psychological levels of reality. It may seem a great distance from Wu Yü-pi, the patriarch of the Ch'eng-Chu school in the early Ming, to the Ch'an monk Te-ch'ing,[bt] discussed by Professor Wu, who wrote probably the first spiritual autobiography of a Buddhist monk at the end of the sixteenth century.[81] There is nothing in Buddhist literature, however, to serve as a precedent for drawing this much attention to oneself in writing, and there is much in Neo-Confucian thought which follows Wu Yü-pi in stressing personal experience and the importance of the self. In the writings of Ch'en Hsien-chang and Wang Yang-ming (who were influenced, directly or indirectly, by Wu), and in the travel journals or records of personal struggles in self-cultivation by Lo Hung-hsien,[bu] Hu Chih (1517-85),[bv] Kao P'an-lung, and others,[82] we see the emergence in literature of that preoccupation with the self which became a dominant trend of Ming Neo-Confucian thought.

In an earlier paper on "Individualism and Humanitarianism in Late Ming Thought," I tried to show that trends of thought usually labeled "nonconformist" or "progressive" actually represented a development of the main tendencies of Neo-Confucian thought, and I concluded that

. . . Confucianism, though the dominant tradition and, to modern eyes, an authoritarian system, proved capable of fulfilling somewhat the same function as that credited by Professor Butterfield to medieval Christianity in the rise of Western individualism. "If the religion produced the authoritarian system, it also produced the rebellion against the system as though the internal aspect of the faith were at war with the external. The total result over the long medieval period may have been a deepening of personality, a training of conscience, and a heightening of the sense of individual responsibility, particularly in the matter of religion itself." [83]

Against this background, we are better able to appreciate the continuities in Neo-Confucian thought from the late Sung into the Ch'ing, and to see how the increase in individual self-consciousness and the heightened religious and moral consciousness reflected in late Ming syncretism, both emerged to a significant degree from the emphasis in earlier Neo-Confucianism on the dominant aim of self-cultivation to achieve sagehood, the individual experience of sagehood as a synthesis of human experience in diverse forms, and the fine balance which was maintained in this synthesis between the competing claims of human individuality, culture, and society.

Changing historical conditions served to actualize and fructify different potentialities of this living synthesis at different times. No tree grows without reaching out—and that means branching out—for the sunlight. Later in this volume, in a separate paper on Neo-Confucian enlightenment, I attempt to show how from the same Neo-Confucian synthesis emerged the strong trend in the seventeenth century toward a kind of Confucian positivism or pragmatism, which has been variously characterized as "practical learning," "empiricism," and "scientific thought."

The culmination of this process was expressed in Neo-Confucian philosophical terms by Huang Tsung-hsi in the late seventeenth century, when he characterized the essence of man's nature as something not to be found in a static state of inward contemplation but in the exercise of virtue, in its own "working out" (*kung-fu so chih*). A major consequence of this shift in outlook consisted precisely in its becoming more of an outlook on the world of human activity and less of an "inlook," introspection or contemplation, on the essential nature of the sage.

This trend, too, may be understood as an outgrowth of the gradual unfolding of Neo-Confucian thought, with its leavening forces of scholarly inquiry and moral concern, its underlying affirmation of both rational order and physical reality, working their way outward from the inner experience and active involvement of generations of Neo-Confucian scholar-officials.

At its inception, what we call Neo-Confucianism was not consciously syncretic, but clearly benefited from an expanded vision and a deeper awareness of the possibilities of human experience. As an "orthodoxy" it represented a process of vital reintegration, the significance of which lay not so much in its explicit rejection of heterodoxy as in its recovery of a sense of balance or poise in reconciling the divergent claims of several methods of self-cultivation.

The Chinese have thought of the Way (or Tao) as a growing process and an expanding force. At the same time, following Mencius, they have felt that this Way could not be real or genuine for them unless somehow they could find it within themselves, as something not external or foreign to their own essential nature.[84] The unfortunate aspect of their modern experience has been the frustrating of that healthy instinct, through a temporary loss of their own self-respect and a denial of their right to assimilate new experience by a process of reintegration with the old. To have seen all value as coming solely from the West or as extending only into the future, and not also as growing out of their own past, has hindered them in recent years from finding that Way or Tao within themselves. The consequences of that alienation and its violent backlash were only too evident in the Cultural Revolution. We may be sure, however, that the process of growth is only hidden, not stopped, and that the new experience of the Chinese people will eventually be seen in significant part as a growth emerging from within and not simply as a revolution inspired from without.

NOTES

1. An exception is found in Carsun Chang's two-volume *Development of Neo-Confucianism* (New York, 1957, 1962). In terms of the problem dealt with here, however, his emphasis is on the degeneration of late Ming thought rather than on its transmutation and renewal. My emphasis is on historical trends in the light of which the thought described by Chang in moralistic terms as "empty," "unhealthy," and "perverted" (II, 28), has new significance and value.
2. Max Weber, *The Religion of China*, translated by Hans H. Gerth (New York, 1951), p. 248.
3. *Ibid.*, p. 164.
4. *Ibid.*, p. 228.
5. *Ibid.*, p. 236.
6. Some of the methodological limitations of Weber's approach to Chinese religion are indicated in C. K. Yang, *Religion in Chinese Society* (Berkeley, 1967), pp. 20, 80, 178, 239.
7. Levenson, *Confucian China and Its Modern Fate* (Berkeley, 1958), I, xvi.
8. *Ibid.*, I, xviii.
9. John King Fairbank, *The United States and China* (new edition; Cambridge, Mass., 1958), pp. 63–64.
10. John King Fairbank, *et al.*, *East Asia, The Modern Transformation* (Boston, 1965), p. 84. It is only fair to say that despite these views Professor Fairbank has been one of the most effective advocates for a deeper study and understanding of traditional China. I am frank to admit also that the quotations given here are not without some qualification in their original context. Nevertheless, I believe they fairly represent the impression widely conveyed to his many readers.
11. For a typical view of Neo-Confucianism as it is seen in popular literature, cf. Liu E., *The Travels of Lao Ts'an*, translated by Harold Shadick (New York, 1952), pp. 98–102.
12. Cf. Hou Wai-lu, *Chung kuo tsao-ch'i ch'i-meng ssu hsiang shih* [bw] (Peking, 1956).
13. T'ang Chun-i, "Ideas of Spiritual Value in Neo-Confucianism," in Charles Moore, *The Chinese Mind* (Honolulu, 1967), p. 208.
14. *Ibid.*, p. 209.
15. Shimada Kenji, *Chūgoku ni okeru kindai shii no zasetsu* (revised edition; Tokyo, 1970).
16. Shimada Kenji, *Shushigaku to Yōmeigaku* [bx] (Tokyo, 1967), especially epilogue.
17. Yü summarizes the alternative interpretations of Chinese writers in his long

article "Ts'ung Sung-Ming ju-hsüeh ti fa-chan lun Ch'ing-tai ssu-hsiang shih," [by] in *Chung-kuo hsüeh-jen* no. 2 (Hong Kong, September, 1970), pp. 19 ff.

18. Cf. my "Reappraisal of Neo-Confucianism" in A. Wright (ed.), *Studies in Chinese Thought* (Chicago, 1954).

19. Cf. W. T. de Bary, *et al.*, *Sources of Chinese Tradition* (New York, 1960), pp. 489–91.

20. See, for example, Kao P'an-lung's case, pp. 178–83, this volume.

21. As reflected in Chu's poetry in the year 1156. Cf. Li Chi, "Chu Hsi the Poet," in *T'oung Pao*, vol. 58 (1972), p. 83. Cf. also J. P. Bruce, *Chu Hsi and His Masters* (London, 1923), pp. 67–8.

22. See pp. 155–57, this volume.

23. *Ibid.*, p. 18.

24. Cf. Hellmut Wilhelm, "Chinese Confucianism on the Eve of the Great Encounter," in Marius Jansen (ed.), *Changing Japanese Attitudes Toward Modernization* (Princeton, 1965), p. 291. Aspects of this "program" are discussed by James T. C. Liu, in "How Did a Neo Confucian School Become a State Orthodoxy?" *Philosophy East and West*, vol. 13, no. 4, pp. 490, 492, 497.

25. See Uno Seiichi (ed.), *Shōgaku* [bz] (Tokyo, 1965), vol. 13 of *Shinyaku kambun taikei*,[ca] pp. 1–4.

26. Chu Hsi's *Chin-ssu lu*, translated by Wing-tsit Chan as *Reflections on Things at Hand* (New York, 1967), especially preface.

27. *Analects*, II, 12.

28. *MJHA* preface; my translation of the passage appears in *Self and Society*, p. 4.

29. Cf. *Chu Wen-kung wen-chi* [cb] 54/962, quoted and discussed in the essay by Yü Ying-shih already cited in *Chung-kuo hsüeh-jen*, II (Hong Kong, September, 1970), 22–23.

30. Cf. *Self and Society*, pp. 8–10.

31. See pp. 162–63, this volume.

32. Okada Takehiko, *Zazen to Seiza* [cc] (Nagasaki, 1965), pp. 82, 92–99. Though not the only method of mind cultivation practiced by Chu or his school, it was the most distinctive exercise and came to typify Neo-Confucian spiritual practice.

33. Ch'en Ti,[cd] in the Ming, pointed out what an inbalance this represented and asked how life could go on if everyone adopted the practice. Cf. Jung Chao-tsu, *Ming-tai ssu-hsiang shih* (Taiwan, 1962), pp. 273–74.

34. Cf. Fung Yu-lan, *A History of Chinese Philosophy*, II, 656–57, 668.

35. Cf. *Chu-tzu wen-chi* [ce] (TSCC edition), 13/471. Hsüeh-hsiao kung-chü ssu-i.

36. *MJHA*, I, 2/1; a fuller study of Hu's religiosity is being undertaken by Anne Meller Ch'ien at Columbia University.

37. Cf. Tu paper, pp. 511–42, this volume.

38. Cf. Enlightenment paper, pp. 141–216, this volume.

39. *MJHA*, II, 10/55–6.

40. See p. 191 (quote from Li Chih), this volume.

41. One such notable exception is Hu Chü-jen. Liu Ts'un-yan, in his study of Taoist influences in Ming Neo-Confucianism, points out Hu's singularity in this respect. See his "Taoist Self-cultivation in Ming Thought," in *Self and Society*, pp. 309–10.
42. *MJHA*, III; 17/84–6; IV, 18/1–4; see also pp. 180–82, this volume.
43. See p. 195, this volume, and *Self and Society*, pp. 12–13.
44. *MJHA*, VII, 34/1a.
45. *Ibid.*, I, 1/1–6.
46. *Self and Society*, pp. 29 ff.
47. Wilhelm, "Chinese Confucianism," in Jansen, *Changing Japanese Attitudes*, pp. 283–303.
48. *Ibid.*, p. 291.
49. See pp. 148–52, 205, this volume.
50. See *Self and Society*, pp. 6–8.
51. *MJHA*, I, 1/1–2.
52. *Ibid.*
53. *Ibid.* According to Chao-ying Fang, in his draft biography of Wu for the Ming Biographical History, there are indications of an estrangement from his father over the latter's willingness to serve the Yung-lo emperor.
54. Weber, *The Religion of China*, pp. 244 ff.
55. *MJHA*, I, 1/7.
56. *Ibid.*, 1/7, 9.
57. *Ibid.*, 1/11.
58. As excerpted in *MJHA*, I, 1/5.
59. *Ibid.*
60. *Ibid.*, 1/Shih shuo 2–3.
61. Chang, *Development*, II, 16.
62. Cf. *Hsüeh Wen-ch'ing kung tu-shu lu* [cf] (TSCC edition), 2/30.
63. Li Chi, "Chu Hsi the Poet," in *T'oung Pao*, vol. 58·(1972), pp. 67, 106–7. On this point Chu Hsi's views resemble those of Wang Shih-chen (discussed by Professor Lynn in this volume), which derive in part from the Ch'an tradition of mastery.
64. Preface to Erh-i nei-i-i, in *Ni Wen-chen kung ch'üan-chi* [cg] (1772 edition), wen-chi 6/13, as translated by Ray Huang in *Self and Society*, p. 435.
65. *Ibid.*, pp. 420–21, 433.
66. *MJHA*, XI, 57/36–37.
67. Cf. Ray Huang, "Ni Yüan-lu: Realism in a Neo-Confucian Scholar-Statesman," in *Self and Society*, pp. 415 ff.
68. Cf. Monica Ubelhör, "Hsü Kuang-ch'i (1562–1633) und seine Einstellung zum Christentum-ein Beitrag zur Geistesgeschichte der Spaten Ming-zeit," *Oriens Extremus*, no. 15 (December, 1968), pp. 191–257; no. 16 (June, 1969), pp. 41–74.
69. *Mean*, 1.
70. *Analects*, XVII, 13.

71. *Analects*, XIII, 21; *Mencius*, VII B, 37.
72. Cf. Julia Ching, "Wang Yang-ming: A Study in Mad Ardour," in *Papers on Far Eastern History* (Australian National University, Canberra, March 1971), p. 91.
73. Cf. de Bary, *Self and Society*, pp. 178–79, 193, 210–13.
74. *Analects*, XVII, 13.
75. Cf. Anna Seidel, "A Taoist Immortal of the Ming Dynasty: Chang San-feng," in de Bary, *Self and Society*, pp. 483, 498–99.
76. de Bary, *Self and Society*, pp. 159–60.
77. Cf. Wing-tsit Chan, "The Ch'eng-Chu School," in *Self and Society*, p. 39.
78. Cf. Jen Yu-wen, "Ch'en Hsien-chang's Philosophy of the Natural," in de Bary, *Self and Society*, pp. 55, 60.
79. de Bary, *Self and Society*, pp. 12–14.
80. Cf. James R. Pusey, *Wu Han, Attacking the Present Through the Past* (Cambridge, Mass., 1969); Clive Ansley, *The Heresy of Wu Han* (Toronto, 1971). In my opinion effective revolutionary action to remedy injustice was just as unrealistic a recourse for Hai Jui in the sixteenth century as it was for Wu Han in the twentieth. The latter recognized this basic similarity in their situation: there was no alternative to each taking the full burden on himself.
81. See Pei-yi Wu, "The Spiritual Autobiography of Te-ch'ing," this volume.
82. E.g., Lo Hung-hsien's *Chin-ling tung-yu chi-lüeh* [ch] (Shuo-fu hsü 25), Hu Chih's *K'un-hsüeh chi*,[ci] excerpted in *MJHA*, V, 22/8–15; and Kao P'an-lung's *K'un-hsüeh chi* in *Kao tzu i shu* [cj] 3.
83. de Bary, *Self and Society*, pp. 223–24.
84. *Mencius*, IV B, 14.

GLOSSARY

a　梁啓超

b　胡適

c　候外廬

d　唐君毅

e　島田虔次，中国に
　　於ける近代思惟
　　の挫折

f　良知

g　王陽明

h　朱熹

i　康有為

j　譚嗣同

k　王安石

l　近思録

m　道学

n　八目

o　小学

p　通鑑綱目

q　司馬光

r　資治通鑑

s　理学

t　性理学

u　気

v　気学

w　心学

x　黄宗羲

y　明儒学案

z　道問学

aa　尊德性

ab　顔元

ac　窮理

ad　居敬

ae　讀書

af　静坐

ag　博学

ah　胡居仁

ai　朱子家禮

aj　陳獻章

ak　王畿

al　王艮

am　泰州

an　李贄

ao　羅汝芳

ap　高攀龍

aq　顔鈞

ar　勞史

as　程在仁

at　性理精義

au　吳與弼

av　伊洛淵源録

aw　醇，誠，澹，静

ax　静

ay　敬

az　上不怨天，下不尤
　　人

ba　日録

bb　李侗

bc　気質

bd　劉宗周

be　薛瑄

bf　倪元璐

bg　金聲

bh　焦竑

bi　方以智

bj　徐光啓

bk　鄉愿

bl　狂

bm　顔鈞

bn　何心隱

bo　德之賊

bp　張刺達

bq　張三丰

br　妻諒

bs　海瑞

bt　德清

bu　羅洪先

bv　胡直

bw　中国早期啓蒙思想
　　史

bx　朱子学と陽明学

by　余英時，從宋明儒
　　学的發展論清代
　　思想史

bz　宇野精一，小学

ca　新譯漢文大系

cb　朱文公文集

cc　坐禪と静坐

cd　陳第

ce　朱子文集

cf　薛文清公讀書録

cg　倪文貞公全集，兒
　　易內儀以

ch　金陵多遊記略，説
　　郛續

ci　困學記

cj　高子遺書

ARAKI KENGO *Confucianism and Buddhism*

in the Late Ming

The most remarkable development in the world of thought in the late Ming was the revival of Buddhism, as it kept pace with the overwhelming popularity of the School of Wang Yang-ming, while at the same time the authority of the School of Chu Hsi rapidly declined. This suggests that the relationship between Buddhism and the School of Wang Yang-ming was quite different from its relationship to the School of Chu Hsi. Why, after the Chu Hsi school had made such an insistent attempt to break with Buddhism, did the development of the School of Wang Yang-ming lead to its revival? What kind of essential connection was there between the School of Wang Yang-ming and Buddhism?

To obtain clear answers to these questions, it is necessary to define the basic character of the teachings of Chu Hsi, Wang Yang-ming, and Buddhism. And to do this, it will be convenient to use the categories of the School of the Mind (*hsin-hsüeh*) [a] and the School of the Principle (*li-hsüeh*),[b] though the concepts represented by these terms cannot be strictly defined. Both the word "mind" (*hsin*) and the word "principle" (*li*) have a variety of meanings and thus it is difficult to render them by any single term.

However ambiguously these terms may have been used, thinkers tended to define their philosophical positions in relation to them; in fact, frequently their use of these terms became the decisive factors in determining their respective positions. That the conflict between the School of Mind and the School of Principle was particularly acute in the Sung period means that the concept of "Mind" and its correlative concept of "Principle" had acquired special meanings and that the relationship between these two had become seriously strained.

The word *hsin-hsüeh* appears in a Buddhist text translated in the Six Dynasties. There the word meant learning about stabilizing the mind, that is, learning of *samādhi* (*ting-hsüeh*) [c] and, thus, the word's usage and meaning differed from that in the later periods. *Hsin-hsüeh* in the Sung period indicates the position that one totally trusts the mind as the integrating and unifying substance of life and believes that by realizing it one can open the gate to enlightenment. This mind is the agent which controls the entire function of human existence. It was Ch'an Buddhism that played a great role in developing the School of Mind and causing it to attain maturity. The mind in Ch'an [d] Buddhism is the unifying substance which embraces both subject and object, spirit and body, internal and external worlds. Ch'an Buddhism tries to grasp this mind as a naked man who has discarded all doctrinal embellishments and traditional norms. Though Ch'an has many branches, they all place supreme emphasis on this mind and stake their existence on attaining its enlightenment. Here lies the reason that Ch'an Buddhism is called the School of Mind.

The characteristics of the Ch'an School are that it concentrates solely on establishing the original root rather than investigating modes of individual phenomena, and believes that as long as the original root is established, individual phenomena can be dealt with intuitively and naturally. "Do not be bothered by minor details so long as you grasp the Source," [1] are the famous words of one Ch'an monk. This caution against paying particular attention to "minor details" (individual phenomena) is because they induce the diffusion of human consciousness and destroy the unitary nature of the mind. To attain enlightenment in Ch'an is to realize at once this unitary nature. This being done, Ch'an claims, the individual, without losing his individuality, can function freely.

Ch'an, however, merely yields the full authority over action to the unitary mind, without establishing any criterion for judging whether an action is proper or improper. Ch'an simply teaches that one should expand the capacity of mind to the fullest and does not propound anything which assures the propriety of individual action. In Ch'an experience there may be a feeling of elation in life, but it may well be said that a sense of the criterion for action is lacking.

According to the Neo-Confucian view, what gives stability and order to all actions is the real principle which "distinguishes clearly what is right from what is wrong." [2] The real principle is the law of action inherent in things in the objective world; to act upon it is good and not to act upon it is evil; in short, it is a concrete standard of value. As the "ought," it directs the subject of action and provides a coherence to the total structure of action. The subject of action, therefore, instead of acting automatically at the dictate of his own one-mind, is expected to investigate the principle (li) inherent in each thing and each action and to act in accordance with that principle. When the principle is neglected, the subject loses propriety in action. In this sense principle directs the subject and transcends the mind. Here the School of Principle recognizes to the highest degree the universal authority of principle.

In contradistinction to the claim of the School of Mind in Ch'an that "all things are constructed by the mind," the School of Principle asserts that "under Heaven nothing is nobler than principle." [3] From the point of view of the School of Principle, Ch'an resembles a markless scale; it ignores the laws governing the objective world and handles things through mere imagination. Thus, Chu Hsi says that "Buddhism knows about emptiness only and does not know that there is a principle in emptiness," [4] and that "in Buddhism there is transcendental brilliance but no Mean." [5] Principle may be regarded as restrictive of the free activity of the mind, but, in reality, it furnishes a moderation and direction. And when the mind comes to function in accordance with principle, significant changes will inevitably be generated in its inner structure.

It goes without saying that in the School of Principle, also, the mind is regarded as the master of one's entire being. The mind, however, is understood as having a quality of invariable stability because of its possession of principle and, on the other hand, a quality of instability because of its potential of acting against principle. The former is called the nature (hsing), [e] and the latter, the feelings (ch'ing). [f] Thus, the mind has a double structure, of nature and of feelings; its core is known as the nature (principle) and the safekeeping of this core is man's greatest obligation. Thus arose the famous maxim that "the nature is identical to principle." The reason Chu Hsi attacked Ch'an Buddhism so violently was that Ch'an ignored completely the authority of principle inherent in the mind.

In the foregoing discussion we have clarified the differences between the School of Mind in Ch'an Buddhism and the School of Principle. In the Sung period, however, there was another group of philosophers that took a middle position between these two schools. This group was satisfied with neither the attitude of Ch'an, which ignored principle, nor the attitude of the School of Principle, which adhered too closely to the primacy and priority of principle. It still held to real principles but subordinated them to the control of the mind. In short, this position differs from that of Ch'an in that it recognizes the real principle, while it also differs from the School of Principle in that it does not recognize the primacy of principle. That it does not recognize the primacy of principle means that it does not admit that the mind has a special zone of inner stability containing principle but holds that the mind itself is endowed throughout with principle.

Why must this be so? In the School of Principle, even if the stability and orientation of the mind may be given by principle, the enhancement of the authority of principle reduces the opportunity for self-reflection on principle itself, thus gradually producing inflexibility. The fact that the term "fixed principle" (*ting-li*) [g] was used in the School of Chu Hsi probably indicates this. Principle so understood suppresses the vitality and spontaneity of the mind and obstructs its positive activities. According to this view, therefore, the relationship that exists between the mind and principle is such that it is not the principle (in terms of a special or separate existence) that directs the mind, as claimed by the School of Principle, but rather it is the mind that is entrusted with the authority to direct the principle, which is supported by the totality of mind. The basic axiom that "the nature is identical to principle" [h] is rejected, and the doctrine that "the mind is identical to principle" [i] is set forth. What is common to these two views is the recognition of the necessity for real principles, but what is different is that one view gives primacy to principle over mind, whereas the other gives primacy to mind over principle. A sharp division of opinion between Chu Hsi and Lu Hsiang-shan developed over this point.

The new philosophical position, which was thus brought forth, should have been identified under another name than the School of Mind or the School of Principle—since it takes a middle position between the School of Mind in Ch'an and the School of Principle—but it has nevertheless generally been called the School of Mind. The reason for this may be that this School of Mind was classified from the standpoint of its being opposed to the School of Principle in that principle was not given such supreme authority as in the School of Principle but was itself subject to the direction of the mind. Therefore, the conflict between the Schools of

Principle and of Mind did not remain as a mere conflict between Confucianism and Ch'an Buddhism, but turned into a three-cornered contest between the School of Mind in Ch'an, the School of Mind in Confucianism, and the School of Principle in Confucianism.

The history of Chinese thought after the Sung period developed with the School of Principle as its pivot, and in the Ming period the School of Chu Hsi was recognized in the civil examination system as orthodox doctrine. In the world of thought, from the beginning to the middle of the Ming period, the particularly noteworthy phenomenon was that the more the orthodoxy of the School of Chu Hsi was emphasized, the more the serious students became tormented by the discrepancy between mind and principle. Ch'en Hsien-chang's [j] (1428–1500) pathetic outcry of "Return to the natural" [k] was evoked by this experience. To break out of this impasse and to create a new philosophical position, there was no other way but to turn from the School of Principle toward the School of Mind. But now it had to be a School of Mind which would transcend the School of Principle and yet would pay due regard to the wisdom it represented. It therefore also had to transcend both the School of Principle and Ch'an. It was Wang Yang-ming's theory of "innate knowledge" (liang-chih) [l] which succeeded in establishing such a new School of the Mind.

There were, therefore, now two types of School of the Mind: the Confucian School, and that of Ch'an Buddhism. Our attempt to understand the relationship between these two will provide us with an important key with which to define the character of the two schools. Wang Yang-ming, as a matter of course, advocated a Confucian School of Mind; but what did he think about the School of Mind in Buddhism?

Until this time there had been almost no exception to the prevailing view of Buddhism as a heterodox teaching, a judgment fixed upon it by the School of Principle, and it was not easy for Wang Yang-ming to free himself from it. To declare that he had nothing to do with Buddhism was a necessary precondition for him to be accepted as an authentic Confucian scholar. Generally speaking, to pass from Confucianism to Buddhism or from Buddhism to Confucianism was almost inconceivable, as the two were thought to run on parallel roads that could never meet. The Confucians claimed that if those who believed in the faultless teaching of Confucianism so much as showed an interest in any other teaching it would disqualify them as Confucians. In this way, a high embankment was constructed between Confucianism and Buddhism. Wang Yang-ming's thinking, however, differed from this. No matter how stout the embankment, or how much the Confucians attacked the Buddhists as heretics, Wang Yang-ming held that if the Confucians themselves were more degenerate than the Buddhists, the latter could just as well attack the Confucians as heretics. They would be like contending mice in the same hole. Thus, he says: "If learned correctly, even a heretical teaching could be useful in the world, but if learned incorrectly, even Confucianism would be accompanied by evils." [6] In short, Wang Yang-ming thought that the problem of orthodoxy and heterodoxy could not be solved by establishing an embankment between the two teachings and that it was rather a matter of mental outlook; depending upon whether one's mind is elevated or degenerated, one would make himself orthodox or heterodox. A Confucian of the Northern Sung, Ch'eng Ming-tao,[m] said: "Avoid Buddhism as you would vulgar music or a charming girl." [7] Wang Yang-ming, however, perceived that even if a man formally broke with heterodoxy, wayward attitudes might still persist in his mind, and nothing would debase Confucianism more than for a man to feel assured that by merely being a Confucian he was less likely to fall into error than if he were a Buddhist. According to him it was the spirit of self-realization that was to be valued in learning, and heretics who strayed from the correct path in searching for self-realization were superior to those who masqueraded as Confucians but did not truly even search for it. [8]

Wang Yang-ming did not build an external embankment against heterodoxy, but sought the solution to the problem in the self-awareness of the inner mind. Later, when his thought fully developed, he called this mind "the innate knowledge" (liang-chih). The distinction between orthodoxy and heterodoxy was eventually made on the basis of whether or not one had awakened to this innate knowledge. Such a view of heterodoxy was criticized because it made the distinction between orthodoxy and heterodoxy ambiguous and it was too liberal toward heterodoxy. It is obvious, however, which attitude reflects a stricter, more self-restrained consciousness: the one which considers the overt disavowal of heterodoxy as sufficient to ensure against falling into it, or the other which is ceaselessly on guard against the danger of falling into it at any moment.

In the Buddhist School of Mind the danger exists that principle may be dissolved into emptiness. In the School of Principle a solid wall of principle is constructed in the mind to avoid this danger, but this invites another danger, of curbing the vitality of the subject. Wang Yang-ming's theory of innate knowledge guarded against both these dangers. The more he became aware of the necessity for real principles, the more clearly he set his position at a distance from Buddhism; but also the more he rejected the fixing of a real principle, the greater the distance he put between his position and that of the School of Principle. Innate knowledge embraced these two mutually opposed tendencies and rose above them in one ever-present moment of consciousness. With this concept, then, a new School of the Mind arose in Confucianism.

Why was it that the School of Wang Yang-ming, which on the one hand criticized the theory of fixed principle in the School of Chu Hsi and on the other hand rejected the idea of emptiness in Buddhism, later came to separate itself further from the School of Chu Hsi while it moved closer to Buddhism?

One characteristic of the theory of innate knowledge is that one should commit oneself on the basis of one's own independent judgment without relying on established values or norms. Along with strengthening the capacity for the autonomy of innate knowledge, the functions of dissolving established principles and creating new ones are swiftly and carefully performed. Innate knowledge does not follow any set rule, but creates its own rule as occasion demands. Innate knowledge, therefore, is good, but at the same time it possesses a dimension beyond both good and evil. This is the reason that Wang Yang-ming advocated the theory that man's inborn nature is both good and, at the same time, beyond good and evil.

To regard the theory that man's inborn nature is neither good nor evil as incompatible with the teaching of Wang Yang-ming is a misconception which arises from a misunderstanding of the theory of innate knowledge. Now, by the expression "neither good nor evil" [n] we are immediately reminded of Ch'an Buddhism, which seeks the formless Self that transcends all concepts, limitations, and discriminations; refuses to adhere to any fixed view of value; and advocates the idea of "neither good nor evil." The dictum of "neither good nor evil" may well give the impression of indifference to the distinction between good and evil and, consequently, of a disregard of morality. In reality, however, it is only meant to encourage the undertaking of any act with one's whole energy, without the loss of vitality which may result from being overscrupulous or too inhibited by preconceived notions about good and evil. In this sense, the theory of "neither good nor evil" in Ch'an and that of the autonomous capability of innate knowledge in Wang Yang-ming point in the same direction. Indeed, to reject the theory of "neither good nor evil" simply on the ground that it comes from a heterodox teaching runs counter to the essence of innate knowledge. Even if it is a theory which grew up in the heterodoxy called Ch'an, as long as it pertains to the essence of human existence it is not subject to judgment in terms of the distinction between orthodoxy and heterodoxy.

Thus, the embankment between Confucianism and Buddhism, constructed so firmly by the School of Chu Hsi, gradually crumbled, for otherwise innate knowledge could not have developed and been true to itself. It would be an exaggeration to say that the entire thought of Wang Yang-ming is predicated on or permeated by the theory of "neither good nor evil," but it would be equally erroneous to attempt to rule out the theory from his thought, as it played an essential role.

As the process of dissolving fixed principle into innate knowledge continued, the theory of "neither good nor evil" became increasingly superimposed on the theory of innate knowledge, a trend which reached its climax in Wang Chi's ° (1498–1583) formulation of the theory of the Four Negatives. Wang Chi replied to those who were concerned about his approach to Buddhism by saying that "Confucians of today do not know that the teaching of Buddhism was originally the great way of Confucianism." [9] When the trend developed to this point, the scaffolding of the doctrine was removed bit by bit and the inquiry into the nature of man himself came to receive the greatest attention. This trend brought the transmutation of Confucianism and a change in its view of man. The argument that something was correct because it was an assertion of Confucianism and incorrect because it was one of Buddhism became no longer tenable. If what is to be regarded as the first premise of investigation is the mind (man himself) instead of doctrine, and if it is held that to be faithful to this mind is the true spirit of Confucianism, then there is no reason to refuse to listen to the claims of Buddhism as a School of Mind. Consequently, close cooperation between the Buddhist School of Mind and Wang Yang-ming's became possible.

It should be stated that this was not a union of the two schools but a manifestation of the self-conscious activity of the original mind in which these two doctrines were completely grasped. As stated by Yang Fu-so [p] (1547–99): "It is an error to think that Buddhism was transmitted to China in the Han period. What was transmitted to China were the outward traces of Buddhism, while its inner spirit was already here from the beginning." [10] Also, Chiao Hung [q] (1541–1620) had these words to say: "The Buddhist texts are commentaries on Confucianism. The contents of Buddhism are the flowers of Confucianism." [11] Wang Yangming's idea that a distinction between orthodoxy and heterodoxy should be made on the basis of what was appropriate to one's innate knowledge itself was further deepened through internalizing the rejection of heterodoxy (by breaking certain attitudes or habits of mind) and was finally formulated into the idea of the mind as existing prior to the arising of any opposition between orthodoxy and heterodoxy.

The evolution of the Confucian School of Mind in this direction further opened the gap between it and the School of Principle, and this development was severely criticized by those who cherished the School of Principle. Ku Hsien-ch'eng [r] (1550–1612) of the Tung-lin [s] (Eastern Grove) school remarked: "If the theory of 'neither good nor evil' signifies a Nothingness apart from being, it will result in the neglecting of good. If it means that Nothing and being are equated, everything will be carried away by evil." [12] The theory of "neither good nor evil" certainly ran the risk of spawning evil through its disregard of the distinction between good and evil, since from the outset it refused to rely upon any established value system. It was, therefore, susceptible—no matter what it did—to attack from the School of Principle. A man who is liberated from the authority of principle, however, continues to follow the path to freedom at an increasing tempo. From the viewpoint of the School of Principle, the word "freedom" was simply another word for "license." It was inevitable that, as the School of Mind developed in this direction, persons who deviated from all norms should have emerged. In the Wan-li era (1573–1620), when the movement of the School of Mind reached a peak, a succession of radical heretics appeared, the most famous of whom was Li Chih [t] (1527–1602).

The thinkers who most influenced Li Chih were Wang Chi and a Ch'an monk named Ta-hui Tsung-kao [u] (1089–1163). Li Chih's sharp criticism of his age was rooted in the attitude toward traditional norms expressed in this theory of "neither good nor evil." He called the pure mind thoroughly imbued with the spirit of true emptiness the "childlike mind." He was deeply indignant over the hypocrisy and falsity reflected from society upon that innocent mind. This heretic, who in the latter part of his life boldly resorted to the step of renouncing the world to become a Buddhist monk, called himself a "devil" but in his own heart took secret pride in thinking "I am a Buddha in the present age." It may be worth noting that the stormy life of Li Chih led to the fatal result predictable for anyone who attempted to promote the theory of "neither good nor evil" in opposition to the establishment. One cannot help but ask if ever in the past the enlightening flame of emptiness introduced by Buddhism had been so briskly kindled as at this time.

The followers of the theory of "neither good nor evil" were not always radicals like Li Chih. On the contrary, it was possible for some to take quite the opposite course. The School of Mind of Wang Yang-ming originally aimed at creating a new philosophy of real principle by breaking out of the inflexible and stagnant position of the School of Principle; the purpose was to urge people who had hitherto accepted established principles, and never questioned their existence at the source, not to be content with a kind of halfway self-reflection. The struggle of *liang-chih* itself led in two directions, one external, one internal—externally, to disclose the ugliness of mind in contemporary intellectuals, and internally, to remove all the dark shadows lurking within one's own mind. In Wang Yang-ming these two opposites were kept in balance, but his followers emphasized one or the other depending on the transmission of the theory of *liang-chih* that they had received.

Unlike Li Chih who led a colorful life fighting external targets, Kuan Chih-tao [v] (1536–1608) was a scholar who advocated internal purification. In the history of Confucianism Kuan Chih-tao has been regarded as a heretic who thoroughly syncretized Confucianism and Buddhism. It is incorrect, however, to view him as having attempted to give a smashing blow to the School of Principle and to destroy Confucian ethics as Li Chih had done. Kuan Chih-tao's intention in synthesizing Confucianism and Buddhism was to establish support for Confucian ethics on firmer ground than the School of Principle provided. It may appear that if he wished to revitalize Confucian ethics, nothing could have been more contradictory than to turn toward Buddhism while attacking the School of Principle. Why then did he choose this course?

According to Kuan Chih-tao, the School of Principle caused harm by attempting to bind people to principle, and principle consequently failed to function as principle, forcing people to turn to the School of Mind. Turning from the School of Principle to that of Mind did not, however, necessarily assure immediate or unconditional liberation, for people, once fascinated by the bewitching appeal of the School of Mind, as typically shown in the claims of Li Chih, indulged in self-complacency, satisfied that man's happiness would be assured if only moral principles were cast down. As there was a pitfall for principle in the School of Principle, so there was a pitfall for the mind in the School of Mind. A way was sought to restrain the radicalization of the School of Mind of Wang Yang-ming. To this end, Kuan Chih-tao gave attention to the School of Mind in Buddhism.

There were various trends in Buddhist thought, as will be described later, but what attracted Kuan Chih-tao's attention was the humble and severe attitude of self-reflection in the Buddhists' practice of asceticism, repentance, and meditation on the Buddha. Buddhism emphasized the cultivation of a keen introspective power which was unknown in the tradition of Confucianism and for which detailed methods of practice were provided. When the trend generated within the Confucian School of Mind seemed to have endlessly increased man's self-indulgence and arrogance, a strong remedy was called for to restore normal standards. No matter how many stones from the School of Principle one might throw into the river in an effort to reerect the embankment destroyed by the swift current, the stones would only be carried away by the current. The best remedy lay in digging the riverbed deeper, or in other words searching into the fountainhead of human evil in the depths of the mind. If one could find no model in Wang Yang-ming's School of Mind, then the only alternative was to turn to Buddhism for help. Buddhist philosophy, which had developed a theory of mind far subtler than that of Confucianism and which had cultivated the ways to ferret out the hidden passions deeply rooted in the mind, was indeed thought to be an excellent medicine with which to treat a stormy, passionate world.

Thus, Kuan Chih-tao, advancing from Wang Yang-ming's School of Mind, reached out to the Buddhist School of Mind. He never left Confucianism, however, for from the beginning his intention was to rescue Confucian ethics, and he only turned to Buddhism as the most effective means of rescue. His pilgrimage from the School of Principle to Wang Yang-ming's School of Mind and from the latter to the Buddhist School of Mind was not a gradual drifting away, but was a definite journey in search of a base on which the unrest within the School of Principle could be stabilized. He therefore repeatedly insisted on the complementarity of Confucian moral norms and Buddhist enlightenment.

When we compare the standpoint of Kuan Chih-tao with that of Li Chih, we notice that, though the School of Mind of Wang Yang-ming was undoubtedly the common ground to both, the directions from which the two men approached Buddhism were diametrically opposed. It was only natural that Kuan Chih-tao spoke ill of Li Chih, calling him "an exploiter of Confucianism" (pa-ju). [w]

So far, we have taken up two polar figures in the relationship between Buddhism and Confucianism in the late Ming. Ranged between these two positions were many others. All had in common that they turned to Buddhist enlightenment for aid in removing the vices firmly established by long-continued custom, thinking that Buddhism would provide the most thoroughgoing method of reform. They did not, however, find in Buddhism a superior way to solve social problems. Indeed, they tended to approve of the bureaucratic system and of class distinctions based on oc-cupation. To them the most important thing in governing the country was to train one's mind while fulfilling one's individual vocational func-tion. For example, Chou Ju-teng [x] (1547–1629), an ardent successor to Wang Chi in espousing the theory of "neither good nor evil," explained his view of society as follows: "Tao has never from the beginning been anything extraordinary. Tao is there wherever students learn, wherever farmers cultivate the soil, wherever monks recite sutras, wherever officials govern, each satisfied with his given status." [13]

Yang Ch'i-yüan [y] (1547–99) was a man who so firmly believed in the unity of Confucianism and Buddhism that he said: "Confucius and Men-cius are the Sākyamunis of China." At the same time, it is said that his daily conduct was exemplary and he was never guilty of violating any of the official regulations. We wonder how those who stood on a similar footing with Yang Ch'i-yüan evaluated Li Chih? Though they responded warmly to the enthusiasm of Li Chih—who perceived the root of the evils of the time and pointed out the hypocrisy and corruption in bureaucratic life—they could not possibly have approved of the unusual step he took in renouncing his official career and becoming a Buddhist monk, nor could they have accepted his violent social criticism. The viewpoint of both Chou Ju-teng and Yang Ch'i-yüan was that, even if the way of purifying the spirit taught by Buddhism might be the most suitable method for saving the world at the time, social reform should be attempted gradually, in keeping with existing social conditions. Accordingly, they remained concerned over the possibility that others might appear to follow and imitate Li Chih.

How, then, did they evaluate Kuan Chih-tao? Kuan Chih-tao—who with passionate sincerity freed himself from the confines of a narrow and intolerant doctrine, who sought in Buddhism an answer to the problem of the fundamental basis of human existence, and who made an effort to break down the inflexible principle-consciousness of the Ch'eng school— would certainly have been entitled to a high evaluation for his sincerity. However, he criticized the popular movement of Confucian lecturing initiated by Wang Ken [z] (1483–1541) among all classes, saying that such a movement presented a danger of throwing the teaching of social morality into confusion; Kuan Chih-tao was extremely fearful that the movement might bring forth a climate of extreme liberalization or even radicalization. And there might indeed have been some risk that the awakening of the populace would bring confusion to the order of the status society. Nevertheless, for him to have attempted to suppress it was a mistake. Thus Kuan Chih-tao's concern to defend traditional norms, which led him to seek help from the Buddhist School of Mind, was not unmixed with a strong gentry-consciousness. Chou Ju-teng and Yang Ch'i-yüan could hardly have approved of that.

It is now clear that the trend to harmonize Confucianism with Buddhism in the late Ming was not a monolinear movement of thought but a manifold one which embraced extremely different views of society. Evidence for this can be found in the fact that the School of Wang Yang-ming was divided into three branches: left, middle, and right. As stated before, the School of Mind originally was characterized by the fact that it allowed each individual to learn and to act on his own initiative without conforming to any set standard. As long as the development of the School of Mind remained faithful to this character, it was inevitable that the movement to harmonize Confucianism with Buddhism should itself split into many groups. Regardless of the existence of such diverse and divisive trends, however, Wang Yang-ming's School of Mind succeeded in enfolding the Buddhist School of Mind within it, thus deepening and strengthening itself, and intensifying its role as a critic of the School of Principle.

The trend toward harmonizing Confucianism with Buddhism was also manifested in various ways in the intellectual life of the time. One noteworthy development was that the interpretations of the Four Books and the Five Classics given by the School of Chu Hsi, which had held the status of a state teaching since the beginning of the Ming, were no longer accepted. The compilation of the Great Compendia of the Four Books and the Five Classics [aa] during the reign of the third emperor of the Ming, Ch'eng-tsu (Yung-lo),[ab] had as their aim the unifying of popular thought through the civil examinations; but, along with the rise and expansion of schools of the Mind, feelings of dissatisfaction with the Great Compendia were continually expressed, and the view that the Books and Classics should not be read and accepted literally, but rather understood through the mind, was repeatedly heard as time went on. The idea that one should not be a slave to the texts had recurred again and again in one corner of the history of Chinese thought since the rise of Ch'an Buddhism in the T'ang period; and in Sung Confucianism it became crystallized in the famous words of Lu Hsiang-shan [ac] (1139–92) that "the Six Classics are the footnotes of the mind." [14]

In the middle of the Ming, when the School of Wang Yang-ming emerged, this feeling became more and more conspicuous. As evidenced by the words of Wang Yang-ming that "the Four Books and the Five Classics merely explain the essence of the mind," [15] Wang Yang-ming's School of Mind established the idea that the mind (innate knowledge) had priority over the Classics (which does not mean that it ignored the Classics) and individual awakening had priority over tradition. Furthermore, Wang Yang-ming thought that, because the commentaries of Chu Hsi on the Four Books then in use for the examinations contained the as yet imperfectly formed opinions of Chu Hsi in his middle age, to adhere to them was to misunderstand Chu Hsi.[16] According to the theory of innate knowledge, to rely on the supreme authority of Books, Classics, and their commentaries was to impair the autonomy of innate knowledge and to compromise the integrity of the individual.

It goes without saying that the School of Wang Yang-ming did not encourage one to ignore the Books and the Classics or to abandon the love of letters. But Wang maintained that unless we understand the Books and the Classics on the basis of our own experience and put their teachings into practice, we are treating them with contempt, acting contrary to their teachings. Freedom in interpreting them, however, once put in the hands of the individual, was gradually expanded along with the popularization of the School of Wang Yang-ming, and finally the individual became free even from the authority of these texts.

With this freedom came the decline in influence of established doctrine and the rise in influence of independent thought. Stereotypes were looked down upon and original ideas appreciated. Thus, the vogue of the School of Mind brought about a decline in the study of the Classics. Not without justification was it said that in the Ming period classical studies fell into the extreme of decadence; and yet, this decline did not mean absence of speculation. On the contrary, the current of free interpretation of the Classics and the Books (particularly the Four Books) was accelerated and the study of the Four Books, independent of tradition, became fashionable. This trend developed for the same essential reasons as the attempt at harmonizing Confucianism with Buddhism discussed above: that Buddhist ideas and attitudes were strongly projected into interpretations of the Four Books. If we take up the section on the Four Books in the *Ssu-k'u ch'üan-shu tsung-mu t'i-yao* [ad] (Essentials of the complete catalog of the Four Libraries), we are surprised at the abundance of commentaries written in the vein of Confucian-Buddhist syncretism. A man of letters in the late Ming, Yüan Tsung-tao [ae] (1560–1600) said: "The sages of the three teachings though they differ from one another in their teachings, remain the same in their fundamental spirit. It is not irresponsible to assert that we can understand Confucianism for the first time only after we have studied Ch'an." [17]

In this manner, commentaries on the Four Books, unrestricted by tradition, were produced in the late Ming. Formerly, during the T'ang and Sung periods when Ch'an was in vogue, Ch'an's disregard of Buddhist sūtras was a shocking thing in religious and scholarly circles. In these periods, under the influence of Ch'an, new interpretations of the Four

Books were attempted, but Buddhism was never openly adopted into them. Its influence was hidden between the lines and the Confucian attitude of moderation was apparent. In the interpretations of the Four Books in the late Ming, however, Buddhist technical terms and concepts were more or less straightforwardly adopted, even to the extent of giving the impression that this was a rather normal practice. The followers of the Chu Hsi School at that time understandably deplored this trend, saying that "people are not only rejecting Chu Hsi but also trying to go beyond Confucius and Mencius." [18]

In the late Ming, as we have said, with the spread of the School of Mind of Wang Yang-ming, there was also a revival of Buddhism. It had long been thought among Confucians in general that when Confucianism flourished Buddhism declined and when Buddhism thrived Confucianism dwindled. This is certainly true in part and can be verified in some periods of the history of Chinese thought. However, as far as the late Ming is concerned, this established opinion cannot be maintained, for in this period clearly both the School of Wang Yang-ming and Buddhism shared popular favor. It may not be wrong to state that for the development of the School of Wang Yang-ming Buddhism was necessary, and for the popularization of Buddhism the School of Wang Yang-ming was indispensable. An eminent monk of the late Ming, Ou-i Chih-hsü [af] (1599–1655), said: "The rise or fall of the Buddha Dharma is contingent upon the rise or fall of Confucianism. The virtuous action and learning of Confucians are the life of Buddhists." [19]

This revival of Buddhism in the late Ming, as we have seen, owed much to Wang Yang-ming's theory of innate knowledge, which undermined the basis of the School of Principle and which went beyond the framework of traditional doctrines. Ch'an Buddhism attained its zenith in the early part of the Southern Sung and then gradually declined. In the Chia-ching (1522–67) and Lung-ch'ing (1567–72) eras of the Ming period it had fallen into extreme decadence without producing any eminent man of ability. The sudden rise of Buddhism, centering around the activities of the so-called three eminent monks in the Wan-li era, is thought to have owed much to developments in the School of Wang Yang-ming rather than to any internal development in Buddhism itself.

The Buddhism of this period of revival was different from that in the

T'ang period. It goes without saying that Buddhists, liberated from the framework of sect and tradition, sought freely for ways to attain individual enlightenment. Under these circumstances a kind of syncretic faith developed. For example, one of the three eminent monks in the Wan-li era, Yün-ch'i Chu-hung [ag] (1535–1615), often preached the idea of the unity of Ch'an and Pure Land Buddhism. Furthermore, in his major work, a commentary on the Amitā Sūtra (*A-mi-t'o ching su ch'ao*), [ah] he utilized the Hua-yen philosophy expounded by Tsung-mi (780–841) to interpret the sūtra. Promoting strict observance of monastic disciplines, he wrote the *Fan-wang ching hsin-ti-p'in p'u-sa-chieh i-su fa-yin*, [ai] and finally advocated even the idea of the identity of Confucianism and Buddhism.

Han-shan Te-ch'ing [aj] (1546–1623) also advocated the idea of the unity of Ch'an and Pure Land Buddhism, and that of doctrinal Buddhism and Ch'an. Breaking away from the pattern for Ch'an monks, he wrote commentaries not only on many Buddhist sūtras but also on non-Buddhist texts such as the *Lao-tzu* and *Chuang-tzu*. Moreover Ou-i Chih-hsü synthesized Ch'an and T'ien-t'ai Buddhism, which were said to have been mortal rivals for many years, and conceived a distinctive religious philosophy.

Seen from the viewpoint of Japanese Buddhist sects, each of which prided itself on a religious purity attained through clarifying its differences with others, the movements of syncretism described above may appear to have been signs of decadence in Buddhist thought. Buddhism in the late Ming gives us the impression that its faith was weak and its followers were satisfied with questionable spiritual reassurances. To treat Buddhist movements in the late Ming from the standpoint of whether they were pure or impure, however, is not very much to the point. People who had been liberated from the School of Principle, and who freely sought a way to consolidate the foundations of their faith, gave priority to their own wishes over sectarian authority. For them, to adhere to sectarian allegiances meant accepting their own spiritual death, while to transcend such allegiances was thought to be a reaffirmation of their own original nature.

Admittedly, Buddhism in the late Ming gave birth to no new sect, as had Sui and T'ang Buddhism, but it produced a new type of Buddhist faith instead. This new type, however, had almost as many forms as it had believers. Accordingly, when an outstanding religious leader died, there was little likelihood of his leaving behind him a well-organized order. Therefore, Buddhism found itself in a condition where the formation of any solid organization as a religious group was difficult and, hence, the revival of Buddhism was bound to be short-lived. But given the differences in the historical circumstances and the spiritual needs of the time, it is probably pointless to adjudge the Buddhist movements of this period as inferior to those in the Sui, T'ang, and Sung periods.

The second characteristic of Buddhism in the late Ming was that the Buddhist faith was closely linked to the everyday world so that Buddhists presented lively opinions on secular problems from their own religious points of view. It was Ta-hui Tsung-kao in the early Southern Sung who established the precedent of trying to solve secular problems in the light of Buddhist thought and to overcome difficulties through the mind of Ch'an. Though this tradition had continued in an unbroken line throughout the Yüan and Ming periods, it had experienced a gradual decline. When the spirit of Ta-hui was almost forgotten, Wang Yang-ming appeared, and under the impetus of the movement of the School of Mind there was a revival of Buddhism after the Wan-li era. In short, it can be said that the spirit of Ta-hui was revived in response to the demands of the new age; Ch'an monks in this period without exception turned toward Ta-hui and even monks belonging to the Ts'ao-tung sect of a different lineage recommended reading the works of Ta-hui.

Now, the challenge of solving the problems of everyday life through the mind of Ch'an could be posed individually in varied ways; naturally, different views of society were expressed just as differences were manifested in the formation of subschools of Wang Yang-ming's School of Mind. If we examine the three eminent monks in the Wan-li era on this point, we find that it was Yün-ch'i Chu-hung who maintained the most moderate view of society. He formed the largest society for the recitation of Buddha's name (nien-fo) [ak] in the late Ming in a small village near Hang-chou. There were profound reasons why he left the cities and chose a mountain village for this. One reason was his fear of Buddhists' losing the purity of the faith by living in cities of great affluence, gaiety, and material consumption, and which were also enmeshed in the bureaucratic system. Another reason was the need he felt to draw a definite line between the established Buddhist world and himself. He who started a new Buddhist society independently, in resistance to the general slackness of the religious and secular worlds, first of all proclaimed as imperative the strict observance of the daily norms of both the religious and secular orders, namely, the disciplinary precepts and regulations. His saying that "the precepts are the original ground of the mind of both Buddhas and sentient beings" [20] expresses the idea that the precepts are to be observed not by any external coercion, but through one's spontaneous initiative. People's minds, liberated from moral norms by the liberal attitudes of the School of Mind, more and more exhibited the unruliness of an untamed horse. There was already an irreversible tide which could not be stopped by politics or punishment. To arrest it, Chu-hung thought, it was urgent to restore man's sense of self-control and to accomplish this there was no more effective and thorough way than observance of the disciplinary precepts.

The ultimate goal of the Buddha Dharma is to transcend good and evil. Yet the precepts require man to conform himself to set rules in specific instances and actions. How could these two views be reconciled? The answer given by Chu-hung was: "The essence of this mind is neither good nor evil, but its function is to practice good and to suppress evil. It is the precepts that give direction to the practice of good and to the suppression of evil." [21] Thus, Chu-hung asserted on the one hand that the self-control of the mind was strengthened by the consciousness of good and evil, while on the other hand he thought that this extraordinary self-control indeed enhanced the value of the Buddhist law. Here the consciousness of self-restraint was rooted in the original source of the mind, transcending the secular law-abiding consciousness. This mind, however, did not look down upon secular norms; rather, it could be expected to support them from a deeper level. On this point Chu-hung's view of the disciplinary precepts was in common with the normative consciousness of Kuan Chih-tao, discussed earlier, which is not strange since Kuan Chih-tao was an enthusiastic follower of Chu-hung. Accordingly, Chu-hung preached that "monks should remember the favors that they have received from the state and should not violate its laws," [22] and that "the laws of Confucianism and those of Buddhism are similar, but they differ in details." [23]

Next, one of the characteristics of Chu-hung's thought was that he earnestly advocated the idea of rebirth in the Pure Land. He clearly believed in the compatibility of Ch'an and Pure Land Buddhism, as evidenced by the fact that he wrote a major commentary on the Amitā Sūtra (A-mi-t'o ching su ch'ao) and also compiled a Ch'an anthology, the Ch'an-kuan ts'e-chin.[al] Chu-hung's aim in uniting Ch'an with Pure Land Buddhism was to have those who were infatuated with Ch'an reflect on their willful and reckless attitude and on their tendency to be satisfied with what they conceitedly believed to be the experience of attaining enlightenment. He also sought to restore this stability of mind by means of nien-fo meditation and prayer. When Ta-hui Tsung-kao in the Sung initiated the movement for relating the mind of Ch'an to the problems of everyday life Ch'an had a formidable, if not frightening, potential energy for the reformation of the actual world. This is because if a man wishes to overcome the difficulties of the actual world, as Ta-hui says, by elevating life into a unity which transcends the differentiation of right from wrong and good from evil, he may cut down the established values one after the other, like a violent wind sweeping over the land and strewing wreckage behind it.

This Ch'an of Ta-hui had been lurking underground for some time, like a sleeping dragon, but as the School of Wang Yang-ming spread its influence in the late Ming, once again the bold figure of Ta-hui Ch'an made its appearance. Kuan Chih-tao, who detected this threatening crisis, criticized the Ch'an of Ta-hui by saying that "it has left behind it the root of arrogance." Chu-hung, too, although attracted to the vigorous spirit of the Ch'an of Ta-hui, had also to consider seriously its tendency to go to excess. To prevent the spread of this demonic Ch'an, the best safeguard was the Pure Land Buddhism which taught nine ways of being born into the Pure Land, and which urged ethical self-examination as a basis for taking refuge in Amitābha Buddha. Chu-hung thought this was the best method by which to bring back to the correct path those who were plunging into decadence and disorder.

By taking Ch'an into the embrace of Pure Land Buddhism and not allowing it to act independently, Chu-hung meant to use Ch'an to revitalize the practice of meditation on rebirth in the Pure Land. He expected no more than this. Thus the possibility existed that Ch'an's wild nature would be tamed by Pure Land Buddhism. Chu-hung's contemporary, T'u Lung [am] (1542–1605), praised him for his quiet self-possession: "His mind is serene like lapis lazuli and his appearance is like jade," [24] while Feng Meng-lung [an] (1574–1646) expressed his dissatisfaction by saying, "There are always several hundred disciples at the side of Chu-hung, but not even half of them are Ch'an monks." [25]

In contrast to Chu-hung, Tzu-po Ta-kuan [ao] (1544–1604) utilized the keen insight inherent in the Ch'an of Ta-hui to deal with actual social problems and to bitterly criticize the bureaucrats for their hypocrisy and self-righteousness. In contrast to Chu-hung's belief that the cause of corruption lay in the selfishness of men who refused to conform to the established order, Ta-kuan thought that it was due to the irresponsibility of those charged with maintaining order, namely, the bureaucrats and eunuchs. To arrive at a fundamental solution to the social crisis, Ta-kuan thought that those in power, instead of making formal gestures of sympathy to the people, should seek a penetrating understanding of the emptiness of nonattachment, cut off the root of self-clinging, and share the sufferings of the people with sincere love.

What were the actual conditions of the bureaucratic life at that time? Li Chih, attacking the corruption of the bureaucrats, said that "they are great robbers clad in official robes and caps," [26] and Ta-kuan said that "thieves are easy to catch because they live in mountains and forests and use weapons, but those who live under the protection of official robes and caps and who take advantage of their names and ranks are difficult to catch." [27] Reproaching for their negligence and irresponsibility those who refused to face up to this reality, Ta-kuan often quoted a passage from the Buddhist text *Pa-ta-jen-chüeh ching* [ap] [28] that stated that "the mind is the source of evils and the body is the abode of sins." The reason for his citing this passage was not to urge people to feel the transiency and corruptibility of all things, but to arouse their anger against their own misery and, in turn, against corruption in the society. For Ta-kuan, therefore, his anger over his own negligence was anger over his not having taken positive steps to cleanse society. Therefore, the characteristic of Ta-kuan's thought as a Buddhist was the extremely high value he set upon activity (*yung*). [aq] The term *yung* had hitherto been used in Ch'an, but its meaning had most often been no more than "response" or "question and answer" within the confines of a closed religious order. Ta-kuan's *yung*, however, meant to work upon the world of historical reality by means of the enlightenment experience. He said: "Nothing exists apart from the self and there is no self apart from things. Since there is no self apart from things, the activities (*yung*) of the self are the activities of things. Since there is no thing apart from the self, the activities of things are those of the self." [29]

This is the theory of the unity (communion) of all things which he expounded. Its lively spirit of love gave him a courage which did not yield to any misfortune. When he became convinced that the difficult problems of the day could no longer be solved by secular rulers and their followers, and when he moved closer to the position of claiming to be a Dharma King, he was clearly destined for future calamity. Finally, when he openly challenged the secular authority to a fight, Ta-kuan, like Li Chih, was imprisoned and committed suicide. His saying that "cutting off our hair is like cutting off our heads; we [monks] no longer have heads to be cut off" [30] reveals his determination to sacrifice himself for his mission as a Buddhist. When Ta-kuan died in prison, a narrow-minded intellectual remarked: "If anyone behaves as a heretic, he will of course be killed. Li Chih and Ta-kuan are good object lessons." [31] Just as Li Chih was considered "a demonic being" by members of the gentry class, so Ta-kuan was regarded as a "heretic" in Buddhist circles. Ta-kuan felt sympathy for the death of Li Chih, but Chu-hung evaluated it coolly, which may reveal the distance between them.

As shown conspicuously in these two figures, the intentions and attitudes of Buddhists varied one from another. And yet, they had one thing in common in that they bitterly criticized Chu Hsi but responded to Wang Yang-ming sympathetically. In short, they thought that one could become a gentleman in the secular world by means of the School of Chu Hsi, but could not reach any higher spiritual stage, while by means of the School of Wang Yang-ming one could attain real enlightenment, breaking through the limitations of Confucianism. Seen from the point of view of the School of Wang Yang-ming, Buddhism could be regarded as an empty and subjective speculation which was ultimately devoid of real principle; on the other hand, seen from the point of view of Buddhism, the School of Wang Yang-ming could be evaluated as a halfway enlightenment yet to be freed from bondage to the secular world. Thus these two Schools of Mind developed, paying close attention to each other's movements. Particularly the Buddhist School of Mind, by pointing out the limitations of the School of Wang Yang-ming, attempted to demonstrate the superiority of the Buddha Dharma and went so far as to claim that the Buddha Dharma was the fountainhead of the Schools of Mind.

Thus, Buddhists, who had long since resigned themselves to the stigma of being "followers of heterodoxy" for many years after the Sung period, came to take pride in themselves for having furnished a philosophy dealing with what they considered the most fundamental principle, and to claim that even movements toward the reformation of Confucianism had followed in the path of Buddhism. Evidence of this is found in the words of Chih-hsü, "The Confucians, the successors of Wang Yang-ming, are without exception turning their minds toward Buddhism." [32]

As we have shown above, the School of Mind differed from the School of Principle in that, rather than producing a fixed doctrine, it called for the formation of thought through the initiative of the committed individual himself in actual practice. Therefore, both the Confucian School of Mind and the Buddhist developed manifold subbranches and their boundaries became vague. The trend of the Schools of Mind, which arose spontaneously and developed freely, without establishing any solid, real principle, was bound to be criticized by the School of Principle as no more than the play of subjective speculation. The more the Schools of Mind tried to be faithful to themselves, the more difficult they found it to settle upon any real principle, for they were strongly disinclined to abide by any fixed standard of value. But without such a standard of value, their creative function in history was left hanging in midair. One method of solving this difficult problem was to attempt to synthesize appropriately the School of Chu Hsi and that of Wang Yang-ming. A typical example of this is found in Ku Hsien-ch'eng of the Tung-lin school. Ku thought, "If we took Chu Hsi as a standard we would be too constrained, and if we took Wang Yang-ming as a standard we would be too self-indulgent." [33] Thus he regarded Chu Hsi and Wang Yang-ming as mere offshoots of the School of Confucius. [34]

The greatest dissatisfaction Ku had with the School of Wang Yang-ming was its theory of absence of good and evil. According to him, this theory, if it drifted into Emptiness (*k'ung*), [ar] would result in the neglect of benevolence, righteousness, and propriety, and, if it drifted into chaos (*hun*), [as] would lead to loss of distinction between good and evil. [35] The standpoint of Ku, who emphasized the core of real principle and aimed at the realization of a vital humanity, had something in common with that of Kuan Chih-tao as far as their motivations were concerned. However, concerning the theory of absence of good and evil, their opinions were sharply at variance. Chih-tao said, "The fact that Wang Yang-ming put forward the theory of absence of good and evil and demonstrated the unity of Confucianism and Buddhism showed his superior discernment." [36] Against this view Ku raised strong objections, saying that "if it [the mind] was seen as neither good nor evil, our inclination to do good could not help but be lessened." [37]

When Ku opened the Tung-lin Academy and set up the basis for his positive educational activities, Chih-tao sent his heartfelt blessings, but the two men may well have felt some frustration over being unable to communicate their true feelings to each other. In time the followers of the Tung-lin school, trying to reconcile their attraction to Wang Yang-ming with their concern over the damage done by the theory of absence of good and evil, concluded that the theory was actually put forward by Wang Chi in contravention of Wang Yang-ming's teachings. How much emphasis Wang Yang-ming put on the theory of absence of good and evil in his teachings merits separate investigation, but to presuppose that the essence of the theory of innate knowledge has nothing to do with the theory of absence of good and evil can hardly be considered a valid approach. As long as the School of Wang Yang-ming remained a School of Mind, like it or not, the theory of absence of good and evil had to be retained in its basic structure. For the harm that came from it Wang Yang-ming cannot be held responsible; it was the responsibility of the innate knowledge of each individual concerned. At the same time the question as to how close the School of Wang Yang-ming should come to Buddhism was not one that awaited the guidance of Wang Yang-ming. It also was one for each individual to put to his own innate knowledge. Indeed, such being the case, there is a fundamental difficulty in any attempt to categorize the relationships of Confucianism and Buddhism in the late Ming.

Translated by Yoshito S. Hakeda and Wm. Theodore de Bary

NOTES

1. Yung-chia hsüan-chüeh: [at] *Chêng-tao ko*. Taishō daizōkyō, 47.
2. *Erh Ch'eng ch'üan-shu*,[au] compiled by Chu Hsi, collated by Hsü Pi-ta, Japanese edition (Edo), 40/30.
3. *Chu Tzu yü-lei ta-ch'üan*,[av] compiled by Li Ching-te, edition of Ch'eng-hua 9 (1473), Chung wen ch'u-pan-she, 4/100.
4. *Ibid.*, 9/252–53.
5. *Ibid.*, 62/2353.
6. *Wang Wen-ch'êng kung ch'üan-shu* [aw] (Hong Kong, 1959), Kuang-chih shu-chü, 31/603, Shan-tung hsiang-shih-lu.
7. *Erh Ch'eng ch'üan-shu*, 2/17.
8. *Wang Wen-ch'êng kung ch'üan-shu*, 7/51, Pieh Chan Kan-ch'üan hsü.[ax]
9. *Wang Lung-hsi ch'üan-chi*,[ay] compiled by Ting Pin, edition of Wan-li 43 (1615), Japanese edition (Edo), 1/18, San-shan-li-tse lu.
10. *Yang Fu-so ch'üan-chi*,[az] compiled by Chao Hou, edition of Wan-li 27 (1599), p. 10, Tung-jih chi (The Cabinet Library of Japan).
11. *Chiao-shih pi-ch'eng hsü-chi*,[ba] Yüeh-ya-t'ang ts'ung-shu, 2/3.
12. *Ku Tuan-wen kung i-shu*,[bb] edition of Kuang-hsü 3 (1877), Ching-li tsung-tz'u ts'ang, 4/3, Hsiao-hsin-chai cha-chi.
13. *Tung-yüeh cheng-hsüeh-lu*,[bc] edition of Wan-li 33 (1605), Wen-hai ch'u-pan she, 10/774.
14. *Lu Hsiang-shan ch'üan-chi*,[bd] Shang-hai Han-fen-lou ying-yin, edition of Chia-ching, 34/1 (SPTK).
15. *Ch'uan-hsi lu*,[be] in *Wang Wen-ch'eng kung ch'üan-shu*, A/10.
16. *Wang Wen-ch'êng kung ch'üan-shu*, 7/57, Chu Tzu wan-nien ting-lun hsü.[bf]
17. *Pai Su-chai lei chi* [bg] (Ming edition), 17/1.
18. *Keng T'ien-t'ai ch'üan-shu*,[bh] edition of Wan-li 26 (1580), Wen-hai ch'u-pan she, 6/661 Yü Hsiao Chi-she.
19. *Ling-feng Ou-i tsung-lun*,[bi] Japanese edition of Kōhō 8 (1723), 2–4/16.
20. *Fan-wang ching hsin-ti-p'in p'u-sa-chieh i-su fa-yin*,[bj] in *Dai Nihon zoku zōkyō*, 5/411.
21. *Ibid.*, 1/325.
22. *Ibid.*, 1/342.
23. *Ibid.*, p. 423.
24. *Fo-fa chin-t'ang lu*,[bk] Japanese edition of Enpō 8 (1680), B/48.
25. *K'uai-hsüeh t'ang chi*,[bl] compiled by Feng Meng-chen, edition of Wan-li 44 (1616), 38/34.
26. *Fen-shu*,[bm] Lo Chin-hsi hsien-sheng kao-wen (Ming edition), 3/65.
27. *Tzu-po lao-jen chi*,[bn] in *Dai Nihon zoku zōkyō*, 21/503, Chieh t'an pao shuo.
28. *Taishō Tripitaka*,[bo] Vol. XVII, no. 779, p. 715.

29. *Tzu-po lao-jen chi, chüan-shou,*[bp] p. 320, Ching Ta-chung.
30. *Tzu-po lao-jen chi, pieh-chi,* in *Dai Nihon zoku zōkyō* 3/63, Yü Feng K'ai-chih.[bq]
31. *Wu-tsa-tsu*[br] Japanese edition of Bunsei 6 (1823), 13/3.
32. *Ling-feng Ou-i tsung-lung,* 4–3/18.
33. *Ku Tuan-wen kung i-shu,* in Hsiao-hsin-chai cha-chi, 3/5.
34. *Ku Tuan-wen kung i-shu,* 11/8, Ching-kao ts'ang-kao.[bs]
35. *Ku Tuan-wen kung i-shu,* 18/3.
36. *Ku Tuan-wen kung i-shu,* A/7, compiled by Cheng Hsing.[bt]
37. *Ibid.,* p. 21.

GLOSSARY

a 心学
b 理学
c 定学
d 禅
e 性
f 情
g 定理
h 性即理
i 心即理
j 陳獻章
k 以自然為宗
l 良知
m 程明道
n 無善無悪
o 王畿
p 楊復所
q 焦竑
r 顧憲成
s 東林
t 李贄
u 大慧宗杲
v 管志道
w 霸儒
x 周汝登
y 楊起元
z 王艮
aa 四書五經大全
ab 成祖(永樂帝)
ac 陸象山
ad 四庫全書總目提要
ae 袁宗道
af 藕益智旭
ag 雲棲袾宏
ah 阿彌陀經疏鈔
ai 梵網經心地品菩薩
　　戒義疏發隱

aj 憨山德清
ak 念佛
al 禪關策進
am 屠隆
an 馮夢龍
ao 紫柏達觀
ap 八大人覺經
aq 用
ar 空
as 混
at 永嘉玄覺，證道歌
　　（大正藏47收）
au 二程全書，朱熹編
　　徐必達和版（江
　　戶）
av 朱子語類大全
　　黎靖德編
　　成化9年刊本影
　　印中文出版社
aw 王文成公全書
　　山東鄉試錄
　　1959年
　　香港廣智書局刊
ax 別湛甘泉序
ay 王龍溪全集
　　三山麗澤錄
　　丁賓等編
　　萬曆43年
　　和版（江戶）
az 楊復所全集
　　冬日記　趙厚編
　　萬曆27年
　　（日本內閣文庫
　　藏）
ba 焦氏筆乘續集
　　粵雅堂叢書收

bb 顧端文公遺書
　　小心齋劄記
　　光緒3年
　　涇里宗祠藏版
bc 東越證學錄
　　萬曆33年刊本影印
　　文海出版社
bd 陸象山全集
　　上海涵芬樓影印
　　嘉靖刊本
　　（四部叢刊收）
be 傳習錄
　　王文成公全書收
bf 朱子晚年定論序
bg 白蘇齋類集
　　明刊本
bh 耿天臺全書
　　與蕭給舍
　　萬曆26年刊本影印
　　文海出版社
bi 靈峰藕益宗論
　　享保8年　和版
bj 梵網經心地品菩薩
　　戒義疏發隱
　　（大日本續藏經
　　收）
bk 佛法金湯錄
　　延寶8年　和版
bl 快雪堂集
　　報密藏師兄
　　馮夢禎撰
　　萬曆44年
bm 焚書
　　羅近谿先生告文
　　明刊本

bn　紫柏老人集
　　戒貪暴說
　　（大日本續藏經
　　收）
bo　大正新修大藏經
bp　紫柏老人集卷首
　　警大衆

bq　與馮開之
br　五雜俎
　　　文政 6 年　和版
bs　涇臯藏稿
bt　證性編

PEI-YI WU *The Spiritual Autobiography*

of Te-ch'ing

Generally considered one of the last great Buddhist monks of the Ming, Te-ch'ing [a] (1546–1623) in many ways exemplifies the contemporary intellectual climate in general and the style of the late Ming Buddhism in particular. He shared with his two equals in critical renown, Chu-hung [b] (1535–1615) and Chen-k'o [c] or Ta-kuan (1544–1604), the adulation of the populace, an easy rapport with the Confucian literati, a profound belief in the syncretism of the Three Teachings, and an insistence on the combination of the Ch'an regimen with the Pure Land practice; but he was more active in worldly affairs than one and more voluminous in exegetical writings than the other. In fact he wrote commentaries not only on most of the major Buddhist scriptures but also on such Taoist and Confucian texts as the *Tao te ching*, the *Chuang-tzu*, the *Tso chuan*, and the *Chung yung*. His exposition of the *Ta hsüeh* was entirely in line with Neo-Confucian practice, without any explicit reference to his religion. For our purpose, however, the most remarkable thing about him is that less than a year before his death he wrote an account of his long and eventful life.[1] This work is the first full-fledged autobiography ever written by a Chinese Buddhist monk.[2]

Autobiography apparently flourished in China during Han times, but for a number of reasons it went into decline after the Six Dynasties. The seventeenth century, on the other hand, witnessed a resurgence of the genre.[3] It is entirely possible that the same factors to which the critics attribute the rise of autobiography in Renaissance Europe were also at work in late Ming China, factors such as rapid social mobility, political turmoil, new interest in genealogy and family history, and, above all, growing individualism and sense of the self.[4] In Te-ch'ing's case, as we shall attempt to establish, both the act of writing an autobiography and the particular shape that his work took had much to do with the intellectual and spiritual climate of his time: his is not the work of a solitary genius but that of a man who was deeply immersed in the mainstream of events.

As such, and even if as nothing more, his autobiography is an invaluable document for its historical and psychological interest and for the light it sheds on the state of Buddhism in his day. A proper appreciation of its originality, both in conception and execution, may perhaps in turn strengthen the new view, which has emerged only in recent years, that the late Ming was a time of great intellectual ferment and creative vitality rather than the lowest level of a long trough.[5]

The format that Te-ch'ing chose for his work is that of a self-edited *nien-p'u*,[d] a subgenre of biography modeled upon the annalistic type of history. First appearing in the Sung period, the *nien-p'u* is a year-by-year account of a man's life. It is, as aptly described by Denis Twitchett, "usually a succession of carefully dated discrete facts, with no attempt to connect them in any meaningful causal pattern; it makes no attempt to provide any explicit interpretation of its subjects, and is best described as materials for a biography rather than biography itself."[6]

The *nien-p'u* format, as described above, does not seem to be a satisfactory medium for recounting a life with shape or unity. But Te-ch'ing is unique among the annalistic autobiographers: he underwent an essential change while all the others, in spite of the vicissitudes of the scholar's tenure and the official's career, remained very much the same men from birth to death. It is this change, continuous but nonlinear—the initial crises, the early conditioning, the subsequent reinforcement, the hesitations and temptations, the backslidings, the strenuous efforts, and the ultimate enlightenment—that gives Te-ch'ing's life up to his thirty-first year a meaningful pattern. Making the most of the natural drift and purport of his life story, he neither strains the plausibility of his conversion nor fails to see the significance of even minor details. When an interesting life is told by a sure-handed master, even the limitations of the *nien-p'u* format cannot prevent the emergence of a distinct and coherent narrative, which may be called in this case the spiritual autobiography of a Buddhist monk.

Te-ch'ing's autobiography begins with the usual account of family and origin, but he keeps that part to a minimum and proceeds to his first spiritual crisis, which occurred in his seventh year. One day when he was out his beloved uncle died and was placed in a bed.

When I came back from school my mother purposely said to me: "Your uncle is asleep. Why don't you go and wake him up?" I tried to call him several times. Then my aunt, looking very sad, cried:

"Alas, he's gone!"
Completely puzzled, I asked my mother:
"Uncle is right here; how can he have gone away?"
"Your uncle is dead," my mother replied.
Where does a dead man go? I was even more puzzled. Shortly afterwards my aunt gave birth to a boy. My mother went to see her and I followed. When I noticed the size of the baby I asked my mother:
"How did this baby enter into Auntie's belly?"
My mother patted me and said:
"Little fool, how did you get into your mother's belly?"
I could not answer. The great puzzle of life and death could not be understood.[7]

Life and death indeed are the ultimate mysteries with which all religions must grapple, and it was only fitting that the future Buddhist master should have been exposed at an early age to the same shattering forces which had set Prince Siddhārtha on his momentous spiritual journey. What is unusual in Te-ch'ing's first crisis is that it was entirely his mother's making. Not only did she not shield her son, as most post-Freudian mothers would have done, from traumatic experiences, but she actually precipitated him, a mere child of seven, into struggles and puzzles of a sort that frequently confronted Ch'an disciples. Indeed, the deliberate and decisive role that the mother played in the development of Te-ch'ing clearly emerges as his childhood and adolescence unfold.

When I was eight I was boarded with a relative across the river so I could attend school. My mother allowed me to come home only once a month. One day while on a home visit I clung to my mother and refused to go back. She became angry and whipped me. When she chased me to the river bank I refused to board the boat. She was so incensed that she grabbed me by the hair and dropped me into the river. She left without looking back. My grandmother happened to notice my plight and cried for help. After I was rescued she took me home. My mother said: "What is the use of saving this stupid boy from drowning!" Relentlessly she again drove me out. Thereupon I thought that my mother was completely heartless, and from that time on I was no longer homesick.[8]

The mother appears in this episode unreasonably harsh, even by seventeenth-century standards, but Te-ch'ing goes on to relate, apparently from hearsay, an incident which puts his mother's behavior in a new light: "My mother often wept by her side of the river. When my grandmother scolded her, she said: "I had to wean him of his attachment to me; otherwise he would never be able to study.' " [9]
In writing this, Te-ch'ing's narration departs from the usual form of

eyewitness account, but the juxtaposition of the two points of view serves to illustrate the complexity and poignancy of his mother's role in the education of a future Buddhist monk. If the first episode shows the mother as a harsh and resolute disciplinarian, the second reveals the heart-rending inner conflicts that must have beset her from time to time. The son was deeply loved, as we shall see from a subsequent account of his childhood, but he was weaned of attachment—this paradoxical relationship might not conform to the expectations of modern child psychology, but it provides, perhaps, a key to the formation of the ideal Buddhist personality: compassion for all beings but attachment to none.

When I was nine I continued my studies in a temple. I heard monks reciting the *Kuan-yin sūtra* which promises relief from the sufferings of this world. Greatly pleased, I got the text from a monk, and memorized it. My mother worshipped Kuan-yin, and I always accompanied her when she burned incense and did obeisances. One day I told her that Bodhisattva Kuan-yin had a sūtra, and she said that she did not know it. I then recited it for her. She was greatly pleased and said: "Where did you get it? Your chanting of the sūtra is like that of an old monk." [10]

From what we have seen, Te-ch'ing's childhood was no ordinary one, but there are a number of other reasons that the childhood segment of Te-ch'ing's autobiography deserves our attention more than any other period. For one thing, no Chinese autobiographer or biographer before Te-ch'ing even gave such a detailed treatment of childhood. Another reason is that every incident in his childhood that he chose to record brought him one step closer to his eventual conversion. Therefore I shall quote two more entries from the early section of his autobiography:

When I was ten my mother supervised my studies with extreme strictness. As I was distressed by it, I asked her:
"What is studying for?"
"For becoming an official," she said.
"What kind of an official?"
"Starting from the bottom, you might get to be the prime minister."
"What's after that?"
"That would be the end."
"It is a pity that after a lifetime of hardship one will come to an end. What's the use of it! I want to be something that will not end."
"A stupid boy like you can only be an itinerant monk."
"Why should I be an itinerant monk? What's good in it?"
"An itinerant monk is a Buddhist disciple who travels all over the world, free and provided for no matter where he goes."

"This is exactly what I would like to be."

"I am only afraid that you won't have such good fortune."

"Why do I need good fortune to be an itinerant monk?"

"People often pass the civil examinations with the highest honors, but there are very few who become great Buddhist masters."

"I do have such good fortune, but I am afraid you could not bear to give me up."

"If you have such good fortune, I surely can bear to give you up."

I silently took mental note of what she said.[11]

One day when I was eleven years old I saw several traveling monks approaching our house, each carrying a pack, a large ladle, and a rain hat made of bamboo. I asked my mother, "Who are those monks?" She said that they were itinerant monks. I was quite happy to hear this and observed them closely. When the monks entered our compound they took down their packs and leaned them against a tree. Greeting my mother, they asked for alms. My mother seated them and went in to make tea and prepare a vegetable meal. She waited on them with much reverence. When they finished they got up and put on their packs. As they were ready to set off they raised their hands, but my mother backed away from them, saying, "Please don't thank me." The monks left without much ado. I said to my mother, "The monks were rude. They ate and left, without thanking you." My mother replied, "If they thanked me, I would not get the blessing." I said to myself: "This shows why the monk is a superior being." I often thought of it, and soon I decided to become a monk. But at that time I did not know how to go about it.[12]

These anecdotes, taken together, constitute an important landmark in the development of Chinese autobiography. When childhood was touched on at all by the predecessors of Te-ch'ing it was usually represented by a few standard *topoi* such as early signs of precocity or commendable acts of filial piety. Te-ch'ing, on the other hand, was interested in a different order of events—events which were not exemplary, or even typical, but crucial to the destiny of one unique person, even though they might not have appeared noteworthy to other autobiographers. Perhaps the elliptical prose of classical Chinese was suitable for representing the exemplary, but now a more robust narrative style was necessary. This seems to me the reason that in Te-ch'ing's narration of his childhood there is an extensive use of dialogue and a plain language bordering on the vernacular. If each event constitutes for him a unique and crucial experience, it must be represented with greater particularity than the historiographical convention usually allows. Conversation must not be summarized but transcribed almost verbatim, and the visit of the traveling monks must be recorded with visual details. "When the monks entered our compound they took down their packs and leaned them against a tree." The packs have no significance as history, but they endow the scene with an individuality and concreteness found only in vernacular fiction.

Te-ch'ing's reconstruction of his childhood affords us, for the first time in Chinese history, a firsthand account of the early education of a future Buddhist master—no divine intervention or sudden outburst of faith, but a slow and gradual process of molding and shaping through the determined effort of a pious mother. No childhood experience that Te-ch'ing remembered and chose to record fails to play a part in this particular education. This selective principle, useful as it is in the mode of spiritual autobiography, might be found objectionable by those who insist that childhood should be treated in its own right, not merely as the full-time preparation for the adult life. Whatever the validity of this objection, we must judge Te-ch'ing's practice in the perspective of the history of human society, mindful of the fact, convincingly established by Philippe Ariès in *Centuries of Childhood*, that the concept of childhood as we know it today is a relatively recent development,[13] and noting too, as stated by Paul Delany, that "we know practically nothing about the childhood and adolescence of most Renaissance men, even quite famous ones." [14] In terms of the proportion of his autobiography allotted to childhood, Te-ch'ing stands comparison with even the best autobiographers of the Renaissance. Cellini's fascinating story in the Penguin translation takes up 381 pages, but only four deal with events that take place before the dashing sculptor reached the age of fifteen.[15]

The first test of Te-ch'ing's early religious education occurred in his twelfth year, when his father, incredibly and unaccountably kept out of his life story until this time, suggested that a betrothal be made for the son.[16] Te-ch'ing not only turned down the idea but decided to leave home and join Abbot Hsi-lin [e] at the Pao-en [f] Monastery. The combined forces of mother and son prevailed over the father's objections, and in 1557 Te-ch'ing was brought to the monastery. The abbot, strange to say, did not admit Te-ch'ing into the order right away, but said, "This child is so exceptional that it would be a pity to let him become an ordinary monk. I shall have him continue his studies with a Confucian teacher, and see how he turns out." A visitor at the monastery was Chao Chen-chi,[g] a prominent member of the T'ai-chou [h] School of Neo-Confucianism, who was so impressed by the young Te-ch'ing that he pronounced that the boy would someday be "the teacher of men and heavenly beings." Chao apparently noticed the equivocal position the boy found himself in, for he asked him, "Would you like to be a high official or a Buddha?" "A Buddha," Te-ch'ing replied without hesitation.[17]

Whatever this seemingly commonplace episode meant to Te-ch'ing, its symbolic significance is clear in the light of the subsequent course of Te-ch'ing's life. The exchange between these two men epitomizes his struggles during the next decade—for a long time, though a monk, Te-ch'ing was torn between the contending claims of the Buddhist and Confucian paths. Chao represents the other type of person he might have become— a prominent Confucian scholar-official with more or less Buddhist sympathies, and also the type with whom Te-ch'ing tended to associate in later life.

During the next few years Te-ch'ing seemed to spend most of his time with Confucian studies.[18] He managed to memorize all the Four Books before proceeding to the *Book of Changes*; he also practiced writing classical prose and poetry. Membership in a literary club brought him into close contact with young Confucian candidates, and he won most literary contests. But such a congenial existence did not go on without interruptions. There were several bouts of an unnamed sickness, and clashes with an inspector of schools. And the real crisis came when he was nineteen. It began with all his close friends in the literary club scoring successes at the local examination, which led him to the temptation of taking the examination himself. As he was wavering, Yün-ku [i] (1500–75), a leading monk of the day, happened to visit the monastery. After hearing Te-ch'ing out, Yün-ku vigorously explained to the young man "the glories of the contemplative life and the promises of enlightenment," and urged him to read books that contained lives of eminent monks. Apparently the perusal of one of the books tipped the scale: "I went through his box of books and got the *Chung-feng kuang-lu*.[j] Halfway through the book I suddenly became exultant and exclaimed, 'This is what delights my heart!' Thereupon I decided to enter the monastic life and asked the abbot to tonsure me."[19]

Te-ch'ing's succinct account of the crisis, although candid, does not delineate the full complexity of his inner struggles, but fortunately it is

possible to obtain further information from other of his writings. Leading
to the crisis was, of course, the temptation of Confucian officialdom, and
the temptation was all the greater to a precocious and self-assured youth
from a poor family, especially as the fortunes of Buddhism had reached
their lowest point at just about this time. Te-ch'ing was very emphatic
about the humble station of the Buddhist clergy in his biography of the
Abbot Hsi-lin, who served in the government for many years as a deputy
undersecretary in the Bureau of Buddhist Affairs (Tso chüeh-i).[k] "The
abbot was frequently aware of the contempt that the scholar-officials had
for the Buddhist clergy. 'When a monk is deficient in education, he invites insults from the Confucians and thus brings shame to the church,'
he said with a sigh." [20] Furthermore, "earlier most monks were so common and uncouth that they could not utter even a word in the company
of the literati. The abbot felt that while the clergy should be concerned
with Meditation and the teachings of the Buddha, they must also learn
from the Confucian teachers in order to be able to read and write as well
as understand the great principles of loyalty and filial piety." [21] Since Te-
ch'ing was the abbot's favorite disciple, perhaps it was inevitable that he
would outdo the abbot in his deprecation of the loutish clerics as he rose
in the esteem of the young Confucian candidates of his region whose ca-
maraderie he enjoyed. In fact, as he revealed in his biography of Yün-ku,
it was precisely his contempt for the monks which brought him to the
verge of defection:

> When I was nineteen I intended to give up the priesthood. When Master Yün-
> ku heard this he asked me:
> "Why do you go against your original commitment?"
> "I am disgusted with the commonness of the monks."
> "If you don't like the commonness of the monks, why don't you learn to be an
> eminent monk? The eminent monks in the olden days were not treated as subor-
> dinates by the emperors, or as sons by their parents. They were even used to the
> respect shown to Gods and Nagas. Just read the Transmission of the Lamp or the
> Lives of Eminent Monks and you'll know."
> I looked through his bookcase and came across a set of Chung-feng kuang-lu.
> When I showed it to him he said:
> "Read it carefully and you'll know the great worth of being a monk."
> Largely owing to his guidance I soon decided to be tonsured.[22]

That the Chung-feng kuang-lu should have proved a timely antidote to
the young novice's doubts and disillusionment lies precisely in the strik-

ing contrast between the exalted career of the author and the sad lot of the late Ming Buddhist clerics. If the records of conversations, correspondence, addresses, and self-eulogies of Ming-pen [1] (1263–1323), also known as Chung-feng, failed to demonstrate amply the universal acclaim that the great Ch'an master enjoyed, the three biographies about him included in the collection—two in the form of memorial inscriptions and one commissioned by the emperor—listed all the honors and favors that Ming-pen received from the royal family and the literati. The King of Korea took a long journey and climbed a high mountain in order to pay personal respects to him; Chao Meng-fu,[m] the great painter and calligrapher, burned incense and did obeisance each time a letter from the master arrived.[23]

Ming-pen, then, represented the embodiment of all the hopes that the young novice had been repeatedly encouraged to entertain ever since his childhood. Considering the subsequent career of Te-ch'ing, there is every reason to believe that his emulation of the great Ch'an master continued for a long time: there were the same close association with the Confucian literati, the same adulation from the imperial family, the same balance between preaching and writing, with not all of the latter limited to religious topics. In fact, the name of the great Ch'an master appears once more in Te-ch'ing's autobiography. When Te-ch'ing visited Peking for the first time in 1574, still a relatively obscure young monk, his arrogance irritated one of the leading scholar-officials of the time. The defense of him by one of the more sympathetic Confucians was that he was no mere monk but would someday prove the equal of Ming-pen.[24] That Te-ch'ing should have remembered this casual remark almost half a century later is one more indication of the indelible place of this model in his consciousness.

But Ming-pen was not the only possible exemplar available: the tradition of the eminent monk who was on easy terms with the literati and enjoyed patronage by the aristocracy was a long and established one, beginning in the fourth century. To the demoralized Buddhist clerics of the middle decades of the sixteenth century, Ming-pen was obviously the most recent and the most dramatic reassurance that all was not yet lost. But even the Abbot Hsi-lin and Master Yün-ku can be seen as latter-day, if somewhat lesser, lights of the tradition; for, as Te-ch'ing made a point of recalling in his biographies of the two, the former distinguished himself by his eloquence and presence of mind before the emperor [25] and the latter never failed to impress the learned and the powerful among the laity.[26] In their own way, these two elders were also models after which Te-ch'ing was to pattern himself.

But, returning to Te-ch'ing's autobiography, we find him burning all his Confucian literary exercises right after he received tonsure. Yet he was not immediately successful in his Buddhist endeavor.

> I gave myself entirely to the daily studies, but made little progress. I then concentrated on the chanting of Amitābha's name, day and night without stop. Shortly afterwards I dreamt one night that Amitābha appeared in person, standing over the horizon where the sun set. His features and aura were all clearly visible. I reached out and greeted him by touching his feet, crying with love and joy. Then I wished that I could also see Avalokiteśvara and Mahāsthāmaprāpta. Both of them appeared instantly. Ever since that time the images of these three have flashed frequently before my eyes, and I came to be confident of my eventual success.[27]

Late that year Te-ch'ing took his final vows (Chü-chieh).[n]

The following year, Master Yün-ku organized a meditation trimester (Ch'an-ch'i) [o] at the T'ien-chieh [p] Monastery, which was to last ninety days. Fifty-five prominent monks from various places were invited to participate. Encouraged by Yün-ku, Te-ch'ing enrolled.

> At first, not knowing how to direct my effort, I was very much distressed. I offered incense and asked the master for instruction. He suggested the approach of thorough contemplation of Amitābha (shen-shih nien-fo).[q] Henceforth I concentrated on the contemplation without a moment of interruption or deviation. Three months passed like a dream: I was never aware of the presence of other participants nor did I notice any daily activities. . . . . When I completed the trimester and came out, I continued to behave for a long time as if I were still sitting on the Meditation seat. Even when I was walking in the marketplace I was not aware of the existence of other people. Everybody was amazed by my behavior.[28]

At a time when the Ch'an School was already extinct in the region of the lower Yangtze valley, Te-ch'ing was fortunate to have received the training in sitting meditation. For the ability of deep concentration and control of the senses, which he acquired during the trimester, was to stand him in good stead ten years later, just before he reached enlightenment. Another significant feature of this training is the instruction he received from Yün-ku at the onset—thorough contemplation of Amitābha. This combination of the Ch'an regimen with a Pure Land practice was to be one of the tenets of the Buddhist ecumenism which all three of the last great Buddhist masters of the Ming embraced.

The final vows, the meditation training, and even the burning of all his Confucian literary exercises still could not keep him away from Confucian activities for very long. In 1567, when he was twenty-two, the Ministry of Rites ordered his temple to establish a charitable school (*i-hsüeh*) [r] for the benefit of young monks and acolytes. Te-ch'ing was appointed teacher, and the enrollment was nearly two hundred. Consequently he "renewed his acquaintance with the *Tso chuan*, the *Dynastic Histories*, and the various philosophers." He continued to teach for the next three years, apparently without any adverse effect on his fundamental Buddhist orientation.[29]

Late in 1571 Te-ch'ing, now twenty-five years old, decided to leave what had become for him a prosaic life of routine and to travel over the vast expanses of central and northern China. Early the following year he arrived in Yangchou. Illness and a snow storm stranded him in the city. He discovered that even in such desperation he was not successful in begging for alms.

> I could not bring myself to enter into any dooryard. Examining myself, I suddenly realized that my reluctance was caused by the possession of a little cash on my person. Thereupon I noticed that several Buddhist monks and Taoist priests were shivering in the snow, apparently even less successful than I in getting food. I invited them all to a meal in a restaurant and used up my last penny. The next day when I walked the street again I found myself able to open my mouth and beg loudly for food at people's doorways.[30]

Utter poverty and frequent distress were no doubt the usual lot of the Buddhist clerics in the Ming, but an eminent monk, even during his apprentice years, had another side to his life. When Te-ch'ing first arrived in Peking, six months after the Yangchou experience, he still sometimes went hungry, but even then he was received by prominent scholar-officials. Two years later when he revisited the capital city he was already in a position to call on all the leading members of the literati and to expect to be treated as an equal. In the exchange of repartee he usually had the upper hand. When Wang Shih-chen [s] (1526–90), for twenty years the proud arbiter of the literary world, slighted him because of his youth, he returned the insult with even greater arrogance. His behavior amidst the rank and fashion certainly conformed in every way to the long-established tradition of the eminent monk, and that he saw himself in such a role is evidenced by his recording, without any demurring, the fact that one leading Confucian compared him to Chih-tun [t] (314–66) while another predicted that he would someday prove the equal of Ming-pen and Tsung-kao [u] (1089–1163).[31]

For a monk of Te-ch'ing's disposition, training, and talent, the greatest temptation during the middle years was the easy path of what Hui-chiao,[v] the author of the *Kao-seng chuan*,[w] called the famous monk. "If men of real achievement conceal their brilliance, then they are eminent (*kao*)[x] but not famous (*ming*); [y] when men of slight virtue happen to be in accord with their times, then they are famous but not eminent." [32] Perhaps continued residence in the capital city would have deflected Te-ch'ing from his spiritual goals. Whether or not this was the reason, early the next year he went to Mount Wu-t'ai [z] with his friend, the monk Fu-teng,[aa] and settled down in a secluded spot near the northern summit. "I was surrounded by ten thousand peaks of snow and ice, precisely the sort of place I had always wanted. Completely gratified, I felt as if I were in Paradise. Soon Fu-teng went to Yen-t'ai and I stayed there alone." [33] Now he began his meditative exercises: "Holding the single thought of Amitābha in my mind, I refused to speak to any visitors but only stared at them. At last people to me were just like things, for I got to the point that I no longer made cognitive distinctions." [34] When spring arrived his meditation was interrupted:

The place was very windy; all the myriad holes and fissures whistled fiercely whenever the wind blew. Then the ice melted and the torrents of water dashing against the rocks in the brook sounded like thunder. In my quietude all the noises appeared to be even louder than they actually were, as if a huge army daily charged by my hut. I was quite distressed. When I asked Fu-teng about it he said:

"Environment [ching] [ab] arises from the mind: it does not come from outside. Have you not heard the ancient saying that if one has been exposed to the sound of a stream for thirty years without its activating the mind, he can bear personal witness to the perfection of Kuan-yin?"

I thereupon chose a narrow wooden bridge over the brook and sat or stood on it every day. At first I heard the sound of the water clearly. After a while I reached the point that the water would become audible only when my thought was activated. One day when I sat on the bridge I suddenly forgot my own person and the water became completely mute. From that time on all sounds were silenced and I was no longer disturbed by them.[35]

The cessation of cognitive and sensory functions, in the light of what was soon to occur, appeared to be no more than a preparation. His simple diet may have been another preparatory element; his daily ration of one-tenth of a pint of rice was supplemented by nothing but bran and wild roots and plants. Before the spring was over he achieved enlightenment.

One day after a meal of rice porridge I began circumambulating. All of a sudden I stopped and could not perceive my body or mind; there was only something huge and bright, something perfect, full, and silent like a gigantic round mirror, with mountains, rivers, and the great earth reflected in it. When I came to I felt very clear. I sought for my body and mind, but they were nowhere to be found. I composed a gāthā:

All of a sudden my wild mind stopped:
Inside and outside, all the roots and dust are cut across.
Turning around I touch and shatter the great empty sky,
All the myriad appearances are nipped before they arise.

From that time on I was clear both internally and externally, and sounds and sights no longer posed obstacles. All the former doubts and confusions were now gone.[36]

The following year Te-ch'ing decided to verify his enlightenment by reading the *Leng-yen ching* [ac] (*Śūraṅgama sūtra*), which he had earlier found quite puzzling. After eight months of application the text became thoroughly comprehensible.[37] This must have laid the foundation for his subsequent exegetical works on the sūtra. He did not explain why he chose this sūtra for a verification of his spiritual experience, but an obvious reason is that his friend Master Fu-teng's admonition, which led him to the threshold of enlightenment, is based on one of the key points of the Buddha's teaching as expounded in the *Leng-yen ching*. To reach Samādhi, the Buddha teaches, one must first learn to control perfectly the six senses, and to learn to control these six senses, one must begin with one.[38] Thus Avalokiteśvara (Kuan-yin) proceeded through meditation by way of the organ of hearing. He declared:

At first by directing the organ of hearing into the stream of meditation, this organ was detached from its object, and by wiping out (the concept of) both sound and stream-entry, both disturbance and stillness became clearly nonexistent. Thus advancing step by step both hearing and its object ceased completely, but I did not stop where they ended. When the awareness of this state and this state itself were realized as nonexistent, both subject and object merged into the void, the awareness of which became all-embracing. With further elimination of the void and its object, both creation and annihilation vanished, giving way to the state of Nirvāṇa which was then manifested.[39]

This passage is crucial to an understanding of Te-ch'ing's enlightenment. Even though at first he did not quite understand the sūtra, his account of the process leading to the great moment and the gāthā he composed after he regained consciousness indicate that he must have followed more or less the procedure suggested in the passage quoted above, although he may not have followed every stage consciously.

The importance of the *Leng-yen ching* goes beyond its role in the enlightenment of Te-ch'ing. The sūtra was read more widely and interpreted more frequently by Ming Confucianists and Taoists than was any other Buddhist text. At least forty works of exegesis are known to have been written during Ming times; among the well-known commentators were the Taoist Lu Hsi-hsing,[ad] the Neo-Confucian Chiao Hung,[ae] the literati Chung Hsing [af] and Ch'ien Ch'ien-i,[ag] as well as Buddhist monks such as Chu-hung and Chih-hsü.[ah] [40] The sūtra's appeal lies, according to Araki Kengo,[ai] in its being quintessentially Chinese; as such it served as a bridge between Chinese Buddhism and Confucianism; and it was the most important force in the syncretism of the Wan-li period.[41] Te-ch'ing's interest in the sūtra, which later produced three exegetical works, must have served as another link between him and the Confucians.

Although Te-ch'ing was now only thirty years old and his ensuing years were replete with color and drama, as a record of education and spiritual progress the autobiography might as well have ended at this point. The mode of the *nien-p'u* now begins to reclaim its usual place in Chinese autobiography: his account becomes a diary of activities rather than a process with shape and meaning. Consequently I shall not deal here with his later life, interesting as it is, except to summarize it briefly.

The most important event in Te-ch'ing's secular life was his involvement in one of the major political controversies of the Wan-li [aj] period. The emperor had three sons, but for many years he refused to designate one as the heir-apparent. The empress-dowager favored her oldest grandson, and her cause was supported by most of the leading officials. The emperor, however, sided with the son borne by the Royal Concubine, Cheng.[ak] Te-ch'ing, as well as his friends Fu-teng and Chen-k'o, was drawn into the controversy because of their close association with the empress-dowager, a devout Buddhist. Te-ch'ing was committed to the cause of the eldest prince from the beginning, as he had been commissioned by the empress-dowager in 1581, when the emperor was only eighteen years old, to pray for the birth of an heir to the throne. He pointedly mentioned in the autobiography that in the fall of the next year "the heir-apparent was born." [42] As the royal princes grew into adolescence, with the emperor still vacillating, the dispute became increasingly acrimonious: many supporters of the eldest prince, who remonstrated unbendingly with the emperor, were harshly punished. The Cheng faction, seeking to weaken the influence of the empress-dowager, decided to undermine her most prominent partisans among the Buddhist clergy. In 1595, Te-ch'ing was arrested and later convicted on a trumped-up charge. Defrocked, he was sent to serve as a common soldier in the garrison army at Lei-chou in the far south. Chen-k'o was more unfortunate. Implicated in the so-called Evil Book (yao-shu) [al] case, one of the many battles over the succession issue, he died in jail. [43]

Te-ch'ing's punishment seems to have solidified his alliance with the leading Neo-Confucians of his day, and the journey south looked more like a triumphant march. The commanders at the garrison were lenient and even respectful to him. In spite of his sentence he was allowed to write, lecture, and travel freely in the south. In 1606 the birth of a son to the oldest prince, who had been formally made crown prince in 1601, occasioned a general amnesty which restored Te-ch'ing to civilian status. However, he continued to live in much the same way as he had during his ten years of exile. In 1622 he wrote his autobiography, and the following year he died—in Ts'ao-ch'i, [am] the place made famous by the Sixth Patriarch Hui-neng. [an]

In the above study we have attempted to chart the spiritual odyssey of Te-ch'ing, taking into account the forces and circumstances that shaped and molded both the man and the autobiography. But a few obvious questions remain unanswered. Why is it that no Chinese Buddhist monk before Te-ch'ing ever wrote about his own spiritual experiences? What were the reasons for Te-ch'ing's doing so? And, finally, why did he go so far as to write an autobiography, the first ever by a Chinese Buddhist monk? Such questions are perhaps ultimately unanswerable, but attempts at plausible explanations might further illuminate both the autobiography and its subject, even if in the end we fail to solve the central mystery.

It is indeed curious that, in view of the proliferation of Ch'an literature since the T'ang and the paramount importance of enlightenment in Chinese Buddhism, no Buddhist monk before Te-ch'ing ever described in writing either the process leading to, or the experience of, his own enlightenment. Many Ch'an masters were, like Hui-neng, allegedly illiterate; they could not have been expected to leave a record in their own hand. But a greater obstacle is the characteristic Ch'an distrust of the written word, and the insistence on not telling things too plainly (*pu shuo p'o*).[ao] What was sought was the immediate, direct, and undifferentiable experience, which, being largely ineffable, could be hinted at or suggested by gestures and metaphors, but not conveyed by declarative prose. Perhaps it was difficult even to talk about one's own intense spiritual experiences. The Sixth Patriarch began his long sermon, which constitutes the bulk of the *Platform Sūtra*, with an autobiographical account, but when it came to his own two instances of enlightenment he was singularly uninformative. The first instance was described as follows: "I happened to see another man who was reciting the Diamond Sūtra. Upon hearing it my mind became clear and I was awakened." [44] The second instance was presented even more tersely: "The Fifth Patriarch saw me off as far as Chiu-chiang Station. I was instantly enlightened." [45] The same reticence seems to have persisted among Ch'an monks for the next nine centuries: when Te-ch'ing's contemporary, Chu-hung, combed through the vast literature of recorded Ch'an conversation for exemplary processes leading to enlightenment, he found only four instances where the enlightened discoursed on his own experiences.[46]

It is certainly paradoxical that a powerful spiritual and intellectual movement which in many ways was so liberating and revolutionary did not lead to more verbal and literary self-revelations. The puzzle is all the greater when we recall such characteristics of the Ch'an school as the total reliance on one's own mind, the belief that the realization of one's own nature should be the goal of all one's endeavors, and the singular behavior of many of the masters—extreme self-assertiveness and sometimes total lack of inhibition. Lu Shih-i [ap] (1611–72), a keen observer of the contrasts between Confucian and Buddhist spiritual experiences, offered the following explanation for this paradox:

When a Confucian sage has experienced enlightenment, he likes to tell others and share it with all people in the world. . . . A Ch'an master upon reaching enlightenment, however, does not like to tell others: he keeps to himself the secret experience. But his exultation is expressed in such wild behavior as leaping up and down, shouting and hitting people with his staff, and cursing loudly.

There is no limit to his unruliness. To the clear-eyed this sort of conduct is nothing but willful eccentricity. Even if a Buddhist is thoroughly enlightened, there is still no reason for going to such extremes. But we must not forget that a Ch'an Buddhist has no alternative. He certainly cannot tell people what he has experienced in his enlightenment, for the very reason that is expressed in the saying: "I told it to you, but you ridiculed me for it." [47]

Even a sampling of the records of Ch'an conversations would support Lu's conclusion, his obvious partiality for the Confucians notwithstanding. No Ch'an monk, after having spent a lifetime in parrying direct queries, would give his potential opponents an opening for attack; his best defense is to utter paradoxes or epigrams, and above all to avoid exposing his flanks by talking about himself in earnest or using plain and denotative language.

Thus Te-ch'ing the autobiographer had few antecedents in the Buddhist tradition. He would have, however, found more congenial company among some of the late Ming Neo-Confucians. Restless, eager, and intensely inquisitive, many of them went through a long search for truth and self from their early youth until, in some cases, quite late in life. In their roaming over the length and breadth of their vast country and their experimenting with diverse schools and regimens they displayed a compulsiveness which went beyond the traditional Confucian sense of measure and sobriety. In fact, most of them, during one or another stage in their perpetual wrestling with the self, betrayed characteristics which are patently identifiable with Ch'an Buddhism. But as Lu Shih-i observed, they differed from Ch'an monks on at least one important point: quite a few of them reported on their passionate quests in letters and discourses; some even wrote autobiographical essays detailing every turn and twist in their spiritual journeys. Of the latter, the most well known are Hu Chih [aq] (1517–85) and Kao P'an-lung [ar] (1562–1626). The most significant feature of their narratives is the description of their intense spiritual experiences which they unabashedly denoted as "enlightenment." [48]

Te-ch'ing was entertained by Kao in 1616. [49] They corresponded and exchanged writings with each other.[50] It is not inconceivable that Te-ch'ing had knowledge of Kao's autobiographical essay which was written in or shortly after 1614. At any rate Te-ch'ing's long and extensive association with the Neo-Confucians must have exposed him to their style of self-examination and their practice of self-revelation. He must have found his own spiritual progress parallel in many ways to theirs. In the climate of the late Ming syncretism, which fostered so many exchanges of ideas and practices between men of the Three Teachings,[51] perhaps all that was needed for the appearance of the first Buddhist autobiography were a few additional personal circumstances, which we shall now explore in detail.

We might begin with Te-ch'ing's choice of format for his autobiography. Since the self-edited *nien-p'u*, or the annalistic autobiography, was still a relatively unknown genre during his lifetime—only nine practitioners of the craft were born between 1470 and 1570—there may be some significance in his telling his life story in this form. Of all the annalistic autobiographies written before Te-ch'ing, which number no more than a dozen, only two can be assumed with any certainty to have been known to him.[52] One was written by Wen T'ien-hsiang [as] (1236–82), the great Sung loyalist, the other by Yang Chi-sheng [at] (1516–55), the Ming official who sacrificed his life in a futile attempt to expose the wicked Senior Grand Secretary Yen Sung.[au] No other works seem to have circulated widely in Te-ch'ing's day, while Wen and Yang were adulated by all in the late Ming as paragons of Confucian heroism. Now the significant fact about these two is that each wrote his autobiography in jail, waiting for his martyrdom, fully aware that the dominant theme of his life—loyalty—would assure him a place in history. Can we then infer, from these facts, that in Te-ch'ing's case the first inspiration for, if not the beginning of the actual composition of, his autobiography occurred during his imprisonment, and that what prompted him to write it was his sense of identification with these models of loyalty to the imperial house, for which he, too, suffered cruel persecution?

Te-ch'ing spent eight months in jail. There was much time for soul searching and self-examination. He was tortured and beaten; his life for quite some time was at the mercy of his tormentors. The frequency with which, in the autobiography, he refers to his role in the service of the heir-apparent clearly indicates his awareness of the depth of his commitment and the magnitude of his contribution. He did not fail to mention his friendship or even slight acquaintance with those scholar-officials who championed the cause of the prince, the most prominent among them being Chang Wei,[av] Tsou Yüan-piao,[aw] Kao P'an-lung, Yüeh Yüan-sheng,[ax] and Fan Yü-heng.[ay] In his other writings he repeatedly compares himself and his friend Master Chen-k'o to Ch'eng Ying [az] and Kung-sun Ch'u-chiu,[ba] the two loyal vassals of the Spring and Autumn Era whose heroic deeds have been celebrated at once in popular drama and in the Confucian moral-historiographical tradition, beginning with the *Shih chi*.[53]

In this regard it was perhaps no accident that Te-ch'ing wrote a commentary on the *Tso chuan*, a book in which the ideal of political loyalty reigns supreme. In fact, in the preface to his commentary he gives us another glimpse of his self-image as a Confucian loyalist: "After I was exiled to Lei-yang and sentenced to serve in the army I no longer dared to consider myself a Buddhist monk. Every time I looked back I realized that I had been destined to be a solitary minister and unloved son (*ku-ch'en nieh-tzu*).[bb] [54] Consequently I examined my faults and studied the facts pertaining to loyal officials and filial sons." [55]

Te-ch'ing's affinity with the *Tso chuan* holds another key to understanding his autobiographical impulse. For one thing, the *Tso chuan* has always been considered the prototype of annalistic history, which in turn provided the model for the *nien-p'u*. Also, it is the *Tso chuan* which formulated for the first time the concept of Confucian immortality, namely that one can live forever on the strength of one's virtue, accomplishments, or words.[56] It is the desire for this kind of immortality, in the opinion of the T'ang historiographer Liu Chih-chi,[bc] that makes men wish to be the subject of a biography.[57] That Te-ch'ing was not unmoved by such considerations can be seen from an entry in his autobiography. When, early in his exile, he was criticized for printing and circulating one of his exegetical works, he defended his action as follows: "Afraid that I might die without being known, I expressed myself in words in the hope that I might thus become immortal." [58] To write an account of oneself would ensure a double kind of immortality, for in doing so one would not only express oneself in words but also become, so to speak, the subject of a biography.

As a frequent biographer of monks—among his twenty-nine subjects are Chu-hung and Chen-k'o—Te-ch'ing was certainly no stranger to the craft of biographical writing. This fact as well as his own views on Buddhist hagiography may have lain behind his decision to write an autobiography. In his reply to a monk who had asked him to write the biography of a recently deceased abbot, he said: "The format of memorial inscription (*t'a-ming*) ^{bd} being what it is, I shall not be able to include all that I know. I can only enumerate what is appropriate; all other deeds of his perhaps should be recorded in another account." [59] On another occasion he declared that there were only four categories of monks whose biographies could be written: Ch'an masters, founding fathers of schools or sects, theurgists, and eminent monks. "Those who do not belong to any of these categories should not have their biographies written, even if they had other great accomplishments." [60] In his youth Te-ch'ing may very well have patterned himself after the model of the eminent monk, but looking back, at the age of seventy-six, and seeing the whole man, he must have realized that he had gone beyond his early exemplar. In a colophon to a series of poems written in his illness during exile he compared himself with Tsung-kao and Chüeh-fan,^{be} the two eminent Sung monks who were, like him, exiled to a southern garrison. He conceded that he was not their equal "in the way of Ch'an and the Law of the Buddha"; but in loyalty and fortitude he believed that he was more like another exile, the Han hero Su Wu.^{bf} [61] Once again his self-image as a Confucian hero seems to have overshadowed his Buddhist identity, for Su Wu is another dramatic figure in both Chinese history and folk literature. This being the case, Te-ch'ing could no longer see himself as falling within any of the four categories of monks mentioned above.

Te-ch'ing's identification with heroic figures such as Ch'eng Ying and Su Wu should be seen in conjunction with his frequent exaltation of himself and his close associates among the Buddhist clergy in terms of courage and valor. He uses such expressions as "great hero," [62] "man of iron," [63] "heroic leader," [64] and "great man." [65] This emphasis on heroism is another link between late Ming Buddhists like Te-ch'ing and Chen-k'o and their Neo-Confucian contemporaries, especially those of the T'ai-chou School.[66] The *hsia* ("knight-errantry") ideal is one point at which the more extreme members of the two sides converge—in this regard Chen-k'o is a better representative even than Te-ch'ing. The two masters never failed to act out their self-definitions, nor were they without detractors. A contemporary criticism of Te-ch'ing's public behavior gives us another glimpse of the master cutting a heroic if somewhat unconventional figure as he moved among adoring crowds.

In every temple when Te-ch'ing ascends to the great hall to preach and receive homage he always sits facing south directly before the high altar, the image of the

Three-World Buddha having been covered by the monks with large sheets. He is treated there with the deference due a visiting governor or magistrate. I have my doubts about his behavior. The Tathāgata Buddha is the teacher in the Buddhist School just as Confucius and Mencius are teachers in the Confucian School. If a great Confucian scholar should lecture on the Classics, he would never usurp the high seat in the Ta-ch'eng Palace and have the statues of Confucius and other sages to his back. I have asked a friend to caution Te-ch'ing on this, but I doubt if he will listen. Recently I have seen several lesser preachers imitating Te-ch'ing in vainglory. They can be said to be completely uninhibited! I have also seen a calling card of Te-ch'ing's with his name written as large as that of a Grand Secretary. This is even more astonishing.[67]

Whether these strictures are justified or not, the account certainly lends further support to the suggestion that Te-ch'ing must have seen himself not so much as an eminent monk but as a unique individual of heroic stature untrammeled by clerical inhibitions. To have had such an image of himself and to know only too well the limitations of Buddhist hagiography may have further contributed to his decision to be his own biographer, for he must have realized that no future biographer of him could possibly understand his unique life story, let alone retell it with all its drama and complexity in an appropriate form.

1. The text of Te-ch'ing's autobiography used in this study was first published in 1651 with annotations prepared by his disciple Fu-cheng.^{bg} Page references are to the modern edition, *Tsu-pen Han-shan ta-shih nien-p'u su-chu* ^{bh} (hereafter abbreviated as NP) Soochow, 1934. A slightly variant text is included in Te-ch'ing's collected works, *Han-shan ta-shih Meng-yu-chi* ^{bi} (hereafter abbreviated as MYC) (Hong Kong: reprint of Chiang-pei edition, 1965), 53/1–54/42.
2. The Sung monk Chih-yüan ^{bj} (976?–1023) wrote what may be called a pseudo-autobiography. Entitled "Chung-yung-tzu chuan," ^{bk} it is in the form of a biography of himself under the alias of Master Chung-yung. The work is largely a spirited argument for Confucian-Buddhist syncretism and says very little about Chih-yüan's life. See *Dai-Nippon zoku-zōkyō*, 1B, 6, 1, 55b–57a.
3. Chinese autobiography is a neglected aspect of sinology. The only article dealing with the subject that I know of is Wolfgang Bauer's "Icherleben und Autobiographie im älteren China," *Heidelberger Jahrbücher*, vol. 8 (1964), pp. 12–40. For a brief discussion of the subject see my paper "Spiritual Progress and Self-Portrait: Two Seventeenth-Century Chinese Autobiographies," presented before the University Seminar on Traditional China (Columbia University, January 20, 1970), pp. 1–4. A portion of the present article was included in the seminar paper, and I wish to thank my fellow seminar members for their useful comments and suggestions.
4. Cf. Paul Delany, *British Autobiography in the 17th Century* (London, 1969), pp. 6–23.
5. Cf. de Bary, *Self and Society*, pp. 1–5.
6. "Problems of Chinese Biography," in *Confucian Personalities*, by Arthur F. Wright and Denis Twitchett (eds.) (Stanford, 1962), p. 37.
7. NP, pp. 9–10.
8. NP, p. 10.
9. *Ibid.*
10. NP, pp. 10–11.
11. NP, pp. 11–12.
12. NP, p. 12.
13. Translated by Robert Baldick (New York, 1962), pp. 128–33.
14. *British Autobiography*, p. 14.
15. *The Autobiography of Benvenuto Cellini*, translated by George Bull (Baltimore, 1964).
16. NP, p. 13. Although we know more about Te-ch'ing's childhood than we know of that of nearly any Chinese before the seventeenth century, nonetheless his silences are sometimes more intriguing than his revelations. One

cannot but wonder, for instance, why he has not said anything about his father until this point. We know from a reference in his collected works (MYC, 49/50) that he had a younger brother, but his autobiography mentions no siblings. The omissions suggest that his mother may have played an even greater role in the formation of Te-ch'ing's personality than one would otherwise infer from the autobiography. We do not, however, have sufficient sources to attempt a psychoanalytical interpretation of the various events in Te-ch'ing's life in the way that Erik H. Erikson did for Martin Luther, who died the same year that Te-ch'ing was born.

17. NP, p. 13.
18. NP, p. 14.
19. *Ibid.*
20. MYC, 30/3.
21. MYC, 30/4.
22. MYC, 30/13–14.
23. *Chung-feng kuang-lu* (Soochow, 1881), 30/8a–26a.
24. NP, p. 27.
25. MYC, 30/1–3.
26. MYC, 30/13.
27. NP, pp. 14–15.
28. NP, p. 17.
29. NP, p. 21.
30. NP, p. 22.
31. NP, p. 27.
32. Quoted in Arthur Wright, "Biography and Hagiography: Hui-chiao's *Lives of Eminent Monks*," in *Silver Jubilee Volume of the Zinbun-Kagaku-Kenkyusyo* (Kyoto University, 1954), p. 393.
33. NP, p. 33.
34. *Ibid.*
35. *Ibid.*
36. NP, pp. 33–4.
37. NP, p. 35.
38. *The Śūraṅgama Sūtra*, translated by Charles Luk (London, 1966), p. 120.
39. *Ibid.*, p. 135.
40. *Fo-hsüeh ta-tz'u-tien*,[bl] edited by Ting Fu-pao [bm] (Shanghai, 1925), II, 1563.
41. "Min-matsu ni okeru ju-butsu chōwa ron no seikaku," [bn] in *Nihon chūgoku gakkai hō*,[bo] no. 18, pp. 213–14.
42. NP, p. 48.
43. For a comprehensive account of the royal succession controversy, see Ku Ying-t'ai,[bp] *Ming-shih chi-shih pen-mo* [bq] (1936 edition), chuan 67. As for Te-ch'ing's role and his subsequent activities, see NP, pp. 45–103.
44. *The Platform Sūtra of the Sixth Patriarch*, translated by Philip Yampolsky (New York, 1967), p. 127.

45. *Ibid.*, p. 133.
46. "Ch'an kuan ts'e chin," [br] in *Yün-ch'i fa-hui* [bs] (Nanking, 1897), 14/10b–12b, 13b–20a.
47. *Lu Fu-t'ing ssu-pien-lu chi-yao* [bt] (Shanghai: Ts'ung-shu-chi-ch'eng edition, 1936), I, 40.
48. For Hu's autobiographical essay, see "K'un-hsüeh chi," [bu] quoted in Huang Tsung-hsi,[bv] *Ming-ju hsüeh-an* [bw] (Taipei: Shih-chieh shu-chü edition, 1965), pp. 222–24. For Kao's, see *ibid.*, pp. 625–27.
49. NP, p. 107.
50. MYC, 15/26–27.
51. Cf. de Bary, *Self and Society*, pp. 12–14. See also *ibid.*, p. 227, n. 26, for a cogent summary of Araki Kengo's view regarding the interactions between Neo-Confucians and Ch'an Buddhists: "It was the intellectual revolution springing from Wang's identification of mind as principle which overcame the intellectual isolation and defensive attitude of Zen Buddhists at this time, and gave them an opportunity to reengage in the intellectual life of the late Ming." Te-ch'ing's writing of an autobiography can be seen in this context as one manifestation of the general trend.
52. All information regarding annalistic autobiographies has been obtained from Wang Pao-hsien,[bx] *Li-tai ming-jen nien-p'u tsung-mu* [by] (Taipei, 1965).
53. MYC, 2/27, 15/20, 27/13. When the House of Chao [bz] fell, the heroic pair plotted to save the only male heir from his merciless enemies. By agreement, Kung-sun sacrificed his life so that Ch'eng could escape with the Chao orphan. When Te-ch'ing made the allusion he obviously had in mind the fact that dedication to the cause of the Ming heir-apparent, who led a precarious life throughout his father's reign, resulted in Chen-k'o's death and his own exile. For an account of the evolution of the Chao story in Chinese theater and its success in eighteenth-century Europe, see Liu Wu-chi, "The Original Orphan of China," *Comparative Literature*, vol. V, no. 3 (summer 1953), pp. 193–212.
54. The phrase is from *Mencius*, VII, 1, xviii. For a more literal translation see James Legge, *The Chinese Classics* (Oxford, 1893), II, 457–58.
55. MYC, 19/31.
56. Cf. Wing-tsit Chan, *A Source Book in Chinese Philosophy* (Princeton, 1963), p. 13.
57. *Shih-t'ung t'ung-shih*,[ca] edited by P'u Ch'i-lung (Taipei: Shih-chieh shu-chü edition, 1962), p. 23.
58. NP, p. 75.
59. MYC, 14/20.
60. MYC, 18/58.
61. MYC, 32/37. For nineteen years Su was held prisoner by the Hsiung-nu, to whom he had been sent as the emperor's emissary. His tormentors, in a futile attempt to obtain his submission, sent him to live in the desolate wilderness near what is now Lake Baykal.

62. *hsiung-meng chang-fu,*[cb] MYC, 27/1.
63. *t'ieh-han,*[cc] MYC, 35/49, 35/54.
64. *hao-chieh chih-shih,*[cd] MYC, 29/1.
65. *chang-fu,*[ce] MYC, 2/27, 15/19, 29/1.
66. For a cogent discussion of Neo-Confucian heroism and its affinity with Buddhism, see de Bary, *Self and Society,* pp. 169–71, and p. 231, n. 82.
67. Shen Te-fu,[cf] *Yeh-huo pien* [cg] (*Fu-li shan-fang* edition), 27.22a–22b. Against this background, Te-ch'ing's recollection of his meeting with Chao Chen-chi on the day that the future master, a boy of eleven, entered the monastery, takes on a new significance, for Chao, a prominent member of the T'ai-chou School and a Grand Secretary in 1569, was well known for his daring exploits during the crisis of 1550 when the Mongol troops were threatening Peking (*Ming-ju hsüeh-an,* p. 332). If Chao was the alternate model for Te-ch'ing in his youth, in his old age the great master seems to have succeeded in being at once an eminent monk and a Confucian grandee.

GLOSSARY

a 德清
b 袾宏
c 眞可（達觀）
d 年譜
e 西林
f 報恩
g 趙貞吉
h 泰州
i 雲谷
j 中峯廣錄
k 左覺義
l 明本
m 趙孟頫
n 具戒
o 禪期
p 天界
q 審實念佛
r 義學
s 王世貞
t 支遁
u 宗杲
v 慧皎
w 高僧傳
x 高
y 名
z 五臺
aa 福登
ab 境
ac 楞嚴經
ad 陸西星
ae 焦竑

af 鍾惺
ag 錢謙益
ah 智旭
ai 荒木見悟
aj 萬曆
ak 鄭
al 妖書
am 曹溪
an 惠能
ao 不說破
ap 陸世儀
aq 胡直
ar 高攀龍
as 文天祥
at 楊繼盛
au 嚴嵩
av 張位
aw 鄒元標
ax 岳元聲
ay 樊玉衡
az 程嬰
ba 公孫杵臼
bb 孤臣孽子
bc 劉知幾
bd 塔銘
be 覺範
bf 蘇武
bg 福徵
bh 足本憨山大師
　　年譜疏註
bi 憨山大師夢遊集

bj 智圓
bk 中庸子傳
bl 佛學大辭典
bm 丁福保
bn 明末における儒佛
　　調和論の性格
bo 日本中國學會報
bp 谷應泰
bq 明史紀事本末
br 禪關策進
bs 雲棲法彙
bt 陸桴亭思辨錄
　　輯要
bu 困學記
bv 黃宗羲
bw 明儒學案
bx 王寶先
by 歷代名人年譜總目
bz 趙
ca 史通通釋
cb 雄猛丈夫
cc 鐵漢
cd 豪傑之士
ce 丈夫
cf 沈德符
cg 野獲編

KRISTIN YÜ GREENBLATT *Chu-hung and Lay*

Buddhism in the Late Ming

The development of the lay Buddhist movement (*chü-shih fo-chiao*) [a] and the combining of the Three Teachings (*san-chiao ho-i*) [b] were two trends in the late Ming Dynasty that stand out in the history of Chinese thought as a whole. The two trends did not, of course, first appear in the Ming. Their earliest manifestation can be traced to at least the Eastern Chin Dynasty (fourth century A.D.). The lively interest in Buddhism taken by the literati as well as their attempt to syncretize Buddhism and Taoism can be seen clearly in two works: The *Hung ming chi* [c] and the *Shih shuo hsin yü*. [d] Nevertheless, even though the Ming movement was not unprecedented, in terms of its pervasiveness and thoroughness it must be regarded as qualitatively different from earlier manifestations.

The rise of lay Buddhism in the Ming is sometimes attributed to the low moral caliber of the priesthood and the attractions of a career in officialdom through the civil service examination system. [1] As a result, the best minds went into official service, and only a few excellent people became monks. The pious, unwilling to join a disreputable *sangha*, chose the practice of lay Buddhism as the only alternative. According to this view, lay Buddhism arose in response to a declining monastic Buddhism. But such an interpretation presupposes an inverse relationship between the two, and such a relationship is open to question, for in fact lay Buddhism has always been intimately linked with monastic Buddhism. Both in the T'ang and the Sung, when Buddhism was a strong institutional religion, eminent monks attracted lay followers. The situation was similar in the Ming, too, as lay Buddhists usually congregated around a few leading monks. The monk Chu-hung [e] (1535–1615) and his lay followers, the subject of this paper, serve as a good example. If there had been no revival of monastic Buddhism in the late sixteenth and early seventeenth centuries, lay Buddhism would not have emerged. Lay Buddhism, then, reflected the new life energy of Buddhism in the late Ming; it did not emerge as a substitute.

To regard lay Buddhism primarily as an "alternative" to the monastic is also to presuppose another widely held view, namely that, since the T'ang, Buddhism had declined continuously and that it reached its nadir in the Ming.[2] The principal reasons advanced for this view are usually that, after the T'ang, no important sūtras were translated, no new Buddhist sect was established, and no great master of originality and doctrinal brilliance appeared. The criteria used to evaluate the growth or the decline of Buddhism in China center on its institutional strength and philosophical creativity. But should the history of Buddhism in China be seen in these terms alone?

This paper deals primarily with the phenomena of the lay Buddhist movement and the so-called Combining of Three Teachings in the late Ming. It is not so much concerned with the question of whether Buddhism declined or degenerated as it is with the fact that the nature of Buddhist practice changed after the T'ang. The main features characterizing this change were an increasing emphasis upon self-enlightenment through a practical methodology and a growing openness toward Confucianism and Taoism. Eschewing doctrinal exclusiveness, post-T'ang Buddhism attempted to become fully integrated with Chinese society. This process of sinification is best exemplified in Buddhism during the Ming Dynasty.

When we probe for causes leading to the rise of lay Buddhism during the late Ming, two stand out for special attention. First, the popularity of the School of Wang Yang-ming, especially its later offshoot, the left-wing Wang school (the T'ai-chou school),[f] undoubtedly contributed in no small measure to the atmosphere of individualism and freedom in religious as well as intellectual inquiry. The nonsectarian approach to spiritual realization as advocated by the Wang school broke new ground for a rediscovery of Buddhism. It kindled a general appreciation of and interest in Buddhism. A second important cause derived from the conscious efforts of monks such as Chu-hung to propagate Buddhism among the educated literati-official class in a form which could be readily understood and easily appreciated. These monks also adopted a conciliatory attitude toward Confucianism and Taoism, although in truth some of them, like Chu-hung, did not really regard either as the equal of Buddhism. The important point here, however, is not so much that Chu-hung did not wholeheartedly welcome Confucianism and Taoism as equals, as that he did seek to accommodate Buddhism to the other two doctrines and to fit all three into a hierarchical pyramid, with Buddhism at the apex. It is important to stress Chu-hung's attitude toward the problem of the Three Teachings, for without this posture of reconciliation it would have been impossible for him to have become the most influential figure in the formation of the lay Buddhist movement in the late Ming, a movement that continued to flourish through the Ch'ing period and is still active among Chinese communities outside mainland China. The lay Buddhist movement and the Combining of Three Teachings laid a theoretical foundation for the absorption of Buddhism into the personal lives of the literati-official class. Conversely, the development of lay Buddhism among this same class was a concrete manifestation of the combination and a tangible index of its success.

As noted above, Chu-hung was the most important figure in the formation of the lay Buddhist movement during the late Ming. Specifically, two of his ideas exerted a great influence on his followers: first, compassion for sentient beings, as manifested in the nonkilling (*pu sha*) [g] and release of animals (*fang-sheng*); [h] second, the promotion of popular morality through the system of merit and demerit outlined in his book, *Tzu-chih lu* [i] (The Record of Self-Knowledge, *Yün-ch'i fa-hui*, XV). As we shall see, Chu-hung was not the originator of these concepts, for both had long been accepted tenets, not only in the Buddhist tradition, but also in Confucianism and Taoism. Nevertheless, his way of interpreting and presenting these ideas yielded great success and won him an immense following among both the educated elite and the common people.

COMPASSION FOR LIFE—THE DOCTRINAL FOUNDATION OF LAY BUDDHISM

The precepts of nonkilling and the release of animals have firm doctrinal bases in Buddhism. They are the first of the "ten grave" (*shih-chung*) [j] precepts and the twentieth of the "forty-eight light" (*ssu-shih pa ch'ing*) [k] precepts. Together, these two groups form the entire set of bodhisattva precepts (*p'u-sa chieh*) [l] as set forth in the second half of the chapter called "Ground of Mind" in the *Sūtra of Brahma's Net (Fan-wang ching hsin ti p'in)*. [m] As the basic precepts of Mahāyāna Buddhism primarily

addressed to lay believers, this set of fifty-eight precepts has always enjoyed great popularity as well as authority in China. There are numerous
commentaries on this sūtra, and that by the T'ien-t'ai master, Chih-i[n]
(538–97), is the most famous. Chu-hung composed a subcommentary on
this work that has the cumbersome title: The Elucidation of the Commentary on the Meaning of the Bodhisattva Precepts as Contained in the
Chapter Entitled: The Ground of Mind in the Sūtra of Brahma's Net
(Fan-wang ching hsin-ti p'in p'u-sa chieh i-shu fa-yin)[o] (5 chüan,
YCFH, I-IV). Since Chu-hung's understanding of and attitude toward
the Buddhist Vinaya are both found in this work, it deserves our special
attention. While his Record of Self-Knowledge is a detailed prescription
for a moral life, this commentary serves as its theoretical rationale,
guided throughout by the spirit of Buddhist compassion.

The scriptural text of the precept of nonkilling reads:

The Buddha said, "All sons of Buddha should neither kill by themselves (tzu
sha),[p] cause others to kill (chiao jen sha),[q] offer others the means to kill (fang-pien
sha),[r] encourage others to kill (tsan-t'an sha)[s] nor help others in killing (chien-tso
sui-hsi),[t] nor kill by uttering a spell (chou sha).[u] There are the primary causes of
killing (sha yin),[v] secondary causes of killing (sha yüan),[w] acts of killing (sha fa),[x]
and the karma of killing (sha yeh).[y] [3] As long as anything has life, you should not
kill it intentionally. Therefore a bodhisattva should abide always in the mind of
compassion (tz'u-pei hsin),[z] the mind of filial obedience (hsiao-shun hsin),[aa] and
always save and protect all sentient beings with expediency of means." [4]

Regarding the last sentence, Chu-hung explains in his commentary
that:

The two things [a bodhisattva] should have are compassion and filial obedience,
and one thing he should do is offer salvation and protection. To kill is to act contrary to Heaven and Principle, therefore it is unfilial and disobedient. Moreover,
since all sentient beings are our parents of many past generations, to hurt and
harm them is to hurt and harm our own fathers and mothers. If one can refrain
from hurting them, one may avoid sin. But, unless one also saves and protects
them, one cannot be called a bodhisattva. Therefore, while practicing nonkilling,
we should also save sentient beings.[5]

Among the injunctions, "nonkilling" heads the list of the ten grave of-
fenses a bodhisattva must avoid. Its importance cannot be overempha-
sized. However, for the advocates of the practice of compassion to animals through such acts as setting them free (fang-sheng) and keeping a
vegetarian diet, the principal rationale is offered by another precept: the

twentieth precept in the group of forty-eight light offences. It is called
"the prohibition against the nonpractice of releasing and saving [sentient
beings]," (Pu-hsing fang-chiu chieh).[ab] It reads:

All sons of Buddha, because of their compassionate hearts, practice the releasing
of sentient beings. All men are my father and all women are my mother. Each
rebirth of mine without any exception, from one rebirth to another, I receive
from them. Therefore all the beings in the six paths of existence are my parents.
If I should kill and eat them, it is the same as killing my own parents. It is also
the same as killing my own self. For earth and water are my former body, while
fire and wind are my original substance. Thus one should always release sentient
beings. Since to be reborn in one existence after another is the permanent and
unalterable law, we should teach people to release sentient beings. When we see
that domestic animals are about to be killed, we ought to save them with expedient means and release them from suffering. We ought always to preach the
bodhisattva precepts and save sentient beings. On the day when one's parents or
brothers pass away, one might ask a Vinaya master to lecture on the doctrine and
rules of the bodhisattva precepts, so that as the dead are aided by the merits they
will be able to see the Buddhas and be reborn in the path of man or heaven.
Those who do not do this commit a venial offense.[6]

In his commentary on this passage, Chu-hung further elaborated the
doctrine. Three main points are emphasized, and they are put in a question and answer format. The questions come from an imaginary interlocuter of decidedly Confucian persuasion. The first question is: "Mo
Tzu advocated impartial love and is regarded as a heretic. Now, how can
one say that all sentient beings are my father and mother?" Chu-hung
answers: "Confucianism only talks of this life, but Buddhism also discusses our previous existences. Since a person is reborn in many lives, he
must receive reincarnation in all the various realms of existence. Then is
it not natural that sentient beings in all six paths of existence are my father and mother? When people only look at the traces which lie nearby
but do not investigate their distant causes, they are naturally prone to find
heresy." [7]

The second question is about the identity between the four elements
(earth, water, wind, fire) and man's physical body. The interlocuter asks,
"The four great (ssu-ta) [ac] elements are external things. How can they be
related to our bodies?" According to Chu-hung, the relationship is illusory. Man's true self is forever "empty" (śūnya) but out of ignorance he
becomes attached to the phenomenal world and regards his temporal existence as real. Once the delusion takes hold, man is trapped in trans-

migration and remains inextricably entangled with the "four elements" which are merely symbols of the phenomena. Thus Chu-hung's answer is:

Sentient beings, being deluded, do not know their true selves which are permanent and real. They regard outside things as their own selves and, taking earth, water, fire, and wind, they make these into their own blood, flesh, body warmth, and breath. They are born when these four great elements are combined, and they die when the elements disperse and disintegrate. Except for death by transformation [ad] [death of beings such as arhāts, who live in realms beyond transmigration], all ordinary mortal dispensations [ae] [death in the three realms of desire, form, and formlessness, as well as in the six paths] cannot survive in a body independent of this condition. [8]

In the third question, anticipating possible doubts on the part of the reader, Chu-hung poses two related problems regarding the correspondence between the physical universe and its human microcosm. He argues his case with analogies and inferences in a manner reminiscent of the fourth-century polemics between the Buddhists and their Confucian opponents, with particular reference to the controversy about the immortality or mortality of the soul. (The foremost of these early polemics, brilliantly presented by the anti-Buddhist Fan Chen [af] [c. 450–c. 515] in the essay "On the Extinction of the Soul," [ag] held the latter view.) [9] The first question in Chu-hung's presentation is: If all creatures are endowed with the same four elements, the natural consequence would be that we should be able to share each other's feeling and sensations. But how is it that when I hurt another being, I do not feel any pain? The answer is:

One's own body and the body of others are both the same and different. The difference is like the case when thousands of flowers grow on one tree, yet each has its own nature. So when one flower is plucked, the rest are not affected. Therefore, the food of one arhāt could not satisfy the rest of the monks, [10] and a loving brother's voluntary cauterization could not lessen another brother's pain. [11] As for their being the same, we have such examples as when the mother bit her finger, the filial son felt it in his heart [12] or when the statue of a rebellious subject was struck, his own head also fell off. [13] When somebody eats a plum, one's own mouth often starts to water in anticipation of the sour taste. When we see another person stand on a cliff, we start to tremble ourselves. This is because all men share the same breath and blood. That is why we can respond to each other. [14]

Chu-hung goes on to raise another question. If our physical body consists of the four elements, then how is it that we are mortally susceptible to their destruction? In other words, why does earth suffocate us, water drown us, fire burn us, and wind freeze us? Chu-hung answers this way:

There are two reasons for this. The first is the mutual antagonism of the elements,[ah] and the second is the self-cancellation of each element.[ai] In the former case, though when earth accumulates, it blocks the wind, when the wind is strong it disperses earth; or when fire is fierce, it dries water, but when there is much water, it extinguishes fire; just so the four elements outside our body are antagonistic toward the four elements inside our body. They check and hold each other in control. In the latter case, just as the collapse of Mount T'ai would wipe out a mound of earth, the waves of the ocean would absorb a spoonful of water, the raging fire eats up a flicker of flame, or the typhoon draws in a light breeze, the external and internal four elements destroy each other because of the similarity of their essence.[15]

Chu-hung, in the commentary, tries to compare the Buddhist attitude toward one's parents with the Confucian and prove the superiority of the former. Since the twentieth precept places the salvation and release of sentient beings before the provision concerning religious services on the anniversary of one's parents' deaths, one may legitimately attack it for its slight against one's own parents. As Chu-hung had his questioner put it, there should be a natural order in expressing one's love and loyalty, that is, one should start with one's immediate family, then extend it to other people, and lastly to inanimate things. Now if, as the precept dictates, one puts others before one's own family, would this not be contrary to nature? Chu-hung answers, "When you put your own before other people, although you are concerned with others, you still make a distinction between yourself and others. This is ordinary compassion. But, when you put other people before your own, you are solely concerned with others, but are no longer aware of yourself. This is compassion par excellence." [16] In other words, Confucian compassion is not as vigorous and thoroughgoing as Buddhist compassion.

On another occasion Chu-hung compared the Confucian moral precepts with the Buddhist and arrived at a similar conclusion. He felt that although they formally resemble each other they were quite different in scope and intensity. Buddhist precepts, according to Chu-hung, were more demanding and far-reaching. They aimed at absolute perfection, whereas Confucian precepts aimed at goodness in moderation.

The precepts of Confucianism and Buddhism are similar, but as the one is limited and the other comprehensive in scope, they are quite different. Take the prohibition against killing, one of the five Buddhist precepts. In Buddhism, it means nonkilling in absolute terms. On the other hand, although Confucianism also teaches compassion, it only says that one should not kill cows, sheep, dogs and pigs without good reason. It does not prohibit killing per se. Confucianism also advocates not fishing with a net or shooting at a nesting bird. Unlike Buddhism, however, it does not prohibit fishing and shooting under all circumstances. Therefore we know that Confucian precepts aim for the good of the secular society, while Buddhist precepts aim for the good in absolute transcendence. It is also not surprising that since ancient times individual Confucians have accepted and observed the Buddhist precepts.[17]

The influence of the precepts of nonkilling and of release of life upon the practice of Chinese Buddhism has always been extensive. Although Chu-hung and his fellow monks emphasized these precepts, this was not the first time that they had been advocated. A brief historical survey of the attempted institutionalization of these ideas may give us some perspective.[18]

HISTORICAL PRECEDENTS FOR THE ADVOCACY OF NONKILLING AND OF RELEASE OF LIFE

During the Sui Dynasty, in A.D. 583, it was legally stipulated that in the first, fifth, and ninth months of the year, as well as in the "six fast days" [aj] (eighth, fourteenth, fifteenth, twenty-fourth, twenty-ninth, and thirtieth days) in every month, no one should kill any living being.[19] The choice of these particular dates was based on the rule set down in the same *Sūtra of Brahma's Net*.[20] It says that during these three months and on these six days of every month a lay devotee should keep the eight precepts, starting with the prohibition against killing and robbery, as well as the rule of not eating after the noon meal. On the six fast days, the four Heavenly Kings would make an inspection of the world, observe the good and evil deeds of men, and make a record of them. Therefore, one should be especially cautious on these days.

During the T'ang Dynasty, in 619, a decree was issued forbidding the slaughter of animals as well as fishing and hunting during the first, fifth, and ninth months of every year.[21] This decree apparently met with varying degrees of success until the Hui-ch'ang persecution (845). As for the establishment of ponds for releasing life (*fang-sheng ch'ih*),[ak] the earliest reference is dated during the reign of Emperor Yüan of the Liang Dynasty (552–55), when a pavilion was constructed for this purpose,[22] but we do not know the exact date or type of design of this institution. During the T'ang Dynasty, Emperor Su-tsung issued a decree in 759 setting up eighty-one ponds for releasing life.[23] The famous calligrapher, Yen Chen-ch'ing [al] (709–85) [24] wrote an inscription on a stone tablet commemorating this event. According to the inscription, the area in which these ponds were established included parts of present-day Shansi, Hupei, Hunan, Szechuan, Yunnan, Kweichow, Kwangtung, Kwangsi, Kiangsi and Chekiang. "Starting from Hsing-tao of Yangchow (Shensi), through the various districts of Shan-nan, Chien-nan, Ch'ien-chung, Ching-nan, Ling-nan, Kiangsi, Chekiang and ending at the T'ai-p'ing Bridge over the Ch'in-huai River at Chiang-ning of Shen-chow (Nanking), every five *li* a pond for releasing life is set up by the river and near the city. Altogether there are eighty-one ponds." [25] Although we have access to governmental decrees and codifications giving some indication of the extent of official compliance, the evidence suggests that the extent of popular practice was very limited. It is not until the Sung Dynasty that we begin to see the pervasive popularization of the release of life.

This eventual result was due mainly to the successful evangelism of outstanding monks. Yung-ming Yen-shou [am] (904–75),[26] the great synthesizer of all Buddhist sects, was an advocate especially of the amalgamation of Ch'an and Pure Land. Before he became a monk, when he was in charge of taxes for the King of Wu-yüeh, he used government money to buy fish and shrimps and set them free. Tz'u-yün Tsun-shih [an] (963–1032),[27] a T'ien-t'ai monk who also advocated Pure Land practice, persuaded many fishermen to change their profession. It is said that when he was lecturing at the K'ai-yüan Monastery "people in the whole city stopped drinking wine, and butchers lost their business." [28] He was also instrumental in setting up new ponds for releasing life. In 1017, Emperor Chen-tsung issued a decree calling for the establishment of ponds along the rivers Huai and Che and in Hunan and Hupei, where fishing was also prohibited.[29] Tsun-shih memorialized the throne in 1019, requesting that the Emperor's birthday be celebrated by having the West Lake established as a pond for releasing life. From then on, every year on Buddha's birthday, the eighth day of the fourth month, "meetings for releasing life" [ao] were organized, and participation in the meetings became fashionable. This custom apparently declined somewhat in later years, for in 1090 Su Tung-p'o [ap] (1036–1101) [30] wrote a memorial asking for its revival.[31]

SOME CHARACTERISTICS OF POST-T'ANG BUDDHISM

During the late T'ang and the Five Dynasties, after the monumental task of sūtra translation, doctrinal elaboration, and sectarian systematization had been finished, assimilation started in earnest. It reached a full flowering during the Sung when Ch'an and Pure Land emerged as the dominant sects of Chinese Buddhism. While superficially different in approach—Ch'an stressed self-realization effected through one's own effort, and Pure Land emphasized faith as expressed in the devotion and worship of the Amita Buddha—they both put practice ahead of doctrine. Religious salvation had to be sought through a religious life. This did not necessarily mean a monastic life, although that continued to be regarded as the preferred state for a person committed to Buddhism. It certainly did entail a definite life-style. The life of a Buddhist devotee was to embody both wisdom and compassion. When a Ch'an practitioner assiduously meditated on a *kung-an* [aq] (in Japanese, *kōan*), he was in fact gradually groping toward the realization of wisdom. Such wisdom could demolish the whole system of false and perverted thought constructions he had inherited as a human condition. In the same way, by performing such small acts of charity as setting a captured fish free or refusing to take meat on certain days, the Pure Land believer hoped to free himself from his innate desire, greed, and hatred. The motivations for such acts were not rooted merely in ethical demands, but had deep religious and psychological underpinnings. When a person killed another sentient being, he broke the hidden bond between all forms of life. Violence alienated the violator not only from a sense of cosmic harmony but ultimately from himself. For although the act of killing was an extreme assertion of the self, the self, which was already so isolated and delimited, became immediately so much more alienated that, ironically, it ceased to have any real life or meaning.

Buddhist vegetarianism, too, was significant only when viewed in this same context. For even if one did not kill an animal oneself, every time one ate its meat, he denied the existence of any meaningful relationship between himself and other beings. By objectifying an animal as "food," he could become insensitive to its suffering and regard it as a mere thing. On the other hand, each time he released a creature from impending death, each time he returned it to freedom, he reaffirmed the original bond between all sentient beings. The act of releasing was a celebration of reunion during which the selfish human will which alienates was momentarily obliterated. The person who released life in fact released himself from human selfishness.

The ordinary person engaged in such acts might not consciously realize their significance. Nor could everyone achieve this qualitative leap of transcendence by the quantitative performance of good deeds. Still, the rationale for this kind of piety was there. It comes as no surprise that the two Sung monks who advocated nonkilling and releasing of life belonged primarily to the Pure Land sect, because of its stress on compassion. What is particularly noteworthy is that this attitude penetrated even to the teachings of the Ch'an masters whose goal was the attainment of enlightenment. The amalgamation of the Ch'an and Pure Land sects started during the Sung and, as the years passed, popular Buddhism, which grew out of their common concern with religious practice, more and more reinforced this syncretic trend.

During the Sung Dynasty, lay associations became increasingly popular in Buddhist circles. Such associations have been traced back to Hui-yüan's (334–416) Lotus Club [ar] [32] and the many organizations whose traces were found in the Tun-huang remains. But as Suzuki Chūsei pointed out in his excellent study on Sung Buddhism,[33] these associations were quite different from their prototypes of the Northern and Southern Dynasties or the Sui and T'ang. In the first place, while the earlier associations were organized mainly for erecting statues of the Buddha excavating caves to store Buddhist treasures, copying and making sūtras, reciting sūtras, or organizing Buddhist feasts and religious festivals, the Sung associations were primarily "associations for reciting the Buddha's name" (*nien-fo hui*).[as] During meetings, members recited together the name of Amitābha Buddha and transferred the merits thus accrued to their speedy rebirth in the Western Paradise. The members also engaged in philanthropic activities, but invocation of the Buddha (*nien-*

fo) was the main purpose. In the second place, members of earlier associations tended to come from the upper classes, but in the Sung, membership was much more diverse and people from ordinary walks of life tended to form the majority. Although these groups were called "associations," we do not find any formal organizational structure or institutional rules. The groups often consisted of indefinite numbers of people, and they met at unspecified times. In sharp contrast to this, the "associations for releasing life" (*fang-sheng hui*) of the late Ming and the Ch'ing were remarkably better organized.

It was also during the Sung that tracts exhorting people to refrain from killing animals for food and to keep a vegetarian diet started to appear in great numbers. The ones I have read [34] are all quite short, and they argue their cases with a general appeal on ethical instead of religious grounds. The piece by Su Tung-p'o, probably the most prominent Sung lay devotee, is a representative example. Su stated that a meat-eater invariably had to violate the five cardinal virtues.

To slaughter another in order to fatten oneself is inhuman (*pu-jen*); to tear it from its kith and kin in order to entertain one's own family is unjust (*pu-i*); to offer its fleshy body to the gods is improper (*pu-li*); to proclaim that what belongs to one as one's proper share must be beheaded is unwise (*pu-chih*); and to set bait and traps to ensnare it is to lack good faith (*pu-hsin*). [35]

CHU-HUNG'S ADVOCACY OF NONKILLING AND RELEASING LIFE IN THE MING

It was in this syncretic tradition that Chu-hung carried out his lay proselytism. His essays "On Refraining from Killing," and "On Releasing Sentient Beings" (*Chieh sha fang sheng wen*) at [36] were reprinted and distributed widely. They were received with such enthusiasm and became so famous that the mother of the emperor sent a special emissary to seek further instruction from him. [37] They also started the vogue in lay circles of organizing "associations for releasing life." These associations tried to raise funds to build "ponds for releasing life" and met at definite intervals to set free captured birds, fish, and other domesticated animals (which they usually bought from fishermen or at the marketplace). In the twenty-eighth year of Wan-li (1600), as a result of Chu-hung's persuasion, his lay followers contributed money, redeemed two abandoned temples in the city of Jen-ho where he was born, and established in each a pond for releasing life. These were the Shang-fang ᵃᵘ and Ch'ang-shou ᵃᵛ ponds.

On the subject of organizing these associations, however, Chu-hung himself was curiously reticent if not outright disapproving. The reason was probably his fear of being connected with the notorious White Lotus Society and other secret societies which appeared periodically and which various governments since the Sung had tried hard to suppress.[38] Chu-hung warned his followers that there were rascals in the society who used the name of the Buddha to do evil things.[39] They proclaimed the imminent coming of the future Buddha Maitreya, and lured adherents with money, fame, material possessions, and women. The only way to disengage oneself from mistaken identification with this discredited group was to try to practice cultivation by oneself. Clubs should be organized with great discretion, and there should not be too many. In his own words:

Associations for the recitation of the Buddha's name (*nien-fo hui*) were started by Master Hui-yüan of Lu-shan, but among the organizers of clubs today, can any be compared to Master Yüan? Can the members be the equals of the eighteen gentlemen of Lu-shan? Therefore, the clubs should be few and not many. This is because people who are really interested in practising the *nien-fo* of the Pure Land are as rare as dedicated monks sitting in the meditation hall. As for women joining an association together with men, this was something unheard of at Lu-shan. Women should practice *nien-fo* at home. Do not mix with men and cause society's criticism and suspicion. If you want to protect the true Law of the Buddha, this is most important. It is also better to have fewer associations for releasing life (*fang-sheng hui*) than many, for people who are really interested in saving sentient beings are as rare as people who participate in recitation groups (*nien-fo hui*). In my opinion, everyone should buy as many creatures as he can afford and release them whenever he sees them. At the end of a season or at the end of a year, everyone may go to one place, the number one has released can be tabulated and his merits assigned. After this let everyone disperse quickly. Do not waste money to prepare offerings and do not waste time in socializing.[40]

The emphasis on flexibility and expediency was characteristic of Chu-hung's approach to problems of religious cultivation. Such organizations were not in themselves undesirable, but because of their tendency to become formalistic, Chu-hung could not endorse them with complete enthusiasm. But, on the subject of releasing life, he was consistently evangelical. In his essay "On Releasing Sentient Beings" (*Fang-sheng wen*) [aw] he argues the case with many examples drawn from historical records, legends, contemporary reports, and personal experiences. More powerful than rational and doctrinal argument, these anecdotes helped to convince not only his contemporaries, but even later readers, of the existence of a law which ensures that a good deed is always rewarded. By using a technique which stressed the working of the numinous in the miraculous, the magical, and the uncommon, he struck a responsive chord among the audiences of that time. The atmosphere of the Ming, as evidenced by the abundance of reported dreams, omens, and other inexplicable events in the *pi-chi* literature of the day, was very receptive to this approach.

Two anecdotes Chu-hung tells in this essay give us a good idea of the type of story he used. Both happened in his own day, one to himself, the other to someone in his native Hangchow.[41] In the fourth year of Lungch'ing (1570), while Chu-hung was staying at a small temple during his wanderings after he had become a monk, he saw that someone had captured several centipedes and was fastening their heads and tails together with a bamboo bow. Chu-hung bought the centipedes and set them free. Only one was still alive and got away, while the rest were nearly dead. Later on, one night while he was sitting with a friend, he suddenly caught a glimpse of a centipede on the wall. After he had tried to drive it away and failed, he said to the centipede, "Are you the one I set free before? Have you come here to thank me? If so, I shall preach the Dharma to you. Listen carefully and do not move." Then, Chu-hung continued, "All sentient beings evolve from the mind. The ones with violent minds are transformed into tigers and wolves, and the ones with poisonous minds are transformed into snakes and scorpions. If you give up your poisonous heart, you can cast off this form." After he finished talking, the centipede slowly crept out the window without having to be driven away. The friend was greatly amazed.

The second incident occurred in the ninth year of Wan-li (1581), to a household named Kan in Hu-lei, Hangchow. A neighbor of the Kan's was robbed and Kan's daughter presented the neighbor's mother with ten eels when she went over to offer condolences. The eels were put away in a big jar and were forgotten. One night the mother dreamt that ten men dressed in yellow gowns and wearing pointed hats knelt before her and begged for their lives. Upon waking, she consulted a fortune teller who told her that some creatures were begging to be released from captivity. She searched all over the house and finally found the jar containing the eels. The eels, which had in the meantime grown to enormous size, numbered exactly ten. She was utterly astonished and set them free at once.

These and other stories were meant to prove that "of the persons who set creatures free, some received honor and prestige, some received added years of life, some were spared from disasters, some recovered from mental illnesses, some achieved rebirth in heaven, and some attained enlightenment in the Way. There is clear evidence that as one releases life, he assuredly receives reward." [42] Although reward should not be the sole purpose in our performance of good deeds, Chu-hung told his readers, nevertheless, as a consequence of a good deed, reward would come even though we should refuse it.

In fact, reward had always served as an important inducement in Chu-hung's advocacy of lay practice. In another article dealing with the same subject, where he offered a complete list of reasons for one to carry out the release of life, reward again occupied a conspicuous position.

As man values his life,
So do animals love theirs.
Releasing life accords with the mind of Heaven,
Releasing life agrees with the teaching of the Buddha.
Releasing life unties the snare of hatred,
Releasing life purifies the taint of sin.
Releasing life enables one to escape the three disasters [of fire, water, wind],
Releasing life enables one to be free from the "nine kinds of untimely deaths"
    (*chiu-heng*).[ax] [43]
Releasing life enables one to live long,
Releasing life enables one to rise high in official career,
Releasing life enables one to have many children,
Releasing life enables one to have a prosperous household.
Releasing life dispels anxieties and worries,
Releasing life reduces sickness and pain.
Releasing life is the compassion of Kuan-yin (Avalokiteśvara),
Releasing life is the deed of P'u-hsien (Samantabhadra).
By releasing life one comes to realize the truth of no birth (*wu-sheng*) [ay]
By releasing life one ends transmigration.[44]

Here Chu-hung tells his readers that releasing life is as much the will of Heaven as a teaching of the Buddha. He attracts his readers with worldly honors and riches, promises them magical protection from disaster and, in the end, holds out the loftiest ideal in Buddhism, "no birth" and release from transmigration. What are we to make of this mixture of religious, magical, moral, and materialistic rationales?

It cannot be denied that Chu-hung consistently used the theme of reward and punishment. But his credentials as a Buddhist master are also beyond doubt. His knowledge and understanding of Buddhist philosophy, especially that of Hua-yen,[az] is excellent. Following the orthodox Chinese Buddhist tradition, he shows his ability as a scholastic commentator on sūtras in the *Fo-shuo A-mi-t'o ching shu ch'ao* [ba] (Phrase by Phrase Commentary on the Buddha's Scripture Concerning the One of Immeasureable Life).[45] Yet both in advocating nonkilling and releasing life, and in propagating the social ethics set forth in the *Record of Self-Knowledge*, Chu-hung displayed remarkably little of his Buddhist learning. He relied much more on practical moral persuasion. This apparent contradiction can be resolved if we examine his purpose for encouraging lay Buddhism: we discover that Chu-hung was not only aiming *for* something; he was also reacting *against* something.

The fact that Chu-hung proselytized in a nonintellectual, nonphilosophical manner was not an accident but a deliberate choice. He was, in fact, greatly distressed by what he considered the failure of Buddhism in his own time. This failure, as he saw it, was due mainly to the degeneration of Ch'an practice and the neglect of monastic discipline. Instead of working seriously on his enlightenment, the Ch'an devotee only talked about it in clever language. Ch'an was no longer a genuine living experience, but was the mimicry of earlier kōans and the fabrication of sophistries. Religious cultivation had come to signify learning by rote and the meaningless display of intellectual cleverness. Neglect of monastic discipline was closely connected with the stultification of Ch'an. Ch'an masters in the T'ang and Sung frequently shocked their disciples by their unconventional behavior and by their refusal to admit the relevance of moral action to spiritual enlightenment. The Truth discovered through enlightenment transcends human morality, and the person in a state of enlightenment regards all moral values as relative. This transcendence of human morality, however, applies only to those who have experienced enlightenment.

Yet in Chu-hung's time, people who had never experienced enlightenment continued to denigrate morality as conventional. It was against this irresponsible attitude that Chu-hung launched an attack. He saw the sense of moral seriousness as most needed. It could take the form of the observance of Vinaya rules in the case of a monk, or the practice of nonkilling, release of life, and social philanthropy in the case of a lay devotee. Under the charismatic inspiration of strong Ch'an masters, Buddhism was able to retain its vitality even if it did not stress moral cultivation. But in the postcharismatic age of the Ming (which Chu-hung, along with other Buddhists, called the "degenerate age of the Law") it would be dangerous to neglect moral discipline. Indeed, moral discipline was the only effective means by which to husband flagging energies and infuse vigor and direction into religious life.

This question arose in Chu-hung's correspondence with Chou Ju-teng,[bb] a member of the T'ai-chou School and a disciple of Lo Chin-hsi,[bc] who introduced him to Buddhist writings.[46] Chou once engaged in a debate with a fellow Confucian concerning the meaning of the famous "Colloquy at the T'ien-ch'üan Bridge." He held to the interpretation then that the mind was neither good nor evil, and he wrote to Chu-hung about it saying, "If we realize the true self, then where is good and evil? It is like the moon shining on the river, how can one say whether it is clear or murky?" To this Chu-hung answered:

Even though the moon is pure, depending on whether the water is clear or murky, the reflection will become dull or bright. Although the mind is originally luminous, yet as one does good or evil deeds, their traces will make the mind soar high or sink to the ground. How can we say that the dirty water is good simply because the moon in its essence cannot be designated as clear or murky? How can one say that evil deeds do not matter simply because the mind in its essence cannot be designated as good or evil? If one is addicted to the biased view of emptiness, he will deviate from perfect understanding. Once you realize that both good and evil are nonexistent, it is all the better that you should stop evil and do good. If you insist on not stopping evil and not doing good, it shows that your understanding is not yet perfect.[47]

"To do good and to stop evil" [bd] was indeed the key to the entire Buddist Vinaya. Chu-hung sought to use Pure Land faith and moral discipline to correct the penchant for "empty talk" current in his day.

Releasing life, then, was intended as a method of moral cultivation. One might wish that Chu-hung, in advocating the performance of good

deeds, had stressed the importance of nonattachment more and the benefits of worldly rewards less. But he was as much a practical missionary as a
Buddhist theologian. He well knew the hopes and aspirations of his audience, and he was concerned above all with providing them with concrete
and practical methods of lay practice. This is demonstrated in the essay
"On Releasing Life," especially at the end where he offered concrete
guidelines. First, everyone was enjoined to buy animals whenever the opportunity presented itself. One should not begrudge the money spent, for
money does not last while the blessedness (fu) [be] created by redeeming
animals lasts forever. If a person does not have money, as long as he has
a compassionate heart and persuades others to buy animals, and as long
as he takes delight in such actions by others, he himself also accumulates
blessedness.

Second, it is the deed of releasing, not the size or quantity of the
animals released, which counts most. The rich man who saves the lives
of many animals, and the poor man who saves only one insect, are
equally praiseworthy. What is most important is that it be done continually and persistently. There are people who do not understand this
principle. They buy many small creatures in the hope of gaining more
merits. This is no more than calculated greed. It is certainly not true
compassion for sentient beings.

Third, in releasing life, one is enjoined to try as much as possible to
perform a religious ceremony at which sūtras are read and Amita Buddha's name is recited. For one should not only save the creature's physical body (se-shen) [bf] but also its spiritual life (hui-ming).[bg] However, if
this cannot be conveniently arranged, one should be flexible. Where
there is not time for sūtra recitation, nien-fo alone is enough. If, for the
sake of the religious ceremony, one keeps the animals overnight and
allows some of them to perish, the consequences surely will negate the
intention.[48]

Despite Chu-hung's reservations about lay associations, he did organize an association himself. The rules he drew up for this association give
us a good picture of its operations. Members of the association were to
meet once a month (on the day before the last day of each month) at the
Shang-fang Temple; hence its name, "The Good Society of Shang-
fang." [bh] At these meetings, accompanied by a monk who beat a wooden
fish, members were to recite first one volume of Vinaya sūtras, then the

name of Amita Buddha five hundred or one thousand times. They were each to contribute five *fen* (one-hundredth of an ounce) toward the preparation of fruit and vegetarian offerings to the Buddha. Members were urged to contribute money for buying captured animals and setting them free, though the amount of money was not fixed. They could also bring fish or birds to the temple and release them there. When members gathered together, no one was allowed to talk about worldly things; they were to discuss only unclear passages of scripture or essential points of cultivation. Discussions were to be short and to the point. Each member took his turn serving as chairman of the monthly meetings, and it was his responsibility to keep the account book for dues received and expenses paid. The chairman was the first to arrive and the last to leave.[49]

Some of Chu-hung's followers organized other associations along similar lines. T'ao Wang-ling,[bi] [50] who was a student of Chou Ju-teng and a close friend to Chiao Hung,[bj] [51] organized a club, together with some friends in the southern part of K'uai-chi (in present-day Shao-hsing, Chekiang), during the summer of the twenty-ninth year of Wan-li (1601). The text of Chu-hung's "Essay on Releasing Life" (*Fang-sheng wen*) appeared at the beginning of the club register.[52] Another lay follower, Yü Ch'un-hsi,[bk] [53] organized a club named the Sheng-lien she [bl] (Luxuriant Lotus) which met on the West Lake. Except for minor details, the rules for this club were identical to those described above.

A companion piece to the "Essay on Releasing Life" was the "Essay on Nonkilling," (*Chieh-sha wen*),[bm] comprised in equal proportions of case histories and methodical directions for practice. Chu-hung believed that the killing and eating of animals was a habit formed gradually and by imitation. If someone ate human flesh, society would be rightly shocked, but if this practice had not been prohibited and had instead been taken over by ever larger numbers of people, then, after a fews years, cannibalism would in like manner have become accepted. Chu-hung was convinced that the custom of killing animals for food had, also, to be stopped. He listed seven occasions whereon the killing of animals would be most common, and in each instance he gave arguments to demonstrate its wrongness or irrationality.[54]

1. On one's birthday one should not kill animals. Parents bear the burden of giving birth to you and bringing you up. From the day you are first born, your parents are already embarked on the slow process of death. Therefore on this day

one should do good deeds in order to help the souls of one's parents achieve a speedy deliverance from suffering. If you indulge in killing, it will not only be disastrous to yourself, but it will also implicate your parents.

2. When you have a son you should not kill animals. Since you know that all men are happy to have sons, is it hard to imagine that animals also love their young? If, to celebrate the birth of your son, you take the life of their sons, can your conscience really be at ease? Furthermore, when a baby is born you ought to accumulate merits for his sake. Now on the contrary, if you create bad karma by killing, this is stupidity beyond belief.

3. When one sacrifices to one's ancestors, one should not kill animals. On the anniversary of the dead as well as during the spring and autumn visits to ancestral graves, one ought to observe the precept of nonkilling in order to assist the dead with good merits. Killing can only bring added karma upon the dead. For the body under the grave, even the choicest delicacies in the world will not be able to reawaken its sense of taste.

4. For the wedding ceremony one should not kill animals. From the preliminary rite of asking names, to betrothal and finally to the wedding, innumerable animals are killed for these ceremonies. But marriage is the beginning of the bringing forth of new life. It is contrary to reason to kill life at the beginning of life. Furthermore, the wedding day is an auspicious day. Therefore it is cruel to perform violent deeds on such a day.

5. For entertaining friends one should not kill animals. Vegetables, fruits, and plain food are equally conducive to friendly conversation. There is no need for slaughtering animals and procuring extravagant dishes. When one realizes that the meat one enjoys came from screaming animals, any person with a heart must feel sad.

6. In praying for avoidance of disaster, one should not kill animals. When a person is sick he often kills animals to sacrifice to the spirits (shen).[bn] But to kill another life in order to ask the spirits for the continuity of one's own life is contrary to the principle of Heaven. Moreover, spirits are upright and just, how can they be bribed? Therefore not only is one unable to prolong one's life, but one commits the evil karma of killing.

7. One should not kill animals in order to make a livelihood. It is said that some people have to fish, hunt, or slaughter cows, sheep, pigs, and dogs for the sake of a livelihood. But people who are not engaged in such professions do not necessarily end up in starvation. To make a living by killing animals is condemned by the spirits, and no one who does this ever achieves prosperity. On the contrary, it surely will lead one to hell and make a person suffer retribution in the next life. Therefore it is imperative for such persons to seek another way of earning a livelihood.

At the end of the essay, Chu-hung once again provided practical instructions [55] for the regular observance of the precept. If a person cannot stop killing on all seven occasions, he should still try his best to reduce the frequency of his violation. If he cannot completely forswear meat, the least he should do is to buy it from the market and not kill the animal himself. Thus, by nurturing the mind of compassion, one may hope to gradually improve one's karmic nature. There are, moreover, two further things one should do. The first is to pass the essay around among one's relatives, friends, and other people. The more persons one converts to vegetarianism the greater is one's own merit. The second is, at the beginning of each year, to paste up on the wall twelve pieces of paper with the name of a month written on each. When one does not kill anything for a whole month, one writes "no killing" on the paper. If a person does not kill for one month, it is "inferior goodness"; [bo] for a whole year, it is "medium goodness"; [bp] for a whole lifetime, it is "superior goodness." [bq]

A CONTROVERSY BETWEEN CHU-HUNG AND MATTEO RICCI

I have devoted considerable space to Chu-hung's ideas on nonkilling and the release of life because these two concepts exerted the greatest impact on lay Buddhism, not only during Chu-hung's own age, but in later generations. However, compassion for animals, vegetarianism, and especially the practice of setting captured animals free, often appear quaint and simple-minded to the modern reader. In fact, resistance to them, based presumably on common sense and rationality, was already being voiced during Chu-hung's lifetime. One attack emanated from Matteo Ricci [br] (1552–1610), the Jesuit missionary who came to China in 1582, became very successful in missionary work, and gained a considerable following among the Confucian gentry. Ricci's attack and Chu-hung's reply started a major controversy between Catholicism and Buddhism. The controversy, which came to be known as the "movement to expose heretical teachings" (*p'i-hsieh yün-tung*), [bs] was carried on energetically around Hangchow and Fukien, and it lasted well into the early Ch'ing Dynasty.[56] Matteo Ricci's main thesis was presented in his book, *The True Meaning of the Lord of Heaven* [57] (*T'ien-chu shih-i*), [bt] written in 1603. In the fifth chapter, Ricci attacked the Buddhist doctrine of transmigration of souls. After listing five arguments against it, he arrived at his main target, namely, his proof that the Buddhist precepts of nonkilling and release of life were absurd.

Those who preach nonkilling fear that the cows and horses one kills might be the reincarnation of one's own parents and therefore they cannot bear the idea of killing them. But if they really think so, how can they bear the idea of forcing cows to till the land or drive the cart?—or they themselves ride on horses? For I think the crimes of killing one's parents and that of enslaving them with physical hardship are not too different.[58]

But, more serious even than his argument that, if one really believes in reincarnation, one should not only not kill animals but should also not use them for farming, was his assertion that the institution of marriage would then have to be outlawed.

If we believe in the theory that a human being can be reborn as another human being, then we have to outlaw marriage and the employment of servants. For how can you know that the woman you are to marry is not the reincarnation of your own mother in your previous life? And how can you be sure that the servant whom you order around and on whom you heap abuse is not the latter-day manifestation of your brother, relative, sovereign, teacher, or friend? The canon governing human relationships will assuredly be wrecked by this.[59]

Citing the Christian concept of Creator-God, Matteo Ricci claimed that everything in this world was created by God for the benefit of man.[60] Similarly, birds and animals were created to nourish the life of man. As long as men used natural resources within limits, killing was not necessarily an evil. In this way, he was in complete agreement with the Confucian conservationist attitude.

The universal law under heaven is to prohibit the killing of man but not animals and birds. For animals, vegetables and plants function in the same way as the economy. As long as we use them with restraint, it is all right. Therefore, Mencius taught the king that in fishing, men should not exhaust the pond, and in cutting down trees there should be a definite time for men to go to the mountains. But he did not say that men should not do such things.[61]

Chu-hung's defense consisted of three short essays entitled "On Heaven" (T'ien-shuo),[bu] which are in his *Jottings Under a Bamboo Window*.[62] The main portion of the argument ran thus:

The *Brahma's Net* only strictly prohibits the taking of life. Since, from time immemorial, we have lived on the wheel of transmigration and in each reincarnation we must have parents, then how can we be sure that they are not our parents of previous existences? But to say that they *might be* our parents is not the same as to say that they definitely *are* our parents. . . . Marriages between men and women, the use of carts and horses, as well as the employment of servants are all ordinary things in the world. They can never be compared with the cruelty of taking the lives of animals. That is why the Sūtra only says that one should not kill any sentient being, but does not say that one should not marry or use any sentient being. The kind of sophistry [used by Matteo Ricci] is a clever play on words. How can it harm the clear teaching of the Great Truth? [63]

In the same year in which he finished this essay (1615), Chu-hung died. His lay disciple, Yü Ch'un-hsi, continued the defense of the Law. He exchanged letters with Matteo Ricci, taking the same position as his master. Yü's letter and Matteo Ricci's reply are contained in a curious book entitled *Posthumous Letters Concerning the Investigation of Knowledge (Pien-hsüeh i-tu)*,[bv] which is attributed to Matteo Ricci and came out twenty years after Chu-hung's death.[64] Besides the two letters, this work also contains a reply supposedly written by Matteo Ricci and directed against Chu-hung's *T'ien shuo*.[65] However, since Matteo Ricci died five years before the appearance of the *T'ien shuo*, he could not have known about it. Therefore, it is clear that at least this part of the book is spuriously attributed to Ricci.[66]

This controversy is significant not only because of its historical interest, but because it illustrated a very important doctrinal difference between Buddhism and other systems of morality. Buddhism requires that a man practice compassion not only toward his fellowmen, but also toward the animal kingdom. What the precepts of nonkilling and releasing life demand, of course, is our extension to animals of the same feeling and sentiments we exhibit toward our fellowmen. This is different from the Confucian concept of *jen* (benevolence) which, though it requires kindness and sympathy toward animals because they share with us the same cosmic process of regeneration and decay, is concerned chiefly with human society. In advocating Buddhist compassion, Chu-hung was trying to effect a form of transvaluation which would reorient the people to a broader value system than that of the traditionally family-centered social consciousness. But while doing this, Chu-hung did not invalidate the Confucian moral schema. Filial piety, loyalty, and other such virtues were accepted intact, which explains Chu-hung's success in proselytizing his Confucian audience. However, he did not merely superimpose Buddhist ethics on a Confucian structure. His method was to take a Confucian virtue, prove that Buddhism also valued it, interpret it according to the Buddhist understanding, give it back to the society, and ask people to value it with this added dimension. Chu-hung's treatment of the concept of *hsiao* [bw] (filial piety) provides a good example. In the *Sūtra of Brahma's Net*, before the Buddha gives the precepts, he says: "You are to perform filial piety to your parents, to the monk who is your teacher, and to the Three Jewels. Filial piety is the law of ultimate truth. It is the discipline (*śīla*)." Chih-i did not comment on this passage, but Chu-hung built a major thesis out of it. He says:

If one is filial to his parents, he will naturally be pleasant in his voice and will not utter crude and unreasonable things. This is the discipline for the mouth. [bx] He is forever solicitous and never disobeys: this is the discipline for the body. [by] He is full of sincere love and his mind will not harbor disloyal thoughts: this is the discipline for the mind. [bz] Filial piety has the power to stop evil, for one fears to disgrace one's parents. This is the discipline of proper conduct. [ca] It can also induce the performance of good, for one wishes to glorify one's parents: this is the discipline of good dharma. [cb] Finally, filial piety also has the power to save others. Because of one's love for one's own parents, other people can often be moved to follow the example. Thus, this is also the discipline for saving the sentient beings. [cc] To sum up, as long as one can be filial, his conduct will naturally be perfect. It is no wonder that the discipline is so interpreted. Aside from filial piety, is there any other discipline? [67]

Chu-hung went even further and subsumed the other five perfections (*pāramitā*) under filial piety.

In accordance with the mind of compassion, one does not indulge in stinginess; this is filial piety as charity. In accordance with the mind of submission, one does not indulge in anger; this is filial piety as patience. In accordance with the mind of perseverance, one does not indulge in laziness; this is filial piety as energy. In accordance with the mind of quietude, one does not indulge in absent-mindedness; this is filial piety as concentration. And finally, in accordance with the mind of luminous knowledge, one does not indulge in delusion; this is then filial piety as wisdom. [68]

CHU-HUNG'S ADVOCACY OF SOCIAL ETHICS: THE RECORD OF SELF-KNOWLEDGE

Before we examine Chu-hung's relationships with his lay followers, we must look briefly at another of his contributions to lay Buddhism, namely his *Record of Self-Knowledge (Tzu-chih lu)*. This book belongs to a class of Confucian-Buddho-Taoist popular books and pamphlets usually designated as "morality books," ^{cd} which were written to inculcate moral values in their readers. Although this form of morality book had been in existence since the Sung, as witnessed by the popularity of another book of this genre, the *Treatise of the Exalted One on Response and Retribution (T'ai-shang kan-ying p'ien)*,^{ce 69} it was not until the late Ming that they really started to exert a strong influence over ordinary people. This change was due mainly to the influence of Chu-hung's *Record* and the work of his contemporary, Yüan Huang (1533–1606).^{cf 70} Yüan wrote the *Record of Silent Recompense (Yin-chih lu)* ^{cg} as a guide to conduct for his own son. It is theoretical and gives only general directions for practice. Chu-hung's *Record*, however, is very detailed in terms of practical application.

The *Record of Self-Knowledge* was modeled after a Taoist work entitled *The Ledger of Merit and Demerit According to the Immortal T'ai-wei (T'ai-wei hsien-chün kung-kuo-ko)*,^{ch 71} which is contained in the Taoist canon *(Tao-tsang)*, preface dated 1171. According to Chu-hung's preface to the *Record of Self-Knowledge*, dated the thirty-second year of Wan-li (1604), he saw *The Ledger of Merit and Demerit* when he was a young man and was so overjoyed that he had it reprinted and distributed free of charge.[72] He seems to have been especially impressed by one method recommended by the author. Chu-hung tells us how the method worked:

The Immortal said that all men ought to have a notebook kept by the side of their beds. When they went to sleep they were to write down both the merits and demerits they had acquired during the day. Accumulating the days to a month, and then accumulating the months to a year, they could either cancel demerits by merits or vice versa. By looking at the number of merits or demerits they would know by themselves if they could expect blessing or punishment.[73]

The book was intended as a model for the ethical life. One might consult it to find out what good deeds one should do and what bad acts one should avoid. *Ko* (ledger) means a frame, a limit, a pattern, or ruled lines for writing. As the passage quoted above makes clear, the practitioner of this system of merit and demerit is urged to keep an account book on his daily behavior. In this sense, *ko* had the meaning of a ledger. The most striking feature of the *Ledger* was its quantification of morality. All acts, both moral and immoral, were assigned a certain number of points. By keeping a daily tally of merits and demerits, by taking monthly and yearly inventories, one could carry out constant self-examination and thus determine how his "merit account" stood. In this way, he could measure how close he was to blessing or disaster.

Chu-hung wrote the *Record of Self-Knowledge* when he was already seventy years of age. By that time, he had long been the leader of both monastic and lay Buddhism. His temple, the Yün-ch'i Ssu, was looked upon as the model of Pure Land meditation and strict Vinaya observance. Why did he turn to the *Ledger of Merit and Demerit* so late in his life and decide to write something similar to it? He never made his reasons clear. It is my belief that he advocated the system of merit and demerit as one more step in his effort to promote a practical lay Buddhism, adding to it many new items, subtracting old ones, and changing others. For instance, the earlier work has thirty-six ledgers for merits and thirty-nine for demerits; Chu-hung enlarged these categories to seventy-nine and ninety-nine, respectively. Since the earlier work was Taoist, its rules covered one's relationship to Taoist deities only. Chu-hung added corresponding rules covering the Buddhist pantheon. By the time he finished his revisions, the *Record* could and did serve to further the cause of lay Buddhism.

The innovative character of the *Record* can be appreciated only after comparing its contents with those of its predecessor, the *Ledger*. The most significant additions Chu-hung made have to do with one of three themes: (1) loyalty and filial piety, (2) social ethics, (3) Buddhist practice. While the *Ledger* mentions loyalty and filial piety only sporadically, the *Record* devotes a whole section to them. Their importance for Chu-hung is undeniable, and this accords well with his general stress on Confucian values. Most of the new entries under social ethics are equally Confucian in orientation. An interesting point is that the *Record* focuses on a few classes of people for special attention. Aside from the good and bad behavior which apply to all, there are specific warnings directed at officials and at gentry-literati. Officials are given detailed legal and administrative guidelines. They are not to take bribes, yield to social pressure, or be unnecessarily harsh when passing sentences. Householders of the gentry class are told not to encroach on other people's property or force others to sell land. They are enjoined to be generous with money and to construct bridges, repair roads, and so forth, for the public weal; to take care of the poor and the helpless; not to mistreat servants, but to try to redeem them and return them to their families; not to use coercion to make the poor return their debts. Since cases of official corruption, legal injustice, and gentry oppression of the common people abounded in the latter part of the Ming, Chu-hung had good reason to give attention to these particular problems.

The prominence given to Buddhist practices sharply distinguishes the *Record* from the *Ledger*. While the *Ledger* is a mixture of Confucian and Taoist values, the *Record* is a mixture of Confucian and Buddhist values. In the section of the *Record* called "Deeds Beneficial to the Three Jewels," as well as in other sections, lay Buddhist practice such as vegetarianism, nonkilling, and releasing sentient beings, appear frequently. In this way, Buddhist values were for the first time formally incorporated into the general sphere of popular morality. The *Record* therefore reinforces those tenets of lay Buddhism which we have discussed earlier in this paper.

In the actual structure of *The Record of Self-Knowledge*, Chu-hung divided all deeds into two categories: meritorious (*shan men*) [ci] and demeritorious (*kuo-men*).[cj] The first category, merits, has four subdivisions: (a) loyal and filial deeds, (b) altruistic and compassionate deeds, (c) deeds beneficial to the Three Jewels, and (d) miscellaneous good deeds. The second category, demerits, also has four subdivisions—the opposites of the four above. Detailed schedules are listed for assignment of merits or demerits to each act under these categories. The maximum number of points for merits or demerits is one hundred; the minimum is one. Between these two extremes, two, five, ten, twenty, thirty, forty, fifty, and eighty points signal the gradations. A very serious offense, such as successfully plotting to have someone sentenced to death, or committing murder, results in the maximum one hundred demerits, but a trivial offense, such as keeping birds in a cage or binding animals with strings for one day, results in only one demerit. It might be instructive to group together all the acts carrying the same number of merits or demerits to see whether one could find any correlation between the number of points and the moral significance of the deed. As it stands, except for the most obvious instances, no strict logic governing assignment of points is immediately discernible for acts that fall between the two extremes.

A few selections from the category of "Altruistic and Compassionate Deeds" will give some idea of how this system worked.

To save a man condemned to death .... 100 merits
To pardon a man condemned to death .... 80 merits
To reduce the number of men condemned to death .... 40 merits

(Demeritorious if done out of bribery or for private reasons.)
To save a baby from being drowned and bring it up oneself ..... 50 merits
To cause others not to drown a baby .... 30 merits
To bring up an abandoned child .... 20 merits
To talk to fishermen, hunters, and butchers in order to make them
   change their professions .... 3 merits
To succeed in making one of them change his profession .... 50 merits
To offically prohibit slaughtering for one day .... 10 merits
To give money to people who cannot afford coffins (for each string
   of cash spent) .... 1 merit
To repair roads (for each string of cash spent) .... 1 merit

We cannot go here into the problem of the possible influence of the penal code on the *Record*. Suffice it to say that the *Record* does emphasize the importance of motivation by making a clear distinction between intentional and unintentional acts and by providing different treatments for each. For instance, to sentence one person to death by mistake counts eighty demerits, but to do so on purpose counts one hundred. The *Record* also differentiates acts according to the means by which or the situations in which they are committed. Thus, any act committed as a result of bribery or because there was no alternative does not count as a merit. If one cancels another's debt only because the court refused to deal with the complaint, again, no merit applies. Or, in a more specific example, when one cooks a living creature in an unusual way and makes it suffer excruciating pain, he gets twenty demerits. The severity of the penalty is apparent when one also reads that to kill a small animal intentionally counts only one demerit. On the other hand, although harming a creature is demeritorious, to harm it in the course of doing good work such as repairing bridges, paving roads, building temples, and so on, brings no demerit. In this way, some flexibility and much rationality is built into an otherwise mechanical system.

The quantification of morality, exhibited by the *Ledger* and the *Record*, could easily have led to the accumulating of "points" without any real commitment to the norms embodied in the system, thus rendering it meaningless. But, given the historical and social context, concretized injunctions of the kind illustrated here did serve a purpose—they made general moral concepts such as justice, integrity, kindness, relate to day-to-day behavior.

It has been observed that great social mobility, both upward and downward, existed in Ming and Ch'ing times.[74] There were constant changes in personal and family fortunes, both political and economic. There were both increased opportunities and more insecurity. If a gentry-official did not find himself reduced to the status of a commoner within his own lifetime, in all likelihood this loss of status would occur by the time of his grandson.[75] Therefore, the same social mobility that created opportunities for the lower classes also induced considerable uncertainty and anxiety. A poor farmer's son, who had newly entered the official ranks by passing the examinations, felt a need for practical guidance in order to reassure himself that he could measure up to people's expectations. Such guidance was offered by numerous sources, and morality books were among them. The contribution peculiar to the *Record of Self-Knowledge* was that it supplied Buddhist values to the general moral schema of the traditional morality books.

THE LAY DEVOTEES

Chu-hung had a wide lay following among the literati-officials of his generation. There are two sources which have particular value for a study of these lay devotees. The first is the *Chü-shih chuan* [ck] (Biographies of Buddhist Devotees) [76] compiled and edited by P'eng Shao-sheng,[cl] also called Chi-ch'ing,[cm] and Ch'ih-mu [cn] (d. 1796), who was the best-known lay Buddhist of the Ch'ing period. Of the three existing collections of biographies of lay Buddhists up to that time,[77] P'eng's was the most comprehensive. The biographies of twenty of Chu-hung's followers appear in this work. The other important source for our purposes is the collected correspondence between Chu-hung and some of his followers which form the *I kao* [co] (Posthumous Papers) section of the *Yün-ch'i fa-hui* (YCFH, XXX, and XXXI). In all, there are about two hundred replies written by Chu-hung, accompanied in most cases by the letters to which he was replying. The number of people involved in the correspondence was about one hundred.

These biographies and the correspondence tell us a great deal about the backgrounds of lay followers, the forms of lay practice in which they engaged, the types of problems they encountered, and Chu-hung's approach to lay Buddhism in general. Several facts about these lay believers emerge immediately. Geographically, the majority came from Kiangsu and Chekiang, although there were also a few from Kiangsi, Fukien, Szechwan, Hukuang, and Shansi.[78] This trend is borne out by Sakai's observations on the general geographical distribution of lay Buddhism.[79] Of the hundred and seven lay Buddhists who appeared in the *Chü-shih chuan*, Sakai found that seventy-two (67.3 percent) came from Kiangsu and Chekiang, while only about 5 percent came from each of the inland provinces of Anhwei, Kiangsi, Szechwan, Hupei, and Hunan. Another significant point is that, except for four, all of this group flourished during some hundred and fifty years spanning the end of the Ming and the beginning of the Ch'ing—the same time span during which Chu-hung and the three other prominent Ming Buddhist monks, Tzu-po Chen-k'o [cp] or Ta-kuan (1544–1604), Han-shan Te-ch'ing [cq] (1546–1623), and Ou-i Chih-hsü [cr] (1599–1655), were active. Thus we learn that the lay Buddhist movement of the Ming was primarily a local phenomenon which sprang up during Chu-hung's lifetime and was centered around the lower Yangtze delta.

Socially, most of the lay followers belonged to the so-called gentry class.[80] From the biographies, we learn that nine held *chin-shih* degrees, and two of these nine achieved such high positions that they merited inclusion in the official history, the *Ming shih* (Yen Min-ch'ing's [cs] biography appears in *chüan* 193 of the *Ming shih*, and that of T'ao Wang-ling in *chüan* 216). About one quarter of all the correspondents held official posts ranging from ranks 2A to 7B.[81] The most commonly held were those of prefect, magistrate, governor, judge, and compiler of the Han-lin Academy. They were thus middle-level officials, predominantly civil, but some military. Among Chu-hung's followers, of both the literati-officials and people who, though educated, did not hold any office, a surprising proportion (about 60 percent) had religious names. These names were given to them by Chu-hung after they had taken the Three Refuges [ct] and received the first set of Buddhist precepts.[cu] In order of seniority, the names could have as their first character Kuang, [cv] or Ta, [cw] or Chih.[cx] The interesting point is that the monks at Yün-ch'i Ssu were given their religious names in the same manner. In this way, Chu-hung made it clear that he regarded his lay disciples as the equals of monks under his direction at Yün-ch'i. The *sangha* and the "householders" (the original meaning of *chü-shih*) were indeed brethren in the faith.

The biographies give us glimpses, but never complete explanations, of the diverse motivations prompting these lay devotees to embrace Buddhism. Some were drawn to it at an early age and in such an inexplicable manner that the Buddhists regarded it as *su-ken* [cy] (a propensity to Buddhism inherited from a previous existence). The more obvious examples were those who suffered from long and incurable diseases. Personal suffering usually helped to draw people to religion, but we find that even a person who led a so-called normal life could suddenly relinquish everything to take up a religious life. This was the case with Wang Meng-su. [cz] [82] After serving as a magistrate and having directed a highly successful military campaign against local bandits, Wang suddenly became disgusted with everything, packed up his clothes, left his post, and started roaming the mountains.

Several other aspects of the biographies catch our attention as well. First, there is the relationship between a man's religious beliefs on the one hand and his official behavior on the other. This is shown with equal clarity in the cases of Yen Min-ch'ing,[83] Ts'ai Huai-t'ing,[da] [84] T'ao Wang-ling, Wang Meng-su, and Ting Chien-hung.[db] [85] Compassion for the suffering of the common people and concern for the proper administration of justice were Confucian as well as Buddhist virtues. However, when Ts'ai Huai-t'ing prohibited the people under his jurisdiction from killing animals in their sacrifices or when Ting Chien-hung gave his prisoners strings of beads and told them to recite the name of the Buddha, this was clearly because of Chu-hung's influence. That they carried out these measures in their capacities as government officials attests to the integration of their inner faith and outward behavior.

Second, there is a close connection between family and friendship ties and the ways in which beliefs were shared and spread. This could take several forms. In the family, it was usually the husband who became converted and the wife who followed his example (as in the case of Wang Tao-an).[dc] [86] It could also be the older brother who introduced the faith to a younger brother (as in the cases of Yü Ch'un-hsi or Wang Jo-sheng) [dd] [87] or the relationship might be one between brothers-in-law (as with Huang Yüan-fu [de] [88] and Wen Tzu-yü).[df] [89] The most common case, of course, was that of the father starting the practice at home and establishing the Buddhist belief as a family tradition (as in the household of Yen Min-ch'ing). As for friendship ties, the teaching was usually introduced to and discussed among friends who either came from the same place or had some common background, as was the case with T'ao Wang-ling and Huang P'ing-ch'ing.[dg] [90] Both men attained the *chin-shih* degree in the same year. Each was closely related to a third friend, Chiao Hung, who also attained the degree in that year. It was with Chiao that T'ao discussed philosophy, and it was also Chiao who introduced Huang to the works of Chu-hung (according to the accounts, during a dream of Huang's). Conversely, a shared belief could also be the basis for a new and lasting friendship. The friendship of Wang Meng-su and Chu Pai-min [dh] [91] is a good example.

The organization of associations of groups for releasing life was a natural extension of these family and friendship ties. They were, in fact, often started by a few like-minded friends (e.g., Yü Ch'un-hsi, T'ao Wang-ling) for the sake of mutual encouragement and consultation and were later enlarged to include others. While the associations had a long historical development, as we have noted, the particular popularity of these Pure Land clubs could also very well have been a reflection of the current vogue in the society at large. We are told that in the late Ming, club organization became widespread.[92]

There were literary clubs for essay writers and poetry clubs for poets. For more than a hundred years (the reigns of Wan-li and T'ien-chi) in the provinces of Kiangsu, Chekiang, Fukien, Kwangtung, Kiangsi, Shantung, Hopei and everywhere we find this trend. . . . Not only did educated men want to establish clubs, but even women took part in literary and drinking clubs to show off their sophistication. [93]

Third, the fluidity and syncretism of religious beliefs in Chu-hung's time are vividly portrayed in these biographies. It was commonplace for a person trained in Pure Land practice (*nien-fo san-mei*) [di] to engage at the same time in Ch'an meditation, Tantric exercises, and doctrinal discussion. Moreover, we find that the boundary line between Buddhism and Taoism was, to say the least, blurred. Thus we read that several of Chu-hung's followers were interested in the Taoist arts for gaining longevity (e.g., Chuang Fu-chen [dj] [94] and Chu Pai-min). Their interest in Taoism was often the path which led them to Buddhism. And after they became Buddhist believers, they did not necessarily end their Taoist pursuits. Perhaps most interesting of all is their easy transition from the secular to the religious. They lived in fact, if not in name, the celibate lives of monks shutting themselves into separate rooms (e.g., Ko I-an); [dk] [95] refusing to take another wife after the first died (e.g., Huang P'ing-ch'ing); living in a monastery (e.g., Wang Tao-an) or traveling around like mendicant monks (e.g., Wang Meng-su and Chu Pai-min). Some of them did, in fact, shave off their hair and become monks just before they died (e.g., Huang Yüan-fu, and Wen Tzu-yü). These tendencies again reflect Chu-hung's approach to religion—his aversion to sectarianism within Buddhist schools, his accommodation to other systems of thought, and his genuine desire to see Buddhism become a secular as well as a religious reality.

When we look into the contents of the correspondence, several themes recur with frequency. Perhaps the foremost is that of religious cultivation. Chu-hung's followers wanted to know when and how to engage in religious cultivation. They were often confused by the multitude of methods available and wanted Chu-hung to recommend the most effective ones. Chu-hung always recommended *nien-fo* although he also discussed the Ch'an approach when someone specifically asked about it. This letter addressed to Hsü Ko-ju [96] is typical of his advice concerning the efficacy of Pure Land meditation:

To achieve an uninterrupted state of *samādhi* [concentration] is not something a person leading a secular life can do. Since it is difficult to achieve *samādhi* this way, it is best that you hold fast to the name of the Buddha. Whenever you have the time, after studying and managing household affairs, you ought to recite it silently. In doing so, you should be careful to articulate each word clearly and to dwell on each utterance with all your heart. If you can continue doing this for a long time without relapsing, your mind will naturally be tamed, and this state is no other than *samādhi*. [97]

To those who started out by following the Ch'an practice of meditating on kōan (*kung-an*) and who held strong belief in the wonders of *hua-t'ou* [dl] (the pithy phrase or the "core" of the *kōan*), Chu-hung suggested that the very act of *nien-fo* could serve as a *hua-t'ou*.

For a long time, Ch'an masters have taught people to ponder over some *hua-t'ou*, whereby mental frustration could be aroused and, out of this, great enlightenment could emerge. They taught people to ponder the word *"wu"* [Nothing] or the word "myriad dharmas." There are many like these. I would say that the phrase: "The myriad dharmas return to the One, and where does the One return to?" dm is extremely similar to this phrase: "Who is the one who is reciting the Buddha's name?" dn If you work hard at this "who," then the former puzzle will naturally become clear. That is why the ancients said that if a Pure Land practitioner who called on Buddha's name desired to practice Ch'an meditation, he did not need any other *hua-t'ou*.[98]

Several followers wrote to Chu-hung complaining about misfortune. In each case, while he offered his sympathy, he also used the opportunity to turn their thoughts to salvation. These are a few examples: A devotee from Chiang-yin, Feng Yü-chü, was in his late seventies and felt depressed. Chu-hung told him that the best time to practice *nien-fo* was in old age.

To live to one's seventies is a rare thing. In these twilight years of your life, you should open your mind and regard everything in the world as events in a play. Say to yourself that as I am reciting the Buddha's name, now I shall definitely be reborn in the West. When you are bothered by something, immediately turn to recitation and say to yourself, "I am a dweller in the world of the Amitābha Buddha. Why should I have the same attitude as ordinary men?" Thinking thus, you will be able to turn anger into happiness.[99]

To Wang Chung-ch'uan from Yü-hang, who had lost his son, Chu-hung wrote:

It must be ordered by fate that you should have only one son. This second one [who died] must have come into this world to seek payment for an old debt. So, after you brought him up, educated him and set him up with a wife, he received whatever he came here for and then drifted away from you like a cloud. Since there is no feeling left between the father and the son, you ought not to torture yourself with further remembrances. Instead, you should read Buddhist scriptures in order to break away from the delusion. Do not live by yourself and harm your health with excessive sorrow.[100]

When another follower, a provincial graduate from T'ai-ts'ang named Wang Tzu-yu, became seriously ill, Chu-hung gave him this advice: "Illnesses usually are the result of much killing. Therefore to release life is especially important. Another thing you ought to know: the efficacy of inviting monks to perform the ritual of repentance is far inferior to that of repentance in one's own heart; so empty your mind, stop all distracting thoughts, and concentrate solely on the one name of Amitābha." [101]

A second, much discussed problem, was that of whether a person educated in Confucianism and active in administrative affairs could conveniently pursue his Buddhist career. Chu-hung's answer was definitely *yes*. He did not see any conflict in a situation which was potentially full of conflicts, and his positive approach certainly encouraged many a doubtful soul and helped the growth of lay Buddhism. The following reply was directed to Wang Jo-sheng, a military commander:

In your letter you mentioned that you are burdened by worldly cares and therefore cannot rid yourself of secular impurities. But we cannot call the secular life a burden. The laws of this world, such as that a son should serve his parents with filial piety, a subject should serve his lord with loyalty, or any other principle governing human relationships, are not basically contrary to the Way. What one should do is follow the circumstances while holding to the principle. The only secret is to respond to the call of worldly duties with a free mind. Now the time for the examination is near. Please study hard. Should you succeed, you ought to make a vow on the day of success that you will never depart from what you have learned because of riches and power. If you can be a good minister in the tradition of the ancients, then this is saving the world. Make a vow that you will never lose your right mindfulness because of riches and power, that you will definitely realize the great cause for Buddha's coming into the world. This is leaving the world. If you can do this, then literati will be able to serve as officials while engaged in meditation, and they will be able to enter the Way while still remaining in the realm of the profane.[102]

In a similar vein, but even more to the point, was his advice to another lay believer who was worried about not being able to fulfill the quota of performing a "thousand good deeds." [do]

If you are pressed for time and cannot fulfill the number of a thousand good deeds, you ought to make this vow with a sincere heart: namely, that after you succeed in the examinations and become an official, you will try with redoubled effort to perform widely all kinds of good deeds. Never accept any request contrary to the principle of Heaven, never do any unjust deed, never harm one innocent man, never hesitate to right a wrong, and never refrain from performing beneficial acts required by duty out of a desire to protect your position. If you can do these, then you will have performed not merely a thousand, but ten thousand, indeed a hundred million good deeds.[103]

Thus the Buddhist requirement for performing good deeds was here skillfully identified with the Confucian ideal of an upright official. Chu-hung's "skillfulness in means" [dp] was shown in another instance when he accommodated the rule of nonkilling to the exigencies of administrative life. One follower made this point: "In carrying out one's official duty, it is sometimes unavoidable that one should have to pass death sentences. But this is forbidden to Buddhists. Now, as I want to take refuge in the Three Jewels, is it then necessary that I retire from office and come to the temple?" [104] The problem of reconciling one's duty with the demands of the religious prohibitions was indeed a perennial problem for the believer's conscience. Chu-hung was well aware of the difficulty and, in fact, anticipated problems of this kind. In his commentary on the first precept of nonkilling, the following passage appears:

Someone asks, "Monks are specialized in the works of compassion, but officials of the Emperor are empowered to let [criminals] live or die. If a person commits a crime, and the official does not kill him, how can he serve the country?" My answer is, as stated in the P'u-sa chieh-pen, [dq] [105] "When a bodhisattva sees a thief or a robber who, because of his greed or profit, is about to kill many people or is about to harm a śravaka of great virtue, he ought to consider this carefully: If I should kill this evil man I will fall into Naraka [hell], but if I do not, he will create unintermitted karma. [dr] I would rather enter hell myself than cause him to suffer the pain of unintermitted punishment. This kind of killing does not constitute any violation, but on the contrary produces much merit." This is to say that one may kill as the occasion demands. [ds] So, if one kills a criminal, one does not violate any rule. The annihilation of the four ferocious tribes (Kung-kung, Huan-tou, San-miao, and K'un) by King Yü and the killing of the two rebels (Wu Keng and Kuang Shu) by the Duke of Chou are examples of this kind. Moreover, if the official always cries after he passes a death sentence, and he carries out the execution only after thinking it over thrice, then he has manifested compassion over the killing, and even though he kills, he does not really kill. In this way, the Law is not abolished, and neither is grace sacrificed. The affairs of the state and the mind of the Buddha do not obstruct each other. [106]

In his interpretation of the precepts, Chu-hung always adopted a flexible approach. He never demanded a literal faithfulness from his followers, nor did he adhere to the letter of the Law without regard to the actualities of a secular life. To this particular follower, he answered in a similar vein: "It is clearly recorded in the sūtras that one may kill if the occasion that demands it is appropriate. As for people who attained enlightenment while they still served the state, you can also find many precedents since ancient times." [107]

Chu-hung did not encourage his lay disciples to enter the priesthood, especially if their parents were still alive or their children were still too young. The carrying out of the obligation of a filial son or a responsible father should come first. This brings us to a third theme running throughout this correspondence. The question was frequently asked: was it true that no matter how diligently a lay believer engaged in self-cultivation, he probably could never compare with the monks? Chu-hung's answer was: "If the lay believer can achieve enlightenment in the midst of the five passions, he is like a lotus flower in the midst of fire. When this kind of lotus receives water, it can grow even taller. But, for those who grow in the water (monks), they will probably wither away when they come into contact with fire." [108]

Chu-hung regarded monastic and lay Buddhism as complementary, but distinct, domains. He assigned equal value to each and made no one-sided judgments. "Those who have shaved off their hair ought to continue their early determination, while those who have not, ought to realize the truth in the midst of worldly existence. Each can progress with single-minded diligence and the purpose of either is to break down delusion and achieve enlightenment. As long as one can realize the nature of his own mind and obtain salvation, it is unnecessary to ask if he has shaved his head or not." [109]

A CASE HISTORY OF A "CONFUCIAN MONK"

We will close this paper with the story of a *chü-jen* degree-holder who eventually became a monk. Chu-hung's influence is clearly seen in each step this disciple took.

There are six letters from Chu-hung addressed to Feng T'ai-ch'ü,[dt] a provincial graduate from Chiang-yin. At first we learn that Feng was contemplating going into retreat for a specific time. But Chu-hung said that since Feng's father was not well, Feng should serve him at home. Besides, contemplation did not necessarily have to be carried out in a definite place or for a definite period. As long as he could calm his mind, he could engage in cultivation even when taking care of his aged and sick father. Otherwise, to insist on seclusion for a set period would be a form of "obstruction." [du] Feng apparently took the advice. In a subsequent letter, Chu-hung said, "Your father suffers from a slight discomfort. This is common with old people. You ought to amuse him all the time. This is most important." He also did not want Feng to waver in his faith in the Pure Land. "In recent times, it has become fashionable to promote Ch'an meditation. I am both glad and worried because of this. There are also people who practice Ch'an but deprecate the Pure Land. I hope that you will be steadfast in your faith and not be weakened by such talk. Only then is there a possibility of success." [110]

Feng eventually became the monk Ch'ang-hsing. But it appears that he did not shave his head right away or go to a monastery for monastic training. In one letter, Chu-hung advised him that he should receive the commandment for a monk (*pi-ch'iu chieh*) [dv] in front of a statue of the Buddha. This was a contingency measure as the normal procedure was to receive it at a monastery with an ordination platform (*chieh-t'ai*). But in the late Ming, all ordination platforms were made inoperative by imperial decree.

If the circumstances do not allow for the regular procedure one may prostrate oneself in front of the Buddha and receive [the precepts] by oneself. If you should doubt this procedure because in the scriptures there is a text saying that one can receive the bodhisattva precepts by oneself, but none about the precepts for a monk, I now tell you this: If under normal circumstances, when the ordination platform is in operation, a person does not go there to receive the precepts on purpose, but performs the rite himself, he is indeed in error. But now, since the law of the land prohibits the operation of the ordination platform, one should indeed perform the rite in front of the Buddha by oneself. You need not doubt this. [111]

Feng's unorthodox way of remaining in the household after announcing his determination to leave the world caused some gossip. Chu-hung defended Feng against such criticism and offered two reasons for his defense: First, Feng's son was only twelve years old, and this was a critical time for the lad's education. Second, Feng's daughter was still unmarried. Chu-hung also had this advice for Feng: "I hope that you will marry off your daughter soon; you and your son are welcome to come to my temple. Your son can then return home every two or three months to visit his mother, and eventually he may take care of the household by himself. Thus you will be able to manage your worldly affairs without causing unnecessary gossip." [112] Feng eventually went to the Yün-ch'i monastery and became one of Chu-hung's most trusted disciples.

CONCLUSIONS

While the essentials of Chu-hung's lay teachings were drawn from Pure Land Buddhism, his movement was syncretic. It emphasized recitation of the Buddha's name (*nien-fo*), nonkilling, compassion both for one's fellow human beings and for animals, and concretized this compassionate attitude in acts of social philanthropy and the release of animals from captivity and slaughterhouses. Although there were precedents for all these, the late Ming movement was far more than just a revival of earlier movements. One principal reason for this was Chu-hung's success in making lay practice as well organized as the monastic order. Not only did he accord the lay believer the same attention as the *sangha*, but he also gave him detailed, programmatic advice on his religious practice. Chu-hung's choice of nonkilling and the release of life as central themes in lay proselytization was another significant development. Since the Confucian tradition also gave great emphasis to the reverence for life, lay Buddhist practice could complement and even deepen the religious consciousness of lay devotees, facilitating the eventual syncretizing of Confucian and Buddhist values in their lives.

A more striking feature of Chu-hung's approach to the lay Buddhist movement was his strong emphasis on moral action and his relative neglect of doctrinal questions. Instead of viewing the human condition as transient, illusory, and painful, Chu-hung regarded it as the best opportunity to realize the Truth. In his eyes, therefore, one should cherish and use this life to achieve enlightenment and should not look at the human condition with horror and disgust. Instead of viewing human relationships and social obligations as obstacles to salvation, Chu-hung regarded them as among the appropriate means leading to salvation. One did not have to reject the world or escape from society to find release. He could find it in the midst of secular activities. To be a filial son and a loyal subject did not bar one from enlightenment. On the contrary, if one failed to be a filial son and a loyal subject, he also failed to be a true Buddhist. The Ch'an saying that to carry water and chop wood was to be in the "marvelous Way," was now brought to its logical conclusion.

The lay Buddhist movement at the end of the Ming was more activist than contemplative, more moralistic than theological, more world-affirming than world-rejecting. All these signify a considerable transformation, if not a complete about-face, from the original Buddhist teaching. Complex social, political, economic, and historical factors were involved in this eventual "Confucianization" of Buddhism. Because Confucians had consistently attacked Buddhists for their alleged suppression of natural feelings and disregard for social and familial obligations, the Buddhists had to come to terms with the realities of a Confucian society in order to survive. It was also undoubtedly true that if Buddhism had not broken away from monastic isolation, doctrinal rigidity, and scholastic obscurity, it would have had a poor chance of reaching the general populace. Chu-hung, in some measure, was responsible for this break, through his innovations in lay Buddhism. Yet precisely because the lay movement did not demand a radical break from the social system in which it existed, it not only survived but continued to flourish throughout the Ch'ing and to some extent into the present time in various overseas Chinese communities, even if not in Mainland China. During this period, the persons who were responsible for the two major attempts at revitalization, Chou Meng-yen ^{dw} (1655–1739), P'eng Shao-sheng (1740–96) in the K'ang-hsi and Ch'ien-lung eras; and Yang Wen-hui ^{dx} (1837–1911) in the late Ch'ing and early Republican, all claimed Chu-hung as their source of inspiration. Thus Chu-hung's work laid the basis for a movement which endured long after its initial popular success.

It would be an oversimplication, however, to view Buddhism's accommodation to Confucianism apart from the influence that Confucianism (and Taoism) also received from Buddhism. If there was a Confucianization of Buddhism in the Ming, there was also a Buddhicization of Confucianism and Taoism, although that is another subject, which we cannot go into here.

This brings us to a final consideration. Syncretism frequently suggests an indiscriminate mixture of disparate elements and, accompanying this, vulgarization of doctrine, weakening of commitment, and corruption of practice. It is perhaps for this reason that purists tend to condemn the syncretic practices of post-T'ang Buddhism as impure and degenerate. Yet I feel that the late Ming development offers a positive example of syncretism. The lay movement proved durable and workable, an important criterion for the evaluation of any religious movement. Similarly, the Combining of the Three Teachings generated an openness and a receptivity in the spiritual, moral, and intellectual spheres of life. More significant, it made separatism among these spheres unnecessary. This fusion, I believe, gave new expression to an already underlying tendency of Chinese thought.

1. Kenneth Ch'en, *Buddhism in China, A Historical Survey* (Princeton University Press, 1964), p. 449.
2. For instance, Kenneth Ch'en uses the subtitle "decline" for his treatment of Buddhism from the Sung on. Arthur Wright terms the years of c. 900–1900 as "the period of appropriation." Cf. Ch'en, ch. 14, and Arthur Wright, *Buddhism in Chinese History* (Stanford University Press, 1970), p. 86.
3. Chu-hung explains the meaning of these terms as follows: "When a thought arises in the mind which materializes into the intent to kill, this is the primary cause (*yin*). The secondary causes are the various factors which lead to the killing (*yüan*). The means and ways which the killing involves constitute the karma (*yeh*)." *Yün-ch'i fa-hui*, II (hereafter referred to as *YCFH*), *Chieh-shu fa-yin*, 3/8a.
4. *Fan-wang ching, Taishō*, 24/1004b.
5. *YCFH*, II, *Chieh-shu fa-yin*, 3/9a.
6. *Fan-wang ching, Taishō*, 24/1006b.
7. *Chieh-shu fa-yin*, 4/47b–48a.
8. *Ibid.*, 48b.
9. *Liang shu*, 48/7a–13a.
10. According to the notes supplied by Chu-hung, this refers to a passage in the *Śūraṅgama Sūtra* (*Leng-yen ching*): "The Buddha says to Ānanda, 'When a monk eats food, do you think the rest of the monks are also satisfied?' Ānanda answers, 'Although the monks are all arhāts, since each of them has a different body, we cannot say that one person satisfies the rest.' " *YCFH*, *Chieh-shu shih-chien*, V/27b.
11. *Ibid.*, 28a. "The younger brother of Emperor T'ai-tsu of Sung, Prince Chin, was sick. The doctor applied cauterization by burning moxa. The prince felt pain and the emperor cauterized himself with moxa in order to share the prince's pain."
12. *Ibid.* "Ts'ai Shun lost his father at an early age and lived with his mother. One day he went out to gather firewood, and a visitor suddenly showed up. When his mother failed to see his speedy return, she bit her finger. Shun felt something in his heart, and casting the firewood on the ground, rushed home."
13. *Ibid.* "In the T'ang Dynasty there was an official who plotted rebellion with An Lu-shan. He was formerly the prefect of Szechwan, and a statue of him remained there. When Emperor T'ai-tsung toured Shu and saw it, he was very angry and he struck its head with a sword. At that time this official was living in Shansi, but his head suddenly fell to the ground."
14. *YCFH*, III, *Chieh-shu fa-yin*, 4/48b–49a.
15. *Ibid.*, 49a–b.

16. *Ibid.*, 50a–b.
17. *YCFH*, V, *Chieh-shu wen pien*, 1b.
18. Cf. Suzuki Chūsei,[dy] "Bukkyō no kinsatsu kairitsu ga Sōdai no minshū seikatsu ni oyoboseru eikyō ni tsuite," *Shūkyō Kenkyū*, 3/1, no. 107 (1941), pp. 115–41.
19. *Fo-tsu t'ung-chi*,[dz] *Taishō*, 49/359c.
20. *Fan-wang ching*, *Taishō*, 24/1007b.
21. *T'ang ta-chao ch'üan-chi*,[ea] 113.
22. "Liang Yüan-ti Ching-chou fang-sheng-t'ing pei," *I-wen lei chü*,[eb] 77.
23. *Fo-tsu t'ung-chi*, *Taishō*, 49/376a.
24. *Hsin T'ang shu*, 153; *Chiu T'ang shu*, 128.
25. "T'ien-hsia fang-sheng-ch'ih pei-ming," in *Ch'üan T'ang wen*,[ec] 339.
26. *Wu-teng hui-yüan*,[ed] 10; *Fo-tsu t'ung-chi*, 26; *Fo-tsu t'ung-tsai*,[ee] 26; *Shih-shih chi ku lüeh*,[ef] 3.
27. *Fo-tsu t'ung-chi*, *Taishō*, 49/207a–209a.
28. *Ibid.*, 208a.
29. *Sung shih*, 8, "Chen-tsung pen-chi."
30. *Sung shih*, 338; *Sung Yüan hsüeh-an*, 99.
31. *Lin-an chih*, 32.
32. T'ang Yung-t'ung,[eg] *Han Wei liang-Chin nan-pei-ch'ao fo-chiao shih* (reprint; Taipei: Commercial Press, 1962), pp. 248–71.
33. Suzuki Chūsei, "Sōdai bukkyō kessha no kenkyū," [eh] *Shigaku zasshi*, vol. 52 (1941), pp. 65–98, 205–41, 303–33.
34. For example: "Tung-p'o chü-shih yin shih shuo," [ei] 135b; "Yu-t'an tsu-shih chieh sha wen," [ej] 136a; "Fo-yin ch'an-shih chieh-sha wen," [ek] 136a; "Chen-hsieh ch'an-shih chieh-sha wen," [el] 136a–b; "P'u-an ch'an shih chieh-sha wen," [em] 136b; all included in *Kuei-yüan chih-chih chi* [en] 2 *chüan*, the preface to which is dated 1570. *Dai-Nippon zoku-zōkyō*, 2.13.2.
35. *Ibid.*, 135b.
36. *YCFH*, XXII, 3–20.
37. His reply exhorting the empress to cultivate both wisdom and blessing is included in a *gātha* entitled "Ts'u-sheng huan-t'ai-hou ch'ien nei-ch'ih wen fa-yao chieh-sung," *YCFH*, XXIX, 21a.
38. Cf. Ogasawara Senshū, *Chūgoku kinsei jōdokyō shi no kenkyū*,[eo] (Kyoto, 1963), section entitled "Byakurenshū no kenkyū," pp. 79–165; Suzuki Chūsei, "Sōdai bukkyō kessha no kenkyū," pp. 303–33; Li Shou-k'ung, "Ming-tai pai-lien-chiao k'ao-lüeh," [ep] *Wen-shih-che hsüeh-pao*, vol. 4 (1952), pp. 151–77.
39. *Chu-ch'uang erh-pi*,[eq] *YCFH*, XXV, 23a–b, "Lien she" (Lotus Society).
40. *Ibid.*, 22a–b, "Chieh she-hui" (organizing associations).
41. *YCFH*, XXII, 16b–a, "Fang-sheng wen."
42. *Ibid.*, 17b.
43. The nine "untimely deaths" are: (1) death by suffering from a disease which

is not attended to by a doctor; (2) death by doing evil and being punished by the law of the land; (3) death by indulging in excessive pleasure causing one to become careless and thus giving ghosts and spirits the opportunity to steal one's energy and breath away; (4) death by drowning; (5) death by burning; (6) death by being eaten by ferocious beasts in the forest; (7) death by falling off a cliff; (8) death by being killed by poison or a curse; (9) death by hunger and thirst. The reference derives from *Yao shih ching*,[er] *Fo-hsüeh ta tz'u-tien* (Taipei, 1961 edition), p. 174bc.

44. YCFH, XXXI, *I kao* 3/78a, "Fang-sheng tu-shuo."
45. The main concepts are discussed in Leon Hurvitz, "Chu-hung's One Mind of Pure Land and Ch'an Buddhism," in de Bary, *Self and Society*, pp. 451–76, esp. pp. 453–69.
46. Lo Chin-hsi gave Chou Ju-teng the Buddhist work, *Fa-yüan chu-lin*[es] (Cyclopedia of the Buddhist System). *Ming-ju hsüeh-an* (Taipei, 1965 edition), 36/372.
47. YCFH, XXXI, *I kao*, 3/14b, "Ta Chou Hsi-meng shao ts'un."
48. YCFH, XXII, 17b–19a, "Fang-sheng wen."
49. YCFH, XXXII, 74a–75a, "Shang-fang shan-hui yüeh."
50. *Ming shih*, 216; *Chü-shih chüan*, 44.
51. *Ming shih*, 283; *Ming-ju hsüeh-an*, 35.
52. Preface to T'ao Wang-ling's "Fang-sheng pien huo,"[et] (Dispelling Doubts Concerning Releasing Life), *Shuo-fu hsü chi*,[eu] p. 30 (1647 reprint).
53. *Chü-shih chüan*, 42.
54. YCFH, XXII, 3b–6b, "Chieh-sha wen." At points I have paraphrased the original in order to avoid unnecessary details.
55. *Ibid.*, 6b–7a.
56. Cf. Ōcho Enichi,[ev] "Min-matsu bukkyō to kirisutokyō to no sōgō hihan," in *Ōtani Gakuhō*, 29/2 (1949), 1–20; 29/3 and 4 (1950), 18–38. Koyanagi Shigeta,[ew] "Rimato to min-matsu no shisōkai," in *Zoku tōyō shisō no kenkyū* (Tokyo, 1943), 83–109. Hou Wai-lu,[ex] *Chung-kuo ssu-hsiang t'ung-shih*, vol. 4B (Peking, 1963), 1189–1213; D. Lancashire, "Buddhist Reaction to Christianity in Late Ming China," in *The Journal of the Oriental Society of Australia*, vol. VI, nos. 1, 2 (1968–69), pp. 82–103.
57. Included in *T'ien-hsüeh ch'u han*,[ey] compiled by Li Chih-tsao (Taipei, 1964 reprint), pp. 351–635.
58. *Ibid.*, pp. 501–2.
59. *Ibid.*, p. 503.
60. *Ibid.*, pp. 505–6.
61. *Ibid.*, p. 509.
62. YCFH, XXVI, 72a–75a.
63. *Ibid.*, 73b–74a.
64. "Yü Teh-yüan ch'üan-pu yü Li Hsi-t'ai hsien-sheng shu," in *Pien-hsüeh i-tu*, *T'ien hsüeh ch'u han*, 2/637–41. "Li hsien-sheng fu Yü ch'üan-pu shu," in *ibid.*, pp. 641–50.

136 KRISTIN YÜ GREENBLATT

65. "Li hsien-sheng fu Lien-ch'ih ta ho-shang chu-ch'uang t'ien-shuo ssu tuan," in *ibid.*, pp. 651–84.
66. In the edition published in Fukien, there was a preface to *Pien-hsüeh i-tu* written by a Mi-ko-tzu (Michael), which was the religious name of Yang T'ing-yün,[ez] (1557–1627). Cf. Fang Hao,[fa] *Chung-kuo t'ien-chu-chiao jen-shih wu chüan*, Vol. I (Hong Kong, 1967), pp. 126–38. He claimed that before Chu-hung died, the latter repented for his wrong faith in the Pure Land. This preface was missing from the Chekiang edition of the same book, which was taken by many Buddhists as proof that the book was a forgery by someone other than Matteo Ricci, used as a shameless polemic against Chu-hung. Cf. "Cheng wang shuo" (Exposing the Wrong), by Chang Kuang-t'ien,[fb] in *Ming-ch'ao p'o-hsieh chi*,[fc] 7.
67. *YCFH*, II, 32b.
68. *Ibid.*, 34a.
69. Authorship is attributed to Li Ch'ang-ling (d. 1008),[fd] *Sung-shih*, 287. Cf. Koyanagi Shigeta, *Rosō no shisō to dōkyō*,[fe] (Tokyo, 1935), p. 385.
70. Sakai Tadao,[ff] *Chūgoku zensho no kenkyū* (Tokyo, 1963), pp. 318–49; Liu-Ts'un-yan, "Yüan Huang and His 'Four Admonitions,' " in *The Journal of the Oriental Society of Australia*, vol. 5, nos. 1, 2 (Sydney, 1967), pp. 108–32.
71. Cf. Takao Giken,[fg] "Mindai ni daizeisareta kōkakaku shisō," in *Ryūkoku daigaku ronsō*, 244/324–337; Shimizu Taiji,[fh] "Mindai ni okeru shūkyō yugo to kōkakaku, in *Shichō*, 6/3 (1936), pp. 29–55; Sakai, ch. 5, entitled "Kōkakaku no kenkyū," pp. 356–400; Yoshioka Yoshitoyo,[fi] "Chūgoku minshū no rinrisho 'kōkakaku' ni tsuite," in *Shūkyō kenkyū*, no. 127 (October, 1951), pp. 72–74; Kenneth Ch'en, *Buddhism*, pp. 436–39.
72. *YCFH*, XV, 5a, "Tzu-chih lu hsü." For a complete translation and analysis of the *Record*, see the author's *Yün-ch'i Chu-hung, the Career of a Ming Buddhist Monk*, Ann Arbor, University Microfilms, 1974.
73. *Ibid.*, 1a.
74. Cf. Ho Ping-ti, *The Ladder of Success in Imperial China* (New York: John Wiley and Sons, 1964).
75. *Ibid.*, pp. 126–68.
76. The work consists of 56 *chüan*, with 228 full biographies, in which 69 additional persons are also briefly mentioned. It was published in 1776.
77. The other two are *Chü-shih fen-teng lü* in two *chüan* by Chu Shih-en,[fj] published in 1632, and *Hsien-chüeh chi* in two *chüan* by T'ao Ming-ch'ien,[fk] published in 1672. P'eng's *Chü-shih chüan* was based on T'ao's work, but he added a great deal of new material. See Ogawa Kan'ichi, "Koji bukkyō no kinsei hatten," [fl] *Ryūkoku daigaku ronshu*, no. 339 (1950), pp. 51–52.
78. Five from Kiangsi, four from Fukien, two each from Hukuang and Szechwan, and one from Shansi.
79. Sakai, *Zensho*, pp. 303–4.

80. While there are as many definitions of the term "gentry" as there are studies about them, I find the classification into official-gentry and scholar-gentry, as outlined by T'ung-tsu Ch'u in his *Local Government in China under the Ch'ing* (Harvard University Press, 1962), pp. 171–73, most helpful.

81. The titles (epistolary or literary) of these positions are: *chün-po* [fm] (prefect, 4B), *i-ling* [fn] (district magistrate, 7B), *chung-ch'eng* [fo] (governor, 2B), *t'ai-shih* [fp] (compiler, 5B). Besides these, the following titles are also found: *tsung-jung* [fq] (brigadier-general, 2A), *fang-po* [fr] (lieutenant-governor or financial commissioner, 2B), *tsung-po* [fs] (director of the court of sacrificial worship, 3A), *ching-chao* [ft] (prefect of the metropolitan prefecture, 3A), *tu-hsien* [fu] (first captain, 4A), *chih-chung* [fv] (subprefect of Shun-t'ien-fu, 5A), *chün-ch'eng* [fw] (first class subprefect, 5A), *chu-cheng* [fx] (second-class secretary of a ministry, 5A), *chung-han* [fy] (secretary of the Grand Secretariat, 7B). The translations of the titles and their grades are made according to Charles O. Hucker, "An Index of Terms and Titles in Governmental Organization of the Ming Dynasty," in *Harvard Journal of Asiatic Studies*, vol. 23 (1960–61), pp. 127–51; and H. S. Brunnert and V. V. Hagelstrom, *Present Day Political Organization of China* (Taipei Book World Co., reprint of the 1910 edition).

82. *Chü-shih chüan*, 48.

83. *Ibid.*, 40.

84. *Ibid.*, 42.

85. *Ibid.*, 48.

86. *Chü-shih chüan*, 38.

87. *Ibid.*, 44.

88. *Ibid.*, 48.

89. *Ibid.*

90. *Ibid.*, 42.

91. *Ibid.*, 48.

92. Hsieh, *Tang-she yün-tung*, pp. 8–13.

93. *Ibid.*, p. 10.

94. *Chü-shih chüan*, 42.

95. *Ibid.*, 41.

96. Whom I cannot otherwise identify.

97. YCFH, XXX 2/25a.

98. *Ibid.*, 46b.

99. *Ibid.*, 34b.

100. *Ibid.*, 26b.

101. *Ibid.*, 47a–b.

102. YCFH, XXX/1/45b.

103. YCFH, XXX/2/24b.

104. YCFH, XXXI, 17a.

105. One *chüan*. There are two versions. One was translated by T'an Wu-ch'an (d. 433) who came from the kingdom of the Northern Liang, *Taishō*,

24/1107–1110. The other was translated by Hsüan-tsang (c. 596–664) of the T'ang, *Taishō*, 24/1110–1115.
106. *YCFH*, II, 10a–b.
107. *YCFH*, XXXI, 17a.
108. *Ibid.*, 26a.
109. *YCFH,07 XXX/2/22a.*
110. *Ibid.*, 35a–36b.
111. *Ibid.*, 36a.
112. *Ibid.*, 36b.

GLOSSARY

a	居士佛教	aj	六齋日	bt	天主實義
b	三教合一	ak	放生池	bu	天說
c	弘明集	al	顏眞卿	bv	辯學遺牘
d	世說新語	am	永明延壽	bw	孝
e	祩宏	an	慈雲遵式	bx	口戒
f	左派王學，泰州學	ao	放生會	by	身戒
	派	ap	蘇東坡	bz	心戒
g	不殺	aq	公案	ca	律儀戒
h	放生	ar	慧遠，蓮社	cb	善法戒
i	自知錄	as	念佛會	cc	攝生戒
j	十重	at	戒殺，放生文	cd	善書
k	四十八輕	au	上方	ce	太上感應篇
l	菩薩戒	av	長壽	cf	袁黄(了凡)
m	梵網經心地品	aw	放生文	cg	陰隲錄
n	智顗	ax	九橫	ch	太微仙君功過格
o	菩薩戒義疏發隱	ay	無生	ci	善門
p	自殺	az	華嚴	cj	過門
q	教人殺	ba	佛說阿彌陀經疏鈔	ck	居士傳
r	方便殺	bb	周汝登	cl	彭紹升
s	讚嘆殺	bc	羅近溪	cm	際清
t	見作隨喜	bd	行善止惡	cn	尺木
u	呪殺	be	福	co	遺稿
v	殺因	bf	色身	cp	紫柏眞可
w	殺緣	bg	慧命	cq	憨山德清
x	殺法	bh	上方善會	cr	藕益智旭
y	殺業	bi	陶望齡	cs	嚴敏卿
z	慈悲心	bj	焦竑	ct	三皈依
aa	孝順心	bk	虞淳熙	cu	受戒
ab	不行放救戒	bl	勝蓮社	cv	廣
ac	四大	bm	戒殺文	cw	大
ad	變易	bn	神	cx	智
ae	分段	bo	下善	cy	宿根
af	范縝	bp	中善	cz	王孟夙
ag	神滅論	bq	上善	da	蔡槐庭
ah	互相刑剋	br	利瑪竇	db	丁劍虹
ai	自相損減	bs	闢邪運動	dc	王道安

dd 王弱生
de 黃元孚
df 聞子與
dg 黃平倩
dh 朱白民
di 念佛三昧
dj 莊復眞
dk 戈以安
dl 話頭
dm 萬法歸一，一歸何處
dn 念佛是誰
do 千善
dp 方便
dq 菩薩戒本
dr 無間業
ds 見機得殺
dt 馮泰衢
du 滯礙
dv 比丘戒
dw 周夢顏
dx 楊文會
dy 鈴木中正，佛敎の禁殺戒律が宋代の民衆生活に及せる影响について
dz 佛祖統紀
ea 唐大詔全集
eb 藝文類聚，梁元帝荊州放生亭碑
ec 全唐文，天下放生池碑銘
ed 五灯會元
ee 佛祖通載
ef 釋氏稽古略

eg 湯用彤，漢魏兩晉南北朝佛敎史
eh 宋代佛敎結社の研究
ei 東坡居士飲食説
ej 優曇祖師戒殺文
ek 佛印禪師戒殺文
el 眞歇禪師戒殺文
em 普庵禪師戒殺文
en 歸元直指集
eo 小笠原宣秀，中國近世淨土敎史の研究，白蓮宗の研究
ep 李守孔，明代白蓮敎考略
eq 竹窗二筆
er 葯師經
es 法苑珠林
et 放生辯惑
eu 說郛續集
ev 橫超慧日，明末佛敎と基督敎との相互批判
ew 小柳氣司太，利瑪竇と明末の思想界，續東洋思想の研究
ex 侯外廬，中國思想通史
ey 李之藻，天學初函
ez 彌格子，楊廷筠
fa 方豪，中國天主敎史人物傳
fb 張廣湉，證妄説
fc 明朝破邪集

fd 李昌齡
fe 老莊の思想と道敎
ff 酒井忠夫，中國善書の研究
fg 高雄義堅，明代に大成された功過格思想
fh 清水泰次，明代に於ける宗敎融合と功過格
fi 吉岡義半，中國民衆の倫理書功過格について
fj 朱時恩，居士分灯錄
fk 陶明潛，先覺集
fl 小川貫弋，居士佛敎の近世發展
fm 郡伯
fn 邑令
fo 中丞
fp 太史
fq 總戎
fr 方伯
fs 宗伯
ft 京兆
fu 都閫
fv 治中
fw 郡丞
fx 主政
fy 中翰

WM. THEODORE DE BARY *Neo-Confucian*

Cultivation and the Seventeenth-Century

"Enlightenment"

The idea of "enlightenment" as the aspiration for freedom from darkness, ignorance, and illusion is one of the most universal of human ideals. In East Asia it has taken two main forms; first, the emancipation of the individual from the fetters of the mind and the sufferings of the world, usually by some religious discipline; and second, a more general cultural movement by which new knowledge would free men from bondage to a benighted past. Our English word "enlightenment" has been applied to both, without, however, presuming or implying that there was any necessary connection between the two. In East Asia, individual enlightenment was a conscious goal of spiritual cultivation or religious practice for centuries, and indigenous terms (Chinese *wu*,[a] Japanese *satori*) existed for it. The broader movement, with emphasis on intellectual and cultural uplift, was recognized as a value, or historical reality, only in comparatively recent times. The Chinese term *ch'i-meng*,[b] or Japanese *keimō*, came into use in this sense only after exposure to the West, first to represent the enlightenment of the modern West and thereafter in reference to Chinese or Japanese approximations of it. Indeed, enlightenment in this latter sense, far from being seen as an outgrowth or extension of the traditional ideal, was generally considered its antithesis. The earlier religious view was regarded as just another form of obscurantism and superstition, to be dispelled and superseded by the new enlightenment.

ENLIGHTENMENT: TRADITIONAL AND MODERN

Subsequent events have not quite borne out that expectation. The traditional ideal of enlightenment has survived and exerts a strong appeal on the offspring of the modern enlightenment, especially in the West. In the meantime, too, there has been a continuing reexamination of the past in China and Japan. Much that was once consigned to "feudal" darkness and oblivion has been progressively reclaimed. "Enlightenment" in the broad social and cultural sense is no longer viewed as exclusively a Western product, but something for which there was considerable precedent and preparation in East Asia. So far, however, there has been little inclination to relate these two developments in any way. The devotees of Zen enlightenment, for instance, whatever their claims for its contribution to Japan's aesthetic culture, have little to say about its role in the historical process which led to the new "enlightenment" and subsequent modernization. On the other hand, those who contend that the modern "enlightenment" was already well under way in East Asia before there was contact with the West rarely ask themselves how such an early development could have emerged in a religious and intellectual atmosphere previously thought so incompatible with it.

These are, of course, large questions, and no study of seventeenth-century Chinese thought can provide us with more than an opening to them. Nevertheless, the seventeenth and eighteenth centuries have often been seen as a time of intellectual awakening in East Asia, and in China the period has been compared to both the Renaissance and the Enlightenment in Europe.[1] That it could be likened to both suggests the crudeness of the comparisons. That they are still commonly resorted to, despite the somewhat contrived nature of such characterizations, suggests that we are confronted with a development of continuing historical significance, however debatable that may still be.

Probably the most substantial effort in Communist China to reassess this period of thought is found in Hou Wai-lu's [c] *History of Chinese Thought in the Early Period of Enlightenment*.[2] Without claiming any close historical parallel to the Enlightenment in the West, Hou finds enough progressive thinking in the seventeenth and eighteenth centuries to justify his view that China, far from being stagnant in these years, was making great intellectual advances. He cites an impressive number of original thinkers whose achievements, judged in their own context, exhibit a noteworthy independence of mind, a high degree of critical intelligence, and some genuine concern for social problems.[3]

Hou's preferences are expressed in somewhat stereotyped "Marxist" terms, but there can be no doubt that the heroes of his "Enlightenment" are men of genuine stature. Whether or not their views can best be described as "progressive," "antifeudal," "materialistic," and so forth, they are on the whole representative of the intellectual climate of the times. By any other name, Hou's "Enlightenment" thinkers, Li Chih,[d] Fang I-chih,[e] Wang Fu-chih,[f] Huang Tsung-hsi,[g] Ku Yen-wu,[h] Yen Yüan,[i] Tai Chen,[j] and so on, would still be the ones to reckon with in any assessment of the period, as they are in the present volume (and, what is more, described by one of our own writers as "Enlightenment" thinkers).[4] In the final analysis, however, the difficulty with Hou's approach is that the more one recognizes the undoubted achievements of these men or the extraordinary level of "Enlightenment" attained, the harder it becomes to explain how such a promising trend could have emerged from such unpromising antecedents or could have exhausted itself by the nineteenth century.

To pose this question is not to imply that, whatever the successes of the Chinese in these years, they must in the end fall short when measured against the eventual demands of Westernization. On the contrary, our point is precisely that no preconceived Western pattern or standard is applicable. A long list of achievements, if recited simply in terms of their alleged approximation to Western developments, whether in "Marxist" terms or any others, is of little avail. Only what can be seen as organic outgrowths of China's own intellectual and spiritual values, the development of which can be established in the light of the whole East Asian cultural complex and its historical growth, can meet the test. So far only the first steps in that direction have been taken, and these falteringly.

Earlier, Liang Ch'i-ch'ao [k] and Hu Shih [l] had attempted to portray this same period as a Chinese Renaissance, and while Hu increasingly recognized the complexities of such a comparison, he continued to reaffirm what for him was central to the rise of "scientific thought" in the seventeenth and eighteenth centuries, namely that it was an outgrowth of the "investigation of things" in the philosophy of Chu Hsi,[m] which had dominated subsequent Neo-Confucian thought. In an essay, "The Scientific Spirit and Method in Chinese Philosophy," [5] Hu described the "great movement in the history of Chinese thought which started out with the ambitious slogan of 'investigation of the reason of all things and the extension of human knowledge to the utmost' but which ended in improving and perfecting a critical method of historical research and thereby opening up a new age of revival of classical learning." [6] Hu is certainly justified in claiming this "investigation of things" as one of the central doctrines of the whole Neo-Confucian movement.[7] There is some basis also for his further claim that this doctrine contributed to the method of "evidential investigation" which first developed fully in the seventeenth century, and that "by the eighteenth and nineteenth centuries practically all first-class minds in intellectual China were attracted to it and were devoting their lives to its application to all fields of classical and humanistic study." [8] It is even understandable why Hu should pay tribute to "a great heritage of scientific spirit and method which makes us, sons and daughters of present-day China, feel not entirely at sea, but rather at home, in the new age of modern science" [9] (though one wonders how the Chinese could expect to feel so completely at home in it when many others are so at sea).

It is not for us to enter here upon the larger questions of the development of science or of a scientific method in China with which Hu is involved. It suffices that the great age of intellectual revival and evidential investigation in the seventeenth and eighteenth centuries may be seen, to some degree at least, as a natural outgrowth of a major trend in Neo-Confucian thought. Hu passes rather quickly, however, over other manifestations of Neo-Confucian thought which cast shadows on his theory. There was not in fact a clear line of development from Chu Hsi in the twelfth century to Chiao Hung[n] (1541–1620) and Ch'en Ti[o] (1541–1617), whom Hu cites as the next great exemplars of this spirit, in the sixteenth and seventeenth centuries.[10] Chiao Hung's feats of critical scholarship fully merit Hu's attention, but far from being a follower of Chu Hsi's Sung Learning, he is one of its most stringent critics. Not only does this raise the question of Chiao's actual indebtedness to Chu Hsi, but it illustrates the more general point that the pragmatic and positivistic spirit which arises in the sixteenth and seventeenth centuries is as much a reaction against Chu Hsi's type of "investigation of things" as it is its further extension.

One must question, then, Hu's acclaim for the "new age of Revival of Learning (1600–1900)" not because this revival failed to "produce an age of natural science," [11] which Hu acknowledges, but because one discerns a certain disingenuous note in his assertion that this spirit of scientific inquiry "succeeded in replacing an age of subjective, idealistic, and moralizing philosophy (from the 11th to the 16th centuries) by making it seem outmoded, 'empty,' unfruitful, and no longer attractive to the best minds of the age." [12] Chiao Hung, actually, is more directly the product of that seemingly outmoded and "empty" philosophy than he is of Chu Hsi's system. Moreover, pressing the point a step further, there is an additional incongruity in that the age so disparaged by Hu was one more directly under the influence of Chu Hsi than was that of Chiao Hung and his contemporaries. From this it might appear, contrary to Hu's whole line of argument, that the further one got from Chu Hsi the better it was for scientific inquiry.

Such points might seem of only historical interest, but they bear in fact upon the whole nature and inner development of Neo-Confucianism, on the different trends which combined to produce this remarkable "enlightenment" in the seventeenth and eighteenth centuries, and on the inherent limits to the growth of that movement. They also bring us back to the meeting place between the old enlightenment and the new. Chiao Hung, who along with Li Chih so well exemplifies the modern temper in sixteenth-century China, was a believer in the essential harmony of the Three Teachings: Buddhism, Taoism, and Confucianism; and as a member of the T'ai-chou [p] branch of Wang Yang-ming's [q] school, who was also influenced by Wang Chi,[r] [13] he almost personifies the miraculous creativity which they so stressed as the fruit of enlightenment. Here, in the supposedly medieval darkness that preceded the new enlightenment, may lie one of the secret keys to the spiritual detachment sought by one age and the degree of scientific objectivity attained by the next.

THE JAPANESE ENLIGHTENMENT

Before pursuing further the twisting trail that leads back from the new "enlightenment" to the old, it may be useful to open up one other dimension of the problem: the Japanese. Japan, in common with Korea and Vietnam, drew heavily on Neo-Confucian thought and culture in the centuries just before the opening of East Asia to the West. While this should not be misunderstood, as it often is, to mean that the higher culture of Japan was largely derivative of China's, students of the subsequent modernization of Japan have not failed to note how importantly the influence of Neo-Confucianism conditioned the reception of Western ideas and practices. These efforts to relate the process of modernization to Neo-Confucianism have sometimes been handicapped by inadequate understanding of the full nature, scope, and permutations of the latter, but there could be no ignoring its crucial role.

In *The Japanese Enlightenment*, Carmen Blacker has described the process of Japan's intellectual modernization in terms which contrast quite sharply with those of Hou Wai-lu or Hu Shih in their interpretation of China's premodern "Enlightenment." [14] Here in mid-nineteenth century Japan, Neo-Confucianism is seen as the great impediment to modernization and the incubus from which Japan had to be delivered if it was to struggle out into the light of modern day. As it was seen by those instrumental in reeducating modern Japan, she would have to make, in Dr. Blacker's words, "strenuous efforts to alter the spirit and habits of thought engendered by two hundred years of feudal and Confucian discipline—and this would mean rethinking many of her most unquestioned assumptions in the sphere of Eastern ethics. Western studies must cease to be an inferior though useful appendage to Chinese learning, and become rather a learning in itself with a dignity and moral purpose not only comparable with but substitutable for Chinese learning." [15] Moreover, "Two hundred years of orthodox Chinese learning, and of the stratified feudal system of which it was the philosophical justification, had entirely smothered any spirit of independence with which the Japanese might naturally be endowed and had encouraged instead a disgraceful tendency to rely, both in thought and action, on others—on the Sages, on the government, on social superiors." [16]

It was, then, the urgent desire to remedy this situation which led Japanese intellectual leaders of the mid-nineteenth century to promote the new enlightenment so desperately needed.

This anxiety to reform the morale and spirit of the Japanese people became the basis of the movement during the 1870's known as the *Keimō* or Enlightenment. . . . *Keimō* meant, in fact, enlightening the darkness of the masses, educating them not merely to a knowledge of new facts, but to an entirely new outlook on the universe, to a rethinking of some of their most unquestioned assumptions about man, nature and value. [17]

Among these unquestioned assumptions a most central one was Chu Hsi's teaching of the "investigation of things and the exhaustive pursuit of principle." To achieve scientific objectivity, according to Dr. Blacker, the leaders of the nineteenth-century Japanese enlightenment found it necessary to reject this doctrine, so permeated was it with a metaphysical and moralistic view of principle, "which bore no relation to a detached scientific exploration of the things of the external world." [18] In place of the "old learning pertaining to the morally organic Nature" and pursuit of the moral Way, they advocated a practical knowledge of the external world which would serve the cause of social progress. [19]

It is clear how much at variance, and almost irreconcilably so, are these two views of Chu Hsi's central teaching, that of Dr. Blacker's Enlightenment leaders who see it as a fundamental obstacle to the new learning, and that of Dr. Hu, who has credited Chu Hsi's "investigation of things" with providing the very essence of a scientific point of view. Further, according to Dr. Blacker, the new practical learning of the Japanese enlightenment which was to replace Chu Hsi's philosophy had, as its prime ingredient, a new attitude of doubt and experimentation. "The spirit of the new *jitsugaku* [s] was . . . essentially one of doubt and experiment. It was only by constant experiment and taking nothing for granted that the laws of nature could be discovered." [20] Compare this to Dr. Hu's: "The Neo-Confucians of the eleventh century often stressed the importance of doubt in thinking." [21] Chu Hsi's "great achievement" was that "he never tired of preaching the importance of doubt in thinking and investigation. . . ." [22] This element of doubt and verification was essential, Dr. Hu contends, to the rise of the age of evidential investigation in the seventeenth and eighteenth centuries. "And for this intellectual revolution of no small magnitude credit must be given to our philosopher Chu Hsi, who in the twelfth century expressed a courageous doubt and proposed a meaningful question which he himself was not yet fully prepared to answer." [23]

By this point the reader himself may well begin to have doubts. Can these two writers be talking about the same thing? Can Chu Hsi and Neo-Confucianism have such completely opposite meanings to different people? The fact is, of course, that they can. Dr. Hu is talking about the more intellectual aspect of Neo-Confucian thought and, as we have seen in his dismissal of Neo-Confucian thought in the twelfth to sixteenth centuries, he too is prepared to dispense with the moralists and metaphysicians Dr. Blacker refers to. On the other hand, there is far more of a basis in Neo-Confucianism for detached scholarly inquiry and a critical

methodology than is allowed for when one identifies it too exclusively
with idealistic metaphysics, ethical knowledge, and a meditative contemplation of Nature.[24]

Thus we are faced with the need to distinguish between the spiritual
and moral aspect of Neo-Confucianism and the intellectual or scholarly,
or between the spiritual and intellectual aspects of both cultivation and
enlightenment. It would be nice if this were all one needed to explain the
great discrepancy between these views. One might suppose then that it
was the merest historical mischance that the enlightenment thinkers of
seventeenth-century China and those of nineteenth-century Japan, or
Doctors Hu and Blacker, had not made each other's acquaintance. But of
course it is not so simple as that, and an additional complication appears
as soon as one juxtaposes the view of Neo-Confucianism found in Dr.
Blacker's nineteenth-century enlightenment with that given in Robert
Bellah's *Tokugawa Religion*.[25] Here, there is no such ambiguity as that
which confuses the issue between Hu and Blacker.

JAPANESE ENLIGHTENMENT: "PRE-MODERN"

The religion Bellah sees as an important force in Japan's preparation for
modernization draws precisely upon that moral and spiritual aspect of
Neo-Confucianism against which the Meiji enlightenment so reacted.
From this standpoint Japan's rapid progress under the "enlightened rule"
of Emperor Meiji was as much the product of a moral and religious
dynamism flowing forth from Neo-Confucianism as it was the achievement of the radical Westernizers' emancipation of Japan from the moralistic learning of the past.

That Bellah's study centers precisely upon the kind of Neo-Confucian
learning which later reformers wished to discard is evident from his discussion of so-called *gakumon*,[t] left untranslated and used in romanized
form because, apparently, there was no exact English equivalent for a
type of learning that so stressed moral commitment and discipline. Bellah
says, "We may distinguish two main directions of process covered by the
term *gakumon*. One is that leading to enlightenment (*kenshō*),[u] 'knowing the nature' or 'knowing the heart.' The other is the ethical practice
following from that enlightenment or knowledge."[26] Bellah allows that

the thought of his prime example, Ishida Baigan ^v (1685–1744), "does not entirely ignore" the more narrow meaning of study or scholarship. He compares the heart to a mirror and considers writings as a polisher to polish the heart. He very often used classical texts as the basis of his lectures. However, when asked whether *gakumon* were anything other than reading books, he replied, "Indeed it is in reading books. However, if one reads books and does not know the heart of the books, it is not called *gakumon*. The books of the sages contain their own heart. Knowing their heart is called *gakumon*. . . ." [27]

Before undertaking a more detailed consideration of the content and method of this religious and moral discipline, which will take us further into the past, I should like to bring out first the significance that Bellah sees in this type of thought for Japan's future modernization. It served, he says, to produce a "this-worldly mysticism," marked by an asceticism that "reinforced the practical frugality which characterized the merchant and peasant ethics," [28] and also a devotion to service "and hard work in one's calling," obviously meant to suggest the inculcation of a kind of "Protestant ethic" in Tokugawa Japan. "The result of enlightenment is not nirvana or any form of withdrawal from the world. Rather it is complete, whole-hearted, and unconflicted action in accordance with morality." [29]

This kind of teaching was known in Japanese as *shingaku*, corresponding to the Chinese *hsin-hsüeh*. ^w I shall return to the significance of this term after one further quotation showing the important role and influence which Bellah believes *shingaku* had in preparing the ground for Japan's modernization:

As a religion it taught enlightenment and the selfless devotion which was both a means toward it and a consequence thereof. Politically it reinforced rationalization and the extension of power by emphasizing the great importance of loyalty and the selflessness of the retainer. . . . Economically it reinforced diligence and economy, it valued productivity and minimized consumption. Further it advocated universalistic standards of honesty and respect for contract and gave them religious underpinnings. In these ways it must be seen as contributing to the growth of a disciplined, practical, continuous attitude toward work in the world among the city classes, important for both entrepreneurs and workers in an economy entering the process of industrialization. In doing all this it utilized one of the oldest and most powerful religious traditions in the Far East, that going back to Mencius. By fashioning this tradition to the needs of the city classes of its day Shingaku brought meaning into the lives of the harried and troubled merchants and channelled their energies in directions which were to have the profoundest consequences for their society.[30]

It is rather striking that Dr. Bellah should attribute so large an influence and such profound consequences to the *shingaku*, when in Dr. Blacker's study of Japan's intellectual modernization, published seven years later, there is not the slightest mention of the movement by either the author or her Enlightenment leaders. How could they have failed to be aware of it? Part of the explanation may lie in the fact that *shingaku* as such was less widespread a movement than *Tokugawa Religion* leads us to believe, and neither commanded attention nor compelled specific comment.[31] On the other hand, the attitudes it exemplified were indeed widespread and certainly known to Meiji thinkers. Thus Enlightenment thinkers were only too conscious of certain intellectual obstacles they had to struggle against in this Neo-Confucian teaching.

NEO-CONFUCIANISM AS A SCHOOL OF THE MIND

This brings us back, then, to the central theme of our own inquiry: the relation between the spiritual and intellectual forces in Neo-Confucianism. We have already noted the terminological correspondence between Japanese *shingaku* and Chinese *hsin-hsüeh*. In actuality, Ishida Baigan's teaching owes little if anything to its apparent Chinese namesake, the so-called School of the Mind identified with the philosophies of Lu Hsiang-shan (1139–92) and Wang Yang-ming (1472–1529). Baigan's school is rather an independent outgrowth of the orthodox Ch'eng-Chu teaching.[32] In this fact alone there is much significance. *Shingaku*, from this standpoint, is more Catholic than Protestant. There is even a sense, as we shall see, in which it is more Catholic than the Pope, i.e., more orthodox than Tokugawa orthodoxy.

Those familiar with Neo-Confucian mysticism in China will find in Baigan's teaching all of its usual earmarks. "The highest aim of *gakumon* is to exhaust one's heart and know one's nature. Knowing one's nature one knows Heaven." Knowing Heaven, at least for Baigan, means that one's own heart is united with the heart of Heaven and earth. However, being darkened by human desires, this heart is lost. Consequently when we speak of exhausting the heart and returning to the heart of Heaven and earth, we are saying to seek the lost heart. If one seeks and attains it, one becomes the heart of Heaven and earth. When one says, "becomes the heart of Heaven and earth," one says "without a heart (*mushin*)." [x] The good person (*jinsha*) [y] "makes his heart united with Heaven and earth and all things. There is nothing which can be said not to be himself. . . . The sage penetrates heaven and earth and all things with his own heart." [33]

Here, allowing for certain variations in the translation of key terms, is the doctrine of Ch'eng Hao [z] concerning the "humanity which forms one body with Heaven and earth and all things." [34] Bellah translates the term *shin* (Chinese *hsin*) as "heart," rather than "mind," no doubt to emphasize the ethical and affective aspects of this very broad concept. [35] This is, nonetheless, the typical Neo-Confucian doctrine of the Mind, which figures so prominently in the thought of the Sung and Ming. Alternatively one can identify it as the Neo-Confucian doctrine of No-Mind (*wu-hsin*), meaning that the humane man has "no mind" of his own but sees and acts toward all things with the mind of Heaven and earth. [36] The psychological and religious phenomena associated with this experience, as described by Bellah for Baigan and his disciples, are likewise almost a stereotype of the mystical experience found especially in Ming thinkers. [37] "As in mysticism generally, what is indicated is some dissolution of the boundary between self and non-self. This union is accompanied by a feeling of great happiness and tranquility, but also a great feeling of power." [38]

What is noteworthy here, as I have put it above, is that this represents "the typical Neo-Confucian doctrine of the Mind." By this I mean to distinguish it from the so-called Lu-Wang School of the Mind, for, as we have already seen, Baigan has no special connection with that. His thinking reflects rather the teaching and cultivation of the mind as it is found in the "orthodox" Ch'eng-Chu school. Though this latter school is usually identified as the "School of Principle," the conventional dichotomy which has developed between "Principle" and "Mind" in describing these two main lines of Neo-Confucian thought tends to obscure the most fundamental role of the Mind in this movement as a whole. [39]

These conventional designations, as Professor Araki's paper in this volume helps to show, serve to differentiate these schools from one another but do not adequately express even more fundamental points of agree-

ment. The School of Principle (li-hsüeh),[aa] as applied to the Ch'eng-
Chu school, focuses attention on what is indeed a basic doctrine of this
school: its belief in fixed moral principles and in the underlying rationality of all things. The significance of the term derives from this
school's rejection of Buddhist "emptiness" as the ultimate reality and its
insistence that there is a "principle in the midst of emptiness," as Chu
Hsi put it.[40] But the principles Chu Hsi was talking about were as much
principles of the mind as principles in things, and the importance of
Mencius to this movement (as brought out in the quotations from Dr.
Bellah) lies in the basis he provided for a Neo-Confucian philosophy of
the mind as an alternative to the Buddhist.[41] Thus in Chu Hsi's system as
it was conveyed to Baigan, there was already a heavy emphasis on cultivation of the mind. It drew upon earlier Sung thinkers like Chou Tun-i [ab]
and the Ch'eng brothers, who, whether they be seen to reflect a strain of
quietism in Sung thought or not, certainly showed the influence of Buddhism in their emphasis on the primacy of mind and the importance of
mental cultivation in forms closely resembling those of Zen Buddhism.[42]

Professor Araki's paper, discussing these designations in the broader
context of Sung thought, which includes the Buddhist School of the
Mind, suggests that use of the same term for the Lu-Wang School tends
to identify it too exclusively with the Mind and fails to bring out how
strongly Wang Yang-ming adhered to the notion of principle, even
though he did not conceive of it as fixed. Precisely the same can be said
in reverse about the Ch'eng-Chu school. It is truly a school of the
Mind, as well as of Principle.

Baigan's shingaku, then, is a School of the Mind or Heart in this
sense. Though it has its own specific Japanese characteristics, including
some direct influence of Zen and a syncretism characteristic of the late
seventeenth and eighteenth centuries in Tokugawa Japan, in a most fundamental sense his teaching of the Mind or Heart faithfully transmits to
this new setting what is known as the orthodox Ch'eng-Chu teaching and
practice in this respect. If one had conceived of its orthodoxy in terms of
adherence above all to "principle," one would be surprised perhaps to
discover that its fidelity to the Ch'eng-Chu school consisted for practical
purposes in its employment of the method of self-examination and contemplation which was as much a fixture in this tradition as examination
of conscience and confession have been to the Roman Catholic. It is in

this specific sense that I have spoken of *Shingaku* as being more Catholic than Protestant, though there are of course other resemblances in it to Protestantism.[43]

Bellah alludes to this in his discussion of the formal practice of meditation by Baigan as a means of "exhausting the heart" and "knowing one's nature." "This exhausting the heart had with the Sung Confucians already become a clearly defined technique. Baigan calls it *kūfu* [ac] or *seiza*. [ad] *Kūfu* implies the expenditure of effort and *seiza* simply means quiet-sitting. What is involved is a sort of concentration of the will. Words and all external things are as much as possible abandoned. Baigan's technique of meditation was, in fact, strongly influenced by the Zen sect of Buddhism." [44]

The term *kūfu*, above, corresponds to the Chinese *kung-fu*, which was already an important term for religious practice in Chinese Ch'an Buddhism before it came into similar use by the Neo-Confucians. *Seiza* corresponds to the Chinese *ching-tso*, a type of quiet-sitting. influenced by Ch'an Buddhism but distinguishable from Ch'an (Zen) "sitting in meditation" (*tso-ch'an*, [ae] Japanese *zazen*). The significant, though often subtle, influences of Ch'an on the Neo-Confucian practice of quiet-sitting in the Sung, as well as the equally significant differences between the two, complicate the question of a separate and direct Zen influence on Baigan; it is a matter requiring some delicacy of treatment and, being secondary to our purpose here, must be held over to a later time.

NEO-CONFUCIANISM AS A FORM OF SPIRITUALITY

Enough has been seen so far to establish that the Neo-Confucianism we are dealing with here is less of a philosophical position or system than it is a type and method of spirituality. Indeed, if there is any purpose in our giving attention to Japanese *shingaku*, which was not that important as an historical movement, it is that it brings out the more religious aspect of orthodox Neo-Confucianism and suggests the need for a reinterpretation of the main line of development in Neo-Confucian thought.

To present this in its most concise form, I turn now to the most important manual of Neo-Confucian teaching, the *Reflections on Things at Hand* (*Chin-ssu lu*) [af] of Chu Hsi.[45] Here one may get a good indication of the relative weight assigned to the different elements in Chu Hsi's synthesis, and also of the central ideal which integrated them and gave them real life. As it happens, too, this was the main text of Neo-Confucianism in the rather scanty library of Ishida Baigan, and one of the principal ones, along with the Confucian Classics, which he expounded.[46]

The first chapter of this anthology, entitled "On the substance of the Way (Tao-t'i)," [ag] begins with a quotation from Chou Tun-i about the Supreme Ultimate and then proceeds to discuss the other key cosmological and moral concepts which provide the metaphysical basis for Neo-Confucian cultivation.[47] Many readers, including Chu Hsi himself, found this summation of Neo-Confucian metaphysics formidable and forbidding. Its coeditor, Lü Tsu-ch'ien,[ah] who was probably most responsible for it, admitted that many people were put off by this abstract formulation, but nevertheless felt that first things should be put first.[48] Chu Hsi's doubts were expressed in his *Classified Conversations:* "The first chapter of the *Chin-ssu lu* is difficult to read. . . . If one reads this chapter only he will be unable to relate to life the principles he finds in it. . . . In reading the *Chin-ssu lu*, if the student does not understand the first chapter, he should begin with the second and the third. In time he will gradually understand the first chapter." [49]

The same experience and reaction, I think, has been had by many in China, Japan, and the West whose introduction to Neo-Confucianism came in this form. Typically, Neo-Confucian philosophy is presented in the same terms and sequence: The Supreme Ultimate, yin-yang, the Five Agents, principle, material force, and so on, as illustrated by Fung Yu-lan's standard *History of Chinese Philosophy*.[50] Thus, the idea has been perpetuated that Neo-Confucianism is primarily a metaphysical system and its significance has been seen as almost exclusively bound up with such a system. Huang Kan, a pupil of Chu Hsi who claimed that the latter had not wanted to include the first chapter "because its abstract character might lead to idle speculation on metaphysics . . . remarked that the book had now become *Reflections on Things Far Away*." [51]

The proper order of chapters and the structure of the whole *Chin-ssu lu* have been matters of debate ever since it first appeared. The most recent scholarly edition and translation into Japanese follows the view that first principles should be put last, and places the first chapter at the end of the book.[52] Those who, unheeding (or, more likely, unaware) of

Chu Hsi's advice, work through this chapter to the others following, wi'l find that the whole atmosphere and spirit of the work change with chapter 2. The remainder of the book is more practical and educational than it is formally philosophical. Perhaps the best analogy for the relation of this concise metaphysical introduction to a work that is otherwise much more human, and often inspirational, are the typical metaphysical settings to the great Chinese novels, such as *Water Margin (Shui-hu chuan)*,[ai] *Monkey (Hsi-yu chi)*,[aj] and *The Dream of the Red Chamber (Hung lou meng)*,[ak] which provide a supernatural or metaphysical setting for the more natural, matter-of-fact world of the main narrative. Abstruse and sometimes rather abstract, they provide a universal framework for the mystery which surrounds and sustains the actions of men.

Chapter 2 of the *Chin-ssu lu*, called "The Essentials of Learning," has as its opening passage (again a quotation from Chou Tun-i): "The sage aspires to become Heaven, the worthy aspires to become a sage, and the gentleman aspires to become a worthy." The aspiration to be a sage, and the method of achieving it, are the grand themes of the work. "The Way of the Sage," we are told in the second quotation, "is to be heard through the ear, preserved in the heart, deeply embraced there to become one's moral character, and to become one's activities and undertakings when it is put into practice." [53] Here is the gate through which, Chu Hsi tells us in his preface, "even a young man in an isolated village" may enter upon the Way.[54] Confucianism had long been called the Way of the Sages. To most people this meant the Way handed down from the sages of the past and received by later generations as a remote ideal to be admired. Rarely had it been thought of as something to which anyone could aspire, as a practical program of cultivation and action by which even "a young man in an isolated village" could hope eventually to attain to the perfection of his own humanity.

Lü Tsu-ch'ien, after defending the first chapter in his preface, says, "As to the contents of the remaining chapters dealing with methods of study and the concrete steps to daily application and personal practice, they involve definite steps." [55] Steps, that is, from the aspiration to sagehood to its final achievement. The last chapter, which deals with the sages and worthies, completes the process and ends with a simple quotation from Chang Tsai: [al] "When they were fourteen or fifteen, the two Ch'engs were already free [from wrong ideas] and wanted to learn to be sages." (Or, as a textual variant in some editions emphasizes, "zealously wanted to become sages.") [56] It is clear that the compilers have deliberately chosen this as the note on which to conclude, to leave as the final impression in the reader's mind the example of the Ch'eng brothers' active commitment to "becoming sages." [57] "You have been shown the Way, now do likewise!"

To a degree the final chapter on the sages and worthies illustrates the authentic line of orthodox transmission as conceived among the Neo-Confucians, and especially by Chu Hsi. But its contents do not state the doctrinal case for orthodoxy or delineate any dogmatic transmission from the early sages. Chan's rendering of the chapter heading is "On the Dispositions of Sages and Worthies" and, though there are differences among the headings in various editions, the most common one calls this "Observing (or contemplating, *kuan*) the Sages and Worthies." [am] [58] In other words, it is their character, personality, manner, and spirit which command attention and admiration, not their philosophical concepts or statements. The Way of the Sage is exemplified above all in the conduct of human life, in the type of personality it produced. What finally is of value is the living of life, the actualization of one's ideals.

In a sense this chapter might be thought to provide the makings of a Neo-Confucian hagiography, and it does indeed serve the same purpose in this tradition of spirituality as do the lives of the saints in the Christian, or, more appositely in this case, as representing the existing alternative, the lives of eminent monks in the Buddhist tradition. There are, however, at least two significant ways in which this Confucian "hagiography" differs from others. First, it gives relatively little attention to the ancient sages and their great achievements. With the wealth of material available in the classics on the sage-kings and the Three Dynasties, the *Chin-ssu lu* draws very sparingly and selectively upon it. By contrast much attention is given to the great Sung masters, and especially to Chou Tun-i and the Ch'eng brothers, whose personalities and activities are presented in intimate, if not extensive, detail. We are reminded of Chu Hsi's comment in the *Classified Conversations* that "Everything in the *Chin-ssu lu* is intimately connected with human life" and that "they are more intimately connected with our own lives" than what is found in the classics. [59]

This, then, is a modern, humanized, and secularized hagiography.

The compilers observe the formal distinction between the original sages and the later worthies, but they make little of it here. The real models presented to the young in vivid, colorful, and inspiring terms are the moderns.

Second, this is not highly stylized hagiography. Differences among individuals are recognized and even highlighted. This is not to suggest that they are all seen as equivalent, for there is still a strong tendency to think in terms of a hierarchy of spiritual ascendancy, but it is nevertheless suggested that the virtues and creativity of Heaven are manifested differently in different men. "Confucius was quite clear and pure in disposition. Yen Tzu (Yen Hui) [an] was quite happy and at ease. And Mencius was quite a vigorous debater." [60] Or again, "Chung-ni [ao] embraced everything. In teaching us the lesson of 'not objecting to anything as if he were stupid' [i.e., not obstinately asserting himself], Yen Tzu showed later generations a disposition of natural harmony, which will silently transform us. Mencius, however, clearly showed his own ability, for, the time in which he lived being what it was, he could not help it." [61] Similarly the differing personalities and situations of the Sung masters are also brought out. This is in contrast to the earlier stereotyping of eminent Buddhist monks, who routinely exhibited the same religious virtues and powers, performed the same supernatural feats, predicted the day of their death, and passed out of the world in an attitude of supreme enlightenment.

Because of this basic respect for individual personality traits, the Neo-Confucian spirituality revealed in the *Chin-ssu lu* cannot be reduced to a single type. Certain characteristic qualities stand out, however. First, there is the reverent attitude toward life, toward Heaven, toward one's fellowmen and all creation. This reverence expresses itself, on the one hand, in taking things seriously, considering one's actions carefully in terms of their effect upon other living beings or of one's responsibilities toward others. Then, along with this basic concern and sympathy for others, there should be a natural and spontaneous joy in life. Seriousness and proper conduct should produce the joy and gladness of spirit which comes from a conscience that is at ease, at peace with itself rather than troubled and confused. Unselfish service of others should free one from the anxieties that beset the self-centered, the egotistical, the ambitious. If one can adhere to a life of strict principle, he can be moral without being moralistic; he can be firm in rejecting evil, without being self-righteous and pompous. He can respond to everything that happens in an appropriate way, which allows for the proper degree of anger or indignation if the evil calls for it, but does not allow one to become obsessed by it. The result of all this is a state of mind or spirit which can neither be appropriated to oneself nor expropriated from oneself. It is a state of poise and serenity achieved through constant effort and self-discipline in the conduct of life, through which the natural powers of Heaven are manifested effortlessly. It is indeed a process of becoming identified with Heaven, with the reality of a moral and creative universe, so that the virtue of Heaven shines through in one's own life.

There is nothing in the *Chin-ssu lu* which quite puts it in words like this. Its authors believe that personal example is more persuasive than discourse. Accordingly, there is a succession of comments such as the following: "Chou [Tun-i]'s mind was free, pure, and unobstructed, like the breeze on a sunny day and the clear moon [at night]." (Chu Hsi explains that this was the result of his being completely at harmony with the Principle of Nature, free of any selfishness or impurity.) "In his governmental administration he was careful and strict, and treated others like himself. He saw to it that he was in complete accord with moral principles." [62]

From this and from what follows one may see that the moral life is guided by a delicacy of conscience and sensitive adherence to the Mean which together maintain a balance between the extremes to which idealism and cynicism so often lead, and avoid the extravagances and excess to which religious zeal is so prone. Balance and poise are among the supreme values in this spiritual tradition. Thus of Ch'eng Hao it is said:

He was liberal but not irregular. He maintained harmony with others but did not drift with them. . . . He was open-minded. He saw penetratingly and made no discrimination between himself and others. As one tried to fathom his depth, one realized that it was as great as a boundless ocean. And as one appraised his virtue at its best, one found that even beautiful words could not describe it. In conducting himself, the Master was serious in controlling himself internally and altruistic in his practice. Whenever he saw any good deed, he felt as if it had issued from himself. He would not do to others what he did not wish others to do to him. There was substance in his words and a proper measure in his deeds. [63]

This type of lofty character and imperturbable spirit was not cultivated in isolation from the world, but provided a means and a model for dealing with it. Again, of Ch'eng Hao it is said:

In his association with people, the Master was discriminating but never set himself apart. When anything acted on him, he always responded. . . . When others were worried lest a thing might be prohibited or handicapped by law, the Master did it freely. And when most people thought that a matter was extremely difficult, the Master did it naturally as the irresistible flow of water. Even when he was hurried or startled, he never showed any expression of disturbance. . . . His self-cultivation was so complete that he was thoroughly imbued with the spirit of peacefulness, which was revealed in his voice and countenance. However, as one looked at him, he was so lofty and deep that none could treat him with disrespect. When he came upon things to do, he did them with ease and leisure, and no sense of urgency. But at the same time he was sincere and earnest, and did not treat them carelessly. His sense of responsibility was so great that he was more concerned about not achieving the objective of learning to be a sage than about achieving fame through any single good deed, and would rather consider it as his own defect if a single person was not benefited by him than consider any temporary benefit to others as his personal success. His conviction was so genuine that if he felt that his belief could be carried out, he would not lightly withdraw from government service for the sake of his own personal purity, and if according to his principles he was satisfied with his situation, he would not be willing to accept even a small position.[64]

The last passage above is quoted from a disciple of the Ch'eng brothers, Lü Yü-shu,[ap] who gives expression to the kind of ideal they inspired in him. His comment on Chang Tsai is similar:

The Master was firm and resolute in nature. His virtue was eminent and his appearance dignified. But in his association with people, he became more and more intimate with them as time went on. In regulating his family and in dealing with others, his basic principle was to correct himself in order to influence others. If people did not believe him, he would examine himself and set himself right but say nothing about the matter. Although some people might not understand his ideas, he would conduct himself naturally and easily without regret. Therefore, whether people knew him or not, they all submitted to him when they heard of his disposition, and dared not do him the slightest wrong.[65]

Such is the example of the fruits of moral and spiritual cultivation set before the readers of the *Chin-ssu lu*. This same ideal and example is presented to the reader just before the final line in which the Ch'eng brothers commit themselves to becoming sages.

In the context of the *Chin-ssu lu* this exposition of Neo-Confucian spirituality is immediately preceded by a critique of the various heresies to be rejected, as if indeed it were a final renunciation before the climactic commitment is made to the Way of the Sage. The exact terms of that critique need not detain us here; [66] suffice it to say that it is in the strongly polemical vein of Mencius or Han Yü,[aq] and not marked by depth of philosophical analysis. Its appeal, like that of the final chapter, is to the heart rather than the mind, if a Western distinction can be made between the two where no Confucian would be likely to make one. It does serve, however, to establish a clear contrast between the Buddhist preoccupation with death and suffering and the Confucian celebration of life and joy; between the Buddhist view of the human order as illusory and the Confucian affirmation of its concrete reality, essential goodness, and rationality; between the Taoist search for immortality and the Neo-Confucian acceptance of the here and now as sufficing for human fulfillment; between the Buddhist preoccupation with the problem of self and identity and the Neo-Confucian unselfish self-realization in the meeting of one's basic human responsibilities.

THE RELEVANCE OF SAGEHOOD

If Vimalakīrti represented the lay ideal of Mahāyāna Buddhism, the Sung masters depicted in the *Chin-ssu lu* were personifications of the ideal of spiritual attainment for the Confucian gentleman. This ideal found its expression in the typical activities of the Confucian *chün-tzu* [ar]—social, political, intellectual, and cultural—and yet raised that activity to a higher spiritual level. The *chün-tzu* himself had represented an ideal, the "noble man" among men, and there is significance in his subordination to the sage, who, as the exemplification of man's union with the Divine (i.e., Heaven), manifests a beatific state of mind and a remarkable charisma in dealing with men.[67]

This beatitude and charisma, however, were to be found in the ordinary pursuits of the scholar, official, ruler, father, and so on. The practice of sagehood was meant not merely to ennoble such prosaic activities but to illumine them with a divine radiance. How to achieve this in everyday life is the very practical concern of the *Chin-ssu lu*. As we examine its contents we find represented there the whole range of Confucian activities, but as we examine still closer, it becomes apparent that the balance between the individual and society so characteristic of the Confucian way has been significantly shifted. The range of topics, interests, and concerns is there, but almost everything is viewed from the stand-point of the individual's moral and spiritual cultivation. Of the fourteen chapters only three deal with political matters, and one of these is wholly preoccupied with the ethical considerations governing—not the state or society—but the question of whether the individual should accept office. The family is disposed of in a single brief chapter which, again, looks at the problem from the viewpoint of the individual's conduct and not the family or household as an independent, objective entity in itself.

Two historical factors lie behind this change, reflecting the religious and political background of Sung Neo-Confucianism. Buddhism, it has long been considered, had a significant influence upon it. This view, however, has stood in marked contrast to the emphatic and explicit rejec-tion of Buddhism we have just seen above. Often this seeming contra-diction has been explained by a distinction between unconscious influ-ence and conscious repudiation of it. That influence could be seen in certain metaphysical concepts, it was thought, and even when it was dif-ficult to identify such concepts as specifically Buddhist, it could be argued that the whole development of a new metaphysics in the Sung was a response to the challenge of Buddhist philosophy.

I would not dismiss this view entirely, but there are difficulties with it. First, it tends to assume that there was little or no Confucian metaphysics before the advent of Buddhism, which certainly takes a narrow and super-ficial view of earlier Confucianism. Second, Buddhist metaphysics was well on the decline by Sung times and unlikely to pose a direct challenge. Indeed, by the eleventh and twelfth centuries the dominant forms of Buddhism were the Ch'an (Zen) and Pure Land sects, usually considered to have replaced the philosophical schools of Chinese Bud-dhism with a new emphasis on faith and practice instead of doctrine. Third, the Neo-Confucian reaction to Buddhism was initially on moral and social grounds, and only later was the metaphysical superstructure elaborated.

For these reasons I would see the predominant influence of Buddhism to lie precisely in the deepening of Neo-Confucian spirituality that we have found so characteristic of the *Chin-ssu lu*. This influence takes the form, not so much of subjective idealism in philosophy, as in a deeper subjectivity in the practice of Confucian self-cultivation. Just as Ch'an Buddhism, the dominant form among intellectuals, was a system of practice rather than a system of metaphysics, so Neo-Confucianism was, I believe, unconsciously emulating the spiritual training and character formation of the Ch'an monk at his best—but, of course, domesticating and secularizing it.

The second factor in this development derives from the original social idealism in the Neo-Confucianism of the early Sung. The great energy and enthusiasm of this movement in its early days was generated by high hopes for a social transformation of China. In the days of Fan Chung-yen,[as] Ou-yang Hsiu,[at] and Wang An-shih,[au] the Way of the Sages was understood primarily as the Way of the Early Kings—the Way of the Sage-kings and sage statesmen of antiquity.[68] They were models for the political and social reform that would bring realization of the Confucian ideal of Heaven-on-earth, the Great Society. Ch'eng I in those days believed that if there were a Great Reform there could be Great Government (ta-chih).[av] [69] But the failure of those reforms had a sobering effect on the next generation of Confucians. Chu Hsi commented on this with a tinge of sarcasm when he was asked about Chang Tsai's belief in the possibility of restoring the ancient well-field system "without having to punish a single person" (i.e., without having to impose the reform in a coercive manner).[70] Chu said: "When one lectures one can say what he likes. But one must wait for an opportunity before one can put the system into practice. Only after a period of great chaos when the population has been reduced [almost] to nothing and all the land has reverted to the government can the land be redistributed to the people." [71]

Again, commenting on the hope for the restoration of feudalism, long the Confucian ideal, Chu said: "Feudalism and the well-fields were institutions of the sage-kings. They were institutions to make the world open to all. How dare I consider them to be wrong? However, I am afraid they are difficult to practice today. Even if they were put into practice there would be many defects." [72]

Or again: "When Master Ch'eng I was young, he repeatedly insisted on the well-field and feudal systems. In his later years, however, he said they were difficult to enforce. . . . I believe [that] Master Ch'eng, having become well experienced in human affairs, realized that circumstances were such that the systems could not be put into practice." [73]

A great faith and optimism concerning the human order, as contrasted to Buddhist pessimism, was one of the distinguishing marks of the Neo-

Confucian movement, expressed in its poetry as well as in its philosophy. With the waning of hope for improvement of society, however, and with the ominous threat of foreign invasion, fulfillment of the Confucian vision devolved more and more upon the individual himself. Failure with the great reforms of the Northern Sung had been a human failure, it was acknowledged, but this proved only that defects in human character (as in Wang An-shih) could vitiate even the noblest ventures, whereas genuine integrity and a lofty spirit (as in the Ch'engs) could survive even the worst social and political disasters.

Hence the political idealism of the noble man (*chün-tzu*), though no less admirable in difficult times, was less plausible and relevant in a deeply troubled and disordered age than was the spiritual transcendence of the sage. Neo-Confucian faith in the goodness of human nature had to call upon deep inner resources of moral strength, and it had to face up to, to learn to deal with, the defects in man. Buddhism, in its own way, had tried to cope with these weaknesses, but had seemed to save man *from* society rather than man *with* society. In the Southern Sung—and indeed in China thereafter—Neo-Confucians would have to save both man *and* society from themselves, but without the expectation of much help from the latter.

This lofty idealism is so pervasive among Sung Neo-Confucians that it becomes a distinctive quality not only of their philosophy but also of their poetry. Chu Hsi's criticism of the great T'ang poet Tu Fu [aw] climaxes the growth of an attitude, already rapturously expressed in Shao Yung's [ax] poetry, of spiritual peace and joy that has triumphed over the vicissitudes of human affairs, and is no longer affected by any selfish involvement in the world, such as concern over life or death, fame or disgrace, disappointment or suffering. Chu Hsi does not hesitate to find fault on this score with even so highly regarded a poet as Tu Fu. Yoshikawa Kōjirō explains:

In appraising the work of Tu Fu, Chu Hsi manifested the highest respect for the great T'ang poet, but criticized Tu Fu's "Seven Songs of T'ung-ku [ay] district" for their utter immersion in sorrow. The Songs, according to Chu Hsi, display heroic strength and tension beyond the capacity of the ordinary T'ang poetry, but their closing sections, in which the poet complains of old age and laments his humble position in life, betray an ignoble attitude and reveal the poet's failure to understand the true nature of the Way. In Chu Hsi's own words, "In these songs Tu Fu is heroic and extraordinary in a way matched by few other poets. But a look at the final section, where he bewails old age and laments his humble station, shows a baseness of will. Can man get along without understanding the Way?" (8:84/8a). By the "Way" Chu Hsi means, it would seem, the philosophy which does not look upon human existence as petty and insignificant.[74]

Actually Chu Hsi's reference to the "Way" is an allusion to Confucius' exclamation in the Analects, "Hearing the Way in the morning, one can die [without regret] in the evening" (IV, 8). To Neo-Confucians this expresses an attitude of religious acceptance, a final reconciliation of life and death, a readiness to meet whatever befalls one.[75] In this case Chu Hsi means that Tu Fu's aim or aspiration somehow fell short of the ideal or he would have achieved a state of mind enabling him to accept old age and humble status without regret. The truly noble man is not disturbed by political failure or personal misfortune. His peace is not the peace of this world in any social sense.[76]

NEO-CONFUCIAN ENLIGHTENMENT AND "HAVING NO MIND"

As set forth in the Chin-ssu lu, the practice of sagehood is an all-embracing system of self-cultivation. To integrate and maintain in balance different vital human activities, so that they foster and nourish each other, is of the essence. The process starts with learning, or as the traditional chapter title puts it, "doing learning" (wei-hsüeh),[az] emphasizing the active aspect rather than the passive, the initiative and commitment of the aspirant to sagehood rather than mere receptivity to traditional teaching.[77] Since this kind of learning sought to mobilize the moral resources of the individual, and was predicated on the active exercise of value judgment, there was a clear contrast to the starting point of Buddhist discipline: disillusionment and skepticism of all received values. As Ch'eng I explains very early in this exposition, "the enlightened person controls his feelings so that they will be in accord with the Mean. He rectifies his mind and nourishes his nature. . . . In the way of learning, the first thing is to be clear in one's mind and to know where to go and then to act vigorously in order that one may arrive at sagehood. This is what is meant by 'sincerity resulting from enlightenment.' " [78] Thus "the control of one's feelings," the achievement of equanimity and poise, is a fundamental aim of the enlightened man, just as control of the desires and emancipation from selfish craving was an aim of the Buddhists. But note here that "enlightenment" for Ch'eng I is a natural condition or quality, something man may employ in his striving for integrity as a man, not Enlightenment as the final and transcendent goal of Buddhism.

The Ch'eng brothers, as quoted in the chapter that sets the tone of Neo-Confucian cultivation, insist that sagehood can be achieved through active moral and intellectual effort, but at the same time one of the prime marks of the sage is spiritual peace, composure, calmness, tranquillity, in the midst of this effort and activity.[79] This state of mind, in which one's will and desires are fully in accord with the principles of Heaven-and-earth so that there is no cause for personal frustration or disintegration, was in Ch'eng Hao's phrase "having no mind [of one's own]." [80] Chu Hsi explained it, ". . . to be in accord with all creation is the same as to be extremely impartial, and to have no mind or feeling of one's own is the same as to respond spontaneously to all things as they come." [81] When someone asked him how Confucius could have been a sage and yet have cried bitterly at the death of his favorite disciple, Chu Hsi answered, "He responded [to his pupil's death] in the way he should have." [82]

This, then, was the kind of enlightenment natural to man, allowing for expression of normal feelings rather than seeking the lofty detachment exemplified by Chuang Tzu's singing at his wife's death. Chuang Tzu's detachment was fake and unnatural. True transcendence allowed a man to give natural expression to his emotions and yet not be carried away by them. At the same time, "having no mind" of one's own was quite different from the idea of simply having "no mind" in the Buddhist or Taoist sense. "For a mind that hates external things to seek illumination in a mind where nothing exists is to look for a reflection on the back of a mirror." [83] "Having no mind" meant emptying it of self and simultaneously allowing it to be completely filled with the mind of Heaven-and-earth, that is, to reflect the moral universe just as it is, rather than assume it to be empty of moral principles. The Tao which filled the mind emptied of self was not as Weber has described it: "simply the embodiment of the binding traditional ritual, and its command was not 'action' but 'emptiness.' " [84] Emptiness was the wellspring of activity in a life that joined the active and contemplative modes, bridging the polarities of religious experience in a manner that defies the categorization of East Asian religion as simply one of quiet acceptance and mystical insight.

Calmness or composure (*ching*) [ba] had to be achieved through moral effort, but this state could be neither an end in itself nor a means used for other ends. In cultivation the key was another *ching*, [bb] "reverence." Other writers have discussed the different meanings of this broad and very basic Confucian concept,[85] which, depending on the context, may convey an attitude of seriousness, earnestness, devotion, and so forth. What is important is that we not lose sight of its original basis in a sense of religious awe and reverence, which is so fundamental to the Confucian's respect for life and acceptance of the world. From this reverence then derives the later, very extensive, use of the term in the moral sense of seriousness and earnestness. It is reverence for life that demands an attitude of seriousness both in respect to what can be known about things and what can be done about them. Unless we recognize this religious basis for Neo-Confucian ethical concern and intellectual activity we may fail to recognize its full range of historical development and its openness not only to other religions but even to science.

In the immediate context of Neo-Confucian cultivation, however, the significance of both reverence and seriousness as complementary aspects of *ching* is essential to recognize, for it links the religious and contemplative aspect of cultivation with the necessary moral effort. As the reader may have begun to suspect, this will prove the key to our earlier problem of the ambiguities of Neo-Confucian enlightenment. In the element of religious quietism was seen the basis for the spontaneous human activity and effort in accordance with Heaven or nature, or in other words the spiritual springs of the moral dynamism which Neo-Confucianism contributed to so many varied historical movements.

The religious attitude of reverence obliged the individual to listen to Heaven's will and to conform to the moral law expressed in the classics. It also called for man to study the principles of nature in all creatures, for Heaven spoke through its creations. But Heaven spoke to man's moral and affective nature as well as to his intellect, and it was a prime concern of Neo-Confucian cultivation that the process of learning in the intellectual sense should not be allowed to preempt the whole man. In the important chapter of the *Chin-ssu lu* variously entitled "Investigation of Things" and "Extension of Knowledge," Ch'eng I is quoted as affirming that "every blade of grass and every tree possesses principle and should be examined," [86] and in the commentary which Professor Chan has conveniently provided from Chu Hsi's writings, the latter reaffirms that everything from the Supreme Ultimate above to a "small thing like a blade of grass, a plant or an insect below, each has its principle . . ." and should be investigated. In principle, then, Neo-Confucian learning was not only open to systematic, rational inquiry into what we call the natural sciences, but actually enjoined it with a religious sanction.

In the same context, however, Chu Hsi and his Sung masters make it abundantly clear that the "humanities" have a priority over the natural sciences because they are the integrative disciplines. There is a well-known passage from Ch'eng I which indicates the relative weight attached to different fields of investigation. "There is principle in everything, and one must investigate principle to the utmost. There are many ways to do this. One way is to read books and elucidate moral principles. Another way is to discuss people and events of the past and present, and to distinguish which are right and which wrong. Still another way is to handle affairs and settle them in the proper way. All these are ways to investigate the principle of things exhaustively." [87] That the first way of investigating things which occurred to him should be reading books is quite natural in the Confucian scholar-official. The relative weight of classical humanistic studies is abundantly illustrated by the remaining contents of this chapter, most of which discusses the study of the several Confucian Classics.

The Neo-Confucians had a strong sense of the need for preserving the unity of mind and heart, but equally so of the delicate balance required for proper control of the mind. Thus, on the one hand they noted the distracting and disintegrating effect of uncontrolled exposure to external influences and sense-knowledge. The mind would literally leak out of the body unless controlled by principle and moral effort.[88] On the other hand too much effort could also be a problem, whether it was excessive rigidity in moral control or too strained an attempt at the acquisition of knowledge. The subtlety and delicacy of the problem is evidenced by the different aspects under which it arose. Ch'eng Hao says, "Now our minds are set on moral principles and yet we are not happy. Why? Precisely because we unnecessarily try to help the mind grow." In an allusion to Mencius' groping with the same problem, he says, although "hold it fast and you preserve it, and let it go and you lose it" [89] is a true statement, yet if one holds it too fast, that will be "always doing something with [selfish] expectation." [90] In controlling the mind, the question can arise whether one remains open to the moral promptings of Heaven and is content with that, or whether one is too morally insistent on the basis of one's preconceived expectations. This is as bad as having no standards or guidelines at all. Another way of putting this is in terms of the goodness of man's nature. That goodness consists in a natural disposition toward moral action or effort. Such effort, however, should be the natural expression of the goodness of the mind. One should not try to "make" the mind be "good" or "moral" according to some extrinsic notion or for any ulterior motive.

Ch'eng I said on this point, "The student should hold fast to the mind with reverence (seriousness). He should not be anxious. Instead he should nourish and cultivate it deeply and earnestly, and immerse himself [in the Way]. Only then can he have a sense of fulfillment and be at ease with himself. If one seeks anxiously, that is merely selfishness. In the end he will not be able to reach the Way." [91] The resemblance here to problems of the spiritual life in the theistic traditions, of spiritual anxiety and trust in Divine Providence, is evident.

There were other problems which linked the larger spiritual life more specifically to the intellectual. Although the intellect was kept under close control and not allowed to overwhelm the moral will in a mass of impressions and facts, this might not be of help if the problem was an overstraining of the intellect itself. The story is told of Ch'eng Hao during his days as a commissary officer that, as he sat at leisure, he looked up at the columns in the corridor and began to count them in his mind. "After he had finished he had no doubt about the number, but when he counted them again, the number did not agree. He could not keep from having someone count them aloud, and found that the number agreed with his original count. From this we know that the more one exerts his mind to hold on to a thing, the more unsure he is." [92] In the same vein Ch'eng I said: "A sage does not make an attempt to remember things. He can therefore always remember. People today forget things because they try to remember them. Both inability to remember and roughness in handling things are the results of imperfect and weak nourishment of the mind." [93]

Other examples abound in the *Chin-ssu lu* and other writings of the Sung masters of the problems of the spiritual life, embracing moral and intellectual problems, as well as those which could best be called religious. Much criticism has been leveled at the Neo-Confucians for the subtleties of their approach to mind control, and such phrases as those of Mencius above have been treated as a kind of theological hairsplitting in which Neo-Confucians became involved under the influence of Buddhism and Taoism.[94]

Mencius' phrase "neither forgetting nor assisting" is a good example. By it he meant to describe the natural way to cultivate one's moral nature and thus achieve an "unperturbed mind" (*pu-tung-hsin*) [bc]—a state of moral health and mental composure in which the exercise of one's conscience and the performance of good deeds contribute to a natural process of self-development and a sense of expanding vitality. Mencius seeks a mean between moral indifference and inaction (i.e., "forgetting," a Taoist expression for freeing oneself from human involvements and leaving everything to nature) and, on the other hand, an insistent moralism which expects immediate results from virtuous conduct and tries to force the outcome by "assisting" nature. The fullness and fulfillment of the moral life is to be achieved by the "steady accumulation of righteous deeds, not by impulsive acts of righteousness." There must, says Mencius, be a constant practice of righteousness, without the object of consciously making oneself good. The need for conscious moral effort to be in keeping with one's natural self-development and workings of the moral order is vividly conveyed by Mencius' metaphor of the man of Sung, who tried to "assist" the growth of his corn by pulling on it but succeeded only in pulling it out. (*Mencius*, IIA, 2.)

It is not strange that this problem should arise in the context of Mencius' discussion of the "unperturbed mind," which is responsive to man's moral impulses and yet is also conscious of the total natural order or process which defines his sphere of moral action. Nor is it far-fetched for Neo-Confucians to find this relevant to their own problem of preserving both serenity of mind and a natural spontaneity in the midst of moral struggle. The opposing claims of quietism and activism, quite possibly also the philosophical challenge of Taoism itself, confronted Mencius well before they did his Neo-Confucian successors. One need not suppose that the latter invoked him simply as a pious gesture to traditional authority. Nor is the recourse to quotations from Mencius simply a contrivance to mask Neo-Confucian acceptance of Buddhist and Taoist ideas and practices.[95] For in citing Mencius, "not forgetting" the Neo-Confucian was explicitly rejecting the Taoist approach to an unperturbed mind and reaffirming that there was a Confucian alternative to the opposing extremes of passive quietism and frenetic activism. The expression describes very well the attitude attributed to Ch'eng Hao in the above-cited characterization of him in the *Chin-ssu lu:* "When he came upon things to do, he did them with ease and leisure, and no sense of urgency. But at the same time he was sincere and earnest, and did not treat them carelessly. His sense of responsibility was so great that he was more concerned about not achieving the objective of learning to be a sage than about achieving fame through any single good deed. . . ."[96]

Such difficulties as these would not arise in a simple quietism, nor in any form of spirituality which wholly subordinates the intellect and morality to spontaneous intuition, nor in the kind of activism that relies on external religious or ideological authority at the expense of one's own conscience. They arise only where the active and contemplative life are intimately joined, where intellect and intuition are seen as partners, and where the conception of man allows equally for the several levels of his existence: moral, intellectual, aesthetic, and spiritual.

QUIET-SITTING

An important adjunct to this kind of spiritual guidance was the practice of quiet-sitting, already referred to in our discussion of Japanese *shingaku.* So far as I am aware there has been no adequate study in a Western language of this typical method of spiritual cultivation, at least not commensurate with its central role in the formal practice of Neo-Confucianism. In the broad range of problems discussed here, we cannot do justice to the subject but must at least draw attention to the significant role it played in the development of Neo-Confucian thought.

The *Chin-ssu lu* does not itself give special attention to quiet-sitting, but it does refer to it in such a way as to approve and encourage the practice. Ch'eng Hao once said to his pupils, "You accompany me here and only learn the way to talk. Therefore in your learning your minds and words do not correspond. Why not practice?" When he was asked what to practice, he said, "Suppose you practice quiet-sitting." It is also reported that whenever Ch'eng I saw someone practicing quiet-sitting, he expressed admiration for such excellence in the pursuit of learning.[97]

The Sung masters, committed to Confucian activism and social concern, were nevertheless conscious that the mind could be carried away by events as well as by its own persistent egotism, thus losing the equilibrium and self-control that keep it in accord with the Mean. No humanitarian action would really help others, or be in accord with their needs and the objective requirements of the situation, if one's own self-interest, passions, or fixations got in the way. Throwing oneself into a good cause was no substitute for self-knowledge.

If the Mean were simply an ideal one admired in the sage, a purely descriptive approach would have sufficed. But if sagehood was something to which everyone should aspire, then some prescription, some definite method of praxis, was necessary. A technique which calmed both body and mind might achieve a composure which could be sustained in action. The essential thing was to get at the roots of human motivation, to establish one's intentions at the very start in conformity with Heaven's will and Heavenly principle. Stability and equipoise would result from eliminating all selfishness or egotism, which are the sources of anxiety, trepidation, and rash conduct. The state of equipoise, or the Mean, was also the state of the original goodness of human nature, and might be described in Mencius' terms as recovering the "lost mind."

Quiet-sitting (*ching-tso*), the form of praxis adopted for this purpose, has been rendered into English as "sitting in meditation." [98] This is not an inaccurate description of the practice itself, but it has the disadvantage of associating it too closely with Buddhist "sitting in meditation." Though *ching-tso* was probably influenced by the latter, the *ch'an* of *tso-ch'an* refers specifically to Buddhist *dhyāna*, or Zen, which has spiritual roots and philosophical associations foreign to quiet-sitting. The significance of what otherwise might seem a petty, terminological distinction, can be seen if one realizes that even all Buddhist meditation is not Zen. How much more misleading it is to identify a quite distinct Neo-Confucian meditation with Zen!

What the two practices share is what the two terms actually have in common: the sitting (*tso*). Sometimes Neo-Confucians practiced this in the "full-lotus" or "half-lotus" position used in Zen sitting, that is, with both legs crossed and both feet drawn up into one's lap, or with only one foot so drawn up. The Neo-Confucian form was generally more relaxed and allowed for greater variation. It could be as strict as Zen posture or could take the form simply of sitting in a chair. (One Chinese Confucian even explained to me that sitting in a chair was more proper because one was in a better position to respond immediately to the needs of his parents, thereby emphasizing that the sitting was not an end in itself but was subordinated to the discharge of one's other responsibilities.) The eyes were generally either fully shut or fully open, not just barely open as in *zazen*. An important ancillary practice was control of the breath (*t'iao-hsi*),[bd] with or without counting of each breath. A manual on this subject, the *T'iao-hsi chen*,[be] was attributed to Chu Hsi.[99] In it, regulation of the breath was recommended as a means of nourishing one's vital spirit, or ether (*ch'i*).[bf]

Neo-Confucian quiet-sitting was practiced in the home or in one's study, not in a separate meditation hall. If one compares the layout (*garan*)[bg] of a Buddhist temple or monastery with the layout of the Confucian school,[100] one notable difference between them is the absence in the latter of any separate meditation hall. This signifies the secularization of meditation as a practice of daily life interspersed with one's normal activities, rather than as a monastic discipline. It was common to begin and end the day with a period of quiet-sitting, but not infrequently this kind of meditation was also practiced as a preparation for study or in alternation with study to refresh and restore the mind. There are instances in which quiet-sitting was pursued more intensively over long periods,[101] but generally it was regarded as a more leisurely pursuit, not something done to the exclusion of the scholar's other duties. Prolonged, intensive sitting, both night and day, and at the expense of sleep, as practiced in Zen Buddhist monasteries, was, so far as I am aware, never encouraged. It was common for the Confucian scholar to light a stick of incense and to time his period of sitting by the burning out of the stick—which must have an extraordinary symbolism here, both of the evanescence of meditation and of Neo-Confucian syncretism.[102]

THE CONTENT AND EXPERIENCE OF
NEO-CONFUCIAN ENLIGHTENMENT

In the content of the meditation fostered by these practices there was a similar range of variation. Before proceeding to discuss this, however, it must be made clear that what we call "Neo-Confucian enlightenment" is not so closely identifiable with quiet-sitting as Buddhist enlightenment has been with meditation or *zazen*. In the first place there was a wider range of Neo-Confucian activities contributing to enlightenment, and doing so under different aspects. Further, quiet-sitting itself, though one of the means conducive to enlightenment, was not bound up with the expectation of achieving a discrete experience of it. It was less structured and less focused than in Zen. Whether such an "experience" was achieved, and whether it was gradual or sudden as in Buddhism, was of less importance than was the spiritual growth of the individual and the deepening of his experience of the Way. We speak then of a moral and contemplative life which included quiet-sitting but extended well beyond it.

Neo-Confucian enlightenment had several aspects, corresponding to the moral, intellectual, aesthetic, and spiritual life of the aspirant to sagehood. As an experience of self-transcendence or of the ground of being it could be mystical and ineffable, but for the most part it was thought of as natural. The Sung masters did not generally stress its total otherness and incomprehensibility but rather its luminous intelligibility. The splendor of truth was what they experienced. Though its wondrous quality might elude description, what it illuminated could often be seen and described with great clarity. This was especially so in the moral and intellectual spheres. The Neo-Confucians had no absolute confidence in the power of words, but neither did they look on truth as being utterly mysterious and to be guarded with great secrecy. On the contrary, they had faith in the power of reason and discussion to open the truth to all.

The Ch'eng-Chu school saw all forms of truth, or all principles, as converging. Hence they would not think to distinguish clearly the various moral and intellectual aspects. Nevertheless, one form of Neo-Confucian mind culture was very much a moral discipline, directed toward the springs of human motivation and greatly concerned with the moral quality in things and ideas. Here the emphasis was upon observing thoughts in the state of "subtle incipient activation (*chi*)" ᵇʰ which issues from quiescence, and bringing one's intentions into accord with the ethical requirements of a situation or affair. Success in such practice brought a feeling of peace and contentment similar to that we associate with having a good conscience.

Mind control in this sense could be seen from two convergent points of view. Chou Tun-i described it in terms of "mastering quiescence" (*chu-ching*),ᵇⁱ suggesting that even in its quiescent state the mind had a kind of moral master or conscience guiding it.[103] Consciousness in this quiescent state was not totally undifferentiated but had active moral direction. Ch'eng I, somewhat distrustful of a tendency toward Taoist quietism in using the term *ching* to mean quiescence or tranquillity, preferred to use the homonyms *chü ching*,ᵇʲ "abiding in reverence." This conveyed the idea of the mind or soul abiding in a state of repose, in an attitude of religious acceptance which at the same time reflected the moral structure and dynamism of Heaven and earth and all things. It avoided both extremes of passivity and agitation. Ch'eng I explained:

The first concern of the student should of course be with his mind and his will. But some people want to discard all sensation and consciousness, and that would be to "abandon sageliness and discard wisdom." [104] Others want to discard all thought, because they fear that it is confusing and disturbing. Then they would have to sit in meditation and enter into calmness. Suppose here is a clear mirror. It is its normal nature to reflect things. It is difficult not to have it reflect them. Similarly the human mind cannot but interact with the myriad things, and it is difficult not to have it engaged in thinking. If one wants to avoid confusion and disturbance, his mind must have a master. What can be its master? Reverence (seriousness) and reverence alone.[105]

Liu Tsung-chou ᵇᵏ (1578–1645) later expressed the Confucian view in comparison to Ch'an Buddhism by citing a Ch'an master who likened the self in Zen meditation to a gourd floating on the water. Liu said the Confucian experience was like riding in a boat with one hand on the rudder, giving direction to its course.[106]

Thus, in Neo-Confucian mind control, there could be a strong emphasis on active moral effort which at the same time expressed a ready acquiescence in the moral imperatives of Heaven and an openness to its providential guidance. As a practical moral discipline, however, the greatest stress would be on self-control. In Ch'eng I and Chu Hsi the purity of principle and of man's nature as an unchanging moral norm (and therefore static, quiescent), was contrasted with the appearance of evil thoughts or intentions in the active mind responding to things and affairs. To distinguish good from evil, or right from wrong, and to ensure that action was properly in accord with principle, was the task of the moral will. To the extent that evil was seen as arising in conjunction with the desires of the bodily self, and the moral will was called upon to exercise strict control over selfish desires, there was a tendency to see the moral nature as in opposition to the physical nature. Hence this discipline was susceptible to puritanical excesses, and also exposed to the reaction against such excesses. Basically, however, it was intended to overcome any dichotomy between self and principle, or self and things, and to produce an experience of freedom in which one had no unsatisfied desires because all were in accord with Heaven's will. (A more detailed discussion of this system of mind culture is presented in Professor T'ang's discussion of the moral mind in Chu Hsi, in *Self and Society in Ming Thought.*) [107]

To many followers of the orthodox Chu Hsi school this discipline, often practiced through quiet-sitting, served essentially as an examination of conscience and was without mystical overtones.[108] In others, however, there was an intense experience of the self's identity or unity of the self with Heaven-and-earth and all things. Often this was described as an experience of self-awareness (*t'i-jen*) [bl] or, as Professor Chan has rendered it, "realization through personal experience," either of some truth or of the underlying reality or ground of one's whole being.[109] The late Tokugawa period Japanese Confucian, Kusumoto Tanzan,[bm] who practiced quiet-sitting and kept a record of his experiences in his *Record of Learning and Practice* (*Gakushū-roku*),[bn] revealed an experience of enlightenment that centered around the saying of Ch'eng Hao concerning the mind which cannot endure the sufferings of others. He described it viscerally in terms used by Mencius as a "breast-full of commiseration" (*man koshi kore sokuin no kokoro*).[bo] [110] He also spoke of it as "experiencing humanity" (*tai-jin*, Ch. *t'i-jen*) [bp] as the life force, the creative force deep in the heart of man and all things, and further in the now-familiar terms of being united with Heaven-and-earth and all things through one's humanity.[111]

In such an experience of the ethical oneness of all creation there is clearly no opposition between the moral will or ideal nature, on the one hand, and the physical self on the other. Nor, despite the "gut feeling" it shares with Zen experience, can this be understood in Zen terms. The predominant ethical tone is Neo-Confucian, and is in keeping with the view of the Sung scholar Chang Chiu-ch'eng [bq] (Heng-p'u) [112] who criticized Zen because it suppressed the natural sense of man's commiseration for others, which should issue in remedial action. The general adoption of such an attitude, he asserts, would undermine humane government, which is based on the idea that the ruler and his ministers cannot endure the sufferings of others. To achieve detachment in such things would make one *able* to bear such sufferings, which is actually contrary to the natural moral order, whereas to be *unable* to bear them is natural and proper. Heaven intends that man should resist some things and take corrective action. [113]

INTELLECTUAL "ENLIGHTENMENT"

At the same time this attitude could find expression in a more intellectual and scholarly way, there being no real discontinuity between the different forms of study. Ch'eng I says, "Things and the self are governed by the same principle. If you understand one, you understand the other, for the truth within and the truth without are identical." [114] The pursuit of this principle could take the form of scholarly investigation. "From the principles in one's own person to those in all things, if one understands more and more, gradually he will naturally achieve a far-reaching understanding." [115]

Concerning intellectual inquiry, the Ch'eng-Chu school may be said to have encouraged broad learning through the "investigation of things" and at the same time to have stressed the integration of this knowledge as the most essential thing in study. There was no precise formula by which to measure the lengths to which study should be carried. "To devote oneself to investigating principle to the utmost does not mean to investigate the principles of all things in the world to the utmost, nor does it mean that principle can be understood merely by investigating one particular principle. It is necessary to accumulate much knowledge and then one will naturally come to understand principle." [116]

On the one hand we find positive injunctions to extend one's study widely and to inquire thoroughly into things, such as became the hall-marks of Chu Hsi's Po-lu tung [br] school,[117] and on the other we have reminders that the significance of this learning must be evaluated in terms of its relevance to the moral self-development of the individual. "Information, however much, is not to enable us to understand why all things in the world are as they are. If we handle the changing events in the world with much information, we can respond to those events about which we already know something. But if we are surprised with something unforeseen we will be at a loss." [118]

The compilers of the *Chin-ssu lu* include quotations from or about the Ch'eng brothers which suggest the range of opinion and degree of emphasis on the value of intellectual inquiry. Ch'eng Hao is said to have deplored memorization, recitation, and acquiring extensive information as "trifling with things and losing one's purpose." [119] Ch'eng I, making the same general point, puts it: "One must investigate one item today and another item tomorrow. When one has accumulated much knowledge, he will naturally achieve a thorough understanding like a sudden release." [120]

On this question A. C. Graham has said, "Thus the investigation of a thing consists of thinking followed by a sudden insight into its principle. This insight reminds one a little of the satori, the sudden and permanent mystical illumination of Zen Buddhism; but it is really quite different, a purely intellectual illumination in which a previously meaningless fact, as we say, 'falls into place.' " [121] This is very well put, except, I think, for the words "quite" and "purely." It is not really possible to speak of such an experience as "purely" intellectual because of the ever-present moral and affective overtones. Even the rationalist Ch'eng I speaks of study in such tones.

In reading the *Analects* and *Mencius*, do so thoroughly and get the real taste of them. Apply the words of the sage to yourself earnestly. Do not treat them as so many words. . . . There are people who have read the *Analects* without having anything happen to them. There are others who are happy after having understood a sentence or two. There are still others who, having read the book, love it. And there are those, who, having read it, unconsciously dance with their hands and feet.[122]

Graham rightly cautions against confusing this kind of illumination with Zen, but it is equally important to recognize the interrelatedness of the different aspects of learning and enlightenment. Only so can we understand how the Neo-Confucian "sage" could be both scholar and saint, and how one of the greatest of them, Wang Yang-ming, danced and shouted with joy at midnight when finally he solved the problem of the "investigation of things" for himself, prosaic though that problem sounds to us. Such emotional intensity, in fact, may well be a distinguishing characteristic of this tradition of spirituality.

The basic point here, however, must certainly be that at the same time it was a tradition of intellectuality and scholarship. The so-called Enlightenment of the seventeenth and eighteenth centuries was heir both to the critical scholarship of Chu Hsi and his humanistic concerns, which combined in the right circumstances to produce critical classical scholarship. That it was not also heir to the same extent to the aspiration for sagehood is a matter which can only be dealt with in the light of the further evolution of Neo-Confucian thought and its own self-criticism. Such a self-critical attitude is evident in Chu Hsi's comments on the passage in the *Mean* (20) exhorting one to "study extensively, inquire accurately, think carefully, sift clearly and practice earnestly." He says:

After one has studied extensively, he can have the principles of all things before him. He can therefore examine them and compare them to get the right questions to ask. Then, as he asks accurately, his teachers and friends will wholeheartedly engage in give-and-take with him, thus stimulating him, and he will begin to think. As he thinks carefully, his thoughts will be refined and free from impurities. Thus he achieves something for himself. He can now sift what he has achieved. As he sifts clearly, he can make decisions without making a mistake. He can therefore be free from doubts and can put his thoughts into action. As he practices earnestly, all he has achieved from studying, asking, thinking, and sifting will become concrete demonstrations and will no longer remain empty words.[123]

Whether or not such an attitude contains all the elements of modern scientific method, it does contain elements of critical self-examination and self-renewal. The outcome of this process is to be found in successive stages of the later Neo-Confucian development.

AESTHETIC ENLIGHTENMENT

The question of the aesthetic development of Neo-Confucian cultivation is less germane to the types of enlightenment with which this essay was initially concerned, but it is important to the development of Neo-Confucian culture as a whole and to overlook it entirely would be to lose sight of a significant element in the total balance for which Neo-Confucianism strove. The Sung was an age in which poetry became an important medium for the expression of Neo-Confucian ideals and spirit.[124] Ou-yang Hsiu, Wang An-shih, Su Tung-p'o, and Chu Hsi are only a few examples of leading scholar-statesmen in the Sung whose poetry is an important source for the study of their thought. Indeed, there are Neo-Confucians for whom poetry is the *most* important source of their thought, a really deep appreciation of which requires a thorough study of the poetry in which it is often best expressed. With particular regard to the aesthetic component in spiritual enlightenment, the poetry of Wu Yü-pi [bs] and Ch'en Hsien-chang [bt] in the early Ming is illustrative. The latter especially expresses sublime sentiments of self-forgetfulness through contemplation of the beauties of nature.[125]

The Sung was also an age in which scholars for the first time became seriously engaged in painting, and regarded it, like poetry, as an important means of self-expression and self-cultivation. In doing this they demonstrated at once their Confucian commitment to culture and their openness to aesthetic experience. At the same time, however, involvement in each new form of cultural activity became a challenge to the "seriousness," the dedication, the reverent concern—all those connotations of the term *ching* representing a basic religious and moral orientation—inasmuch as any of these activities might tend to become an end in itself and lose its sense of human relevance and proportion. It was in this spirit that Ch'eng Hao spoke of his practice of calligraphy. "When I practice calligraphy," he said, "I am very serious (or reverent). My objective is not that the calligraphy must be good. Rather my practice is the way of moral training." [126]

The Neo-Confucian attitude toward literature and art has been criticized in modern times as excessively moralistic, but often from a superficial point of view, assuming that moral meanings were arbitrarily imposed on things in a didactic and doctrinaire manner, without appreciating how much in fact Neo-Confucian "reverence" was open to the discovery of significance in things rather than simply imposing it upon them. In this case Ch'eng Hao did not seek to make the calligraphy "teach a moral lesson" to others. Its moral value lay in the beneficial effect of the aesthetic activity upon his own mind and spirit, in the creative interaction of outward activity and inner personality. It involved a morality with an aesthetic dimension, no less than an aesthetic with a moral dimension.

This is spirituality of a high order. Until we have more adequate studies of the relation between Chinese painting and Neo-Confucian thought we shall not be able to do justice to either.[127] Even without that, however, we may recognize the one-sidedness, at the other extreme, of the Weberian characterization of the Confucian as above all the aesthetic gentleman, whose concern was for style and refinement, for the "beautiful and polite gesture as an end in itself." [128] The narrowly moralistic view of the Confucian life orientation, on the one hand, and the predominantly aesthetic view on the other, serve not so much to refute each other as to demonstrate the remarkable balance achieved by Neo-Confucianism between the competing claims of both. Neo-Confucians had tendencies toward both puritanism and aestheticism, as indeed did Christianity, and neither the Puritan nor the aesthete can fairly be taken as the dominant representative of either.

For the present I shall confine myself to giving an example of how the aesthetic element entered into the "enlightenment" of one Neo-Confucian thinker who was in many ways typical of this still-developing tradition in the late Ming. He is Kao P'an-lung,[bu] a member of the Tung-lin [bv] school of neoorthodoxy in the late sixteenth and seventeenth centuries, who was identified with its strong moral and political reformism. Kao, along with other Tung-lin leaders, and most notably Ku Hsien-ch'eng,[bw] practiced quiet-sitting as part of his orthodox training. By "orthodox" I mean "traditional" and "standard"—not a slavish adherence to past authority. Kao and Ku have left valuable records of their experiences, which reveal an independent and critical approach combined with a concern for the restoration of basic moral principles in a skeptical and dissolute age. Ku tended to favor Chou Tun-i's method of "mastering quiescence," about which Ch'eng I and Chu Hsi had reservations as being perhaps too quietistic. Busch, in his study of the Tung-lin Academy, gives a passage from Ku explaining his view of "quiet-sitting":

The quiescence advocated by Master Chou (Tun-i), which is doubtless deduced from the "limitless" (wu-chi) [bx] is the final aim; the "sitting quietly" which Master Ch'eng [I] likes to see is a preliminary exercise. But "sitting quietly" is extremely difficult. If the mind has something to dwell on it stagnates; if it has nothing to dwell on it drifts. The state "antecedent to the activation of affection, anger, grief, and pleasure," of which Li T'ung [by] [129] speaks, is just in the middle between having and not having something to dwell on. It offers an entrance to the interior. If one methodically and continuously [makes use of it], the life force (*ch'i*), after a while, gradually becomes calm and the mind settled, and [one can be] in this state when one is alone, when one is occupied, when one is with people, and even when affection, anger, grief, or pleasure suddenly overtake us. When one is always and completely in this state antecedent to the activation [of the emotions], so that there is no distinction whatsoever between interior and exterior, quiescence and motion, then the preliminary phase becomes the final stage. [130]

Kao P'an-lung left an even more extensive record of his views on and experiences with quiet-sitting, including a short treatise entitled *On Quiet-Sitting (Ching-tso shuo)* [bz] and a spiritual autobiography, *A Record of Difficulties in Learning (K'un hsüeh chi)*.[ca] Busch gives an excellent account of this in his study, which is recommended to readers interested in particulars. [131] Of significance for our purposes is Kao's synthesis of the different strains of quiet-sitting and Neo-Confucian enlightenment. He joins together "mastering quiescence" and "abiding in reverence," and describes "reverence" as a state in which the mind is "without affairs" (*wu-shih*) [cb] and "not set on anything" (*wu-shih*).[cc] Busch explains Kao's view of the quiescence of mind as "a restful return of the mind to itself, a passive awareness of its nature, wherein the mind clears itself from all selfish desires and the heavenly norm, embodied in it, emerges." [132] The quietistic tendency is further brought out in Kao's advice not to try to regulate the mind in any way, or forcibly to expel unruly thoughts, but simply to allow the inner self to emerge. "The 'intimate awareness' of the original state is nothing but a 'returning' in profound silence to it. As soon as one attaches oneself to it by the slightest intention or thought, the original state is lost. One should pass from contemplation to activity in the mood of quiescence, thus making contemplation fruitful for activity; then activity will in turn make contemplation more fruitful." [133]

There is further significance in Kao's emphasis on enlightenment, and his description of his experience of enlightenment. It was in the rather free-wheeling left wing of the Wang Yang-ming school that much was made of an experience of enlightenment having a strong affinity to that of Buddhism. The Tung-lin reacted strongly against the very free morality that went with this among some of the followers of Wang Chi and Wang Ken,[cd] but significantly did not associate enlightenment with moral laxity or vice versa. The combination of Confucian moral concern with a quietistic enlightenment is strikingly exemplified in Kao's account of his own spiritual struggles. Enlightenment came to him on a journey undertaken because of an inner unrest which Kao describes as finding "in my breast the heavenly norm and selfish desires in conflict with each other." This dissatisfaction with himself eventually led to a kind of crisis, when he found no surcease in the usual social diversion with intellectual friends. At a drinking party "the rivers and mountains looked charming, and with friends urging one another to drink, I should have had a most enjoyable time. Yet I felt discontented and downcast and inexplicably restrained. I tried to enter into the spirit of the occasion but could not." [134]

Brooding over his own state of mind Kao finally made a resolution: "If during this journey I do not gain a thorough understanding of this point, the life in me will have been found wanting in duty toward the mind." [135] He thereupon set up a strict routine for himself, spending half the day in quiet-sitting and half the day in study. While sitting, he tried to carry out the instructions of Ch'eng I and Chu Hsi to the letter. For two months he kept this up intensively while traveling by boat, having no other business to preoccupy him. Then finally came the experience of enlightenment described in these terms:

The scenery was beautiful; I was alone with my servant, and so everything was completely tranquil. One evening I ordered some wine; we stopped the boat at a green hill and let it drift about in the blue brook. For awhile I sat down on the rocks. The sound of the creek, the singing of the birds, the luxuriant trees, and the high bamboo, were many things to delight the mind, but my mind did not get attached to these surroundings. Passing by T'ing-chou in Fukien we went by land to an inn. To the inn belonged a small tower which faced the mountains and in the rear was close to a mountain creek. I mounted the tower and felt very happy. [In this mood] I happened to read the words of Master Ming-tao.[ce] "In the midst of the many thousand affairs of the various offices, in the midst of millions of tools of war, one can still have joy, though one drinks water and uses the bended arm as a pillow. The myriad changes are all man's own creations; in reality there is not a thing." I had a sudden awakening and said: "So, that is the way it is! Indeed, there is not a thing!" Thereupon, as if cut off, all the entanglements of my worries were gone, and suddenly something like a burden of a hundred pounds fell with a crash to the ground. It furthermore penetrated my body and my soul like a flash of lightning, and thereupon I became fused with the Great

Change. There was no longer a separation of heaven and man, interior and exterior; now I saw that the six points are all [my] mind, that the breast is its realm, and the square-inch [of the heart] is its proper seat. If one understands it deeply one cannot speak of a location at all. I had always despised scholars who spoke boastingly of enlightenment; now I regarded it as something ordinary. It was a conviction that from now on I was in the right position to work on my moral perfection.[136]

I have included this rather long excerpt because it seems the only way to convey the strong aesthetic element in Kao P'an-lung's enlightenment. Clearly this coexists in his mind quite easily with a strong ethical commitment. It represents what one would have to call, I think, a nature mysticism, with the beauty and serenity of the natural surroundings contributing much to an experience of union with the cosmos.[137] In the Chinese context one would tend to identify this aesthetic element or nature mysticism with Taoism, and indeed the Neo-Confucian "enlightenment" was open to the Taoist experience as much as to the Buddhist. This was one of the principal bases of the religious syncretism of the Late Ming, and it accounts also for the fact that in Japan the Neo-Confucianism of so many Tokugawa scholars, such as Ishida Baigan himself, was likewise open to the aesthetic and religious experience of Shinto and produced a similar syncretism.

But more fundamentally this was a "nature" mysticism which saw nature, Heaven-and-earth, as united to man through one all-embracing order that was moral, rational, aesthetic, and religious all at once. It was with this in mind that Chu Hsi chose the White Deer Grotto near Mount Lu [cf] as the sylvan setting for his school, and expressed in a prose-poem (fu) [cg] his elation over having found a scene of such great natural beauty to inspire lofty thoughts and the recognition of high principles.[138] Kao P'an-lung's predilection for scenic sites and the leisurely enjoyment of nature as conducive to spiritual struggle and supportive of moral commitment is perfectly in line with Chu Hsi's own view.

Thus, illumination of the mind and heart may take a variety of forms in Neo-Confucianism. Though often described as enlightenment (wu or chüeh),[ch] it may range from a new intellectual awareness or moral intuition to a religious experience of sublime peace and joy.[139] Again, it may represent simply a new stage (among several) in the growth of one's intellectual or spiritual life, or a single transforming experience, a religious conversion, that changes the direction of one's life.[140] Quite often among Neo-Confucians this experience may result from prolonged study of books, something quite rare in the contrasting case of Ch'an Buddhism.[141] In other instances man's life may be deeply affected by a dream experience, which is seen as having a deep significance or is taken as a sign from Heaven.[142]

Wu Yü-pi's *Jih-lu* [ci] [143] and other "journals" of daily learning experience suggest, as in the instances above, some of the forms such experience may take in a thinker or scholar regarded as a highly orthodox Ch'eng-Chu school man. They also indicate the content of that learning experience in a way quite in contrast to Ch'an. The lesson learned, or the significance derived from it, is intelligible even if it cannot be reduced to a simple intellectual process. In some cases what is learned may be highly specific to a certain intellectual or aesthetic discipline, as in poetry and painting. R. J. Lynn has expressed the view that, in the "orthodox" poets of the sixteenth and seventeenth century (the so-called Former and Latter Seven Masters),[cj] the enlightenment experience represented controlled intuition or intuitive mastery of the creative process in poetry.[144] In this case the enlightenment concept and the strong emphasis on authority and discipline may derive from Ch'an Buddhism, but as a spiritual discipline it can be lifted from the context of Buddhist philosophy and appropriated for cultural purposes more identifiable with Confucian tradition. The study of past masters and their writings to the point that one has thoroughly assimilated their styles and qualities, and the natural manifestation of these as part of one's own self-expression, represent a style of self-cultivation and cultural activity even more characteristic of Neo-Confucianism than of Buddhism.[145]

NEO-CONFUCIAN "EMPTINESS"

When Kao P'an-lung speaks of the mind in the state of quiescence as being "without affairs" (*wu shih*) and "not set on anything" (*wu-shih*), he describes a meditation which is not directed toward moral control itself, but is antecedent to it. He also calls it a state in which the mind is not attached to anything. Such characterizations are reminiscent of the Buddhist meditative state of "emptiness" (*k'ung*), [ck] and yet Kao was strongly anti-Buddhist on moral grounds. There is also a question as to how being "without affairs" (or, more freely, "not busying the mind with anything") relates to the doctrine of "having no mind" of one's own. Since Sung and especially Ming thought were attacked for their "emptiness," this is a crucial problem in the development of Neo-Confucian thought.

Wu-shih, in the sense of "not being set on anything," comes from the *Analects* (IV, 10) where Confucius speaks of the noble man as being "neither for nor against anything under Heaven. He follows what is proper [in the context of his actions]." "Having no mind" of one's own meant for the Ch'eng brothers that the mind was empty of all selfishness and was completely receptive and responsive to the principles of Heaven-and-earth and all things. These were ethical principles, and so the "emptied" human mind was, like an unobstructed mirror, automatically filled with these principles. The Ch'eng brothers, however, spoke of this state in somewhat ambiguous language. For instance, Ch'eng Hao said in response to a question as to how worries could be driven from the mind:

This is just like resisting robbers in a ruined house. Before you chase away the one who has entered from the east, another one comes from the west. They come in from all directions and there is no time to chase all of them away. The reason is that the house is exposed on all sides so that robbers can come in easily and there is no way for one to be the master of his own house and keep the situation under control. It is like water coming into an empty vessel. Naturally the water comes in. But if the vessel is filled with water, even if you put it under water, how can water get in? For whatever has a master inside is no longer empty. Since it is not empty, external troubles cannot come in. Then there will be nothing to worry you.[146]

The word for "empty" here is *hsü,*[cl] and it indicates an undesirable state of mind. To avoid it the mind should be filled (*shih*)[cm] with moral principles. Now consider Ch'eng I's observation which concludes the passage quoted earlier to the effect that it is the nature of the mind to reflect all things and unnatural to expect that it could be disengaged from thought. The only solution to the problem is to make reverence (seriousness) the master. "With a master the mind will be vacuous and if it is vacuous depravity cannot enter. Without a master, the mind will be filled. To be filled means that external things will seize it."[147]

The word rendered as "vacuous" here by Chan is the same word *hsü* translated as "empty" above, though in the first instance it is an undesirable state and in the second quite the reverse. Similarly the same word "to be filled" (*shih*) has opposite values in the two cases. I believe this ambiguity was fundamentally a fruitful one for the development of Neo-Confucianism, though it also provided the grounds for the critique of Sung and Ming thought by the enlightenment thinkers of seventeenth- and eighteenth-century China and Japan. The significance of "vacuousness" in Ch'eng I is that it represents a state of concentration or seriousness in a mind from which all distractions have been removed. W. T. Chan defines it as "absolutely pure and peaceful, and not disturbed by incoming impressions." In Ch'eng Hao's terms, on the other hand, the presence of a master in the mind ensures that it is solid, filled, real, and not empty.

It seems to me that the ambiguity here may correspond to two related values in Neo-Confucian reverence: religious openness or self-transcendence, and moral seriousness or concentration which issues in action. Hsüeh Hsüan cn (1389–1464), a Ch'eng-Chu follower in the early Ming, who was concerned with promoting "real" learning (*shih hsüeh*), saw quiescence and emptiness as the ground of such "real" learning. "The mind that is empty [or open] can contain all principles." [148] Lo Ch'in-shun co (1465–1547), a leading Ch'eng-Chu school figure, speaks in the same way of knowing as being empty in the sense of being indeterminate, and of what is known as being "real" in the sense of giving definite or solid content to that emptiness. [149] For that reason I translate *hsü* in the former sense as "openness" or "receptivity," and see it as the basis for a thoroughgoing objectivity achieved through self-transcendence, which was increasingly manifest in the Neo-Confucian experience of the Ming. In one sense this could be understood as almost a "value-free objectivity," but under another aspect its mirrorlike receptivity was understood to reflect perfectly the value-full nature of Heaven-and-earth.

Joseph Needham, in his discussion of Chinese thought as it contributed to or conditioned the rise of Chinese science, has asserted that the potentiality for scientific observation existed in early Taoism. "The observation of nature, as opposed to the management of society, requires a passive receptivity in contrast to a commanding activity, and a freedom from all pre-conceived theories in contrast to an attachment to a set of social convictions." [150] He speaks eloquently of Chuang Tzu's rising to great heights of spiritual transcendence and describing "the sense of liberation which could be attained by those who could abstract themselves from the trivial quarrels of human society and unify themselves with the great world of Nature." [151] "The philosophy of Taoism . . . developed many of the most important features of the scientific attitude . . . [but] failed to reach any precise definition of experimental method or any systematization of their observations of nature." [152] He therefore sees a cleavage in Chinese thought between the rationalists (as represented by the Confucians) and the logicians, on the one hand, and the experimental empiricists as represented by the Taoists. [153] This cleavage, however, was largely overcome by the Neo-Confucian philosophy of organicism, which afforded a world view "extremely congruent with that of the natural sciences." [154] In this synthesis of Confucianism and Taoism "there would be as much room for experimental and observational science as for humanistic philosophy." [155]

For this favorable development and its conduciveness to scientific thought and investigation Needham gives great credit to the Sung Neo-Confucianists, and particularly Chu Hsi. He sees Ming thought and especially the "metaphysical idealism" of Wang Yang-ming as "most inimical to the development of natural science." [156] The influence of Buddhism in this regard he also sees as unfortunate for science, [157] and it was only in the face of the challenge of Buddhism that Confucianism and Taoism joined forces to evolve a "unitary world-picture." [158]

We have already observed some of the elements in the critical outlook and method which the Ch'eng-Chu school contributed to the intellectual enlightenment emerging in the seventeenth and eighteenth centuries, and have no reason to dissent from Needham's very high estimate of Chu Hsi in this regard. On the other hand, he may be doing less than justice to the full range of Neo-Confucian thought, to Ming thought especially, and to Buddhism. What he has said concerning early Taoism would be applicable as well to much of Ming thought, particularly in the sixteenth century when there was a remarkable drive toward transcendence of the kind he describes, combined with "great freedom from all pre-conceived theories in contrast to an attachment to a set of social conventions." Both the Tung-lin school, exemplified above by Kao P'an-lung, and its major opposing movement, the T'ai-chou school, show these characteristics and share in the Neo-Confucian "enlightenment" explained above.

Such receptivity or objectivity could be of great significance in the "investigation of things." Religion or contemplation in this sense might provide a detachment from things and affairs which would free the mind from conventional views. An example of "emptiness" as openness is found in Chiao Hung. His combination of religious openness and philosophical skepticism provided the basis for objective evidential investigation through its rejection of the rationalistic and moralistic commentaries of Chu Hsi in favor of precise philological glosses on the classics. On the other hand, moral seriousness stressed relevance to human life, to the solid realities of man's everyday condition. Between the two—seriousness and openness—there was a constant interplay in the development of Neo-Confucianism, with its intense moral concern complemented by spiritual transcendence and intellectual detachment, and the latter at times providing a lofty perspective on the narrowness and rigidities of the moralistic approach. From this point of view the new learning or "enlightenment" of the seventeenth and eighteenth centuries, with its great stress on practicality and its distinctive "humanistic pragmatism," can be seen in part as the offspring of underlying tendencies in Neo-Confucianism, while at the same time it rebelled against its parent, using the very weapons of intellectual objectivity and practical concern which the latter had put into its hands.

In different ways Ch'en Ti, Chiao Hung, Li Chih, Huang Tao-chou,^{cp} Ni Yüan-lu,^{cq} Huang Tsung-hsi, and many others of the late sixteenth and early seventeenth centuries influenced by Wang Yang-ming, also contributed to or participated in the rise of the new realism, critical scholarship, and intellectual objectivity. Several of them also had a significant involvement with Buddhism, the influence of which must be understood in terms of the dynamic humanism which inspired the intellectual and spiritual life of that time.[159] The radicals of the T'ai-chou school, whom Hou Wai-lu has heralded as pioneer progressives and contributors to the New Enlightenment, were also known as the Wild Ch'an sect. Thus the views of Needham and Hou fail to take sufficiently into consideration the role of both Wang Yang-ming and Ch'an in this development. Certainly one cannot assume that the role of Buddhism on the eve of the new enlightenment was simply obscurantist.

BUDDHISM AND THE NEW "ENLIGHTENMENT"

How then do we assess the influence of Buddhism on the new "Enlightenment"? Despite the claim sometimes made for Buddhism today that it is more compatible with modern science than any of the other world religions, little, if anything, has been done to assess its historical contribution to the development of any of the sciences or of a "scientific outlook." The present state of our knowledge about China does not justify drawing definite conclusions; more detailed studies must be made of the late Ming forerunners of the seventeenth-century enlightenment. But the problem is there, and some of our recent studies may help us to formulate it more clearly.

For one thing, I believe that the state of Buddhism at the end of the Ming warrants no claim that it was a vital *intellectual* force in the seventeenth century. The Buddhist revival at the end of the sixteenth century appears to have been in part a religious phenomenon reflecting the insecurities of rapid social change and political decay, and in part a moral revival in the face of an unprecedented disintegration of the traditional fabric of personal ethics and social mores. It was not, however, as represented by its putative leaders, an intellectual or philosophical movement. From Yün-ch'i Chu-hung,[cr] Han-shan Te-ch'ing,[cs] Tzu-po Ta-kuan,[ct] and Ou-i Chih-hsü,[cu] emerged nothing in the way of ideas, concepts, or methods that entered into the studies of the "Enlightenment." They were moral and social reformers, spiritual guides, or reinvigorators of monastic discipline, but not intellectual leaders or seminal thinkers.

On the other hand, as we have seen, many members of the educated class were attracted to Buddhism. Professor Araki's paper, "Confucianism and Buddhism in the Late Ming" (chapter 2), gives some revealing examples of those who turned to Buddhism, but their thinking seems to represent side currents, leading away from the mainstream of Neo-Confucian thought, not into it. A possibility exists, however, that Buddhist skepticism and detachment did affect the intellectual climate—negatively and subtly, rather than positively and tangibly. It is an influence difficult to assess, since the general atmosphere in the sixteenth century was already permeated by the "emptiness" of Neo-Confucianism, which itself may have owed something originally to Buddhism, and in turn fused again almost imperceptibly in thinkers like Wang Chi, Chou Ju-teng,[cv] Kuan Chih-tao,[cw] Chiao Hung, and Li Chih, with Buddhist "emptiness."

Granting the elusiveness and complexity of the situation, however, I believe that Buddhism as we find it in Li Chih and Chiao Hung contributed to a strong sense of philosophical skepticism in the late Ming. The usual view of this has been of a vapid and airy metaphysics in the Ming that finally yielded to more solid and utilitarian thinking in the Ch'ing. In reality, however, it was not metaphysics that held sway in the late Ming, but rather a reaction against the speculative metaphysics of the "Ch'eng-Chu system." In other words there was an "emptiness" of metaphysics. The existentialist strain in the Wang Yang-ming school furthered this trend, and the prevalent forms of Buddhism, Pure Land and Ch'an, stressing faith and intuition respectively, and sharing the skepticism of the Mādhyamika toward all rational philosophy, could only add to the growing dissatisfaction with Neo-Confucian metaphysics.

The enigmatic writings of Li Chih and Fang I-chih in Buddhist matters, which may be intelligible if at all only to the Ch'an initiate, remain unexplored by modern scholarship.[160] Still, there can be little doubt that the attitude of cultural transcendence implicit in Buddhism fostered a pluralistic standpoint and a critical detachment toward Confucian tradition. Li Chih's radical and debunking attitude was no doubt exceptional for his times but it nonetheless had wide effect. His sharp challenge to Neo-Confucianism could not be ignored. This was not simple disaffection but a profound rationalist critique of prevailing tradition. Thus his critical and iconoclastic writing shook the intellectual world of late Ming Confucians as nothing had before. Later, with the added shock of dynastic collapse and the damage to Chinese self-confidence of subjection to alien rule, the intellectual despair of the Confucian at midcentury was such as to generate both a deeper questioning of tradition and an effort to reestablish it on more solid foundations.

At this point Buddhist skepticism could reinforce the questioning attitude which we have already found in Neo-Confucianism itself. Yet in the end, whatever its contribution spiritually, intellectually Buddhism left only a vacuum. Emptiness could be a penetrating solvent, but once Heaven-and-earth had collapsed, cement not solvent was needed to rebuild. For clearing the way there may have been Nothing like Emptiness, but for reconstruction Emptiness was Nothing without the life-affirming and culture-generating power of Neo-Confucianism.

THE REASSESSMENT OF NEO-CONFUCIANISM

The critical reevaluation of Neo-Confucianism which took place in the seventeenth century may be illustrated by comparing the disillusionment of Li Chih in the late sixteenth century with Huang Tsung-hsi's questioning in the seventeenth century of the process of canonization in the official Confucian temple. In the free-thinking atmosphere of the late Ming a skeptic like Li Chih could whimsically cast doubt on the criteria of orthodoxy and the ideal of sagehood:

People all think Confucius a sage and so do I. They all think Lao Tzu and Buddha are heretics and so do I. But people don't really know what sagehood and heterodoxy are. They have just heard so much about them from their parents and teachers. Nor do their parents and teachers really know what sagehood and heterodoxy are; they just believe what they hear from the scholars and elders. And the scholars and elders don't know either, except that Confucius said something about these things. But his saying "Sagehood—of that I am not capable" [as quoted in *Mencius*, IIA, 2] they take just as an expression of modesty, and when he spoke of "studying strange teachings [as] harmful" (*Analects*, II, 16) they interpret this as referring to Taoism and Buddhism. The scholars and elders have memorized these things and embroidered on them; parents and teachers have preserved and recited them, and children have blindly accepted them.[161]

Li's doubts about orthodoxy and sagehood arise from a deep questioning of the values enshrined in the earlier Neo-Confucian ideal of sanctity and serenity. He exposes the pretentions of those who pursue the orthodox path to sagehood in a passage which seems almost a caricature of Weber's Confucian "gentleman":

In ordinary times when there is peace, they only know how to bow and salute one another, or else they sit the day long in an upright posture [practicing quiet-sitting] like a clay image, thinking that if they can suppress all stray thoughts they will become sages and worthies. The more cunning among them participate in meetings to discuss innate knowledge, secretly hoping to gain some recognition and win high office. But when a crisis comes, they look at each other pale and speechless, try to shift the blame to one another, and save themselves on the pretext that "the clearest wisdom is self-preservation." Consequently if the state employs only this type of scholar, when an emergency arises it has no one of any use in the situation.[162]

Though Huang Tsung-hsi, in the next century, is the ideological archenemy of the Wild-Ch'an iconoclast Li Chih, his thoughts on the subject are no less critical than Li's, and reveal the evolution of Neo-Confucian realism and practicality as they have strained against Neo-Confucian idealism and spirituality. Li Chih's contempt for those who pretend to sagehood is based on their inability to fulfill the Confucian obligation to serve society or the ruler in critical times. Huang Tsung-hsi's conception of orthodoxy insists on the same criterion of social relevance, perhaps even further intensified by his disgust with the aberrant individualism of Li Chih and the social decadence he believed it to have spawned. In an essay on enshrinement in the Confucian temple which is part of a larger discussion of orthodoxy and heterodoxy written around 1692, Huang questions whether canonization should be confined to those identified in the "legitimate" Ch'eng-Chu succession, such as Chou Tun-i, the Ch'eng brothers, Chang Tsai, Chu Hsi, and their heirs. "The Way of Confucius is not the teaching of one school or period . . ."

If an age is well ordered there is no clerk or flunkey in the government who does not know the beauty of humanity and righteousness. But if an age is disordered the scholar-official must guard his honor strictly, and is determined not to sacrifice the high standards to which he has dedicated his life, no matter what the tortures and punishments visited on him by the ruler. For him it does not suffice to the fulfillment of duty simply to write commentaries on the Four Books, compile philosophical dialogues, or open a school and gather students. Throughout the ages, past and present, there have been those like Chu-ko Liang ^{cx} of the Han, Lu Chih ^{cy} of the T'ang, Han Ch'i,^{cz} Fan Chung-yen, Li Kang,^{da} and Wen T'ien-hsiang ^{db} of the Sung, and Fang Hsiao-ju ^{dc} of the Ming—these seven public-spirited gentlemen, eminently devoted to the public weal and sincere unto death, who accepted the responsibility for all-under-Heaven and labored undaunted in stormy seas. In them the world had a clear standard of rectitude—men who could actually practice the teachings of Confucius . . .

These seven gentlemen had nothing beyond the teachings of Confucius to guide them in their actions. How could they have been privy to some other transmission, outside of that coming down from Confucius, or seek to maintain a school of their own? How could the school of Confucius be so pedantic and narrow that it would be concerned with nothing but self, have nothing to do with order and disorder in the world, and be ready to cast into the ditch all those heroes of past and present who have tried to shake the world into action? How incredible then that these seven gentlemen remain unenshrined [in the Confucian temple].

It may be argued that those enshrined are distinguished for their refinement in the discussion of mind and human nature, not for the mark they have left on the conduct of affairs. I reply: These gentlemen held fast to one teaching and did not turn back no matter how many reverses they suffered. Their courageous spirit filled Heaven-and-earth; no trace of selfish desire remained in them. If what you want are those who close up their eyes, dull their senses, and reduce the mind to a state of unimaginable purity—a never-never land of consciousness—that is the teaching of Buddha and your candidates for enshrinement would have to be found among those who transmit the lamp [of the Ch'an masters].¹⁶³

Huang's critique of the official orthodoxy embodied in the enshrinement process is significant for more than its voicing of an independent, more liberal view. In making the case for these Confucian activists, his aim is not so much to win a broader tolerance for divergent opinions (which he could have done by making room for other metaphysicians of the Sung and Ming), as the Confucian Temple of the Ming was already quite eclectic in this respect. What he sought was to reassert a basic principle of the Confucian tradition: that true virtue cannot be cultivated in isolation but must be made manifest in actions benefitting the people. Though Huang would not go so far as to destroy the temple or cast out the Ch'eng-Chu schoolmen, he insists that room be found in the Confucian pantheon for those who in later times exemplify a practical teaching. For these heroes not to be enshrined is less of a disservice to them than to Confucianism, which is diminished when it forfeits its claim to their achievements and allows itself to be isolated from the world.

Huang speaks, then, as the exponent of a living Confucian tradition, not as a rebel against orthodoxy or as a champion of innovation. And in this he speaks with unexcelled authority. As the direct heir to the neoorthodoxy of the Tung-lin and Liu Tsung-chou, who attempted to reintegrate Chu Hsi and Wang Yang-ming into a traditional, but revitalized, Confucianism, Huang could speak for the past—for the philosophy of human nature and mind—while at the same time he decried a narrow and socially sterile view of it. He speaks also as a leading scholar and thinker of the seventeenth-century "Enlightenment." Not only was his greatness as a spokesman for Confucian scholarship acknowledged in his own time, but he has been identified as a pioneer in the "evidential research" of the so-called Han learning in the early Ch'ing "Enlightenment." [164] If we consider further that the ideal type he acclaims here is an earlier embodiment of some of the basic values of the "Enlightenment"—with its stress on social utility, concrete practicality, and tangible evidence—then we have a case made implicitly by Huang for the Confucian character of the "Enlightenment" itself. We may be sure that this pivotal figure in the seventeenth century would resist just as strongly today the exclusion or removal of the notion of "Enlightenment" from Confucianism as well as protest the view that it sprang fullblown from a new age and owed little to its Neo-Confucian predecessors. It was to establish this link, and to assert the continuing relevance of Ming thought to Ch'ing developments that he compiled his survey of Neo-Confucian thought in the Ming, the *Ming-ju hsüeh-an.*[dd][165]

Nevertheless, if some of the basic values are similar, the historical situation is different from the earlier period of Neo-Confucianism. There is, for one thing, a greater distance in time from the great age of Buddhism. The secularizing tendencies in Neo-Confucianism have worked to liberate it from the more ascetic and transcendental influences of Buddhism which had been part of the air Sung thinkers breathed, whereas in the Ming era Buddhism too had become more secularized, partly through the influence of Wang Yang-ming. Also, the new age had undergone unparalleled social ferment, political upheaval, and intellectual questioning, in the course of which many Confucians had come to reject earlier forms of Neo-Confucian thought and practice as unsuited to the fulfillment of their original ideals, while they turned to other Neo-Confucian ideas and activities more appropriate to their needs.

NEO-CONFUCIAN VITALISM AND THE REACTION TO MING "IDEALISM"

Neo-Confucianism from the start had seen the Way, or Tao, as a dynamic life force. Sung thinkers quoted the *Book of Changes* to the effect that the essence of the Tao was "vitality" or "creativity" (*sheng sheng*).[de][166] Chu Hsi's discussion of humanity (*jen*)[df] spoke of this key virtue and power as "having a mind that fosters the life of Heaven-and-earth and all things." [167] Shimada Kenji,[dg] in a major contribution to the understanding of Ming thought, has shown how Wang Yang-ming's teaching strongly reasserted this value in relation to the mind. The Tao as seen by Wang and many of his followers was constantly manifesting its vital power in the impulses of the mind and heart, in creative thought and emotional drives. To them any quietistic tendency which stilled the mind or suspended thought also stifled the life force.[168]

Mind here was understood as a spiritual faculty embodied in physical form, a manifestation of the dynamic life force, or ether (*ch'i*). Often in the Wang Yang-ming school mind (*hsin*) and ether (*ch'i*) were spoken of in the same terms, as "alive," "living," "life-giving," or "life-renewing" (*sheng*, or *sheng-sheng*), and as such were identified as the basis of man's nature *(hsing)*.[dh] [169] This follows Wang's effort to conceive of man's nature not as abstract principle or norm, but as active principle in a dynamic mind. Frequently the essential reality was described in the assertion that "Throughout Heaven-and-earth, all is ether *(ch'i)*" or "Throughout Heaven-and-earth all is mind *(hsin)*," where *hsin* and *ch'i* were used interchangeably to represent the vital force in man and the universe.[170] Lo Ju-fang, a major figure in the Wang Yang-ming school and its T'ai-chou branch, greatly stresses this idea of *sheng*, equating mind with creativity or vitality.[171] Others emphasized the dynamic force *(ch'i)* and became forerunners of the trend toward a monism of *ch'i* in the seventeenth century.[172]

The significance of this development in the late Ming is manifold, but a major element lies in its stress on the actualities of life and human nature. There is a note of realism here in accepting man as he is, with his physical desires, affections, and emotional drives. Lo saw these as good, as being essential to the expression of human nature. Indeed, he virtually consecrated them as manifestations of cosmic creativity. A modern existentialist might believe "realism" to consist in facing the starker realities of the human condition which would, if anything, correspond more closely to the tendency within the Ch'eng-Chu school to dwell on the evil propensities in human desires and contrast them to man's inborn Heavenly nature. Lo is more optimistic, and one might even say typically Chinese, in his affirmation of the present life and the essential goodness of man's actual nature.

I draw attention to Lo Ju-fang [di] not only because he is a major thinker and influential teacher, but because he exemplifies attitudes both typical of the late Ming and influential in the seventeenth century. The "Enlightenment" of the seventeenth and eighteenth centuries has frequently been seen as a reaction to late Ming thought, and in one sense the analysis offered above would appear to confirm this, since it points to the reassessment of Neo-Confucianism after the fall of the Ming. That reaction, however, has been seen too much as a reaction *against* Wang Yang-ming or *against* Neo-Confucian thought as a whole. The misleading contrast is then drawn between the practical and utilitarian character of the new thought as compared to the abstruseness of the old; the "materialistic" or "naturalistic" emphasis on *ch'i* in the one as compared to the idealistic tendency of the other; the critical temper and "evidential research" of the

Ch'ing as compared to the lofty and detached speculation of the Sung and Ming.

The supposed Ch'ing reaction to Ming idealism is referred to by Joseph Levenson in his study "The Abortiveness of Empiricism in Early Ch'ing Thought." [173] Speaking of Huang Tsung-hsi as a "materialist" who led the attack in the early Ch'ing on Ming idealism and the Lu-Wang school, Levenson describes Huang as "finding the fatal stain of Zen on Lu and Wang," thus stigmatizing the latter again with Buddhist obscurantism. In fact, however, Huang Tsung-hsi, though a determined opponent of Zen (Ch'an), strongly upheld Wang Yang-ming against it and would be the last to find in him any stain of Zen. What is more to the essential point, Huang would have had no reason to attack either the Lu-Wang school or "Ming idealism" in behalf of a new "materialism." On the contrary he personifies the evolution of the old *into* the new, which is to say, of Ming vitalism into a new naturalism or realism. Like others in the Wang Yang-ming school, he sees mind (*hsin*) as virtually equivalent to ether or the vital force (*ch'i*). His preface to the *Ming-ju hsüeh-an* begins with the familiar assertion that "throughout Heaven-and-earth all is mind," and elsewhere makes it clear that there is no mind apart from ether (*ch'i*), and that "throughout Heaven-and-earth all is ether and there is no principle apart from it." [174]

Thus Huang's anti-idealist position is manifest, but he sees this "idealism"—the idea that principle exists apart from ether or things—as an aberration of the Sung school, not of Wang Yang-ming. His critique, indeed, follows in line with Yang-ming's position that principle or the nature (*hsing*) does not exist apart from mind or ether.

LIVING IN THE PRESENT AND THE NEW HISTORICAL AWARENESS

Just as the vitalism in late Ming thought stressed the actualities of life and the immediacy of the present, it gave new attention and significance to the ideas of present utility and immediate practicality. In one sense these can be taken as constant values in Neo-Confucianism, which from the onset stressed contemporary relevance and applicability—in the Northern Sung as political and social reform, and in Chu Hsi's teaching as personal cultivation for the here and now (or the "near" in time, place, and priority, as the title *Chin-ssu lu* implies). But in the late Ming, the cumulative effect of its reiteration in Neo-Confucianism and its role in Ming history is noticeable. The founder of the dynasty had set a tone of simplicity and practicality in administration and in the men he employed; and the growing popular literature of the Ming answered to an interest in what was of daily utility, *jih yung.* [dj] [175] Wang Yang-ming's thought with its stress on personal experience and, as today it might be put, "what one could use" of received ideas, was both congenial and contributory to this trend, while the decline in metaphysics further prepared the stage for "contemporaneity," "practicality," and "utility" to come to the fore. Even in late Ming Buddhism there was an unusual emphasis on present usefulness. [176]

The contemporary interest was expressed in a broad range of literature, especially popular fiction, drama, and poetry, which felt no need to reminisce on the past or to treat classic themes. Lo Ju-fang and his vitalism were a powerful stimulus to this popular literature, through T'ang Hsien-tsu, [dk] Li Chih, and others. [177] Equally significant was the stimulus to recent or contemporary history. Chiao Hung, Lo's student, assiduously collected quantities of biographical materials for the study of recent Ming history. [178] Huang Tsung-hsi did the same for Ming literature and philosophy as well as for history, consciously asserting the value of this new growth and rejecting the idea that the classical tradition alone was worth preserving. [179] Huang's conception of "living in the present" involved no repudiation of the past and was worlds apart from Li Chih's libertarian spontaneity, but their interest in the contemporary they shared with other scholars of the late Ming who were touched by this vital current.

Contemporary history gave expression to a related value in the cluster of meanings that surround the Chinese term *sheng* and the Neo-Confucian idea drawn from the *Changes* of the renewal of life (*sheng sheng*). This is the sense of new growth, especially of what we could call historical growth. Huang's survey of Ming thought was the first in China to focus on the history of ideas in a separate period, seeing that period as having a significant growth in itself and not simply as restating eternal verities or perpetuating a traditional orthodoxy. Again one can point to Sung precedents, insofar as works like the *Chin-ssu lu* and *I-Lo Yüan-yüan lu* [dl] focused attention on Sung models and not solely on classical prototypes. But that attitude is carried significantly forward by Huang's tracing of the historical growth from one master and school to another, delineating the specific contribution of each and likening the whole process to the spreading, proliferating vine, seeking the sunlight and bearing flower and fruit in profusion.[180] Even more noteworthy is the absence of any résumé of the sages' teaching or geneaology of the orthodox succession as a preface to the whole. Huang took the unprecedented step for a historian of working back from the present into the past, rather than the reverse, treating the Ming first and only later reaching back into the Sung and Yüan periods in his *Sung-Yüan hsüeh-an.*[dm]

Thus the Neo-Confucian emphasis on renewal and growth, enhanced by the value given to life experience and present realities in the school of Wang Yang-ming, helped to produce a new attitude toward history, seeing it as more than the endless repetition of dynastic cycles or degeneration from an ideal past. This attitude became a major ingredient of the new "Enlightenment," which made great strides in both historical research and interpretation, recognizing and accepting change, facing facts and not just reiterating principles, and indulging much less in moralistic judgments as a substitute for conclusions based on evidence.

These attitudes carried over also into other branches of study, and especially the textual study of the classics, where the consciousness of the present, as well as of historical change and growth, helped to produce a more critical attitude. The questioning of accepted texts had already been dramatized by Wang Yang-ming's challenge to the Chu Hsi version of the *Great Learning,* a controversy which could only be mediated and settled on the basis of textual evidence, as Lo Ch'in-shun insisted.[181] In the historical and classical studies of the seventeenth century, scholars such as Ku Yen-wu and Wang Fu-chih were to share in this new consciousness without feeling any debt to Wang Yang-ming for it. But the heightened awareness of present and past, the questioning attitude and critical method in classical phonology, textual criticism, and exegesis of earlier scholars such as Ch'en Ti, Chiao Hung, Ni Yüan-lu, and later Huang Tsung-hsi—as contrasting cases identified with the Wang Yang-ming school or influenced by it—demonstrate that scholarly objectivity and evidential research had already made its appearance in the school Ku criticized for its airy subjectivity.

One of the most revealing questions in the study of the classics arises from the view of Ch'en Ti and Chiao Hung that centuries of commentaries should not stand in the way of a direct reading and understanding of the original texts themselves.[182] Chiao further believed that anyone with something to say about one of the Classics should do so in a work of his own, issuing directly from his personal knowledge and experience, rather than putting his ideas forward surreptitiously as commentary on a classic.[183] Chiao's attitude, which resembles the modern "Great Books" approach of John Erskine, asserted the autonomy of individual experience and reason in a manner clearly reflective of Wang Yang-ming.[184] Ni Yüan-lu's approach to the *Changes*, cited earlier, is similar. He does not deny history or tradition, but seeks to be its master. A generation later Huang Tsung-hsi combined these approaches—the direct encounter with the classics and a critical reading of the commentaries (which he recommended for the civil service examinations) and direct quotation of later philosophers together with appropriate commentary (which he combined in his accounts of Neo-Confucian thought)—to exemplify both the broad learning and the critical mastery which were to become hallmarks of the Han Learning.[185] There could be perhaps no more striking example of how Neo-Confucian scholarship—"book learning"—was brought to new levels of accomplishment by the interaction of rational reflection and personal experience to produce a higher rationality and new "Enlightenment."

THE NEW NATURALISM OR "MATERIALISM"

Thus far our discussion has focused on new trends in the seventeenth-century "Enlightenment" which emerged in part from within, and not simply in reaction to, the dominant Wang Yang-ming school in the late Ming. It may seem even less likely that the new era should have owed something also to the Ch'eng-Chu school, but that is nonetheless the case. Moreover, since the historical climate and context do much to define concepts in current use, the evolution of other Neo-Confucian ideas from within the Ch'eng-Chu school helped to shape and direct the trends already mentioned.

The centrality and multivalency of *ch'i* (ether, vital force, material force) have already been noted. In the Wang Yang-ming school its dynamic aspect was evoked in association with mind (*hsin*) and life-renewal (*sheng-sheng*). Another important aspect of *ch'i* in the seventeenth century was the physical and material, figuring prominently in relation to concrete objects and their study. Where this aspect of *ch'i* was emphasized, the Confucian "investigation of things" could stress physical objects rather than "matters" and "affairs" (i.e., moral and social questions). The insistence on *ch'i* as the underlying substance of all things has led some to characterize a monism of *ch'i* as "materialism," though this involves difficulties where the spiritual and "ethereal" aspect is no less important. The incongruity is apparent in the application of such terms to the School of Wang Yang-ming, labeled "idealist" as a School of the Mind and yet, as a School of *ch'i*, presumably "materialist." [186]

In this volume Professor Cheng's study of *li-ch'i* relationships uses the term "naturalism" for the developing philosophy of *ch'i* in the seventeenth century, and cites Wang Fu-chih as a prototypical case. Professor McMorran's investigation of the Neo-Confucian roots of Wang Fu-chih's thought shows it to have emerged from the soil of the Sung school, and, for all of Wang's undoubted originality and independence of thought, not to be a radical break with the past. There is in fact a considerable development in the Ch'eng-Chu school of the Ming which contributes to the philosophy of *ch'i* and reconverges with the Wang Yang-ming school's vitalistic emphasis on *ch'i* in the seventeenth century.

Even among the early leaders of the Ch'eng-Chu school in the Ming there was uneasiness over a tendency in Chu Hsi and some of his followers to assign a higher value and metaphysical status to principle (*li*) than to ether (*ch'i*). They remained "orthodox" in their adherence to the *li-ch'i* dualism, stressing *ch'i* in order to counteract the view that *li* was the regulative principle over *ch'i* and had priority over the physical element in man. Hsüeh Hsüan (1389–1464), whose concern for "real learning" we have already observed, cautioned against a teaching which spoke of principle in too lofty terms, and insisted that "real principles and real ether have neither a hair's breadth of space nor an instant of time separating them." [187] "Principle is only found in ether. It is impossible to speak of the one as anterior or the other as posterior." [188] "Under Heaven there is no thing without principle and no principle apart from things." [189] "Principle and ether are not to be confused but neither are they to be separated. Under Heaven there is no principle without ether and no ether without principle. There is no nature apart from ether and no ether apart from nature. They cannot be separated into two." [190]

Within the Ch'eng-Chu school the issue was further pressed by Lo Ch'in-shun (1465–1547) as a matter of doubt concerning Chu Hsi's own ambiguous and sometimes infelicitous handling of it. Lo's reputation as a defender of Ch'eng-Chu orthodoxy was established through his controversies with Wang Yang-ming, but in regard to the status of *ch'i* his and Wang's views were closer than either was to Chu. Lo expressed his own reservations about Chu Hsi's view of principle and ether in his *K'un-chih chi* [dn] ("Knowing-Pains" or "Knowledge Attained Through Painful Effort"). Though affirming the inseparability of principle and ether, Lo leaned toward a monism of the latter by asserting that "principle is just the principle of ether." [191] Lo attributed Chu's metaphysical view of principle to the influence of Ch'eng I and expressed his own preference for Ch'eng Hao's view of the Way as made manifest in physical objects, the only difference between ether and principle being that one has form and the other has not. Lo thus accentuates the actual and the physical as does Wang Yang-ming, but he also insists against Wang on the study of principle through its manifold manifestations in things and objects—implying a somewhat more objective approach even than Ch'eng I and Chu Hsi. [192] Moreover, Lo denies that the physical desires are evil, emancipating himself from a puritanical attitude which extended from the Sung school down even to Wang Yang-ming. Thus an important element in the new outlook that was to dominate the seventeenth century—the reality of the actual, physical natures of man and things—emerges directly from within the Ch'eng-Chu "orthodoxy" at the same time that it goes beyond it by developing further the empiricism implicit in the view of principle as inhering in things.

The views of Hsüeh and Lo were influential on Tung-lin thinkers in the early seventeenth century, and especially on Kao P'an-lung. There had been a marked decline in the direct influence of the Ch'eng-Chu school in the late fifteenth and sixteenth centuries, as compared to the flourishing of Wang Yang-ming's, but by this time ideas circulated freely among thinkers and schools, and the Tung-lin, though championing a neoorthodoxy, drew eclectically from sources supportive of firm moral principles and action. The integration of objective norms, subjective motivations, and actual conduct figured prominently in their thinking. Hence it is not surprising to find Hsüeh Hsüan and Lo Ch'in-shun invoked alongside of conservative members of the Wang school such as Wang Shih-huai [do] (1522–1605), who stressed both the physical reality of ether and traditional moral standards.[193]

The effort to redefine orthodoxy and reestablish a common ground between Chu Hsi and Wang Yang-ming, which is characteristic of both the leading late Ming philosophers Kao P'an-lung and Liu Tsung-chou, brought them to the same combination of elements: a monism of ether, a dynamic view of man's moral nature, and the effort to reestablish a bridge between subjective and objective morality. Though both still practiced quiet-sitting, there was a subtle shift under way toward a more outward and outgoing view of the cultivation of one's nature, and away from the view of principle or nature as an immutable inner essence to be perceived in a quiescent state and expressed in exemplary conduct. From this it was only one step to Huang Tsung-hsi's definition of the substance of man's nature as being indistinguishable from its effective exercise or application,[194] which is grounded in the dynamic process of ether (ch'i) and manifest in a far broader range of human activities. For Hsüeh Hsüan in the fifteenth century all reality had been embodied in ether, but "real learning" (shih hsüeh) was defined primarily in moral terms. Valid study and action were adjudged by the criterion of relevance to man's moral and spiritual essence.[195] By the seventeenth century that conception of relevance had been notably expanded so that a wider variety of studies and activities, together with a more critical and objective approach to them, was possible.

The problem of relevance remained for the Neo-Confucian, but in a new and larger context for the pursuit of "real learning." Practicality or utility, for instance, were no longer conceived so much in terms of personal morality, but neither was "real learning" defined solely in terms of what was "practical." An important area for the new evidential research—phonological studies in classical poetry—was not eminently practical at all but was rather bookish, and was one in which the aesthetic and cultural interests of the Confucian were on the defensive against moral and social claims. Here the new critical temper and historical consciousness operated in the mind of a Ch'en Ti or Chiao Hung, which had been opened to new experience and knowledge that was not valued simply by the standard of social utility or practicality (though these were in their own right values stressed by Ch'en and Chiao). A process of cross-fertilization was at work to produce the new growth, and not just a deeper plowing of old furrows.

Indeed the argument can be made that both the practicality and a certain critical distance or detachment were necessary to the new learning; that its most original minds were survivors from the Ming, whose contributions arose from this confluence of practical concern (seriousness) and detachment (openness) discussed earlier; and that the more practical and relevant studies became in the Ch'ing, the farther away they grew from the spontaneous sources of their original inspiration and the more limited became their horizons. In this view, if Ch'ing thought ceased to be philosophically creative and became simply classical and practical (classical studies being practical because rewarded and supported by the state, and "practical" being given a traditional definition in terms of social utility), the reason may be that it had become totally relevant to the immediate needs of the state, society, and culture that supported them and had largely lost sight of the original complement to practicality and utility—the Ming openness to the irrelevant, its "not being set on anything."

In any case the long development of Neo-Confucian thought from the twelfth century had reached a new stage by the seventeenth century. From the inner enlightenment of the sage had emerged the new "enlightenment" of critical scholarship and thought in the seventeenth century. In this process a crucial transformation had taken place in the original unifying conception of the sage. As the Neo-Confucian became a better scholar he also became less of an aspirant to sagehood. As his secular preoccupations grew—the natural outgrowth of the original Neo-Confucian commitment to this world as opposed to Buddhism's renunciation of it—and as his learning produced an ever more complex culture, it became more difficult for the Confucian to sustain the all-embracing ideal of sagehood. Li Chih's skepticism concerning it we have already seen. It was shared by others less iconoclastic than he, and Huang Tsung-hsi's candidates for canonization were heroic leaders—men of action—not sitting sages.

Commitment to the ideal of the sage remained a distinguishing mark of the so-called Sung school, but by its very identification with the original Ch'eng-Chu school in the Sung, this movement stood as something of an anachronism in the Ch'ing. It was a Ch'ing school but not *the*

Ch'ing school. It was indeed only one symptom of the tendency for Ch'ing scholars to look back toward different schools or stages in the past as a means of identifying themselves. The Sung learning, the Han learning, the return to the original fountainhead in Confucius' teaching, each bespoke an effort to remain true to one or another of the tendencies in the original Neo-Confucian synthesis, as they had come to a parting of the ways.

Few of the great early Ch'ing thinkers consciously strove for sagehood, but the case of Yen Yüan, described in this volume by Professor Tu, is particularly illuminating in this regard. His early struggle to attain sagehood bears many resemblances to that of Wang Yang-ming in its religious intensity and its aversion to book learning. But his resolution of the problem is more "practical" in the ordinary sense, more programmatic and formulaic, while it is also much less philosophical and transcendental.

From the growing Ch'ing criticism of the Ch'eng-Chu teaching as having been perverted by Buddhism, we can see it being purified of those influences which had unconsciously taken hold, in an age permeated by Buddhist spirituality, of even its Neo-Confucian critics. The secularization of Chinese thought, begun anew in the Sung, had moved on to yet another stage in the seventeenth century. Thus was advanced still further one of the elements of "modernity" which had manifested itself before the modern period. Sagehood as a goal of spiritual attainment had become almost as rare as had sainthood in the twentieth-century West.

CONCLUSION

My aim here has been to show both the variety and interrelations of the forms of Neo-Confucian enlightenment and experience which contributed to the so-called Enlightenment of the seventeenth and eighteenth centuries. The continuities are clear enough to warrant seeing that "Enlightenment" as an outgrowth of Neo-Confucian thought, and as reflecting Neo-Confucian attitudes which were not uncongenial to the development of scientific inquiry or critical thought in fields relevant to Confucian concerns. My purpose has not been to attempt any overall assessment of the scientific character of that "Enlightenment" in Western terms, but only to show that Neo-Confucianism was not inherently antipathetic to scientific study or resistant to new ideas. With Levenson I would agree that the leaders of this "Enlightenment" "were not aiming at science and falling short, but living out the values of their culture." [196] If, however, we recognize here "a Chinese taste for a style of culture not the style of the modern West," [197] we may yet have to suspend the further judgment of Levenson that it is not the style of modern China. That latter style is still in the process of formation, and it would be premature for us to equate it simply with the style of the modern West, or to assume that the Chinese today are not still living out, in important ways, the values of their own culture.

There are also grounds for questioning whether the Neo-Confucian potential can be judged solely on the basis of the cultural configuration of seventeenth- and eighteenth-century China. In different historical and cultural circumstances certain potentialities of Neo-Confucian thought were more fully realized in Tokugawa and Meiji Japan than in Ch'ing China, a possibility raised in our earlier discussion of Ishida Baigan and the Meiji "Enlightenment."

A single example may suggest how new researches can alter our view of the matter. The pioneering studies of Professor Abe Yoshio [dp] in the transmission of Neo-Confucian philosophy through Korea to Japan reveals how much more influence Lo Ch'in-shun's version of Ch'eng-Chu orthodoxy had in the development of Tokugawa thought than it had in China. [198] Lo's stress on *ch'i* and on the study of principle in things gave a more naturalistic direction and intellectual cast to the Neo-Confucianism espoused by the Hayashi family, the official Tokugawa school, and by others like Kaibara Ekken, [dq] whose thought, influenced by Lo, leans strongly to a monism of *ch'i* and to studies in the natural sciences. This official orthodoxy in Japan, encouraging the scholarly and to some extent the "objective" study of principle in history and nature, contrasts with the independent Ch'eng-Chu orthodoxies represented by Yamazaki Ansai [dr] and Ishida Baigan, with their strong religious and moral commitment.

From this viewpoint, the modern "Enlightenment" in Japan was neither a wholly modern importation nor the product of an indigenous "protestant" movement, but something that began to emerge in the Tokugawa period itself and that (leaving aside many other historical factors) involved a significant interaction of several orthodoxies. Thus the differences from one strain of Neo-Confucian orthodoxy to another can significantly alter our interpretation and evaluation of thought trends, for not only do they put individual trends and movements in a new perspective, but they may also invalidate simplistic characterizations of Neo-Confucian thought, orthodox and heterodox, in studies concerning its role in the modernization of China and Japan. As more becomes known about the diverse outgrowths of Neo-Confucian thought, and its cultural manifestations in China, Japan, and Korea, we shall come to appreciate more fully the past and potential contribution of their peoples to the enlightenment of the modern world.

NOTES

1. Liang Ch'i-ch'ao. *Intellectual Trends in the Ch'ing Period*, translated by Immanuel Hsü (Harvard University Press, 1959), pp. 21 ff.
2. Hou Wai-lu, *Chung-kuo ts'ao-ch'i chi-meng ssu-hsiang shih* (Peking, 1956).
3. *Ibid.*, pp. 26–36.
4. See Chung-ying Cheng, this volume, p. 503.
5. In Charles Moore (ed.), *The Chinese Mind* (Honolulu: East-West Center Press, 1967), pp. 104–181. (Hereafter referred to as Hu, "Scientific Spirit.")
6. *Ibid.*, p. 115.
7. *Ibid.*
8. *Ibid.*, p. 128.
9. *Ibid.*, pp. 130–31.
10. *Ibid.*, p. 124.
11. *Ibid.*, p. 128.
12. *Ibid.*
13. Cf. de Bary, *Self and Society*, pp. 121 ff., and Edward Ch'ien's paper, this volume.
14. Carmen Blacker, *The Japanese Enlightenment, A Study of the Writings of Fukuzawa Yūkichi* (Cambridge, Mass., 1964; hereafter referred to as Blacker, *Enlightenment*).
15. *Ibid.*, p. 29.
16. *Ibid.*, p. 31.
17. *Ibid.*, p. 32.
18. *Ibid.*, p. 22.
19. *Ibid.*, p. 51.
20. *Ibid.*, p. 56.
21. Hu, "Scientific Spirit," p. 117.
22. *Ibid.*, p. 118.
23. *Ibid.*, p. 120.
24. Blacker, *Enlightenment*, pp. 22, 46, 54.
25. Robert Bellah, *Tokugawa Religion, The Values of Pre-Industrial Japan* (Glencoe, Illinois: The Free Press, 1957; hereafter referred to as Bellah, *Tokugawa Religion*).
26. *Ibid.*, p. 148.
27. *Ibid.*, p. 149.
28. *Ibid.*, p. 152.
29. *Ibid.*, p. 153.
30. *Ibid.*, pp. 175–76.
31. Cf. R. P. Dore, *Education in Tokugawa Japan* (Berkeley, 1965), pp. 236–38, for a more realistic indication of its role and influence.

32. Bellah, *Tokugawa Religion*, p. 177.
33. *Ibid.*, pp. 150–51.
34. Cf. Chan, *Source Book in Chinese Philosophy* (Princeton, 1963), p. 523; and de Bary, *Self and Society*, pp. 14, 26–27 (n. 26–27).
35. *Ibid.*, p. 20.
36. Cf. de Bary (ed.), *Sources of Chinese Tradition* (New York, 1960), p. 561; Chan, *Source Book*, p. 525; de Bary, *Self and Society* (New York, 1960), p. 200.
37. *Ibid.*, p. 14.
38. Cf. Bellah, *Tokugawa Religion*, p. 150; de Bary, *Self and Society*, p. 12. See also p. 165, this volume; W. T. Chan, "The Ch'eng-Chu School in the Early Ming," in *Self and Society*, pp. 29 ff.
39. Cf. Professor Araki's paper, pp. 39–66, this volume.
40. *Ibid.*, pp. 39–40, this volume.
41. Fung Yu-lan, *History of Chinese Philosophy*, II (Princeton, 1953), 551–58, 566–71; J. P. Bruce, *Chu Hsi and His Masters* (London, 1923), pp. 245–60.
42. Cf. de Bary, *Self and Society*, pp. 15–16.
43. In its tendency toward popularization, use of the vernacular, adaptation to middle-class values, "this-worldly asceticism," nationalism, and so on. Some pertinent factors are considered in the section of this paper entitled "Aesthetic Enlightenment."
44. Bellah, *Tokugawa Religion*, p. 151.
45. Chu Hsi and Lü Tsu-ch'ien (compilers), *Chin-ssu lu*, in *Chu Tzu i-shu*,[ds] I-wen yin shu kuan (Taipei, reprint of K'ang-hsi edition), 1/2a; translated by Wing-tsit Chan, *Reflections on Things at Hand* (Columbia University Press, 1967), p. 3. Unless otherwise indicated I have followed Professor Chan's translation, giving the page number in *Reflections* after each passage quoted. In some cases I have adapted the translation slightly in order to bring out a meaning relevant to the question at hand. For instance, I have had more reason and occasion to translate *ching* as "reverence" than he. He renders it as both "seriousness" and "reverence" (in that order of preference), whereas I reverse the priority. At the same time I must renew the thanks expressed in my foreword to this book for the scholarly aids Professor Chan has provided us for the understanding of this work. It is far more than just a translation, though the translation itself is an impressive contribution.
46. Cf. Shibata Minoru[dt] (ed.), *Ishida Baigan zenshū* (Tokyo, 1956), p. 617. Cf. Bellah, *Tokugawa Religion*, pp. 143, 203.
47. *Ibid.*, 1/1a; Chan, p. 5.
48. Chan, *Reflections*, p. xl.
49. *Ibid.*, 1/2a; Chan, p. 3.
50. Fung Yu-lan, *History of Chinese Philosophy*, translated by Derk Bodde (Princeton, 1953), Vol. II, ch. 11, 12, 13.
51. Chan, *Reflections*, p. 324, quoting *Huang-mien chai chi*,[du] 2/2a.
52. Cf. Yamazaki Michio, *Kinshiroku*[dv] (Tokyo, 1967). An abridged translation with commentary.

53. *Chin-ssu lu*, 2/1a; Chan, p. 35.
54. *Ibid.*, 1/preface, 1b; Chan, p. 2.
55. *Ibid.*, 1/2a; Chan, p. 3.
56. *Ibid.*, 14/6a; Chan, p. 308.
57. Yamazaki, *Kinshiroku*, p. 276.
58. *Ibid.*, p. 257.
59. Chan, *Reflections*, xl.
60. *Chin-ssu lu*, 14/1a; Chan, p. 291.
61. *Ibid.*, Chan, p. 290.
62. *Ibid.*, 14/2b; Chan, pp. 298–99.
63. *Ibid.*, 14/2b; Chan, p. 299.
64. *Ibid.*, 14/4a, 5a; Chan, pp. 301–2, 305–6.
65. *Ibid.*, 14/5ab; Chan, pp. 307–8.
66. Cf. A. C. Graham, *Two Chinese Philosophers* (London, 1958), pp. 83 ff.; Fung, *History*, II, 566 ff.; de Bary, *The Buddhist Tradition* (New York, 1968), pp. 240–51.
67. I mean here to stress the religious attitude and not necessarily to imply a theistic devotion, though it was so understood by some later Neo-Confucians, especially in Korea and Japan. Cf. Ichirō Ishida, "Tokugawa Feudal Society and Neo-Confucian Thought," in *Philosophical Studies of Japan*, I (1964), 1–32, esp. pp. 4–6; 24–29, 32; John T. Meskill, *Ch'oe P'u's Diary: A Record of Drifting Across the Sea* (Tucson, 1965), pp. 34–36, *passim.* Weber's discussion of the life style of the "gentleman" and the "central concept of propriety" is quite apt, except for his tendency to regard this propriety as wholly conventional and predicated on a pious acceptance of the established order. The real depth of the Confucian commitment to struggle and sacrifice, which found its fullest expression in the Ming, is missing to Weber. Cf. his *Religion of China*, pp. 156, 228.
68. Cf. de Bary, *Sources of Chinese Tradition*, ch. xix.
69. Quoted by Itō Jinsai [dw] in a calligraphic scroll in my possession. The same sentiments are expressed in memorials by the Ch'engs translated in de Bary, *Sources of Chinese Tradition*, pp. 450–58.
70. Cf. de Bary, "A Reappraisal of Neo-Confucianism," in A. F. Wright, *Studies in Chinese Thought* (Chicago, 1953), pp. 105–6.
71. Chan, *Reflections*, p. 236.
72. *Ibid.*, p. 237.
73. *Ibid.*
74. Kōjirō Yoshikawa,[dx] *An Introduction to Sung Poetry*, translated by Burton Watson (Harvard University Press, 1967), p. 28; his *Sōshi gaisetsu* (Tokyo, 1962), p. 39.
75. Cf. de Bary, *Self and Society*, p. 190.
76. Cf. *Chu tzu ta ch'üan* [dy] (SPPY edition), IX, 84/8a. The translation "baseness of will" in the preceding passage from Yoshikawa conveys perhaps too strong a feeling of moral contempt. Tu Fu is accused of no culpable intent or failure. Also, Yoshikawa's explanation of the "Way" in terms of a "philosophy

which does not look on human existence as petty or insignificant" makes the passage serve his own interpretation of Sung poetry better than it expresses Chu Hsi's attitude. The latter's acceptance of life also has a transcendent and even mystical aspect.

77. Yamazaki, *Kinshiroku*, p. 65.
78. *Chin-ssu lu*, 2/1b, Chan, pp. 36–37.
79. *Ibid.*, 2/2a; Chan, p. 39.
80. *Ibid.*, 2/2ab; Chan, p. 40.
81. Chan, *Reflections*, p. 40, citing *Chu Tzu Yü-lei*, 95/28a.
82. *Ibid.*, 95/27ab.
83. *Chin-ssu lu*, 2/2b; Chan, p. 40.
84. Weber, *Religion of China*, p. 236.
85. See Chan, *Source Book*, p. 785; *Reflections*, p. 361; Graham, *Two Chinese Philosophers*, pp. 68–69.
86. *Chin-ssu lu*, 3/3a; Chan, p. 93.
87. *Ibid.*, 3/2ab; Chan, pp. 91–92.
88. *Ibid.*, 4/4b; Chan, p. 137.
89. *Mencius*, VII A, 3.
90. *Ibid.*, II A, 2; *Chin-ssu lu*, 4/2b–3a; Chan, p. 129.
91. *Ibid.*, 4/2b; translation adapted from Chan, p. 128.
92. *Ibid.*, 4/3a; Chan, pp. 130–1.
93. *Ibid.*, 4/3b; Chan, p. 133.
94. de Bary, *Self and Society*, pp. 1–3.
95. Cf. Liu Ts'un-yan, "Taoist Self-Cultivation in Ming Thought," in *Self and Society*, p. 313.
96. *Chin-ssu lu*, 14/5a; Chan, p. 305.
97. *Ibid.*, 4/8b; translation adapted from Chan, p. 151.
98. *Ibid.*
99. Okada Takehiko, *Zazen to seiza* [dz] (Nagasaki, 1965), pp. 28, 33.
100. At least such as I have been able to observe in Japan, Korea, and Taiwan, especially the Yushima seidō in Tokyo, Shizutani gakkō in Okayama; Kōdōkan in Mito; Ashikaga gakkō in Ashikaga-shi; and the Sang gyung kwan in Seoul.
101. For instance, by Ch'en Hsien-chang. Cf. *Self and Society*, p. 57.
102. Cf. Okada, *Zazen to seiza*, pp. 27, 114.
103. *Ibid.*, pp. 53–54.
104. *Lao Tzu*, p. 19.
105. *Chin-ssu lu*, 4/6a; translation adapted from Chan, pp. 143–44.
106. Okada, *Zazen to seiza*, p. 67.
107. T'ang Chun-i, "The Development of the Concept of Moral Mind from Wang Yang-ming to Wang Chi," in de Bary, *Self and Society*, pp. 93–120.
108. Julia Ching, in a personal communication, adds the comment concerning this "examination of conscience": "not so much in making discursive, moral judgments on oneself, as to let 'inner calm' prevail, so that *hsin* (the

mind) becomes mirror-like, reflecting what is good and evil in oneself. In this sense it remains a contemplation (i.e., intuitive, natural, pre-reflective)." While this may be generally true, and especially so of the earlier Neo-Confucians in the Sung and Ming, Wilhelm draws attention to those Sung school men in the Ch'ing who kept a very precise record of their thoughts and deeds as an aid to self-correction. Cf. Jansen (ed.), *Changing Japanese Attitudes Toward Modernization*, pp. 292–93. Professor Tu's study of Yen Yüan in this volume confirms the point (see pp. 511–39).

109. See Chan, *Reflections*, p. 368; and his "Synthesis in Chinese Metaphysics," in Moore, *The Chinese Mind*, p. 145. This was the teaching of Li T'ung (Yen-p'ing), 1088–1163, a pupil of the Ch'eng brothers and teacher of Chu Hsi. His doctrine and practice passed down to the Tung-lin school of the late Ming and through its writings to Japanese Confucians in the Tokugawa period.

110. *Mencius*, IIA, 6; VIA, 6.

111. Okada, *Zazen to seiza*, pp. 76–77.

112. Chang Chiu-ch'eng (Heng-p'u), 1092–1159. A disciple of Yang Shih,[ea] who had studied under the Ch'eng brothers. *Sung-Yüan hsüeh-an* 40.

113. Okada, *Zazen to seiza*, p. 60.

114. *Chin-ssu lu*, 3/2b–3a; Chan, p. 93.

115. *Ibid.*, 3/3a; Chan, p. 93.

116. *Ibid.*, 3/2b; Chan, p. 92.

117. *Ibid.*, 2/10a; Chan, p. 69.

118. *Ibid.*, 2/14a; Chan, p. 84.

119. *Ibid.*, 2/6a; Chan, p. 52.

120. *Ibid.*, 3/2b; Chan, p. 92.

121. Graham, *Two Chinese Philosophers*, p. 78.

122. *Chin-ssu lu*, 3/6a; Chan, p. 103.

123. Chan, *Reflections*, p. 69, citing *Chung-yung huo-wen*,[eb] 20/105b–106a.

124. See Yoshikawa, *Sung Poetry*, pp. 21 ff. There were, however, different views among leading Neo-Confucians on the value of poetry itself. Ch'eng I thought much poetry frivolous and not serious writing, but his view of the beneficial effects of poetry in self-cultivation is expressed in *Chin-ssu lu*, 3/6b; Ch'an, p. 105. An excellent study of *Chu Hsi, the Poet* by Dr. Li Chi of the University of British Columbia, illuminates the tension experienced between the commitment to moral philosophy, on the one hand, and his poetic sensibility and love of nature and art, on the other. Cf. T'oung Pao, 58 (1972), 55–119.

125. Cf. Jen Yu-wen "Ch'en Hsien-chang's Philosophy of the Natural," in *Self and Society*, pp. 53, 58, 83.

126. *Chin-ssu lu*, 4/3b; Chan, p. 133.

127. A useful contribution in this direction is David Mungello's "Neo-Confucianism and wen-jen aesthetic theory," PEW, Vol. XIX, no. 4 (October, 1969), pp. 367 ff.

128. Weber, *Religion of China*, p. 245.
129. Chu Hsi's teacher.
130. Heinrich Busch, "The Tung-lin Academy and Its Political and Philosophical Significance." (Hereafter referred to as Busch, *Tung-lin*), MS, XIV (1949–55), p. 119.
131. *Ibid.*, pp. 124–30.
132. *Ibid.*, p. 125.
133. *Ibid.*, pp. 126–27.
134. *Ibid.*, p. 128.
135. *Ibid.*
136. *Ibid.*, p. 129. A similar experience with both aesthetic and moral dimensions is recorded by Ch'en Hsien-chang and translated in Chang, *Development*, II, 20–21.
137. I use the term "nature mysticism" with some diffidence here. There is a question as to whether nature enters into the actual experience of enlightenment or whether the natural setting merely provides the occasion for an experience that transcends it. That the aesthetic element should be seen as a mere adjunct to the enlightenment experience is the view expressed by Julia Ching in a personal communication to me. She says: "The beautiful nature was only an occasion which helped to give rise to this experience. The experience brought the realization 'the myriad changes are all man's own creations; in reality there is not a thing'; i.e., his mind became quite detached from visible beauty; the peace it acquired implied the experience of a more transcendent beauty. . . . In my opinion the aesthetic component is not an intrinsic part of the experience, but only an occasion giving rise to it."

A full examination of the question is beyond the scope of this paper. I must confine myself to the point most relevant to our inquiry: that the Neo-Confucian view was open to a wide range of experience and that the "orthodoxy" we deal with here laid claim to these as different dimensions of human experience which were not mutually exclusive. Kao could share the nature-mysticism of the Taoist without renouncing his Confucian moral concern, and could even interpret the experience as a renewal of his moral life, as had Chu Hsi and others before Kao. Compare the experience as described by Kao with that of Te-ch'ing (pp. 76, 78, this volume), whose enlightenment followed prolonged concentration to achieve insensibility to his surroundings.
138. *Chu tzu ta ch'üan*, III, 1/1b–2b, cited by Li Chi in *Chu Hsi*.
139. Cf. *MJHA*, I, 1/8, 11, where Wu Yü-pi recounts experiences reflecting several of these aspects.
140. Cf. de Bary, *Self and Society*, pp. 12–24, 57.
141. *Ibid.*, p. 60.
142. *Ibid.*, p. 158.
143. Cf. (Wu) *K'ang-chai hsien-sheng wen-chi*,[ec] preface dated Wan-li 18 (1590), *chüan* 11 (microfilm of copy in National Library of Peking).

144. See paper by Lynn, this volume.
145. Cf. James Cahill, "Confucian Elements in the Theory of Painting," in A. F. Wright, *The Confucian Persuasion* (Stanford, 1960), pp. 115–40; Roderick Whitfield, *In Pursuit of Antiquity; Chinese Paintings of the Ming and Ch'ing Dynasties from the Collection of Mr. and Mrs. Earl Morse* (Princeton University Art Museum [1969]; and Rutland, Vermont: Charles E. Tuttle, 1969), pp. 19–49.
146. *Chin-ssu lu*, 4/2a; Chan, p. 126.
147. *Ibid.*, 4/6a; Chan, p. 144.
148. *MJHA*, II, 7/10.
149. *Ibid.*, IX, 47/53.
150. Joseph Needham, *Science and Civilisation in China*, II (Cambridge, England, 1956), 57.
151. *Ibid.*, p. 67.
152. *Ibid.*, p. 161.
153. *Ibid.*, pp. 162–63.
154. *Ibid.*, p. 493.
155. *Ibid.*, p. 494.
156. *Ibid.*, p. 510.
157. *Ibid.*
158. *Ibid.*, p. 494.
159. Cf. de Bary, *Self and Society*, pp. 22–24, 156, 176–77, 233 n. 114.
160. Shimada Kenji has been concerned about this question but remains, he confesses, unable to solve it. Cf. *Shushigaku to Yōmeigaku*, ed pp. 183–86 for his latest comment.
161. *Hsü fen-shu* ee (Peking, 1959); de Bary, *Self and Society*, p. 212.
162. *Fen-shu* ef (Peking, 1961), 4/159; *Self and Society*, pp. 204–5.
163. *P'o hsieh lun*, eg 1a–b in *Li-chou i-chu hui-k'an*, edited by Hsieh Teng-ch'ang (Shanghai, 1910), XIII.
164. By Chiang Fan in his *Han hsüeh shih-ch'eng chi*. eh
165. Cf. *Self and Society*, p. 4.
166. *I Ching*, Hsi tz'u A (Shanghai: Commercial Press, 1934), I, 40.
167. Cf. Chu Hsi, "Treatise on Jen," ei in Chan, *Source Book*, pp. 593–96.
168. Shimada Kenji, "Mindai shisō no ichi kichō," in *Tōhō gakuhō* ej no. 36 (October, 1964), pp. 580–82.
169. *Ibid.*, p. 586.
170. *Ibid.*
171. *Ibid.*, p. 583; *MJHA*, VII, 34/1–2.
172. Yamanoi Yū, "Min-Shin jidai ni okeru 'ki' no tetsugaku," ek in *Tetsugaku zasshi*, vol. 66 (1951), no. 711; and Shimada Kenji, "Subjective Idealism in Sung and post-Sung China: The All Things are One Theory of Jen," in *Tōhō gakuhō*, el no. 28 (March, 1958), p. 43.
173. Joseph Levenson, "The Abortiveness of Empiricism in Early Ch'ing Thought," in *Confucian China and Its Modern Fate*, I, 4–5.
174. *MJHA*, I, 1/1; X, 50/2.

175. Cf. Sakai Tadao, "Confucianism and Popular Educational Works," in *Self and Society*, pp. 332–35.

176. See the Araki paper, this volume.

177. Cf. C. T. Hsia, "Time and the Human Condition in the Plays of T'ang Hsien-tsu," in *Self and Society*, pp. 249–51.

178. See the Ch'ien paper on Chiao Hung, this volume.

179. In his *Ming wen hai*, *Ming wen an*, the unfinished *Ming shih an*, and contemporary historical works collected in the *Hsing-ch'ao lu*.[em]

180. *MJHA*, I, 1/1–2 (personal preface).

181. On this, see Yü Ying-shih, "Ts'ung Sung-Ming . . ." pp. 27–29, 32.

182. Cf. Jung Chao-tsu, *Ming-tai ssu-hsiang shih*[en] (Taipei, 1966), pp. 278–83, and Yü, "Ts'ung Sung-Ming . . . ," p. 40, n. 4.

183. See the Ch'ien paper, this volume.

184. See the Araki paper, this volume.

185. Cf. his *Ming-i tai-fang lu*,[eo] chü shih, shang, *Wu kuei lou* edition 15a–17a.

186. Discussed by Shimada in his "Subjective Idealism, etc.," in *Tōhō gakuhō*, no. 28, pp. 41, 43, 68; *Shushigaku to Yōmeigaku*, pp. 193–201; de Bary, *Self and Society*, pp. 20–21.

187. *MJHA*, II, 7/10.

188. *Ibid.*, II, 7/8.

189. *Ibid.*, II, 7/9.

190. *Ibid.*, II, 7/11.

191. *MJHA*, IX, 47/34–51; Abe Yoshio, "Nissen shi no shushigaku jō no mondai josetsu," in *Tōyō gakujutsu ronsō*,[ep] no. 3, p. 7; Chang, *Development*, II, 80–87.

192. Cf. Abe Yoshio "Ra Kin-jun," in *Chūgoku no shisōka*.[eq] Compiled by Research Office in Chinese Philosophy (Tokyo University, 1963), pp. 577–78.

193. *MJHA*, IV, 20/66–67; Cf. Busch, *Tung-lin*, pp. 108–17; Shimada, "Ichi kichō," in *Tōhō gakuhō*, no. 36, p. 585.

194. *MJHA*, I, 1/1, preface.

195. *Hsüeh Wen-ch'ing kung tu-shu lu*[er] (TSCC edition), 2/28–30; *MJHA*, II, 7/3–4, 7–11. At that, Hsüeh had to argue the case for the relevance of book learning to moral cultivation, since it was viewed in the Ch'eng-Chu school as sense-knowledge and hence both external and potentially distracting.

196. Cf. Levenson, *Confucian China*, p. 13.

197. *Ibid.*, pp. 13–14.

198. Abe Yoshio, "Ra Kin-jun," and *Nihon Shushigaku to Chōsen*[es] (Tokyo, 1965), pp. 149–238, 489–557.

GLOSSARY

a	悟	aj	西遊記	bs	吳與弼
b	啓蒙	ak	紅樓夢	bt	陳獻章
c	侯外盧，中國早期	al	張載	bu	高攀龍
	啓蒙思想史	am	觀聖賢	bv	東林
d	李贄	an	顏子 (顏回)	bw	顧憲成
e	方以智	ao	仲尼	bx	無極
f	王夫之	ap	呂與叔	by	李侗
g	黃宗羲	aq	韓愈	bz	靜坐說
h	顧炎武	ar	君子	ca	困學記
i	顏元	as	范仲淹	cb	無事
j	戴震	at	歐陽修	cc	無適
k	梁啓超	au	王安石	cd	王艮
l	胡適	av	大改則大治	ce	明道 (程顥)
m	朱熹	aw	杜甫	cf	盧山
n	焦竑	ax	邵雍	cg	賦
o	陳第	ay	同谷	ch	覺
p	泰州	az	爲學	ci	日錄
q	王陽明	ba	靜	cj	前七子後七子
r	王畿	bb	敬	ck	空
s	實學	bc	不動心	cl	虛
t	學問	bd	調息	cm	實
u	見性	be	調息箴	cn	薛瑄
v	石田梅岩	bf	氣	co	羅欽順
w	心學	bg	伽藍	cp	黃道周
x	無心	bh	幾	cq	倪元璐
y	仁者	bi	主靜	cr	雲棲袾宏
z	程顥	bj	居敬	cs	憨山德清
aa	理學	bk	劉宗周	ct	紫柏達觀
ab	周敦頤	bl	體認	cu	藕益智旭
ac	工夫	bm	楠本端山	cv	周汝登
ad	靜坐	bn	學習錄	cw	管志道
ae	坐禪	bo	滿腔子これ惻隱の	cx	諸葛亮
af	近思錄		心	cy	陸贄
ag	道體	bp	體仁	cz	韓琦
ah	呂祖謙	bq	張九成 (橫浦)	da	李綱
ai	水滸傳	br	白鹿洞	db	文天祥

dc	方孝儒	dv	山崎道夫，近思錄	el	中国近世の主觀
dd	明儒學案	dw	伊藤仁齋		唯心論について—
de	生生	dx	吉川幸次郎		萬物一体の仁の
df	仁	dy	朱熹：朱子大全		思想，東方学報
dg	島田虔次	dz	岡田武彦：坐禪と	em	明文海，明文案
dh	性		靜坐		明史案，行朝錄
di	羅汝芳	ea	楊時	en	容肇祖，明代思想
dj	日用	eb	中庸或問		史
dk	湯顯祖	ec	吳康齋先生文集	eo	明夷待訪錄
dl	伊洛淵源錄	ed	朱子學と陽明學	ep	日鮮支の朱子學上
dm	宋元學案	ee	續焚書		の問題序説，東
dn	困知記	ef	焚書		洋學術論叢
do	王時槐(塘南)	eg	破邪論，梨州遺著	eq	羅欽順：中國の思
dp	阿部吉雄		彙刊		想家
dq	貝原益軒	eh	江藩：漢學師承記	er	薛文清公讀書錄
dr	山崎闇齋	ei	仁説	es	阿部吉雄，日本朱
ds	朱子遺書	ej	島田虔次：明代思		子學と朝鮮
dt	柴田實：石田梅岩		想の一基調，東		
	全集		方學報		
du	黃勉齋集	ek	山井湧，明清時代		
			における氣の		
			哲學		
			哲學雜誌		

RICHARD JOHN LYNN *Orthodoxy and*

Enlightenment: Wang Shih-chen's Theory of Poetry

and Its Antecedents

From the latter part of the fifteenth century until the early eighteenth century, there is, in various critical writings on poetry (*shih-hua*),[a] frequent use of the terms "orthodoxy" or "orthodox" (*cheng*)[b] and "enlightenment" or "enlightened" (*wu*).[c] For the most part this happens in the *shih-hua* of some of the so-called Former Seven Masters (*ch'ien-ch'i-tzu*)[d] and Latter Seven Masters (*hou-ch'i-tzu*)[e] and, later in the Ch'ing, in those of Wang Shih-chen [f] (1634–1711) and his immediate followers. In the earlier part of this span of time we are most concerned with the criticism of Li Meng-yang [g] (1473–1529), one of the Former Seven Masters, and a slightly earlier figure—Li Tung-yang [h] (1447–1516). Three of the Latter Seven Masters wrote considerable amounts of poetry criticism— Hsieh Chen [i] (1495–1575), Li P'an-lung [j] (1514–70), and Wang Shih-chen [k] (1526–90). However, Li and Wang seem to have based most of their theories of poetry upon certain key critical concepts stated earlier by Li Tung-yang and Li Meng-yang, and were not particularly original critics of poetry themselves. For our purposes, therefore, we can disregard them and concentrate upon Hsieh Chen and a slightly later figure who is sometimes associated with the Latter Seven Masters—Hu Ying-lin (1551–1602).[1] Of all the Ming critics associated with an "orthodox" school or tradition of poetry, Hsieh Chen and Hu Ying-lin seem to be the most sophisticated and thoughtful theorists, and their theories of poetry appear to be the most balanced and comprehensive. Wang Shih-chen [f] in the Ch'ing is perhaps the last prominent figure associated with this "orthodox" tradition, and his theory of poetry climaxes its whole development—a development which reaches back through all the Ming critics and beyond.

Actually, to understand what "orthodoxy" and "enlightenment" meant to all these critics we have to examine the critical concepts and practices of two earlier figures—Yen Yü,[m] (1180–1235) whose *Ts'ang-lang shih-hua* [n] heavily influenced all of them, and Kao Ping [o] (1350–1423), whose *T'ang-shih p'in-hui* [p] practically attempted to differentiate T'ang poetry according to Yen's "orthodox" views. All the Ming critics and Wang Shih-chen [f] acknowledge their debt to the *Ts'ang-lang shih-hua*; they must have read it very carefully since much of their own criticism is concerned with the same problems and even uses much of the same critical terminology. Yen Yü's influence upon them resulted in three basic features common to their theories of poetry: (1) their identification with an "orthodox" (*cheng*) tradition of poetry which they believed had to be followed to the letter for one to become a master of poetry himself; (2) a belief in poetic "enlightenment" (*wu*) which meant that the enlightened poet achieved perfect intuitive control over the poetic medium; (3) a realization that enlightenment can only come from a thorough assimilation—a complete internalization—of the orthodox tradition. As Yen Yü provided the theory, so Kao Ping supplied the practical guidebook to orthodoxy and all the secrets of enlightened poetry. Inevitably, however, all this led to an inordinate emphasis upon the formal dimensions of poetry and the belief that imitation of past masters constituted the basis of poetic training. Much of Ming and Ch'ing poetry is characterized by excessive formalism and slavish imitation, and the blame for this can be laid ultimately at Yen Yü's door. Countless run-of-the-mill poets learned their craft in the *Ts'ang-lang shih-hua* and the *T'ang-shih p'in-hui*, and their mediocre achievements have done much to discourage modern scholars both from examining the theoretical bases of their poetic activity and from appreciating the few poets among them who are in fact worthy of appreciation.

While many Ming and Ch'ing personalities composed *shih* [q] poetry as a mere social convention, many others took it very seriously. Some of these serious poets (for example, the figures mentioned above) wrote criticism, and their critical remarks sometimes contain statements which express their ideas about the function of poetry—why they wrote poetry and what they expected it to "do" for them. Although the outward signs of the poetry of the Former and Latter Seven Masters and the later Wang Shih-chen [f] might be formalism and imitation, its real significance for them lay elsewhere: all of them, and the best of their followers, looked upon poetry as one important means or medium of self-cultivation (others of this same period regarded painting and calligraphy in much the same light). In formal terms enlightenment (*wu*) meant the achievement of perfect intuitive control over the poetic medium, but in psychological or spiritual terms it meant the attainment of a state of being where subjective self, medium of communication, and objective reality became one. The ultimate aim of self-cultivation was self-transcendency, and in this important aspect poetry as a discipline closely resembles quiet-sitting, mind control, and other activities usually associated with Neo-Confucian self-cultivation proper.[1] It should also be emphasized that poetry did not just provide an objective correlative (in this case linguistic) for the individual's state of self-cultivation—something by which he and others could gauge his spiritual progress. The act of writing poetry *itself* was an act of self-cultivation. Poetry provided the framework or context within which the individual came to grips with himself and his environment. It not only gave him knowledge of self; it also provided him with a means to know the world outside himself—and, perhaps most important, it supplied the link between the two.

We shall see that these poets were committed to words in the sense that they insisted that experience be interpreted in linguistic terms. This very insistence upon words helps us to place the whole phenomenon in the Neo-Confucian camp rather than identifying it with either philosophical Taoism or Ch'an Buddhism—both of which abhorred words as impediments to truth and enlightenment. This tradition of poetry—like the larger sphere of Neo-Confucianism itself—owes much to Ch'an as a source of inspiration (or stimulation), ideas, and terminology, but in the final analysis its ultimate aims lie entirely within the boundaries of Neo-Confucian discipline and aspirations.

We can now turn to a consideration of Yen Yü's *Ts'ang-lang shih-hua*, that mainspring of critical impulse and theoretical direction which so influenced the course of Chinese poetry over the next five hundred years. I have made a selection of passages from it which seem to have most influenced the Former and Latter Seven Masters and Wang Shih-chen and which, as we shall also see, excited such opposition among their adversaries: [2]

For the student of poetry, judgment is the most important thing: his introduction must be correct (*cheng*), and his ambitions must be set high. He takes Han, Wei, Chin, and High T'ang (*sheng*-T'ang)[r] as his teachers, and he does not wish to be someone who lived after the K'ai-yüan [713–41] and the T'ien-pao [742–55] eras. If he yields, he will have the inferior-poetry-devil (*hsia-lieh shih-mo*)[s] enter his bosom—this because he did not set his ambition high. If one has not yet reached the end of his journey, he can increase his efforts, but as soon as he goes off the road, the more he hurries the more he goes astray—this because his introduction was not correct. . . . First one must thoroughly recite the *Ch'u-tz'u*[t] and sing them morning and night so as to make them his basis. When he recites the Nineteen Ancient Poems,[u] the "Yüeh-fu in Four Sections,"[v][3] the five-syllabic poetry of Li Ling and Su Wu[w] and of the Han and the Wei, he must do them all thoroughly. Afterward, he will take up the collected poetry of Li [Po] and Tu [Fu][x] and read them [the poems] in dovetail fashion as people of today study the Classics. Next he will take up comprehensively the famous masters of the High T'ang. Having allowed all this to ferment in his bosom for a long time he will be enlightened spontaneously (*tzu-jan wu-ju*).[y] Although he might not attain the ultimate of study, still he will not go off the correct road.[4]

This passage is reminiscent of certain Neo-Confucian writings:

The Way of the sage is as level as a highway. The trouble with students is that they do not know how to enter it. If they know, they will reach it no matter how far away it is. Are not the Classics the way by which to enter it? . . . I hope you will search for moral principles through the Classics. If you make more and more effort, someday you will see something [the Way] lofty before you. You will be as if you were dancing with your hands and feet without knowing it. Then without further effort you cannot help but keep going.[5]

The general sense of Yen Yü's statement is so close to that of Ch'eng I that one wonders if it is not in some way based upon it. Of course, in Neo-Confucian writings the "great road" or "highway" is a common metaphor for the orthodox tradition of the Confucian school, and it ultimately derives from the *Mencius*: "The way of truth is like a great road. Is it difficult to know? The trouble is that men do not follow it."[6] This metaphor was also not restricted to the Sung Neo-Confucianists; Wang Yang-ming[z] used it some three hundred years later:

When you become familiar with it [innate knowledge], the lack of clarity will vanish of itself. It may be compared to driving a vehicle. You are driving it on a broad highway. . . . You are already on the broad highway itself and will not mistakenly go into sidetracks or crooked paths. Of late, only a few of our like-minded friends in the country have reached this stage of progress. This is good fortune for the Confucian doctrine.[7]

Hsü Ai[aa] (1487–1518) regarded Confucian orthodoxy in the same light and of course considered that his teacher's (Wang Yang-ming) philosophy was its latest true successor:

. . . I gradually realized that his [Wang's] teachings are to be applied to one's life and to be concretely demonstrated, and then I came to believe that they represent the direct heritage of the Confucian school, and that all the rest is but byways, small paths, and dead ends . . . after I thought them over long enough, I was so happy that I danced with my hands and feet.[8]

All these statements suggest that enlightenment (in poetry and in moral truth) depends upon the assimilation of an orthodox tradition, and the orthodox tradition is represented as a broad highway. Heterodoxy, as Wang Yang-ming and Hsü Ai pointed out, is nothing other than "sidetracks" and "dead ends," or, as Yen Yü phrased it:

In the tradition of the Ch'anists there is a Lesser and a Greater Vehicle (*sheng yu ta hsiao*),[ab] there is a Southern and a Northern School (*tsung yu nan pei*),[ac] and there is a heterodox and an orthodox Way (*tao yu hsieh cheng*).[ad] The student must follow the very highest Vehicle, embody the Correct Dharma Eye (*cheng-fa-yen*),[ae] and experience enlightenment of the first order (*wu ti-i i*).[af] If it is Lesser Vehicle Ch'an, the attainment of the Śrāvaka [ag] or Pratyeka,[ah] it is never orthodox (*cheng*). Discussing poetry is like discussing Ch'an. The poetry of the Han, Wei, Chin, and the High T'ang is enlightenment of the first order. Poetry of after the Ta-li [766–79] era is Lesser Vehicle Ch'an and has already fallen into enlightenment of the second order (*ti-erh i*).[ai] The poetry of the Late T'ang is Śrāvaka or Pratyeka. He who studies the poetry of the Han, Wei, Chin, and High T'ang is an adherent of the Lin-chi [aj] School, and he who studies post-Ta-li era poetry is an adherent of the Ts'ao-tung [ak] School. . . . If one tries to take up the poetry of the Chin and the Sung and thoroughly identify with it, then tries to take up the poetry of the Southern and Northern Dynasties and thoroughly identify with it, then tries to take up the poetry of Shen [Ch'üan-ch'i],[al] Sung [Chih-wen],[am] Wang [Po],[an] Yang [Chiung],[ao] Lu [Chao-lin],[ap] and Lo [Pin-wang] [aq] and thoroughly identify with it, then tries to take up the poetry of the masters of the K'ai-yüan and T'ien-pao eras and thoroughly identify with it, then especially tries to take up the poetry of Li [Po] and Tu [Fu] and thoroughly identify with it, then tries to take up the poetry of the Ten Talents of the Ta-li Era [ar] and thoroughly identify with it, then tries to take up the poetry of the Yüan-ho era [806–820] and thoroughly identify with it, then tries to take up the poetry of all the masters of the Late T'ang and thoroughly identify with it, and finally tries to take up the poetry of Su [Shih] [as] and Huang [T'ing-chien],[at] of the present dynasty, and of their followers and thoroughly identify with it—then truly what is right and what is wrong will not be able to remain hidden. If there is still any poetry which is not seen among all of these, then it is wild-fox heterodoxy (*yeh-hu wai-tao*) [au] which obscures true knowledge. One can not save himself from it and will never reach enlightenment.[9]

Many critics of Yen Yü have accused him of confusing poetry with Ch'an—and with a Ch'an that he did not really understand. Ch'ien

Ch'ien-i [av] (1582–1664), for instance, dismissed Yen as someone who possessed only "half-baked intelligence" [aw] and who thoroughly misunderstood Ch'an, [10] and Feng Pan [ax] (1614–71) had this to say about him: "Ts'ang-lang said that to use Ch'an as a metaphor for poetry was precise and illuminating. However, I regard this as mere unintelligibility and confused nonsense." [11] Then Ch'ien and Feng go on to say that Ch'an is an inappropriate metaphor for poetry since poetry deals with words and personal emotion and Ch'an lies beyond both. They are so dissimilar that only harm will result if one tries to understand one in terms of the other. [12] Also, the charge has been leveled at Yen that it is improper for a Confucian gentleman to talk about Buddhism anyway—and to introduce Ch'an into a discussion of serious literary art is really unthinkable. [13] Of course this all misses the point. Yen never said that poetry was Ch'an or Ch'an poetry. He merely borrowed the Ch'an tradition (as he, a layman, saw it) as an analogy for the tradition of poetry, as he said: "Therefore, I have casually fixed the general scope of poetry and have borrowed Ch'an as an analogy. Having made a careful analysis, from the Han and the Wei on, I decisively say that we must take High T'ang as law (or *dharma*) (*fa*)" [ay] [14]

The idea persisted, however, that Yen Yü tried to identify poetry with Ch'an and that the theory of poetry espoused in the *Ts'ang-lang shih-hua* was based upon some notion of Ch'an mysticism. [15] Actually, Yen was probably no more committed to Ch'an than any Neo-Confucian philosopher who used Ch'an terminology in his dissertations (and probably less, considering how little he knew about the historical Ch'an tradition), and we should, I think, take his explanation at face value—he was making an analogy between poetry and Ch'an and used Ch'an terminology for the sake of convenience. This also holds true for the other critics with whom we shall be dealing later on; their critical writings are often filled with Ch'an terminology and concepts, but we should not confuse any of them with Ch'an proper.

Orthodoxy, then, is orthodoxy, and the student of poetry bears the same kind of relation to the tradition of poetry as the student of Ch'an bears to the Ch'an tradition, or, for that matter, the aspiring sage bears to the Confucian orthodox tradition. The student is introduced to what is proper or correct (*cheng*), he assimilates it all, and then with practice he hopefully achieves spontaneous control over it—enlightenment. Above all, however, study for the student of poetry means imitation of correct or orthodox models, and success means a complete identification with them: "There is no need to argue about what is right and what is wrong in poetry. All one has to do is take his own poetry and place it among the poetry of the ancients. If, upon showing it to a connoisseur he is unable to notice that it is any different, one is then a true man of antiquity."[16] We saw how Yen Yü declared that the poetry of the High T'ang was "law." In this he meant that it was the supremely proper model for the student to emulate. Although the student of poetry had to internalize all stages of the poetic tradition in order to attain enlightenment, in addition he had to aspire to the "very highest Vehicle" and have enlightenment of "the first order." Yen, in fact, believed that there existed different levels or depths in poetry just as in Ch'an:

However, there are different depths and different scopes of enlightenment (*wu*). There is thoroughly penetrating enlightenment (*t'ou-ch'e chih wu*),[az] and there is enlightenment which only reaches partial understanding (*i-chih pan-chieh chih wu*).[ba] The Han and the Wei are indeed supreme! They did not depend upon enlightenment at all! Those masters from Hsieh Ling-yün [bb] down to the High T'ang had thoroughly penetrating enlightenment. Although there were also others who achieved enlightenment, it was not that of the first order.[17]

One statement in the above passage is particularly intriguing: The Han and the Wei did not "depend upon enlightenment at all!" Yen elaborates upon this elsewhere:

People of the Southern Dynasties [420–587] excelled at phraseology (*tz'u*) [bc] but were weak in reason (*li*).[bd] People of our present dynasty [i.e., the Sung] excel in reason but are weak in idea (*i*) [be] and inspiration (*hsing*).[bf] The people of the T'ang excelled at idea and inspiration, and reason was inherently there. However, in the poetry of the Han and the Wei no outer sign of phraseology, reason, idea, or inspiration can be found.[18]

The poetry of the Han and the Wei is then beyond craft since it is thoroughly spontaneous and exhibits no sign of conscious effort. As in perfect enlightenment in Ch'an, these poets were able to eliminate all distinctions between themselves as subjects and the topics of their poetry as objects, and they also became one with the medium of expression. They did not "depend upon enlightenment at all" because in their perfectly naive and unself-conscious state they were enlightened by nature and did not have to go through any training or discipline to achieve it.

The poetry of Hsieh Ling-yün down to the poetry of the masters of the High T'ang, on the other hand, at best only achieves "thoroughly penetrating enlightenment," and as such is of lower quality. Even though some of these later poets, Li Po and Tu Fu for instance, were able to transcend self-conscious craft, they still had to pass through a stage of training before they were able to *unlearn* all the rules of conscious poetic craft. By the thorough internalization of the rules they were finally able to approach the perfectly naive and unself-conscious poetry of the Han and the Wei. However, they never quite reached it since they had to *depend* upon enlightenment. The poetry of the Han and the Wei is then beyond reach of all later emulators since the Chinese poetic tradition developed in such a way that rules and conventions made learning how to write poetry a formally conscious affair. The best that a student could hope to achieve is "thoroughly penetrating enlightenment"—a suppression of self-conscious design and a recovery, at least to some extent, of naive spontaneity.

Although the poetry of the Han and the Wei was beyond the reach of the student, the poetry of the High T'ang was not, and it represented the supreme model for him to follow. Li Po and Tu Fu were the best of the High T'ang, but Tu Fu was the most worthy of study: "In poetic method (*shih-fa*) [bg] Shao-ling [Tu Fu] is like Sun [Wu] [bh] and Wu [Ch'i], [bi] and T'ai-pai [Li Po] is like Li Kuang. [bj] Shao-ling resembles a teacher who goes by the rules." [19] Sun Wu and Wu Ch'i, of the Spring and Autumn and Warring States eras respectively, were famous military strategists and generals who gained their victories through the careful application of rules and procedures. Li Kuang, on the other hand, won more than seventy victories over the Hsiung-nu, at the beginning of the Han, by his brilliant and unconventional actions conceived of "on the spot." Yen Yü here declares that if one carefully studies the poetry of Tu Fu, he will be able to see how it succeeds, but that the poetry of Li Po is beyond rational analysis—and so an inappropriate model to try to emulate. This is very much like what Ch'eng Hao [bk] advised the student of sagehood: "Mencius' natural endowment is on a very high level. For students who want to learn from him, there is nothing to hold on to. They should learn from Yen Tzu. As a way to enter sagehood, his learning is nearer at hand and there are in it definite places for the student to make his effort." [20] However, there is another good reason to make Tu Fu the best model to study: "The poetry of Shao-ling finds its rules and regulations in the Han and the Wei and obtains its materials from the Six Dynasties. As for the marvelousness which he himself achieves, this is what earlier generations have called the synthesis of the great achievements of others." [21] Tu Fu, as the great synthesizer, sums up the best that the tradition has to offer, and so makes the ideal teacher.

Yen Yü describes "thoroughly penetrating enlightenment" in this manner:

There are three stages in the study of poetry: At first one does not know good from bad and writes one thing after another as quickly as his brush will go. Next he is ashamed and begins to feel timid; it is extremely difficult to write then. But when one is thoroughly penetrating (*t'ou-ch'e*) [bl] then, in an all encompassing fashion, he trusts his hand to do as it pleases, and everything goes smoothly. [22]

This is enlightenment of "the first order," and only Li Po and Tu Fu had ever achieved it. Nevertheless, this is still the goal for which all poets should strive. However, the student must make his way to enlightenment through one who has become enlightened (Tu Fu) and should not attempt to emulate those poets who never had to rely upon enlightenment at all (poets of the Han and the Wei). The same kind of distinction existed in the tradition of Confucian sagehood. Ch'eng Hao once remarked: "Yao and Shun were beyond comparison. When it came to T'ang and Wu, they were different. Mencius said that [Yao and Shun] 'were what they were by nature' whereas [T'ang and Wu] 'returned to their nature.' . . . We know therefore that Yao and Shun were born with the knowledge [of Virtue], whereas T'ang and Wu learned and acquired the ability to practice it." [23] After Yao and Shun, only King Wen and Confucius were sages by nature. All the rest, from Yen Tzu and Mencius on down, had to learn sagehood, or, as Ch'eng Hao put it: "Chung-ni [Confucius] left no trace; Yen Tzu left a small amount. In Mencius, the traces are clearly visible." [24] Chu Hsi [bm] in his commentary on this passage observed: "Compared with Confucius, Yen Tzu was still conscious of his good qualities and his labor. But in Confucius, there was no trace [of this self-consciousness] to be seen." [25] Therefore, just as the student of sagehood could only aspire to the perfection of the sage-kings and Confucius through Yen Tzu and Mencius, so the student of poetry could only aspire to the perfection of the poets of the Han and the Wei through Tu Fu and Li Po. Yen Yü admitted that he used Ch'an as an analogy for poetry; he could have said just as much for Neo-Confucianism.

Yen Yü, in his *Ts'ang-lang shih-hua*, always spoke of the orthodox

tradition of poetry in rather general terms and never clearly differentiated
T'ang poetry into all its component parts. Although he did distinguish between the High T'ang, Middle (post-Ta-li) T'ang, and Late T'ang, he did
not say anything about the Early T'ang or how poets other than Tu Fu or
Li Po ought to be ranked on the ladder of enlightenment. Kao Ping's
collection of T'ang poetry, the *T'ang-shih p'in-hui*, attempted to supplement these deficiencies and to present the student of poetry with a convenient and practical guide to enlightenment. Kao divided T'ang poetry in
the following way. First he divided it into seven categories: five-syllabic
ancient verse (*ku-shih*),[bn] five-syllabic regulated verse (*lü-shih*),[bo] five-
syllabic quatrains (*chüeh-chü*),[bp] five-syllabic "regulated verses in a row"
(*p'ai-lü*),[bq] seven-syllabic quatrains, seven-syllabic regulated verse, and
seven syllabic ancient verse. Then he subdivided these categories chronologically according to this sequence: Early T'ang,[br] the "Orthodox
Beginning" (*cheng-shih*); [bs] High T'ang—divided among "Orthodox Patriarchs" (*cheng-tsung*),[bt] "Great Masters" (*ta-chia*),[bu] "Famous Masters"
(*ming-chia*),[bv] and "Assistants" (*yü-i*); [bw] Middle T'ang,[bx] the "Immediate
Successors" (*chieh-wu*); [by] and Late T'ang [bz]—divided between "Orthodox
Innovation" (*cheng-pien*) [ca] and "Lingering Echoes" (*yü-hsiang*).[cb] [26] Kao
meant his collection of T'ang poetry to be the literal manifestation of the
concept of poetic orthodoxy expounded by Yen Yü. In the *T'ang-shih
p'in-hui*, he put it this way: "If the student would enter the gate and establish his ambition, he can obtain what is orthodox from this." [27] This,
of course, is a close paraphrase of the opening lines of the *Ts'ang-lang
shih-hua*,[28] and it is obvious that Kao's collection of poetry is the anthology he thought Yen Yü would have made had he ever been so inclined.

So far we have discussed Yen Yü's theory of enlightenment in terms of
intuitive control over the poetic medium. Now we can turn to a consideration of its implications for psychological or spiritual self-cultivation.
Perhaps the most significant passage in the *Ts'ang-lang shih-hua* which
deals with this is the following:

The people of the High T'ang were only concerned with inspired interest (*hsing-
ch'ü*).[cc] They were antelopes who hung by their horns leaving no trace by which
they could be found.[29] Their marvelousness (*miao-ch'u*) [cd] lies in being as transparent as crystal (*t'ou-ch'e ling-lung*) [ce] and being free from blocking (*ts'ou-
p'o*).[cf] [30] Like a sound in the void, color in appearances, like the moon reflected
in water or an image in a mirror—their words come to an end, but their ideas (*i*)

are limitless. Modern writers make bizarre interpretations. Consequently they consider language to be poetry, talent and learning to be poetry, or disquisitions to be poetry. They certainly are not unskillful, but their poetry will not be up to the poetry of the ancients. . . . Moreover their writings involve much working over of allusions, and they do not concern themselves with inspired atmosphere (*hsing-chih*).^{cg} [31]

"Inspired interest" and "inspired atmosphere" probably refer to the same thing—an inspired awareness of the ultimate reality of things. Since this awareness transcends both sense and reason, the kind of poetic language required to render it into words must have the capacity of limitless suggestion, connotation, and implication. The passage seems to indicate a cognitive function for poetry—poetry defined as a means by which one knows, or gains an intuitive awareness of, things as they really are. Immediately preceding this passage is the statement:

Poetry is concerned with a different kind of talent, which is not concerned with books; it involves a different kind of meaning, which is not concerned with principles. [32] However, if one does not widely read books and thoroughly investigate the principles of things (*to ch'iung li*),^{ch} he will not be able to reach its [poetry's] ultimate meaning (chih).^{ci} That which has been called "don't travel on the road of principles, don't fall into the fish trap of words" [33] is the superior way. [34]

The above passages strongly suggest that, while book learning and rational investigation are prerequisites for poetry, poetry itself is concerned with intuitive apprehension—something that lies beyond words. Words themselves are connotative signs which, while limited entities in their own right, have the potential to suggest limitless ideas. They have value, but they are not ends in themselves. Although we can discern strong influence from Ch'an here, Neo-Confucian writings also advised the student to have a balanced appreciation of the value and limitation of words: "Among students, those who do not rigidly adhere to the literal meanings of words turn away from them completely, while those who understand the literal meanings of words adhere to them so rigidly that their minds become blocked. . . . In reading books, we should not rigidly stick to one meaning because the words are the same or similar. Otherwise every word will be a hindrance." [35] This much is clear, but we still have to determine what the object of this verbalized intuitive apprehension is—to what, after all, is it directed, and what does it really mean?

The key to this problem lies, I think, in unraveling what Yen Yü meant by "like a sound in the void, color in appearances, like the moon reflected in water or an image in a mirror." This has puzzled many later commentators and actually antagonized some.[36] At first glance it merely looks like a string of metaphors for the limitless capacity of verbal connotation and suggestion, all dressed up in fanciful, if not mystical, imagery. However, it means more than that, and if we turn to texts where similar imagery is employed, the meaning becomes clear. Probably the first mention of the mirror image occurs in the *Chuang Tzu*: "The mind of the perfect man is like a mirror. It does not lean forward or backward in its response to things. It responds to things but conceals nothing of its own. Therefore it is able to deal with things without injury to [its reality]." [37] Perfect knowledge, then, occurs when the mind reflects things as they are—when one is able to completely eliminate all distinctions between self and object, knower and known, and "look" at things from their point of view. Water functions in the same way as a mirror, and the *Chuang Tzu* also compares it to the mind of the sage: "When water is tranquil, its clearness reflects even the beard and the eyebrows. It remains definitely level, and master carpenters take it as their model. If water is clear when it is tranquil, how much more so is the spirit? When the mind of the sage is tranquil, it becomes the mirror of the universe and the reflection of all things." [38]

Tranquillity of mind does not mean mindless unconsciousness but rather a state in which personal elements are missing. The mind takes things as they are, not as it wishes them to be. It operates passively, without the demands of preconception and prejudice or any other manifestation of ego. Both W. T. Chan and P. Demiéville have pointed out that these passages with their mirror and water metaphors had considerable influence upon Neo-Confucianism as well as Ch'an,[39] and probably both schools of thought contributed to the passage in question in the *Ts'ang-lang shih-hua*. However, I think that Yen Yü also had another passage in mind from the *Chuang Tzu*:

Men of the world who value the Way all turn to books. But books are nothing more than words. Words have value; what is of value in words is meaning. Meaning has something it is pursuing, but the thing it is pursuing cannot be put into words and handed down. . . . What you can look at and see are forms and colors; what you can listen to and hear are names and sounds. What a pity!—that the men of the world should suppose that form and color, name and sound, are sufficient to convey the truth of a thing.[40]

In effect, Yen Yü accepts the challenge of the *Chuang Tzu* and declares
that what words, through meaning, are pursuing can convey the truth of
a thing. He says that the poets of the High T'ang wrote poetry which is
like a sound in the air or color in appearances, like water or a mirror
which reflects things as they really are. In Yen's view, this poetry of
"thoroughly penetrating enlightenment" or "enlightenment of the first
order" represents the verbal equivalent, the objective correlative, of the
mind of the perfect man, the tranquil mind of the sage, and these great
poets used their poetry as a means to perfect knowledge and self.

Of course, it is rather unlikely that Yen Yü derived this view of poetry
and sagehood solely from a firsthand reading of the *Chuang Tzu*. Undoubtedly he was also aware of passages in contemporary Neo-Confucian
texts which treat sagehood in similar terms—though nowhere in these
texts does there occur even the slightest precedent for Yen's extravagant
claims for poetry itself.[41] A brief survey of occurrences of the water/mir-
ror = mind of the sage metaphor in Sung and post-Sung Neo-Confucian
writings might be in order at this point since so much of the general
theory of poetry of the Former and Latter Seven Masters and the Ch'ing
Wang Shih-chen depends upon it. Reference to Sung occurrences is
especially appropriate because Yen Yü may have been directly influenced
by them, and Ming occurrences are worthy of our attention because we
should be aware of the persistence of this metaphor into Ming times,
when critics such as Hsieh Chen and Hu Ying-lin used it in their *shih-
hua*. By this time it seems to have become a fairly common figure of
speech since it turns up in the writings of other later Ming figures as
well—for example, Wang Chi [cj] (1498–1583) and Li Chih [ck] (1527–
1602).[42] However, we should not insist that these Ming critics and the
Ch'ing Dynasty Wang Shih-chen [f] were directly influenced by Wang
Yang-ming and his later followers in this regard.[43] It is more likely that
they had the Sung Neo-Confucians in mind since they all used the metaphor with an accurate sense of its contextual meaning as it occurs in such
writings as those which are preserved in the *Chin-ssu lu*.

Ch'eng Hao uses the mirror metaphor to help define the mind as agent
of response to the external world:

Everyone's nature is obscured in some way and as a consequence he cannot
follow the Way. In general the trouble lies in the resort to selfishness and the exercise of cunning. Being selfish, one cannot take purposive action to respond to

things, and being cunning, one cannot be at home with enlightenment. For a mind that hates external things to seek illumination in a mind where nothing exists is to look for a reflection on the back of a mirror.[44]

Neo-Confucianism did not deny the existence and value of external things, but it did advocate that one should not attach himself to things through selfishness and cunning.[45] If the mind is tranquil and calm, it is in a state of selflessness and can reflect the true nature of reality as though it were still water: "Someone said, 'Concentration on one thing means complete singleness of mind.' Vacuity in tranquility means that the mind is comparable to a clear mirror or still water, without an iota of selfish desire in it." [46] "Brilliance and intelligence result if the mind is tranquil and calm. Still water can reflect, but running water cannot. The principle is the same." [47] However, for the mirror of the mind to be clear, it must be polished: "The mind is like a mirror and seriousness is like polishing. When the mirror is polished, the dust will be removed and brightness will grow. When the mind becomes serious, human selfish desires will disappear and the Principle of Nature will become brilliant." [48] With the rise of Wang Yang-ming's School of Mind, the mirror-of-the-mind image begins to play an even more central role; in Wang's Ch'uan-hsi lu,[cl] for instance, no less than five lengthy passages are concerned with it.[49] This is to be expected since the focal point of his whole philosophy is the cultivation (polishing) of the mind as repository of Universal Principle. For Wang, the innate knowledge (liang-chih) [cm] which resides in the mind is the key to wisdom and sagehood:

The mind of the sage is like a clear mirror. Since it is all clarity, it responds to all stimuli as they come and reflects everything. . . . The only fear is that the mirror is not clear, not that it is incapable of reflecting a thing as it comes. The study of changing conditions and events is to be done at the time of response. However, a student must be engaged in brightening up the mirror. He should worry only about his mind's not being clear, and not about the inability to respond to all changing conditions.[50]
    . . . innate knowledge always knows and always shines. Always knowing and shining, it is like a suspended brilliant mirror. As things appear before it, none can conceal its beauty or ugliness.[51]

Hsü Ai (1487–1518) went so far as to say that the essential difference between the ordinary man and the sage is that the mind of the ordinary man is like a dull mirror, where as the mind of the sage like a clear mirror.[52]

Enlightenment for the Ming Neo-Confucian Wang Chi meant a recovery of the original substance of the mind (*pen-hsin*),[cn] and here, in a passage which in parts is strikingly reminiscent of Yen Yü's discussion of the marvelousness of the poets of the High T'ang,[53] he explains how difficult enlightenment is:

If we seek it apart from being, we will sink into emptiness. On the other hand, if we attempt to cultivate it through being, we will fall into relativism. It is somewhere between being and Nothing and therefore difficult to pinpoint. It is like the trace of a bird flying in the air or the moon in water. It appears to exist and at the same time it appears not to exist. . . . The original substance is empty. There are no definite steps or tracks to follow.[54]

The mirror-of-the-mind image also occurs in the writings of the late Ming philosopher Li Chih, where it is used to symbolize innate knowledge (*liang-chih*), but here Li draws upon the Mahāyāna Buddhist idea of perfect, undifferentiated consciousness, as well as upon Wang Yang-ming's idea of perfect, intuitive moral wisdom: "All men possess the mirror of Great Perfect Wisdom (*ta-yüan-ching chih*),[co] which is the 'illustrious virtue' of the *Great Learning* shining within. It is one with Heaven above and earth beneath, and with thousands of sages and worthies in between. They do not have more of it nor I less." [55] Li Chih was indicative of a general syncretic movement in thought toward the end of the Ming which attempted to reconcile various aspects of Buddhism and the Neo-Confucianism of the School of Wang Yang-ming.

None of the Ming critics with whom we are dealing here nor the Ch'ing Wang Shih-chen [f] were professional philosophers, so we do not know exactly what their attitudes, as individuals, were to all this. Although their critical writings are filled with Buddhist terms and concepts, still the basic drift of their arguments seems to be Neo-Confucian. It is impossible, however, to ascertain the exact proportion of their relative commitments to the Ch'eng-Chu and Wang Yang-ming schools. My general impression is that they were, as a group, strongly oriented toward the Ch'eng-Chu school. Their basic commitment to the internalization of (or identification with) a vast tradition of poetry suggests a parallel to the Ch'eng-Chu commitment to large-scale book learning. To put it in W. T. de Bary's terms, they accepted the "great burden of culture" which had accumulated by Ming times, and they firmly rejected any shortcut to enlightenment, poetic or otherwise.[56] As educated, thoughtful men they were undoubtedly aware of the main features of Wang Yang-ming's philosophy. While they surely rejected the extreme individualism of Wang's followers, they may well have been attracted to his concept of innate knowledge since intuition—that is, intuitive response and intuitive control—plays such an important parallel role in their own critical thinking. This is getting us into the realm of speculation, however, and we should now turn to a direct consideration of the critics in question and let them speak for themselves.

Li Tung-yang (1447–1516) was the first Ming critic to discuss poetry largely in terms of formal features and sound qualities, and as such he sets a whole "formalistic" tone for much of the rest of Ming criticism. The following passage is typical of his interests and his terminology:

In writing poetry, one must have a perfect eye and one must have a perfect ear. The eye is concerned with form, the ear with sound.[57] If, when you hear the zither stop, you know which string it ended on, you have a perfect ear. If you can distinguish among five different-colored threads out in the moonlight from inside your window, you have a perfect eye. . . . Try to take some poems which you have never seen, and if you can tell the time of their ko-tiao [cp] and not miss one out of ten, you then are someone who understands poetry.[58]

Here the term ko-tiao seems to designate both formal features (ko) and sound qualities (tiao), and as such could be translated as "formal style"— the sum total of the linguistic dimensions of poetry.[59] In fact, as far as Li Tung-yang is concerned, form and sound are the only things which distinguish poetry from prose.[60]

Li Meng-yang (1473–1529) was a great advocate of imitation as the way to become a master of poetry, and, like Yen Yü, he thought that Tu Fu made the best model:

In writing poetry, one must imitate Tu Fu. His poetry is like a perfect circle that can dispense with the compasses, or a perfect square that can dispense with the rulers.[61]

Words must have methods and rules before they can fit with musical laws, just as circles and squares must fit with compasses and rulers. The ancients used rules, which were not invented by them but actually created by Nature. Now when we imitate the ancients, we are not imitating them but really imitating the natural laws of things.[62]

The Ming-shih [cq] attributes to Li Meng-yang the famous slogan: "Prose must be Ch'in or Han, and poetry must be High T'ang—anything outside this is not worth talking about." [63] This is very much like what Yen Yü said: ". . . we must take High T'ang as law" and "if there is still any poetry which is not seen among all of these, then it is wild-fox heterodoxy." [64] The orthodox masters, especially Tu Fu, realized in their poetry the very truth of the workings of Nature itself. Therefore, imitation of them is not only justifiable—it is absolutely necessary. [65] However, these rules exist in order to be transcended. Tu Fu's poetry is perfect because, although composed according to rules, it looks as if it had completely dispensed with them ("like a perfect circle that can dispense with the compasses"). Here, very clearly, is the idea that intuitive control over the poetic medium derives from a complete assimilation of the orthodox poetic tradition, rules and all.

Hsieh Chen (1495–1575) was the eldest of the Latter Seven Masters. He left behind a considerable amount of poetry criticism which was collected together as the *Ssu-ming shih-hua* [cr] in four *chüan*. Hsieh's criticism abounds in Ch'an terminology, and in many places his remarks seem to be direct commentaries or elaborations on Yen Yü's *Ts'ang-lang shih-hua*. For instance:

In writing poetry, there are those who specialize in using learning and pile it up, and there are those who do not use learning and are level and smooth. These two approaches signify the difference between enlightenment (*wu*) and nonenlightenment. Only intuition (*shen-hui*) [cs] can determine what should be taken and what should be discarded—thus enabling one to hasten along the great highway and to avoid side paths. . . . This means that one should avoid specializing in learning, but it is not something which someone who has no learning can achieve. [66]

The ancients' writing of poetry is analogous to walking upon the great highway to Ch'ang-an and not going off on side paths. They considered orthodoxy (*cheng*) as the most important thing and so reached everywhere in the world without the slightest hindrance. Men such as T'ai-pai [Li Po] and Tzu-mei [Tu Fu] both moved with great strides—differing only in that [Li] was transcendently free and [Tu] was concentrated and intense. We can formulate rules for Tzu-mei, but it has never been easy to do so for T'ai-pai. [67]

Again we have the formula: internalization of the orthodox poetic tradition via its greatest master(s) = poetic enlightenment (intuitive control). The idea of intuitive control occurs throughout Hsieh's writings [68] and was obviously a cornerstone of his theory of poetry. However, the key to poetic excellence is still imitation:

We value what lies between being the same [as the past masters] and being different. If one is the same, [his poetry] is too familiar, but if it is different, it will be too strange. These two things seem easy but actually they are difficult. One holds it in his hand and concentrates on it in his mind. If it is so secure that he cannot remove it, he will be able to be near but not too familiar, far but not too strange. Only those of transcendent enlightenment (*ch'ao-wu-che*) [ct] attain this.[69]

One, therefore, "learns" enlightenment through imitation of appropriate models—models which represent enlightenment achieved in their own right.

So far this has all been concerned with intuitive control of the formal poetic medium, but, unlike Li Tung-yang and Li Meng-yang, Hsieh Chen balances his theory of poetry with superformal considerations. Hsieh had a great deal to say about the relationship between self-expression and cognition of the external world; he saw poetry as the fusion of internal emotion or sensibility (*ch'ing*) [cu] with external scene (*ching*): [cv]

> The writing of poetry is based upon emotion and scene. Each by itself is incomplete, and the two do not conflict. . . . Some emotions and scenes differ and some correspond. Some descriptions are easy and some are difficult. Poetry has these two essential features; nothing is more important. One looks and [his impression] is the same as that which is external to him. He experiences emotion and [the scene] is different from that which is inside him. He must then exert his strength and make what is internal and what is external into something which seems to be the same thing. There must be no discrepancy between what leaves and what enters his mind. Scene is the go-between of poetry, and emotion is its embryo—they fuse and become poems.[70]
>
> Ten thousand scenes and the seven emotions fuse when one climbs up high and looks into the distance. If you set up a group of mirrors before your face, every reflection will be true—sadness or happiness will not present two different appearances. Whether from the side or from straight on, there will be only one mind [behind the face]. From the side you will get only half of it, and from straight on you will get all of it. The mirror is like the mind, and light is like the spirit (*shen*).[cw] When thought (*ssu*) [cx] enters infinity (*ju yao-ming*),[cy] there is no I (*wo*),[cz] no things (*wu*).[da] This is indeed the magical power of poetry![71]

The mind of the sage and the mind of the master poet are like mirrors—perfect mirrors which reflect reality as it is. In doing this, the subjective self fuses with objective reality and they become one, and the poetry which results is the scene intuitively grasped by the poet and charged with his emotions and sensibilities.

Hu Ying-lin (1551–1602) was greatly influenced by both Yen Yü and Li Meng-yang:

> From those who have, after the Han and the T'ang, discussed poetry, I have obtained the word enlightenment (*wu*) from Yen Yü-ch'ing [Yen Yü] of the Sung

and the word law *(fa)* from Li Hsien-chi [Li Meng-yang] of the Ming. These two words have constituted the great pivot of the realm of poetry for a thousand ages. One cannot emphasize the one and disregard the other. To have law without enlightenment is to be like a young novice monk fettered by the rules, but enlightenment which does not derive from law is the wild fox of heterodoxy.[72]

The student of poetry must *transcend* the rules of orthodoxy, not disregard them and go off on his own. Here, in a nutshell, Hu presents the exact relationship between orthodoxy and enlightenment. However, his debt to Yen Yü was particularly great, as these two passages testify:

> The great essentials of writing poetry do not go beyond two principles: form and sound *(t'i-ko sheng-tiao)* [db] and inspired imagery and personal tone *(hsing-hsiang feng-shen).*[dc] Form and sound have rules which can be followed, but inspired imagery and personal tone have no methods which can be learned. Therefore the poet tries to make his structure *(t'i)* correct *(cheng)* and his form *(ko)* lofty, his sound *(sheng)* vigorous and his tone pattern *(tiao)* rich. After a long time of accumulated practice his concentrated efforts will undergo a complete transformation and formal features will be metamorphosed. Inspired imagery and personal tone will become spontaneously transcendent. It is analogous to flowers seen in a mirror or the moon seen reflected in water: form and sound are the mirror and the water, and inspired imagery and personal tone are the flowers and the moon. The water must be clear and the mirror bright—only then can the flowers and the moon present their true likenesses. How could we ever hope to see them contained in dingy mirrors or murky water? Therefore law comes first and enlightenment must not be forced.[73]
>
> Mr. Yen uses Ch'an as a metaphor for poetry—how excellent! In Ch'an, once one has experienced enlightenment, the myriad rules all become void, and even banging and bawling and shouting in anger become the most proper principles. In poetry, once one has experienced enlightenment, he mystically comprehends *(ming-hui)* [dd] the myriad images of objective existence, and his moans and sighs, made in response to stimuli, are spontaneous and real.[74]

Until now, in the Neo-Confucian texts and in the writings of Yen Yü and Hsieh Chen, mirrors and water have always been used as symbols for the mind. Here, however, Hu Ying-lin seems to say that they should be regarded as symbols for the medium of communication or expression of mind. Like mirrors or water the poetic medium (form and sound) must clearly (i.e., perfectly) reflect both the poet's inner world of emotions and sensibilities and his outer world of perception and cognition. *Feng-shen* ("personal tone") represents the sum aggregate of this inner world, and *hsing-hsiang* ("inspired imagery") represents the outer. Hsieh Chen called the inner world "emotion" *(ch'ing)* and the outer world "scene" *(ching)*, but he and Hu seem to have had the same basic view of poetry—poems are the fusions of the inner psychological reality of the poet and his inspired awareness of the outer world. However, I think we can say that form and sound do not constitute just a medium of communication. The capacity of mirrors and water to reflect *perfectly* implies a complete, perfect identification of mind or consciousness (the sum total of the inner and outer worlds) with its verbal equivalent. In other words, the mind can only come to know itself through verbal articulation, and consciousness needs the linguistic medium of poetry for true, complete realization.[75] This leads to a further implication: Hu must have regarded poetry as a central means of self-cultivation—perhaps the only means. If the mind can only know itself through poetry, the study of poetry—that assimilation of poetic "law"—means much more than the "mere" acquisition of formal poetic skill; it means, in effect, the acquisition of the means of self-realization—sagehood itself.

We must remember that one basic attribute of the sage is his ability to identify self with things and resolve the false distinction between the internal and the external. As Ch'eng Hao expresses it:

To regard things outside the self as external, and force oneself to conform to them, is to regard one's nature as divided into the internal and the external. Furthermore, if one's nature is conceived to be following external things, then, while it is outside, what is it that is within the self? To conceive one's nature thus is to have the intention of getting rid of external temptations, but to fail to realize that human nature does not possess the two aspects of internal and external. Since one holds that things internal and external form two different bases, how can one hastily speak of calmness of human nature? [76]

Here is another indication that these Ming critics, despite their fondness for Ch'an terminology, are essentially Neo-Confucian in their outlook: Hu Ying-lin declares that poetry can be the bridge between the inner and the outer worlds of the individual—a means of identifying each with the other. As such he not only acknowledges the existence of both but also affirms the value of each. This is something which sets him clearly apart from the Buddhists.[77]

The world of poetry during the last fifty years of the Ming and the first two decades of the Ch'ing (from about 1590 until the 1650s) saw a great reaction to this allegiance to an "orthodox" tradition and its insistence upon imitation, and the influence of the Former and Latter Seven Masters and their theoretical mentor Yen Yü went into a long decline. They were revived later (and only temporarily) by Wang Shih-chen [f] (1634–1711). If this tradition consisted of only poet-critics like Hsieh Chen and Hu Ying-lin, with their sophisticated and vital theories of poetry, it probably would have maintained its position of preeminence. However, lesser men only understood and appreciated the role of imitation in the tradition and, by the hundreds if not thousands, they wrote poetry "in the style of" Li Po or Tu Fu or of any number of other T'ang masters. Imitation took the place of creativity and inspiration, and the idea arose that any hack could become another Tu Fu if he only learned to follow the rules.

Unfortunately the critics we have been studying here were held responsible for all this, and they, their poetry, and criticism were soundly condemned. Opposition to them was first raised by the Kung-an [de] school, led by Yüan Hung-tao [df] (1568–1610). The most comprehensive statement of the basic tenets of this school is found in two essays by Yüan Hung-tao: *Hsüeh-t'ao-ko chi hsü* [dg] (Preface to the Literary Collection from the Snowy Waves Pavilion)—that is, of Chiang Ying-k'o [dh] (*chin-shih* of 1592) [78]—and *Hsü Hsiao-hsiu shih* [di] (Introduction to the Poetry of Hsiao-hsiu)—that is, of Yüan Chung-tao [dj] (1570–1624). [79] In these two essays Yüan Hung-tao asserts four basic principles: (1) Literature is a developing phenomenon, and each age has a particular character, style, or set of distinguishing features. Both creative writing and criticism should manifest this. (2) Imitation destroys the life of literature and makes writers lose their own individual character of expression. (3) One should therefore concern himself with the expression of "native sensibility" (*hsing-ling*) [dk] and should not be bound by the rules and conventions of accepted literary forms. Individuality and the direct expression of strongly felt emotion are the most important things in poetry. If a writer imitates other writers, either past or contemporary, he subverts all this. (4) Drama and vernacular fiction have true literary value, and critics should try to elevate them to the same exalted position as T'ang poetry.

Instead of affirming an "orthodox" tradition with its center in T'ang poetry, the Kung-an school attempted to destroy it. Every one of these four tenets is a reaction to some aspect of the theory of poetry espoused by Yen Yü and amplified by the Former and Latter Seven Masters. The first tenet denies the supremacy of the poetry of the Han, Wei, and High

T'ang and declares that poetry is, or should be, a continually developing phenomenon, significant in every age. The second tenet, in rejecting imitation, strikes directly at the heart of orthodoxy; it affirms that each poet must find for himself his own "correct" means of expression. In effect, it champions the cause of unorthodoxy—"enlightenment"—which does not derive from orthodoxy. The third tenet denies, or at least ignores, the role of self-cultivation in poetry. The orthodox tradition regards poetry as the verbal equivalent of perfected consciousness (or the process of achieving such a state); the Kung-an school declares that poetry should be the direct expression of "native sensibility"—each poet's emotional dimension in all its individualized peculiarity. In fact, the poetry of the Kung-an school is a glorification of ego; it takes man as it finds him and delights in the expression of sensual, natural man. The fourth tenet denies the supremacy of *shih* poetry itself. The literati has always regarded the *shih* as the mainstream of the Chinese poetic tradition and had viewed the later developments in the *tz'u* [dl] and *ch'ü* [dm] as inferior forms, but the Kung-an school raises them, and vernacular fiction as well, to the same level as the *shih* and regards all forms as significant—the significance of each determined by its relative vitality as a genuine medium for spontaneous self-expression. The Kung-an school's view of poetry is poles apart from that of the Former and Latter Seven Masters; in fact, they are as dissimilar as Li Chih's Neo-Confucianism and Ch'eng-Chu orthodoxy.[80]

This opposition to the orthodox poetic tradition did not end with the fall of the Ming, but was carried over into the early Ch'ing by Ch'ien Ch'ien-i (1582–1664). Ch'ien was surely the foremost poet in the empire in his day, and his influence as a critic was tremendous; it goes without saying that he was the "grand old man" of poetry when Wang Shih-chen (1634–1711) was beginning his own career in the 1650s. The two were close friends; as the mature giant of poetry and its most promising student, Ch'ien and Wang were inevitably drawn together. Writing in 1704, toward the end of his life, Wang declares that Ch'ien had been the best friend he had ever had (*p'ing-sheng ti-i chih-chi*). [dn] [81]

For his part, Ch'ien had a profound respect for Wang's poetry and praised him both in a preface he wrote to Wang's first large published collection of poetry [82] and in his own poetry itself.[83] This might suggest that a teacher-student relationship existed between them and that Wang derived his theory of poetry from Ch'ien. Nothing could be further from the truth. Ch'ien's view of poetry is in large part similar to that of the Kung-an school, while Wang's is directly in the tradition of the Former and Latter Seven Masters. Ch'ien, as we have already seen, had nothing but contempt for Yen Yü and the *Ts'ang-lang shih-hua;* [84] Wang had nothing but the highest praise for both and defended Yen against Ch'ien's harsh criticism: "Mr. Ch'ien . . . did not approve of Yen's theory of marvelous enlightenment *(miao-wu).* [do] The chronic shortcoming he suffered all through his life resides exactly in this." [85] Much of Ch'ien's criticism was also directed against the Former and Latter Seven Masters, and here too Wang rose to their defense. [86]

Ch'ien's theory of poetry, like that of the Kung-an school, was essentially expressionistic: he regarded poetry as the spontaneous and direct expression of real, strongly felt emotion. As such he deplored the practice of imitation and believed that Yen Yü's and Kao Ping's idea of an orthodox tradition was a grievous affliction from which poetry had suffered long enough:

During the past three hundred years, the illness which the study of poetry has suffered has been very severe. From preceptors in the Hanlin Academy to those who give lessons in village schools, all have come under the influence of Mr. Yen's "Poetic Method" *(shih-fa)* [dp] [a section of the *Ts'ang-lang shih-hua*] and Mr. Kao's *[T'ang-shih] p'in-hui.* People have become thoroughly indoctrinated by them and have literally committed them to memory. . . . As far as the poetry of the entire T'ang period is concerned, each poet has his own individual spirit and his own individual atmosphere. Now they [Yen and Kao] fix boundaries according to Early, High, Middle, and Late T'ang, and even dissect it further and say: "This is 'marvelous enlightenment,' that is 'Lesser Vehicle'; this is 'orthodox patriarch,' and that is 'assistant.' " They have so divided and cut it up that the true likenesses of the people of the T'ang are obscured so that later students will have wrongly fixed ideas about them for 1,000 years. How terrible! [87]

Ch'ien also dismissed the idea that poetry had anything to do with "enlightenment" and the search for sagehood: "Poetry is where the heart's wishes go. [88] One molds his native sensibilities *(hsing-ling)* and wanders amidst scenery. Every person says what he wants to say—that's all there is to it!" [89]

It is no surprise that Ch'ien had little sympathy for Yen Yü and his essentially impersonal view of poetry; instead of enlightenment and the negation of self, Ch'ien regarded poetry as the celebration of self. He despised the Former and Latter Seven Masters because he believed that

they did not write "true" (chen) [dq] poetry but only "phony" (wei) [dr] poetry—
or, as he also put it: they were "without poetry" (wu-shih) [ds] and not "with
poetry" (yu-shih). [dt] By this he meant that "true" poetry or "with poetry"
designated the spontaneous expression of real emotion and that "phony"
poetry and "without poetry" designated imitative poetry based upon
false emotion. [90] Ch'ien's straightforwardly expressionistic theory of poetry
was at the bottom of his antipathy for Yen Yü, Kao Ping, and the Former
and Latter Seven Masters. It does not appear that he ever understood
what their tradition was all about; he saw only the bad effects that imitation had upon contemporary poetry as a whole—less gifted individuals
took shelter and sustenance in imitation because they could not compose
poetry in their own right, and truly talented people, who might have
become really creative, were beguiled by the easier option that imitation
offered. To be fair to Ch'ien, however, we should wonder if anyone outside a few people like Hsieh Chen and Hu Ying-lin really understood
what the orthodox tradition meant. Perhaps there were as few enlightened
poets around then as there were enlightened sages!

Like the Former and Latter Seven Masters, Wang Shih-chen [f] derived a
great deal of his theory of poetry from Yen Yü. But unlike them he based
his theory as well upon another, earlier critic—Ssu-k'ung T'u [du]
(837–908):

Yen Ts'ang-lang discussed poetry and said: "The people of the High T'ang were
only concerned with inspired interest. They were antelopes who hung by their
horns leaving no traces by which they could be found. Their marvelousness lies
in being as clear as crystal and being free from blocking. Like a sound in the void,
color in appearances, like the moon reflected in water or an image in a mirror—
their words come to an end, but their ideas are limitless." Ssu-k'ung Piao-sheng
discussed poetry and said: "It's the flavor beyond sourness and saltiness." [91] At the
end of the wu-ch'en year of K'ang-hsi [1688] I daily took up the poetry of the men
of the K'ai-yüan and T'ien-pao eras [the High T'ang] and read them, and then I
had a different flash of insight into what these two masters had said. I set down
those poems which especially possessed intriguing interest and transcendent
meaning (chün-yung ch'ao-i) [dv] and came up with forty-two poets, from Wang
Yu-ch'eng [Wang Wei [dw] (699–759)] on down, as the T'ang-hsien san-mei chi [dx]
("Collection of Samādhi of T'ang Worthies"). [92]

Both Yen Yü and Ssu-k'ung T'u advocated a kind of poetry which embodied transcendent cognition or insight in language that has a limitless
capacity for connotation and suggestion. Wang Shih-chen seems to have

taken over this view as his own and has labeled the poetry which possesses these qualities as *samādhi* (*san-mei*) [dy] poetry. The term *samādhi* in Sanskrit means "putting together," "composing the mind," "intent contemplation," "perfect absorption," "union of the meditator with the object of meditation." [93]

In any event, Wang's use of the term *samādhi* indicates his essential concern with the relationship between the self and objective reality. It is significant that he associated *samādhi* with a certain tradition of poetry— something often loosely termed the "school" of Wang Wei. When they discussed the poetry of the High T'ang, Yen Yü and the Former and Latter Seven Masters never associated enlightenment with any particular poet or school of poetry and simply said that all the poets of the High T'ang had it. Formal considerations and the concept of an orthodox tradition so dominated their thinking that most if not all of them overlooked the fact that one group of poets "led" by Wang Wei "specialized" in rendering flashes of intuitive insight and transcendent vision into poetry. More than any other tradition in Chinese poetry, the Wang Wei "school" of contemplative landscape poetry attempted to bridge the gap between the inner psychological reality of the individual and the outer reality of nature at large. However, Wang Shih-chen was well aware of this and shaped his theory of poetry, otherwise almost entirely based upon Yen Yü and his followers in the Ming, to fit the actual historical tradition of the Wang Wei "school"—a school to which he himself believed he largely belonged.

Wang apparently derived the theoretical basis for his own identification with the Wang Wei kind of landscape poetry from Ssu-k'ung T'u. Wang once remarked that what Ssu-k'ung meant by "the richness and excellence which lies beyond saltiness and sourness" was the "pure placidity and essential delicacy" (*ch'eng-tan ching-chih*) [dz] of the poetry of Wang Wei and Wei Ying-wu.[ea] [94] In fact, Wang so appreciated Wang Wei and some of those associated with him that he declared that such men were actually better poets than Li Po and Tu Fu. He renders this opinion in a critique he made of Kao Ping's *T'ang-shih p'in-hui*:

When Kao T'ing-li's [*T'ang-shih*] *p'in-hui* appeared, what he called "Orthodox Beginning," "Orthodox Tones," "Great Masters," "Famous Masters," "Assistants," "Immediate Successors," "Orthodox Innovation," and "Lingering Echoes" is all very neat and tidy. However, for seven-syllabic ancient verse he makes Li

T'ai-pai [Li Po] the "Orthodox Patriarch," Tu Tzu-mei [Tu Fu] a "Great Master," and Wang Mo-chieh [Wang Wei], Kao Ta-fu [Kao Shih],[eb] and Li Tung-ch'uan [Li Ch'i] [ec] merely "Famous Masters." This is not correct. These last three masters all ought to be "Orthodox Patriarchs," and Li and Tu should be "Great Masters." . . . This is an exact certainty which cannot be altered! [95]

From the point of view of the poetic tradition, it is not too extreme for Wang Shih-chen to have considered Wang Wei a better poet than Li Po and Tu Fu, but his opinion that Kao Shih and Li Ch'i were better than Li and Tu would have appalled such critics as Yen Yü, Li Meng-yang, and Hsieh Chen. Wang Wei was perhaps often held in the highest esteem, but Kao and Li were hardly ever accorded similar status.

Although Wang departed from the general theory of poetry of the Former and Latter Seven Masters in identifying "perfect" poetry with the Wang Wei school, he still remained close to them on the issues of poetic orthodoxy and enlightenment (perfect intuitive control over the poetic medium), and like these Ming critics he realized the intimate relationship between them:

" 'Abandon the raft and climb the bank'—the followers of Ch'an consider this to be the realm of enlightenment (wu-ching),[ed] and poets consider it to be the realm of intuitive control (hua-ching).[ee] In poetry or in Ch'an it ultimately comes to the same thing; there is not the least bit of difference." Ta-fu [Ho Ching-ming [ef] (one of the "Former Seven Masters")] brought this up in a letter he wrote to K'ung-t'ung [Li Meng-yang].[96]

In Ch'an the "raft" is a symbol for the rules and regulations of the monastic community and the sūtras and other teachings of the tradition; in poetry it is the symbol for the rules and regulations, the conventions, of the formal poetic medium sanctioned by the orthodox tradition. In both cases when one has "arrived" at enlightenment he can abandon the means of transportation. As the ultimate meaning of enlightenment in Ch'an lies beyond rules and regulations, so perfect intuitive control in poetry lies beyond the actual conscious practice of poetic craft. This is exactly what Yen Yü meant when he said that the student of poetry will be spontaneously enlightened after having allowed the tradition to "ferment in his bosom for a long time." Since Wang Shih-chen quotes this passage favorably, we can assume that he accepted Ho Ching-ming's opinion as his own.

However, Wang's major influence came from Yen Yü, and the follow-

ing passage seems to be a commentary upon an already familiar passage
in the *Ts'ang-lang shih-hua:*

In the Way of poetry there is basis (*ken-ti*) ᵉᵍ and there is inspired apprehension
(*hsing-hui*).ᵉʰ However, in general these two things cannot be obtained at the
same time. Images in a mirror, the moon in water, the color in appearances, the
antelope hangs by its horns and leaves no trace by which it can be found—this is
inspired apprehension. Base yourself upon the *Feng* and *Ya* [the *Book of Odes*]
and so find the source; go upstream to the *Elegies of Ch'u* and the *Li Sao*, to the
yüeh-fu and the poetry of the Han and the Wei and so keep up with the flow;
broaden yourself with the *Nine Classics*, the *Three Histories*, and the various philosophers and so familiarize yourself thoroughly with all possible variations—this
is basis. Basis has its origin in study, but inspired apprehension comes from one's
intuitive powers of discernment (*ch'ing-hsing*).ᵉⁱ When one puts these two things
together and supports them with his own personal temperament (*feng-ku*),ᵉʲ
nourishes them with red and green [i.e., embellishment], and harmonizes them
with metal and stone [i.e., music], he will be able to hold beauty in his mouth
and hang substance at his girdle, free himself from the words of others, and
become a master in his own right.⁹⁷

For his concept of orthodoxy, Wang includes not only the mainstream
of the poetic tradition but the grand tradition of Confucian letters at
large. By assimilating this enlarged orthodoxy the poet provides a basis for
his own intuitive powers of apprehension. Hu Ying-lin also divided the
essentials of poetry into those things which can be learned and those
which cannot.⁹⁸ Wang may well have had that in mind when he wrote
the above passage. In another part of his critical writings Wang records a
conversation he once had with Wang Yüan-ch'i ᵉᵏ (1642–1715)—one of
the foremost painters of the seventeenth century. Here the poet and the
painter discuss orthodoxy and intuitive control, and it is worth our while
to present the conversation in its entirety:

The Junior Censor [Wang Yüan-ch'i] came by to see me. . . . We therefore
thoroughly discussed the principles of painting. He considered that we should call
those painters, beginning with Tung [Yüan] and Chü [Jan] the Southern
School—just as there is a Southern School in the Ch'an Sect. He said that the
ones who continued this tradition were the Four Masters of the Yüan—of whom
Ni [Tsan] and Huang [Kung-wang] were the best. During the 270 years of the
Ming, of those who were prominent, he praised men like T'ang [Yin] and Shen
[Chou] for their thoroughly accomplished styles, but he considered President
Tung [Ch'i-ch'ang] to be the best of them. If it were not this tradition, then it
could be nothing other than either heterodoxy or devilish deviation. He also said
that whoever would be a painter in the beginning takes care about being able to

get in and, after a time, takes care about being able to get out, and must consider profundity and thorough expressiveness as the ultimate aim of painting. For the sake of argument I said, "My dear sir, in the Yüan you advocate Yün-lin [Ni Tsan] and in the Ming Wen-min [Tung Ch'i-ch'ang]. These two painters belong to what people call the transcendent or other-worldly category (*i-p'in*).[el] As for the profundity and thorough expressiveness of which you speak—where are they in respect to them?" The Junior Censor smiled and said, "Wrong! Wrong! Look at what you consider to be 'antique-and-placid' or 'serene-and-distant' and you will find that profundity and thorough expressiveness actually inhere in it. But this is not something which commonplace ways of thinking can understand." I then said, "Your discussion of painting is indeed superb, however it should not just apply to painting. Throughout ancient and modern times, the ramifications of the Way of poetry, which begin with the *Feng* [*Book of Odes*] and the [*Li*] *Sao*, certainly do not go beyond this. Is not the development which took place from Yu-ch'eng [Wang Wei] to Hua-yüan [Tung Yüan], Ying-ch'iu [Li Ch'eng], Hung-ku [Ching Hao], and Ho-yang [Kuo Hsi] the equivalent of the development in poetry from Hsieh [Ling-yün] through Shen [Ch'uan-ch'i], Sung [Chih-wen], She-hung [Ch'en Tzu-ang], Li [Po] and Tu [Fu]? Moreover, are not Wang [Wei], Meng [Hao-jan], Kao [Shih], and Ts'en [Shen] the Tung [Yüan] and Chü [Jan] of the Kai-yüan era? Coming down to Ni [Tsan], Huang [Kung-wang] and the others of the Four Masters, and extending further on to President Tung of the modern era, is this not the equivalent of the poetry of the Ta-li and Yüan-ho eras? If it is not this, then it is heterodox development. Is there not a system of legal progeny and an orthodox patriarchate among the poets? Getting in and getting out—is this not the discarding the raft and climbing the bank of the poets? As for profundity and thorough expressiveness, not just Li [Po], Tu [Fu], and Ch'ang-li [Han Yü] possessed them—Hsieh [Ling-yün], Wang [Wei], Meng [Hao-jan] and their followers had them as well. Although your discussion is concerned with painting, it applies equally well to poetry." [99]

Although both Wang Shih-chen and Wang Yüan-ch'i must have been thinking about Yen Yü's conception of orthodoxy, Wang Yüan-ch'i surely based his own arguments directly upon certain passages in the art criticism of Mo Shih-lung [em] (an older contemporary of Tung Ch'i-ch'ang [en] [1555–1636] and of Tung himself.[100]

Besides the concepts of orthodoxy and enlightenment (intuitive control) another idea is presented in this conversation—that landscape can and should be used as a vehicle for the expression of emotion. This idea has a long tradition in China, and we cannot attribute its origin to any particular individual or any particular school—for either painting or poetry. However, the presentation of profundity and thorough expressiveness in the "antique-and-placid" and "serene-and-distant" modes can generally be attributed to a tradition of poetry which begins with T'ao Ch'ien [eo] (365–427) and a tradition of painting which begins with Wang Wei. Wang Wei, of course, wrote poetry largely in the same modes. While it is beyond the scope of this paper to trace the full development of the idea that landscape is a fitting vehicle for the expression of emotion and personal character, [101] we should be aware of the sources of influence which made Wang Shih-chen commit himself to it. There appear to be three such sources.

The first source came from Wang's eldest brother, Wang Shih-lu [ep] (1626–73), who seems to have had a personal preference for the Wang Wei kind of poetry—so much so that he made sure that Wang's own introduction to the study of poetry was entirely in terms of the Wang Wei school. On one occasion, when Wang Shih-chen was probably not yet ten, his brother had him copy out from a collection of T'ang poetry the poems of people like Wang Wei, Meng Hao-jan, and Wei Ying-wu, [102] and some years later we know the same sort of thing happened again:

My eldest brother . . . liked to compose poetry, so my brothers and I all liked to compose poetry too. Once, at the end of the year, there was a great snowfall. That night we gathered in a pavilion and set out wine. When we had finished half the wine, he brought out Wang [Wei's] and P'ei [Ti's] [eq] *Wang-ch'uan chi.* [er] We agreed to write poems echoing its rhyme schemes, and as soon as someone finished a poem, we were quick either to praise it or to point out its faults. [103]

By the time Wang had become a serious poet his tastes in poetry were already settled on the Wang Wei school; it was probably then that he discovered his second source of influence: the criticism of Ssu-k'ung T'u, which not only provided a theoretical justification for them but also deepened his own concerns with poetic theory. Later in life Wang was fond of quoting from Ssu-k'ung's criticism, as such passages as the following show:

Ssu-k'ung Piao-sheng arranged his *Shih-p'in* [es] in twenty-four modes (*p'in*). Concerning the one he calls "serene-and-placid" he says, "Come upon it and it isn't deep; the closer you draw near the more tenuous it becomes." Concerning the one he calls "natural" he says, "If you bend over it's right there; don't take it from your neighbor." Concerning the one he calls "pure-and-extraordinary" he says, "Spirit comes from what is antique and rare; placidity is not something to amass." These are the very highest of poetic modes. [104]

In Piao-sheng's discussion of poetry he proposes twenty-four modes. I like most the phrase: "Without writing down a single word, completely get the spirit of it."

He also said, "Sparkling, sparkling is the flowing water; glittering, glittering is far-reaching Springtime." These two phrases are particularly marvelous for describing the realm of poetry. They mean precisely the same thing as when Tai Jung-chou cited the phrase: "When the sun is warm at Lan-t'ien, fine jade produces smoke." [105]

Such qualities as these all suggest that poetry can express something transcendental. Ssu-k'ung's whole theory of poetry seems to be based on the assumption that poetry can communicate the incommunicable; words can convey more than they actually mean.

The third influence upon Wang came from that trend of critical thought which regarded poetry as the fusion of the poet's inner consciousness and his view of objective reality. We have already seen two Ming critics, Hsieh Chen and Hu Ying-lin, committed to this idea; [106] a much earlier reference to it actually occurs in the writings of Ssu-k'ung T'u, who once wrote to a friend: "What you have achieved in five-syllabic poetry is the fusion of thought with scene; this is what poets consider most important." [107] However, the most important influence surely came from the actual artistic realization of this in the painting and poetry of the Wang Wei "school". It is apparently no accident that Wang and Wang Yüan-ch'i talked about the oblique expression of profound emotion in the guise of serene, placid landscape: just as Wang Yüan-ch'i subscribed to the Wang Wei tradition of painting, so Wang Shih-chen subscribed to the Wang Wei tradition of poetry.

Much of Wang Shih-chen's criticism is concerned with the role of the poet's inner consciousness in poetry—something he usually designated "personal tone" (yün).[et] Someone once asked Wang: " 'Concerning the poetry of Meng Hsiang-yang [Meng Hao-jan], people of the past have remarked that its ko [eu] and its yün are superlative. May I presume to ask what the difference is between ko and yün?' Wang replied, 'Ko means p'in-ko [ev] and yün means feng-shen." [ew] [108] This contrast between p'in-ko and feng-shen should immediately remind us of that passage in Hu Ying-lin's critical writings where he contrasts t'i-ko ("structure") and sheng-tiao ("sound qualities") with hsing-hsiang ("inspired imagery") and feng-shen ("personal tone").[109] It is quite probable that Wang had this passage in mind (at least unconsciously) when he formulated his own distinction between ko and yün. The great similarity in terminology must be more than mere coincidence. Therefore, p'in-ko must refer to formal poetic features and *feng-shen* must refer to superformal features. *Ko* in *ko-tiao* (Li Meng-*yang*), *ko-li* (Yen Yü), and *t'i-ko sheng-tiao* (Hu Ying-lin) always refers to form—it must also in *p'in-ko*. As a critical term, *p'in* first comes into important usage in both painting and poetry criticism at about the same time, at the end of the fifth century A.D., in Hsieh Ho's [ex] *Ku-hua p'in-lu* [ey] and Chung Jung's [ez] *Shih-p'in*.

Each of these works attempts to categorize or evaluate the various painters and poets, largely on the basis of formal considerations. The influence of these texts upon later people interested in aesthetic judgment was tremendous; it is not unlikely that Wang drew upon them (and others as well, to be sure) for some of his critical terminology. If he did, then *p'in-ko* would mean something like the level of formal excellence in poetry: *level* of excellence expressed by *p'in* and *formal* expressed by *ko*. *Feng-shen* here probably means the same thing it did in Hu Ying-lin's passage—"personal tone"—or that superformal quality of an individual's poetry which, aside from an individual formal style, distinguishes one man's poetry from another. Therefore, Wang, in this passage, distinguishes between technical expertise and personal tone; elsewhere he deals with this same distinction and uses slightly different terminology: "In the past . . . Po Lo-t'ien [Po Chü-i] composed a verse which said, 'I dare say my literary art could surpass that of . . . [Wei Ying-wu].' However if you take a look at it today, although Lo-t'ien's *chin-yün* [fa] is great and expansive and not inferior to that of Mr. Wei's, in *shih-ko* [fb] he is definitely inferior to him." [110] Here, instead of contrasting *p'in-ko* with *feng-shen* (*yün*), Wang contrasts *shih-ko* with *chin-yün*. *Shih-ko* clearly refers to poetic form, and *chin-yün*, which literally means "the tone in one's bosom," signifies personal tone. On another occasion Wang quotes with approval from the criticism of the Sung poet Chiang K'uei: [fc] "The poetry of each master has its own flavor (*feng-wei*) [fd] just as each of the twenty-four modes of music has its own tone,' on which the music depends for its character (*ko yu yün-sheng*).[fe] Imitators, though their words may resemble the master's, have lost the tone (*yün*)." [111] It is obvious from all these passages that Wang had a keen interest in personal tone, the inner consciousness and character of the poet, and that he often employed the term *yün* to express it.

Yün, of course, occurs in the term *shen-yün* [ff]—the term which contemporary and later students of poetry say characterizes Wang's whole theory of poetry (Wang's "school" of poetry is, in fact, known as the *shen-yün p'ai*).[fg] Extensive reading in the Chinese critical tradition before Wang and in his own critical writings has led me to the conclusion that this term signifies three essential concepts. As we have already seen, *yün* surely refers to personal tone—the interior world of individual poetic consciousness. *Shen*, on the other hand, refers not to just one but two things: the poet's intuitive vision, his cognition, of the world around him, and his intuitive control over the poetic medium. Since Wang never seems to have explicitly defined what he meant by *shen-yün*, we have to examine various occurrences of it in his critical writings and try to infer from the contexts the full range of its meanings.

Wang once remarked that he had used the term *shen-yün* before he knew that it had actually been so used before:

K'ung Wen-ku from Fen-yang [K'ung T'ien-yün [fh] (*chin-shih* of 1532)] said, "Poetry is for the expression of one's personal character, but, to be worthy of esteem, it must be pure and distant (*ch'ing-yüan*)."[fi] Hsüeh Hsi-yüan [Hsüeh Hui [fj] (1489–1541)] had a high opinion only of Hsieh K'ang-lo [Hsieh Ling-yün], Wang Mo-chieh [Wang Wei], Meng Hao-jan, and Wei Ying-wu. He once said, " 'White clouds envelop dark rocks; green bamboos enhance the beauty of clear brooks' [by Hsieh Ling-yün]—this is purity (*ch'ing*). 'The advent of supernatural things doesn't excite esteem; who will pass on what holds truth?' [also by Hsieh]— this is distance (*yüan*). 'Why must it be strings and woodwinds; mountains and streams have their own pure sounds' [by Tso Ssu] 'The scene darkens and singing birds gather; water and trees provide pure and brilliant beauty' [by Hsieh K'un]— these last two represent the fusion of purity and distance, and the summation of this marvel lies in *shen-yün*." In the past, when I began to use the term *shen-yün* while discussing poetry for my students, I did not realize that it first had appeared here.[112]

Since Wang does not qualify Hsüeh's statement in any way, we can assume that his interpretation of *shen-yün*, at least in part, came to the same thing, and he must also have agreed with K'ung that one major function of poetry was to express personal character in an oblique and distant manner. Hsüeh's concept of purity (*ch'ing*) seems to signify "pure" landscape, "untainted" by the poet's personality, thought, or emotions, and his concept of distance seems to signify an other-worldly atmosphere or transcendental tone with which some poems are charged.

The first couplet quoted is "pure" landscape, and the second is charged with an other-worldly atmosphere (the oblique expression of Hsieh's noble desire to be used for great things and his poignant regret that he has been ignored). Ideally the best poetry should combine both these features. It should incorporate an other-worldly tone in the presentation of pure landscape. The last two couplets (by Tso Ssu and Hsieh K'un) supposedly succeed in doing this, and the kind of poetry which has resulted seems, on the surface, to lack any personal reference to the poet, but somehow his presence is still felt there. Interior mood fuses with exterior scene; one so merges with the other that they are indistinguishable. Notice also that this kind of poetry is associated with a particular tradition— that of Hsieh Ling-yün, Wang Wei, Meng Hao-jan, and Wei Ying-wu; Wang Shih-chen made this association himself on other occasions, as we have already seen.

Elsewhere in his critical writings Wang discusses the poetry of various Ming and early Ch'ing masters, which "contains" *shen-yün*, and concludes that the poems concerned (all of "pure" and "distant" type) are examples of *shen-tao*[11] and freedom from "blocking" (*tsou-p'o*).[113] We have already met the term *tsou-p'o* in the *Ts'ang-lang shih-hua*, and we concluded that it referred to the transcendental nature of suggestive, connotative poetic language—"words come to an end, but . . . ideas are limitless." The term *shen-tao* occurs in another of Wang's critical statements:

People commonly say that Wang Yu-ch'eng [Wang Wei] painted bananas in the snow and that his poetry was just the same. For example . . . he strings together various place names . . . all of which are far apart and do not belong together. However, for the most part the painting and the poetry of the ancients were only concerned with inspired apprehension (*hsing-hui*) or *shen-tao*.[114]

For Wang Shih-chen, poetry and painting should not be concerned with realistic description or rational discourse but with the poet's intuitive and imaginative faculties. *Hsing-hui* ("inspired apprehension") and *shen-tao* ("what the spirit reaches") characterize these faculties. The *shen* in *shen-tao* must then refer to the poet's intuitive powers of cognition, the special powers that enable him to see through appearances into the essence of reality and to reconstruct that vision as poetic scene. Remember that Wang used the term *hsing-hui* to characterize the poet's intuitive powers of discernment which lie innate in him.[115] The *shen* in the *shen-yün* of these last few passages seems, therefore, to belong to the scene half of the scene-emotion fusion.

For a long time in China, the word *shen* has meant, or at least has been associated with, the concept of spiritual, transcendent, or intuitive cognition. The *Chuang Tzu*, for instance, contains two passages in which *shen* occurs with this meaning:

> The bright-eyed man is no more than the servant of things, but the man of spirit (*shen-che*) knows how to find real proofs. The bright-eyed man is no match for the man of spirit. . . . Yet the fool trusts to what he can see and immerses himself in the human.[116]

> He [the man of kingly Virtue] sees in the darkest dark, hears where there is no sound. In the midst of darkness, he alone sees the dawn, in the midst of the soundless, he alone hears harmony. Therefore in depth piled upon depth he can spy out the thing; in spirituality (*shen*) piled upon spirituality he can discover the essence.[117]

The bright-eyed man uses sharp senses and clear reason to know and discern things, but he ultimately fails to comprehend them. The man of spirit uses his spiritual (*shen*) faculties and thus arrives at true understanding. The object of spiritual cognition is the essence of reality—the spiritual (*shen*) dimension which lies beyond both sense and reason. The term *ju-shen* [fk] occurs in the so-called Ten Wings of the *Book of Changes*: "Investigate the principles of things with care and refinement until we enter into their spirit (*ju-shen*), for then their application can be extended, and utilize that application and secure personal peace. . . . To investigate spirit (*shen*) to the utmost and to understand transformation is the height of virtue." [118] Spirit here seems to mean something like the essence or essential being—that dimension of existence which lies above or beyond the physical appearance of things. Liu Hsieh [fl] (*c.* 465–522), the author of the famous *Wen-hsin-tiao-lung*, [fm] actually thought that *ju-shen* constituted the essential feature of the *Book of Changes*: "The *Book of Changes* does nothing but discuss Heaven; it enters into the spirit of things (*ju-shen*) in order to extend their application." [119] Liu Hsieh himself used a different word, *ch'i*, [fn] to express much the same idea: ". . . the men who wrote the *Odes* [*Book of Odes*] responded to things and their association of ideas was without limit. . . . They depicted the spirit (*ch'i*) of things and described their appearances." [120] The binome *shen-ch'i*, again meaning spirit, occurs in the late fifth-century text, the *Ku-hua p'in-lu*: "Although he [Emperor Ming of the Chin] was haphazard in his form and coloring, he was rather successful at obtaining the spirit (*shen-ch'i*) of things." [121] Moreover, the *Ku-*

hua p'in-lu also uses the term *ju-shen:* "They [Chü Tao-min and Chang Chi-po] . . . in their painting of men and horses were never wrong in their proportions by so much as a hair, and the marvelousness of their other genres also enters the spirit of things (*ju-shen*)." [122] Finally, perhaps the most important occurrence of the term *ju-shen* for our understanding of Wang Shih-chen's theory of poetry, is in the *Ts'ang-lang shih-hua:* "The ultimate excellence of poetry lies in one thing: entering the spirit (*ju-shen*). If poetry can succeed in doing this, it will have reached the limit and cannot be surpassed." [123]

Shen has also a long tradition of being associated with the concept of intuitive control. The first occurrence of this deals not with the refined arts of painting or poetry, but with the earthy task of butchery:

Cook Ting laid down his knife and replied, "What I care about is the Way, which goes beyond skill. When I first began cutting up oxen all I could see was the ox itself. After three years I no longer saw the whole ox. And now—now I go at it by spirit (*shen*) and don't look with my eyes. Perception and understanding have come to a stop and spirit moves where it wants." [124]

Later on during the Han Dynasty, the *fu* writer, Ssu-ma Hsiang-ju [fo] (179–117 B.C.) is supposed to have achieved marvelous intuitive control over the poetic medium—a quality which Yang Hsiung [fp] (53 B.C.–A.D. 18) praised as a result of "spiritual transformation" (*shen-hua*).[fq] [125] One occurrence of *shen* in the *Wen-hsin-tiao-lung* seems to refer to both intuitive cognition and intuitive control:

The marvelousness of the configurations of thought is that spirit (*shen*) roams about with things. When spirit resides in one, the will and the vital force (*ch'i*) constitute its latch and pivot. When things stimulate the eyes and the ears, verbal expression controls the latch and pivot. When latch and pivot work smoothly, things have no aspect which remains unrevealed. As soon as spiritual thought (*shen-ssu*) goes into operation, a myriad roads come to light, rules and regulations are unsubstantial, and carving and engraving leave no external traces. . . .[126]

It is also possible that the term *ju-shen* as it occurs in the *Ts'ang-lang shih-hua* indicates perfect intuitive (spiritual) control over the poetic medium [127] as well as perfect intuitive (spiritual) cognition. There is a passage in Wang Shih-chen's criticism which, while using much new Buddhist terminology, seems to be based, at least in part, upon these last three quoted passages—however, instead of "enters the spirit" (*ju-shen*), Wang says "enters Ch'an" (*ju-ch'an*): [fr]

Five-syllabic quatrains of the people of the T'ang often enter Ch'an (ju-ch'an). They have the marvelous quality of making one forget the words as soon as he gets the idea. This quality constitutes the very same axis or pivot as Vimalakīrti's doctrine of absolute silence or Bodhidharma's doctrine of obtaining the essence.[128] Look at the Wang-ch'uan chi of Wang [Wei] and P'ei [Ti] . . . although it is only of dull capacity (tun-ken) [fs] and merely the first step to enlightenment, still it is capable of effecting sudden enlightenment (tun-wu).[ft] [129]

Perfect intuitive control means the ability to realize in verbal form the intuitive cognition of states of existence which lie beyond both rational analysis and ordinary verbal expression. It appears that Wang considered cognition and control to be two complementary aspects of the same thing—two sides of the same coin—and that he considered poetic enlightenment (wu) to signify the achievement of spiritual (shen) access to both. As cognition, shen is directed outward to things, and as control, it provides the perfect verbalization of the poet's "spiritual" vision of external reality. However, we must not forget the other half of the shen-yün binome. Just as shen as intuitive control deals with the verbalization of the external, so it also provides the means of perfect (shen) expression of the poet's internal state of personal being (yün). Wang actually sometimes employs the whole term shen-yün to signify exclusively the poet's personal tone. For example:

> People used to say that in the Elegies of Ch'u and in the poems which are mentioned in the Shih-shuo [hsin-yü,[fu] fifth century] there is beautiful material (chia-liao).[fv] This is because their mood or atmosphere (feng-tsao) [fw] or shen-yün is not far removed from the Feng and the Ya [Book of Odes].[130]

> People who evaluate poetry have always either held forceful vigor (hsiung-hun) [fx] in high esteem and slighted personal tone (feng-tiao) [fy] or appreciated personal tone (shen-yün) and disparaged forceful vigor (hao-chien).[fz] Moreover each type ridicules the other.[131]

Personal tone, whether it is rendered as shen-yün,[132] feng-tsao, feng-tiao, feng-ku,[133] or feng-wei,[134] always seems to indicate that quality in poetry which expresses, in an indirect and tenuous way, personal mood, atmosphere, or tone. In this last passage this quality is contrasted with "forceful vigor"—the direct expression of strongly felt emotion. Wang advocated the former, and Ch'ien Ch'ien-i, for instance, advocated the latter.[135] While Wang preferred poets like Wang Wei or Meng Hao-jan, Ch'ien preferred Li Po or Han Yü. Although both "personal tone" and "forceful vigor" indicate expressionism in poetry, there is considerable difference in respect to the nature of expression. In *shen-yün* poetry the presence of the poet is felt in only an oblique and tenuous way; in *hsiung-hun* or *hao-chien* poetry the poet's strongly felt emotions are directly displayed. In the former an attempt is made to achieve a delicate balance between personal states of being and inspired visions of reality; in the latter the poet as personality dominates scene—it is self- or ego-oriented, whereas *shen-yün* poetry attempts to express a state in which the reality of self merges in submission to the larger reality of Nature as a whole.

Shen-yün, then, seems to be a catchall term in Wang's criticism. Sometimes it seems to refer only to personal tone, sometimes to the fusion of intuitive cognition with personal tone, sometimes to intuitive cognition and intuitive control, sometimes to intuitive control and personal tone, and sometimes to all these at once. Only a careful reading will indicate how this term should be interpreted in each instance. We should also be aware that the other key term in Wang's criticism, *samādhi* (*san-mei*), is used, apparently, largely as a cognate, an alternate expression, for *shen-yün*, and its range of meanings must also be interpreted from the context.[136] *San-mei*, as enlightened poetry, however, usually seems only to refer to intuitive cognition and intuitive control, and personal tone seems to be included in it only by implication. Wang's account of his compilation of the *T'ang-hsien san-mei chi* [137] largely deals with *san-mei* as intuitive cognition; in the following passage it seems to refer to intuitive control:

The Maiden of Yüeh, when discussing the art of swordsmanship with Kou-chien, said, "I did not receive it from anyone; I just suddenly got it." Ssu-ma Hsiang-ju, when asked about the art of writing the "exposition" (*fu*), replied, "The mind of a *fu*-writer can be achieved from within but cannot be conveyed in words." The Zen Master Yün-men said to his disciples, "You do not try to remember your own words but try to remember mine. Are you going to sell me in the future?" All these remarks have hit the secret (*san-mei*) of poetry.[138]

Although *san-mei* is a Buddhist term, here it not only refers to Ch'an but also to things which occurred before Buddhism was introduced into China. The concept of poetic enlightenment (here the perfect identification of the poet with his medium of expression) was apparently such a parallel idea to spiritual enlightenment in Ch'an that Wang, as others before him, could not help but borrow Ch'an terminology and anecdotes to express it. The famous seventeenth-century dramatist, Hung Sheng [ga]

(1646?–1704), who considered himself one of Wang's students of poetry, could not avoid using Ch'an terminology in this way either:

Hung Sheng . . . asked Shih Yü-shan [Shih Jun-chang **gb** (1619–83)] about the method of composing poetry. . . . Yü-shan said, "Your teacher says that poetry is like an exquisite towering pagoda which appears at the snap of the fingers or like the twelve towers of the five cities of the immortals which ephemerally exist at the edge of Heaven. I do not agree. To use a metaphor, poetry is like someone building a house out of tiles, glazed bricks, wood, and stone—he must put them all together, one by one, on solid ground." Hung replied, "This constitutes the difference between the meanings of sudden and gradual enlightenment of the Ch'an sect." [139]

Wang and his disciples, as Yen Yü and the Ming critics before them, used Ch'an as an analogy for poetry—for the idea of poetic orthodoxy—but most of all for the concept of poetic enlightenment and how it emerges from the rules and regulations of orthodoxy:

It is recorded in the *Seng-pao-chuan* **gc** that the Shih-men Ts'ung Ch'an Master once said to the Ta-kuan T'an-ying Ch'an Master, "This matter [Ch'an] is like learning calligraphy. When the strokes and dots can be imitated, one is skillful—otherwise he is clumsy. Why is this so? It is because the person involved has still not forgotten the rules (*fa*), and, since he is still bound by rules, he cannot help but stop and start [i.e., be hesitant]. However, once the brush forgets the hand and the hand forgets the mind, it will be perfectly all right." These are words about the way a man attains the Way, but they can also serve as an axiom for people like us who write poetry and prose.[140]

It is to Yen Yü, of course, that we have to attribute this practice of using Ch'an as an analogy or metaphor for poetry. The critics among the Former and Latter Seven Masters seem to have adopted this practice from him without any noticeable change. We saw above how Wang, in identifying with the Wang Wei school of landscape poetry, differed from these Ming critics. It is also in this respect that Wang amended Yen Yü's analogy between Ch'an and poetry:

Yen Ts'ang-lang employed Ch'an as an analogy for poetry. I profoundly agree with what he says. However, the five-syllabic line is especially close to it [Ch'an]. For example, the quatrains in Wang [Wei's] and P'ei [Ti's] *Wang-ch'uan* [*chi*], word after word, enter Ch'an (*ju-ch'an*). . . . These quatrains are marvelous truths and subtle words—they are not any different from "Śākyamuni picked a flower and Kāsyapa gently smiled." [141] Those who thoroughly understand this can talk about the Great Vehicle.[142]

CONCLUSION

From this survey of the critical writings of Yen Yü, various "orthodox" critics from the Ming, and Wang Shih-chen in the Ch'ing, we can draw these tentative conclusions:

1. The kind of poetry associated with the "orthodox" tradition can be viewed largely as an aesthetic counterpart to the Neo-Confucian discipline of self-cultivation and search for enlightenment. Although the poetic theory behind this poetry is filled with Ch'an terminology and ideas, it is essentially directed toward promoting a kind of poetry which attempts to integrate individual man and objective reality. Unlike the Buddhists, who deny the value and very existence of objective reality and who concentrate only upon the perfection of the inner realm of consciousness, the orthodox tradition of poetry balances inner man with his perception and conception of external reality. In this view poetry is the bridge between self and the world at large.

2. This conception of poetry differs remarkably from that espoused by the Kung-an school at the end of the Ming and by Ch'ien Ch'ien-i, for example, in the early Ch'ing. The orthodox tradition did not consider poetry to be primarily a medium for the direct expression of individuality and strongly felt emotion, as did the Kung-an school and Ch'ien. As a form of self-cultivation, poetry in the orthodox tradition attempted to suppress individuality and strong, personal emotion. Following largely the tenets of Ch'eng-Chu Neo-Confucianism or "Sung Learning," it deplored the "unorthodox" adulation of the self, the ego-centered philosophy of someone like Li Chih—with whose world view people like Yüan Hung-tao, one of the most ardent foes of the Former and Latter Seven Masters, largely concurred. Wang Shih-chen left no formal philosophical writings, but since he so identified with the general theory of poetry of the Former and Latter Seven Masters, we can assume that he was, as they appeared to have been, essentially inclined to Ch'eng-Chu thought. Also, since this "Sung Learning"—with all its emphasis upon orthodoxy and orthodox enlightenment—was still very much alive throughout the seventeenth century,[143] there is no reason to doubt Wang's general familiarity with it.

3. Despite the bad effects of this tradition upon the great mass of lesser talents throughout Ming and Ch'ing times (that is, their uncritical dependence upon superficial imitation of past masters), the theory behind the tradition is a vital and significant attempt to define the role of poetry in the moral and intellectual life of the individual. Like Ch'eng-Chu philosophy, the orthodox tradition, as an assemblage of "enlightened" specimens, offered the student a concrete program of study—a set of "perfect" models to emulate—and, as a body of theoretical principles, it offered him a vision of the goal to be won. Enlightenment, in either philosophy or poetics, meant much the same thing: the achievement of perfected knowledge of self and of one's objective environment, and the ability to integrate one with the other. Poetry attempted to verbalize this integration, and in so doing actually served as a means for integration itself.

Wang Shih-chen is remembered more for his theory of poetry in modern Chinese scholarship than for his poetry. His theory of *shen-yün* occupies a prominent place in Kuo Shao-yü's [gd] *History of Literary Criticism in China,*[ge] for instance, but his poetry, like most Ming and Ch'ing poetry, has been largely ignored in China—as it has also been, of course, in the West.[144] The major trend of literary scholarship in this century in China has been to view literature largely in "organic" terms, as an evolution of genres, each one inevitably succeeding the other. In this view genres are regarded as living organisms in nature. As one evolves, matures, and dies, a new one succeeds the old and the process is repeated again and again as the whole literary tradition makes its way through history. Therefore there is T'ang *shih*, Sung *tz'u*, Yüan *ch'ü*, and Ming and Ch'ing vernacular fiction. Since there is no place in this scheme for *shih* poetry of the Ming and Ch'ing eras, it has been largely dismissed as an unfortunate historical anachronism.[145] Coupled with this "organic" view of literature is the general modern propensity to judge literary works solely in terms of "originality." Here also Ming and Ch'ing *shih* poetry has fared badly. However, the development of new genres and the exercise of originality make up only a part of any national literature. Innovation can only have meaning in the context of tradition, and if a tradition is broad and deep enough—as I believe the Chinese tradition continued to be in Ming and Ch'ing times—exceptional individuals such as Wang Shih-chen could continue to work inside it and produce works of real creative value. However, Wang's significance for us here is as a critic. Essentially he was a synthesizer who adopted the best from Yen Yü and the Ming critics associated with orthodoxy and amended it with a keen commitment to the Wang Wei school of landscape poetry. As such his criticism serves as a focal point for much of the later tradition of Chinese poetry as a whole.

NOTES

1. Cf. de Bary, "Neo-Confucian Cultivation and Seventeenth-Century 'Enlightenment,' " this volume, especially pp. 170–72.
2. Cf. pp. 221–22, this volume.
3. It is a mystery what this refers to since no collection of *yüeh-fu* by this title is known to have existed.
4. Yen Yü, *Ts'ang-lang shih-hua chiao-shih*,[gf] edited and annotated by Kuo Shao-yü (Peking, 1962; hereafter referred to as *Ts'ang-lang*), p. 1.
5. Ch'eng I [gg] quoted in Chu Hsi and Lü Tsu-ch'ien [gh] (compilers), *Chin-ssu lu* [gi] (*Chu-tzu i-shu* [gj] edition); translated by W. T. Chan, *Reflections on Things at Hand* (New York, 1967; hereafter referred to as *Reflections*), pp. 47–48.
6. *Mencius*, 6B/2.
7. *Ch'uan-hsi lu*, in *Wang Wen-ch'eng kung ch'üan-shu* [gk] (SPTK edition), 2/122b; translated by W. T. Chan, *Instructions for Practical Living* (New York, 1963; hereafter referred to as *Instructions*), p. 172.
8. *Ch'uan-hsi lu*, 1/64a; Chan, *Instructions*, p. 24.
9. *Ts'ang-lang*, pp. 10–11.
10. Ch'ien Ch'ien-i, *Yu-hsüeh chi* [gl] (SPTK edition), 15/127a.
11. Feng Pan, *Tun-yin tsa-lu* [gm] (*Pi-chi hsü-pien* [gn] edition), 5/1a.
12. Cf. pp. 239–40, this volume.
13. This view of the Ch'an elements in the *Ts'ang-lang shih-hua* was espoused even in Yen Yü's own time. A maternal relative of his, a certain Wu Ling,[go] told Yen that "Ch'an is not something a Confucian literatus should discuss": *Ts'ang-lang*, p. 234.
14. *Ibid.*, pp. 24–25.
15. One of the few modern critics who have tried to correct this erroneous view is James Cahill: "Since Yen Yü was referring to poetry produced before the rise of Ch'an in China, there is certainly no suggestion of a Ch'an aesthetic being involved. The author, in fact, ends his discussion with the statement that in determining the schools of poetry, he has merely 'borrowed Ch'an as an analogy.' " Cf. his "Confucian Elements in the Theory of Painting" in A. F. Wright (ed.), *The Confucian Persuasion* (Stanford, 1960), pp. 115–16 and n. 5.
16. *Ts'ang-lang*, p. 127.
17. *Ibid.*, p. 10.
18. *Ibid.*, p. 137.
19. *Ibid.*, p. 156.
20. Chan, *Reflections*, p. 49.
21. *Ts'ang-lang*, p. 157.

22. *Ibid.*, p. 121.
23. Chan, *Reflections*, p. 289.
24. *Ibid.*, p. 291.
25. *Ibid.*
26. Chu Tung-jun [gp] *Chung-kuo wen-hsüeh p'i-p'ing shih ta-kang* [gq] (Shanghai, 1946), pp. 219–20.
27. Quoted in Kuo Shao-yü, *Chung-kuo wen-hsüeh p'i-p'ing shih* (Shanghai, 1964), p. 289.
28. Cf. p. 219, this volume.
29. The image of the antelope (*ling-yang*) [gr] which hangs by its horns from a tree branch and leaves no tracks was often employed by certain Ch'an masters of the T'ang. The Ch'an Master I-ts'un [gs] (822–908) said to his disciples: "If I speak of this and that, you pursue my words and chase my phrases, but if I become an antelope and hang by my horns, where will you go to catch me?" *Ching-te ch'uan-teng lu* [gt] (*Taishō shinshū daizōkyō* [gu] edition no. 2076), 16/328b7. The Ch'an Master Tao-ying [gv] (d. 902) also addressed his disciples: "You are like good hunting dogs who only know how to find animals which leave tracks—suddenly you come across an antelope which hangs by its horns; not only are there no tracks, you don't even recognize its scent!" (*Ching-te ch'uan-teng lu*, 17/335b8). What these Ch'an masters are saying is: "If you want to learn anything, you cannot get caught up in the precise, literal meaning of what we have been saying. Sense and reason are useless since we leave no such tracks for you to follow." Yen Yü here implies that the poets of the High T'ang were like these Ch'an masters—the real meaning and significance of their poetry lies beyond sense and reason and the literal meaning of language.
30. "Blocking" originally referred to boats becalmed or "blocked" in backwaters. In Ch'an this term came to be used to describe the mind when it engages in rational calculation or reflection that leads nowhere. Just as boats are "blocked" in backwaters, the mind is "blocked" in the backwaters of rational thought. Cf. Kuo Shao-yü's remarks on this in *Ts'ang-lang*, p. 25, n. 5, and P. Demiéville's review of G. Debon, *Ts'ang-lang's Gespräche über die Dichtung. Ein Beitrag zur chinesischen Poetik* (Wiesbaden, 1962), *T'oung Pao*, vol. 49 (1961–62), p. 471.
31. *Ts'ang-lang*, p. 24.
32. Translation by James J. Y. Liu, *The Art of Chinese Poetry* (Chicago, 1962), p. 82.
33. This is an allusion to a passage in the *Chuang Tzu*, 26/48: "The fish trap exists because of the fish; once you've gotten the fish, you can forget the trap. . . . Words exist because of the meaning; once you've gotten the meaning, you can forget the words. Where can I find a man who has forgotten words so I can have a word with him?" Translated by B. Watson, *The Complete Works of Chuang Tzu* (New York, 1968), p. 302.
34. *Ts'ang-lang*, pp. 23–24.

35. Ch'eng I quoted in the *Chin-ssu lu.* See Chan, *Reflections,* p. 98.
36. Cf. Ch'en Yen ᵍʷ (1856–1937), *Shih-i-shih shih-hua* ᵍˣ (Shanghai, 1929), 10/2a. Ch'en denounces such expressions as "antelopes hanging by their horns" as so much meaningless verbosity—deliberately abstruse remarks designed to hide Yen Yü's ignorance.
37. *Chuang Tzu,* 7/32; translated by W. T. Chan, *A Source Book in Chinese Philosophy* (Princeton, 1963), p. 207. (Hereafter referred to as Chan, *Chinese Philosophy.*)
38. *Chuang Tzu,* 13/3; Chan, *Chinese Philosophy,* p. 208.
39. Cf. Chan, *Chinese Philosophy,* pp. 207–8, and P. Demiéville, "Le miroir spirituel," *Sinologica,* vol. 1 (1948), pp. 117–19.
40. *Chuang Tzu,* 13/64; Watson, *Complete Works,* p. 152.
41. The Sung Neo-Confucians in general did not have a very high regard for poetry, and except for occasional references to the *Book of Odes* they had little to say about it. Ch'eng I went so far as to say that the composition of poetry was a waste of time and even a hindrance to self-cultivation. Cf. *I-shu* ᵍʸ (*Erh-ch'eng ch'üan-shu* ᵍᶻ), 18/42b.
42. Cf. p. 231, this volume.
43. In fact, it is *very* unlikely that they were so influenced. The kind of extreme individualism that the so-called left wing of the Wang Yang-ming school advocated appealed not to the Former and Latter Seven Masters, but to their "opponents" at the end of the Ming—the three Yüan brothers, Yüan Tsung-tao ʰᵃ (1560–1600), Hung-tao (1568–1610), and Chung-tao (d. 1624). The Yüan brothers and their associates formed the Kung-an school of poetry, named after their home district in Hupeh, and their close association with Li Chih is well documented; cf. Kuo Shao-yü, *Chung-kuo wen-hsüeh p'i-p'ing shih* (Shanghai, 1964), pp. 348–51. The Ming Wang Shih-chen, who might be regarded as spokesman for the Latter Seven Masters in this regard, had nothing but contempt for the followers of Wang Yang-ming and accused them of "unrestrained selfishness" and of nearly causing a disaster as bad as the Yellow Turban movement at the end of the Han; cf. de Bary, "Individualism and Humanitarianism in Late Ming Thought," in de Bary, *Self and Society,* p. 178. The basic difference between the views of poetry of the Former and Latter Seven Masters and of the Kung-an school is discussed below.
44. Chan, *Reflections,* p. 40.
45. James Cahill has discussed the problem of nonattachment in *wen-jen* ʰᵇ (*literati*) theories of painting in "Confucian Elements in the Theory of Painting," A. F. Wright (ed.), *The Confucian Persuasion* (Stanford, 1960), pp. 132–34. Neo-Confucianism affected the Former and Latter Seven Masters–Wang Shih-chen tradition of poetic theory in much the same way.
46. Chu Hsi, *Chu-tzu yü-lei* ʰᶜ (1880 edition), 94/38b; Chan, *Reflections,* p. 123.
47. Yeh Ts'ai ʰᵈ (fl. 1248), *Chin-ssu lu chi-chieh* ʰᵉ (Kambun taikei edition 1916), 4/20; Chan, *Reflections,* p. 153.

48. Hsüeh Hsüan [hf] (1389–1464), *Tu-shu lu* [hg] (*Cheng -i-t'ang ch'üan-shu* edition), 5/13b–14a; cf. W. T. Chan, "The Ch'eng-Chu School of Early Ming," in de Bary, *Self and Society*, p. 38.
49. *Ch'uan-hsi lu*, 1/65a (Chan, *Instructions*, p. 27), 1/71b (*Instructions*, p. 45), 1/74a–74b (*Instructions*, p. 52), 2/112b–113a (*Instructions*, p. 148–49), 2/116a–116b (*Instructions*, p. 157).
50. *Ch'uan-hsi lu*, 1/65a; Chan, *Instructions*, p. 27.
51. *Ch'uan-hsi lu*, 2/116a; Chan, *Instructions*, p. 157.
52. Cf. *Ch'uan-hsi lu*, 1/71b; Chan, *Instructions*, p. 45.
53. Cf., pp. 226–27, this volume; especially "the moon (reflected) in water" and "no tracks to follow."
54. Quoted and translated in Takehiko Okada, "Wang Chi and the Rise of Existentialism," de Bary, *Self and Society*, p. 135.
55. Li Chih, *Hsü Fen-shu* [hh] (Peking, 1959), 1/3–4; cf. de Bary, "Individualism and Humanitarianism in Late Ming Thought," p. 194.
56. Cf. de Bary, "Introduction," *Self and Society*, pp. 8–12.
57. Liu, *The Art of Chinese Poetry*, p. 79.
58. Li Tung-yang, *Lu-t'ang shih-hua* [hi] (*Li-tai shih-hua hsü-pien* [hj] edition), 2a–2b.
59. In his dharma, or law of poetry, Yen Yü postulated five principles or dimensions: "structure" (*t'i-chih*),[hk] "formal strength" (*ko-li*),[hl] "personal style" (*ch'i-hsiang*),[hm] "inspired interest" (*hsing-ch'ü*), and "sound qualities" (*yin-chieh*); [hn] cf. *Ts'ang-lang*, p. 157. These five divide into two groups: "personal style" and "inspired interest" are on one side as superformal dimensions and "structure" (generic poetic form), "formal strength" (individual formal style), and "sound qualities" are on the other side as formal dimensions. "Personal style" looks inward to the internal world of the poet's character, emotions, and sensibilities—to a "personal tone"—and "inspired interest" looks outward to the external world and represents the faculty or function of the poet's vision—his intuitive cognition. "Structure" probably refers to generic form (seven-syllabic ancient verse has a different "structure" than five-syllabic regulated verse, for instance), and "formal strength" probably refers to the formal variations possible within each "structure." "Sound qualities" as a term is self-explanatory. Li Tung-yang's *ko-tiao* seems to be based upon the three formal dimensions of Yen Yü's law: *ko* represents *t'i-chih* ("structure") and *ko-li* ("formal strength"), and *tiao* represents *yin-chieh* ("sound qualities"). Although a *ko-tiao p'ai* ("formalistic school") did not actually emerge until the Ch'ing (Feng Pan is an early proponent), the groundwork for it was laid by some of the Former and Latter Seven Masters—especially Li Meng-yang, Li P'an-lung, and Wang Shih-chen [k]—all of whom based themselves upon Yen Yü's concept of poetic law and Li Tung-yang's idea of poetic form (which he always expressed as *ko-tiao*).
60. Cf. Liu, *The Art of Chinese Poetry*, p. 79.
61. *Ibid.*
62. *Ibid.*, p. 80.

63. *Ming-shih* (Kaiming edition), 286/7794.2.
64. Cf. p. 221, this volume.
65. Cf. Liu, *The Art of Chinese Poetry*, p. 80: "This is an ingenious and plausible defense of imitation, for it identifies imitation with learning metrical rules, which are in turn identified with the natural laws of rhythm and euphony."
66. *Ssu-ming shih-hua* (*Li-tai shih-hua hsü-pien* edition), 3/17a; cf. *Ts'ang-lang*, pp. 23–24; and p. 227, this volume.
67. *Ssu-ming shih-hua*, 3/5a; cf. *Ts'ang-lang*, p. 156; and p. 224, this volume.
68. Cf. *Ssu-ming shih-hua*, 1/11a, 2/4b, 4/18b, for example.
69. *Ibid.*, 3/3b.
70. *Ibid.*, 3/2b.
71. *Ibid.*, 3/3b.
72. Hu Ying-lin *Shih-sou nei-pien*,[ho] *chüan* 5; quoted in Kuo Shao-yü, *Chung-kuo wen-hsüeh p'i-p'ing shih*, p. 333.
73. *Ibid.*
74. *Ibid.*, p. 334.
75. Benedetto Croce's identification of intuition with its expression is a concept strikingly similar to what we are discussing here; cf. *Aesthetic: As Science of Expression and General Linguistic*, translated by D. Ainslie (New York, 1965), p. 8: "Intuitive activity possesses intuitions to the extent that it expresses them."
76. Chan, *Reflections*, p. 39.
77. Chu Hsi, *Chu-tzu yü-lei*, 96/14b; Chan, *Reflections*, p. 282: "They [the Buddhists] have some enlightenment, which enables them to be serious to straighten their internal life. But they differ from us Confucianists. They are essentially impatient, and therefore want to do away with everything. We Confucianists treat existing things as existent and nonexisting things as nonexistent. All we want is that when we handle things we shall manage them in the correct way."
78. Yüan Hung-tao, *Yüan Chung-lang ch'üan-chi* [hp] (Taipei, 1965), pp. 6–7.
79. *Ibid.*, pp. 5–6.
80. Cf. de Bary, "Individualism and Humanitarianism in Late Ming Thought," pp. 188–225.
81. Wang Shih-chen, *Tai-ching-t'ang shih-hua* [hq] (1872 reprint of 1760 edition; hereafter referred to as *Tai-ching*), 8/12b.
82. Ch'ien Ch'ien-i, *Yu-hsüeh chi*, 17/153b.
83. *Ibid.*, 11/95b–96a.
84. Cf. p. 222, this volume.
85. *Tai-ching*, 6/4a.
86. *Ibid.*, 2/9b–11a.
87. Ch'ien Ch'ien-i, *Yu-hsüeh chi*, 15/127b–128a.
88. This is the first line of the "Preface to the Book of Odes" (*Mao-shih hsü*); [hr] Liu, *The Art of Chinese Poetry*, p. 70.

89. Ch'ien Ch'ien-i, *Ch'u-hsüeh chi* [hs] (SPTK edition), 31/332a–332b.
90. Cf. *Yu-hsüeh chi*, 17/150b and 47/464b. Perhaps Ch'ien derived this distinction between true and phony poetry from Li Chih's discussion of the "childlike mind" and "phony men"; cf. de Bary, "Individualism and Humanitarianism," pp. 195–96.
91. Cf. Ssu-k'ung T'u, *Ssu-k'ung Piao-sheng wen-chi* [ht] (SPTK edition), 2/9a: "Prose is difficult, but poetry is even more difficult. There have been many symbolic ways of expressing this in ancient and modern times, but I think if we make distinctions according to flavors, we can then discuss poetry. South of Chiang-ling [beyond the pale of Chinese culture proper] whatever can be eaten, such as sour things, are certainly sour, but they are only sour and nothing more, and salty things are certainly salty, but they are only salty and nothing more. These are things which proper Chinese stop eating as soon as their hunger is satisfied—since they know that these things lack the richness and excellence which lie beyond saltiness and sourness." The straightforward, literal meaning of prose is to the subtle "meaning beyond meaning" of poetry as the crude, primary flavors of aboriginal cooking are to the subtle "overtones" of proper Chinese cuisine.
92. *Tai-ching*, 4/6a.
93. W. E. Soothill and L. Hodous, A *Dictionary of Chinese Buddhist Terns* (Taipei, 1968), pp. 66–67. Monier-Williams explains *samādhi* as "concentration of the thoughts, profound or abstract meditation, intense contemplation of any particular object (so as to identify the contemplator with the object meditated upon) . . . with the Buddhists *Samādhi* is the fourth and last stage of Dhyāna or intense abstract meditation." See Sir Monier Monier-Williams, A *Sanskrit-English Dictionary* (Oxford, 1966), p. 1159.
94. *Tai-ching*, 1/14b; Meng Hao-jan [hu] is another poet closely associated with Wang Wei.
95. *Ibid.*, 1/15a.
96. *Ibid.*, 3/11a.
97. *Ibid.*, 3/7b.
98. Cf. p. 235, this volume.
99. *Tai-ching*, 3/12a–12b.
100. Cf. Mo Shih-lung, *Hua-shuo* [hv] (Mei-shu ts'ung-k'an [hw] edition) and Tung Ch'i-chang, *Hua-ch'an-shih sui-pi* [hx] (Shanghai, 1911), 2/15a–15b and 3/18a. Nelson Wu discusses Mo's idea of a "we-group" or orthodox tradition and his influence upon Tung Ch'i-ch'ang in "Tung Ch'i-ch'ang (1555–1636): Apathy in Government and Fervor in Art," A. F. Wright and D. Twitchett (eds.), *Confucian Personalities* (Stanford, 1962), pp. 270–73.
101. For a treatment of this problem, cf. James Cahill, "Confucian Elements in the Theory of Painting," in Wright, *The Confucian Persuasion*, pp. 115–40.
102. *Tai-ching*, 7/8b.
103. *Ibid.*, 7/6a.

264 RICHARD JOHN LYNN

104. *Ibid.*, 3/4a.
105. *Ibid.*, 3/4a–4b. Cf. Ssu-k'ung T'u, *Ssu-k'ung Piao-sheng wen-chi*, 2/15a: "Tai Jung-chou said, 'The scene of the poet, such as "When the sun is warm at Lan-t'ien, fine jade produces smoke," is something which one can view from a distance but which he cannot place right before his eyebrows and eyelashes.' How indeed could we easily talk about the appearance beyond appearance and the scene beyond scene?"
106. Cf. pp. 234–35, this volume.
107. *Ssu-k'ung Piao-sheng wen chi*, 1/8a.
108. *Tai-ching*, 29/13a.
109. Cf. p. 235, this volume.
110. *Tai-ching*, 5/2b.
111. *Ibid.*, 3/6b; Liu, *The Art of Chinese Poetry*, p. 83.
112. *Ibid.*, 3/4b. Professor Pei-yi Wu of Columbia University has drawn my attention to the fact that the term *shen-yün* had also occurred in the writings of the Ming critic Lu Shih-yung [hy] (*chin-shih* of 1523); see, for instance, the preface to his anthology of T'ang poetry, *T'ang-shih ching* [hz] and *Shih-ching tsung-lun* [ia] (*Li-tai shih-hua hsü-pien* edition), 1b and 14b. Professor Wu also points out that Lu seems to have anticipated Wang in another respect in that he deprecates the poetry of Li Po and Tu Fu in the *T'ang-shih ching*—just as Wang omitted them from his compilation of the *T'ang-hsien san-mei chi*. However, Wang mentions neither the *T'ang-shih ching* nor Lu Shih-yung anywhere in his writings, and it is unlikely that he was influenced by him in either respect. The term *shen-yün* had been known for many centuries before Lu Shih-yung and Hsüeh Hui (cf. below, notes 121 and 132), and Wang Shih-chen's use of it probably has little if anything to do with these Ming critics. On the other hand, Lu and Wang both seem to have been latter-day adherents of the Wang Wei school of landscape poetry; this would account for the similarity of taste they displayed in compiling their respective anthologies.
113. *Tai-ching*, 3/3b.
114. *Ibid.*, 3/1b–2a.
115. Cf. p. 243, this volume.
116. *Chuang Tzu*, 32/51; Watson, *Complete Works*, p. 361.
117. *Ibid.*, 12/16; Watson, *Complete Works*, p. 128.
118. *Book of Changes*, hsi-hsia/4; Chan, *Chinese Philosophy*, p. 268.
119. Liu Hsieh, *Wen-hsin-tiao-lung hsin-shu fu t'ung-chien*,[ib] Wang Li-ch'i [ic] (ed.) (Centre franco-chinois d'études sinologiques publication no. 15; reprint; Taipei, 1968), 1/6/3.
120. *Ibid.*, 10/120/7.
121. Hsieh Ho, *Ku-hua p'in-lu* (*Ts'ung-shu chi-ch'eng chien-pien*, ts'e 499), p. 11. Just as *shen* and *ch'i* seem to be used interchangeably in the *Ku-hua p'in-lu*, so do the terms *ch'i-yün* [id] and *shen-yün*, and we can translate them both as "spirit-tone." *Shen-yün* occurs briefly just once (*ibid.*, p. 4), but

ch'i-yün is the key concept in Hsieh Ho's first law of painting (*ibid.*, p. 1):
"The first (law) is—spirit-tone; this is how one engenders animation (*sheng
tung* [ie])." This bears comparison with the opening line of the *Shih-p'in* of
Chung Jung (later fifth-early sixth centuries): "Spirit (*ch'i*) animates things
(*tung-wu* [if]), and things stimulate man." (*Ssu-pu pei-yao* ed., A/la).

Chung Jung's *ch'i* is the life force which animates the whole physical
universe; the *ch'i* of the *ch'i-yün* of Hsieh Ho is the life force of the individual painter, and *yün* is the configuration or pattern, the *tone* of his life force
or "spirit." Hsieh's first law says, in effect, that the painter endows his subjects with life force, "spirit," through his personal *ch'i* in the same way as
things in nature are animated by the universal *ch'i*. Since the personal *ch'i*
of the painter has an individual *yün* ("tone"), the "spirit" or life force his
paintings contain will also have this "tone." *Ch'i-yün*, and its cognate *shen-
yün*, signify the capacity of the artist to function as "spiritual" expressor—in
that he endows his subjects with a sense of life through the expression of his
own "spirit"—and as "spiritual" knower—in that he perceives and articu-
lates the "spirit" of things which lies beyond or above simple physical
appearances.

122. *Ibid.*, p. 10.
123. *Ts'ang-lang*, p. 6; Liu, *The Art of Chinese Poetry*, p. 81.
124. *Chuang Tzu*, 3/5; Watson, *Complete Works*, p. 50.
125. *Hsi-ching tsa-chi* [ig] (*Han Wei ts'ung-shu* edition), 3/6a. Although this work is
      now generally regarded as probably a T'ang forgery, Wang Shih-chen would
      have regarded it as authentic.
126. Lui Hsieh, *Wen-hsin-tiao-lung*, 6/80/1.
127. Cf. p. 225, this volume.
128. "Absolute silence" refers to the nature of the dharma as something which is
      inexplicable in speech and unrealizable in thought; cf. Chan, *Chinese Phi-
      losophy*, p. 368. "Obtaining the essence" refers to obtaining the essence of
      the truth of the dharma—something which lies beyond words and rational
      thought; *ibid.*, pp. 425–26.
129. *Tai-ching*, 3/2a.
130. *Ibid.*, 3/8a.
131. *Ibid.*, 6/18b.
132. *Shen-yün* seems to occur with this particular meaning in Hsieh Ho's *Ku-
      hua p'in-lu*, p. 4.
133. Cf. p. 243, this volume.
134. Cf. p. 247, this volume.
135. Cf. pp. 238–40, this volume.
136. Cf. *Tai-ching*, 3/7a, 3/11b, 3/12a—for example.
137. Cf. p. 240, this volume.
138. *Tai-ching*, 3/10b; Liu, *The Art of Chinese Poetry*, p. 85.
139. *Ibid.*, 3/8a.
140. *Ibid.*, 3/10a.

141. This is supposedly the beginning of the *Dhyāna* (Ch'an) tradition; cf. Ch'ü Ju-chi,[ih] *Chih-yüeh lu* [ii] (1868), 1/11a: "Once Sākyamuni presided over an assemblage at Spirit Mountain. He picked a flower and showed it to them, but they all remained silent—only the sage Kāsyapa broke into a gentle smile. Sākyamuni said, 'I have the secret of the Correct Dharma Eye (*cheng-fa-yen*) . . . it is not set down in words and constitutes a separate teaching. I entrust it to the Great Kāsyapa.'"

142. *Tai-ching*, 3/10b–11a.

143. Cf. Helmut Wilhelm, "Chinese Confucianism on the Eve of the Great Encounter," in M. Jansen (ed.), *Changing Japanese Attitudes Toward Modernization* (Princeton, 1965), pp. 289–303.

144. I have undertaken a consideration of Wang Shih-chen's poetry in my unpublished doctoral dissertation, "Tradition and Synthesis: Wang Shih-chen as Poet and Critic" (Stanford, 1970), pp. 157–208.

145. This theory of the evolution of genres was first developed in the West by the French critic and historian Hippolyte Taine (1828–93) and was closely modeled upon Darwin's concept of the evolution of species in plants and animals. When Chinese scholars began to write histories of their own literature in the 1920s, the influence of Taine often played a great role in their critical thinking. Cheng Chen-to,[ij] for instance, was greatly influenced by him; cf. his *Ch'a-t'u-pen Chung-kuo wen-hsüeh shih* [ik] (Hong Kong, 1965), p. 2; Cheng's work was finished in 1932.

GLOSSARY

a	詩話	ak	曹洞	bu	大家
b	正	al	沈佺期	bv	名家
c	悟	am	宋之問	bw	羽翼
d	前七子	an	王勃	bx	中唐
e	後七子	ao	楊炯	by	接武
f	王士禎	ap	盧照鄰	bz	晚唐
g	李夢陽	aq	駱賓王	ca	正變
h	李東陽	ar	大曆十才子	cb	餘響
i	謝榛	as	蘇軾	cc	興趣
j	李攀龍	at	黃庭堅	cd	妙處
k	王世貞	au	野狐外道	ce	透徹玲瓏
l	胡應麟	av	錢謙益	cf	湊泊
m	嚴羽	aw	一知半見	cg	興緻
n	滄浪詩話	ax	馮班	ch	多窮理
o	高棅	ay	法	ci	至
p	唐詩品彙	az	透徹之悟	cj	王畿
q	詩	ba	一知半解之悟	ck	李贄
r	盛唐	bb	謝靈運	cl	傳習錄
s	下劣詩魔	bc	辭	cm	良知
t	楚詞	bd	理	cn	本心
u	古詩十九首	be	意	co	大圓鏡智
v	樂府四編	bf	興	cp	格調
w	李陵, 蘇武	bg	詩法	cq	明史
x	李白, 杜甫	bh	孫武	cr	四溟詩話
y	自然悟入	bi	吳起	cs	神會
z	王陽明	bj	李廣	ct	超悟者
aa	徐愛	bk	程顥	cu	情
ab	乘有大小	bl	透徹	cv	景
ac	宗有南北	bm	朱熹	cw	神
ad	道有邪正	bn	古詩	cx	思
ae	正法眼	bo	律詩	cy	入杳冥
af	悟第一義	bp	絕句	cz	我
ag	聲聞	bq	排律	da	物
ah	辟支	br	初唐	db	體格聲調
ai	第二義	bs	正始	dc	興象風神
aj	臨濟	bt	正宗	dd	冥會

de	公安	eo	陶潛	fy	風調
df	袁宏道	ep	王士祿	fz	豪健
dg	雪濤閣集序	eq	裴廸	ga	洪昇
dh	江盈科	er	輞川集	gb	施閏章
di	敍小修詩	es	詩品	gc	僧寶傳
dj	袁中道	et	韻	gd	郭紹虞
dk	性靈	eu	格	ge	中國文學批評史
dl	詞	ev	品格	gf	校釋
dm	曲	ew	風神	gg	程頤
dn	平生第一知己	ex	謝赫	gh	呂祖謙
do	妙悟	ey	古畫品錄	gi	近思錄
dp	詩法	ez	鍾嶸	gj	朱子遺書
dq	眞	fa	襟韻	gk	王文成公全書
dr	僞	fb	詩格	gl	有學集
ds	無詩	fc	姜夔	gm	鈍吟雜錄
dt	有詩	fd	風味	gn	筆記續編
du	司空圖	fe	各有韻聲	go	吳陵
dv	雋永超詣	ff	神韻	gp	朱東潤
dw	王維	fg	派	gq	中國文學批許史大
dx	唐賢三昧集	fh	孔天允		綱
dy	三昧	fi	清遠	gr	羚羊
dz	澄淡精緻	fj	薛蕙	gs	禪師義存
ea	韋應物	fk	入神	gt	景德傳燈錄
eb	高適	fl	劉勰	gu	大正新修大藏經
ec	李頎	fm	文心雕龍	gv	道應
ed	悟境	fn	氣	gw	陳衍
ee	化境	fo	司馬相如	gx	石遺室詩話
ef	何景明	fp	揚雄	gy	遺書
eg	根底	fq	神化	gz	二程全書
eh	興會	fr	入禪	ha	袁宗道
ei	情性	fs	鈍根	hb	文人
ej	風骨	ft	頓悟	hc	朱子語類
ek	王原祁	fu	世說新語	hd	葉采
el	逸品	fv	佳料	he	近思錄集解
em	莫是龍	fw	風藻	hf	薛瑄
en	董其昌	fx	雄渾	hg	讀書錄

hh 續焚書
hi 麓堂詩話
hj 歷代詩話續編
hk 體製
hl 格力
hm 氣象
hn 音節
ho 詩藪內編
hp 袁中郎全集
hq 帶經堂詩話
hr 毛詩序
hs 初學集
ht 司空表聖文集
hu 孟浩然

hv 畫說
hw 美術叢刊
hx 畫禪室隨筆
hy 陸時雍
hz 唐詩鏡
ia 詩鏡總論
ib 新書附通檢
ic 王利器

id 氣韻
ie 生動
if 動物
ig 西京雜記
ih 瞿汝稷
ii 指月錄
ij 鄭振鐸
ik 插圖本中國文學史
il 神到

EDWARD T. CH'IEN *Chiao Hung and the Revolt*

against Ch'eng-Chu Orthodoxy

THE LEFT-WING WANG YANG-MING SCHOOL
AS A SOURCE OF THE HAN LEARNING
IN THE EARLY CH'ING

The apparent failure of Chinese rule under the Ming, and the re-
emergence of the Manchu "barbarians" as conquerors of China in 1644,
posed a difficult problem for Chinese thinkers of the late seventeenth
century—who were only too vividly aware of alien conquests in the past
and were deeply disturbed by the repetition of history. To Ku Yen-wu [a]
(1613–82), for instance, the overthrow of the Ming by the Ch'ing in 1644
was comparable to the barbarian occupation of North China during the
Six Dynasties, and he found in scholars' "pure discussions" (ch'ing-t'an) [b]
the reason for China's repeated failures in resisting the foreign invasion:

It is known to everyone that the disturbance of China by Liu [Yüan] [c] and Shih
[Le] [d] came about primarily as a result of pure discussions. But who is it that
knows that the pure discussions of today are worse than those of the past? While
the pure discussions of the past talked about Lao Tzu and Chuang Tzu, those of
today dwell on Confucius and Mencius. [The pure discussions today] leave out the
crude, although they have yet to attain the refined. They reject the branch even
before they investigate the root. They do not study the texts of the Six Classics, nor
do they examine the codes of the hundred kings. They do not arrange for contemporary affairs. They totally fail to ask about the essential teachings of Confucius on
learning and government, but rather speak of the "one thread" (i-kuan) [e] [1] and
"wordlessness" (wu-yen). [f] [2] They substitute empty talk on illumining the mind and
seeing into one's nature for the real learning of self-cultivation and governing the
people. . . . The dynasty was overthrown and the nation lay in ruins. Previously, Wang Yen [g] prided himself on clever speech, comparing himself to Tzu
Kung. [h] However, when he was going to his execution at the hand of Shih Le and
was about to die, he looked up and said, "Alas! We are certainly no match for the
ancients. Still, we would not have come to a situation like this, had we not

pursued the vain and illusory but rather had exerted ourselves to buttress the empire." Should not the gentlemen of today feel a sense of shame at these words! [3]

In thus condemning scholars given to "pure discussion," and those of the late Ming period in particular, as being essentially responsible for the barbarian triumphs in Chinese history, Ku came out most strongly against Wang Yang-ming [i] (1472–1529). Wang's doctrine of "original-good-knowing" (liang-chih),[j] according to Ku, started Ming intellectuals on the track of empty speculation on the mind and nature and ultimately caused the destruction of the Ming empire.[4]

Ku's diagnosis of China's weakness in regard to the barbarian invasion, his condemnation of late Ming ch'ing-t'an, and his specific attribution to Wang Yang-ming of the Ming's failure in resisting the Manchus, find concurrence in many of his contemporaries who also viewed the Ming's collapse as being a result of the moral decline and intellectual disorder at the end of this period and attributed it to Ming Neo-Confucianism.[5] Judgments of this sort would no doubt appear to us now as oversimplifications of what was actually a very complex situation. They represent the kind of soul-searching and self-criticism that was carried on among loyalist scholars in the wake of the Ming's overthrow by the Ch'ing. Few modern scholars would accept them without modification, and some have in fact tried to trace the early Ch'ing growth of Han Learning back to the late Ming period. Liang Ch'i-ch'ao [k] (1873–1929), for instance, is certainly no great admirer of late Ming Neo-Confucianism, the "defects" of which he compared to "those of Christianity in Europe during the Middle and Dark ages." [6] He is, however, more discriminating than the Ming loyalist scholars of the early Ch'ing in not lumping Ming thinkers together as "wild Ch'anists" (k'uang-ch'an).[l] He was careful to distinguish Wang Yang-ming from his later adherents, recognizing the former's eminence as a philosopher.[7] He was also obviously aware of the diversity of late Ming thought and detected in the last two or three decades of the Ming dynasty certain "new phenomena" which presaged the later development of Ch'ing "evidential research" (k'ao-chü).[m] Liang alluded to late Ming achievements in astronomy and mathematics and to "scientific inquiries" into the natural world as represented by Hsü Hsia-k'o's [n] (1585–1680) Hsia-k'o yu-chi [o] and Sung Ying-hsing's [p] T'ien-kung k'ai-wu. [q] He noted Liu Tsung-chou's [r] (1578–1645) efforts to rectify the left-wing corruption of the Wang Yang-ming school of Mind by emphasizing "vigilance in solitude" (*shen-tu*).[s] And he further contrasted what he considered to be the general Ming aversion to reading books with the large-scale printing and collecting of books by the two libraries, T'ien-i ko [t] and Chi-ku ko,[u] during the late Wan-li period.[8]

But Liang was a member of the Modern Text school and regarded himself as a lineal descendent of the early Ch'ing School of Han Learning whose spirit of "objective inquiry" he applauded as "progressive." He had little sympathy for Neo-Confucianism, which he characterized as "subjective speculation" in diametrical opposition to the "evidential research" of Han Learning. Indeed, he interpreted the early Ch'ing growth of Han Learning as a "great reaction" against Sung-Ming Neo-Confucianism, particularly against the left-wing Wang Yang-ming School of Mind.[9] The "new phenomena" of the late Ming period to which he referred as the origins of Han Learning were thus considered by him as "initial indicators" of a "great reaction." As such, they not only were unrelated in any positive way to the Neo-Confucian past of the Sung and Ming dynasties but, surprisingly enough, did not possess for Liang much significance in comparison to the flourishing Han Learning of the Ch'ing period. The printing and collecting of books by the T'ien-i ko and the Chi-ku ko seemed to Liang significant mainly in that they performed a "beneficial" service for early Ch'ing critical scholarship by preserving rare books which might otherwise have become lost.

Liu Tsung-chou's advocacy of "vigilance in solitude" was, on the other hand, to Liang a mere reaction against the "empty talk" of the left-wing Wang Yang-ming School of Mind. It performed the necessary function of clearing up obstacles in order to facilitate a new movement which was yet to be born, and was regarded by Liang as the death throes of an old era, bearing little positive relation to the growth of the critical scholarship of Han Learning.[10] The latter, according to Liang, was essentially a new development of the Ch'ing period, and the one person who was most instrumental in setting the patterns of the new scholarship was Ku Yen-wu, whom he honored as the founding father of Han Learning.[11]

In contrast to Liang's high valuation of Ch'ing "evidential research," Ch'ien Mu [v] deplored the lack of concern among the scholars of Han Learning for the political and social affairs of their times, and he condemned their antiquarian interests as an "escape into piles of ancient paper shreds." He appreciated the intrinsic value of Neo-Confucianism as philosophy and found in the late Ming reaction against speculation not only indications of an old era coming to an end, but serious efforts of certain scholars for intellectual reconstruction.[12] With great deference, he spoke of the Tung-lin [w] Neo-Confucianists who tried to arrest the *fin de siècle* degeneration of the Wang Yang-ming School of Mind and to bridge the gap between the intellectuals' pursuit of knowledge in private academies and the officials' conduct of politics at court.[13] Ch'ien also challenged Liang's exaltation of Ku Yen-wu as the founding father of Han Learning. Ku's thesis that "classical study is the study of rational principle" (*ching-hsüeh chi li-hsüeh*) [x] was, according to Ch'ien Mu, first propounded by Ch'ien Ch'ien-y [y] (1582–1664), and Ku's two well-known studies of the phonetics of the *Book of Odes* and the *Book of Changes*, the *Original Pronunciations of the Book of Odes* (*Shih pen-yin*) [z] and the *Original Pronunciations of the Book of Changes* (*I pen-yin*),[aa] were largely anticipated by Ch'en Ti's [ab] (1541–1617) *An Inquiry into the Ancient Pronunciations of the Book of Odes* (*Mao-shih ku-yin k'ao*) [ac] and *On the Ancient Pronunciations of the Rhymed Songs by Ch'ü Yüan and Sung Yü* (*Ch'ü-sung ku-yin i*) [ad] of the late Ming period.

Ch'en Ti, Ch'ien Mu pointed out further, also preceded Ku in formulating the methodological theories of "internal evidence" (*pen-cheng*) [ae] and "collateral evidence" (*p'ang-cheng*) [af] which Liang mistook to be a special contribution by Ku Yen-wu.[14] Ch'ien Mu therefore disputed Liang's interpretation of Han Learning as a distinctly Ch'ing development. Instead, he stressed late Ming accomplishments in phonetics and philology as positive manifestations of the endeavors of certain thinkers, especially those of the Tung-lin school, to integrate the "study of the classics" with the "study of rational principle," which Ch'ien viewed as a late Ming continuation of the emphasis in Ch'eng-Chu Neo-Confucianism on "managing the world and brightening the Way." [15]

Like Ch'ien Mu, Hu Shih [ag] also regarded the early Ch'ing development of Han Learning both as a negative reaction against the degeneracy of the left-wing Wang Yang-ming School of Mind [16] and as a positive outgrowth of the Ch'eng-Chu school of the Sung period. But, unlike Ch'ien Mu, what Hu Shih considered as significant about Ch'eng-Chu Neo-Confucianism was not its concern with the "management of the world and the brightening of the Way" but its concept of "investigation of things" (*ko-wu*) [ah] which, with its emphasis on "doubt" and "verification by evidence," led eventually to the early Ch'ing growth of "a 'Higher

Criticism' in the form of investigations of the authenticity and dating of a part of the classical texts" and to "the development of a scientific study of the problems of Chinese phonology." [17]

It is not without reason that Ch'ien and Hu viewed the early Ch'ing critical scholarship as a reaction against the left-wing Wang Yang-ming School of Mind and as an extension of Ch'eng-Chu Neo-Confucianism of the Sung period. Most late Ming and early Ch'ing scholars of "evidential research," such as Ch'en Ti and Ku Yen-wu, were highly critical of the left-wing movements within the Wang Yang-ming School, and almost all of them demonstrated a keen concern for the social and political problems of their time. By contrast, the concept of "investigation of things" as interpreted by the Ch'eng brothers and Chu Hsi [ai] does seem to contain a kind of "scientific spirit" congenial to the "objective inquiries" of "evidential research." However, this interpretation by Ch'ien and Hu of the origins of Han Learning involves a few obvious difficulties. First, early Ch'ing scholars of Han Learning were not necessarily partisans of Ch'eng-Chu Neo-Confucianism. Yen Yüan [aj] (1635–1704) and Tai Chen [ak] (1724–77) were at least as critical of the Ch'eng brothers and Chu Hsi as they were of the left-wingers of the Wang Yang-ming school. Second, the Ch'eng brothers and Chu Hsi do not seem to have been in particular favor of textual criticism as an undertaking and some of their followers in the Ming dynasty were actually opposed to it. In discussing the *Odes*, Ch'eng Hao [al] "would not utter a word of literal explanation (*hsün-ku*)." [am] "He would only brood over the odes leisurely to get the real taste of them, softly chanting them in a rising and falling voice. In that way he enabled one to achieve something." Ch'eng I [an] spoke of "literary composition," "textual criticism" (*hsün-ku*), and "Confucianism" as three kinds of learning and was of the opinion that "if one wishes to advance toward the Way, nothing other than Confucianism will do." This description of Ch'eng Hao's approach to the *Book of Odes* and Ch'eng I's attitude toward textual criticism appeared in the *Chin-ssu lu* [ao] and was followed by Chu Hsi's commentaries which showed his wholehearted approval.[18] Likewise, as an early Ming Neo-Confucian of the Ch'eng-Chu persuasion, Hu Chü-jen [ap] (1434–84) had little use for textual criticism and denounced it as a "petty" (*mo*) [aq] pursuit which, he said, was what "Master Ch'eng [Hao] referred to as 'trifling with things and losing one's purpose.' " [19]

Finally, there is the problem of Chiao Hung [ar] (1540?–1620) [20] who, as

we shall see later, made important contributions to Ch'ing critical scholarship in the classics and history but who was a "wild Ch'anist" of the
T'ai-chou [as] school. He was an avowed critic of Ch'eng-Chu orthodoxy
and a sincere believer in the oneness of the Three Teachings. Both
Ch'ien Mu and Hu Shih acknowledged Chiao Hung's achievements in
critical scholarship [21] but ignored his membership in the T'ai-chou
school. Liang also took notice of Chiao Hung's erudition as a scholar and
was obviously embarrassed by Chiao as a left-winger when he said,
"Chiao Jo-hou [at] [i.e., Chiao Hung] was also a vigorous leader of the
Wang school. But he was fond of reading books." [22]

The apparent contradiction of Chiao Hung as a left-winger and as a pioneer of Ch'ing critical scholarship, which Ch'ien and Hu failed to note
and which Liang was unable to explain, would thus seem to challenge
their view of Han Learning as a reaction against the left-wing degeneracy
of the late Ming period or as an extension of Ch'eng-Chu Neo-Confucianism. It raises the possibility of the left-wing Wang Yang-ming
School of Mind being a positive source from which the early Ch'ing development of Han Learning may properly be viewed as a logical outgrowth. With these problems in mind, I shall try in the following paragraphs to analyze some of Chiao Hung's ideas with reference to the
problem of "evidential research" which was a central concern of early
Ch'ing critical scholarship and which has been taken by a contemporary
Chinese scholar as a synonym for Han Learning. [23]

CHIAO HUNG: A BIOGRAPHICAL SKETCH

The *Ming Shih* [au] described Chiao Hung as a man of Chiang-ning [av] [24]
(modern Nanking), although he seems to have thought of himself as a
native of Jih-chao [aw] in Shantung, from where his ancestors had migrated
early in the Ming dynasty. After passing the Palace Examination as op-
timus (*chuang-yüan*) [ax] in 1589, he addressed a letter to his clansmen at
Jih-chao in which he acknowledged his ancestral origin from Jih-chao
but declined their offer of a monument of celebrity. The money, Chiao
Hung suggested, should instead be set aside to purchase a piece of land,
the revenues from which would be used to maintain his ancestral temple
and to provide for his poor relatives at Jih-chao. [25]

At the time Chiao Hung was born, his family seemed well settled in Nanking where his father held a position as Ch'i-tu-wei.[ay] [26] His childhood education consisted mainly of private tutoring in the classics by his elder brother, Po-hsien,[az] who once served as magistrate of Ling-shan [ba] in Kuangtung.[27] In 1555, Chiao Hung was selected to attend the Metropolitan Prefectural School (*ching-chao hsüeh*)[bb] in Nanking.[28] In the meanwhile, he was also studying at the two temples of T'ien-chieh ssu [bc] and Pao-en ssu.[bd] [29] But he did not seem to be particularly conscientious or to want to make Neo-Confucian studies an active pursuit in his life until he met Keng Ting-hsiang [be] (1524–96). The latter was then the Educational Commissioner (*hsüeh-cheng*)[bf] of Nan-Chihli [bg] and held informal meetings with the young students in Nanking, which in 1566 became institutionalized as the Ch'ung-cheng Academy.[bh] Chiao Hung later recalled his experience at these meetings:

The teacher [i.e., Keng] came [to us] from time to time and we brought up our doubts and difficulties to question him. He opened us [as though] with the key to the springs [of the mind]. There were none of us whose minds were not awakened and whose vision was not made clear. And so we jumped and leapt for joy. Sometimes it was without a word of explanation and only with a look that he made us understand. There were often cases of those who came [to the meetings as though] empty and went away fulfilled.[30]

Chiao Hung was soon accepted by Keng as a disciple and thus became identified with the T'ai-chou school. He participated in the organization of the Ch'ung-cheng Academy and was chosen by Keng to take charge of it when the Academy was formally founded in 1566.[31] He expressed great admiration for Wang Ken [bi] (1483–1541) whose disciples he said "divided the country of Lu equally" with the followers of Wang Yang-ming.[32] He was a close friend of Ch'en Ti to whose *Inquiry into the Ancient Pronunciations of the Book of Odes* he wrote a preface.[33] He maintained firm connections with Li Chih [bj] (1527–1602), who, he said, could shoulder the word *k'uang* (wild) and might sit next to the sage.[34] Because of his association with the members of the T'ai-chou school, and with Li Chih in particular, he was labeled by his contemporaries as a "Ch'anist," [35] an accusation he seems to have accepted with equanimity.

Chiao Hung's official life did not start until 1589 when, after repeated failures, he finally obtained his *chin-shih* degree and was made a Hanlin Compiler (*pien-hsiu*).[bk] [36] In 1592, he was appointed Co-Examiner (t'ung-k'ao-kuan)

(*t'ung-k'ao-kuan*) [bl] for the Metropolitan Examination (*hui-shih*),[bm] [37] after which he was sent out by the Emperor to confirm the succession of the district princes at Ku-yüan [bn] (in modern Kansu), Shang-jao [bo] (in modern Kiangsi), and Shen-ch'iu [bp] (in modern Honan), and so on.[38] In 1594, he was appointed Lecturer (*chiang-kuan*) [bq] to the eldest son of the Wan-li Emperor [39] for whose education Chiao Hung was said to have employed the favorite Neo-Confucian method of question and answer to stimulate the Prince's thinking.[40] For the Prince's moral edification, Chiao Hung compiled the *Yang-cheng t'u-chieh*,[br] an illustrated thesaurus of golden sayings and noble deeds drawn from history, which was, however, never presented to the Prince because of the jealousy and opposition of Chiao Hung's fellow lecturers.[41]

Also in 1594, and through the recommendation of the then Minister of Rites, Ch'en Yü-pi,[bs] Chiao Hung became Official-Compiler (*tsuan-hsiu-kuan*) [bt] in charge of the compilation of the Ming state history.[42] However, Ch'en's death in 1596 and a palace fire in the same year—which damaged materials collected for this project—brought it to an end.[43] In the meanwhile, Chiao Hung had completed the bibliographical section in six *chüan* which was later published independently as the *Bibliographical Treatise of the [Ming] State History (Kuo-shih ching-chi chih)*.[bu] [44] The *Imperial Catalogue (Ch'in-ting ssu-k'u ch'üan-shu tsung-mu)* [bv] criticized Chiao Hung's *Bibliographical Treatise* as the most unreliable work in the entire history of Chinese bibliography because it failed to distinguish the books that were extant from those that were lost at the time of its compilation. This criticism by the *Imperial Catalogue* is still maintained by some contemporary Chinese scholars who continue to dismiss the work as unreliable and insignificant.[45] But, as Naitō Tora-jirō [bw] has pointed out in his *Shina shigaku shi*, [bx] the same criticism can be directed against many bibliographical works before Chiao Hung's *Bibliographical Treatise*, the bibliographical treatises in the *T'ang-shu* [by] and *Sung Shih* [bz] being such examples. Besides, Chiao Hung revived in this work the practice of writing prefaces to each section, which had been interrupted since the *Chiu T'ang-shu*. [ca] In both these prefaces and the one supplementary *chüan* of corrections, Chiao Hung demonstrated a good sense of criticism and independent judgment. Naitō considered this work to typify the best bibliographical tradition in China as exemplified by Cheng Ch'iao's [cb] *Chiao-ch'ou lüeh*. [cc] [46]

Also for the abortive project on the Ming state history, Chiao Hung compiled 120 *chüan* of biographies known as *A Record of the Worthies of the Reigning [Ming] Dynasty (Kuo-ch'ao hsien-cheng lu)* [cd] which includes biographies of men from the beginning of the Ming dynasty down to the end of the Chia-ching period.[47] This work corrects and supplements the *Ming shih-lu* in many cases and was relied upon by Wan Ssu-t'ung (1638–1702) as a basic source in compiling his version of the *Ming shih*.[48] It is also significant as a work which, according to Naitō, marked the beginning of the change in Ming *chang-ku* [ce] [49] from hearsay-based gossip literature to serious writing of history, and which also served as the model for the *Pei-chuan chi* [cf] of the Ch'ing dynasty.[50]

In 1597, Chiao Hung was appointed Deputy Chief-Examiner (*fu-chu-k'ao*) [cg] for the metropolitan area of Shun-t'ien [ch] [51] and, as such, was held responsible by his political enemies for the heterodox expressions which were said to have appeared in the papers of some of the successful examinees. He was consequently exiled to Fukien where he served for about a year as Vice Magistrate (*t'ung-chih*) [ci] of Fu-ning Subprefecture.[cj] In 1599, he tendered his resignation and terminated his career as a government official.[52] He lived in retirement until his death in 1620, devoting himself entirely to teaching and writing.

CRITICISM OF CHU HSI AND HIS
NEO-CONFUCIAN PREDECESSORS

Considering Chiao Hung's background as a member of the T'ai-chou school, which is known for its radical spirit of iconoclasm, and as a disciple of Keng Ting-hsiang, whose attitude toward Buddhism Huang Tsung-hsi [ck] (1610–95) described as one of "half belief and half disbelief," [53] it is perhaps not surprising that we should find Chiao Hung in serious disagreement with Chu Hsi on the interpretation of the classics, which in turn involved Buddhism. The basic problem with Chu Hsi, as Chiao Hung saw it, was his fear of Ch'an Buddhism being unorthodox and, thus, his unwillingness to use ideas that would have served well to elucidate the truth of Confucianism but might have been suspect because of their Ch'an derivation. As a result, Chu Hsi's commentaries on the classics, though not totally without value, had nevertheless missed the "cardinal meaning" of the sages' teachings which, according to Chiao Hung, could best be explained by the mystical doctrines of Ch'an Buddhism.[54] This fear of Chu Hsi's, Chiao Hung noted, was shared by many other Confucianists who had accepted and even cherished for generations such foreign weapons and precious stones as Su-shen's [cl] arrows and Ch'üan-fu's [cm] jade, but who had persistently rejected Buddhism just because it was foreign. These Confucianists, Chiao Hung grumbled, "are truly to be marveled at!" [55]

In spite of the Buddha's having been an Indian prince, Chiao Hung does not seem to have regarded his teaching as a foreign doctrine. Buddhism, as Chiao Hung understood it, could in fact be considered as part of the heritage of China's ancient philosophical tradition since it dealt with the problems of "nature" (hsing) [cn] and "destiny" (ming) [co] which, according to Chiao Hung, had also been concerns of Confucius and Lao Tzu. Confucius, of course, never pursued problems of this sort to great lengths. In Chiao Hung's words, he "rarely spoke about them." But, as Chiao Hung also tried to argue, Confucius did this only because he was waiting for a qualified person to emerge with whom it would be appropriate to discuss these problems. "That was why," Chiao Hung explained, "[Confucius] said, 'To those who are less than mediocre, the highest subjects may not be revealed.' " [56] Confucius had obviously waited in vain. Still, as Chiao Hung was quick to point out, the Analects contained quite a few more-than-casual remarks on "nature" and "destiny," which Buddhism had made its special field of inquiry.[57] As such, Buddhism was viewed by Chiao Hung as "a commentary on [the teachings of] Confucius and Mencius." "Once the Buddhist scriptures are penetrated," Chiao Hung said, "the sayings of Confucius will be understood immediately. There are not two [separate] principles [in Buddhism and Confucianism]." [58]

At first glance, Chiao Hung's argument that Buddhism pursued the kind of problems which had also concerned Confucius and Lao Tzu, and that it was "a commentary on [the teachings of] Confucius and Mencius," may seem an appeal to Chinese nativist sentiments. Chiao might thus appear to be an example of what Professor Cohen has described as the gentry-dominated tradition of "Sinomania," which had first looked down on Buddhism as a mere corruption of native Taoism and which later accused Christianity of plagiarizing the then relatively domesticated

Buddhism.[59] However, the imputation to Chiao Hung of such "Sino-mania" would be unwarranted. Chiao Hung was advocating the acceptance and not the rejection of Buddhism. Though in a sense he viewed it as part of China's own philosophical heritage, he did not claim Buddhism as uniquely Chinese. For him it was simply a doctrine helpful in elucidating the truths of "nature" and "destiny." He said,

"Nature" and "destiny" are the treasures of our own household. We [Chinese] have an inexhaustible deposit of these treasures which long have been buried while we have been poor and with nothing to live on. There then comes a barbarian merchant [i.e., the Buddha] who points them [the treasures] out to us. Can we reject his words because he is not Chinese? Although that man is a barbarian merchant, the treasures are our own possession. There may be differences among men between aliens and Chinese. But the treasures recognize no such differences. [60]

He thus appropriated Buddhism as a Confucian commentary not so much to deny its Indian source of origination as to affirm its universal validity as a teaching.

Lying behind Chiao Hung's acceptance of Buddhism as a teaching is his belief in the infinite Way (*tao*) [cp] as a dynamic, existential process, the truth of which it is impossible to state adequately in words. He said, "It is not that there is a Way which cannot be talked about. What cannot be talked about is the Way." [61] The teachings, since they are composed of verbal statements about the Way, are necessarily imperfect representations of its truth. They were regarded by Chiao Hung as "traces" (*chi*) [cq] or "images" (*hsiang*) [cr] which are suggestive of what the Way is but which cannot be held onto as the Way itself. "That which is the Way stands prior to the images and transcends the surface of the [verbal] appurtenances." [62] This mystical conception of the Way as ineffable truth implies the essential difference between the Way and the teachings, the former being completely independent of the latter. "What the sages had spoken of as the Way," said Chiao Hung, "is like what the people have called Heaven. While the Chinese people call it Heaven, the Hsiung-nu [cs] people call it Ch'eng-li.[ct] Could it be that there were two Heavens? Heaven itself certainly does not know what it is being called. It is only the people who have forcibly given it a name." [63]

This distinction between the Way and the teachings also postulates the Way as the sole reality of ontological ultimacy. The teachings as merely verbal representations of the Way's inexplicable truth are not only imperfect but are ultimately unreal. "Ink and paper," Chiao Hung said, "are originally empty, and words and literature are not real." [64] They are like the "fish trap" (ch'üan) [cu] or the "rabbit snare" (t'i) [cv] which, though useful as instruments for fish-catching or rabbit-snaring, are to be forgotten as soon as the fish or the rabbit is caught. Chiao Hung described the proper attitude toward the teachings through the analogy of a horse. A good horse, on seeing the mere shadow of a whip, gallops forward instantaneously. [65] The pursuit of the Way's inexplicable truth is therefore a perennial process of marching onward, led by the shadows, but going beyond them. There can be no stopping or standing still even for a moment; no attachment to the teachings and still less any engagement in ideological controversies about the various teachings which have only a shadowy, transitory existence and no enduring identity in and of themselves.

The sages in ancient times, Chiao Hung seemed to believe, understood well this difference between the Way and the teachings. He was therefore convinced that they, though of different schools of thought, never wrangled among themselves for the claim to orthodoxy. Instead they embraced the Way in its entirety and, being aware of the inadequacy of any one teaching, tried to learn from one another in spite of their differences in ideological affiliation. "The history of scholarship from the ancient past to the present," Chiao Hung said, "may be compared to that of the states. Just as there were times when the lords went to the meetings with jade and silk, so the period of the Three Dynasties and before witnessed the states circulating the goods of all under Heaven to provide for the needs of all under Heaven. There then was no exclusiveness due to differences in locality." [66] To contrast this open-mindedness of the ancient sages with the exclusiveness of later generations, Chiao Hung cited the great Yü [cw] and Lao Tzu. The former, Chiao Hung pointed out, happily doffed his clothes when he ventured into a country of nudists and the latter imitated what was obviously a barbarian language while he was staying in the land of the Western Barbarians (hsi-jung). [cx] [67] It was on the supposed authority of Confucius, Chiao Hung noted, that later Confucianists waged their campaigns against Buddhism and Taoism. But, Chiao Hung argued, Buddhism had not yet been introduced to China in Confucius' time, and he could not possibly have attacked it as heterodox.

Nor would he have been likely to do so, since he never attacked Lao Tzu as unorthodox. "Why do people today," asked Chiao Hung, "attack what Confucius himself did not attack?" [68]

For Chiao Hung, therefore, a genuine spirit of intellectual open-mindedness had prevailed in ancient China until the late Chou period when Mencius launched his overly zealous crusade against Mo Ti [cy] and Yang Chu,[cz] and denounced them as beasts. "For the most part," Chiao Hung said, "the teachings of the two philosophers [i.e., Mo Ti and Yang Chu] had their origins [in the ancient sages]." [69] Mohism was based on Yü's teachings and the philosophy of Yang Chu was derived from the traditions of the Yellow Emperor and Lao Tzu. Mencius, Chiao Hung conceded, had certainly inquired deeply into the teachings of the early sage-kings and could hardly be accused of being ignorant of the sources of the ideas of Mo Ti and Yang Chu. Nevertheless Mencius denounced the latter as beasts and must therefore be said to "have held his views with extreme rigidity." [70] The scholarly world had since become increasingly partisan and Confucians of later generations, taking their cue from Mencius, often attacked Buddhism and Taoism as unorthodox without really knowing what these two teachings were about. This, according to Chiao Hung, was the case with Han Yü [da] (789–824) and Ou-yang Hsiu [db] (1007–70). Han Yü, Chiao Hung noted, was much impressed by his acquaintance with the monk Ta-tien,[dc] whom he described in his letter to Meng Chien [dd] as "having no impediments in his breast" and "indeed being able to transcend the bounds of the body, thereby conquering the self by means of reason and not permitting himself to be invaded or thrown into confusion by things and events." [71]

What thus impressed Han Yü about the monk Ta-tien was, according to Chiao Hung, the great possible benefit to be derived from the "field of blessings" [72] (*fu-t'ien*).[de] And yet, in this same letter to Meng Chien, Han Yü denied any personal interest in Buddhism as such, saying, "It is not that I worship or believe in his [Ta-tien's] dharma or seek benefits from the field of blessings." Han Yü, Chiao Hung taunted, must therefore have gotten involved in Ta-tien's teachings without himself being aware of it. Ou-yang Hsiu, on the other hand, was said by Chiao Hung to be "particularly stubborn." Toward the end of his life, he heard about Fu Pi's [df] obtaining the dharma from the monk Ching Tz'u [dg] and was obviously impressed, as he always trusted and admired Fu Pi as a man of independent mind. He himself therefore started making inquiries into the teachings of Hua-yen ^{dh} Buddhism. But he never got very far in these inquiries because he died shortly afterward. For Chiao Hung, therefore, Han Yü and Ou-yang Hsiu had not even so much as "touched the ground with their heels" and there was no need to take seriously their opposition to Buddhism and Taoism, which they took up out of the mere desire to imitate Mencius in his crusade against Mo Ti and Yang Chu.[73]

But if Han Yü and Ou-yang Hsiu, in their opposition to Buddhism and Taoism, seemed to Chiao Hung to be partisan and yet not quite certain of themselves, the rejection of these two teachings by the Ch'eng brothers and Chu Hsi was both firm and deliberate. It was almost like an intentional cultivation of ignorance and prejudice. Ch'eng Hao's criticisms of Buddhism were, according to Chiao Hung, quite without foundation. They were based on his own "surmises" and not on any genuine understanding of Buddhism—which Ch'eng Hao advised his followers not to investigate thoroughly but to judge only by its practice.[74] Like a judge handling a lawsuit, Ch'eng Hao had thus rendered an arbitrary decision without giving the defendant a chance to speak out. "Being the judges [ourselves]," Chiao Hung asked, "shall [we] say that there ought to be no following of the conventional world and that the sentence ought to be reversed to make it a happy thing for both the past and the present?" [75] Actually, Chiao Hung pointed out, Ch'eng Hao was not entirely unaware of the "silent correspondence" between Buddhism and Confucianism. He once expressed great admiration for the manners of a reverential monk whom he chanced to see, and said, "Herein lies all the majesty and decorum of the Three Dynasties." Nevertheless, Ch'eng Hao insisted on the incompatibility of these two teachings and "confined himself to the practice of partiality, narrow-mindedness and obstinacy." In this regard he was like all other "Confucianists of the world" who "were entangled with the names without investigating the facts." [76]

"Extreme rigidity" and "narrowness" also characterized the outlook of Chu Hsi, whom Chiao Hung criticized for having claimed for himself the right of succession to the orthodox teachings of Yao,^{di} Shun,^{dj} Confucius, and Mencius and for having rejected Ch'an and all other teachings except his own as heterodox. In thus arrogating to himself the right to orthodoxy as something of a monopoly, Chu Hsi was being as foolish and senseless as Chuang Tzu's "noises of the multitudinous holes" (*chung-ch'iao chih-hao*),[dk] each of which, though caused by the same wind, disputed against the other for the exclusive claim to being identified with the wind.[77] During the Ming dynasty, some scholars came out openly to advocate "union of the Three Teachings in one" (*san-chiao ho-i*),[dl] which they held to be the correct approach to understanding the Way. From Chiao Hung's point of view, however, they failed to realize that "the Way does not exist as three. It does not become three [in spite of our attempt to] make it three. [On the other hand,] the Way is not one. It does not become one [in spite of our attempt to] make it one." It is like the great void which it would be absurd either to divide or to integrate.[78] For Chiao Hung, therefore, the Way always exists unto itself as the truth, regardless of the teachings. To grasp it, one does not become concerned with the contentions of the various teachings which are made to disappear in the Way's infinity. This, according to Chiao Hung, was the message that Chuang Tzu had tried to convey in his essay "*Ch'i wu lun*." [dm]

According to Chiao Hung there had long been a misunderstanding of Chuang Tzu's "*Ch'i wu lun*" which was traditionally read as "*Ch'i-wu lun*" and thus interpreted as "an essay on the equality of things." This way of reading the essay, Chiao Hung noted, had come about by rendering the second word, *wu*, in the same sense as the *wu* in the statement by Mencius that "it is the nature of things [*wu*] to be of unequal quality," [79] and by dismissing the third word *lun* as inconsequential. The first two words, *ch'i* and *wu*, thus formed an expression by which Chuang Tzu was said to have demonstrated his will to equalize things. On this account, Chuang Tzu had often been criticized. The critics quoted Mencius as saying to Ch'en Hsiang [dn] that "it is the nature of things to be of unequal quality," [80] and considered Chuang Tzu wrong in trying to equalize intrinsically unequal things. According to Chiao Hung, however, the critics were mistaken in their understanding of the text, as a result of misreading the three characters of "*Ch'i wu lun*." The third character, *lun*, far from being inconsequential, was rather of crucial importance. With the second character, *wu*, it formed the term *wu-lun*, "theories about things," which Chuang Tzu had used to designate the divergent views of the various teachings. Therefore, what Chuang Tzu really wanted to do in this essay was not to equalize intrinsically unequal things but to demonstrate the senselessness and futility of being self-righteous. In doing this, Chuang Tzu had hoped that the scholars would stop their petty ideological squabbles and "together forget themselves in the art of the Way." [81]

In thus challenging what he considered to be the traditional Way of interpreting the *"Ch'i wu lun,"* Chiao Hung cannot be considered original. The idea was apparently well known already during the Sung dynasty. As Ch'ien Ta-hsin [do] (1728–1804) has noted in his *Shih-chia-chai yang-hsin lu,* [dp] it was first proposed by Wang An-shih [dq] (1021–86) and Lü Hui-ch'ing [dr] (1031–1111) and was later picked up again by Wang Ying-lin [ds] (1223–86) as a problem for special analysis. [82] Wang An-shih's two essays on the *Chuang Tzu* were copied in toto into Chiao Hung's *Wing to the Chuang Tzu (Chuang-tzu i),* [dt] [83] which also listed Lü Hui-ch'ing's commentaries for reference. [84] Chiao Hung would thus seem to have been well acquainted with these two men's ideas on this problem, although he made no acknowledgment to that effect.

One may also question the soundness of this reinterpretation. As Chang Ping-lin [du] (1868–1936) has pointed out, the new reading of the chapter's heading as *"Ch'i wu-lun"* does not really gibe with the contents of the text, which seems to stand for a lot more than the heading would then suggest. [85] The content of the chapter clearly indicates that the "equality of things" was indeed a major problem of Chuang Tzu's concern. It cannot be eliminated from Chuang Tzu's mind by merely changing the reading of the chapter's heading, however imaginative that may be.

There is perhaps no need further to pursue the problem of Chiao Hung's reinterpretation of Chuang Tzu's *"Ch'i wu lun,"* since he probably did not take it very seriously himself. It does not appear in the *Wing to the Chuang Tzu,* which Chiao Hung compiled from the commentaries of forty-nine scholars—including himself—on the *Chuang Tzu.* The reinterpretation was offered by him in his critique of Chu Hsi, and is therefore significant mainly in connection with the latter's thought. Chu Hsi's rejection of Ch'an as heterodox, along with all other teachings except his own, was a mark of his "extreme rigidity" and "narrowness" [86] which are not only morally deplorable but, when viewed in the context of Chiao Hung's *"Ch'i wu-lun"* theory and his concept of the Way as ineffable truth, are also philosophically untenable. They are morally unacceptable because Chu Hsi thereby demonstrated his failure to recognize in other teachings what was lacking in his own, and indulged, as the sages in ancient times never had, in petty ideological squabbling. Worse still, by appropriating for his own teachings the pretentious claim to orthodoxy, Chu trapped himself in the mere "images" of a Way which is itself imageless. Truly to apprehend the Way, one would ultimately have to go beyond all the teachings and discover what "stands prior to the images." To try to comprehend it merely in terms of its "images" is an impossibility.

CLASSICS AND COMMENTARIES

Reflected in the above criticisms of Chu Hsi and his Neo-Confucian predecessors is an element of syncretist thinking which was very common among the left-wing members of the Wang Yang-ming School of Mind and for which these left-wingers were often condemned as "wild Ch'anists." The influence of Buddhism, and, for that matter, of Taoism also, on the development of left-wing Neo-Confucianism during the late Ming period can certainly not be denied. Chiao Hung's conception of the Way as ineffable truth and his skepticism about the teachings as mere "images" of the imageless Way indicate strong influence from the mystical doctrines of Buddhism and Taoism to which indeed he constantly referred in his argument. But, in the tension-charged atmosphere of sixteenth- and seventeenth-century China, when "wild Ch'an" scholars were being most vehemently denounced as corrupted by the heterodoxies of Buddhism and Taoism, it was often not emphasized that they retained certain basic Confucian values which justified their still being considered Confucians.

Chiao Hung, for all his uncertainties about the teachings being merely imperfect representations of the ultimately unrepresentable Way, did not regard them as something to be dispensed with. He emphasized the Way's ineffability but also affirmed the positive value of words and teachings. He said, "As the fish and the rabbit have yet to be caught, the fish trap and the rabbit snare cannot be done away with." [87] "Intellectual discussion" (*chiang-hsüeh*) [dv] was, as a matter of fact, a favorite teaching method of Ming Neo-Confucianists and, as noted earlier, when Chiao Hung was appointed Lecturer in 1594, he even tried to introduce it for the education of the eldest son of the Wan-li Emperor. For Chiao Hung, therefore, to transcend the teachings did not require their negation. His mystical sense of the Way as ineffable truth was invoked not to justify the rejection of the teachings but to stress the need to consider the equal, though qualified, validity of manifold teachings. Intellectually this reflected his basically Confucian valuation of learning. It also served as the basis of his philosophical pluralism, which made it possible to engage in dialogue with schools of thought other than Confucianism.[88] Even more important for our purposes, it enabled him to challenge the state-imposed orthodoxy of Ch'eng-Chu Neo-Confucianism and to advocate independent studies of the Classics in disregard of the standard commentaries.

Chiao Hung criticized the state's practice of imposing upon the people a set of officially sanctioned commentaries as orthodox interpretations of the classics. The thrust of his criticism was mainly directed at the T'ang government, and understandably so, since earlier dynasties, in spite of their patronage of Confucianism as a state ideology, lacked the institutional means to maintain such an orthodoxy until T'ang times, when the Confucian-oriented system of civil service examinations became the most important route to political success. Moreover, as Chiao Hung pointed out, during the T'ang dynasty the state commissioned K'ung Ying-ta [dw] to write commentaries on the Classics which were then promulgated throughout the country as the standard interpretations of these canonical works and which the scholars of the time were obliged by the emperor's fiat to follow meticulously. This measure by the T'ang government was regarded by Chiao Hung as "grossly inappropriate." The truth contained in the teachings of the ancient sages was considered by Chiao Hung to be multifaceted and could not be molded into definitive form in terms of a single school of interpretation. The proper attitude toward the various schools of commentaries was therefore not to make a commitment to just one of them but to become thoroughly exposed to all. Hopefully, the student of the classics would emerge from his study of the commentaries with his doubts resolved and would find truth in the classics as a result of the exercise of his own judgment. There could be no fixing of one school of commentary as standard, or forcing of the whole nation to adapt its views to accord with it.[89]

The problem involved here is not merely one of opposing the authoritative interpretations of the state-imposed orthodoxy and of getting acquainted with the multiplicity of commentaries. As a critic of Ch'eng-

Chu Neo-Confucianism, Chiao Hung would not seem a very likely champion of "comprehensive learning" (*po-hsüeh*), one of the chief aims of the Sung school. Ch'eng I and Chu Hsi, according to Chiao Hung, misinterpreted the "investigation of things" and the "extension of knowledge" (*chih-chih*),[dx] and their followers "exhausted their energies in searching for the principles in things in utter disregard for their minds and bodies." [90] "To study," Chiao Hung said, "is to restore man's nature" which "is the same in every person regardless of whether he is a Shun or a Chih [dy] or whether he lives in the past or the present." [91] Man's nature is also self-illuminating and self-sufficient. And yet, it cannot remain so if the person involved does not study, for "its brightness would then be mistaken for obscurity and its sufficiency for inadequacy." [92]

Learning for Chiao Hung, as for many other Ming thinkers, was therefore primarily and ultimately a process of realization in consciousness of one's innate moral nature. As such, it was to be done by and within one's self. There could be no "reliance on searching without." [93] Accumulation of "comprehensive learning" might be of value as a procedure toward self-realization. It was like knitting the mesh without which there could be no net to use in catching fish.[94] Nevertheless, the net was not the fish, and "comprehensive knowledge" was not true knowledge unless it was cultivated in relation to one's self, the reality of which lends truthfulness to all knowing.[95]

Chiao Hung does not feel ashamed when he seems to be lacking some piece of specific knowledge.[96] Nor does he hesitate to stand up to the scholars of the past and say, "I am as much a man of spirit as they were. Why should I be contemptuous of myself and beat a retreat [in front of them]? The student of the Way should sweep away all the straw-dogs of the ancients and create a universe from within his own mind." [97] Thus concerned with the self's independence and the mind's autonomy, Chiao Hung was ready to liberate the student of the classics from not only the coercion of the one-school commentaries of official orthodoxy but also from whatever limitations might attach to studying the commentaries in and of themselves. He proposed to study the classics apart from the commentaries.

The close association of the commentaries with the classics was not, according to Chiao Hung, originally the practice in high antiquity. In ancient times, Chiao Hung maintained, when people wished to comment on the sages' teachings, they did so by writing a book of their own without attaching it to one of the classics that it pretended to interpret. Confucius, therefore, in order to elucidate the truth in the *Book of Changes*, composed the "Ten Wings" (*shih-i*) [dz] which he kept separate from the former as a work in its own right. The same practice was observed by Tzu Ssu,[ea] Mencius, and Chuang Tzu when the first two wrote the *Doctrine of the Mean* and the *Mencius* to develop further the philosophy of the *Analects* and the last wrote the *Chuang Tzu* to clarify the ambiguities in the *Lao Tzu*.[98]

It was not until the Han dynasty when Mao Ch'ang [eb] and K'ung An-kuo [ec] ceased producing works on their own account and merely offered interpretations of the two classics, the *Odes* and the *History*, that the formal association of the commentaries with the classics became first established. This association was then made a firm practice during the Three Kingdoms period, by Wang Pi,[ed] [99] who incorporated the "Ten Wings" into the text of the *Book of Changes* without realizing that the latter had been written with rhymed literature with an integrity of its own and that it should not be confused with writings of other sorts. Wang Pi, Chiao Hung further pointed out, had apparently also forgotten that the three versions of *Changes* by Fu Hsi,[ee] King Wen and the Duke of Chou, and Confucius, were in many respects different from one another and could not be lumped together and treated as one consistent whole.[100]

However, the practice of associating the commentaries with the classics persisted and, as time passed, grew in intensity until, as in the case of the *Spring and Autumn Annals*, the commentaries finally overshadowed the Classics in importance and became the main subjects of study while the classics were pushed into the background as something merely subsidiary.[101] Chiao Hung deplored this excessive emphasis on the commentaries and held it responsible for the superficialities of Confucian scholarship in later ages. "As the commentators explain more," Chiao Hung said, "the student of the Classics thinks less. Negligent and unmindful, [he] no longer engages in deep reflection. It is like meeting a person in the street [when one] recognizes the person's outward appearance without knowing his inner thoughts and behavior." [102]

Chiao Hung suggested that the scholars go straight to the classics without first consulting the commentaries. Speaking specifically of the historical connections of the three commentaries of Kung Yang,[ef] Ku Liang,[eg] and Tso Shih[eh] with the *Spring and Autumn Annals*, Chiao Hung pointed out that the latter work was composed by Confucius with no anticipation of the three gentlemen commenting on it and that it ought to be perfectly intelligible as a classic by itself. There should be no need to refer to the commentaries in order to understand it.[103] Moreover, the commentaries could sometimes be misleading and obscure the true meaning of the classics which would otherwise have been clear to the reader. This, according to Chiao Hung, was true of the *Doctrine of the Mean*, the significance of which as a work of "Confucian mystical teaching" was not always adequately appreciated because the scholars so far "had not known to interpret the *Doctrine of the Mean* through the *Doctrine of the Mean*." [104]

In thus objecting to reading the commentaries as a necessary aid to the study of the Classics, Chiao Hung's aim was not to preclude scholars from commenting or discoursing on the meaning of the classics. He himself in fact ventured into extensive discussions on the meaning of various works, including such canonical scriptures as the *Analects*, the *Mencius*, and the *Doctrine of the Mean*.[105] However, he remained true to the ancient tradition as he visualized it and kept his comments on these three classics as separate notes collected in his own work, the *Chiao-shih pich'eng*.[ei] He thus renounced any claim to speak for someone other than himself.

It is also noteworthy that Chiao used the terms *ch'üan* and *i* as titles for his three other commentary works on the *Book of Changes*, the *Lao Tzu*, and the *Chuang Tzu*. We have encountered the term *ch'üan* in the previous discussion. It is drawn from the *Chuang Tzu* and refers to a kind of fish trap which is used in catching fish but which one is supposed to forget as soon as the fish is caught.[106] The word *i* (wing) has been used to designate Confucius' commentaries on the *Book of Changes* which, as noted above, Chiao Hung believed to be originally a separate work. By using these terms, Chiao Hung leaves no doubt about the nature of his own works as commentary according to his own view of it: secondary when used as an aid to studying the original works but primary and independent of the latter as books in their own right expressing a part of his own self.

On the other hand, Chiao Hung did not reject out of hand the reading

292 EDWARD T. CH'IEN

of all commentaries. What seemed to him objectionable in commentaries was not their being used as guides to the classics but the fact that most of the commentaries which had been used as guides to the classics were discursive commentaries of a type which claim to speak for the sages rather than for oneself and which, in the guise of classical commentary, actually propound a philosophy. Chiao Hung contrasted the *Erh Ya* [ej] with the commentaries which Wang Pi had attached to the *Book of Changes* and pointed out that the *Erh Ya*, as a collection of glosses taken from the *Book of Odes*, bore to the *Odes* the kind of relationship which exemplified the true and ideal connection between the classics and the commentaries as it had existed in ancient times.[107] "The ancient commentators," Chiao Hung said, "explain the words and the language without trying to unravel the meaning of the classics which the reader would have to perceive for himself through deep reflection."[108] This, according to Chiao Hung, was still the practice largely maintained by the Han Confucianists, and the change in practice in later times from linguistic analysis to philosophical exposition was, as noted earlier, considered by Chiao Hung to be the chief cause of increasing superficiality in Confucian scholarship.[109]

In thus rejecting discursive commentaries and redefining what proper commentaries ought to be in terms of the *Erh Ya* as a historical model, Chiao Hung anticipated the development of "evidential research" which was distinctly philological in tone. He also enunciated a principle for the direct study of classics which later became the central tenet of Han Learning. "The *Book of Odes*," Chiao Hung said, "should be discussed in terms of its sound and the rest of the classics be understood by way of their language."[110]

CONCLUSION

One of the constant accusations that has been made against Ming thought is that it neglects classical studies to an unprecedented degree. P'i Hsi-jui [ek] (1850–1908), for instance, who, as a late Ch'ing Classicist of the Modern Text School, was a fine product of the nearly three hundred years of classical scholarship in the Ch'ing dynasty, wrote in his *A Lecture on the History of Classical Scholarship* (*Ching-hsüeh li-shih chiang-i*): [el]

The Yüan continued [the Sung practice of testing the civil service examinees in the meaning of the Classics] and prescribed a set of questions about the Four Books and the Five Classics. In the early Ming period, questions of this type were still being used. Later on, however, they were given up for the essays [that the examinees were supposed to write] on the meaning of the Four Books and the Five Classics. The method of writing such essays was derived from Wang Ch'ung-yün's [em] *Shu-i ching-shih* [en] of the Yüan dynasty and also from the written examination forms drawn up by Wang P'ang [eo] (1044–76). [This Ming examination system] claimed to be selecting officials on their understanding of the Classics. In reality, it was a way of neglecting the Classics and insulting the ancients at its worst. The so-called Classical sholarship of the Ming dynasty was no more than [the pursuit of] the ignorant and the shallow-minded. A few indeed wrote books [on the Classics]. But, as Ku Yen-wu said, Ming scholars, while writing books, were merely plagiarizing, and the commentaries on the Classics produced since the Hung-chih [ep] period were mostly written by removing the names of previous scholars whose ideas [Ming scholars] thus appropriated as their own.[111] The ones that have been taken notice of by the Imperial Catalogue are strange and absurd. They are not worth our further inquiry. It is during this period that the trailing of the Classics in the dust was carried to the extreme.[112]

Like many other criticisms of Ming thought, P'i's disparagement of Ming classical scholarship can be traced back to the early Ch'ing period when scholars, in the immediate years after the Ming's failure, launched damaging attacks on Ming intellectual life. Thus Fei Mi [eq] (1625–1701) condemned Ming scholars for conforming to the Sung classical commentaries as required by the examination system with the result that "the ancient meaning [of the Classics] was completely abandoned" and "the practical learning as transmitted by the seventy disciples of Confucius and preserved by the Han and T'ang scholars became almost lost."[113] This early Ch'ing disapprobation of Ming classical scholarship has apparently persisted into our modern scholarship on Chinese thought, which also tends to view the Ming's neglect of classical studies as a reflection of a general Ming trend toward anti-intellectualism. Liang Ch'i-ch'ao quoted Fei Mi as saying, "So far as the commentaries on the thirteen Classics are concerned, [during the Ming] there existed only the Fukien edition."[114] He concluded from this that "it became a habit among Ming people that they did not like to read books."[115] Professor Yü Ying-shih,[er] who in his recent article tried to analyze the problem of Han Learning in the Neo-Confucian context of the Sung and Ming dynasties, also characterized Ming Neo-Confucianism as "anti-intellectual" and considered the development of Han Learning to be a result of the reassertion of "intellectualism" which he identified as an essential characteristic of Ch'eng-Chu Neo-Confucianism.[116]

Excessive involvement in book learning and belles-lettres, as Professor de Bary has pointed out, was indeed a major concern of Ming intellectuals who, like Wang Yang-ming, yearned for "the simplicity of the ancient sage." [117] This attitude toward book learning sometimes led to libertinism among certain individuals who rejected intellectuality in favor of naturalness and spontaneity. But, in what has always been described as the corrupt and degenerate atmosphere of late Ming China, there was no lack of serious scholars trying to reorder the society by rebuilding the Chinese intellectual tradition on a solid basis of Confucian learning. What these scholars tried to emphasize with regard to book learning was not so much the harmful effects of excessive involvement in it as its relevance or utility to the human problems of their time.

This late Ming concern with the practicality of knowledge was reflected most notably in the efforts of Tung-lin scholars to relate their intellectual pursuits in the academy to political and social reforms in government. It was also manifest in the left-wing Wang Yang-ming school when some of its members such as Chiao Hung emphasized the need to cultivate "comprehensive learning" in relation to one's self. Therefore, while he was concerned over the problems of book learning and comprehensive knowledge, he was at the same time a prolific writer and bibliophile who memorialized the throne to send out commissioners to collect rare books in ancient editions [118] and who compiled a monumental work of Chinese bibliography. For late Ming intellectuals like Chiao Hung, resistance to book learning did not smack of "anti-intellectualism" and did not reflect a tendency to disregard books. It was an effort "to redress the Confucian balance in the direction of moral cultivation in practice, as opposed to cultural activity and the accumulation of learning" [119] as ends in themselves.

Fei Mi, however, if understood properly in context, was actually telling a truth about the state of Ming classical scholarship when he said, "So far as commentaries on the thirteen Classics are concerned, [during the Ming] there existed only the Fukien edition." Liang Ch'i-ch'ao is certainly misleading, however, when he presents this statement in total isolation from its context, thus creating the impression that, according to Fei, the classical commentaries of the Fukien edition were the only classical commentaries produced during the Ming dynasty. In reality, Fei was not speaking of classical commentaries written in the Ming but of the commentaries done by scholars of the Han dynasty that were still extant during the Ming period. In making the above-quoted statement, Fei was therefore not suggesting that the Ming had only one edition of classical commentaries. He was rather criticizing Ming scholars for neglecting the commentaries of the Han dynasty and conforming to those of the Sung which, as noted earlier, he viewed as a surrender by Ming scholars to the pressure of the civil service examinations. Fei is certainly justified in complaining that Ming classical studies were largely governed by Sung commentaries. But, if Sung commentaries dominated the classical scholarship of the Ming dynasty, there was also during the Ming a revolt against their authority which had its significant beginning during the Wan-li period when scholars such as Chiao Hung rejected the discursive commentaries of Ch'eng-Chu orthodoxy and reoriented classical scholarship toward philological analysis.

This late Ming revolt against Ch'eng-Chu orthodoxy as witnessed by Chiao Hung had some notable achievements in critical scholarship on the classics and history. We have already mentioned Chiao Hung's accomplishment as a bibliographer and his contribution as a critical historian to the historicization of Ming *chang-ku* learning. However, he also made the discovery of "rhyming pronunciations" (*hsieh-yin*)[es] in the ancient odes. Being dissatisfied with Chu Hsi's use of the term "rhyming pronunciation," he set out to analyze the rhymes in the ancient odes and came up with the theory that the end rhymes in the ancient odes, which no longer fitted into the modern rhyming schemes, were all natural rhymes whose pronunciations happened to have changed in the course of time.[120] This same theory of "rhyming pronunciation" was also held and propounded by Ch'en Ti in an even more elaborate fashion in his *Inquiry into the Ancient Pronunciations of the Book of Odes* and *On the Ancient Pronunciations of the Rhymed Songs by Ch'ü Yüan and Sung Yü* which, as pointed out above, had in many respects anticipated Ku Yen-wu's two famous works on the phonetics of the *Book of Odes* and the *Book of Changes*. These late Ming achievements in critical scholarship, though not comparable in magnitude to the accomplishments of the early Ch'ing period, were nonetheless significant as the basis of later developments in "evidential research." That the early Ch'ing growth of Han Learning occurred in one sense as a revolt against Ch'eng-Chu orthodoxy is relatively well known. It is seldom recognized, however, that this revolt actually began in the late Ming period. It is therefore worth noting that Fei Mi, unsparing in his criticism of Ming intellectual life, criticized it for its conformity to Sung commentaries and that he traced the reorientation in classical scholarship back to the Wan-li period [121] and acknowledged Chiao Hung's contribution as a forerunner. [122]

That this late Ming reorientation in classical scholarship was positively related to the left-wing speculations on mind and nature is vividly illustrated by Chiao Hung's life, work, and intellectual associations. As pointed out earlier, though he was a leading member of the T'ai-chou school, Chiao pioneered in the development of critical scholarship. While maintaining firm connections with Li Chih, who was probably the most notorious "wild Ch'anist" of the T'ai-chou school, he also maintained a close friendship with Ch'en Ti, the great late Ming master of "evidential research." These seeming inconsistencies, however, are perfectly understandable in the light of his thought, which is remarkably consistent. As I have tried to demonstrate, Chiao Hung synthesized his Buddhist- and Taoist-tinged concept of the Way as ineffable truth with his basically Confucian valuation of learning, and established in his thought a philosophical pluralism which, together with his stress on the self's independence and the mind's autonomy, led logically to his rejection of the authority of Ch'eng-Chu orthodoxy and to his advocacy of linguistic analysis as a method for the direct study of the classics. His pioneering in critical scholarship is thus deeply rooted in the philosophy of the T'ai-chou school and is not a result of his "intellectualism" as Professor Yü Ying-shih has suggested. [123] Though a left-winger, Chiao Hung may not be accused of "anti-intellectualism." But neither can he, for all his erudition and scholarship, be considered a follower of Chu Hsi's "comprehensive learning." A representative in some ways of important trends in late Ming thought, he was, nevertheless, not merely a product of his age, but as one who thought for himself, a producer of the age to follow.

NOTES

1. *Analects*, 4/15, cf. W. T. Chan, *A Source Book in Chinese Philosophy* (Princeton University Press, 1963), p. 23.
2. *Analects*, 17/19; cf. *ibid.*, p. 47.
3. Ku Yen-wu, *Jih-chih lu* [et] (Taipei: Commercial Press, 1965), III, 7/32.
4. *Ibid.*, VI/8/121.
5. Cf. Liang Ch'i-ch'ao, *Chung-kuo chin-san-pai-nien hsüeh-shu shih* (hereafter referred to as *Hsüeh-shu shih*) (Taipei: Chung-hua shu-chü, [eu] 1962, pp. 5–7.
6. Liang Ch'i-ch'ao, *Intellectual Trends in the Ch'ing Period*, translated by Immanuel Hsü (Harvard University Press, 1959), p. 28.
7. Liang, *Hsüeh-shu shih*, p. 3.
8. *Ibid.*, pp. 7–10.
9. *Ibid.*, pp. 1–5.
10. *Ibid.*, pp. 7–10.
11. *Ibid.*, pp. 52–53.
12. Ch'ien Mu, *Chung-kuo chin-san-pai-nien hsüeh-shu shih* (hereafter referred to as *Hsüeh-shu shih*) (Taipei: Commerical Press, 1957), "Preface," pp. 1–3.
13. *Ibid.*, pp. 7–21.
14. *Ibid.*, pp. 135–38.
15. *Ibid.*, 1–21.
16. Hu Shih, "Chi-ko fan li-hsüeh ti ssu-hsiang chia," *Hu Shih wen-ts'un* (Shanghai: Ya-tung t'u-shu-kuan, [ev] 1930), III, 2/111–185.
17. Hu Shih, "The Scientific Spirit and Method in Chinese Philosophy" (hereafter referred to as "Scientific Spirit"), in Charles A. Moore (ed.), *The Chinese Mind* (University of Hawaii Press, 1967), pp. 104–31. The quotation is taken from p. 127.
18. *Chin-ssu lu chi-chu*, Ssu-pu pei-yao ed., [ew] (Taipei: Chung-hua shu-chü, 1966, 3/8a–b, 2/14a; W. T. Chan, *Reflections on Things at Hand* (hereafter referred to as *Reflections*), (Columbia University Press, 1967), pp. 63–64, 105–6.
19. Hu Chü-jen, *Hu Ching-chai chi*, in Chang Po-hsing (ed.), *Cheng-i t'ang ch'üan-shu*, [ex] (preface dated 1708), 2/39a. For Hu's quotation of Ch'eng Hao, see *Chin-ssu lu chi-chu*, 2/9a; Chan, *Reflections*, p. 52.
20. Chiao Hung's year of birth has variously been given as 1539, 1540, and 1541; cf. Jung Chao-tsu, "Chiao Hung chi ch'i ssu-hsiang" (hereafter referred to as "Chiao Hung"), *Yen-ching hsüeh-pao*, [ey] XXIII (1938), 1–2.
21. Ch'ien, *Hsüeh-shu shih*, p. 136; Hu, "Scientific Spirit," p. 124.
22. Liang, *Hsüeh-shu shih*, pp. 9–10.
23. Tu Wei-yün, "Ch'ing sheng-shih ti hsüeh-shu kung-tso yü k'ao-chü hsüeh ti

fa-chan," *Shih-hsüeh chi wai-kuo-shih yen-chiu lun-chi*, Ta-lu tsa-chih she [ez] (1967), pp. 144–53.

24. *Ming shih*, Wu-ch'ang: Hu-pei ch'ung-wen shu-chü [fa] (1877), 288/5b.
25. Chiao Hung, *Tan-yüan chi* [fb] (Library of Congress microfilm), 13/1b–2a.
26. *Ibid.*, 13/1b.
27. Jung Chao-tsu, "Chiao Hung," pp. 2–3.
28. *Tan-yüan chi*, 25/17a.
29. *Ibid.*, 16/10a.
30. *Ibid.*, 20/15b.
31. *Ibid.*, 33/7b.
32. I.e., the two Wangs were equally influential in the realm of Confucianism.
33. *Ibid.*, 14/2b–3b.
34. Huang Tsung-hsi, *Ming-ju hsüeh-an* [fc] (Taipei: Commercial Press, 1965), 7/46.
35. *Ming shih*, 288/6b.
36. *Ming shih-lu*,[fd] 105/209/8b, 10b.
37. *Tan-yüan chi*, 15/22b.
38. *Ming shih-lu*, 107/247/10a.
39. *Ibid.*, 108/269/1b–2a.
40. *Ming shih*, 288/6a–b.
41. *Ibid.*, 288/6b.
42. *Ibid.*, 288/6a. Actually, Ch'en proposed this project in 1593 (*Ming shih-lu*, 107/264/1b–4a) but it was not approved by the emperor until 1594 (*ibid.*, 108/271/5a, 8a–b). To assess the full significance of this project in terms of Chinese historiography is beyond the scope of this paper. Suffice it to note that Ch'en Yü-pi, in making this proposal on the Ming state history, cited as precedent similar projects during the Sung dynasty (*ibid.*, 107/264/2a–b). Actually, the T'ang dynasty preceded the Sung in launching projects of this kind and the tradition of compiling histories by the reigning dynasties for their own times can be traced back to the *Han Record of the Eastern Library* (*Tung-kuan han-chi*) [fe] of the Eastern Han (cf. Li Tsung-t'ung, *Chung-kuo shih-hsüeh shih*,[ff] 1953, pp. 34–35, 71–73; Chin Yü-fu,[fg] *Chung-kuo shih-hsüeh shih* [Taipei, 1960], pp. 44–47, 108–9). These works are different from the *Shih-lu* in that they were written in the composite style (Li Tsung-t'ung, *Chung-kuo shih-hsüeh shih*, p. 93; Yang Lien-sheng, "The Organization of Chinese Official Historiography: Principles and Methods of the Standard Histories from the T'ang through the Ming Dynasty," in Beasley and Pulleyblank (eds.), *Historians of China and Japan* [Oxford University Press,1961], p. 56). They are usually known as "state" or "national histories" (*kuo-shih*),[fh] although both Ch'en Yü-pi and the *Ming shih-lu* referred to his projected work as "Standard History" (*cheng-shih*).[fi]
43. Sun Ch'eng-tse, *Ch'un-ming meng-yü lu*, Ku-hsiang chai [fj] (1883), 13/4a. Officially the project was only suspended temporarily (*Ming shih-lu*, 110/311/7a), but it was never resumed.

44. *Imperial Catalogue* (Shanghai: Ta-tung shu-chü,[fk] 1930), 87/1b–2a.
45. E.g., Hsu Sze-in (Hsü Shih-ying), *Chung-kuo mu-lu-hsüeh shih* [fl] (Taipei, 1954), pp. 149–53.
46. Naitō Torajirō, *Shina shigaku shi, Kōbun dō* [fm] (1950), pp. 368–70.
47. *Imperial Catalogue*, 62/3b.
48. Wolfgang Franke, *Preliminary Notes on the Important Chinese Literary Sources for the History of the Ming Dynasty*, 1368–1644, Ch'engtu: The Chinese Cultural Studies, Research Institute (West China Union University, 1948), pp. 24–25; Huang Chang-chien, "Kuo-ch'ao hsien-cheng lu ying-yin-pen hsü," in *Kuo-ch'ao hsien-ch'eng lu* (Taipei: Taiwan hsüeh-sheng shu-chü,[fn] 1965), pp. 1–5.
49. A branch of learning dealing with historical precedents and anecdotes.
50. Naitō, *Shina shigaku shi*, pp. 343–47.
51. *Ming shih-lu*, 110/313/2a.
52. *Ming shih*, 288/6b. For Chiao Hung's self-defense, see his memorial to the throne which was printed in his *Tan-yüan chi*, 3/7a–10b.
53. Huang Tsung-hsi, *Ming-ju hsüeh-an*, 7/35.
54. Chiao Hung, *Chiao-shih pi-ch'eng* (hereafter cited as *Pi-ch'eng*) (Shanghai: Commercial Press, 1935), 4/103.
55. Chiao Hung, *Chiao-shih pi-ch'eng hsü-chi* [fo] (hereafter referred to as *Pi-ch'eng hsü*) (Shanghai: Commercial Press, 1935), 2/169–170.
56. *Analects*, 6/19. Translated by James Legge.
57. *Pi-ch'eng hsü*, 2/169.
58. *Ibid.*, 2/170.
59. Paul A. Cohen, *China and Christianity* (Harvard University Press, 1963), pp. 3–60.
60. *Pi-ch'eng hsü*, 2/170.
61. *Tan yüan-chi*, 22/25b. The antithesis in this statement is not very clear. Chiao Hung was apparently playing on words to emphasize the Way's ineffability.
62. Chiao Hung, *Chuang-tzu i*, in the *Chin-ling ts'ung-shu* [fp] (1914), preface/1a.
63. *Pi-ch'eng hsü*, 2/169.
64. *Tan-yüan chi*, 22/3b.
65. *Ibid.*
66. *Pi-ch'eng*, 4/104.
67. *Tan-yüan chi*, 12/18b.
68. *Pi-ch'eng hsü*, 2/169.
69. *Pi-ch'eng*, 4/103.
70. *Ibid.*, 4/103-104.
71. For Han Yü's letter to Meng Chien, see *Han Ch'ang-li chi* [fq] (Taipei: Commercial Press, 1953), 4/83–86. This translation of the quotation is adapted from Derk Bodde, *A History of Chinese Philosophy* (Princeton University Press, 1953), II/411.

72. I have followed Professor Yampolsky in the translation of this term. As Professor Yampolsky has explained, the term implies that "by good works in this world a person prepares the ground (*t'ien*) which will produce the fruits and flowers (*fu*) of the next world," cf. Philip B. Yampolsky, *The Platform Sutra of the Sixth Patriarch* (Columbia University Press, 1967), p. 128n.
73. *Tan-yüan chi*, 47/13a–13b.
74. This advice is usually attributed to Ch'eng I. It appeared in *chüan* 15 of the *Ho-nan Ch'eng-shih i-shu* [fr] which was ascribed by some to Ch'eng Hao. Cf. A. C. Graham, *Two Chinese Philosophers* (London: Lund Humphries, 1958), p. 141.
75. *Tan-yüan chi*, 12/19a–b.
76. *Ibid.*, 12/18b–19a.
77. *Pi-ch'eng*, 4/103–104. The analogy was drawn from the *Chuang Tzu*, the opening paragraph of the "*Ch'i wu lun*" chapter.
78. *Pi-ch'eng hsü*, 2/171.
79. *Mencius*, III A, 4 : xviii. Translated by James Legge.
80. *Ibid.*
81. *Pi-ch'eng*, 4/103–104.
82. Ch'ien Ta-hsin, *Shih-chia-chai yang-hsin lu* (Shanghai: Commercial Press, 1935), 19/457.
83. *Chuang-tzu i*, 24th *ts'e*, pp. 5b–7b.
84. *Ibid.*, Bibliography/1a.
85. Chang Ping-lin, *Ch'ung-ting ch'i-wu lun shih*, in *Chang-shih ts'ung-shu* (Shanghai: Yu-wen she,[fs] 1916), 12th *ts'e*, p. 1a.
86. *Pi-ch'eng*, 4/104.
87. *Tan-yüan chi*, 22/3b.
88. The problem of Chiao Hung's syncretism will be explored further in my next research, "The Late Ming Neo-Confucian Synthesis in Chiao Hung."
89. *Pi-ch'eng hsü*, 3/202–203.
90. *Tan-yüan chi*, 12/11a.
91. *Ibid.*, 4/1a.
92. *Ibid.*
93. *Pi-ch'eng hsü*, 1/163.
94. *Ibid.*, 1/154.
95. *Tan-yüan chi*, 49/7b–8a.
96. *Pi-ch'eng hsü*, 1/153.
97. *Ibid.*, 2/171.
98. *Ibid.*, 4/214.
99. *Ibid.*, 3/202.
100. *Ibid.*, 4/214.
101. Chiao Hung, *Kuo-shih ching-chi chih* (hereafter cited as *Ching-chi chih*) (Ch'ang-sha: Commercial Press, 1939), 2/25–26.
102. *Pi-ch'eng*, 1/27–28.
103. *Ching-chi chih*, 2/26.

104. *Pi-ch'eng hsü*, 1/165.
105. *Ibid.*, 1/147–168.
106. *Chuang Tzu*, ch. 26, last paragraph.
107. *Pi-ch'eng hsü*, 3/202.
108. *Pi-ch'eng*, 1/27.
109. *Ibid.*
110. *Ching-chi chih*, 2/20.
111. Ku Yen-wu, *Jih-chih lu*, VI/18/123. Not an exact quotation.
112. P'i Hsi-jui, *Ching-hsüeh li-shih chiang-i* (Shanghai: Ch'ün-i shu-she,[ft] 1911), pp. 82–83.
113. Fei Mi, *Hung-tao shu*, in *Fei-shih i-shu san-chung* [fu] (1927), I/20a.
114. *Ibid.*, I/20b.
115. Liang, *Hsüeh-shu shih*, p. 9.
116. Yü Ying-shih, "Ts'ung Sung-Ming ju-hsüeh ti fa-chan lun Ch'ing-tai ssu-hsiang-shih (1)" (hereafter referred to as "Sung-Ming ju-hsüeh"), *Chung-kuo hsüeh-jen*,[fv] II (September, 1970), 19–41.
117. de Bary, *Self and Society*, pp. 8–12.
118. For the memorial, see *Tan-yüan chi*, 5/10a–11a.
119. de Bary, *Self and Society*, p. 10.
120. *Pi-ch'eng*, 3/63. Cf. Hu Shih, "Scientific Spirit," pp. 123–25.
121. *Hung-tao shu*, I/21b.
122. *Ibid.*, I/22b.
123. Yü Ying-shih, "Sung-Ming ju-hsüeh," pp. 34–37.

GLOSSARY

a 顧炎武
b 清談
c 劉淵
d 石勒
e 一貫
f 無言
g 王衍
h 子貢
i 王陽明
j 良知
k 梁啓超
l 狂禪
m 考據
n 徐霞客
o 霞客遊記
p 宋應星
q 天工開物
r 劉宗周
s 慎獨
t 天一閣
u 汲古閣
v 錢穆
w 東林
x 經學卽理學
y 錢謙益
z 詩本音
aa 易本音
ab 陳第
ac 毛詩古音考
ad 屈宋古音義
ae 本證
af 旁證
ag 胡適
ah 格物
ai 朱熹
aj 顏元

ak 戴震
al 程顥
am 訓詁
an 程頤
ao 近思錄
ap 胡居仁
aq 末
ar 焦竑
as 泰州
at 焦弱侯
au 明史
av 江寧
aw 日照
ax 狀元
ay 騎都尉
az 伯賢
ba 靈山
bb 京兆學
bc 天界寺
bd 報恩寺
be 耿定向
bf 學政
bg 南直隸
bh 崇正書院
bi 王艮
bj 李贄
bk 編修
bl 同考官
bm 會試
bn 固原
bo 上饒
bp 沈邱
bq 講官
br 養正圖解
bs 陳于陛
bt 纂修官

bu 國史經籍誌
bv 欽定四庫全書總目
bw 內藤虎次郎
bx 支那史學史
by 唐書
bz 宋史
ca 舊唐書
cb 鄭樵
cc 校讎略
cd 國朝獻徵錄
ce 掌故
cf 碑傳集
cg 副主考
ch 順天
ci 同知
cj 福寧州
ck 黃宗羲
cl 肅慎
cm 權扶
cn 性
co 命
cp 道
cq 跡
cr 象
cs 匈奴
ct 撑犁
cu 筌
cv 蹄
cw 禹
cx 西戎
cy 墨翟
cz 楊朱
da 韓愈
db 歐陽修
dc 大顛
dd 孟簡

de	福田	ej	爾雅	fc	明儒學案.
df	富弼	ek	皮錫瑞	fd	明實錄.
dg	淨慈	el	經學歷史講義	fe	東觀漢紀
dh	華嚴	em	王充耘	ff	李宗侗. 中國史學
di	堯	en	書義矜式		史
dj	舜	eo	王雱	fg	金毓黻
dk	衆寡之號	ep	宏治	fh	國史
dl	三教合一	eq	費密	fi	正史
dm	齊物論	er	余英時	fj	孫承澤. 春明夢餘
dn	陳相	es	叶音		錄. 古香齋.
do	錢大昕	et	日知錄	fk	大東書局.
dp	十駕齋養新錄	eu	中國近三百年學術	fl	許世瑛. 中國目錄
dq	王安石		史, 中華書局		學史
dr	呂惠卿	ev	﹁幾個反理學的思	fm	弘文堂
ds	王應麟		想家﹂. 胡適文	fn	黄彰健. ﹁國朝獻
dt	莊子翼		存. 亞東圖書舘.		徵錄影印本序﹂.
du	章炳麟	ew	近思錄集注,		臺灣學生書局.
dv	講學		四部備要.	fo	焦氏筆乘續集
dw	孔穎達	ex	胡敬齋集. 張伯行.	fp	金陵叢書
dx	致知		正誼堂全書.	fq	韓昌黎集
dy	跖	ey	容肇祖. ﹁焦竑及	fr	河南程氏遺書
dz	十翼		其思想﹂. 燕京	fs	重訂齊物論釋. 章
ea	子思		學報.		氏叢書. 右文社.
eb	毛萇	ez	杜維運. ﹁清盛	ft	群益書社.
ec	孔安國		世的學術工作與	fu	弘道書. 費氏遺書
ed	王弼		考據學的發展﹂.		三種
ee	伏羲		史學及外國史研	fv	﹁從宋明儒學的發
ef	公羊		究論集.		展論清代思想
eg	穀梁		大陸雜誌社.		史﹂. 中國學人.
eh	左氏	fa	明史. 武昌. 湖北		
ei	焦氏筆乘		崇文書局.		
		fb	滄園集.		

TANG CHUN-I[a] *Liu Tsung-chou's*[b] *Doctrine of Moral Mind and Practice and His Critique of Wang Yang-ming*[c]

In early seventeenth-century China, at the end of the Ming dynasty, there were various criticisms of the thought of Wang Yang-ming and his school. The winds of learning had still not turned "back to Han dynasty learning" and away from "Sung-Ming learning," as many scholars of the Ch'ing dynasty would later insist. Such eminent scholars as Wang Fu-chih,[d] who revived the teachings of Chang Tsai,[e] and Ku Yen-wu,[f] who was actually a descendant of the Chu Hsi school, were just at the stage of turning "back to Sung dynasty learning." However, the most important criticism of Wang Yang-ming's thought came from developments within the Wang Yang-ming school itself.

The thought of the Tung-lin school[g] and of Liu Tsung-chou originated from the teachings of Wang Yang-ming and other thinkers of the Ming dynasty. Their criticisms of Wang Yang-ming and his school may be taken as the inner criticism of developments within the school, and as one turning point in the intellectual history of the last period of the Ming dynasty. Compared with the Tung-lin school's criticism of Wang's thought, Liu's criticism was deeper and more constructive. Nevertheless, they were all concerned with the central problem of man's inner moral life and found something ambiguous and suspect in Wang Yang-ming's thought, especially as it was developed by Wang Chi[h] of the Che-tung school[i] and by thinkers of the T'ai-chou school.[j]

Wang Chi, like thinkers of the Chiang-yu school,[k] considered *liang-chih*[l] as an ontological reality. Yet the Chiang-yu school thought of *liang-chih* itself as a substance which was a quiet and tranquil reality beyond its function, more like a metaphysical being. Wang Chi never separated the substance and function of *liang-chih*; he thought the substance and reality were wholly immanent in its function. To him, *liang-*

chih, as the function of a pure knowing which is also pure substance, transcended ordinary empirical good and evil. It was beyond good and evil, and thus absolutely good. Surely this type of thinking is subtle and profound, yet it is also most dangerous in the ordinary ethical sense. Because if the absolute good is beyond good and evil, then how is it differentiated from the no-good of ordinary life? Every man can make an excuse and persuade himself that his no-good is the absolute good and his evil is no-evil as well.

The idea of beyond good and evil was also propounded by later thinkers such as Chou Ju-teng [m] of the T'ai-chou school. In the T'ai-chou school, the idea of "natural life" or "cosmic life" was stressed, as in the thought of Wang Ken,[n] the founder of this school, and of Lo Ju-fang,[o] his eminent successor. In the T'ai-chou school, man's spiritual or moral life is rooted and embodied in the natural life. The idea of natural life as such may also be taken as beyond any ethical ideas of "good" or "evil." In this school, the realization of *liang-chih* or the practice of morality is coextensive with man's natural life or ordinary life. Thus any type of human life could be pervaded with the light of *liang-chih* and could become an embodiment of it. Therefore the scholars of the T'ai-chou school could take up any profession in the community and engage in any form of action with a sense of moral enterprise or moral heroism. The type of personality developed in this school is usually not classical, as with traditional Confucianists, but more chivalrous and romantic.

T'ai-chou teachings spread rapidly among laymen and ordinary people. The disciples of the school, who took morality as existing in any kind of life, looked upon its practice as an easy thing. They did not realize how serious it was, or how morality can be perverted by personal emotions and desires.

In opposition to them, the Tung-lin school thinkers and Liu were classical Confucianists who took the practice of morality seriously. Their central philosophical ideas of morality stressed the ideas of goodness, moral reason, and moral will in the ethical sense. These ideas were differentiated from Wang Chi's ontological ideas of *liang-chih* on the one hand, and from the T'ai-chou school's cosmological idea of life on the other hand. Tung-lin school thinkers and Liu admired man's sacrifice of the natural life for the dignity of his moral reason and moral will, with a sense of the realization of good as good. As a result of their learning and teaching, there were many more from the Tung-lin school who were martyred in their political struggles with powerful men in the government, and Liu himself committed suicide by fasting for twenty-one days when the Ming dynasty collapsed.

Their actions of self-sacrifice are the everlasting glories of Confucianism in the late Ming. Yet in the following sections I shall limit my discussion to the philosophical idea of good as the thinkers of the Tung-lin school stressed it, and to their criticism of Wang Yang-ming on this point. This discussion will serve as an introduction to Liu's ideas of moral will and to his own criticism of Wang Yang-ming, which were more profound even than the Tung-lin.

THE TUNG-LIN SCHOOL'S CRITICISM OF WANG YANG-MING AS A PREFACE TO LIU TSUNG-CHOU'S CRITICISM OF WANG YANG-MING

The ideas of good as propounded in the Tung-lin school by Ku Hsien-ch'eng [p] and Kao P'an-lung [q] were centered on the "priority of goodness" over Wang Yang-ming's "*liang-chih* as pure knowing." Surely Wang's *liang-chih*, which is an original-conscientious-consciousness that knows what is good and evil, also likes what is good and dislikes what is evil, and can do what is good and avoid what is evil. It is not merely a theoretical consciousness but a moral consciousness or moral mind. However, when Wang Yang-ming talked about the substance of this consciousness or mind, he pointed out that the substance of mind is beyond good and evil.

I have explained elsewhere what he means: that when evil is avoided, no evil remains; when good is done, one passes beyond anything good as well and one does not look upon himself as good. Therefore, the substance of mind or *liang-chih* as the origin of man's capacity for passing through evil and good should be seen as a pure knowing which is beyond good and evil.[1] In Wang Chi's thought, the idea of *liang-chih* as pure knowing, which is ontologically beyond good and evil, was developed to the extreme. It was itself both the function and substance of original mind. It was like a pure light which is also void; thus it is both being and nonbeing. It is serene and quiet, as a mirror; yet when it is active, it is responsive to things without attachment. Hence it is not attached to the goodness of the responsive action, either inner or outer. The sage, whose *liang-chih* is fully realized, responds to everything in the right way and his responsive action is always good. However, as the sage never attaches to the goodness of his action, his mind as the full realization of his *liang-chih* is in a state beyond good as well as beyond evil. He also realizes that *liang-chih* itself is beyond good and evil. All good actions, inner or outer, are just out-flowings from *liang-chih*, like reflections of the moon in the water, or the trail of a bird's flight in an empty sky.[2] It is full of light and also void; it is both being and nonbeing.

Surely Wang Chi's development of the idea of "beyond good and evil" in Wang Yang-ming came from a very lofty ontological vision. Such a vision is attainable when man's mind reaches transcendent heights, and man should have this vision, at least in certain stages of the development of his spiritual life or moral life. However, if we say that we should have such a vision or we should have such a state of mind, we already presuppose such a state of mind as "good"—because whatever should be, or ought to be, is always looked upon as good. A state of mind which is beyond good and evil must be considered as good. Here the idea of good is predicative of the "state beyond good and evil" as its subject. The predicate "good" goes beyond even this "state" as well. Here the priority of the idea of good comes in, as it does in the criticism by the Tung-lin school of the idea of "beyond good and evil."

The writings of Tung-lin thinkers who criticize the idea of "beyond good and evil" are numerous. In connection with what has been said above, I shall quote one paragraph from Ku Hsien-ch'eng's writing:

What modern men are talking about when they speak of "beyond good and evil" . . . just means that man in his moral life should not be attached to whatever is good. . . . One says that the substance or reality of the nature of mind is itself void, luminous (full of light), transparent, serene and tranquil . . . and therefore the word good is not sufficient to describe the reality of the nature of mind. However, to my way of thinking, the good is the name of ten thousand virtues (of the mind). Voidness, luminosity, transparency, serenity, and tranquility (of mind) are each a special name of a special virtue which is good.[3]

Here Ku's criticism of the idea of "beyond good and evil" is most penetrating. It means that when we say that the reality of the nature of mind is void or luminous, and so on, and that one should realize the reality of the nature of mind as Wang Yang-ming and Wang Chi have taught it, we presuppose that one's nature and the virtues are already good. Thus if the reality of the nature of mind can be thought of as void or luminous, it has to be thought of as good as well. It is then impossible for us to escape the term "good" when we think about the reality of the nature of mind. So Ku said that good is the original color of mind itself.[4] This means that the mind always tends to be good and thus to be good is the original nature of mind or the reality of the nature of mind.

In the above paragraph by Ku, the sentence "the good is the name of ten thousand virtues, and voidness, transparency . . . are each a special name of a special virtue" is most significant. It means that there are many other virtues of mind besides voidness and transparency, and that there are other sides of the mind's nature which, when realized, become man's virtues as well.

What are the other virtues? Some are, for example, filial piety to parents, loyalty to country, duty to the community, and responsibility to the age and to historical and cultural heritage. In the same essay, Ku related a story of Wang Yang-ming, in which Wang said frankly that it was impossible for him to detach himself from his parents when he was affected by the feeling of filial piety. Ku said that this is proof that detachment of mind, and such virtues as voidness, transparency, and serenity, which originate from detachment of mind, are not the only virtues, and that there are ten thousand other virtues which are good as well. Thus the idea of good has a much wider connotation than just the ideas of voidness, transparency, and serenity of mind, and the idea of good is also logically prior to them.

The priority of the idea of good is insisted upon by the thinkers of the Tung-lin school, but from the ethical point of view. It is quite different from Wang Chi's thought, which insists from an ontological point of view on the priority of *liang-chih* as pure knowing that transcends the ideas of ordinary good and evil.

The priority of the idea of good as insisted upon by the Tung-lin school is different also from the priority of the idea of natural life or cosmic life as emphasized by the T'ai-chou school from the cosmological point of view. When thinkers of the T'ai-chou school talk about the coextensiveness of morality with the natural or cosmic life, they surely make morality more active and alive. However, when morality is submerged into the exuberance of natural life, there is a danger of its losing itself.

The sense of morality should be a sense of "being a master of the flowing of natural life" as well. Man has to "stand still on the good" amidst the flowing life in order to have a genuine ethical life. Therefore, thinkers of the Tung-lin school used the term *chih-shan*,ʳ which means "to stand still on the good," to differentiate their teaching from both the T'ai-chou school and Wang Chi's teaching. The term originated with the Great Learning (*Ta-hsüeh*).ˢ The importance of *chih-shan* was also propounded by Li Ts'ai (Chien-lo),ᵗ who saw the same defects in Wang Yang-ming's thought. However, it was through the thinkers of the Tung-lin school that it became a more popular slogan.

What does it mean, "to stand still on the good"? In the Great Learning it means to stand still on the ultimate good in special existential situations with other men, as filial piety is an ultimate good when one is in an existential situation with one's parents. Life flows from one occasion to another, yet each is special and definite. What is good for any definite occasion is also definitely good. There may not be an ultimate good in the flowing of life as a whole, yet there is ultimate good in any definite occasion of life for the realization of the reality of the nature of mind. Though the occasions are relative and temporal, this realization has its absolute and eternal significance for man's becoming a sage, and it is good. Thus the good is connected with the nature of our mind on one side, and with the objective occasions of life on the other. Hence the thought of the Wang Yang-ming school—which took the good as belonging just to the mind—should be supplemented by the Ch'eng-Chu school idea of moral reason, that the good is "whatever things should be" and belongs to things as well.⁵ This way of thinking actually aims at a synthesis of the Wang Yang-ming and the Ch'eng-Chu schools.

THE IDEA OF MORAL WILL AS IMPLICITLY PRESUPPOSED IN WANG YANG-MING'S THOUGHT AND THE AMBIGUITY OF WANG'S IDEA OF WILL

In comparison with the Tung-lin school, Liu Tsung-chou opposed the "idea of beyond good and evil," and emphasized "mastering the natural life" and "standing still on the good," as Tung-lin thinkers did. Yet Liu Tsung-chou went a step further to center his criticism of Wang Yang-ming and his school on the "nature of mind revealed through the will in connection with the idea of good." In the Tung-lin school, the idea of good was sometimes taken as being prior even to the nature of mind.[6] As the good is what a man is striving to be, it is an ideal the mind knows and aspires to realize; thus it may be described as prior to the *nature* of the mind which merely knows the mind's ideal and does not aspire to realize it. Yet if the mind's nature consists not essentially in "knowing the good as ideal," but in "willing to realize the good and to be good," then "the good and to be good" must be immanent in the willing itself, and the good should not be taken as prior to the mind's nature as will. Liu Tsung-chou saw the mind's nature as essentially a good will, and his idea of good was combined with his idea of will. "To stand still on the good" was for him nothing more than the "self-sustaining of good will."

The importance of will had been proposed by Wang Tung,[u] a thinker of the T'ai-chou school, and Wang Shih-huai (T'ang-nan),[v] of the Chiang-yu school, before Liu propounded it. Wang Tung had said that "the mind as knowing is void, luminous, and sensitive," and that "the will is that which has orientation and is contained therein." [7] Wang Shih-huai said that the constant creativity of spirit in its secrecy is called the will.[8] The will is different from *nien*,[w] or volitional ideas. These sayings anticipated Liu's thought of will. We may say that Liu's idea of will has also been implicitly presupposed in Wang Yang-ming's theory of *liang-chih* as conscientious consciousness, something above our ordinary will which consists just of volitional ideas. In our ordinary will, some ideas are good or right and some are evil or wrong. Yet *liang-chih* as a conscientious consciousness knows what is good, and favors or likes and does it; it knows what is evil, and disfavors or dislikes it and avoids it. It is of course transcendental to the ordinary will, stands above its goodness or evil, and may be taken as "beyond good and evil."

However, when Wang says that *liang-chih* always favors or likes the good and disfavors or dislikes the evil, simultaneously with its knowing good and evil, and passes on to doing the good and avoiding the evil, then *liang-chih* is not merely cognitive but also affective. It is not merely a knowing, but also a feeling and a will which tends to do the good only and to avoid the evil. The avoiding of evil is also good. Thus *liang-chih* as will is an absolute good and transcends the ordinary good and evil, willing or volitional ideas. Because *liang-chih* as will is inseparable from its knowing, and its will is absolute good, its knowing is also absolute good. Therefore the idea of will as an absolute good is implicitly presupposed in Wang Yang-ming's thought. Hence Liu Tsung-chou's thought may be taken as a development of Wang Yang-ming's, which makes explicit what is implicit in Wang's thought and so completes Wang's teaching. This is the reason, I think, that Huang Tsung-hsi,[x] who admired both his master, Liu, and Wang Yang-ming, did not think there was any fundamental incompatibility between them.

However, though the idea of will, as Liu propounded it, may be taken as implicitly presupposed in Wang Yang-ming's thought, Wang still did not realize this and usually talked about the "will" in an ambiguous way. When Wang talked about ch'eng-i,[y] "making the will authentic or sincere," as a way for the realization of liang-chih, he meant only the will which is absolute good and exists on the same level as liang-chih as the substance and function of knowing. Yet in his four-sentence teaching, he said simply that there are volitional ideas which are either good or evil and are known by liang-chih as a knowing of a higher level, standing above and beyond ordinary good and evil. Liang-chih, when taken as absolute good, was not seen through the absolute goodness of its "willing to do good only and avoiding evil," and then its absolute goodness was just taken as identical with its "going beyond ordinary good and evil." Thus there was much confusion, and the development of Wang's thought was diversely interpreted as Wang Chi's ontological idea of liang-chih, which emphasized it as primarily beyond any good or evil, and Wang Ken's idea, which tended to identify it with cosmic life. They all neglected the primordial importance of the ethical idea of good, and lost the spirit of ethical idealism in Confucianism. Yet from Liu Tsung-chou's point of view, all these interpretations originated from the teaching of Wang Yang-ming himself, who, though an ethical idealist in practice, was not aware of what was missing in his own teaching and taught in an ambiguous and misleading way.

Liu's criticism of Wang's teaching of liang-chih is centered on the idea of "will as absolute good," which he saw rightly as what was missing. In the four-sentence teaching, Wang took the will or volitional idea as ordinary empirical will which may be either good or evil, but he also talked about the authenticity of the will which was assumed to be of absolute good. Here the word "will" is plainly ambiguous. So Liu said, If the will is either good or evil, then, if we make the good will authentic, it is surely a better will; but if we make the evil will authentic, it is a worse will. Then, what use is the teaching of authenticity of will? [9] On the other hand, if the will in the teaching of "the authenticity of will" is good, and without it the realization of *liang-chih* is impossible, why talk about *liang-chih* or conscientious consciousness as merely a function of knowing good and evil, and not as a function of "willing the good only"?

POSTERIORITY OF KNOWING AND THE PRIORITY
OR PRIMACY OF WILL

In Liu Tsung-chou's critique of Wang Yang-ming's thought, it is a contest for the "priority or primacy" of conscientious consciousness as "willing only the good" over "the primacy or priority" of the same consciousness as "knowing good and evil." In Wang's thought, this consciousness starts with knowing good and evil; then, second, liking the former and disliking the latter; and, third, doing the former and avoiding the latter. This seems to be a psychological order conforming to common experience. However, according to Liu, this order must be converted into one which recognizes the primacy or priority of the good will as an original function of mind which is connected with another original function of mind—feeling. The knowing function is essentially determined by the orientation of the original will and its accompanying feeling, and is posterior to the will and feeling in an ontological order.

Nevertheless, this was not considered by Liu as a theoretical problem only, but was taken as most crucial for the moral practice of becoming a sage. According to him, for example, when I take the knowing of good and evil as of primary importance and as the first step for my moral practice, ordinary good and evil ideas or wills and actions must already be there. Thus the knowing is actually posterior to such good or evil things as are done by me. My moral knowledge and choice between good and evil, even in connection with moral feelings, as favoring and liking the good and disfavoring and disliking the evil, and with moral actions of doing what is good and avoiding what is evil, are all just my activities which run after the good or evil I have already done. Even though what is good is all preserved and what is evil is all checked, I still have no guarantee that I will do no evil hereafter. Thus I shall never be a moral being with the confidence that I can be a sage, for all my moral struggles follow after evils already done. My struggles for my moral cultivation are one step behind the evils already done, and the pursuit of my moral career is just to catch the tail of those evils. Where then, is the guarantee that I shall eradicate the roots of evil and become a sage?

The problem of Wang Yang-ming's thought about moral practice, as Liu points it out, is a universal problem of human moral thought. When man finds out that he has no guarantee of not-doing-any-evil-again, he realizes the limitation to his moral career and usually prays to a transcendental being, as God, to help him. Yet man still has no guarantee that God will accept his prayer. Therefore, man seems destined to worry about his future, including the future of his moral career.

In the tradition of Neo-Confucianism this problem had been seriously considered since Ch'eng I [z] and Chu Hsi and answered in different ways by different thinkers. In Wang Yang-ming's thought the problem was also raised and answered in another way. This is self-confidence about the existence of *liang-chih* or conscientious consciousness as an eternal being. The knowing of good and evil as a function of *liang-chih* is surely posterior to the good and evil already done, as Liu Tsung-chou had asserted in his criticism of Wang. Yet the substance of *liang-chih* is prior to anything in the world; it is eternally self-existing and beyond ordinary good and evil. Therefore, when man is self-conscious about the eternity of *liang-chih*, and has such self-confidence or self-faith, he need not be afraid of whatever evil he has done and need not worry about his moral future.

If we view Wang Yang-ming's thought from this side, Liu Tsung-chou's criticism can be met and answered to some degree. Nevertheless, if we take the approach of Liu Tsung-chou, we may still ask, What is the self-confidence of *liang-chih?* We shall find that it is a persisting state of mind which is not merely a knowing but also a willing. Wang Yang-ming talked about *liang-chih* as the substance of pure knowing and not the substance of pure willing. He never asserted the primacy or priority of will as essential to the very idea of *liang-chih*. His thought is still inadequate, and must be revised and reconstructed.

From Liu's point of view, if one realizes the primacy or priority of will, then the way for moral practice to be a sage does not start from knowing the good and evil already done, complemented with the self-confidence in the existence of *liang-chih* as eternal substance. It should start with a deeper understanding that our original mind, or *liang-chih*, which is oriented only toward the good after its knowing good and evil, can be thought of ontologically from the very beginning as consciousness having a primary pure will accompanied by a primary pure feeling in the very life of pure consciousness as pure knowing itself. It is absolute good before any ordinary empirical good or evil arises and is known. Therefore, the most direct way for our moral practice to be a sage is to have a self-respect or self-reverence for such an original mind or *liang-chih* in itself. When we have such an understanding in a genuine sense, we stand in a place which is absolute good and can start our moral practice from there; then all other goods follow naturally.

ORIGINAL MIND AS PURE CONSCIOUSNESS WITH PURE KNOWING, PURE FEELING, AND PURE WILL, AS THE ORIGIN OF ALL GOODS

The original mind as a pure consciousness is a philosophical idea understood by thinkers of Wang Yang-ming's school and by Wang Yang-ming himself, as well as by Liu Tsung-chou and such others as Chu Hsi. Consciousness is not pure when it is object-oriented to get empirical impressions or ideas from objects, and is mixed with them. Consciousness is pure when it withdraws itself from outer or inner empirical objects, purifies itself from what it is mixed with, and sees itself as a pure subjectivity or a pure spiritual light. Chinese thinkers usually use the words *chüeh* [aa] or *ling-chüeh* [ab] to describe this pure consciousness. *Chüeh* may be translated as "awareness" or "sensibility" or "consciousness." In the West, when people talk about awareness or sensibility, they think of objects to become aware of or to be sensed. When consciousness is mentioned, it is usually associated with being conscious of something. However, in such Western philosophies as Kant's or Husserl's, there is the idea of pure consciousness—consciousness as pure subjectivity without connection with the object. So I use the words "pure consciousness" as a translation of the Chinese word *chüeh* when it does not imply any connection with the objects and is not mixed with impressions or ideas gotten from the objects.

In Chinese thought, when thinkers talk about mind as empty (hsü),[ac] luminous (ming),[ad] and transparent or sensitive (ling),[ae] the words denote pure consciousness. The meaning of "mind" is "original mind" and is identical with pure consciousness. When Wang Yang-ming and Wang Chi talk about knowing chih,[af] it is originally a pure consciousness as pure knowing beyond good and evil, and has no connection with objects. When Liu Tsung-chou talks about chüeh or tu-chüeh,[ag] he means also a pure consciousness as pure knowing. The word tu[ah] means solitary, unique, and absolute. The pure consciousness as pure knowing, in contrast to its objects, is itself solitary, unique, absolute, and transcendental. Here we have a genuine philosophy beyond ordinary empirical thought, which is agreed to in principle by many great philosophers of the West and India as well as by Chinese Taoists, Buddhists, and many Neo-Confucianists. One who does not understand the existence of such a consciousness is still outside the gate of genuine philosophy.

However, passing through the gate, one finds that there are still different kinds of philosophy and many things to say. In Liu Tsung-chou's thought, as a climax to the development of Neo-Confucianism, pure consciousness is taken not merely as a pure knowing, like a light, but also as a pure feeling and a pure willing, like the heat of light. Thus, pure consciousness has a life. This life is usually described by Liu in terms of the succession of the four seasons from spring to summer, autumn, winter, and to spring again, around a heavenly axis, to symbolize the rotation of the four feelings from delight to anger, sorrow, enjoyment or happiness, and to delight again. In the pure consciousness, there is no object of delight, anger, sorrow, or enjoyment, as there is nothing produced and passed through the four seasons.[10] What Liu has said is that there is a continuous living and creative process in pure consciousness. Sometimes he called this process "primordial change," or "change before Heaven" (hsien-t'ien chih i),[ai][11] which means a transcendental inner change of the pure consciousness itself, before it has objects and a universe. Here the pure consciousness is not taken as a static entity, a pure function, or anything established once and for all. It is always in a living, creative process and has its own inner rhythmic vibration. From its vibration, consciousness springs forth, grows up, regresses, and finally withdraws to its source and becomes self-consciousness. When it springs forth, it is at the stage of spring, with a feeling of delight; when it grows, it is at the stage of summer, with a feeling of anger; when it regresses, it is in the stage of autumn, with a feeling of sorrow; and when it withdraws and becomes self-consciousness, it is winter, with a feeling of enjoyment or happiness. Thus the pure consciousness, if taken as a pure light, is not radiating its light of knowing straight from the inner world to the outer; its light is originally vibrating back and forth within itself, through a curved way, as the rotation of heaven around its axis with its rotations of four seasons or four feelings.

The life of pure consciousness in its four seasons or four feelings is always anticipating its successive stages. It is intentional and has a constant will which is always willing. The constant will keeps the orientation of the mind from stopping in one stage or being partial, and always keeps it turning around and back. Thus the process of the life of pure consciousness is spiral, when viewed from outside. Yet when viewed from inside it is intentionally oriented by "will" to one creative process, and the spiral form is the expression of the creative will in the life of pure consciousness itself. Here Liu Tsung-chou called the creative will the "master" (*chu-tsai*) [aj] of pure consciousness. The nature of will, as creative, is the essential nature of our minds, and this nature (*hsing*) [ak] is continuously revealed through the creative will as the self-governing principle of the pure consciousness in its creative process.

Liu Tsung-chou's subtle explication of the inner life of pure consciousness is also an ontological conception of the original mind as pure consciousness which is transcendental to ordinary empirical consciousness. The distinctive feature of his thought is that the original mind as pure consciousness still has its inner life. So he spoke of the inner state of *tu-chih* [al] or *tu-chüeh*, which is an absolute solitary and pure consciousness, as a sphere full of the flowing of the creative will (*sheng-i*), [am] or creative force (*sheng-ch'i*), [an] or original force (*yüan-ch'i*), [ao] and said that there is a self-turning of the axis of Heaven in the very solitary, absolute, and pure consciousness, in order to describe the self-turning life of the consciousness around the axis of will as rooted in Heaven. Here we may say that the idea of life which was emphasized by T'ai-chou school thinkers was also emphasized by Liu Tsung-chou. However, the "life" of the T'ai-chou school usually means cosmic or natural life which may be neither good or evil in itself. Liu's "life" is one of the pure inner consciousness or original mind which is oriented by its creative will and is essentially good.

As essentially good, Liu's pure consciousness is also different from Wang Chi's, which just took the pure consciousness as pure knowing beyond ordinary empirical good and evil.

The reason the life of pure consciousness is essentially good can be seen from the fact that in all men, as Liu explains, evil begins with partiality and solidification of the activity of consciousness. The partiality and solidification come from the fact that there is something remaining when the activity of consciousness is gone. Liu called this "remaining something" *yü-ch'i*. [ap] [12] The word *ch'i* [aq] may be translated as material force; *yü-ch'i* means a residual force left or remaining when an activity is gone. Actually, what the *yü-ch'i* denotes is the potentiality of an activity when it is gone. This is the origin of habits. Every habit, as it comes from man's past activity of consciousness, has some residual effect to compel the present consciousness to take the habitual form, called *hsi*. [ar] *Hsi* may be quite different from nature. [13] When the present consciousness takes the habitual form of its past activity, which is different from nature, it withdraws itself backward to the habitual form and solidifies in that form, becoming partial and noncreative. This is the origin of error and evil.

People usually say that evil comes from egoism or selfishness. This is a superficial way of thinking. Actually, egoism or selfishness is just a sense of the solid-being of one's ego or self. This sense is nothing other than a solidification of consciousness controlled by partial habitual form. From this, the consciousness mechanizes itself and becomes a hard-being with a kernel inside and a shell outside. Thus man develops the sense of the solid-being of his ego or self and becomes egoistic and selfish. All faults, evils, and sins, naturally follow. Therefore, if one hopes to eradicate these, one must have the wisdom which goes to the root or origin of all faults, evils, and sins. The solidification of pure consciousness controlled by the partial habitual form is this very root or origin. Yet the pure consciousness is not originally a being so controlled. The essential nature of pure consciousness is always creative and lively. Thus when we have understanding about the life of such a pure consciousness and have a self-respect or self-reverence for its life, we shall find the way for our moral practice to become a sage which starts from an origin which is absolute good and beyond all evil.

THE PRACTICE OF SELF-REVERENCE, THE
SPONTANEITY OF GOOD ACTION, AND THE
IMMANENCE OF KNOWING IN THE WILLING

To have such self-respect or self-reverence, we must withdraw from our ordinary consciousness which, as object-oriented, is mixed with the impressions that come from the objects, and must then purify it until it becomes pure consciousness. When the present consciousness withdraws itself from what it is mixed with, it becomes pure, self-creative, and meets also the coming pure-consciousness from its source. Here the present consciousness, as self-creative, also intentionally wills the coming-consciousness to be. Through the willing as the connection of the present consciousness and coming-consciousness, they are all just one pure consciousness. The source of this pure consciousness, as unseen, may be taken as ultimate mystery, and Liu used the word *mi*, [as] which means mystery, secret, hidden, or unseen, to describe it. When the present consciousness meets the coming-consciousness with a sense of intimacy or gratitude, it is self-reverence of the consciousness itself. In this self-respect or self-reverence, the mystery, as it were, shines forth its light toward the light which shines backward toward the mystery. Then the mystery is also manifested in the process.

The word self-respect (or self-reverence) is my translation of the single word *ching*, [at] which may also be translated as just respect or reverence. "Respect" or "reverence" in English usually have objects to be respected or revered. This corresponds to the original meaning of *ching*, which also has an object. However, since the Ch'eng brothers talked about "abiding in reverence" (*chu-ching*), [au] it has come to mean to cultivate a state of mind which has no other object to be respected or revered. Thus it is better to add the word "self" to make clear that this is a "respect" or "reverence" which has no other object. This is similar to "being conscious of one's own dignity." Actually, consciousness of one's own dignity and the sense of self-respect or self-reverence have one origin, or are actually the same thing. That is, man realizes that "he is essentially a self-conscious subject, and not an [external] object one [he] is being conscious of, but above all objects." Thus, a man who has a sense of self-dignity is a subject who is always self-conscious and does not have a "consciousness mixed with objects." Such a subject—*qua* subject—is nothing other than pure consciousness. Hence man's sense of self-dignity originates from this pure consciousness.

Yet the ordinary man may feel only that he has self-dignity and may not know what has been discussed above. Therefore, when he is asked where his dignity comes from, he is usually perplexed. However, when man has self-reflection enough, I believe he will realize that his dignity as man comes from the fact that he has a consciousness which is above all objects, and, when not thought of as mixed with its objects, is a pure consciousness. According to Liu's teaching, to know the existence of such a consciousness, of course, one has to withdraw his ordinary consciousness from its object-orientation—and yet after the withdrawal, what he finds is not merely a pure consciousness as pure knowing which is both being and nothing, as is Wang Chi's *liang-chih*. It is a pure consciousness which is creative in its pure feeling and pure willing as well, and full of life. Hence, man's sense of self-dignity or self-respect or self-reverence should be itself a feeling and a will to realize the nature of pure consciousness as feeling and willing.

The practice of this self-reverence or self-respect to keep one's self-dignity is called *kung-fu*. [av] What is realized through practice is the reality (*pen-t'i*), [aw] substance, or nature (*hsing*), the sources of man's dignity. The practice is the realization of the reality or substance or nature—or, in other words, the realization of the reality or substance or nature of pure consciousness. Hence, Liu Tsung-chou talked about the "identity of practice and substance" (*chi kung-fu chi pen-t'i*) [ax] just as Wang Yang-ming and Wang Chi had, though Liu's understanding about the pure consciousness is deeper and more comprehensive than theirs.

When Liu takes self-reverence (or self-respect) as the origin of all good virtues in man, his thought is very similar to Chu Hsi's. However, Chu Hsi usually took both self-reverence and "investigation of things and searching out of their reasons" as parallel ways for moral practice. In Liu's thought, the latter is included in the very practice of self-reverence; there is only one way. Wang Yang-ming's theory of the realization of *liang-chih* is actually developed from Chu Hsi's theory of the investigation of things. [14] Liu disagreed with Wang's theory of the realization of *liang-chih* as well as with the theory of Chu Hsi, in that both men thought that there are ways of moral cultivation outside of self-reverence. In Liu's theory, self-reverence is the only way to realize the pure consciousness as knowing, feeling, and willing, which is itself absolute good and the origin of all ordinary good virtues and good actions.

From self-reverence all ordinary good actions follow naturally and spontaneously, somewhat as with a man who has a high sense of personal dignity, who naturally tends to do noble and good things, and is ashamed to do base or evil things. The good things are always done with noble and good feeling and willing, and here the mind's function as knowing just subsists in the feeling and willing. This will be explained below.

MORAL PRACTICE WHICH STARTS FROM "KNOWING" OUTSIDE THE "GOOD AND EVIL KNOWN" AND ITS RELATION TO MORAL WILL SUBSISTING

In Liu's thought, the best action of man is that which originates spontaneously and naturally from good will and good feeling and not from the deliberate choice between good and evil. The choice between good and evil begins with knowing good and evil. Here Wang Yang-ming said that to know the good, favor it, and do it, and to know the evil, disfavor it, and avoid it, is the way to the realization of *liang-chih*. However, in Liu Tsung-chou's thought, the knowing process itself is outside of what is known to be good and evil. The knowing does not subsist in what is known. Thus even the knowing itself is good. If what is known includes one's evil, one is still not completely good but partly bad. Therefore, the man who just knows both good and evil, and, practicing the way of the realization of *liang-chih*, starts with the choice between good and evil, is not good enough. On the other hand, if his action or behavior is completely good, there is no such thing as a choice between good and evil and there is no "knowing outside what is known as good or evil." Here the "knowing" only subsists in good willing, good feeling, and good action, and illuminating the willing, feeling, and action from within, so the "knowing" can never be taken as something above the good willing, feeling, and action.

Here Liu detected the fundamental defect in Wang Yang-ming's thought, which stresses that *liang-chih* is originally a knowing outside the good and evil known, and said that Wang's understanding of *chih,* or knowing, does not conform to the teaching of Confucius and Mencius. For example, Mencius said that a child knows to love his parents and to respect his elders. This kind of love and respect is spontaneously and naturally expressed by the child without a sense of choice. Here the word "to know" is not something outside of or above love or respect. The knowing function of mind just subsists in the very love and respect. It is not like Wang Yang-ming's "knowing" in "knowing good and evil" [15] which is a knowing above or outside of what is known as good and evil. This is proof that Wang Yang-ming's idea of knowing is not faithful to the Confucian tradition and also neglects the knowing which subsists in the willing and feeling. Spontaneous or natural good actions, such as to love and to respect, are the direct expression of our good nature, and may be taken as directly following from this nature. Its good is intrinsic to the action and is absolute good, as it is not related to evil.

In comparison with the goodness of the creative life of pure consciousness, as we have said before, the goodness of willing and feeling in the action of love and respect is still secondary goodness. The goodness of creative life in pure consciousness with its pure knowing, pure feeling, and pure willing, is the primary and absolute good and the origin of all good actions and good virtues. In comparison with our moral goods, which come from deliberate choice between good and evil, and which start with "knowing the good and evil from outside and relative to the evil," it is still an intrinsic and absolute goodness. It is a goodness that has more intimate relation to the "origin" and it is on a higher level than that which comes from the choice between good and evil and starts from knowing good and evil.

From what has been said above, it is plain that when Wang Yang-ming talks about "knowing good and evil" as the beginning of moral practice, it is moral practice starting from the lowest level. Since in "knowing good and evil" the knowing is outside and above the good and evil known, it is quite possible that the knowing itself is purely contemplative or theoretical and is neither good nor evil. In this case, the knowing is nonmoral. If one has only nonmoral knowing and then just thinks of all moral things contemplatively and theoretically, that is also immoral and becomes the very first step in man's falling into evil. Therefore, knowing good and evil from the outside is a dangerous thing.

However, when Wang Yang-ming talked about knowing good and evil, this "knowing" was not merely contemplative or theoretical. Wang knew also that "knowing good and evil things as external objects" is dangerous. So he opposed Chu Hsi's investigation of things which might include the investigation of things good or evil as external objects. In Wang Yang-ming's thought, the knowing in "knowing good and evil" is itself a knowing originally connected with feeling and willing, as we said before, and his theory of the identity of knowledge and action actually connected "feeling" and "willing" with "knowing." He realized as well as Liu Tsung-chou that mere knowing does not concern our moral life. Thus some of Liu's criticism is not fair. However, Wang still did not say that will accompanied by feeling is the very root of knowing, and that it is primary and prior to knowing. Wang did not realize that the good which comes from a choice between good and evil is a good relative to evil, a good of the lowest order, and not absolute and intrinsic good. It is far from the goodness of the life of pure consciousness as the origin of all good actions and good virtues.

Of course, the goodness realized after the choice made between good and evil as known, is still a moral good. Spontaneous and natural actions which are absolute good, though most precious, are rare. After man has left his childhood, it is only the sage who has the heart of a child and whose good actions flow from the heart of his original nature spontaneously and naturally. However, from the stage of child to the stage of sage, man has to be neither child nor sage, and just a man with both good and evil actions. A man aspiring to become a sage must know the good and evil and choose the good. This is the ordinary way of man's moral practice. Here, Chu Hsi talked about the self-examination of one's goodness and evil, and Wang Yang-ming talked about the realization of *liang-chih*, which knows the difference of good and evil. Liu Tsung-chou did not deny this kind of moral practice as understood by Chu Hsi and Wang Yang-ming. However, Liu stressed one point even in this kind of moral practice. That is, we have to know that in the choice between good and evil, the "knowing-liking-doing-the good" and the "knowing-disliking-avoiding the evil" are not two separate things but originate from "one single will" subsisting.[16]

This will is single, because to do the good is the positive will and to avoid the evil is the negative of the negative, which is also a positive will.

When one understands this point with inner intimacy, then he will not look upon his doing this and that good, and avoiding this and that evil, as moral piecework. He will realize that when he does the good, there is a will subsisting which is intentionally tending to avoid all evils which are in opposition to good. The will, like the needle of a compass, always moves from the wrong direction, which is evil, to the right direction, which is good. Thus it is absolute good. When one knows that this will is always subsisting, and practices *shen-tu*,[ay] [17] or "taking care of the absolute good will in solitude," to make this will sincere and authentic, then through mutual enhancement of doing good and avoiding evil one can have the genuine sense of integrity and unity of personality which make him a real individual with moral grandeur, an absolute and solitary being in the universe. The ultimate stage of this individual is a sage who has no evil to avoid, and then all his good flows from his nature spontaneously and naturally as a child of Heaven. This is the way from the relative good to the absolute and original good in Liu's teaching.

LIU'S FOUR-SENTENCE TEACHING VERSUS WANG'S FOUR-SENTENCE TEACHING

In conclusion, all of Liu's criticisms of Wang Yang-ming come from his idea of pure consciousness as primarily a will which is original good in an absolute sense and is always oriented toward the absolute good in its knowing of all the ordinary goods and evils. Thus the will is originally a sincere and authentic will, and Liu took self-reverence as the most direct way for our moral practice and insisted that to "make the will sincere and authentic, when it is mixed with insincerity or inauthenticity," should be taken as the central kernel even in the teaching of the realization of *liang-chih* as Wang Yang-ming propounded it. Therefore, Liu changed the four-sentence teaching of Wang Yang-ming into the following four sentences: [18]

> Sometimes good and sometimes evil, is where the mind moves.
> Liking the good and disliking the evil, is where the will rests.
> Knowing good and evil, is *liang-chih* or conscientious consciousness.
> "Good without evil" is the ruling principle of things.

What the first sentence describes is the state of our ordinary empirical consciousness which has ordinary volitional ideas or wills, feelings, and actions, which may be either good or evil. This sentence corresponds to the second sentence of Wang Yang-ming's "Four sentences." Wang took all of these as coming from the movement of will, meaning ordinary will. Here Liu used the term "mind" to replace Wang's "will," and in his second sentence he talked about the will which likes the good and dislikes the evil as the will of mind. It is a will which is transcendental to the ordinary volitional ideas or wills, and is purely a moral will existing on a level above the ordinary wills or volitional ideas Wang talked about in his second sentence. In Liu's second sentence, as the "will" likes only the good and dislikes the evil and abides in such liking and disliking, it is the center of mind which is oriented only toward the good. It is opposed to the first sentence of Wang, which says that beyond good and evil is the substance or reality of mind, and which does not realize that there is the will as the center of mind which is oriented to the good and never goes beyond good.

Liu's third sentence has the same words as Wang's. This is proof of Liu's agreement with Wang on the existence of conscientious consciousness. However, as this sentence follows the above two sentences, its significance in Liu's four-sentence teaching is different from that in Wang's. In Liu's four-sentence teaching, the will is taken as the center of mind, and thus is also the center of mind-knowing-of-good-and-evil, which is *liang-chih*. Thus in the *liang-chih* of the third sentence of Liu, the good will is implicated.

Liu's fourth sentence, corresponding to Wang's, talks about things. Wang used the word "things" to mean all our actions or doings, and not just external things. Liu's "things" should have the same meaning. In Wang's fourth sentence, "to do good and avoid evil" is the "investigation of things." Good and evil are assumed to be already there, and good and evil are relative. In Liu's fourth sentence, " 'good without evil' is the ruling principle of things" means: "good things tend to have being and evil things tend to have no-being when they are seen through the ruling principle of our doing and actions, which is directed by will." Therefore, the ruling principle is good without evil. The ruling principle of our doings or actions and will is the very nature of our mind which is revealed and expressed in the moral will of our mind. Thus the nature of mind is good. Hence the fourth sentence indicates the ultimacy of the good of the nature and will of mind, which knows and is conscious of things. This sentence points the way to understanding the mind itself as pure consciousness, which is pure knowing, pure willing, and pure feeling as good in an original sense, and also points to the practice of self-reverence as explained before, although they are not explicitly included in Liu's words.

Generally speaking, Liu's insistence on the ultimacy of goodness is very much like the thought of thinkers in the Tung-lin school. They were in the same current of late Ming thought, which took the view that the idea of good should preside over the idea of the natural life which the T'ai-chou school stressed, as well as over the pure consciousness as pure knowing which Wang Chi had stressed. We have said that the idea of natural life is cosmological and the idea of pure consciousness as knowing which is being and nonbeing is ontological. The idea of good is ethical. Yet Liu did not merely stress the priority of good in the ethical sense; he also had ontological statements about the status of good in the original mind, and connected the "good" with the innermost part of mind which is a "will" having its source in an unseen Heaven. Thus Liu's thinking went a step further than that of thinkers of the Tung-lin school.

When the Ming dynasty fell, Liu committed suicide through fasting. He did not use poison or a knife to end his life suddenly because he did not want to destroy the integrity of his body which he had received from his parents. He had to be both loyal to the country and filial to his parents. His suicide is not like that of the many martyrs of the Tung-lin school who became martyrs through engagement in struggle and combat. This is proof that his learning and thinking were fruitful in his whole personality and worthy forever of our admiration.

THE HISTORICAL SIGNIFICANCE OF LIU'S CRITICISM
OF WANG YANG-MING IN CONTRAST TO THAT
OF OTHER SEVENTEENTH-CENTURY CRITICS

From what has been said above we may understand the depth of Liu Tsung-chou's thought, his contribution to the philosophical development of Neo-Confucianism, and the moral grandeur of his personality. Liu's life, ending in martyrdom, was a life of pure spiritual inwardness, of pure subjectivity of which we can say nothing more. More can be said, however, about the significance of Liu's criticism of Wang's teachings to the intellectual history of the late Ming dynasty or of seventeenth-century China. This can easily be seen from Liu's teaching as a Confucian scholar and moral teacher, and from the difference between his criticisms of Wang Yang-ming and those of other thinkers of his time.

It is noteworthy that Liu as a Confucian scholar and moral teacher emphasized the reading of the traditional Confucian classics and books of history much more than Wang and his direct disciples had. Liu edited a bibliography of the classics [19] and wrote an important book called *Jen-p'u* [az] (Manual of Man). It is a book of moral instruction just as is the *Chin-ssu lu* [ba] edited by Chu Hsi. Yet the contents of the two books is quite different. The *Chin-ssu lu* begins with Chou Tun-i's [bb] discussion of the ultimate principle of the objective universe, and follows with chapters on moral principles and maxims for moral cultivation. The *Jen-p'u* begins with a chapter about the reality of mind as the foundation for the establishment of "man as the ultimate" (*jen-chi*),[bc] and follows with chapters about methods of moral cultivation as exemplified by great historical personages. The moral behavior of these great personages originated with their "moral will," which is always intentional and directed to the concrete social and cultural situation in which men live in each historical age. Thus Liu's emphasis on the "moral will" also implied an emphasis on the knowledge of different historical ages. Here we can easily understand the transition from Liu's thought as a moral teacher to the work of his disciple Huang Tsung-hsi as a historian, a critic of past and recent history and politics.

In contrast to Liu's criticism of Wang, which is almost like a self-criticism and a further development of Wang's teaching, there is the criticism of Wang made by Ku Yen-wu, who was a follower of Chu Hsi.[20] Ku was a friend of Huang Tsung-hsi and had almost the same ideal of political reconstruction and the same high moral sense of loyalty to the Ming dynasty. But he criticized Wang's disciples severely as men given to "pure talk" about "mind and nature" without making an effort to search out the manifold aspects of knowledge, and without a sense of moral responsibility answering to the crisis of the age and the miseries of the people. Ku's criticism of Wang's disciples as not searching out the manifold aspects of knowledge is true to the line of Chu Hsi's criticism of Lu Hsiang-shan.

The other type of criticism of the Wang Yang-ming school came from Wang Fu-chih. Wang Fu-chih called himself a disciple of Chang Tsai. Like Chang, he showed a religious piety toward the natural universe as objective reality and thus respected men's natural desires as the expression of heavenly principle. He also viewed the economic and political aspects of human existence as of equal importance to the cultural and moral aspects. Moreover, he had a strong sense of the continuity of culture among the Chinese people as a historical reality. Hence he rejected the thought of Wang Yang-ming and his disciples as subjective and romantic idealism, lacking a sense of objective reality in nature and history.

There were two other schools of Chinese thought and learning in the late Ming which also differed from Wang's school. Yet whether they emerged mainly as countercurrents of thought is doubtful. One type of thought and learning was represented by Fang I-chih.[bd] Fang was a theoretically oriented man and anxious, like the modern scientist, to get theoretical knowledge about physical nature. The other type of learning was represented by Yen Yüan [be] and Li Kung.[bf] Yen and Li were practically oriented and anxious to get technical knowledge for the maintenance of man's natural and social life on earth.

Yet it is doubtful that the Yen-Li type of thought and learning arose just in opposition to Wang's learning. Yen and Li severely criticized the book learning of the Ch'eng-Chu school. By comparison their criticisms of Wang's theory of knowledge and action were rather restrained and sometimes they even made statements in favor of Lu Hsiang-shan and Wang Yang-ming.[21] It is not difficult to see that there is an ideological link between Wang's idea of moral action and the Yen-Li idea of practical action.

It is also questionable whether the type of learning represented by Fang I-chih was opposed to Wang's type of learning. Here we must recognize that Wang's teaching of *liang-chih* is not logically incompatible with a broad knowledge of culture, history, and nature. Of course, some disciples of Wang may indeed have been given to "pure talk" about "mind or human nature" and lacked a sense of objective reality, as Ku Yen-wu and Wang Fu-chih asserted. Yet the idea of *liang-chih* or mind in Wang Yang-ming can be understood as an objective mind and not merely as a subjective one. This is what Huang Tsung-hsi suggested in his preface to the *Ming-ju-hsüeh-an.* [bg] When the mind is understood as objective, all things in the universe are what the spiritual light of the mind shines upon. Then the understanding of the facts of culture, history, and nature is learning that is not apart. Thus Huang Tsung-hsi could be a scholar of great erudition and still be a disciple of Liu Tsung-chou and Wang Yang-ming. There is no reason to say that an emphasis on scientific knowledge about nature, such as we find in Fang I-chih, stands in opposition to Wang's teaching.

If we do not take the thought of the Yen-Li school and Fang I-chih as being in opposition to Wang's teaching, then there remain just three types of criticism of Wang's teaching, represented by Liu Tsung-chou, Ku Yen-wu, and Wang Fu-chih. The latter two types came from traditions of thought different from Wang Yang-ming's, and were directed mainly at abuses that arose in his school. Their criticisms were external to it and negative, and not without some misunderstandings of Wang's teaching as a whole. By contrast, Liu's criticism was internal and positive, and resulted in a development of that teaching. Huang Tsung-hsi understood this point very well and identified himself as a disciple of both Liu and Wang. As a scholar of enormous erudition, he realized perfectly well that there was no logical incompatibility between the moral idealism of Liu and Wang and a many-sided knowledge of culture, history, and nature. Hence, there are clear links from Wang to Huang's scholarship, and a definite historical continuity in the thought of the late Ming and early Ch'ing. At the same time we should not overlook the importance of Ku Yen-wu and Wang Fu-chih as alternatives to Liu and Huang in this period of Chinese intellectual history.

NOTES

1. See my earlier paper, "The Development of the Concept of Moral Mind from Wang Yang-ming to Wang Chi" in de Bary, *Self and Society*, pp. 108–13.
2. *Wang Lung-hsi yü lu* ᵇʰ (Taipei: Kuang-wen Bookstore reprint, [n.d.]), 7/13.
3. *Ming-ju hsüeh-an* (Chung-hua edition), 58/12.
4. *Ibid.*, 58/13.
5. Cf. My paper, "Yang-ming hsüeh yü Chu-Lu i-t'ung chung pien" ᵇⁱ (The Learning of Wang Yang-ming and an Evaluation of Similarities and Differences between Chu Tzu and Lu Hsiang-shan's Thoughts) in *Hsin-ya hsüeh-pao*, ᵇʲ Vol. VIII, no. 2, pp. 114–18.
6. *MJHA*, 58/25.
7. *Ibid.*, 32/19.
8. *Ibid.*, 20/4.
9. *Liu Tzu ch'üan-shu*, ᵇᵏ edition of Tao-kuang 15 (1835), 21/10.
10. *Ibid.*, 2/9, 11/8–10, 9/15, 10/28.
11. *Ibid.*, 2/13.
12. *Ibid.*, 8/19, 2/11.
13. *Ibid.*, 7/8, 19/53.
14. See the article mentioned in note 5; Vol. IX, no. 1, pp. 1–16.
15. *Liu Tzu ch'üan-shu*, 8/25.
16. *Ibid.*, 19/51, 10/24–25.
17. For examples see *ibid.*, 1/3, 8/9–11, 18/24–25.
18. *Ibid.*, 10/26.
19. Cf. Yao Ming-ta, ᵇˡ *Liu Tsung-chou nien-p'u* ᵇᵐ (Shanghai: Commercial Press, 1934), p. 268.
20. See the essay on Chu and Lu by Chang Hsüeh-ch'eng ᵇⁿ in his *Wen-shih t'ung-i* ᵇᵒ (Peking: Hsin-hua Press edition, 1956).
21. Cf. Tai Wang (ed.), ᵇᵖ *Yen-shih hsüeh-chi*, ᵇᑫ (Shanghai: Commercial Press edition, 1933), pp. 31–32.

GLOSSARY

a	唐君毅	x	黃宗羲	av	工夫
b	劉宗周	y	誠意	aw	本體
c	王陽明	z	程頤	ax	卽工夫卽本體
d	王夫之	aa	覺	ay	慎獨
e	張載	ab	靈覺	az	人譜
f	顧炎武	ac	虛	ba	近思錄
g	東林學派	ad	明	bb	周敦頤
h	王畿	ae	靈	bc	人極
i	浙東學派	af	知	bd	方以智
j	泰州學派	ag	獨覺	be	顏元
k	江右學派	ah	獨	bf	李塨
l	良知	ai	先天之易	bg	明儒學案
m	周汝登	aj	主宰	bh	王龍溪語錄
n	王艮	ak	性	bi	陽明學與朱陸異同
o	羅汝芳	al	獨知		重辨
p	顧憲成	am	生意	bj	新亞學報
q	高攀龍	an	生氣	bk	劉子全書
r	止善	ao	元氣	bl	姚名達
s	大學	ap	餘氣	bm	劉宗周年譜
t	李材，見羅　嘉靖	aq	氣	bn	章學誠
	41年進士	ar	習	bo	文史通義
u	王棟	as	密	bp	戴望
v	王時槐，塘南	at	敬	bq	顏氏學記
w	念	au	主敬		

WILLIAM S. ATWELL *From Education to Politics:*

The Fu She

In traditional China, as elsewhere, educated men often formed small groups to discuss literature, philosophy, history, and other topics of mutual interest. Frequently these organizations were known as *wen-she*,[a] a term which for convenience' sake will be used throughout this paper to refer to all groups sharing this general quality. Although it was during the late Ming period that *wen-she* reached the height of their popularity, they had enjoyed a long history of development: "It is highly probable that the *Analects* is basically a summary of various small group discussions presided over by Confucius and a few of his important disciples. The *Book of Mencius* is essentially of a similar nature."[1] It is not surprising, then, that the unofficial motto of many *wen-she* was "*i wen hui yu, i yu fu jen.*"[b][2] This passage is from the *Analects* (XII, 24) and has been translated as "[The gentleman] by his culture collects friends about him, and through these friends promotes Goodness."[3]

As is often the case, however, the classical ideal was difficult to maintain, and later *wen-she* frequently engaged in activities which were quite different from those encouraged in the above quotation. During the chaotic period following the fall of the Han dynasty, for example, many leading intellectuals turned to Taoism and Buddhism in their frustration over the failure of Confucianism to stabilize Chinese society. One of the most interesting developments during these years was the proliferation of small groups of thinkers who engaged in *ch'ing-t'an*, [c] or "pure conversation," conversation which was "highly witty, refined, and concerned with philosophical matters transcending the concerns of the mundane world."[4] The most famous of the groups was the Seven Sages of the Bamboo Grove:

Not far from Chi K'ang's luxurious estate . . . was a grove of bamboo where he and certain Taoist friends used to walk . . . making up poetry, drinking a little wine, and playing the lute. Here . . . they indulged themselves in "pure conversation" which would end . . . when they reached the Unnameable and then "stopped talking and silently understood each other with a smile." Their strolls invariably wound up at the local tavern. . . . By the end of the evening they would be in a stupor of glorious indifference to the world and intimacy with Tao.[5]

Although not as colorful as their Taoist counterparts, Buddhist study groups also flourished during this period. Perhaps the most important of these was the Pai-lien She [d] of Lu-shan, in modern Kiangsi, which was led by the eminent monk Hui-yüan [e] (334–416). This group included both monks and laymen, and Lu-shan became famous as a place where literati could escape the pressures and dangers of public life.[6] One of Hui-yüan's friends and a frequent visitor to Lu-shan was T'ao Ch'ien [f] (365–427), who has long been considered a classic example of the disillusioned official who turns his back on government service to seek solace in wine and poetry.[7] And while it is obvious that the emphasis of these Taoist and Buddhist groups on "other-worldly" matters was hardly in keeping with typical Confucian concerns, they have nevertheless been regarded as the forerunners of wen-she, Confucian and otherwise, of later periods.[8]

During the T'ang and Sung dynasties wen-she continued to be popular. Prominent figures such as Po Chü-i [g] (772–846) and Yüan Chen [h] (779–831), for example, gathered friends together to discuss literature, engage in writing contests, and criticize each others' compositions.[9] These activities were continued by later groups such as the Ch'i-ying Hui [i] of Loyang, which counted Ssu-ma Kuang [j] (1019–86), Fu Pi [k] (1004–83), and Wen Yen-po [l] (1006–97) among its members.[10] In southern Sung times wen-she were common in both urban and rural areas, and leading intellectuals even built special studios in which philosophical discussions with friends and students were held.[11]

With the fall of the Sung and the establishment of Mongol rule over China, a new element was added to the traditional conceptions of wen-she, as some groups took on a distinct political character. This is not to suggest that politics had been unimportant to the members of earlier wen-she; perhaps in no other society have thinkers and writers been so intimately involved with government and its workings. Nevertheless, the Yüan period was different from earlier ones in several important respects. During the first years of the dynasty, for example, Neo-Confucian ideas of loyalty prevented many ex-Sung officials from serving their conquerors. Instead, these loyalists and their supporters organized *wen-she* and wrote poetry filled with obscure references to the Sung. Perhaps the most important of these early Yüan groups was the Yüeh-ch'üan She,[m] which flourished in the late thirteenth century.[12]

As the Yüan period wore on, memories of the fallen Sung naturally grew dim, and many Chinese found it possible and even rewarding to serve in the Mongol government. Nevertheless, there were also scholars who, for various reasons, chose not to serve. Not a few of these men grouped together with friends out of a sense of frustration and a desire to have some outlet for their creative abilities. The poet Kao Ch'i[n] (1336–74) was a member of one such group and described its activities as follows:

With nothing to do, I spend day and night with these several gentlemen, sometimes arguing philosophical points and refining definitions for the sake of improving our learning, perhaps responding to each others' poems in order to set forth our ambitions, sometimes strumming lutes and lyres to express our innermost feelings, or perhaps just sitting together at the banquet table, joining in the pleasures of the feast. Although it is a time of chaos and disorder, and we have long been forced to withdraw into seclusion, yet together we have found lighthearted joys, so that there is none of us who has not benefited from our association.[13]

During the Ming, and particularly during the latter years of the dynasty, the character of *wen-she* changed significantly. Previously these groups seem to have been organized as a diversion from, or an alternative to, official life. For men like Po Chü-i and Ssu-ma Kuang, *wen-she* afforded an opportunity to relax among friends and to engage in pursuits they perhaps had little time for as officials.[14] For others, such as the Seven Sages, the members of the Yüeh-ch'üan She, and Kao Ch'i's coterie, the groups served as a kind of refuge from government service which had become distasteful or even dangerous. In late Ming times, however, this rather passive orientation away from the concerns of government gave way to a more active one as many *wen-she* became involved in education and in politics.[15]

One of the reasons Ming *wen-she* assumed a role in education was the notoriously poor quality of the prefectural and county schools. Despite the desire of Ming T'ai-tsu to establish a national school system with qualified teachers, "gradually school posts came to be reserved for deadwood *chü-jen* and *kung-sheng*, who from mid-Ming times onward began to glut the lower stratum of officialdom, and the value of the schools as local centers of serious studies became less and less." [16] There were, of course, other educational institutions to which students might turn. Most prominent among these were the private academies (*shu-yüan*) ° which had been the real centers of learning in China since southern Sung times. Nevertheless, it is also true that Ming *shu-yüan* frequently became embroiled in political controversies, and at various times during the dynasty they were even suppressed by the central government, which feared their potential for independent political activity. Of particular interest here is the fact that two important prohibitions on *shu-yüan* occurred during the Wan-li [P] and T'ien-ch'i [q] periods (1572–1627), with the result that the rate of establishing, repairing, and restoring academies fell to its lowest point since the Cheng-te [r] reign (1506–21).[17] In light of this, it should be noted that it was precisely during the Wan-li and T'ien-ch'i eras that *wen-she* began to be organized in unprecedented numbers.[18] The implication is that since government schools and private academies were unable to provide the necessary instruction, young scholars were forced to find other ways to satisfy their educational requirements.[19] One way was to organize *wen-she*, where it was possible to gather together with teachers and fellow students in order to improve each others' learning.[20]

Other factors influencing the development of Ming *wen-she* should also be mentioned. Ho Ping-ti has estimated that in 1600 China's population was approximately 150 million, about double the figure he suggests for the beginning of the fifteenth century.[21] Given the peace and prosperity of the times, this growth in population was not particularly rapid, but when combined with other factors it takes on new significance. During the sixteenth century, for example, the teachings of Wang Yang-ming [s] (1472–1529) and his followers triggered a revolutionary development in Chinese education. Proclaiming that within every man there is the potential for sagehood, members of the Wang Yang-ming school such as Wang Chi [t] (1498–1583) and Wang Ken [u] (1483–1541)

carried the intellectual torch to the masses. Here and there in Kiangsu and Anhwei . . . we find agricultural tenants, firewood gatherers, potters, brick burners, stone masons, and men from other humble walks of life attending public lectures and chanting classics. . . . Never before and never afterward, in traditional China, were so many people willing to accept their fellowmen for their intrinsic worth or did they approach more closely the true Confucian ideal that "in education there should be no class distinctions." Whatever the evil consequence of the intensified Ming autocracy, the Ming period as a whole must be regarded as one of remarkable intellectual and social emancipation.[22]

It seems clear, therefore, that more people were being exposed to basic Confucian education during late Ming times than ever before, and it would not be unreasonable to postulate that this increasing interest in learning, coupled with the pressure of the steadily growing population, eventually created an unprecedented demand for instruction above the elementary level. As has been mentioned, however, the county and prefectural schools were inadequate and *shu-yüan* were periodically suppressed. For this reason, it is significant that during the 1620s and 1630s certain important *wen-she* began to expand greatly and to include on their membership rolls substantial numbers of students from humble backgrounds. In addition, some of the most influential *wen-she* leaders were deeply concerned with problems of education and took pains to help disadvantaged students in their studies.[23]

The nature of the civil service examinations also helped to change the focus of *wen-she* activities. During the Ming the form of the examinations hardened and questions had to be answered in *pa-ku* [v] or "eight-legged" essay style:

A typical specimen takes the announced topic . . . and analyzes it into two subthemes. . . . In the main body of the essay, an extended sentence or group of sentences will be put forward on one of the themes; they are in loose, "ancient prose" style . . . at once followed by an exactly similar sentence or set of sentences on the other theme, which mirror the earlier ones character for character. This game will be played several times before the essay reaches its close.[24]

Compounding the difficulties inherent in this kind of writing was the fact that there were also different styles within the *pa-ku* genre, one of which might be more popular with the examiners at one time than another. Consequently, many young scholars joined or organized *wen-she* in order to have their essays read and criticized by their fellow students and by teachers who were *pa-ku* experts.[25]

Ming *wen-she* also helped their members by collaborating with bookstores to publish collections of their writings. These collections, generally known as *she-kao*,[w] are said to have aided the authors by bringing their names and writing styles to the attention of future examiners.[26] In previous dynasties, patronage had been a fact of life and it had not been unusual for individual students to seek help from those in positions of power. For groups of students to do so en masse, however, was perhaps a new departure, and indicates that all was not well with the examination system. This may have indeed been the case, given the conditions which existed in late Ming times, particularly in Nan-Chihli.[27] It has been noted that from 1400 to 1600 the population of China approximately doubled. At the same time the number of *sheng-yüan*, or holders of the first degree, increased from about 30,000 to perhaps as many as 600,000.

Several factors contributed to this spectacular rise, including the growth in population and the interest in education fostered by the Wang Yang-ming school. Most important, however, was the disinclination of the government to control the number of *sheng-yüan*. In culturally advanced areas, for example, there were virtually no limits on the number of people permitted to hold the first degree. The government did, on the other hand, maintain strict quotas for *chü-jen* and *chin-shih*. Of particular relevance here is the fact that in terms of the area's population and cultural advancement, the *chü-jen* quota for Nan-Chihli was much lower during late Ming times than it should have been.[28] Consequently, counties with wealth, high population, and marked cultural development, such as those in Soochow, Sungkiang, and Ch'ang-chou prefectures, had large numbers of *sheng-yüan* who were unsuccessful in their attempts to pass the provincial examinations. In their frustration, it was only natural for these scholars to seek ways to influence examiners. Significantly, it was in Nan-Chihli that *wen-she* and *she-kao* enjoyed their greatest popularity.

As might be expected, the greater the success a *wen-she* had in helping its members pass the examinations, the more powerful the group became. First, other scholars would join to share in the success, and this, in turn, would increase "grass-roots" support and perhaps enable the group to exert even more influence on examiners and other officials. Second, and more importantly, after members had obtained official positions they could help other members to pass the examinations and move into the government. Here, then, was fertile ground for political activity, and, in an age noted for factional strife, it is not surprising that some *wen-she* became deeply involved in politics. The most prominent of all *wen-she* in this area was the Fu She.[x]

THE FOUNDING OF THE FU SHE

The Fu She had its origins in a group called the Ying She [y] which was organized in 1624 by young scholars from the Soochow area.[29] Among its founders were Chang P'u [z] (1602–41), Chang Ts'ai [aa] (1596–1648), and Yang T'ing-shu [ab] (1595–1647), all of whom were later to be important figures in the Fu She. During the first several years of the group's existence, Ying She members busied themselves with their studies in preparation for the examinations. In one of their projects, for example, they divided themselves into five small groups, each of which did detailed research on one of the Five Classics. They then held meetings, exchanged information, and ultimately published collections of essays based on their findings.[30]

Despite their interest in scholarship, however, the Ying She members were eventually drawn into the political disputes then raging in China. From 1624 to 1627 the notorious eunuch Wei Chung-hsien [ac] (1568–1627) was the veritable ruler of the country, consolidating his power through brutal purges of his political opponents, particularly those associated with the so-called Tung-lin Movement.[31] In 1626 Wei's reign of terror came to Soochow and to the doorstep of the Ying She.[32] The Soochow affair centered around Wei's desire to eliminate an eloquent and respected opponent, Chou Shun-ch'ang [ad] (1584–1626), who was then living in the city. Chou had connections with the Tung-lin movement and had become increasingly critical of Wei from 1622 to 1626. Finally the eunuch ordered Chou's arrest on spurious charges. When this news was made public, Chou's friends and admirers, including a number of Ying She members, began a campaign to raise money for his release. After several days of negotiations, however, the attempt to free him failed and he was sent under guard to Peking. There ensued in Soochow a massive and violent demonstration in which governmental personnel were attacked and even killed by the outraged citizenry.[33] As might be expected, Ying She members also had an active role in this incident. And although the affair ended with Chou's murder in prison, it had important consequences for these young scholars. They had been taken away from their books and thrust into the world of politics, a world with which they became ever more familiar.

Until 1626 the Ying She's membership remained limited in both numbers and geographical distribution. About that time, however, several members began advocating its expansion. The others agreed and soon men were enrolled from Kiangsi, Chekiang, Fukien, and modern Anhwei as the group took on aspects of a broad regional organization. From the eleven or twelve founders, the membership rose to more than forty.[34] The Ying She also made strides in other areas as a number of members did well in various examinations. The group had its finest hour in 1628 when at least five members won their *chin-shih*.[35] Some of this success can probably be attributed to the new political climate in the country created by the death in 1627 of the T'ien-ch'i emperor and the accession of Ch'ung-chen. After some hesitation, Ch'ung-chen removed Wei Chung-hsien and his cohorts from power, and opponents of the eunuch, as the Ying She members had proven themselves to be, were temporarily free of political opposition.

Ch'ung-chen's enthronement also had happy consequences for Ying She leader Chang P'u, as he was selected to be an *en-kung-sheng* [ae] in celebration of the occasion. In 1628 this honor took him to Peking, where he was able to establish good relations with students of the Imperial Academy, and with older officials who had been forced out of office by Wei Chung-hsien and who were just then being brought back into the government. Chang spent long hours talking with these people, and, encouraged by the warm reception he received, he took the opportunity to organize a branch of the Ying She in the north.[36]

After returning home to T'ai-ts'ang near Soochow, Chang and several friends decided that the time was ripe for an even greater undertaking. Having obtained financial support from certain wealthy families in the area, they sent invitations to scholars throughout the country to attend a meeting at Yin-shan in Wu-chiang County in early 1629. When the meeting was convened, people from modern Kiangsu, Anhwei, Hupei, Hunan, and Chekiang were in attendance, and letters expressing interest came from Shensi, Shansi, Fukien, and Kwangtung. Chang convinced this assembly to organize a giant *wen-she* which he hoped would unite like-minded scholars all over the empire, and it was agreed that the new group would be called the Fu She.[37]

Following this initial success, Chang worked hard to expand his organization. In 1630 he and other influential Fu She members took advantage of the congregation of scholars in Nanking for the provincial examinations to organize a second large meeting. This gathering was also successful as the group acquired a number of new recruits including Huang Tsung-hsi af (1610–95).38 Huang was the son of Tung-lin martyr Huang Tsun-su ag (1584–1626), and his name on the membership roll undoubtedly added to the Fu She's prestige.

The results of the 1630 examinations gave the group further cause for rejoicing. In Nanking, Yang T'ing-shu distinguished himself and the Fu She by placing first while Chang P'u, Ch'en Tzu-lung ah (1608–47), Wu Wei-yeh ai (1609–72) and at least twenty-nine other members also passed. In addition, Fu She scholars from other provinces were successful in their examinations. The next year, then, found Chang P'u and a number of his colleagues in Peking to sit for the *chin-shih* examinations. And, as was to be common for the next decade, members of the Fu She were near the top of the list of successful candidates. In the metropolitan examination Wu Wei-yeh placed first, and in the palace examination which followed he was second. Other scholars who received their *chin-shih* that year included Chang P'u, Hsia Yüeh-hu aj (d. 1637), and more than fifty other men who were Fu She members or who later actively supported the group in its political battles.39

Chang P'u's first official assignment after the examinations was to routine clerical work in the Hanlin Academy. It was at about this time that he made the acquaintance of one of the most powerful men in the capital, the grand secretary Chou Yen-ju ak (*chin-shih* 1613, 1588–1644). Although Chou liked Chang and treated him well, his patronage proved to be a mixed blessing, for it involved Chang in the reemerging factional disputes at court. Chou's leading political opponent, Wen T'i-jen al (*chin-shih* 1598, d. 1638), soon accused Chang of being unsuited for his post and demanded that he be ousted from the Academy. Through Chou's intervention Chang's position was saved, but he became more and more uncomfortable as the animosity between him and Wen's faction grew. Finally, in late 1632 Chang asked for and was granted leave from the government. After returning home, he once again organized a meeting of the Fu She which was held in the spring of 1633 at Tiger Hill (Hu-ch'iu) am near Soochow.40 This gathering attracted more than a thousand scholars and "there were none who did not sigh [with admiration] and feel that for three hundred years there had not been [a meeting] like this."41

THE FU SHE ORGANIZATION

At the Yin-shan meeting of 1629, Chang P'u produced an oath for the Fu She by which all members agreed to abide:

Do not follow that which is contrary to established norms. Do not flaunt the Classics. Do not disregard [the wisdom of] old and experienced men. Do not boast of your own abilities. Do not reveal the shortcomings of others. Do not use clever words to disrupt the government. Do not disgrace yourself by seeking advancement [improperly]. Henceforth, those who are guilty of minor violations [of the oath] will be admonished; those guilty of major violations will be expelled. . . .[42]

The language of this oath should not be misinterpreted nor should its significance be underestimated. First, it should be noted that in a shrewd political maneuver, Chang tailored the oath almost word for word after a famous edict of Ming T'ai-tsu, thus making it difficult for enemies to attack the group on ideological grounds.[43] Second, the very existence of such an oath indicates a group consciousness in the Fu She which its predecessor, the Tung-lin Movement, lacked.[44] Moreover, Chang ordered that a membership list be published with the group's she-kao, a move undoubtedly designed to advertise its power and prestige. At the same time, it guaranteed that in the subsequent political battles there would be little question of who was friend and who was foe.

The organizational structure of the Fu She also contained some interesting innovations. What might be termed the group's "national office" was located in T'ai-ts'ang with Chang P'u at its head. From there he directed a sizable staff in activities such as fund raising, the recruitment of new members, and the publication of the she-kao which he edited. Situated below Chang in the Fu She hierarchy were representatives for each prefecture and county in which members resided. Although it is not clear how these representatives were chosen or what their exact duties were, they appear to have had the responsibility of maintaining group discipline, suggesting other scholars for membership, and recommending essays for publication in the she-kao.[45] They also furnished a link between the leadership and the rank and file, thus creating a rather sophisticated network for group communications.

On the local level many Fu She members also belonged to smaller *wen-she* which functioned as branches of the larger organization. In fact, the Fu She could be described as simply a federation of these local groups: "Within the large *she* [i.e., the Fu She], there were numerous small organizations [i.e., the local *wen-she*]. With regard to external matters [i.e., politics], all used the name Fu She: [but] with regard to internal affairs [education, scholarly research, etc.], each [smaller organization] pursued its own line of interest."[46] Hsieh Kuo-chen [an] has identified sixteen of these smaller *wen-she* as having been affiliated with the Fu She, the most important of which were located in modern Kiangsu and Chekiang.[47]

Working from two seventeenth-century Fu She membership lists, the Japanese scholar Ono Kazuko [ao] has arrived at the following figures for the group's geographical distribution:[48]

Area	List A	List B
Nan-Chihli	856 (38.3) *	1230 (40.9)
Pei-Chihli	33 (1.5)	50 (1.7)
Chekiang	440 (19.7)	520 (17.3)
Kiangsi	330 (14.8)	386 (12.8)
Fukien	173 (7.8)	270 (9.0)
Hukwang	227 (10.2)	242 (8.1)
Shantung	74 (3.3)	97 (3.2)
Kwangtung	42 (1.9)	150 (5.0)
Honan	38 (1.7)	27 (0.9)
Shansi	7 (0.3)	14 (0.5)
Shensi	0 (0.0)	5 (0.2)
Szechwan	8 (0.4)	8 (0.3)
Kwangsi	1 (0.0)	1 (0.0)
Kweichow	1 (0.0)	4 (0.1)
Yunnan	0 (0.0)	1 (0.0)
Totals	2232	3005

* The numbers in parentheses represent the percentages of the respective totals.

From these figures, two significant facts should be noted. Although the Fu She drew members from all parts of China, approximately 40 percent were from Nan-Chihli alone. And when the totals for Nan-Chihli, Chekiang, Kiangsi, Fukien, and Hukwang are added, more than seven-eighths of the Fu She members are found to have been natives of those areas. In addition, Ono's work on these two lists has revealed that roughly one-third (34.3 percent in List A, 34.6 percent in List B) of the members came from just five neighboring prefectures: Soochow, Sungkiang, Hang-chow, Chia-hsing, and Hu-chou.[49] In contrast to Hucker's findings for the Tung-lin Movement, therefore, the strong regional character of the Fu She is undeniable.[50]

AIMS AND IDEALS OF FU SHE LEADERS

In his study of Tung Ch'i-ch'ang [ap] (1555–1636), Nelson Wu has written: "Late Ming China presents a picture of a society so heterogeneous as to make the term relatively meaningless outside the chronological frame. The diversity of political and intellectual movements and the wide range of individual attitudes toward life and court, set in a landscape rich in regional differences, produce a complex composition whose divergent elements all may be called typically late Ming." [51] Much of what Professor Wu says about late Ming society in general may be applied to the Fu She in particular. As might be expected with such a large number of members, the group included people with widely varying backgrounds, interests, and ambitions. There were struggling students as well as established scholars, painters as well as experts on military strategy, and carefree men-about-town as well as serious, dedicated officials.

Despite this diversity, however, there were certain ideas which served to unify the Fu She. First of all, it is important to understand what a shattering blow the Tung-lin debacle of 1625–26 was to the young men who became the group's organizers and leaders. Within the space of those two years, Wei Chung-hsien succeeded in eliminating a sizable number of the country's ablest political leaders. Of particular interest here is the fact that of the fourteen best-known Tung-lin people to die in the purges, seven were from Nan-Chihli, two from Chekiang, and one each from Hukwang and Fukien.[52] It was from these areas, of course, that the Fu She drew its greatest support. To Chang P'u, Ch'en Tzu-lung, Huang Tsung-hsi, and their friends, these Tung-lin martyrs were not merely political leaders but also teachers, relatives, friends, and heroes.[53] Their reaction to the purges was understandably one of shock and outrage, and they delighted in demonstrating their disdain for Wei and his supporters. The participation of future Fu She members in the 1626 Soochow affair has been mentioned, but this was not an isolated incident. In a foolhardy but symbolically significant act, young scholars in

Sungkiang led by Ch'en Tzu-lung made a straw effigy of Wei and shot arrows at it, thereby terrifying their more cautious elders who had visions of eunuch-inspired reprisals.[54] Huang Tsung-hsi's actions to avenge his father's murder were even more spectacular. He stabbed two of his father's enemies as they were being questioned at their trial, cut the hair of another political opponent and buried it as an offering to his father, and led the sons of other Tung-lin martyrs in a memorial service at the gates of the imperial prison.[55] Chang P'u and Chang Ts'ai are also known to have led a group of young scholars from the T'ai-ts'ang area in a violent demonstration directed against one of Wei's most important compatriots.[56]

Despite the attention and support gained by such actions, however, the position of these young scholars was a precarious one. Although Wei and his supporters were removed from power by Ch'ung-chen, Fu She members still lacked friends in the higher echelons of the government, and, since their leaders had died in the purges, they had nowhere to turn for guidance and protection. Consciously or unconsciously, then, Chang P'u and the others came to see what Ho Hsin-yin [aq] (1517–79) had seen more than fifty years earlier: "a need for the scholars to organize in some kind of association that gives them collective strength, and not just personal intimacy." [57] Using the existing local *wen-she* as a foundation, Chang P'u built the Fu She into a formidable organization dedicated to aiding its members in the seemingly never-ending factional struggles.

The Fu She leaders were not interested in political power for its own sake, however.[58] They were perhaps even more aware than their Tung-lin predecessors that their dynasty was in trouble and that political and social reforms were of the utmost importance. Of their aims, Étienne Balazs has said: "I think [the] idea of *renewal* or *renaissance* is a leading one, because one of the foremost clubs bore the name of *Fu She* [the character *fu* means, among other things, to return or to renew]. This originally referred to the renewal of ancient learning, but it is fairly certain that members of the *Fu She* . . . interpreted renewal in the sense of a general renaissance, implying the regeneration of society as a whole." [59] The statement of purpose written for the group by Chang P'u generally supports Balazs' contentions:

From the time education [began to] decline, scholars have not understood the wisdom embodied in the Classics. Instead they plagiarize what they have heard and seen and call it their own. Some have been lucky enough to become officials. [But] those at court are incapable of advising the emperor [and] those who are local officials do not know how to help the people. There are fewer and fewer talented men and the government gets worse every day. This is all because [of the decline in education]. I do not want [to attempt] to measure [my own] virtue nor calculate [my own] ability. I [only] hope to join with many scholars from all over the empire to revive the ancient teachings so that future generations will be able to provide useful service [for the country]. For this reason, [our group's] name is the Fu She.[60]

Chang P'u's call "to revive the ancient teachings" (*hsing-fu ku-hsüeh*)[ar] should not be misconstrued. It was not a call for a blind, archconservative attempt to restore ancient institutions. To the contrary, it symbolized the belief that men should make creative use of the lessons of the past to solve contemporary problems.[61] The members of the Fu She understood that times and conditions had changed and that new problems required new and innovative solutions. Nevertheless, they were also convinced that these solutions must be grounded in a thorough understanding of history and the Confucian tradition.[62]

One of the first goals of the Fu She leaders, therefore, was to do something about what they saw as the sorry state of scholarship and education. Much of their dissatisfaction in this area was centered on certain practices connected with the use of *pa-ku* essays in the examinations. Because style rather than content was emphasized in this type of writing, it was common for students to study model essays on the classics instead of the classics themselves, a fact which caused one Fu She member to lament: "What men in former times needed ten years to accomplish can now be finished in one; what once required a year to learn can now be finished in a month. . . . But if by chance you ask someone about a classic he has not read, there are those who will be so confused they will not know what book you are talking about. . . ."[63] For this man and his Fu She compatriots there were no shortcuts to knowledge, and their commitment to the "revival of ancient learning" carried with it the recognition that true education required dedication and hard work. The most outstanding examples of this no-nonsense approach to scholarship in the group were Huang Tsung-hsi and Ku Yen-wu[as] (1613–82), men whose contributions to the study of Chinese civilization were of the highest quality. Nevertheless, their brilliance should not obscure some of the other members. Chang P'u's diligence as a young student was legendary,[64] and despite his later involvement in Fu She affairs and teaching, he still found time to write and edit an impressive number of works on the classics and to become a leading expert on the literature of the Han, Wei, and Six Dynasties periods.[65] In addition, he was well read in history and wrote important commentaries to the *Sung-shih chi-shih pen-mo* [at] and the *Yüan-shih chi-shih pen-mo,* [au] among other things.[66] Fang I-chih [av] (1611–72) had an extremely wide range of interests and produced significant works in several fields.[67] Although he has perhaps been best known for his literary accomplishments, Ch'en Tzu-lung was also highly regarded by his contemporaries for his research into problems of "practical statesmanship" (*ching-shih chih-yung*).[aw] [68] It is hardly an exaggeration to say that many of the best minds of the late Ming period were members of the Fu She.

These men were not interested in simply writing books and obtaining scholarly reputations, however. Believing that social and political reform depended upon improvements in education, they worked hard to continue the revolution in this field begun by Wang Yang-ming and his followers. As recent research has revealed, one of the reasons the Fu She grew to such enormous size was that the established members accepted large numbers of people from humble backgrounds as their students.[69] During the 1630s, for example, Yang T'ing-shu was perhaps the most famous teacher in the Soochow area. He is said to have had two thousand students and his idealistic commitment to education earned him the highest praise from his friends.[70] So many people studied with Ch'en-Tzu-lung and Hsü Fu-yüan [ax] (1599–1665) in Sungkiang that their doorways were "filled with sandals."[71] In T'ai-ts'ang, Chang P'u and Chang Ts'ai were heavily engaged in teaching and have received special attention for their protection and sponsorship of a talented indentured servant in defiance of certain wealthy families. The two Changs and other members also took their message directly to the people. In a spirit somewhat reminiscent of Wang Ken and his disciples, they organized public lectures at which the listeners were exhorted to obey the law and adhere to the high moral standards laid down by the speakers.[72]

It was also clear to the Fu She leaders, however, that peasants who were plagued by unfair taxes, corrupt officials, and the constant threat of natural calamities required more than a moral revival to improve their lives; they needed material help as well. Acting in the role of gentry leaders, then, Fu She members helped local officials draft proposals for tax reforms, directed and financed public works projects, effected the removal of rapacious government workers, and, in times of famine, provided food for the hungry and burial money for the dead.[73] Fu She members who themselves became local officials were also known for their support of humanitarian projects.[74]

As might be expected, their interest in practical problems led some Fu She people to examine the question of reform in a scholarly manner. The leaders in this field were Ch'en Tzu-lung and other members of the Chi She,[ay] the Fu She's branch organization in Sungkiang. In 1638 Ch'en and two friends edited a work of more than five hundred *chüan* entitled *Huang Ming ching-shih wen-pien*,[az] which was a collection of essays and memorials on political and economic problems written by leading scholar-officials of earlier Ming reigns.[75] One of the interesting things about this compilation is that it not only includes writings by Tung-lin leaders such as Ku Hsien-ch'eng [ba] (1550–1612) and Tsou Yüan-piao [bb] (1551–1624), but also pieces by several Tung-lin enemies including Chang Chü-cheng [bc] (1525–82) and Wang Hsi-chüeh [bd] (1534–1611). This open-mindedness indicates that Ch'en and the others were much more interested in what scholars had to say about important problems than in their political affiliations. In 1639 Ch'en edited Hsü Kuang-ch'i's [be] (1562–1633) influential treatise on agriculture, the *Nung-cheng ch'üan-shu*,[bf] which contained information he believed would provide "the basis for enriching the country and transforming the people." [76] In the same year he also published a selection of writings on statecraft by certain T'ang dynasty officials he admired.[77]

Other Fu She leaders pursued similar lines of study. Chang Ts'ai worked on problems related to the grain transport system.[78] The intense and talented Wu Ying-chi [bg] (1594–1645) wrote on numerous political, military, and economic topics.[79] At the metropolitan examination of 1631, Hsü Kuang-ch'i was greatly impressed by Chang P'u's performance and called the younger scholar in to urge him to study things which might be of use to the country. Chang took this advice to heart and in 1635 was responsible for the publication of a new edition of the *Li-tai ming-ch'en tsou-i*,[bh] a collection of memorials on government by famous pre-Ming officials. In his own writings he covered a wide range of practical topics and seems to have been particularly interested in the institutional problems and reform attempts of earlier dynasties.[80] As has been noted, two of the giants of *ching-shih chih-yung* studies in the early Ch'ing period, Huang Tsung-hsi and Ku Yen-wu, were both members of the Fu She and undoubtedly profited from the group's awareness of, and involvement in, political, social, and economic questions. Works like Huang's *Ming-i tai-fang lu* [bi] and Ku's *T'ien-hsia chün-kuo li-ping shu* [bj] represent the culmination of the kind of scholarship so important in Fu She circles during the 1630s and 1640s.

For all their idealistic hopes and plans, however, the Fu She leaders understood quite well the fundamental political reality of imperial China: little could be accomplished without kindred spirits in positions of power. To meet this need, therefore, they worked hard to establish connections with sympathetic officials and, above all, to get their own people into the government.

THE FU SHE IN OPERATION

In the years between the group's founding in 1629 and the fall of the dynasty in 1644, the Fu She had a remarkable record in the civil service examinations. Although a detailed statistical account of its successes cannot be attempted here, a brief review of several of the high points will help to illustrate this point. In the 1630 Nanking provincial examination (for Nan-Chihli), more than thirty Fu She members won their *chü-jen*, with Yang T'ing-shu having the additional honor of placing first. The next year in Peking at least fifty men with Fu She connections were awarded their *chin-shih*, including Wu Wei-yeh who was first in the metropolitan examination and second in the palace examination. Hsia Yüeh-hu was third in that same palace examination. The group's most impressive showing was in 1637 when Fu She people finished first, second, and third in the palace examination and at least thirty-four other members also obtained their degrees.[81]

Since the Fu She included a number of distinguished scholars and teachers, there is probably no question that many of these examination successes were honestly deserved and honestly won. Nevertheless, it is also clear that the group was not prepared to leave its fate to chance and scholarship, and various methods were employed to help Fu She candidates. In addition to publishing *she-kao* and membership lists so that Fu

She people would become better known, the leaders also wrote letters to examiners urging them to help those scholars who met with the group's approval.[82] The best guarantee of success, of course, was to have examiners who were ready and willing to help. In this context, it is significant that the chief examiner for the 1630 Nanking provincial examination, Chiang Yüeh-kuang [bk] (chin-shih 1619, d. 1649), had been a staunch opponent of Wei Chung-hsien and was known for his Tung-lin leanings.[83] Although it is impossible to document whether or not Chiang went out of his way to help Fu She candidates, it is intriguing that they had such success in an examination he administered. And it should also be remembered that because of the low chü-jen quota imposed upon Nan-Chihli, the provincial examinations held in Nanking during the late Ming period were probably the most competitive in the entire country.

At other times during the 1630s, Fu She members are said to have been directly involved in influencing examination results. There is some evidence, for example, that Chang P'u's good relationship with examiners led to favorable treatment for Fu She candidates in the metropolitan examinations of 1634.[84] Perhaps the most colorful story of Fu She examination intrigues concerns an incident which took place during the metropolitan examination of 1637. At that time Hsia Yüeh-hu was helping to supervise the examination with a certain Lo Ta-jen.[bl] Lo, it should be noted, had received his chin-shih in 1631 along with Hsia, Chang P'u, and Wu Wei-yeh, and the four had served together in the Hanlin Academy.[85] After the papers were collected, Hsia is said to have become very ill. According to Lu Shih-i [bm] (1611–72), "[when his] fellow examiners saw that he was ill, Yüeh-hu was already unable to speak. They saw that beside his pillow there was an examination paper. Ta-jen checked it and saw that it still had not been graded. Everyone said: 'This must be the one he likes best.' It was taken and recommended. . . ." [86] The paper, of course, turned out to be that of another Fu She member. Whether this story can be believed is a matter of conjecture. Nevertheless, the man in question did receive his chin-shih that year along with many other Fu She members, including the first-, second-, and third-place finishers in the palace examination.

Despite this record of success, the Fu She was not a significant force in national politics during the early 1630s. For one thing, most of the members were quite young, and even those who had become officials were just beginning their careers, held only minor positions, and were therefore incapable of exerting any real influence in the capital. In addition, the most powerful man in the government at that time was Chang P'u's nemesis from his days in the Hanlin Academy, Wen T'i-jen, who kept a close watch on potential threats to his power. The early 1630s, then, saw the Fu She bide its time, waiting for its people to move up the official ladder. What influence it did have was largely confined to the local level. On this local level, however, its influence was often considerable, for its prestige, growing contacts in the government, and sheer numbers enabled it to bring pressure to bear on low-ranking officials. Aware of the group's power, some officials assigned to Fu She strongholds made a point of frequently consulting with members in order to maintain good relations with them. For those who did not cooperate with the group, life could be quite unpleasant. At least one official is known to have resigned his post because of Fu She–initiated student protests.[87]

Also of value to the Fu She were members who had themselves become local officials. In the early 1630s, for example, a relative of Wen T'i-jen's, living in Chekiang, published a satirical work which was very critical of the Fu She, its leaders, and particularly its recruitment policies. When they heard about this piece from their followers, Chang P'u and Chang Ts'ai traveled to Chekiang to see a Fu She member who was serving in the area as an educational official. This man immediately stopped the sale of the work and had the printing blocks destroyed.[88] In areas exposed to its power, criticism of the Fu She was risky.

The growing influence of the group did not go unnoticed nor unchallenged, however, for "[as] its power increased so did the number and hatred of its enemies."[89] Of all the enemies the Fu She made, none was more formidable than Wen T'i-jen who rose to power during the 1630s through his extraordinary political skill. One of his favorite ploys was to periodically attack men associated with the Tung-lin movement, and since the Ch'ung-chen emperor was opposed to factionalism of any variety, these attacks apparently fell on receptive ears.[90] In any event, by 1633 Wen had ousted most of his rivals from court and had emerged as the most powerful man in the government.

Because of its strong Tung-lin connections, Wen's dislike for the Fu She is understandable, and it is not surprising that he did his best to discredit the group and its leaders. The first open conflict between Wen and the Fu She occurred in 1631–32 when Chang P'u was serving in the Hanlin Academy and Wen attempted to have him removed from office. Although this maneuver was unsuccessful, the animosity between the two men was intense and the affair was an indication of what was to come. In 1634, for example, Wen used his influence to effect the demotion of the Fu She member who had earlier prevented Wen's relative from publishing his work critical of the group.[91] The next several years saw Wen win victory after victory as he was responsible for the resignation from the government of Wen Chen-meng [bn] (1574–1636), the impeachment and "involuntary retirement" of Ni Yüan-lu [bo] (1594–1644), the arrest of Cheng Man [bp] (1594–1638), and the demotion of Huang Tao-chou [bq] (1585–1646).[92] All these men had connections with the Tung-lin Movement and Huang was one of the Fu She's special heroes.

In 1636–37 Wen once again attacked the Fu She directly when one of his underlings submitted a memorial accusing the group of disrupting local government and harassing peasants. At the same time this charge was under investigation, another case involving the Fu She was brought to the attention of the court. In this instance, the main figure was the official mentioned earlier who had resigned his post under Fu She pressure. Supported by Wen's faction, this man memorialized the throne, accusing the Fu She of interfering in local government, of tampering with the examinations, and of forcing his resignation. The emperor again ordered an investigation. Much to the surprise of Wen and his clique, however, the investigating officials in both cases completely exonerated the Fu She of any wrongdoing. And although several of these officials were later demoted by Wen's henchmen, no action was ever taken against the group. The cases were finally closed in 1641–42, when men sympathetic to the Fu She occupied positions of power.[93]

In 1637, for reasons other than his conflicts with the Fu She, Wen T'i-jen resigned from the government and returned home to Chekiang where he died the following year. Since members of his faction still held important positions in the government, however, this turn of events did not signal the emergence of an administration favorable to the Fu She. Nevertheless, the group was rid of its most powerful enemy, and with the members increasingly confident of their own power, the Fu She soon became involved in more overt political activity. Perhaps the best known example of this involvement was the group's 1639 attack on Juan Ta-ch'eng [br] (1587–1646).[94]

This affair had its origins in the disputes between the Tung-lin faction and supporters of Wei Chung-hsien. During the early 1620s, Juan Ta-ch'eng had had friendly relations with some Tung-lin people and particularly with Tso Kuang-tou bs (1575–1625). In 1624, however, Juan was angered when the Tung-lin group supported another man for a position which he coveted. To thwart this he aligned himself with the eunuch faction and was finally rewarded by being given the disputed position. Nevertheless, after a short time in office Juan became apprehensive about possible Tung-lin reprisals and resigned. In 1627 when it became apparent that Wei Chung-hsien's career was finished, "Juan wrote memorials excoriating both the Tung-lin group who despised him and the eunuchs who had helped him." [95] In so doing, Juan hoped to conceal any connections he had had with either of the contending groups. This bit of subterfuge was temporarily successful, for in 1628 he was once again given an official position. The next year, however, Juan's dealings with Wei were revealed and he was stripped of official rank. He returned home to Anhwei in disgrace, but when peasant unrest there became acute several years later, he left to seek refuge in Nanking.

Unfortunately for him, however, the 1630s had seen Nanking become a center of Fu She activities. Because of its beautiful scenery, varied entertainments, and renown as a cultural center, Fu She members from all parts of the country flocked to the city to live and study. [96] Juan was conscious of the group's reputation, and, in an attempt to play down his past, he sought to establish good relations with some of the members. This effort met with complete failure. Undismayed, Juan then spent a great deal of money to form a *wen-she* of his own which he hoped would be able to compete with the Fu She. He also gathered about him a group of unemployed soldiers with whom he discussed "military strategy and swordsmanship, secretly hoping to be summoned [to court] on account of his knowledge of frontier affairs." [97] As might be expected, Juan's ostentatious display of wealth and his involvement in military affairs outraged the members of the Fu She, many of whom believed him to have been at least partially responsible for the victory of Wei Chung-hsien over the Tung-lin faction. They were particularly incensed by Juan's boasts that his removal from office was merely temporary and that friends at court would soon secure a new position for him. Consequently, in 1638 several Fu She members drafted a harsh attack on Juan for his past and present activities. This document was known as the *Liu-tu fang-luan kung-*

chieh, [bt] or the "Proclamation to Guard Against Disorder in the Subordinate Capital." Finally published in 1639, the proclamation was actually an open letter to the emperor charging Juan with everything from bribery to treason.[98] It was signed by 140 young scholars then present in Nanking, the majority of whom were members of the Fu She.[99]

The proclamation achieved the desired result. Juan went into hiding as public opinion against him in Nanking rose to a high level and he did not reappear on the political scene for five years. In retrospect, however, it may seem difficult to understand just why the proclamation has attracted so much attention. Although the attack was successful both in terms of Juan's humiliation and the favorable publicity received by the Fu She, it might be argued that the affair actually did little to enhance the group's political power. Juan had been discredited by the disclosure of his connections with Wei Chung-hsien, and when the proclamation was published he held no official position whatever. While the Fu She enjoyed a spectacular victory, therefore, it was over a relatively weak opponent.

Nevertheless, this incident is significant for other reasons. For one thing, it represented a complete rejection of Ming T'ai-tsu's dictum that students must concentrate on their studies and refrain from discussing politics or affairs of state.[100] The signers of the proclamation, most of whom were *sheng-yüan*, obviously believed that even scholars without advanced degrees or official rank had the right and the obligation to speak out on important public issues. And while this point of view was not unknown in earlier times,[101] it was something of a heresy in a dynasty in which governmental intimidation of intellectuals was an established tradition.

The proclamation is also noteworthy as a symbol of the Fu She's determination to dominate the political scene in Nanking. By the early seventeenth century, Nanking had come to be regarded by many people as an apolitical city, a delightful alternative for those scholar-officals who had no taste for the brutal political in-fighting so typical of Peking.[102] As the Fu She gained in strength throughout the 1630s, however, its members began to view the city in a new light. Nanking was, after all, the empire's second capital, it was an important cultural and educational center, and the crucial provincial examinations for Nan-Chihli were held there. Since most Fu She members were young and as yet unable to wield power in Peking, they simply made Nanking their political base. For them Nanking was still an alternative to the capital, but now it was a political alternative, and they wanted to hold it until they could move into the upper echelons of the government. While the attack on Juan Ta-ch'eng rid them of a hated but weak foe, therefore, it also served notice that any threat to the Fu She's political ascendancy in Nanking would be strongly resisted.

During the 1640s the factional struggles at court raged on. When Wen T'i-jen resigned from office in 1637, he left behind in the government several associates, the most important of whom was Hsüeh Kuo-kuan [bu] (*chin-shih* 1619, d. 1641). With Wen's support and recommendations to the emperor, Hsüeh enjoyed a rapid rise to power. By 1639 he had succeeded in ousting several rivals from the government, been promoted to grand secretary, and become one of Ch'ung-chen's favorite advisors.[103] This was hardly welcome news for the Fu She, which had a history of enmity with Hsüeh dating to 1631, when he attempted to implicate Wu Wei-yeh in examination irregularities.[104] In 1640, however, the situation changed suddenly when Hsüeh was charged with corruption. After an investigation the emperor became convinced of Hsüeh's guilt and ordered him to commit suicide. And although the Fu She's role in this case is not completely clear, it is known that member Wu Ch'ang-shih [bv] (*chin-shih* 1634, d. 1643) was then serving in Peking and was deeply involved in political maneuvering. Significantly, Hsüeh's last words are reported to have been: "Wu Ch'ang-shih is killing me." [105]

Hsüeh's fall from power was accompanied by the recall of Chou Yen-ju to office, a turn of events in which the Fu She again had a hand. Chou was the grand secretary who had befriended Chang P'u when the latter was serving in the Hanlin Academy in the early 1630s. Since Chou himself had been forced out of the government by Wen T'i-jen, Chang and other Fu She members thought him to be the ideal man to replace Hsüeh and lobbied to have him reinstated. How much the emperor was influenced by this lobbying is difficult to determine, but in 1641 he ordered Chou to return to Peking.[106]

It is ironic that in the spring of that year, just when substantial political power seemed within reach, Chang P'u suddenly became ill and died. Since 1629 Chang had been at the center of Fu She activities, and it was his reputation and strong leadership which had made the organization thrive. It is doubtful, however, whether even Chang could have accomplished much in the chaotic years which followed. Although some Fu She members continued to do well in the examinations and to receive governmental promotions, the administration for which Chang had such high hopes became so divided by factionalism as to preclude any hope for reform. One clear indication of the confusion which reigned at that time is the fact that between 1641 and the fall of the dynasty, eighteen different men served in the Grand Secretariat.[107] Weakened by such instability, the Ming slipped into defeat.

The Fu She did not give up easily, however, as a number of the group's leaders joined and even led the struggle to restore Ming rule. The first attempt at restoration centered around a grandson of the Wan-li emperor who, in June, 1644, established his court in Nanking, taking the reign-title Hung-kuang.[bw] Unfortunately for the Ming cause, Hung-kuang's court was just as torn by factionalism as any at Peking had ever been. Generally speaking, there were two groups which vied for control. One of these was under the nominal leadership of Shih K'o-fa [bx] (chin-shih 1628, d. 1645) and included such Fu She people as Wu Wei-yeh, Ch'en Tzu-lung, and Ch'en Chen-hui [by] (1605–56). Allied with this group were several men who had been associated with the Tung-lin Movement—Huang Tao-chou, Chiang Yüeh-kuang, and Liu Tsung-chou [bz] (1578–1645). The opposing faction was led by Ma Shih-ying [ca] (1591–1646), an official who was a close friend of Fu She enemy Juan Ta-ch'eng. Through Ma's influence, Juan was given a position in Hung-kuang's government and the two wasted little time consolidating their power. Their first move was to effect the transfer of Shih K'o-fa to Yang-chow to direct preparations for the defense of Nanking. With Shih out of the way and Ma in control at court, Juan began to settle some old scores. Officials with Tung-lin and Fu She backgrounds were forced out of the government, and when a wholesale purge became imminent, they had no choice but to flee the city.

Following this turn of events, the Ming loyalist position rapidly deteriorated. Armies supposedly loyal to Hung-kuang fought among themselves and Shih K'o-fa was unable to obtain sufficient men and materials for his defensive operations. Yangchow finally fell to the Manchus in May, 1645, followed by Nanking a month later. With the loss of these strategic cities, it was just a matter of time before the rest of China was brought under Ch'ing control. Nevertheless, many Fu She members continued to resist, some of them paying dearly for their courage and determination.[108] Yang T'ing-shu, Wu Ying-chi, and others were captured by the Ch'ing forces and executed, while Ch'en Tzu-lung, Hsia Yün-i, and Hsü Ch'ien ^{cb} (*chin-shih* 1628, d. 1645) were among those who preferred suicide to the humiliation of defeat.[109] And while some Fu She people did serve the Ch'ing,[110] the most important of the surviving leaders went into seclusion and refused to have anything to do with their conquerors.

CONCLUSION

At the Fu She's first great meeting in 1629 there was brave talk of benefiting the people and helping the emperor solve the country's problems. The corrupt and the incompetent were to be turned out of office and replaced by men of talent and integrity who were determined to rectify the wrongs in government and society. Less than twenty years later, however, these idealistic plans were all but forgotten as the Ming house had collapsed, an alien conqueror was on the throne, and the Fu She had ceased to exist. Nevertheless, study of the group is still valuable for the light it can shed on several important aspects of late Ming history. For example, research by Fu She members into various economic and governmental problems and their active support of famine relief, canal and dike maintenance, and other public welfare projects were part of an interesting attempt to translate the humanitarian and pragmatic ideals of late Ming thought into a meaningful reality. Inspired by those ideals and by the steadily worsening domestic situation in the 1620s and 1630s, men like Ch'en Tzu-lung, Hsü Fu-yüan, and Chang P'u became leaders in the search for solutions to the pressing problems of the day. It is not without some justification, therefore, that one modern scholar has credited the Fu She with "laying the foundation" for the great development of "practical" studies in Ch'ing times.[111]

In a recent discussion of late Ming society, W. T. de Bary has written: "The striking feature of the new humanitarianism which developed out of the Wang Yang-ming school was that, drawing on the latter's liberal view of man, it brought together the upper and lower classes, deepening the level of social consciousness in the former and raising the level of moral consciousness in the latter, while also releasing new political and cultural energies throughout the society." [112] This blurring of class lines was also a notable characteristic of the Fu She. Although most of the leaders seem to have come from at least moderately wealthy families, the group demonstrated its social commitment by championing education for poor students, sponsoring public lectures, and accepting large numbers of members from humble backgrounds. The people responded by giving the group active support in several key political battles, including the 1626 Soochow affair and the 1639 attack on Juan Ta-ch'eng.

The Fu She leaders were also realists, however. While welcoming public support, they understood that to effect significant and long-lasting changes the exercise of political power at the highest levels was essential. But with the tragic Tung-lin experience fresh in their minds, they also knew that to obtain and hold such power was both difficult and dangerous. Partially for their own protection, therefore, they formed probably the largest and most sophisticated political organization in the history of traditional China, an organization whose influence at times ranged from grand secretaries to impoverished students. With its "national office," local branches, publications, and unconventional political tactics, the group had a strikingly modern flavor. [113] Nevertheless, the Fu She's fundamental goals were far from revolutionary. Like their Tung-lin heroes, they wanted to reverse the trend toward despotism in China and restore the scholar-official to a position of dignity and responsibility. Before they had a chance to wield significant power in the government, however, the Ming dynasty collapsed and this intriguing experiment came to an abrupt end. And while men like Huang Tsung-hsi continued to examine and write about many of the ideas current in Fu She circles, the watchful Ch'ing rulers made sure their work remained exercises in theory.

NOTES

1. Ping-ti Ho, "Salient Aspects of China's Heritage," in Ping-ti Ho and T'ang Tsou (eds.), *China in Crisis* (Chicago, 1968), Vol. I, Bk. I, p. 32.
2. Lu Shih-i, *Fu She chi-lüeh*,[cc] in *Tung-lin shih-mo* [cd] (Taipei, 1964; hereafter referred to as Lu, FSCL), 1/171; Tu Teng-ch'un, *She-shih shih-mo*,[ce] in *Chao-tai ts'ung-shu* [cf] (Tao-kuang edition; hereafter referred to as Tu, SSSM), 1b–2a.
3. Arthur Waley (trans.), *The Analects of Confucius* (London, 1949), p. 170.
4. Wm. Theodore de Bary, Wing-tsit Chan, and Burton Watson, *Sources of Chinese Tradition* (New York, 1960), p. 287.
5. Holmes Welch, *Taoism: The Parting of the Way* (Boston, 1966), p. 124.
6. E. Zürcher, *The Buddhist Conquest of China* (Leiden, 1959), pp. 204–19.
7. T'ao never became a formal member of the Pai-lien She, however. He was invited to join by Hui-yüan, but declined. See Chang Chih, *T'ao Yüan-ming chuan-lun* [cg] (Shanghai, 1953), pp. 81–82.
8. Tu, SSSM, 1a–2a; Chang Yin-lin, "Shu she," [ch] *Ch'ing-hua hsüeh-pao*, III (December, 1926), 297.
9. Cheng Chen-to, *Chung-kuo wen-hsüeh shih* [ci] (Taipei, 1970), pp. 359–61; Ch'en Shou-yi, *Chinese Literature: A Historical Introduction* (New York, 1961), p. 306.
10. Wang Ch'eng, *Tung-tu shih-lüeh* [cj] (Taipei: facsimile reproduction, 1967), 67/7a; Tu, SSSM, 1b.
11. Wu Tzu-mu, *Meng-liang lu*,[ck] in *Hsüeh-chin t'ao-yüan* (Pai-pu ts'ung-shu chi-ch'eng edition), 19/8a–11a. Cf. Chang Yin-lin, "Shu she," p. 297; and James T. C. Liu, "How Did a Neo-Confucian School Become a State Orthodoxy," *Philosophy East and West*, Vol. XXIII, no. 4 (October, 1973), pp. 491–95.
12. Ch'en Hao-ch'u, "Liang Che chieh-she k'ao," [cl] in *Che-chiang sheng-li t'u-shu-kuan yüeh-k'an*, Vol. IV, no. 1 (January–February, 1935), pp. 1–4; Frederick W. Mote, "Confucian Eremitism in the Yüan Period," in A. F. Wright (ed.), *The Confucian Persuasion* (Stanford, 1960), p. 235.
13. Kao Ch'i quoted by Frederick W. Mote, *The Poet Kao Ch'i* (Princeton, 1962), pp. 95–96.
14. It was not unusual, for example, for retired officials to organize groups to discuss and study Buddhism and Taoism. See *ibid.*, pp. 197–200; and Liu Ta-chieh, *Chung-kuo wen-hsüeh fa-ta shih* [cm] (Taipei, 1968), p. 472.
15. It should not be inferred that the traditional activities of *wen-she*, such as philosophical debates, literary discussions, the writing of poetry, and wine drinking, were dispensed with entirely. To the contrary, these activities were popular even among the most serious-minded of the late Ming *wen-she*. See

Hsieh Kuo-chen, *Ming Ch'ing chih chi tang-she yün-tung k'ao* [cn] (Taipei, 1967; hereafter referred to as Hsieh, MCCC), pp. 10–11, 176–77, 185; Hsieh Kuo-chen, *Huang Li-chou hsüeh-p'u* [co] (Taipei, 1965; hereafter referred to as Hsieh, HLCHP), pp. 98–99; Chou Li-an, *Ch'ing Ming chi* [cp] (Shanghai, 1939), pp. 20–21; and Suzuki Tadashi, "Minmatsu ni okeru Shōkō no Ki Sha ni tsuite," [cq] *Shikan*, nos. 57–58 (March, 1960), p. 72.

16. Ping-ti Ho, *The Ladder of Success in Imperial China* (New York, 1964; hereafter referred to as Ho, *Ladder*), p. 171. Cf. Ch'en Teng-yüan, *Chung-kuo wen-hua shih* [cr] (Taipei, 1966), II, 161–62.

17. John Meskill, "Academies and Politics in the Ming Dynasty," in Charles O. Hucker (ed.), *Chinese Government in Ming Times: Seven Studies* (New York, 1969; hereafter referred to as Meskill, "Academies and Politics"), p. 169.

18. Ch'en Teng-yüan, II, 160–64; Chang Liang-ts'ai, *Chung-kuo feng-su shih* [cs] (Taipei, 1969), p. 194; Hsieh, MCCC, pp. 9–10.

19. It is significant that private academies in southern Kiangsu were particular targets of the T'ien-ch'i suppression and that it was in this area that *wen-she* were organized in the largest numbers. See Meskill, "Academies and Politics," p. 173; Heinrich Busch, "The Tung-lin Academy and its Political and Philosophical Significance," in *Monumenta Serica*, XIV (1949–55), 66; and Li Chieh, *Ming-shih* [ct] (Taipei, 1965), p. 403.

20. Lu, FSCL, 1/171.

21. Ping-ti Ho, *Studies on the Population of China, 1368–1953* (Cambridge, Mass., 1967), p. 277.

22. Ho, *Ladder*, p. 199. Cf. de Bary, "Individualism and Humanitarianism in Late Ming Thought," in de Bary, *Self and Society* (hereafter referred to as de Bary, "Individualism"), pp. 171–78.

23. Tu, SSSM, 13a–14b; Chang P'u, *Ch'i-lu-chai chi* [cu] (facsimile reproduction of Ch'ung-chen edition), 1/10a–b; Ōkubo Hideko, "Minmatsu dokushojin kessha to kyōiku katsudō," [cv] in Hayashi Tomoharu (ed), *Kinsei Chūgoku kyōiku shi kenkyū* [cw] (Tokyo, 1958), pp. 193–98.

24. David S. Nivison, "Protest Against Conventions and Conventions of Protest," in A. F. Wright (ed.), *The Confucian Persuasion* (Stanford, 1960; hereafter referred to as Nivison, "Protest"), p. 194.

25. Tu, SSSM, 2b; Lu, FSCL, 1/171.

26. Li Chieh, p. 403; Yang T'ing-fu, *Ming-mo san ta ssu-hsiang chia* [cx] (Shanghai, 1955), p. 21; Yokota Terutoshi, "Ki Sha no setsuritsu ni tsuite," [cy] in *Shina gaku kenkyū*, XIV (March, 1956), 34.

27. The following discussion relies heavily on Ho, *Ladder*, pp. 173–85, 232–34.

28. From 1600 to 1630, for example, Nan-Chihli averaged 141 *chü-jen* per provincial examination. Kiangsi, with less than one-half of Nan-Chihli's population, averaged 115 *chü-jen* per examination over that same period. For these figures see *Chiang-nan t'ung-chih* [cz] (1736 edition), 129/27b–130/18a; and *Chiang-hsi t'ung-chih* [da] (1880 edition), 31/14a–39b. An estimate of Ming population by province is given in Ho, *Ladder*, p. 225.

29. For a detailed though disorganized discussion of the Ying She, see Chu T'an, *Ming-chi she-tang yen-chiu* [db] (Chungking, 1945), pp. 159–207.

30. *Ibid.*, p. 165. Cf. Chang P'u, *Ch'i-lu-chai chi*, 1/36a; Hsieh, MCCC, pp. 160–61; and Ono Kazuko, "Minmatsu no kessha ni kansuru ichi kōsatsu," [dc] in *Shirin*, XLV (March, 1962), 41–42.

31. For information on the Tung-lin political battles, see Charles O. Hucker, "The Tung-lin Movement of the Late Ming Period," in J. K. Fairbank (ed.), *Chinese Thought and Institutions* (Chicago, 1967; hereafter referred to as Hucker, "Tung-lin", pp. 132–62; Charles O. Hucker, *The Censorial System of Ming China* (Stanford, 1966), pp. 152–74; and Ulrich Hans-Richard Mammitsch, "Wei Chung-hsien: A Reappraisal of the Eunuch and the Factional Strife at the Late Ming Court" (unpublished doctoral dissertation, University of Hawaii, 1968).

32. For this affair see Charles O. Hucker, "Su-chou and the Agents of Wei Chung-hsien: A Translation of the K'ai-tu ch'uan-hsin," in *Silver Jubilee Volume of the Zinbun-Kagaku-Kenkyuso* (Kyoto, 1954; hereafter referred to as Hucker, "Su-chou"), pp. 224–56; Yang T'ing-shu, *Ch'üan Wu chi-lüeh*, [dd] in *Ch'ung-chen ch'ang-pien* [de] (Taipei, 1964), pp. 3–4; and Chu T'an *Ming-chi she-tang*, pp. 179–80.

33. In retaliation for this demonstration, five Soochow commoners were later executed on Wei's orders. In 1627 Ying She leader Chang P'u wrote an essay praising the five and describing the efforts of the Ying She to have their tombstones properly engraved. This essay, entitled "Wu-jen mu-pei chi," [df] became something of a minor classic and may be found in *Ku-wen kuan-chih* [dg] (Taipei, 1966), pp. 591–93; and *Ming wen-hui* [dh] (Taipei, 1958), pp. 1094–95. Cf. Hucker, "Su-chou," p. 255 n. 4.

34. Chang P'u, *Ch'i-lu-chai chi*, 1/32a–33a; Chu T'an, *Ming-chi she-tang*, p. 167; Hsieh, MCCC, pp. 151–52.

35. Lu, FSCL, 1/167, 174.

36. *Ibid.*, 1/174–175. Cf. Hsieh, MCCC, pp. 153–54; and Ono, *Minmatsu no kessha*, pp. 46–47.

37. Wu Wei-yeh, *Fu She chi-shih*, [di] in *Tung-lin shih-mo* (Taipei, 1964; hereafter referred to as Wu, FSCS), p. 158; Chang Ts'ai, *Chih-wei-t'ang wen-ts'un* [dj] (facsimile reproduction of K'ang-hsi edition), 8/3a–b; Lu, FSCL, 1/180–181; Chu I-tsun, *Ming shih-tsung* [dk] (Taipei, 1962), 76/1a–b.

38. Hsieh, HLCHP, p. 99.

39. Lu, FSCL., 1/181–205; *Ming-Ch'ing li-k'o t'i-ming pei-lu* (Taipei, 1969), II, 1265–82; Tu Lien-che, *Ming-Ch'ao Kuan-hsüan lu* [dl] (Taipei, 1966), p. 86.

40. This date is in dispute. Tu Lien-che and Hsieh Kuo-chen say the meeting was held in 1632. Lu Shih-i and Chiang I-hsüeh, on the other hand, place it in 1633. If, as Chiang says, Chang P'u left the government in late 1632, the 1633 date would appear to be correct. See Arthur W. Hummel (ed.), *Eminent Chinese of the Ch'ing Period* (Taipei, 1964; hereafter referred to as Hummel, *Eminent Chinese*), p. 52; Hsieh, MCCC, p. 164; Lu, FSCL, 2/207; and Chiang I-hsüeh, *Chang P'u nien-p'u* [dm] (Shanghai, 1946), pp. 30–31.

41. Lu, FSCL, 2/207. Similar large-scale meetings of literati were not unknown in earlier Ming reigns, however. See Meskill, "Academies and Politics," pp. 158–59.

42. Chang P'u quoted in Lu, FSCL, 1/181. This passage has also been translated by Wm. Theodore de Bary, "A Plan for the Prince: The Ming-i tai-fang lu of Huang Tsung-hsi, Translated and Explained" (unpublished doctoral dissertation, Columbia University, 1953; hereafter referred to as de Bary, "Plan"), p. 14; and Robert B. Crawford, "The Biography of Juan Ta-ch'eng," in Chinese Culture, IV (March,1965), 56.

43. Sheng Ch'eng, "Fu She yü Chi She tui T'ai-wan wen-hua ti ying-hsiang," [dn] in T'ai-wan wen-hsien, XIII (September, 1962), 198.

44. Hucker has said, for example, that it "is probable that many men whose names appear on Tung-lin blacklists had no group consciousness whatever, no sense of belonging to any political entity," See Hucker, "Tung-lin," p. 161.

45. Lu, FSCL, 1/181 2/207–208; Hsieh, MCCC, p. 163; Jung Chao-tsu, Ming-tai ssu-hsiang shih [do] (Shanghai, 1941), p. 327.

46. Hsieh, MCCC, p. 161.

47. Ibid., p. 162. Cf. Lu, FSCL, 1/181; and Chu, Ming shih-tsung, 76/1a–b.

48. This chart is adapted from Ono, Minmatsu no kessha, p. 62.

49. Ibid.

50. For Hucker's views on this question see his "Tung-lin," p. 157–58.

51. Nelson I. Wu, "Tung Ch'i-ch'ang (1556–1636): Apathy in Government and Fervor in Art," in A. F. Wright and D. Twitchett (eds.), Confucian Personalities (Stanford, 1962), p. 262.

52. This information is taken from Hucker, "Tung-lin," pp. 142, 374–76, notes 81, 82, 92, 94, 96, and 97.

53. In addition to Huang Tsung-hsi, the sons and grandsons of a number of other Tung-lin martyrs were active members of the Fu She. See Ch'ai Te-keng, "Ming-chi Liu-tu fang-luan chu-jen shih-chi k'ao," [dp] in Shih-ta shih-hsüeh ts'ung-k'an, I (June, 1931), 9–11; and Hsieh, MCCC, p. 174.

54. Wang Yün (ed.), Ch'en Chung-yü nien-p'u, [dq] in Ch'en Chung-yü ch'üan-chi [dr] (1803 edition; hereafter referred to as Wang, CCYNP), 1/8a. Cf. Hu Ch'iu-yüan, Fu She chi ch'i jen-wu [ds] (Taipei, 1968), p. 19.

55. Huang Ping-hou, Huang Li-chou hsien-sheng nien-p'u, [dt] in Hai-wai tung-k'u chi [du] (Taipei, 1962), pp. 186–87. Cf. de Bary, "Plan," pp. 7–8.

56. Lu, FSCL, 1/174. Cf. Jung Chao-tsu, p. 342.

57. de Bary, "Individualism," p. 185.

58. This is not to suggest there were no opportunists in the group. Nevertheless, among the leaders there does seem to have been a sincere desire for reform.

59. Étienne Balazs, Political Theory and Administrative Reality in Traditional China (London, 1965), p. 14. Emphasis Balazs'.

60. Chang P'u quoted in Lu, FSCL, 1/181. Cf. Crawford, Juan Ta-ch'eng, p. 56; and de Bary, "Plan," p. 14.

61. In a general discussion of this point, F. W. Mote has written: "There is an

apparent anomaly in Chinese civilization with regard to the uses of the past: the defining criteria for value were inescapably governed by past models, not by present experience or by future ideal states of existence. Yet the entire purpose of civilization and men's individual lives was to realize the maximum from this present moment, not to blindly repeat some past, nor to forego the present in preparation for some anticipated future." See F. W. Mote, "The Arts and the 'Theorizing Mode' of the Civilization," in *Artists and Traditions: A Colloquium on Chinese Art* (Princeton University Department of Art and Archaeology, May, 1969), p. 4.

62. This interest of Fu She members in both classical scholarship and "practical" learning was shared by a number of other late Ming scholars. For general discussions of this subject, see Jung Chao-tsu, *Ssu-hsiang shih*, pp. 270–83; Chi Wen-fu, *Wan Ming ssu-hsiang shih lun* [dv] (Chungking, 1944), pp. 98–106; and Yü Ying-shih, "Ts'ung Sung Ming ju-hsüeh ti fa-chan lun Ch'ing-tai ssu-hsiang shih," [dw] in *Chung-kuo hsüeh-jen*, II (September, 1970), 19–41.

63. Ku Yen-wu quoted by Nivison, "Protest," p. 197.

64. *Ming-shih* (Kuo-fang yen-chiu yüan edition; hereafter referred to as MS), V, 288/3241; Chang Ts'ai, *Chih-wei-t'ang wen-ts'un*, 8/1b–2a; Lu, FSCL, 1/174.

65. For a bibliography of Chang P'u's works see Chiang I-hsüeh, *Nien-p'u*, pp. 50–51. Cf. Chang Ts'ai, *Chih-wei-t'ang wen-ts'un*, 8/7b–8a.

66. These commentaries are attached to most editions of the *Sung-shih chi-shih pen-mo* and the *Yüan-shih chi-shih pen-mo* and may also be found in Chang P'u, *Li-tai shih-lun* [dx] (Kuang-hsü edition).

67. Hummel, *Eminent Chinese*, pp. 232–33.

68. This translation of the term *ching-shih chih-yung* is from Liang Ch'i-ch'ao, *Intellectual Trends in the Ch'ing Period*, translated by Immanuel C. Y. Hsü (Cambridge, Mass., 1959), p. 4.

69. Ōkubo, *Dokushojin kessha*, pp. 193–98.

70. Hucker, "Su-chou," p. 228 n. 3; Chu T'an, *Ming-chi she-tang*, p. 180; Chang P'u, *Ch'i-lu-chai chi*, 1/10a–b.

71. Wang, CCYNP, 1/15a–b; Wang Yün, *Tung-hai hsien-sheng chuan*, [dy] in *Hsü An-kung hsien-sheng nien-p'u* [dz] (Taipei, 1961), p. 64. Cf. Tu, SSSM, 13b–14a.

72. Ōkubo, *Dokushojin kessha*, pp. 177–84, 194–95. Cf. Chang Ts'ai, *Chih-wei t'ang wen-ts'un*, 8/4a, 10/1a–3a; and Ch'ien Pao-ch'en, *Jen-kuei chih kao* [ea] (1881 edition), 2/53b.

73. Ōkubo, *Dokushojin kessha*, pp. 177–84.

74. See, for example, the description of Ch'en Tzu-lung's activities in Chekiang in the early 1640s in Wang, CCYNP, 1/30a–b, 1/32a.

75. For a brief description of this work, see Chu Hsi-tsu, "Huang Ming ching-shih wen-pien pa," [eb] in *Pei-ta t'u-shu-pu yüeh-k'an*, I (January, 1928), 41–42.

76. Ch'en Tzu-lung quoted in Wang, CCYNP, 1/25b.

364 WILLIAM S. ATWELL

77. *Ibid.*, 1/25a–26b.
78. Chang Ts'ai, *Chih-wei-t'ang wen-ts'un*, 11/18a–20b; Lu FSCL, 2/209–211.
79. See his *Lou-shan-t'ang chi*,[ec] in *Kuei-ch'ih hsien-che i-shu*[ed] (1920 edition), especially 7/1a–10/8a.
80. Chiang I-hsüeh, pp. 28–29; Hu Ch'iu-yüan, p. 23; Chang Ts'ai, *Chih-wei-t'ang wen-ts'un*, 5/15a–16a, 8/8a. Cf. Chang P'u's *Lun-lüeh*[ee] in his *Ch'i-lu-chai chi*.
81. Lu, FSCL, 1/181–205, 4/248–49; Wu, FSCS, p. 159; *Ming-Ch'ing li-k'o t'i-ming pei-lu*, II, 1265–1314.
82. Lu, FSCL, 2/207–208. Cf. Hsieh, MCCC, pp. 165–66.
83. MS, V, 274/3081.
84. Lu, FSCL, 2/214–215.
85. Tu Lien-che, *Ming-ch'ao kuan-hsüan lu*, p. 86.
86. Lu, FSCL, 4/249.
87. *Ibid.*, 2/209–214, 4/242; Wu, FSCS, p. 160; Jung Chao-tsu, *Ssu-hsiang shih*, p. 342.
88. Lu, FSCL, 2/208.
89. Hummel, *Eminent Chinese*, p. 52.
90. MS, V, 308/3492–3494; Hsieh, MCCC, p. 78–80.
91. Lu, FSCL, 2/216–217.
92. Hummel, *Eminent Chinese*, p. 113; Ray Huang, " 'Realism' in a Neo-Confucian Scholar-Statesman," in de Bary, *Self and Society*, pp. 419–20.
93. MS, V, 288/3242; Lu, FSCL, 4/242–255; Wu, FSCS, pp. 160–61; Chiang P'ing-chieh, *Tung-lin shih-mo*[ef] (Taipei, 1964), p. 51.
94. For the following section I have relied upon Crawford, *Juan Ta-ch'eng*, pp. 36–48; and Hsieh, MCCC, pp. 172–85.
95. Hummel, *Eminent Cpinese*, p. 398.
96. See, for example, Wu Ying-chi's description of Fu She activities in Nanking in *Lou-shan-t'ang chi*, 17/2b–3b.
97. MS quoted by Crawford, *Juan Ta-ch'eng*, p. 38.
98. For the text of the proclamation, see Hsieh, HLCHP, pp. 100–2.
99. According to the *Ming-shih*, all of the signers were Fu She members. While this may be true, I have been able to identify only 108 of them as definitely being members of the group. The identification was made by matching the list of signers in Hsieh, HLCHP, p. 103, and incomplete lists of Fu She members found in Lu, FSCL, 1/181–204, and Wu Tseng, *Fu She hsing-shih lu*[eg] (facsimile reproduction of 1832 edition).
100. For Ming T'ai-tsu's views on this subject, see *Ming hui-tien*[eh] (Kuo-hsüeh chi-pen ts'ung-shu edition), 78/1808–1809. Cf. Jung Chao-tsu, *Ssu-hsiang shih* pp. 335–36.
101. See, for example, descriptions of student protest in Sung times in Lin Yutang, *A History of the Press and Public Opinion in China* (Chicago, 1936), pp. 46–57. Cf. Hu Shih, "Huang Li-chou lun hsüeh-sheng yün-tung,"[ei] in *Hu Shih wen-ch'ao*[ej] (Hong Kong, [n.d.]), pp. 183–85.

102. F. W. Mote, "The Transformation of Nanking—1350–1400" (unpublished manuscript cited with permission of the author), pp. 66–68.
103. MS, IV, 253/2868–2869.
104. For this incident see Lu, FSCL, 2/205.
105. MS, IV, 253/2869–2870. Cf. Wu, FSCS, p. 162; and Hsieh, MCCC, pp. 168–69.
106. For slightly varying accounts of this affair, see MS, V, 308/3491; Wu, FSCS, p. 163; Tu, SSSM, 10b–11a; and Wen Ping, *Lieh-huang hsiao-chih* ek (Taipei, 1964), 7/187.
107. Tu Nai-chi, *Ming-tai nei-ko chih-tu* el (Taipei, 1969), pp. 313–16. Cf. Meng Sen, *Ming-tai shih* em (Taipei, 1957), pp. 347–50.
108. Mr. Jerry Dennerline of the Yale University Department of History is presently completing a detailed study of the resistance movement entitled "The Mandarins and the Massacre of Chia-ting: An Analysis of the Local Resistance to the Manchu Invasion of Kiangnan, 1645."
109. Descriptions of these and other Fu She members' deaths may be found in Hsü Tzu, *Hsiao-tien chi-chuan* en (Taipei, 1963).
110. The most famous of these was probably Wu Wei-yeh, who had a brief and unhappy career in the Ch'ing government.
111. Li Chieh, *Ming shih*, p. 404.
112. de Bary, "Introduction," in de Bary, *Self and Society*, pp. 22–23.
113. These factors have even led several scholars to call the Fu She China's first political party. See Hu Ch'iu-yüan, *Fu she*, p. 28; Li Chieh, *Ming shih*, p. 404; and Chou Li-an, *Ch'ing Ming chi*, p. 17.

GLOSSARY

a	文社	ak	周延儒	bu	薛國觀
b	以文會友以友輔仁	al	溫體仁	bv	吳昌時
c	清談	am	虎邱	bw	弘光
d	白蓮社	an	謝國楨	bx	史可法
e	慧遠	ao	小野和子	by	陳貞慧
f	陶潛	ap	董其昌	bz	劉宗周
g	白居易	aq	何心隱	ca	馬士英
h	元積	ar	興復古學	cb	徐汧
i	耆英會	as	顧炎武	cc	陸世儀，復社紀略
j	司馬光	at	宋史紀事本末	cd	東林始末
k	富弼	au	元史紀事本末	ce	杜登春，社事始末
l	文彥博	av	方以智	cf	昭代叢書
m	月泉社	aw	經世致用	cg	張芝，陶淵明傳論
n	高啓	ax	徐孚遠	ch	張蔭麟，述社
o	書院	ay	幾社	ci	鄭振鐸
p	萬歷	az	皇明經世文編		中國文學史
q	天啓	ba	顧憲成	cj	王俌，東都事略
r	正德	bb	鄒元標	ck	吳自牧，夢梁錄
s	王陽明	bc	張居正	cl	陳豪楚
t	王畿	bd	王錫爵		兩浙結社考
u	王艮	be	徐光啓	cm	劉大杰
v	八股	bf	農政全書		中國文學發達史
w	社稿	bg	吳應箕	cn	謝國楨，明清之際
x	復社	bh	歷代名臣奏義		黨社運動考
y	應社	bi	明夷待訪錄	co	黃黎洲學譜
z	張溥	bj	天下郡國利病書	cp	周黎庵，清明集
aa	張采	bk	姜日廣	cq	鈴木正，明末にお
ab	楊廷樞	bl	羅大任		ける松江の幾社
ac	魏忠賢	bm	陸世儀		について
ad	周順昌	bn	文震孟	cr	陳登原
ae	恩貢生	bo	倪元璐		中國文化史
af	黃宗羲	bp	鄭鄤	cs	張亮采
ag	黃尊素	bq	黃道周		中國風俗史
ah	陳子龍	br	阮大鋮	ct	黎傑，明史
ai	吳偉業	bs	左光斗	cu	張溥，七錄齋集
aj	夏日瑚	bt	留都防亂公揭		

cv 大久保英子，明末
　　讀書人結社と教
　　育活動

cw 林友春，近世中國
　　教育史研究

cx 楊廷福
　　明末三大思想家

cy 橫田輝俊，幾社の
　　成立について

cz 江南通志

da 江西通志

db 朱倓，明季社黨研
　　究

dc 小野和子，明末の
　　結社に關する一
　　考察

dd 楊廷樞，全吳紀略

de 崇禎長編

df 五人墓碑記

dg 古文觀止

dh 明文彙

di 吳偉業，復社紀事

dj 張采，知畏堂文存

dk 朱彝尊，明詩宗

dl 杜聯喆
　　明朝館選錄

dm 蔣逸雪，張溥年譜

dn 盛成，復社與幾社
　　對臺灣文化的影
　　響

do 容肇祖
　　明代思想史

dp 柴德賡，明季留都
　　防亂諸人事蹟考

dq 王澐，陳忠裕年譜

dr 陳忠裕全集

ds 胡秋原
　　復社及其人物

dt 黃炳垕
　　黃黎洲先生年譜

du 海外慟哭記

dv 嵇文甫
　　晚明思想史論

dw 余英時，從宋明儒
　　學的發展論清代
　　思想史

dx 張溥，歷代史論

dy 王澐，東海先生傳

dz 徐闇公先生年譜

ea 錢寶琛，壬癸志稿

eb 朱希祖
　　皇明經世文編跋

ec 樓山堂集

ed 貴池先哲遺書

ee 論略

ef 蔣平階，東林始末

eg 吳翻
　　復社姓氏錄

eh 明會典

ei 胡適，黃黎洲論學
　　生運動

ej 胡適文鈔

ek 文秉，烈皇小識

el 杜乃濟
　　明代內閣制度

em 孟森，明代史

en 徐鼒，小腆紀傳

WILLARD J. PETERSON *Fang I-chih:*

Western Learning and the "Investigation of Things"

From the twelfth century, one of the central issues in Chinese thought was the interpretation of the phrase *ke wu*.[a] At the beginning of the *Great Learning* there is the pregnant passage which reveals that for men in antiquity *ke wu* was the means by which their knowledge was extended (*chih chih*),[b] from which could follow a series of steps, each in turn prerequisite to the next—giving integrity to their intentions, correcting their hearts, improving their selves, properly regulating their families, putting the state in order, and, finally, realizing their wish of making "bright virtue plain to the world." [1] This implicitly prescriptive chain of activities in itself provides a Confucian explanation of *why* we should *ke wu*, lying as it does at the base of moral and social action. *How* we should *ke wu* was subject to varying interpretations. Fang I-chih [c] (1611–71) was part of a movement under way in the seventeenth century which directed the attentions of scholars away from prevailing interpretations of *ke wu* to what became known as Ch'ing learning.

Fang I-chih came from a prominent family of T'ung-ch'eng,[d] An-hwei.[2] His great-grandfather, Fang Hsüeh-chien [e] (1540–1616), declining official appointment achieved a reputation through his writings and activities as a follower of the Lu Hsiang-shan/Wang Yang-ming school such that he was honored in 1611 at a meeting sponsored by the Tung-lin Academy. Hsüeh-chien's eldest son, Ta-chen [f] (1558–1631), ended a long career in various censorial and judicial capacities by resigning in 1625 from the Grand Court of Revision because of the factional attacks on his friends associated with the Tung-lin movement. At the same time Fang K'ung-chao [g] (1591–1655), Ta-chen's only son and I-chih's father, was dismissed from his post as a bureau director in the Ministry of War, where he was serving after two terms as local magistrate. Fang I-chih, who had moved with his father's career to Szechwan, Fukien, and Peking, thus had ample opportunity to observe the vicissitudes of holding office and the vulnerability of righteous officials.

As a young man, Fang I-chih was talented, gregarious, and ambitious. For a decade following his father's reappointment to the Ministry of War, when the Ch'ung-chen emperor took the throne in 1627 and Wei Chung-hsien was ousted, I-chih's life-style was similar to that of other well-fixed young men with intellectual pretensions. He had undergone the standard educational fare of Classics and histories, had developed an interest in music, military matters, astrology, and the yin-yang tradition, and had become competent in such "extraneous amusements" as calligraphy, playing chess (wei-ch'i), brandishing a sword, and performing on the lute (ch'in). "Whatever he saw, he immediately wanted to do." [3] He wrote that in his early twenties "I increasingly read widely from the various philosophers, but by nature I preferred to write poetry and songs (shih ke)." [h][4] During this decade from 1628–38 I-chih's attention and energies were concentrated on activities associated with the literary societies which were so popular and influential. At the beginning of the Ch'ung-chen reign he had organized a small, informal group called the Tse-she.[i][5] He and his friends read and discussed books, medicine, and principles of things (wu li).[j][6] They wrote poems and sang the songs of lamentation of which they were fond. "Frequently we would get a little drunk and wander into the mountains [near T'ung-ch'eng] at night. Sometimes we would start singing in the market place as if there were no one around. People thought we were a bit nuts, but on the other hand we said the rest of the world was a bit nuts." [7] Fang's interest and talent in poetry involved him with several of the more prominent members of such politically influential societies as the Chi-she and Fu-she.[k][8] In the 1630s, then, Fang I-chih moved among the leaders of the young men of the lower Yangtze valley and involved himself in the literary societies, with their attendant drinking and poetry as well as serious discussion of intellectual and political matters.

While Fang I-chih was making a name for himself by his literary and social activities, he could not altogether avoid the troubles that were becoming more prevalent in the empire. In 1634 his home district, T'ung-ch'eng, experienced a "popular uprising" in which the households of prominent families were attacked.[9] His father, K'ung-chao, helped organize the suppression of the dissidents and was instrumental in making preparations for the successful defenses of the walled city against repeated threats by marauding "bandit" armies.[10] After the first incident, however,

Fang I-chih removed himself to Nanking.[11] Perhaps as a result of the T'ung-ch'eng troubles, sometime in the mid-1630s Fang began to have doubts that found expression in a fictional account, written in 1637, of a self-conscious, frustrated young man's sorting through the alternatives that seemed available to him for a meaningful life when he was not in accord with the times. Rejecting uncritical pursuit of success in the civil examinations, unscrupulous accumulation of wealth, association with others for the purpose of taking action in the corrupt world, submission of lofty recommendations to the emperor, retirement to a refuge in the mountains, and escape through drugs or magical arts that promised longevity, riches, and pleasure, the fictional protagonist (and Fang I-chih?) resolved his frustrations by realizing he should use his superior talents in scholarship so as to leave a legacy for later men.[12]

Fang did not, however, withdraw from the world in the late 1630s to study and write. Whatever his intentions, events pressed in on him. In 1639 when he was in Nanking to sit (successfully) for the triennial provincial examination, he was at least marginally involved in the so-called Manifesto against Juan Ta-ch'eng,[1] by which a group of young men led by Fang's friends in the Fu-she heaped abuse on their collective enemy.[13] Along with the others, in 1645 Fang was to suffer Juan's revenge. Of more immediate consequence for him in 1639, however, was his father's imprisonment. K'ung-chao, appointed governor of Hukuang (modern Hunan and Hupei) in 1638, had had a string of eight victories with various rebel bands and had memorialized against the military commander's accepting the surrender of the rebel leaders. When the leaders rose up again in mid-1639 and Ming troops, including some under Fang K'ung-chao's control as governor, were routed, he was impeached and imprisoned in Peking.[14] Going to the capital to assist his father, I-chih submitted a memorial in the third month of 1640 in which he pleaded to be allowed to receive any punishment for which his father was judged liable.[15] By crawling and wailing outside of the gate of the court as officials passed by, Fang I-chih supposedly even attracted the emperor's attention as an exemplary son.[16] Moved by the display of filial devotion as well as by K'ung-chao's record of service to the dynasty, the emperor reduced his punishment from execution to banishment to Shaohsing.[17]

While K'ung-chao was undergoing imprisonment and banishment,

Fang I-chih was doing much of the work for two of his most important books, the T'ung ya [m] and the Wu li hsiao chih.[n] He had been making notes of what he learned by reading, listening, and observing since the late 1620s,[18] and he seems to have brought some of the material together into a final form during the first few years of the 1640s. The preface and first three sections of the introductory chüan of the T'ung ya were dated 1641, while the fan-li [o] was dated the summer of 1643. Fang also dated the Wu li hsiao chih preface 1643, although the two books were not completed before the fall of the Ming dynasty. A section of the T'ung ya was dated 1650 (shou 3.1a), and in the Wu li hsiao chih reference was made to the Jesuit Smogolenski, who did not arrive in China until 1646. But Fang did not continue to work on the two books until their publication in the 1660s. His son, Chung-t'ung,[p] in remarks prefatory to the Wu li hsiao chih, wrote: "My father's draft of the T'ung ya was brought back from the capital; the Wu li hsiao chih originally was appended to it." [19] This statement implies that the manuscript was completed before Fang I-chih left Peking for the last time in 1644. However, Chung-t'ung continued: "When my father in 1650 was among the Miao,[q] he sent back a hamper [of manuscripts]; I sorted and arranged them." [20] It would seem, then, that although material was added to the two books after Fang I-chih had fled to the south, much of the T'ung ya and Wu li hsiao chih was completed while he was in the capital to aid his father and then while he was waiting for and holding an official appointment.

Fang had been successful in the chin-shih examination of 1640.[21] He was appointed a corrector in the Hanlin Academy with assignment as tutor to the emperor's third son.[22] Fang K'ung-chao, relieved of his banishment in 1642, returned to the capital and, early in 1644, was appointed an assistant censor-in-chief and charged with general supervision of military posts in Shantung and Hopei.[23] I-chih, still a corrector in the third month of 1644, vainly requested to be allowed to leave Peking to raise troops.[24] Later that month, when Li Tzu-ch'eng's forces occupied the city, Fang apparently paid the required ransom in silver to the new "government" and escaped to Nanking in the fifth month.[25] Conditions were not much better at the new seat of the Ming court. The Fu-she's old enemy, Juan Ta-ch'eng, was allied with those who were in ascendence at Nanking and the factional controversies of the preceding reign were revived. In Fang's words, Juan "sought to exterminate the good men and famous scholars of the empire," [26] that is, those who had denounced Juan in the Manifesto of 1639. Fang knew that he, too, was scheduled for reprisals, but his punishment—banishment—was commuted to a money payment, and then he was even pardoned from that. [27]

The situation in Nanking being what it was, Fang I-chih could not hold an official appointment there. Before the capture of the southern capital by Ch'ing troops in the fifth month of 1645, he went to the south, where, dressed as a commoner, he sold medicine to support himself. [28] Fang declined a summons to serve the new Ming emperor, Lung-wu,[r] enthroned at Foochow in mid-1645, [29] but by some accounts he did join the court of Lung-wu's successor, who was established as the Yung-li [s] emperor at Chao-ch'ing, Kwangtung, in the eleventh month of 1646. Supposedly Fang accepted an appointment as a Hanlin academician [30] and was with the court in the first month of 1647 when the emperor and his entourage, moving up the river from Chao-ch'ing in retreat from Ch'ing troops, reached Wu-chou [t] in eastern Kwangsi. [31] It is also reported that the following month, as the emperor was progressing up the river from Wu-chou through P'ing-lo [u] to Kueilin (provincial capital of Kwangsi), [32] Fang I-chih was promoted to Grand Secretary, but, realizing the task was impossible, he shortly left the government. [33]

However, Fang's own account of his activities during the period 1645–47 seems to suggest that he did not take any office under the Yung-li emperor. In a letter he wrote that, even before the Lung-wu emperor had taken the throne,

. . . my father, knowing that great turmoil was forthcoming, ordered me to go and serve in our deeply troubled lands, but the southern capital fell. I traveled to friends in Yüeh [i.e., Kwangtung and Kwangsi], but Yen-p'ing and Ting-chou [in Fukien] both fell [i.e., the Lung-wu emperor was captured]. The Yung-li reign was then initiated. Eunuchs holding power and the government being in turmoil, I declined the command from the Grand Protector. [34] Being ill I remained behind in Wu-chou [as the emperor moved on to P'ing-lo], but Chao-ch'ing and Kuang-chou [Canton] fell. The imperial banners progressed farther west, and, although ill, I went to the mountains at Fu-i.[v] [35]

There is an understandable ambiguity in Fang's letter as to whether he had served the Yung-li emperor. To have admitted having held office would have explicitly acknowledged his involvement in the anti-Ch'ing effort at a high level. What is clear from even Fang's own testimony is that he declined an appointment at the Ming court in early 1647. He wrote that when the emperor had been forced to proceed to southern Hu-kuang, "I thereupon sorrowfully declined a cabinet title." [36]

After declining to continue to serve in the Yung-li emperor's govern-ment, Fang remained in the mountains. He wrote that he lived in retire-ment for two years in a village in eastern Kwangsi, and he repeatedly declined appointment to office. [37] That he remained in contact with his former associates in the southern Ming court is further evidenced by his exchanging poems even as late as New Year's Day, 1649, with Ch'ü Shih-ssu, the loyalist who defended the provincial capital, Kuei-lin, until the eleventh month of 1650. [38]

In the winter of 1650 a friend of Fang's from T'ung-ch'eng arrived in P'ing-lo and Fang came from the village where he was living to share in a banquet with the friend. They parted company the next day, and imme-diately were endangered by the sudden presence of Ch'ing troops. To es-cape the cavalrymen sent after him, Fang tonsured himself and put on Buddhist robes. [39] It is told that Fang was arrested, taken before a Ch'ing general, and ordered to choose between donning the garments of an of-ficial, thus manifesting his willingness to surrender and accept an ap-pointment from the Manchu government, or being killed with the sword held ready. Even though he had voluntarily retired from the service of the Yung-li emperor, Fang refused to submit to the threat. Impressed, the general then treated Fang with respect and agreed to allow him to live as a monk. [40] In spite of his unwillingness to surrender to the Ch'ing, as a monk at Wu-chou Fang advised the same general to receive with magnanimity the captured grandson of Ch'ü Shih-ssu, Fang's former col-league. [41] Thus, even while withdrawing Fang remained involved, al-though for the last twenty years of his life he lived as a Buddhist monk.

Fang's seeking refuge as a monk raises the question of how deep his commitment was to a religious life. Given the revival of Buddhism's intellectual and social respectability in the last four reigns of the Ming, Fang as a young man must have been at least passingly familiar with Buddhist literature, some of which he quoted in the Wu li hsiao chih and T'ung ya. However, the circumstances under which he became a monk might be interpreted as casting doubt on his motivations. As the Ming cause collapsed in the south, Buddhism was a recourse taken by many who wished to manifest their determination not to serve the new dynasty,[42] and, perhaps not incidentally, to escape retribution from the Ch'ing for participating in the southern Ming courts. As a friend of Fang's who was a Ch'ing official observed, although Fang I-chih "was not a monk, in the end he grew old as a monk, yet there was not a moment in which in speech or conduct he forgot that he was a Confucian."[43] However we interpret Fang's motivations, he did *act* as a monk from the early 1650s to the end of his life. Going north to the Yangtze valley, he studied for some three years in Nanking under the eminent master Chüeh-lang Tao-sheng.[w] He then traveled to various religious establishments in the south to receive instruction and to visit his family home in Anhwei.[44] After short periods of residence with administrative responsibilities at temples in Kiangsi, in 1664 Fang accepted an invitation to take charge of a temple at Ch'ing-yüan mountain, south of Chi-an,[x] in Kiangsi. He was not a recluse, but received a stream of visitors, including officials of the area and influential local figures as well as his sons and men who declined to serve the Ch'ing.[45] Such involvements perhaps contributed to precipitating his death.

As a monk, Fang did not pursue his former interests in scholarship, but he did continue to write. Two manuscripts from the last twenty years of his life are crucial to any attempt to evaluate his thought as a whole. In 1652, shortly after becoming a monk, he prepared a draft that he revised the next year.[46] The manuscript, entitled *Tung-hsi chün*,[y] was not published until 1962, when it was presented as an important example of materialist thinking in the seventeenth century. The other work, written about 1660, is the *Yao-ti p'ao Chuang*,[z] a critique of the *Chuang tzu* in which Fang selected items from earlier commentators and added his own as well as the ideas of Chüeh-lang Tao-sheng, under whom he had studied.[47] In both works Fang was exploring—on a more philosophical plane—ideas that he had been developing while compiling the *Wu li hsiao chih* and *T'ung ya*. Hou Wai-lu has gone so far as to say that, although there are contradictions in orientation and substance between the books of Fang's earlier and later periods, his basic approach was unitary.[48] In an exchange that took place on his birthday in 1665, Fang minimized the dichotomy between his former (Confucian) and present (Buddhist) intellectual interests.[49] It is noteworthy that the *T'ung ya* was published in 1664 and the *Wu li hsiao chih* in 1666. The point is that

Fang as a monk had not repudiated his former endeavors even though he did not continue to pursue them.

The details of Fang I-chih's death remain shrouded in mystery, but it has been established that, after half a dozen years at Ch'ing-yüan, in the late 1660s he became implicated in a legal proceeding apparently arising in Kwangtung. In 1671, Fang apparently committed suicide on a boat going south, in Kiangsi.[50] Thus, while Fang had adopted the garb of a monk at least in part to remain loyal to the Ming and to avoid serving the new dynasty, he was not able to escape the entanglements of society. His life illustrates the tensions and troubles of mid-seventeenth–century China. Local, governmental, and dynastic upheavals all had their impact on him and helped determine the context in which he worked out his ideas.

Fang was also influenced by the presence of Jesuit missionaries, who, by the beginning of the seventeenth century, were further contributing to an already fluid intellectual milieu. Pursuing a strategy of establishing themselves as the peers of the literati, the missionaries published books on Western knowledge in addition to religious works. Once they had discerned an interest on the part of the Chinese in Western mathematics, astronomy, and natural philosophy, they catered to it, and so stimulated curiosity for more such works. Fang I-chih was well acquainted with the books published in the Ming by the Jesuits. He cited two of their books by title, quoted without acknowledgment at least three others, and knew of most of the rest. Fang's father prepared a summary account of the imperially sponsored collection on Western astronomy entitled *Ch'ung-chen li-shu.*[aa][51] The other important collection of Jesuit books was the *T'ien-hsüeh ch'u han,*[ab] published in 1628 and including all of the significant titles by Jesuits prior to 1625. Fang I-chih recalled that "they wrote a book called the *T'ien-hsüeh ch'u han.* I have read it, but there is much I did not understand."[52] Thus Fang was demonstrably cognizant of most of the Jesuits' books in Chinese about Western natural philosophy published before the fall of the Ming dynasty.

Fang I-chih's approach to the natural philosophy which Jesuit missionaries published in the seventeenth century derives ultimately from the first section (in Chu Hsi's rearrangement of the text) of the *Great Learning.*

The men of old who wished to make bright virtue plain to the world first put their countries in order, for which they had first to regulate their families, and for that to improve themselves as individuals, and for that to correct their hearts, and for that to give integrity to their intentions, and for that to extend their knowledge. The extension of knowledge lies in the investigation of things (*ke-wu*).[53]

The crucial endeavor, *ke-wu*, which was held to lie at the base of moral action, was subject to interpretations that varied with philosophical predispositions.

In the Sung the Ch'eng brothers, who gave greater stress than their predecessors to the *Great Learning* as a philosophical text, explained *ke wu* as follows: "*Ke* means 'arrive at.' *Wu* means 'activities.' In all activities there are principles; to arrive at their principles is *ke-wu*." [54] In their explanation the Ch'engs significantly expanded the meaning of the statement. Their gloss of *ke* is undoubtedly supportable,[55] and explaining *wu* as activities (*shih*) [ac] is not incongruent with the *Great Learning* passage as a whole. What was added was the assumption that there are principles (*li*) in all activities and that comprehending these principles is the purpose of our inquiry. Emphasis thus shifted from "investigation of things" to fathoming principles. Chu Hsi, reinforcing the shift, commented that *ke wu* means "to reach to the utmost [the] principles of activities and things" (*ch'iung chih shih wu chih li*).[ad] [56] This interpretation of *ke wu*, which became orthodox, implies that principles are particularized aspects of the one Principle which is the basis of moral action, so that our goal in knowing Principle is to know what to do. Also latent in this interpretation is the possibility that the process of "investigation of things" itself can be taken as a type of moral endeavor, even as an end in itself. In either case, exerting mental effort day after day in order to accumulate knowledge relevant to moral principles entailed a relative neglect of the study of natural phenomena.[57] While Chu Hsi allowed that *wu* refers to "objects" as well as to "affairs," the moralistic interpretation of *ke wu* remained one of the central concerns in the subsequent development of the Ch'eng-Chu school.

At the beginning of the sixteenth century Wang Yang-ming developed a reading of *ke wu* that was an extension of the interpretation deriving from Chu Hsi. Wang's famous passage about investigating bamboo in 1492, when he and his friend became ill trying to fathom the principles in some growing bamboo, can be taken to mean that he was frustrated in seeking to follow Chu Hsi's doctrines literally. Wang's experience showed him that the concept that the principles which should guide our conduct can be discerned in what is "out there," even in a blade of grass, was meaningless. It was only after the lapse of several years that Wang "realized that there is really nothing in the things in the world to investigate, that the effort to investigate things is only to be carried out in and with reference to one's body and mind. . . ." [58] In other words, Wang's breakthrough was that Principle, the basis of moral action, had to be found within the mind rather than "out there." Thus Wang was led to conclude that *ke wu* meant nothing more than "to do good and remove evil." [59] This entailed putting a new interpretation on the "extension of knowledge," which in the *Great Learning* is the immediate reason for us to *ke wu*: "The extension of knowledge is not what later scholars understand as enriching and widening knowledge. It is simply extending one's innate knowledge of the good to the utmost." [60]

Going beyond the Ch'eng-Chu interpretation of *ke wu*, Wang stressed that the moral purpose of *ke wu* is to be accomplished solely within our minds. By locating Principle in our minds, and thus making what was "out there" irrelevant for the purposes of moral self-cultivation, Wang laid the ground for the flowering of intuitionalism in the sixteenth century. But for all their differences, Wang was not doing violence to Chu Hsi's intent in holding that *ke wu* was both a moral effort in itself and the means whereby we come to be aware of the principles which are our sure guide to what should be.

In what must be understood as a reaction to the interpretations of *ke wu* stemming from Ch'eng-Chu and from Wang Yang-ming, Fang I-chih advanced an inclusive definition of *wu*.

Things (*wu*) are that which fill the space between heaven and earth. Here is where human beings attain life. Life being contained in our bodies and our bodies being contained in the real world, all that we experience are events (*shih*). Events [or activities] are a class of *things*. The sages [of antiquity] made implements (*ch'i*) and developed useful methods so that the lives of human beings would be eased, and then made principles (*li*) manifest so that their minds would be ordered. Particular physical objects (*ch'i*) certainly are *things*, and mind (*hsin*) is a *thing* as well. On a more profound level, the nature (*hsing*) and fate (*ming*) [ae] [associated with any particular being] together are a *thing*. Viewed comprehensively, heaven and earth together are a *thing*. [61]

Coming more than a century after Wang Yang-ming had dismissed "things in the world" as unworthy of investigation compared to what was to be found "within our minds," Fang's definition of *wu* is part of his attempt to reinvest "things" with intellectual significance.

The first sentence of the definition is a close paraphrase of a passage at the beginning of the "Hsü kua" [af] commentary of the *Book of Changes* and represents a commonsense notion that the totality of physical objects are "things." By this statement of the "obvious," Fang was defining *wu* as, at least in part, external to our minds, a concept implicitly held by Wang Yang-ming to be irrelevant. Next, Fang included in his definition "all that we experience," or events, which was the gloss of *wu* stressed by the Ch'eng-Chu school, but which Wang had taken at best in a very narrow sense. By using *ch'i* with the ordinary meaning of "implements" or "utensils," and then with the meaning of "particular physical objects," Fang shifted from what are easily regarded as external "things" to a philosophical term that was contrasted to "that which is without form." He then went on to assert that three other philosophical terms—"mind," "nature," and "fate"—also denoted "things." By associating these four terms denoting aspects of "things" which are external to our minds, Fang was preparing the way for his contention that higher knowledge can be sought in "things." As the final layer in his definition, Fang asserted that the cosmos itself can be regarded as a "thing," with the implication that it, too, can be understood through intellectual inquiry which was not intuitive.

In addition to advancing an inclusive definition of *wu*, Fang used other ways to reestablish the intellectual importance of "things." He disparaged his contemporaries who neglected them.

Nowadays, when the level of culture is so advanced, there nevertheless are those who [claim to be able to] fathom principles (*li*) and perceive human natures (*hsing*), but who are, contrary to what ought to be the case, incapable of knowing in detail about any single *thing* [in the sense of "object"]. It is laughable that when one speaks of [the sages of] antiquity having ordered *things* so as to extend their usefulness and speaks of the [sages'] principle (*li*) of treating each *thing* in a manner consonant with it as a *thing*, they laughingly regard these matters as impractical and without benefit. [62]

Fang repeatedly reminded his readers that the sages, by understanding and thus becoming capable of manipulating "things" in the sense of physical objects, had contributed so importantly to mankind's physical well-being. Since cultural achievements were the beneficial results of the willingness of some superior men of more recent as well as ancient times to direct their attention to the physical world, Fang urged his contemporaries to show the same concern. In stressing the importance of external "things," Fang was not negating the goal of fathoming "principles." He merely contended that such knowledge had to be rooted in a detailed understanding of *wu*. As his definition of *wu* asserts, the sages who gave us cultural objects also made principles manifest. Fang asked rhetorically, "Unless one formulates guidelines about heaven and earth and categorizes the essentials of the myriad *things*, how can he know the reasons behind all these?" [63] The answer, that one cannot know without giving due attention to the "myriad things," was a denial of claims that one can intuitively apprehend an external world, universal values, or whatever.

Fang had two main arguments, then, for our focusing on "things." "With regard to fundamentals and ramifications, sources, and developments, if one understands them all then he is better at exercising control over them. If one disregards *things*, then he cannot grasp principles (*li*), and what is there for him to investigate (*ke*)!" [64] By juxtaposing the two arguments, Fang would have his readers equate the "things" which are of material benefit to man and at man's disposal with the "things" we investigate in order to fathom "principles" which have a moral relevance. Under Fang's view, our investigations must be directed at "things," and at least in part those "things" must be external and not merely the products of our own mental processes.

In addition to "things," Fang was concerned with words because they are the primary means by which the past is known and by which information and ideas are conveyed. (Much of Fang's scholarly product, notably his *T'ung ya*, was devoted to explicating the meanings and pronunciations of words and phrases.) An essay dated 1641, in which he considered types of knowledge, began by stressing the importance of words. "The three types of knowing all end up involving the understanding of words. This [realization] is of great usefulness in investigating (*ke*) oneself and others, inner and outer, ancient and modern [phenomena]. If one is unable to understand words, how is he able to grasp that to which they refer?" [65] Fang's point was that the study of words is a necessary concomitant to studying their objective correlatives.

The "three types of knowing" (*san chih*) [ag] as set forth in the *Analects* (16/9) are knowledge held from birth, knowledge gained from study, and knowledge gained by those who seek to learn only after undergoing duress. Fang distinguished three types, using different criteria from Confucius. In the first place, there are the various sets of practical, day-to-day knowledge which are to be studied along with the words used in each. "There are specific ways of speaking [i.e., technical vocabularies] in such fields as ethics, economics, literature, crafts, law, textual studies, chronicles, and metaphorical speech; in general, there is no one of these fields that is not involved with the Way and with the nature (*hsing*) and fate (*ming*) [of its respective phenomena]." [66] This first type of knowledge concerns aspects of human affairs, which are part of Fang's definition of *wu*. By asserting that these sets of mundane knowledge are "involved with the Way and with the nature and fate" of their respective sets of "things," Fang was arguing that they are worthy of our attention, though he does not claim we can learn of "principles" through such knowledge. "But," Fang continued with regard to a second type of knowledge, "there [also] are specific ways of speaking of the Way *of* nature and fate which disregard events and rules in order to illuminate one's mind and advance one's own blinkered assumptions." The advocates of this second type concern themselves with, in effect, unverifiables, such as life hereafter, genii, "nourishing life," and the like. [67] Fang recognized the appeal of this type of knowledge, aiming at transcendence, but it was not based on "things" and thus was inferior to the third type, by which we might fathom "principles."

For those who seek to fathom heaven and earth without passing beyond materialistic *and* comprehensive discussions (*chih lun t'ung lun*),[ah] there are theories in such fields as [prognosticating on the basis of] "image" (*hsiang*) and "number" (*shu*),[ai] music, calendars, phonetics, and medicine. These [fields of learning] are all comprehensive with regard to what is material (*chih*) [aj] [within their respective fields]; they are all concerned with principles of *things* (*wu li*). To speak in specific ways of governing is to be concerned with principles of social order (*tsai li*).[ak] To speak in specific ways of "comprehending seminal forces" (*t'ung chi*) [al] is to be concerned with the wherefore of extended principles of *things* (*wu chih chih-li*).[am] Both of these fields, being comprehensive, comprehend what is material [within their fields].[68]

According to Fang, then, in fields of limited subject matter within the third type of knowledge, there was nevertheless a comprehensive aspect to the theories which distinguished the fields from the first type of knowledge; they were not prevented by being based on "things" from reaching a higher level of understanding—that is, "principles of things." In the field of learning that dealt with governmental affairs there was a separate set of

principles to be discerned, although in his own work Fang was little concerned with these. As the title of the *Wu li hsiao chih* (Notes on the Principles of Things) suggests, Fang's attention was on "things" and their
principles, both of the middle range (as contained in music, astronomy,
medicine, and the like) and, at least in theory, the encompassing, or "extended," ones derived from "comprehending seminal forces" (*t'ung chi*).

Fang made a distinction in methodology which reflects the difference
between the first and third types of knowledge.

On a more abstruse level [than that of observable phenomena], what is known is
of assistance in dealing with the unknowable. The recondite, which we know by
means of what is of broad applicability, together with the unitary reality underlying layers of mysteries are the profound "seminal forces" (*chi*) of every material
thing and immaterial impulse. Profoundly searching out from whence comes the
web of imperceptible influences is called "comprehending seminal forces" (*t'ung
chi*). What is called "material investigations" (*chih ts'e*) [an] is the substantial examination of the particular causes of *things* (*wu*), ranging from epochs of time down
to plants and minute insects, categorization of their characteristics, assessment of
their merits and defects, and determination of their changes and constancies.[69]

Fang was at pains to point out that these two approaches are concomitant. Neither can be neglected, although "material investigations" has
primacy by being based more immediately on "things." "[The method of]
'material investigations' encompasses 'comprehending seminal forces.' To
sweep aside 'material investigations' and blindly advocate 'comprehending
seminal forces' so as to [pretend to be able to] make manifest the immaterial impulses of what is profound and mysterious results in leaving *things* out
of consideration altogether." [70] The opposite extreme, according to Fang,
is just as misguided. "The knowledge from the Far West which entered
[China] in the Wan-li period is detailed in 'material investigations' but
deficient in speaking of 'comprehending seminal forces.' This being so,
in the estimation of truly knowledgeable scholars their 'material investigations' still are not adequate." [71] Thus Fang I-chih was almost as critical
of the Westerners' having usable knowledge about phenomena without
adequate general theories as he was of those who sought to extend their
knowledge without reference to "things" in the sense of objective phenomena.

Then how did Fang come to draw so much material for his *Wu li hsiao
chih* from books published by Jesuits in the late Ming? [72] One reason is

simply that the bulk of his information on "things" was derived from books. Inspection of the *Wu li hsiao chih* reveals this. Moreover, Fang's speculation about the ideal scholarly situation shows that collecting material from other books was a desirable intellectual pursuit.

If I had worldly riches, I would set up a rude place of study and provide stipends to the most talented minds of the empire. We [or they?] would systematically categorize (*lei*) [ao] excerpts from ancient and modern books. We would utilize the strong points and get to the heart of the ultimate ramifications of causes in each of such fields as classical exegesis, principles of natures (*hsing li*), principles of things (*wu li*), literature, economics, philology, technical skills, music, calendrical knowledge, and medicine. We would arrange the important points and make details known about specific phenomena. Hundreds of *chüan* could thus be realized. [73]

In line with this scholarly ideal, Fang I-chih's son Chung-t'ung commented that in his work his father "assembled the arguments of ancient and modern men so as to give rise to his own arguments; he collected the wisdom of the empire so as to give rise to his own wisdom. This is called 'selecting what is good' (*tse shan*)." [ap] [74]

"Selecting what is good" entails investigating and understanding the past and its wisdom, but Fang warned against wholly submitting to it. As he explained at the beginning of the *T'ung ya*, "The data about ancient and modern times are accumulated through our knowledge, and living in the latter period we inquire into the ways in which the past determines the present. Yet we cannot become bogged down in the past." [75] Fang was self-consciously a "modern." Criticizing uncritical conservatism in holding to theories about historical pronunciations of characters, he wrote, "Since it is wrong to adhere to the ancient and disregard the modern, it is even more unnecessary to adhere to the *errors* of the past." [76] He saw his task not simply as the preservation or recovery of past knowledge, but as the systematization and clarification of all that is and can be known. "How can we not be pleased that, being born in the present age, we are able, by inheriting the achievements of past sages and sorting through the explanations of past worthies, to sit in judgment of the knowledge of the past thousands of years and reach balanced decisions [about particular points]?" [77] Fang I-chih's claim for the capacity of scholars of the present to judge past ideas is not unprecedented, and may even grow out of Wang Yang-ming's point that each man's own intellect can be his own standard. By valuing his contemporaries' as well as his own views more highly, Fang was free from any need to disparage Western learning simply because it was new.

Merely the newness, however, of the Western learning could not justify Fang's selecting information from the Jesuits' books. The rationale was more subtle. Fang held that one cannot limit his knowledge to that of which he has personal experience. One should be aware of what is "over there" as well as what is at hand. To this point Fang quoted Teng Yüan-hsi (1529–93), author of the *Wu hsing chih.* [aq]

Even within our land the soils are slightly different and the production of things accords with these differences, so how much more so in the distinction between Chinese (*hua*) and barbarian (*i*). With seas and mountains as the boundaries, how could the variations of great oddity all be recorded? How do we know that what formerly did not exist is not created in the present? How do we know that what is now known familiarly will not be obliterated in the future? [78]

But recognizing that there is a spatial as well as a temporal dimension to knowledge still does not justify using another people's wisdom.

In a passage in the *Wu li hsiao chih* Fang partly met this problem by referring to the notion that the temperate zone is the most conducive to the development of civilization.

China being situated north of the equator between 20 degrees and 40 degrees, the sun is wholly to the south, so [China] does not endure violent heat. On the other hand, not being excessively distant from the sun [China] enjoys warmth and its normal climatic condition is temperate. Because of its carts, writing, rites and music, its sages and heroes, [China] is paid court by barbarians on all sides. The far south, near to the sun and very hot, is only fit for southern barbarians beyond the seas to inhabit. The far north, distant from the sun and very cold, is only fit for desert peoples beyond the passes to inhabit. The site of the men of the West being beyond the North Pole, and on the same latitude as China, their people as well [as China's] all take pleasure in studying and understand the principles of astronomy. It is a general rule that in Moslem countries, which are not of the same latitude [as China and the Western countries, the people], are violent and are prone to murder. [79]

In this passage, then, Fang seemingly admitted the Western countries' culture to a rough parity with the Chinese.

Fang found a symbolic justification for quoting from Westerners' books in a classical precedent. His argument was most fully developed in his discussion of the shape of the earth.

[The notion that] heaven is round and earth is square refers to their characters (*te*).[ar] The body of the earth actually is spherical and it is in the center of the heavens. They are analogous to a bladder and bean. In the case of a bladder and bean, if one puts a bean inside of a bladder and blows to inflate it, then the bean will be placed precisely in the center [of the bladder]. Someone might say that this is the theory of the Far West. I say that the Yellow Emperor asked Ch'i Po,[as] Is the earth below? Ch'i Po said the earth is below man and in the midst of the heaven. The emperor said, How is it suspended? He replied that a great *ch'i* supports it.[80] Shao Yung and Chu Hsi were both clear that the physical form of the earth floats in emptiness and never falls down. But the present age does not have the likes of Chang Heng [at] (78–139), Tsu Ch'ung-chih [au] (429–500), [the Buddhist monk] I-hsing [av] (682–727), and Shao Yung [all famous for their contributions to natural philosophy]. Confucius said, "When the officers of the Son of Heaven are not properly arranged we may learn from the wild tribes all round about. The remark seems to be true." The men of today are in error in not examining the matter but transmitting [the *Kai-t'ien* theory] that the earth floats on water and the heavens enclose the water. The physical form of the earth [actually] is like the meat of a walnut; the convexities are mountains and the concavities are seas.[81]

Although associated with and somewhat obscured by the addition of related Chinese ideas, the concept of a spherical, central earth that Fang was conveying was Western in origin.

By following what would appear to his readers as the Westerners' theory about the shape of the earth, Fang was open to the criticism that he was adhering to a non-Chinese idea, as is implied by his sentence, "Someone might say that this is the theory of the Far West." Fang attempted to mitigate this criticism by citing Ch'i Po's answers and by recalling Shao Yung's and Chu Hsi's views, all of which might be taken to support the "modern" view. Going beyond this to justify using a foreign idea, Fang first pointed to the contemporary absence of men comparable to those in the past who made exemplary contributions to our fund of knowledge about nature and from whom he might learn. Then he cited Confucius' learning from a barbarian when there was no one else to turn to. The precedent is recorded in the *Tso chuan*.

When the viscount of T'an came to our court (of Loo in the autumn of 524 B.C.) . . . Ch'aou-tsze asked what was the reason that Shaou-haou named his officers after birds. The viscount replied, "He was my ancestor, and I know (all about) it. . . ." Chung-ne having heard of this, he had an interview with the viscount of T'an, and learned from him. Afterward he said to people, "I have heard that, when the officers of the son of Heaven are not properly arranged, we may learn from the wild tribes all round about. The remark seems to be true." [82]

The viscount of T'an (T'an tzu) [aw] on whom Confucius called was a barbarian (*i*) in a very restricted sense, for the small state of T'an was located just to the southeast of Lu. Nevertheless, the lesson the incident illustrated for seventeenth-century purposes was that it is sometimes justified to learn from outsiders, as Confucius had done. Fang I-chih several times referred to his "using the Far West as a Viscount of T'an." [83]

What did Fang learn from his "Viscount of T'an"? There are numerous examples of Fang's tacitly accepting Western explanations of natural phenomena. The ones cited here will illustrate his assumptions in selecting as well as in rejecting ideas advanced in books published by Jesuits in China. Let us first consider how Fang handled the problem of the structure of the universe.

In the *T'ung ya* as in some passages in the *Wu li hsiao chih*, Fang seemed to accept without qualification the Western concepts that the earth is spherical in form, that it occupies the central place in the sphere of the heavens, and that it is very small in relation to the encompassing heavens. [84] To illustrate the Westerners' theory Fang drew an analogy between the series of concentric heavens and the layers of an onion. He reported their idea that the sun, moon, and stars, though in motion, are fixed in their respective heavens like knots in a plank; each moves in accordance with the movement of its heaven. The substance of these heavens is clear and perfectly penetrable by light. [85] In the *Wu li hsiao chih*, however, Fang included material in which can be discerned the contemporary debate in Europe over whether the structure of the universe is geocentric.

Fang presented the Aristotelian concept of concentric heavens in an entry entitled "Nine Layers" (*chiu ch'ung*). [ax] The *locus classicus* for *chiu ch'ung* is the poem associated with Ch'ü Yüan's name, *T'ien wen* [ay] (Questions about the Heavens), written in about 300 B.C. [86] The term was subsequently used in discussions about the heavens; Chu Hsi, for instance, viewed the *chiu ch'ung* as layers of *ch'i* which are harder as they increase with distance from the earth's surface. [87] The Jesuits adopted this term for "layers" to describe their vision of a system of concentric crystalline spheres; Diaz's *T'ien wen lüeh* [az] (Catechism on the Heavens) speaks of "twelve layers" (and the title itself is a reference to Ch'ü Yüan's poem). Fang's entry in the *Wu li hsiao chih* on the "nine layers" recorded the Western calculations of the periodicity of the moon, Mercury, Venus, the sun, Mars, Jupiter, and Saturn, and then continued: "The heaven of the constant stars *(ching-hsing t'ien)* [ba] completes one circuit in 49,000 years. The *primum mobile* heaven *(tsung-tung t'ien)* [bb] makes one circuit each day. What is called the 'quiescent heaven' *(ching t'ien)* [bc] is named in terms of the accepted conception [of the Aristotelian cosmological system]." [88] Without explaining the celestial mechanics entailed in the model or acknowledging its Western origins, Fang let these details of the Aristotelian system of concentric heavens which appeared in Jesuit books published before the late 1620s stand in juxtaposition to the rather vague tradition suggested by the term *chiu ch'ung*. It was the tenth heaven, the "quiescent heaven," which occasioned an implied criticism of the Jesuits' cosmology (and its religious overtones) and an overt criticism of their philosophical orientation. Fang assumed a negative response when he asked rhetorically: "Is what is called the 'Lord of Creation' then in that majestic, limitless [tenth] heaven? They [referring to the Westerners] are detailed in 'material investigations' *(chih ts'e)* but not good in speaking of 'comprehending seminal forces' *(t'ung chi)*. Frequently their meanings are encumbered by their words." [89] By his having raised this criticism at this point, we can see where Fang drew the line in accepting Western ideas.

Fang did not, however, simply present the theory of concentric spheres. To emend the theory in favor of a limited heliocentrism, Fang cited a Jesuit's view for support.

I judge it to be like this: Venus and Mercury, near to the sun, make a single circuit [in one year]. Mr. Mu [bd] [i.e., Nicolas Smogolenski] said that this method [i.e., the Aristotelian model] is not exact, and that "In my country there was someone [presumably Copernicus] who clearly understood Mercury." [He argued that] since Venus and Mercury, near to the sun, have small revolutions like a solar halo, then the Nine Layers [theory] is not acceptable. [90]

In this ambiguous passage Fang seems to be accepting the assertion that the theory of concentric heavens is wrong because of Venus' and Mercury's orbiting the sun (if that is indeed the meaning Fang had in mind). In the succeeding entry in the section on astronomy in the *Wu li hsiao chih* Fang presented one of the most consequential results of seventeenth-century astronomical observation, the fact that Venus is observed to have phases. The entry is entitled "A Detailed Discussion on the Distances of the Orbits," and Fang drew his material from Schreck's *Ts'e t'ien yüeh-shuo* [be] (A General Account of Investigating the Heavens), which was completed in the late 1620s and included in the *Ch'ung-chen li shu*. (Fang did not acknowledge his source, nor did he give any indication when he was quoting and when he was paraphrasing.)

The moon, being near to the earth, is able to block [our sight of] the sun and the five planets. These six luminaries sometimes block the fixed stars. The distant ones of the luminaries move more slowly, the nearer ones move more quickly. The old theories on whether Venus and Mercury are below or above the heaven of the sun are all without substantiation. If one seeks to prove [whether Venus and Mercury are above or below] by which blocks which, then [in transit across or behind the sun, the planet] no longer can be seen in the brightness [so we cannot see whether it is above or below the sun]. If one seeks to argue from the speeds [of Venus, Mercury, and the sun], the movements of the three luminaries have always been the same. Both methods [i.e., observation and deduction from the relative speeds] are useless, and therefore we know they are both opinion [rather than proofs]. Recently in the Western countries they have investigated Venus by means of a telescope. Sometimes it is dark, sometimes it has first or last quarters. It is reckoned that Venus is near to the sun but when it moves to a distance it is scarcely one-eighth [illuminated], so it is of a different principle than the moon. Therefore, we realize that when [Venus] is beyond the sun it consequently is full and its size is small, when it is below the sun [i.e., between the sun and the earth] it is dark, and when on either side it consequently is in a first or last quarter. Mercury's size is small and it is nearer to the sun so to see its dark and bright [phases] is difficult, but in its movement it is not different from Venus. Its speed also is of the same principle as Venus. I say, do these [two planets] not make their orbits near to the sun! [91]

While the planetary system discussed here is not unambiguously Tychonic, the report of the telescopic observation of the phases of Venus and the qualitative description of Venus' orbit as moving around the sun can only be associated with Tycho Brahe's and not Ptolemy's system (that is, if the Copernican hypothesis is not admissible).[92] Thus Fang presented one of the more telling empirical arguments for accepting the limited heliocentrism of Tycho's theory, but without seeking to reconcile it with the cosmology he had presented in the entry entitled "Nine Layers."

Another problem in astronomy with which Fang dealt concerned the size of the sun. He began by referring to Ricci's *Ch'ien-k'un t'i i* [bf] (On the Structure of Heaven and Earth): "Matteo Ricci said that the circumference of the Earth is 90,000 *li*, its diameter is 28,666 *li* and 36 *chang*, the diameter of the sun is 165-3/8 times as large as the earth's (The distance [of the sun] from the center of the earth is more than 16,055,690 *li*) . . . ," and continued with the Western figures for the distances and relative diameters of the planets and moon.[93] What particularly concerned Fang about these figures was Ricci's assertion that the sun's diameter is more than 160 times as large as the diameter of the earth.[94] The figure was palpably preposterous, but rather than dismiss it out of hand Fang reproduced the arguments of two of his contemporaries before offering his own criticism.

The first critic, Hsiung Po-kan,[bg] who was a friend of Fang's father, proposed a theory that there is a one-to-one relation between the diameter of a flame and the distance to which its heat is "unbearable." Hsiung sought to use this theory to demonstrate the absurdity of the Westerners' idea of the size of the sun. According to Fang,

Hsiung Po-kan said that as for a light the size of a finger, its heat is unbearable at half an inch or less. The heat of a torch the size of a fist is unbearable at three inches or less. The heat of a brush fire the size of a cartwheel is unbearable at three feet or less. As for the measurement of the sun's disc according to the Western method, if it [the diameter] is twice the empty space between the sun and the earth, how could we bear the scorching heat on the earth's surface? [95]

Hsiung's attempt to render absurd the Westerners' idea of the sun's diameter falls down because the Jesuits never made the claim for its size that he imputes to them. More interestingly, Hsiung explained *why* the Westerners were mistaken by suggesting an ingenious analogy between the lenses of a telescope and the crystalline spheres which Ricci and some other Jesuits maintained formed the heavens. The analogy was to be understood in terms of a distinction made by Chu Hsi. Hsiung continued,

Chu said that rays are the substance [or embodiment, *t'i*] of brightness and brightness is the manifestation (*yung*) of rays. In the concept of substance there is inner substance, which is "true" substance, and there is outer substance, which is manifestation considered as substance. The Westerners' measurements of the sun are discussed in terms of a combination of inner and outer substance. In the West they use a telescope. Its four layers [i.e., lenses] all protrude on the outer side [i.e., are convex] but are depressed on the inner side [i.e., are concave]. By being depressed [on the side] near the eye [each lens] is able to enlarge a small image. Each layer passes on what it receives, so the multiplying [of the image] must continue to build up. Since the sun is in the fourth heaven, or layer, how can the crystalline material [which constitutes the substance of the encircling heavens] not enlarge [the image]? This is like a light hanging at a temple on a mountain. It is even seen from more than one *li* away. If the substance [in the sense of size] of the light is like a date, on observing it from a distance it is like a bushel basket [would appear in size at that distance instead of being imperceptible, as a date would be]. Is not this combining the lantern frame with the light itself to see them both as the substance of the light? [96]

Thus Hsiung explained the Westerners' error over the size of the sun in terms of their not comprehending Chu Hsi's distinction between the "substance" and "manifestation" of rays of light.

The second contemporary whom Fang quoted was Ch'iu Wei-p'ing [bh] (1614–79), whose *tzu* was Pang-shih. Ch'iu dismissed Hsiung's criticism of the Westerners' theory as ill-founded, but was able to show that there was a real contradiction in the Jesuits' theory of the diameter of the sun which discredited their contention that it was more than 160 times the diameter of the earth.

Ch'iu Pang-shih of Ning-tu (Kiangsi) said that it is true about the heat [varying with] the distance and size [of the flame] of the light, torch, and brush fire, but the size of the sun's disc according to the Western method is not at all twice the empty space between the sun and the earth. If the diameter of the earth's sphere is 28,636-4/9 *li* and the diameter of the sun is 165-3/8 times that of the earth, then the sun's diameter is 4,735,752-5/9 *li*. The distance of the sun from the center of the earth is more than 16,000,000 *li*, which is over triple the sun's diameter [according to Ricci's figures]. However, the diameter of the sun's heaven is double the more than 16,000,000 *li* that the sun is from the center of the earth. Calculated by the ratio of a diameter's seven to a circumference's 22, the circumference of the sun's heaven is over 100,000,000 *li* [i.e., 22/7 times 32 million *li*]. As for [the circumference's] 360 degrees, each degree is more than 270,000 *li*, and thus the diameter of the sun is barely more than 130,000 *li* [according to the Western theory that the sun's diameter is equal to one-half degree of its orbit]. So how do they arrive at its being more than 160 times [the diameter] of the earth! [97]

Thus, in a piece of logical argumentation that would no doubt have pleased them, Ch'iu has shown that the Jesuits cannot maintain that the sun is 160 times the diameter of the earth *and* that its diameter is one-half degree of its orbit.[98] After his logical demonstration of the contradiction, Ch'iu chose the figure of 130,000 *li* as the more sensible one for the diameter of the sun. It remained for Fang I-chih to explain the error of the Jesuits' thinking that the sun is 160 times the size of the earth. But first Fang added his agreement to Ch'iu's dismissal of Hsiung's refutation of a view the Westerners had not even propounded. "I say that this calculation that the sun is triple [the sun's diameter in its] distance from the earth is sufficient to refute the previous statement [by Hsiung] that the size of the sun's disc is twice the empty space between the sun and the earth, and the notion that the fire of the sun would desiccate the earth cannot be maintained." [99]

Fang sought to explain why the contradiction exposed by Ch'iu Wei-p'ing had arisen, and how some Westerners had arrived at an erroneous notion about the size of the sun. According to Fang, the use of geometrical methods to determine the diameter of the sun neglects the important principle that light rays are fat, by which he seems to have meant that they diffuse.

All of the [controversy] is because Western studies are not all of one school. Each by means of its techniques derives an ingenious calculation but still ignores the principles involved, so how can [their results] be relied upon? [The Westerners] make a detailed examination and thus obtain the vanishing point of the sun's image by setting the earth in the middle of an acute angle and extended straight lines. [100] Therefore, the size of the sun is like that [which they say it is, i.e., 165 times the diameter of the earth]. They do not realize that the sun's rays are always fat. The earth's image, of itself thin, cannot be obtained by acute angles and straight lines. Why? Material things being obstructed by form, their image is easily made to vanish. Sound and light rays are always more subtle than the "number" (*shu*) of things. Sound cannot be seen. Rays can be seen and measured, but the measuring is not accurate. [Seen through the comparatively] small hole of a courtyard well, the sun's image is like a bowl [i.e., it seems larger than when we are standing in the open]. I have tested this by means of a piece of paper. Pierce a small hole and cause the sun [light] to pass through [the hole] to illumine a stone which happens to be like [the light] in size. As the hand gradually moves [the paper] upward the ray [passing through the hole] gradually becomes larger than the stone. Pierce four or five holes, then the earth reflects them [the rays passing through the holes]. The four or five each make the image of a ray. As the hand gradually moves [the paper] upward the [four or five] rays unite to become one [spot of light] and the images of the four or five holes cannot be restored [so long as the paper is held high]. Rays are always fat and images are thin. [101]

Fang was objecting to the Jesuits' assumption that light rays constitute a geometrically straight line and he advanced an example of an observable phenomenon to show that the assumption was unwarranted. Thus he employed a result obtained experimentally to explain the fallacy of a result obtained deductively from mathematical assumptions.

I have not exhausted the passages in the *Wu li hsiao chih* which include Western ideas on celestial phenomena, but it should already be clear that Fang was dealing with astronomy in mainly descriptive terms. He did not attempt to reproduce the Westerners' mathematical models of the skies. Such details about the heavens as orbital times, the existence of the *primum mobile* sphere, the relative positions of the celestial bodies, the phases of Venus, and the dimensions and distances of the celestial bodies other than the sun, were reported and apparently accepted by Fang from Western sources. Where he did not follow them was in such matters as their calculations of the diameter of the sun, or their positing a tenth, "quiescent" heaven, or their commitment to cosmological models with philosophical implications. He was able both to elaborate the Aristotelian conception of the heavens as a series of geocentric spheres and to include statements which implied a Tychonic system involving limited heliocentrism.

In addition to drawing on Western astronomy, Fang's *Wu li hsiao chih* included explanations of terrestrial phenomena in terms of the Western theory of four elements. The theory, deriving from Aristotle, was the keystone of scholastic natural philosophy, for with it all sublunar phenomena could be explained as functions of the dynamic interaction of fire, air, water, and earth, and their respective primary and secondary qualities. Fire's primary quality, according to the theory, is heat, and its secondary quality dryness; air's qualities are dampness and, secondarily, heat; water's are cold and dampness; and earth's are dryness and cold. The theory was so integral to Western conceptions of the natural world that it remained dominant in Europe until the end of the seventeenth century. In his separate entries on each of the traditional Chinese elements (water, fire, wood, metal, and earth), Fang did not discuss the Western theory of four elements.

However, Fang did consider the problem of how many elements there are in a separate entry entitled "The Theories of Four Elements and of Five Elements." Fang began, "It has been asked how we decide between China's speaking of five elements and the Far West's speaking of four elements. I ask how it could only be a matter of different parts of the world." [102] Thus Fang denied that the difference in the number of elements was a cultural one due to geography. To support this point, Fang first cited Sung scholars' views on the elements. Shao Yung, according to Fang, spoke of water, fire, earth, and stone but glossed over metal and wood. Chu Hsi said that "four is substance (*t'i*) and five is function (*yung*)," while Chou Tun-i emphasized the role of water and fire and held that metal and wood are produced from the element earth.[103] These three Sung scholars were not specially disposed toward the number five. Fang also cited pre-Sung examples in which the number five was accorded a lesser or even no role in theories about "elements." The Yellow Emperor's book said that what is within the six directions is not disparate from [the number] five. Also, the book mentioned the "five transpositions" and distinguished the six types of *ch'i*.[104] These, according to Fang, illustrate the equal roles of five and six. The sentence (from the *Book of Rites*), "The five elements are distributed through the four seasons," is an example of using the number four.[105] Fang also glossed the sentence from the Hsi Tz'u Commentary in the *Book of Changes*, "One *yin* and one *yang* is called the Way"[106] so as to relate it to the problem of the number of elements:

Is this [sentence] not using [the number] two? It is possible to say that these [two, *yin* and *yang*] are the two elements water and fire. It is possible to say that they are the two [concepts], intangible *ch'i* (*hsü ch'i*)[bi] and tangible form (*shih hsing*).[bj] Intangible [*ch'i*] certainly is *ch'i*. Tangible form is *ch'i* which has coalesced. These are one and the same *ch'i*, a pair of elements (*hsing*)[bk] which are interdependent.[107]

From this argument Fang would have us understand that the concept of two elements, represented by *yin* and *yang*, or water and fire, or formed and formless *ch'i*, is also deeply rooted in Chinese thought. To bring his discussion back to the point which touched it off, the Jesuits' contention that there are four elements, Fang referred to a sūtra, the *Śūrangama*, translated as the *Leng-yen ching*.[bl] The *Leng-yen ching* spoke of earth, water, fire, wind, emptiness (or space), vision, and understanding as the "seven greats" (*ch'i ta*)[bm] and Fang noted that the first four are similar to water, fire, earth, and air (*ch'i*), without adding that these latter four are the four elements according to the Westerners.[108] Later in the same *chüan*, however, Fang again noted the parallel between four of the *Leng-yen ching's* "greats" and the West's "four elements."[109]

In his brief review of the literature on conceiving the number of elements to be other than five, Fang demonstrated that there are precedents which contradict the assertion that China spoke only of five elements. Moreover, although he did not seek directly to confound the Jesuits' persistent contention, beginning from Ricci's *Ch'ien-k'un t'i i*, that there are only four elements and that to think there are five is to be mistaken, Fang implicitly argued against them by his agnostic view that it does not matter much which number one stresses.[110]

It was this lack of commitment to any systematic, comprehensive theory which enabled Fang to quote segments of Western theories about particular phenomena without becoming involved in the ramifications of the four-elements theory. For example, Fang drew selectively on Western explanations of meteorological phenomena. The explanations were founded on the assumption that the atmosphere is divided into three strata in which moist air and dry air interact. Fang began an entry in the *Wu li hsiao chih* entitled "The Three Strata" with a statement on the assumed configuration: "As for the three strata, the one nearer the earth is the warm stratum, the one nearer the sun is the hot stratum, and the one in the space in between is the cold stratum." [111] In Fang's presentation the Jesuits' explanations of forms of precipitation were emended by substituting *yin* and *yang* for "moist air" and "dry air." With regard to rain he wrote: "The same air, whether ascending or descending, of itself is *yin* or *yang*. When [*yin*] air goes out [i.e., ascends from the earth's surface] and is impeded by the cold stratum, it [the moist air] unites to form rain. . . ." [112] Other atmospheric phenomena were also explained in terms drawn from the Westerners.

When *yang* air is caught inside *yin* air and cannot pass out but explodes, then it is thunder. If the fire and air issued forth [from this explosion] happen to illuminate a section of clouds, the [resulting] brilliant flash of the rays is called lightning. In the summer months the extreme heat of fire *ch'i* dashes against moist air and it becomes agitated. This [air] rises up to the more remote parts of the cold stratum and suddenly congeals into hail.[113]

Fang did not include only the Westerners' explanations of precipitation. He quoted an extended passage from Tung Chung-shu's "Yü pao tui" [bn] (A Dialogue concerning Rain and Hail), in which Tung argued that atmospheric phenomena were the result of the interaction of *yin* and *yang* air. Fang commented, "At the beginning of Han, Tung had already penetrated to the essence of the [meteorological] principles and therefore I have recorded it." [114] While the statement might suggest that Fang would have his readers accord equal status to Tung's and the emended (and thus similar) Western explanation, his final sentence of the entry forces a different conclusion: "In terms of material investigations using the three strata [theory] of the present day, hail, being formed very quickly, encloses some air inside of it and therefore hail always is hollow." [115] This explanation of an observed phenomenon, going a step beyond what Tung had written, demonstrates the advantage of being a modern man surveying past and present knowledge.

An explanation which Fang presented almost intact in its Western form was that of comets. In his discussion in the *Wu li hsiao chih* he wrote:

The uppermost [sublunar] space is all fire. Near to the [enclosing lunar] heaven is excessive heat. As in an oven there is no light [i.e., flame], but if something is put in, then a light is manifested. These [comets] are a result of earth *ch'i* scattering upward and carrying "something" into the hot stratum so that fire and light shoot forth. As for [comets] of long duration, the *ch'i* is bound together to form a thing which is dense and large and which follows the revolution of the encircling heaven. Their distance from the earth is comparatively close; they are not in the heaven of the constellations. [116]

By referring to the concepts of a layer of fire encircling and heating the upper stratum of the atmosphere, of comets being formed upon the penetration of earth into the hot stratum, of comets moving with the rotating heavens, and of comets being an atmospheric rather than a celestial phenomenon, Fang followed in detail the Western interpretation which Tycho Brahe had refuted at the close of the sixteenth century but which continued to be advanced by, among others, the Jesuits in China. This may have been because, as Needham points out, "Few elaborate theories about comets seem to have been produced in China." [117]

The geographical knowledge which the Jesuits published was, in contrast to their meteorological explanations, not burdened by theories and Fang found it easy to quote a wide variety of items. He did criticize their division of a great circle on the earth's surface into 360 units rather than 365¼ degrees, which was the Chinese convention, but he reproduced the Jesuits' calculation that movement 250 *li* due north raises the pole star one degree farther above the horizon, a fact from which the earth's circumference can be calculated. [118] To illustrate that it is possible to stand anywhere on a spherical earth without falling off, Fang noted that ants on a leaf consider "down" where their feet are, and that Mr. Li [bo] (i.e., Ricci) had experienced the sphericity of the earth in traveling far south of the equator when coming to China.[119] Fang reported that the southern tip of Africa was on the opposite side of the sphere from China, but added a note that some Western books said South America was on the opposite side.[120]

Fang's main source of Western material on world geography was Aleni's *Chih-fang wai chi* [bp] (Memoir on Countries Not Listed at the Record Office). By mentioning transliterated place names from Western Asia, Europe, the Americas, and Africa, Fang acknowledged the unprecedented expansion of geographical knowledge which resulted from the Jesuits' presence in China. Fang reproduced more than fifty passages from the *Chih-fang wai chi* to present examples of phenomena which were out of the ordinary.[121] He was not at variance with contemporary European geographers in not distinguishing fact from fiction, observation from rumor. Consider the reports of certain natural phenomena which Fang quoted from Aleni's geography. In Arabia there is a sea some 800 *li* in length, the water of which is so salty that there are no waves, things cannot be sunk in it, nor living creatures survive in it; this sea is called the "Dead Sea" (*Ssu hai*).[bq] [122] On an island (referring to Florida?) near America there is a spring, and if an old man washes his face one hundred times with water drawn from this spring his youth is restored.[123]

Fang also quoted from the *Chih-fang wai chi* on such animals as lions (they are numerous in Africa and they only fear roosters and the sound of cart wheels),[124] the ostrich (the king of all birds, it is long-lived, causes its young to look at the sun without blinking, and reciprocates any kindness accorded it by a man),[125] and the phoenix (which, after living four or five hundred years, immolates itself on a pyre of aromatic wood; its ashes turn into a worm, which is transformed back into the bird itself).[126] Examples of strange products of human ingenuity were also quoted by Fang. In Persia there was a garden built up into the sky,[127] while the capital city of Mexico is built on wooden posts over a lake.[128] And in Sicily there was a clever gentleman named Chi-mo-te [br] who cast an immense mirror with which he set fire to the ships of an enemy.[129] The *Chih-fang wai chi* was also the source of examples of unusual people. In Holland a woman was captured from the sea. She ate the food given her and was willing to act as a servant, but she was unable to speak; moreover, her body from the waist down was formed like a gown, reaching to the ground.[130] In Tartary there is a nation of women called Amazons, whose custom it is to invite men to their territory only in the spring, and they immediately kill any male baby.[131]

These examples, of course, do not exhaust Fang's use of Aleni's book, but they indicate the range of material Fang used and demonstrate how easy it was for him to take disparate facts, arranged by region in contemporary European geographers' style, and place them under entries of his own fashioning in the *Wu li hsiao chih*. All these items further support the notion that in other lands there are phenomena which are unfamiliar to us and about which we can learn.

The only field in which Fang presented the conceptual framework as well as the details of a Western theory with apparent acceptance on his part was physiology. He quoted extended passages from Schall's *Chu chih ch'ün cheng* [bs] (A Host of Evidence that God Rules), which represented the scholastic version of Galen's teachings about the human body. Fang began with the explication of the two basic forces of moisture and heat, by which life is sustained, and the role of blood in dissipating the body's heat. He then quoted the description of the venal system stemming from the liver and by which "natural spirits" (*t'i-hsing chih ch'i*) [bt] are distributed throughout the body.[132] He continued with the details of the arterial system stemming from the heart and through which the heat force and "vital spirits" (*sheng-yang chih ch'i*) [bu] course. Third, there is the network of nerves by which "animal spirits" (*tung-chüeh chih ch'i*),[bv] so called because of their association with *anima* or soul, are dispersed from the brain.[133] Fang quoted the *Chu chih ch'ün cheng's* account of the processes by which food is transformed in the stomach, blood made in the liver, and the three "spirits" produced in the liver, heart, and brain.[134]

Thus Fang reproduced in the *Wu li hsiao chih* the main ideas about physiology in the Western tradition, ascribed to Galen, even though Chinese knowledge in this field was well developed. Fang provided his readers with an explanation of this apparent anomaly. "I say that as this discussion of the theory of the liver, heart, brain, and nerves does not arise either from the *Yellow Emperor's Inner Classic: The Spiritual Pivot* or *The Plain Questions*, I therefore have included it in order to make complete [the material in this book] for reference." [135] Fang would have his readers recognize the divergence of the Westerners' theory from traditional explanations of the principles of body processes. At the same time, the quantity of material quoted from Schall's book without any critical remarks suggests that Fang would have these passages stand as a contribution to the fund of knowledge about the physiology of the human body.

Fang also quoted a number of passages from the *Chu chih ch'ün cheng* on topics other than physiology. For instance, in the *Wu li hsiao chih* he included the description of the disposition and number of the bones (3.11b, quoted from A.11b), and the rationalistic account of the proportions of the human body (3.11b–12a, quoted from B.2b–3a). These passages, like the ones about physiology, were part of a theological argument in Schall's book. The theological considerations were omitted by Fang. He did not quote Schall's statement of *why* the bone structure was discussed: "Wanting to evidence God's rule, one far-reachingly draws [evidence] from all things, and more narrowly draws [evidence] from our own bodies. Since no thing is purposeless, how could the body alone not [be purposeful in design]?" [136] Schall's contention that the design in nature is proof of God's existence was rejected by Fang. His excision of such passages is revealed in his handling of Schall's summary of the discussion of the types of human flesh. (The italicized sections in parentheses were omitted from Fang's quotation.)

These [types of flesh] all have their own function and are in accord with the numerous and varying movements of one's body. This is their general purpose. (*In the West there was a famous medical man who has investigated*) the purposes of each of the bones; there are approximately forty. As for [the purposes of] each of the types of flesh, there are approximately ten. (*By examining the purposes of each of the parts and portions of the human body*) one can count several tens of thousands. (*Alas! Without omnipotence and omnicompetence, who could devise all of this?*) [137]

The theological assumptions that lay behind much of the Jesuits' published material on natural philosophy were part of the target in Fang's appraisal of them. "The knowledge from the Far West which entered [China] in the Wan-li period is detailed in 'material investigations' but deficient in speaking of 'comprehending seminal forces.' " [138]

In one concise statement in the *T'ung ya*, Fang I-chih disparaged what he felt to be the contemporary alternatives to his own mode of intellectual endeavor and explained, again, why the Westerners' knowledge could be used in spite of its shortcomings.

The scholars of this age chafe at the encumbrances of the world. If one is pleased to cultivate his "self," then he holds to "constant" [i.e., nonphenomenal] principles. If he has [literary] talent, then he gives himself over to stylistic elegance. If he is of far-ranging intelligence, then he finds his pleasure in self-indulgence. But who is willing to develop, and extend in its essentials, our knowledge so as to resolve what has been causing doubt? It is indeed difficult to come across a Chang Heng, a Tsu Ch'ung-chih, an I-hsing, or a Shao Yung [to show the way of extending knowledge]. The "material investigations" of the Westerners somewhat get to the essentials. Their [approach to] "comprehending seminal forces" is insupportable, but they are [even] drawn upon as a Viscount of T'an by those who would seek to understand matters involving spirit (*shen-ming*).bw 139

Here Fang was criticizing his contemporaries who neglected the importance of the notion that "the extension of knowledge lies in the investigation of things," and at the same time was criticizing the Westerners for passing beyond "material investigations" into other realms, particularly religious. Nevertheless, Fang had found a new store of knowledge about the external world in the writings of the Jesuits. He could disregard their Aristotelian cosmology, with its theological content, to pick through their books to select facts and opinions about "things" on the basis of which our knowledge might be further extended.

Fang I-chih's handling of the Western natural philosophy published by Jesuits is a substantive example of his practical understanding of the term *ke wu*. By concentrating on descriptive "principles" associated with astronomy, certain sets of natural phenomena, the human body, and medicine, he was slighting the interpretation that *ke wu* is primarily the means by which we can come to know and implement the normative "principles" which are our guide to moral conduct. The shift in focus was reinforced by Fang's not explaining "seminal forces" even while arguing that "comprehending seminal forces" (*t'ung chi*) and understanding the "extended principles of things" (*wu chih chih-li*) had to be founded on "material investigations" (*chih ts'e*). It was "principles of things" (*wu li*) in a narrow sense that he sought to uncover. The effect of what Fang was doing in the *Wu li hsiao chih* was to relegate "comprehending seminal forces" to the supportive role of validating our pursuit of "material investigations," much as "fathoming principles" gave meaning to the "extension of knowledge" for the more pedantic followers of Chu Hsi. Fang was implicitly making the *process* of "investigation of things" sufficient in itself. *Ke wu* for Fang I-chih could thus serve as a form of intellectual self-discipline and moral training, as in Wang Yang-ming's interpretation, but directed at that which is external to our minds, as in Chu Hsi's interpretation.

In addition to redirecting the goal of *ke wu*, Fang was involved in the development of a new interpretation of the proper means of acquiring knowledge. His stress on accumulating items of knowledge and his opposition to introspection as a method anticipate two of the characteristics of the School of Evidential Research (*k'ao cheng hsüeh*) bx which rose to prominence in Ch'ing. The eighteenth-century editors of the *Ssu-k'u ch'üan-shu* singled out Fang as the only author in the latter half of the Ming dynasty who was wholly devoted to evidencing assertions and who anticipated the scholarship of Ku Yen-wu by (1613–82) and others in early Ch'ing who promoted *k'ao cheng*.[140] There are many similarities between Fang and Ku. Ku disparaged the Ming fashion of substituting introspection for building knowledge item by item and of substituting pedantry bogged down in the past for broad learning. Ku's best known work, the *Record of Knowledge Gained Day by Day* (*Jih-chih lu*),bz manifests this emphasis. He explained:

I have often said that men of today compile books in the same way that they mint coins. Whereas men in antiquity dug copper from the hills, men of today buy old coins and call them copper scrap simply to supply the mints. The coins which are minted are coarse and bad, and moreover the precious coins which have come down from antiquity are broken up and will not be preserved for subsequent generations. Is this not a loss both ways? You inquired how many further *chüan* of the *Record of Knowledge Gained Day by Day* have been completed. Presumably you think of it as copper scrap. In the year that we have been separated, morning and evening I have read, deliberated, and searched, and I have scarcely completed a dozen items. Thus I have some hopes that what I write is comparable to copper dug from the hills.[141]

This was to become the new scholarly fashion: original, carefully researched, fully verified items of information presented in the form of notes.[142] In all of this, Ku and Fang were alike.

The crucial difference between Fang and Ku was not their methodology but their view of the content of the word *wu*, "things," as the object of intellectual inquiry. Both held that knowledge had to be rooted in the objective world, external to our minds. But Ku Yen-wu and the School of Evidential Research largely focused on matters relating to human affairs, and thus channeled energies into historical and textual studies and, ideally, statecraft. Fang's scholarship, on the other hand, is representative of the possibility in the seventeenth century that the realm of "things" to be investigated would center on physical objects, technology, and natural phenomena. By providing a justification for taking the investigation of "things" as implicitly worthy in itself, by contributing to the establishment of a methodology which stressed evidence, and by applying his new orientation even to his selective use of Western learning, Fang I-chih was offering to his contemporaries a mode of endeavor which was parallel to the secularization of natural philosophy in seventeenth-century Europe.

1. *Ta hsüeh*, section 1 (in the "modern" arrangement of the text). I have followed the translation of the passage in A. C. Graham, *Two Chinese Philosophers* (London: Lund Humphries, 1958), p. 74.
2. The *T'ung-ch'eng Fang shih ch'i tai i-shu* ᶜᵃ (1888) (hereafter referred to as *Ch'i tai i-shu*), 1a, notes that "Our family, the Fangs, has lived in T'ung-ch'eng since the end of Yüan." Detailed references for this paragraph on Fang's family will be found in Chapter I in my *Fang I-chih's Response to Western Knowledge* (Harvard University, unpublished dissertation, 1970). An adequate biography of Fang I-chih has yet to be published. There is an entry concerning him in A. W. Hummel (ed.), *Eminent Chinese of the Ch'ing Period* (Washington, D.C.: U.S. Government, 1943–44). There is some biographical material in Hou Wai-lu, "Fang I-chih—Chung-kuo te pai-k'e-ch'üan-shu p'ai ta che-hsüeh chia," *Li-shih yen-chiu* ᶜᵇ (1957), 6, 1–21; 7, 1–25; and in Sakade Yoshinobu, "Hō I-chi no shisō," in Yabuuchi Kiyoshi (ed.), *Min-Shin jidai no kagaku gijutsu shi* ᶜᶜ (Kyōto: Kyōto daigaku jinbun kagaku kenkyūjo, 1970), pp. 93–134.
3. Fang I-chih, "Ch'i chieh," *Chi-ku-t'ang wen-chi*,ᶜᵈ in *Ch'i tai i-shu*, 1/30b.
4. *Chi-ku-t'ang wen-chi*, in *Ch'i tai i-shu*, 2/29a.
5. *Chi-ku-t'ang ch'u chi*, in Fang I-chih, *Fu-shan wen-chi*,ᶜᵉ 1a.
6. Fang I-chih, *T'ung ya*, Yao Wen-hsieh (ed.), shou 2/5b.
7. *Chi-ku-t'ang wen-chi*, in *Fu-shan wen-chi*, 2/27a.
8. Hsü Tzu, *Hsiao-t'ien chi-chuan* ᶜᶠ (Peking, 1958), pp. 189, 249.
9. The author of K'ung-chao's tomb inscription claimed that the Fang household "was not destroyed because of their generations of virtue"; 2a, in *Ch'i tai i-shu*.
10. *Ibid.*, 2a, 5a–b; *Ming shih* (Po-na pen),ᶜᵍ 260/20b; and *Fu-shan wen-chi*, 8/11b.
11. *Fu-shan wen-chi*, 9/13a.
12. "Ch'i chieh," 1/31b–39b.
13. Hsieh Kuo-chen, *Ming Ch'ing chih chi tang-she yün-tung k'ao* ᶜʰ (Taipei, 1967), pp. 179, 184.
14. *Ming shih*, 260/20b–21a.
15. *Fu-shan wen-chi*, 4/8a–b.
16. *Ming shih*, 260/21b; Li Yao's biography of Fang I-chih in *Nan chiang i shih* ᶜⁱ (Taipei, 1968), pp. 1876–77.
17. *Ming shih*, 260/21b.
18. *Fu-shan wen-chi*, 2/35a.
19. Fang Chung-t'ung, "Wu li hsiao chih pien-lu yüan-ch'i," ᶜʲ 1b, in *Wu li hsiao chih* (1666).
20. *Ibid.*

21. Wang Fu-chih, "Fang I-chih chuan," ^{ck} la, in *Ch'i tai i-shu*.

22. *Ch'ing shih lieh-chuan* ^{cl} (Shanghai, 1928), 68/5b, and Hummel, *Eminent Chinese*, under Fang I-chih.

23. *Ch'ung-chen ch'ang-pien* ^{cm} (Shanghai, 1917), 2/1b.

24. Hsü Tzu, *Hsiao-t'ien chi-nien fu-k'ao* ^{cn} (Peking, 1957), p. 84.

25. *Fu-shan wen-chi*, 8/9a.

26. *Ibid.*

27. *Ibid.*

28. Hsü Tzu, *Hsiao-t'ien chi-chuan*, p. 250.

29. *Ibid.*, and *Fu-shan wen-chi*, 8/10a.

30. Hsü Tzu, *Hsiao-t'ien chi-chuan*, p. 250. Hummel, *Eminent Chinese*, under Fang I-chih, says, "Fang I-chih accepted appointment as junior secretary of the Supervisorate of Instruction."

31. Hsü Tzu, *Tsiao-t'ien chi-nien*, p. 251. Chi Liu-ch'i, *Ming chi nan lüeh*.^{co} (Taipei, 1968), 12/18a, records that in the fourth month of 1647 Fang offered advice on military strategy, but it is not clear that he held an official appointment at the time.

32. Hsü Tzu, *Hsiao-t'ien chi-nien*, p. 523.

33. Hsü Tzu, *Hsiao-t'ien chi-chuan*, p. 250. Hummel, *Eminent Chinese*, under Fang I-chih, says, "In 1647 he was made concurrently Vice-President of the Board of Ceremonies and Grand Secretary, but was soon dismissed." Ch'ien Ch'eng-chih, *So chih lu* (Taipei: Shih-chieh, 1971), "Yung-li chi-nien," ^{cp} 5b, records that Fang was a Grand Secretary. Ch'ien (1612–93) was from the same district (T'ung-ch'eng, Anhui) as Fang, and in the 1630s Fang had persuaded him not to remain allied to an enemy of the Fu-she. (Hsieh Kuo-chen, *Ming Ch'ing chih chi tang-she yün-tung k'ao*, pp. 172–73.) Ch'ien met with Fang in Kwangsi in 1650 and 1651 (*So chih lu*, "Yung-li chi-nien," 62a, 67b), and presumably had direct knowledge of Fang's involvement in the Yung-li court. The implication of *Ming chi nan lüeh*, 14/32b, is that Fang did not decide the situation at the court was hopeless and retire until 1648.

34. Fang I-chih used the title *Chung-yün* ^{cq} to designate the source of the command. *Chung-yün* was a post established in the Han dynasty and connected with the person of the heir apparent. In the first month of 1647 Ch'ü Shih-ssu,^{cr} who was a Grand Secretary and one of the mainstays of the Yung-li emperor's government, had been named Grand Protector of the Heir-Apparent. (Hsü Tzu, *Hsiao-t'ien chi-nien*, p. 523.) Therefore, I assume that Fang meant the command had come from Ch'ü Shih-ssu.

35. *Fu-shan wen-chi*, 8/10a. "The mountains at Fu-i" apparently refers to the area on the Kwangsi-Hukuang border, north and east of Kuei-lin.

36. *Ibid.*

37. *Ibid.*, 9/21a; 10/1a ff. The village, P'ing-hsi,^{cs} was near P'ing-lo in eastern Kwangsi, south of Kuei-lin (*ibid.*, 8/37a). Ch'ien Ch'eng-chih, *So chih lu*, "Yung-li chi-nien," 62a, said P'ing-hsi was forty *li* from P'ing-lo.

38. Ch'en Chi-sheng, *T'ien-ch'i Ch'ung-chen liang ch'ao i-shih* [ct] (Peking, 1958), p. 420.

39. Ch'ien Ch'eng-chih, *So chih lu*, "Yung-li chi-nien," 62a–63a.

40. Hsü Tzu, *Hsiao-t'ien chi-chuan*, p. 250. A different account of the interview between Fang and the general is given in Wen Jui-lin, *Nan chiang i shih*, in *Wan Ming shih-liao ts'ung-shu* [cu] (Tokyo, 1967), p. 304. It should be noted that Ch'ien Ch'eng-chih recorded that Yen Wei,[cv] to whose house Fang was going when the troops were sent after him, was arrested, interrogated, tortured, and brought before the same general who, according to Wen Jui-lin, confronted Fang I-chih. Moreover, the same alternatives of either official garb or an executioner's sword were offered to Yen, who, like Fang I-chih, refused to submit and was released by the general with permission to become a monk. (*So chih lu*, 63a. Cf. Hsü Tzu, *Hsiao-t'ien chi-chuan*, p. 601.) Thus, in some of its details this story about Yen, recounted by Ch'ien Ch'eng-chih, corresponds with Hsü's, Wen's, and others' accounts of events involving Fang I-chih. Fang became a monk in the tenth or eleventh month of 1650. The chronology of Ch'ien Ch'eng-chih's contemporary account differs from that in Hsü Tzu's study. It would seem from Ch'ien that his meeting with Fang, the fall of Kuei-lin, and Fang's becoming a monk all took place at the beginning of the tenth month. Hsü Tzu, in the *Hsiao-t'ien chi-nien*, p. 650, recorded that Kuei-lin was taken at the beginning of the eleventh month. (The difference cannot be attributed to Ch'ien's use of the Ming calendar—which he makes clear had an intercalary eleventh month in 1650—and Hsü's use of the Ch'ing calendar—which added the intercalation after the second month of 1651.)

41. Hsü Tzu, *Hsiao-t'ien chi-nien*, p. 655. There is a problem with this account, too, in that the incident purportedly took place in Wu-chou in the twelfth month of 1650, although Hsü Tzu and Ch'ien Ch'eng-chih agree that Wu-chou was not occupied by Ch'ing troops until the intercalary second month of 1651. Ch'ien Ch'eng-chih also recorded that he met Fang in Wu-chou toward the end of 1651. (*So chih lu*, 67b.)

42. Ch'en Yüan, *Ming chi Tien Ch'ien fo-chiao k'ao* [cw] (Peking, 1962), pp. 108, 238. Cf. Hsü Tzu, *Hsiao-t'ien chi-nien*, p. 653.

43. Shih Jun-chang, *Shih Yü-shan wen-chi*, in *Shih Yü-shan ch'üan chi* (Lien-t'ing tsang),[ex] 5/8b; also quoted in Yü Ying-shih, *Fang I-chih wan chieh k'ao* [cy] (Hong Kong, 1972), p. 67. Wen Jui-lin, *Nan chiang i shih*, p. 304, records that Fang entered three years of mourning for his father's death in 1655.

44. Li Yao's biography of Fang I-chih in *Nan chiang i-shih*, p. 1874; Yü Ying-shih, *Fang wan chieh k'ao*, pp. 7–9, 27, 126–27.

45. Yü Ying-shih, *Fang wan chieh k'ao*, pp. 55, 57–58. The *Ch'ing-yüan shan chih shu* (Fang Chang lou),[cz] published in 1669, includes dozens of poems written for the monk Fang I-chih. See especially *Ch'ing-yüan shan chih shu*, 10/15b.

46. For these dates, see Hou Wai-lu's introduction to the *Tung-hsi chün* (Peking, 1962), p. 1, and the editor's postface, p. 167.
47. Hou Wai-lu, *Chung-kuo ssu-hsiang t'ung-shih* [da] (Peking, 1960), vol. 4, p. 1152. Yü Ying-shih, *Fang wan chieh k'ao*, p. 123, suggests the *Yao-ti p'ao Chuang* was begun in 1660 and completed in 1663. The book, long unavailable, has recently been republished in Taiwan.
48. Hou Wai-lu, p. 1151. All the titles, including manuscripts, attributed to Fang are listed in Hou Wai-lu, pp. 1123–24. Yü Ying-shih, too, has discussed the continuities in Fang's thought. (See *Fang wan chieh k'ao*, ch. 3, esp. pp. 90–91.)
49. Hou Wai-lu, pp. 1133–34.
50. Yü Ying-shih, *Fang wan chieh k'ao*, pp. 94, 103, 108. Yü's findings on the circumstances surrounding Fang's death are the most complete now available.
51. *Wu li hsiao chih*, 1/25a–b. The *Ch'ung-chen li-shu* was compiled on imperial command in the 1630s at the Calendrical Bureau under the direction of Adam Schall and Jacobus Rho.
52. Fang I-chih, "Hsi-yü hsin pi," [db] 26a, in *Ch'i tai i-shu*.
53. Translated in Graham, *Two Chinese Philosophers*, p. 74.
54. Quoted in *ibid.*, from *Erh Ch'eng ch'üan-shu* (SPPY edition), "Ho-nan Ch'eng shih wai-shu," [dc] 2.4a.
55. Cf. D. C. Lau, "A Note on *Ke wu*," *Bulletin of the School of Oriental and African Studies*, vol. 30 (1967), pp. 353–57.
56. Quoted in *ibid.*, p. 353.
57. For Chu Hsi, "the whole purpose of the Investigation of Things is moral self-development; the principles which really matter are moral principles, and investigation is mainly concerned with uncovering them in human affairs." (Graham, *Two Chinese Philosophers*, p. 79.) In the recorded dialogues of the Ch'engs and Chu there are, of course, numerous references to the natural world as an object of interest, but the references are incidental rather than central.
58. Wang Yang-ming, *Instructions for Practical Living and Other Neo-Confucian Writings*, translated by Wing-tsit Chan (Columbia University Press, 1963), p. 249; cf. *Wang Wen-ch'eng kung ch'üan-shu* (Taiwan, reprint SPTK edition), "Ch'uan-hsi lu," [dd] 153b–154a.
59. Chan, *Instructions*, p. 244; cf. "Ch'uan-hsi lu," 152A.
60. Chan, *Instructions*, p. 278; cf. *Wang Wen-ch'eng kung ch'üan-shu*, 26, "Ta-hsüeh wen," [de] 739a.
61. Fang I-chih, *Wu li hsiao chih*, "Tzu hsü," la. This preface has also been translated in Mark Elvin, *The Pattern of the Chinese Past* (Stanford University Press, 1973), p. 230. The English word "thing," which I have used to translate *wu*, [df] like it includes two main areas of meaning. The meaning in English of "things" as "affairs" (developed from the root meaning of "thing" as a public or judicial assembly) is similar to the gloss in Chinese of *shih* for

wu. The further meaning of "thing" as "entity" (i.e., that which exists, whether as an object of perception or thought) is parallel to the modern gloss of *wu* as *tung-hsi.* [dg] Fang's definition of *wu* included "affairs" (or events, or activities, or *shih-ch'ing*),[dh] physical (or material) objects, and objects of mental effort. However, in the *Wu li hsiao chih* and *T'ung ya,* Fang's concern was primarily with "things" as "objects," including technological and natural processes as well as physical "entities" and our conceptions of them, rather than with "affairs." Here, the word "things" should be read with Fang's predisposition in mind.

62. *Wu li hsiao chih,* "Tsung lun," 7b.
63. *Ibid.,* 8a.
64. *Ibid.,* 3a.
65. Fang I-chih, *T'ung ya,* shou 3/11b.
66. *Ibid.*
67. *Ibid.,* 11b–12a.
68. *Ibid.,* 12a.
69. *Wu li hsiao chih,* "Tzu hsü," 1a.
70. *Ibid.,* 1a–b.
71. *Ibid.,* 1b.
72. In quantitative terms approximately 5 percent of the *Wu li hsiao chih's* pages are taken up with Western ideas, which makes the Jesuits' books collectively one of Fang's most fruitful sources. The *T'ung ya* also contains scattered references to Western ideas.
73. Fang I-chih, "Hsi-yü hsin pi," 24b–25a.
74. Fang Chung-t'ung, *P'ei ku chi,*[di] quoted in Hou Wai-lu, "Fang I-chih," *Li-shih yen-chiu,* 1957, 6, 9. The idea of "selecting what is good" comes from the *Analects* (7:27), where Confucius said he selects what is good from that which he learns from others and follows it, and he records (in his mind) that which he witnesses.
75. *T'ung ya,* shou 1/1a.
76. *Ibid.,* shou 1/27b.
77. *Ibid.,* shou 1/2a. This was dated 1641.
78. *Wu li hsiao chih,* "Tsung lun," 4a.
79. *Wu li hsiao chih,* 1/3a–b. It may be noted that both the notion of degrees of latitude and of two temperate zones are Western and were expounded by the Jesuits. For example, Aleni, *Chih-fang wai chi* (first published in 1623; reference is to the copy in the Vatican Library, Rome), "Tsung shuo," 2a–b.
80. Fang was paraphrasing a passage in the *Huang-ti nei-ching su wen.* It may be that he was following a different text than that in the SPTK edition, but it must be noted that the SPTK edition says that the earth "is in the middle of the great emptiness" (*t'ai-hsü chih chung*) [dj] rather than "in the midst of the heavens" (*t'ien chih chung*),[dk] as Fang has it. *Ch'ung kuang pu-chu Huang-ti nei-ching su wen* [dl] (Shanghai: SPTK edition, 1929), 19/9b.

81. *Wu li hsiao chih*, 1/25a. The *Kai t'ien*, or Hemispherical Dome, theory and the *Hun t'ien*, or Celestial Sphere, theory are discussed in Joseph Needham, *Science and Civilisation in China*, vol. 3 (Cambridge University Press, 1959), pp. 210–19.

82. James Legge (trans.), *The Chinese Classics*, vol. 5 (Hong Kong University Press, 1960), pp. 667–68.

83. For example, *Wu li hsiao chih*, "Tsung lun," 4a; *T'ung ya*, shou 2/5a. For a general account of the Western knowledge on which Fang was drawing, see W. J. Peterson, "Western Natural Philosophy Published in Late Ming China," *Proceedings of the American Philosophical Society*, vol. 117, no. 4 (1973), pp. 295–322.

84. *T'ung ya*, 11/15b.

85. *Ibid.*

86. David Hawkes (trans.), *Ch'u Tz'u: The Songs of the South* (Oxford, 1959), p. 47, renders the passage as, "Who planned and measured out the round shape and the ninefold gates of heaven?"

87. Cf. Alfred Forke, *The World Conception of the Chinese* (London, 1925), p. 104; Needham, *Science and Civilisation*, vol. 2, p. 483; vol. 3, p. 222; and Chu Hsi, *Chu tzu ch'üan-shu* [dm] (Ku-hsiang chai), 49/25b.

88. *Wu li hsiao chih*, 1/26a–b. I have not determined from which book Fang drew his figures, but similar ones appeared in Matteo Ricci's *Ch'ien-k'un t'i i* (first published in 1614; reference is to the copy in the Bibliothèque Nationale, Paris).

89. *Wu li hsiao chih*, 1/26b.

90. *Ibid.*

91. *Ibid.*, 1/27a; drawn from Johannes Schreck, *Ts'e t'ien yüeh-shuo* (first published in 1637; reference is to the copy in the Vatican Library, Rome), A/16a–17a.

92. Cf. Thomas Kuhn, *The Copernican Revolution* (Harvard University Press, 1966), pp. 222–24.

93. *Wu li hsiao chih*, 1/32b–33a. The figures were taken by Fang from Ricci's *Ch'ien-k'un t'i i*, A/4b–5b, and B/3a.

94. This discussion of Fang's handling of the problem of the sun's size is based on the *Wu li hsiao chih*, but Fang also raised the problem in *T'ung ya*, 11/16b–17a.

95. *Wu li hsiao chih*, 1/33a.

96. *Ibid.*, 1/33a–b.

97. *Ibid.*, 1/33b–34a. I have not located Ch'iu's argument in his *Ch'iu Pang-shih wen-chi* [dn] (1875).

98. An instance of the Jesuits' asserting that the diameter of the sun is one-half of a degree is found in Schreck, *Ts'e t'ien yüeh-shuo*, B/14b.

99. *Wu li hsiao chih*, 1/34a.

100. Fang's son Chung-t'ung appended a note which explained in more detail the geometrical method to which his father was here referring. "Chung-

t'ung says that as for what is called 'obtaining the image,' from the fact that the earth's image blocks [the light from] the sun and eclipses the moon but not Mars, Jupiter, Saturn, or the twenty-eight 'lunar mansions,' it must be that the earth's image does not extend that far. If the sun's disc were smaller than or equal to the earth, then the earth's image would have no vanishing point. Therefore, by setting the earth between two straight lines from the moon, one determines [the diameter of] the disc of the sun." From *Wu li hsiao chih*, 1/34b.

101. *Ibid.*

102. *Wu li hsiao chih*, 1/14a.

103. *Ibid.*

104. "Wu yün hsing" [do] is the title of *chüan* 19 of the *Huang-ti nei-ching su wen*. On the six types of *ch'i*, see *Ch'ung-kuang pu-chu Huang-ti nei-ching su wen*, 19/3b–4a.

105. *Wu li hsiao chih*, 1/14a. I have followed the translation in James Legge (trans.), *The Sacred Books of the East: The Li Ki* (Oxford, 1885), p. 381.

106. I am not certain how Fang I-chih thought the passage should be read. Cf. the translations by R. Wilhelm, *The I Ching* (London, 1951), vol. 1, p. 319, and by J. Legge, *Sacred Books of the East: The Yi King* (Oxford, 1882), p. 355.

107. *Wu li hsiao chih*, 1/14a–b.

108. *Ibid.*, 1/14b. In Buddhist literature, earth, water, fire and wind (*feng*) [dp] are commonly referred to as the "four greats" (*ssu ta*).[dq]

109. *Ibid.*, 1/21b.

110. Cf. his concluding sentences, *Wu li hsiao chih*, 1/15a.

111. *Ibid.*, 1/27b.

112. *Ibid.*

113. *Ibid.*, 1/27b–28a.

114. *Ibid.*, 2/7a.

115. *Ibid.*

116. *Ibid.*, 2/8b.

117. Needham, *Science and Civilisation*, vol. 3, p. 432.

118. *T'ung ya*, 11/16a.

119. *Ibid.*

120. *Ibid.* The latter, of course, is correct.

121. I have found and verified fifty-four quotations from Aleni's book (*Chih-fang wai chi*) in the *Wu li hsiao chih*.

122. *Wu li hsiao chih*, 2/17b; Fang also mentioned the Dead Sea on 1/16b. He quoted from *Chih-fang wai chi*, 1/10a.

123. *Wu li hsiao chih*, 2/24a.

124. *Ibid.*, 10/12b, quoted from *Chih-fang wai chi*, 3/1b.

125. *Wu li hsiao chih*, 10/5b, quoted from *Chih-fang wai chi*, 3/2a–b.

126. *Wu li hsiao chih*, 11/23a, quoted from *Chih-fang wai chi*, 1/9b.

127. *Wu li hsiao chih*, 12/22a, quoted from *Chih-fang wai chi*, 1/7b, where the structure was reported as one of the seven wonders of the world.

128. *Wu li hsiao chih*, 12/22a, quoted from *Chih-fang wai chi*, 4/10a.
129. *Wu li hsiao chih*, 2/24b, quoted from *Chih-fang wai chi*, 2/20a, where the
     gentleman's name is given as A-erh-chi-mo-te,[dr] i.e., Archimedes (287–12
     B.C.).
130. *Wu li hsiao chih*, 3/28b, quoted from *Chih-fang wai chi*, 6/6a–b.
131. *Wu li hsiao chih*, 3/26a, quoted from *Chih-fang wai chi*, 1/3a.
132. *Wu li hsiao chih*, 3/9b–10a, quoted from Adam Schall, *Chu chih ch'ün
     cheng* (first published in 1636; reference is to the copy in the Vatican
     Library, Rome), A/12b–13a.
133. *Wu li hsiao chih*, 3/10a–b, quoted from *Chu chih ch'ün cheng*, A/13a–14a.
134. *Wu li hsiao chih*, 3/12a–13a, quoted from *Chu chih ch'ün cheng*, A/12a–b.
135. *Wu li hsiao chih*, 3/11a.
136. *Chu chih ch'ün cheng*, A/10b.
137. *Wu li hsiao chih*, 3/11b, and *Chu chih ch'ün cheng*, A/11b.
138. *Wu li hsiao chih*, "Tzu hsü" 1b.
139. *T'ung ya*, shou 2/5a.
140. *Ssu-k'u ch'üan-shu tsung-mu t'i-yao* [ds] (Shanghai: Commercial Press,
     1934), p. 2501.
141. Ku Yen-wu, *Ku T'ing-lin shih-wen chi* [dt] (Peking, 1959), pp. 97–98.
142. Much of Ku's efforts, like Fang's, went into determining the meaning, or-
     thography, and pronunciation of words as the medium of our knowledge.
     And, like Fang, Ku denied that words should capture our attention. "To
     take 'investigation of things' as 'widely knowledgeable in the names of fauna
     and flora' is to be concerned with the insignificant." Ku Yen-wu, *Jih-chih
     lu*, 6, "Chih chih" t'iao.[du] Ku, it may be noted, was alluding to *Analects*,
     17:9. Cf. Graham, *Two Chinese Philosophers*, p. 79.

GLOSSARY

a	格物	ak	宰理	bu	生養之氣
b	致知	al	通幾	bv	動覺之氣
c	方以智	am	物之至理	bw	神明
d	桐城	an	質測	bx	考證學
e	方學漸	ao	類	by	顧炎武
f	方大鎮	ap	擇善	bz	日知錄
g	方孔炤	aq	鄧元錫．物性志	ca	桐城方氏七代遺書
h	詩歌	ar	德	cb	侯外盧．方以智．
i	澤社	as	岐伯		中國的百科全書
j	物理	at	張衡		派大哲學家．歷
k	幾社，復社	au	祖冲之		史研究
l	阮大鋮	av	一行	cc	坂出祥伸．方以智
m	通雅	aw	郯子		の思想
n	物理小識	ax	九重		藪內清．明清時
o	凡例	ay	天問		代の科學技術史
p	方中通	az	天問略	cd	七解．稽古堂文集
q	苗	ba	經星天	ce	浮山文集．初集
r	隆武	bb	宗動天	cf	徐鼐．
s	永曆	bc	靜天		小腆紀傳
t	梧州	bd	穆	cg	明史（百納本）
u	平樂	be	測天約說	ch	謝國楨．明清之際
v	夫夷	bf	乾坤體義		黨社運動考
w	覺浪道盛	bg	熊伯甘	ci	李瑤．南疆繹史
x	青原山，吉安	bh	丘維屏．邦士	cj	物理小識編錄緣起
y	東西均	bi	虛氣	ck	王夫之．方以智傳
z	藥地炮莊	bj	實形	cl	清史列傳
aa	崇禎曆書	bk	行	cm	崇禎長編
ab	天學初函	bl	楞嚴經	cn	小腆紀年附考
ac	事	bm	七大	co	計六奇．明季南略
ad	窮至事物之理	bn	雨雹對	cp	錢澄之．所知錄．
ae	器，心，性，命	bo	利		永曆紀年
af	序卦	bp	職方外紀	cq	中允
ag	三知	bq	死海	cr	瞿式耜
ah	質論通論	br	幾墨德	cs	平西
ai	象，數	bs	主制群徵	ct	陳濟生．天啓崇禎
aj	質	bt	體性之氣		兩朝遺詩

cu 溫睿臨. 南疆逸史.
　　晚明史料叢書

cv 嚴煒

cw 陳垣. 明季滇黔佛
　　教考

cx 施閏章. 施愚山文
　　集，全集.
　　棟亭藏

cy 余英時
　　方以智晚節考

cz 青原山志書，方丈
　　樓

da 中國思想通史

db 滕寓信筆

dc 二程全書，河南程
　　氏外書

dd 王文成公全書.
　　傳習錄

de 大學文

df 物

dg 東西

dh 事情

di 陪古集

dj 太虛之中

dk 天之中

dl 重廣補注黃帝內經
　　素問

dm 朱子全書

dn 丘邦士文集

do 五運行

dp 風

dq 四大

dr 亞而幾墨得

ds 四庫全書總目提要

dt 顧亭林詩文集

du 致知條

IAN MCMORRAN *Wang Fu-chih and the*

Neo-Confucian Tradition

The picture of Wang as the solitary scholar of Shih-ch'uan shan [a] [1]—so dear to his biographers (and to Wang himself)—would be misleading if it were to deceive one into thinking that his was a philosophy evolved independently in the silence of the mountains, or that it was simply the product of a recluse's pondering over the books of his forebears. Wang was in fact very much a man of his age and was throughout his life keenly aware of, and passionately concerned about, the events taking place in the world around him. For him Confucianism was nothing if not the philosophy of those morally committed to action relevant to the problems of the present, and much of the vehemence of his writing was undoubtedly born of the desperation of a thinker who was also a frustrated man of action. In even the most abstract of his philosophical works the realities of the contemporary situation are never far from his mind, and, indeed, it would have been strange if it had been otherwise in the case of a man who is considered one of the harbingers of the *shih hsüeh*, [b] the Neo-Confucian form of realistic pragmatism which flourished in the early Ch'ing period. Nonetheless, in any discussion of the trends and influences in the intellectual history of this period, it is well to remember that, although Wang is now recognized as one of the major philosophers of his time, he made virtually no impact on either his contemporaries or his immediate successors, due to the isolation in which he lived from the early 1650s onward, and the fact that his most important works were not published until the nineteenth century. (In the late nineteenth and early twentieth centuries these were, of course, to exert considerable influence among both reformers and revolutionaries, but this aspect of Wang's position in the history of Chinese thought, important though it is, does not fall within the scope of this paper.) To this extent then, he was a peripheral figure.

In terms of understanding the direction in which late Ming and early Ch'ing thought was moving, however, a study of Wang Fu-chih may prove useful not only for the evidence it may reveal concerning the problems which confronted thinkers of the period, and the influences to which they were subjected, but also for the example which his philosophy provides of the type of solution proposed by the earliest proponents of the new Neo-Confucian realistic pragmatism. This philosophical phenomenon was, I believe, the consequence of a situation in which the forces at work—Wang himself would have spoken of the *shih* [c]—were extremely complex, and not confined to the philosophical sphere. The sheer impact of the dual catastrophe of peasant armies toppling the dynasty and the Manchu invasion, together with a confused but nonetheless profound reaction against the predominance of what were regarded as the decadent forces in Ming society and ideology, were certainly major factors.[2] This reaction can be traced back as far as the Tung-lin movement, and Wang's own philosophical standpoint is best understood if, for example, one first appreciates that he was living in the aftermath of the Tung-lin movement and following in the footsteps of its leaders. In this paper I shall therefore try to throw some light on the background against which Wang developed his philosophy and examine certain of his basic philosophical positions.

Wang Fu-chih was born in 1619 in Heng-yang, Hunan, into a rather insignificant family of scholars with military antecedents, which seems by Fu-chih's time to have isolated itself on the fringe of local gentry society.[3]

For information about his early life and family background one must depend almost entirely on Wang's own accounts.[4] The picture which emerges of his father, Ch'ao-p'in,[d] is, even allowing for filial platitudes, one of a scholar of stern moral principles and strong personality whose influence on his three sons—Fu-chih was the youngest of the three—was considerable. We are given little direct substantial information about Ch'ao-p'in's brand of Neo-Confucianism as such. The emphasis is on its incarnation in his style of life which is described at length and illustrated with anecdotes. In both respects, however, the reflection of the father in the writing of the son reveals something about both of them.

In the first lines of his biography of his father, Fu-chih mentions that Ch'ao-p'in was known among scholars as Master Wu-i [e]—because he attached so much importance to the mountain where Chu Hsi had attained enlightenment that he named his studio after it, and cherished an ambi-

tion to make a pilgrimage there. This fits in well enough with Fu-chih's
further description of him as one who "honored the orthodox tradition of
Lien and Lo [f] [i.e., Chou Tun-i and the Ch'eng brothers] and set great
store by practical action, not concerning himself with perverse abstrac-
tions." Indeed, according to Fu-chih, Ch'ao-p'in's official career suffered
as a result of this orthodoxy and his refusal to compromise his moral integrity. It is to Ch'ao-p'in's orthodoxy at a time when "new doctrines
spread throughout the world, carving up the sacred classics, and, having
recourse to Buddhism, forced upon them an interpretation according to
the theory of innate knowledge (*liang-chih*)," [g] that Fu-chih ascribes his
father's lack of success in the provincial examinations. It was not until
1621, when he was already over fifty years old, that Ch'ao-p'in's efforts
were crowned with some success. After reaching the "reserve list" for the
second time, he benefited from an act of grace, following on the accession of the T'ien-ch'i emperor, and was admitted to the Imperial Academy in Peking. This should normally have led to an appointment in the
civil service proper. However, as Fu-chih puts it, "At that time the process of selecting officials was exceedingly corrupt, and office was secured
through bribes." Ch'ao-p'in spent two periods in the Academy without
being offered a post, one from 1621–26, and the other from 1628–31.
The first coincided with the life and death struggle for power between
Wei Chung-hsien and the Tung-lin party, and the second saw the eclipse
of both Wei Chung-hsien and Tung-lin elements by the unscrupulous
grand secretaries Chou Yen-ju and Wen T'i-jen.

In 1631 Ch'ao-p'in was finally offered a minor post, but when it was
made clear to him that he must grease the palms of the officials in the
Board of Civil Office or forego all hopes of appointment, he decided to
retire, saying: "I have lands to plow and sons to educate. I should never
try to cheat Heaven by purchasing an appointment with bribes." In any
case it is doubtful whether Ch'ao-p'in could have afforded to bribe any-
body. The small amount of land the family held seems to have been of
little or no value. He tutored the sons of the local gentry in order to support his family, and, even so, as Fu-chih recounts, the Wangs were
reduced to real hardship, and his mother had great difficulty making ends
meet. Finding the money to enable Ch'ao-p'in to travel to Peking in the
first place had proved almost impossible.

Thus from 1631 onward Ch'ao-p'in, pronouncing himself completely disillusioned with the government and society of his day, cut himself off from all contact with the outside world, thereafter seeing only his family, his students, and an occasional old friend.

From the above it would appear that Ch'ao-p'in was a pillar of strict Ch'eng-Chu orthodoxy. Yet it becomes quite clear from other statements by Fu-chih that Ch'ao-p'in's philosophical formation owed something to the Chiang-yu [h] wing of the Wang Yang-ming school. Fu-chih does not insist on this point, and one feels that he would have been reluctant to do so. He simply says that Ch'ao-p'in had, in his youth, studied under Tsou Te-p'u,[i] from whom he received the tradition of Tung-k'uo [j] (i.e., Tsou Shou-i), [k] and devoted himself to the study of true knowledge (*chen chih*) [l] and actual practice (*shih chien*).[m] At the same time he adds that Ch'ao-p'in kept aloof from the controversies which divided contemporary Neo-Confucianists, and adopted *ch'eng-i* [n] (make the intentions sincere) as his discipline of self-examination. In another passage Fu-chih writes that Ch'ao-p'in had, since his youth, been the leading disciple of a local scholar, Wu Ting-hsiang,[o] who had taught him not only about metaphysics but also about economic and military matters, but here Fu-chih is primarily concerned with showing Ch'ao-p'in's loyalty and devotion to his old teacher. He relates how, when Wu died of a contagious disease in 1626, Ch'ao-p'in was the only person to tend him and remain with him till the end.

Tsou Te-p'u was a descendent and follower of Tsou Shou-i and emphasized the importance of man's relationship with the world around him.[5] A similar concern with the practical world was a prominent feature in the teaching of Wu Ting-hsiang, which also seems to have been inspired by the Chiang-yu school.[6] In this context Fu-chih's brief remarks on Ch'ao-p'in's thought take on additional meaning. One begins to suspect that the emphasis on "true knowledge and actual practice" indicates a position closer to that of Wang Yang-ming and the Chiang-yu school than one would expect from one who "honored the orthodox tradition of Lien and Lo." This suspicion is strengthened when one considers the importance which Ch'ao-p'in accorded to *ch'eng-i*. Although other Neo-Confucianists, including Chu Hsi, had treated this concept,[7] it was of course Wang Yang-ming who laid particular stress on it and identified the task of making the intentions sincere with *ko-wu*. [p] [8] Unfortunately, however, so sparse is the information concerning Ch'ao-p'in's philosophy that it is difficult to reach any hard and fast conclusions about the exact degree of his indebtedness to the Chiang-yu school—particularly if one bears in mind that a tendency away from the intellectual and toward the moral, away from rational metaphysics and toward personal introspection, was, as Professor Chan has recently demonstrated,[9] already present in the Ch'eng-Chu school of the early Ming period. There is one further aspect of Ch'ao-p'in's scholarship which would seem to redress the balance somewhat in favor of the Sung tradition. He was, Fu-chih makes clear, a lifelong student of history who expounded his own views on the *Spring and Autumn Annals* to his sons, and also made a practice of analyzing and explaining the course of events in Ming times for their benefit.

Fu-chih's selection of what was significant in his father's philosophy probably coincided with what he himself most admired in it, but there is no reason to doubt his honesty in presenting the evidence. The same is true of his reporting of the events of Ch'ao-p'in's life and his choice of anecdotes to illustrate his father's character. The result is a biographical account which corresponds to a remarkable extent with what Professor de Bary, in his contribution to this volume, has to say about Neo-Confucian "hagiography" in the *Chin-ssu lu*.[10] Here is the same image of Confucian ideals incarnate, the same emphasis which we have already noticed on the actual realization of these ideals in the character and way of life of a *chün-tzu* rather than on philosophical dogma.

Ch'ao-p'in, according to Fu-chih's description, exemplifies the same reverent attitude toward life, the same unselfish readiness to serve others, the same commitment to a life of strict moral principle, and above all the same spiritual equilibrium. He is shown as a filial son, galloping across country at dead of night to be at his sick father's bedside, and (as we have already seen) a faithful follower of Wu Ting-hsiang. He is a stern father who eschews all luxury and frivolity and expects his sons to do likewise. He is a resolute anti-Buddhist whose only excursion into public controversy is to win a debate over the meaning of *shuai-hsing* [q] with a Buddhist monk, but afterward declines to discuss it with his sons, dismissing Fu-chih's questions with a smile. Despite his self-effacing modesty, he exerts an awe-inspiring moral influence in the local community. Corrupt and immoral people—including officials—are shamed into mending their ways or keeping well away from Ch'ao-p'in, although he was never roused to anger and showed compassion even for those who offended against him. He practiced quiet-sitting and achieved a spiritual equilibrium which no external misfortune could destroy: he remained equally calm whether assaulted by a soup peddler or taken prisoner by peasant rebels.

This portrait is, despite its hagiographic aspect, a convincing one, and, together with the philosophical blend of Ch'eng-Chu and Chiang-yu elements which the available evidence indicates, suggests the sort of influence to which Fu-chih was exposed at home, particularly from the age of twelve onward when his aging father retired and personally took charge of educating him. During Ch'ao-p'in's absence Fu-chih's brother, Chieh-chih,[r] who was thirteen years his senior, had acted as his tutor. Chieh-chih, although he later took some part in Fu-chih's youthful activities, was on the whole much closer to their father than to Fu-chih, and his career was almost a carbon copy of Ch'ao-p'in's.[11] In 1639, after spending years teaching locally, he was summoned to the Imperial Academy in Peking, but resigned almost immediately, declaring himself unable to endure his colleagues' vicious struggle for advancement. According to Fu-chih, he clung to the family tradition of scholarship, and due to his unfashionable orthodoxy found himself isolated in the prevailing intellectual climate. Eventually Chieh-chih in his turn retired from public life altogether, echoing his father's criticisms of contemporary scholars.

Fu-chih's relationship with his father involved no such simple emulation. One of the more piquant aspects of his account of Ch'ao-p'in is that this picture of the *chün-tzu* according to the criteria of Ch'eng-Chu orthodoxy is drawn by one who had himself come to find the teachings of this school inadequate to the exigencies of his own life, and there is more than a hint of conflict between them. Significantly, this conflict concerned Fu-chih's involvement in contemporary politics.

The young Fu-chih's preoccupation with the contemporary political situation is much in evidence in the poems he wrote in the last years of the Ming dynasty, bitterly criticizing the intrigues of court officials and the ineptitude of the administration in the face of steadily deteriorating conditions in the country at large.[12] It was this preoccupation which led him to frequent the private academies of a literary, philosophical, and increasingly political nature which sprang up everywhere in the Ch'ung-chen period. When he and Chieh-chih began to take part in the activities of these academies, Ch'ao-p'in at once made his disapproval clear, and Chieh-chih seems subsequently to have complied with his father's wishes. Fu-chih, however, despite his father's opposition, proceeded to organize the founding of a *K'uang-she*,[s] or Reform Club, with his friends in Heng-yang, in 1639.[13] A possible influence on Fu-chih in this sort of activity was Kao Shih-t'ai,[t][14] the nephew of a leading member of the Tung-lin party, Kao P'an-lung.[u] Shih-t'ai, who was assistant provincial director of studies at this time in Hukuang, and for a while Fu-chih's teacher, returned to Wu-hsi in 1642 where he presided over the Academy until his death in 1676. Certainly Fu-chih marked the foundation of the *K'uang-she* in Heng-yang with a poem acknowledging the Tung-lin as the source of inspiration behind the undertaking.

Fu-chih again incurred Ch'ao-p'in's displeasure when, in 1642, after succeeding in the provincial examinations, he was preparing to leave for Peking to take the *chin-shih* examinations and told his father that on arriving at the capital he intended to pay his respects to various notable gentlemen of the day (no names are mentioned) and ask for their guidance. Ch'ao-p'in saw this as the first step toward involvement in political factions, and his reaction was typical of his attitude toward such involvement. "I would not presume to know what is meant by a gentleman these days," the old man said,

but if one wishes to put one's own ideas into practice there are primary and secondary considerations to bear in mind. If one gives priority to other people's ideas and treats one's own as secondary one is bound to end up sacrificing oneself for the ideals of others. How can this compare with sacrificing oneself for one's own ideals! Be careful! Once you involve yourself you will be unable to stop. Eventually even though you may wish to sacrifice yourself for your own ideas you will no longer be able to do so.[15]

Whereas Ch'ao-p'in was concerned with the danger of compromising one's moral integrity—a position which stemmed from his concept of *ch'eng-i*—Fu-chih was convinced of the need for some practical action. Although Fu-chih was, on this occasion, prevented from following his plan by the peasant insurgents who blocked the road northward from Nan-ch'ang, his desire to take some positive action only increased with the gravity of the situation, and after the fall of the dynasty he was to plunge into the factional strife at the Yung-li court.

By 1642 the position of the Ming dynasty was already desperate, threatened as it was by armed enemies from both within and without, and what Fu-chih saw on his journey from Nan-ch'ang back to Heng-yang left him even more distressed for the country's future, as his poetry once again shows.[16] Late the same year Chang Hsien-chung's peasant army took Heng-chou, and in the subsequent drive to recruit support from the local gentry both Fu-chih and Chieh-chih were summoned to serve with the rebels, who seized their father as hostage. Chieh-chih was for committing suicide, but Fu-chih managed to secure Ch'ao-p'in's release and evade the summons by inflicting several spectacular knife-wounds on himself and having himself carried into the rebel camp where he reported that his brother was already dead.[17]

After the fall of Peking, Fu-chih built himself a hut in Heng-shan which he called "The Refuge for Continuing Dreams." For awhile he remained there studying the I-ching, and it was at this time that his ailing father, feeling death imminent, enjoined him to compile a commentary on the Spring and Autumn Annals, embodying the family interpretation of this Classic.[18] As far as Fu-chih was concerned, this life of scholarship in no way signified an abandonment of the Chinese cause. Both his study of the Book of Changes—undertaken at this period of momentous change—and his commentary on the Spring and Autumn Annals were inspired with the same will to understand more fully the course of history and draw the appropriate lessons for the present. For him these books, far from being Classics of academic interest only, were repositories of a truth vitally relevant to the present.[19]

One passage in the Spring and Autumn Annals which caught his attention was that which narrates how the state of Lu was defeated when it embarked on a punitive expedition in support of a pretender to the throne of Ch'i, whose ruler had been murdered. In this he saw a parallel with the present situation, in which "the [Chinese] armies have also been defeated, because when the snipe and the oyster are locked in combat the only one to profit from the situation is the fisherman." "The Spring and Autumn Annals," he writes, "do not shrink from recording this defeat at Kan-shih,[v] indicating thereby that if one can engage the enemy in battle even defeat is still honorable." "But," he concludes, "how could retirement from the world after defeat cause one anything but chagrin? . . . It is all very well to say that in doing battle with the enemy defeat is no disgrace, but if one subsequently loses the will to act what is there honorable in that?" Consequently he "sought out true comrades and made hazardous journeys in a constant state of armed readiness in order to serve the cause actively." [20] His companions in the *K'uang-she* formed the nucleus of a group of such comrades, while Kao Shih-t'ai, Chang K'uang,[w] [21] and Tu Yin-hsi [x] [22] were all associated with them in varying degrees. These men were united by their patriotic concern for the nation,[23] and this common bond was strengthened by the special relationships which, under the traditional examination system, developed both between examiners and examinees and between fellow candidates.[24]

Chang K'uang, who had first come into contact with Fu-chih as his examiner in 1642, served under Ho T'eng-chiao [y] [25] who, with Tu Yin-hsi, commanded the Ming forces in Hukuang. These forces had combined with the remnants of Li Tzu-ch'eng's peasant armies in an anti-Manchu alliance, and in 1646, when this alliance seemed in danger of breaking up, Fu-chih set forth from his refuge to put concrete proposals to Chang for remedying the situation.[26] He met with no success, but the following year set off again with one of his "comrades," Hsia Ju-pi,[z] [27] in an effort to join the Yung-li emperor who was then in Wu-kang,[aa] where he had fled under pressure from Manchu attacks which were penetrating deep into Hukuang. Once again he suffered a setback, with torrential rain stranding him and his friend in the mountains.

In 1648, after he and a fellow-member of the *K'uang-she*, Kuan Ssu-ch'iu,[ab] [28] had raised troops in Heng-shan and been defeated by the Manchu forces,[29] Fu-chih finally succeeded in making his way to the Yung-li court which was then in Chao-ch'ing.[ac] Although Tu Yin-hsi recommended him for office, Ch'ao-p'in had died the previous year, and Fu-chih declined on grounds of mourning.

Fu-chih returned to Hunan, passing through Kuei-lin [ad] in the spring of 1649, and it was at about this time that he came to the attention of the Imperial Custodian of Kuei-lin, Ch'ü Shih-ssu,[ae] [29] who recommended him for the palace examinations when he returned to the Yung-li court later that year. Fu-chih was, however, still in mourning for his father and was once more excused on these grounds.

On these journeys Fu-chih made the acquaintance of Fang I-chih,[af] who was to remain a lifelong friend.[30] Fang, who was living in P'ing-lo,[ag] refused to take up an appointment as president of the Board of Rites and grand secretary at the beginning of 1649, and despite Ch'ü Shih-ssu's exhortations would take no further part in what he considered to be a lost cause, but, instead, subsequently became a monk.[31]

Fu-chih's first brief visit to the Yung-li court in 1648 had left him with no illusions about it,[32] but when at last his period of official mourning came to an end, early in 1650, he accepted a post as *hsing-jen* (imperial messenger), saying, "These times are very different from those of recluses such as Yen Kuang [ah] and Wei Yeh.[ai] It is my duty to leave my mother and go far away to share my ruler's fate in life and death." [33]

The Yung-li court depended for most of its short existence on a curious amalgamation of groups whose conflicting interests frequently threatened to destroy their precarious alliance around the Prince of Kuei. At this time its armies comprised the regular Ming soldiers, the remainder of Li Tzu-ch'eng's peasant armies, and the troops of such as Li Ch'eng-tung [aj] and Chin Sheng-huan [ak] who rallied to the Ming cause early in 1648 after vigorously collaborating with the Manchus in putting down previous Ming resistance.[34] In addition, the bureaucrats of the régime formed numerous cliques, some based on regional and others on personal loyalties. The two dominant factions were those known as the Ch'u [al] and Wu parties,[am] each of which worked in collaboration with its own allies among the military commanders in the provinces.[35] The primary concern of each of the parties was to draw or keep the emperor under its influence. In practice this coincided with persuading the emperor to accept the protection of residing in the territory which fell within the sphere of influence of their respective military allies, for, with the breakdown of the old administration, the provincial commanders ruled like warlords over the regions they occupied. At the center of this power struggle the Yung-li emperor, a weak and vacillating figure, incapable of acting as an arbiter but easily led, became little more than a pawn in the hands of those who held the real power.

The struggle between the two parties involved, as Fu-chih himself understood,[36] a struggle between the "inner court" and the "outer court," similar to that which had been a feature of the last years of the dynasty in Peking, with the Ch'u party and its allies in the role of the Tung-lin party of that period. There were of course important differences, notably in the part played by the military backers of the Ch'u and Wu parties, but the Ch'u party—like the Tung-lin before it—certainly had the support of those sincerely devoted to the moral reform of the political administration as well as to the preservation of national interests,[37] while its opponents seem to have been more concerned with securing internal political advantage and were either oblivious or indifferent to the external dangers. Fu-chih vigorously supported the cause of the Ch'u party, but paid the penalty when the Wu clique got the upper hand. He was impeached on trumped-up charges and only escaped with his life due to the intercession of the peasant general, Kao Pi-cheng.[an] [38] He was forced to resign and retire from the court, and although he was still only thirty-one, this was the end of his active public life.

For the rest of his life he was a refugee in his own country, mortified to stand helplessly by while the last areas under Chinese control disappeared. His refusal to cut his hair or compromise in any way with the Manchu authorities obliged him to live in hiding, and at one time he took refuge among the people of the local Yao tribe.[39] He was not, however, as much of a recluse as he is sometimes made out to have been. Despite his isolation he kept in touch with some old comrades, such as Fang I-chih, who tried to persuade Fu-chih to join him in the monastery.[40] He also attracted a few followers, including the sons of his erstwhile comrades in the *K'uang-she*,[41] and the last forty years of his life were spent in expounding his teachings both to them and in a prodigious number of books, while also living in poverty. That he regarded himself as a practical failure is clear from the numerous passages in his writings in which he reflects dismally on his situation and from the epitaph which he composed for himself: "I have nursed the solitary wrath of a Liu Yüeh-shih,[ao] but found no way of sacrificing my life. I have sought after the true doctrines of Chang Heng-ch'ü,[ap] but not been strong enough to attain to them. Fortunate as I am to have come safely to this grave, surely I shall carry my sorrow with me throughout the ages!" [42]

On the evidence available, Wang Ch'ao-p'in's philosophical position would seem to have been fairly close to that of the scholars of the Tung-lin. His philosophical formation, drawing as it did on both the Ch'eng-Chu and Chiang-yu schools, reflects the same limited eclecticism, which in the face of the extremism of the Che-chung and T'ai-chou schools [aq] took on the appearance of a conservative orthodoxy. He shared with the Tung-lin scholars an abomination for crypto-Buddhistic Confucianism, and his emphasis on the moral and practical has a Tung-lin air about it.

He must surely have been basically in sympathy with the Tung-lin scholars insofar as they stressed morality in public service, but he must just as surely have been opposed to the political machinations of the Tung-lin *tang*. The latter was at the height of its activity during the years Ch'ao-p'in spent in Peking, and he must have come into contact with its supporters and been exposed to their ideas, but although the Tung-lin is never mentioned in Fu-chih's account of his father, Ch'ao-p'in's advice to Fu-chih about the dangers of compromising oneself through involvement in factions leaves little doubt about his attitude toward it.[43]

It was on this point that father and son differed. Fu-chih was, as we have seen, already consciously emulating the example of the Tung-lin when he founded the *K'uang-she* at the age of twenty. In the course of his subsequent activities he encountered several figures associated with the Tung-lin, and these contacts were invariably characterized by mutual respect. Kao Shih-t'ai praised the compositions which Fu-chih submitted, while preparing for the provincial examinations, with the words, "In his writings one sees the expression of the loyalty and righteousness of a brave nature." [44] At the Yung-li court, Ch'ü Shih-ssu, who had participated in the factional struggles in Peking along with Ch'ien Ch'ien-i [ar] twenty years earlier, conferred his patronage on Fu-chih, who then aligned himself with Ch'ü and the Ch'u party, whose supporters included several members of the Fu-she which had earned itself the title of "the junior Tung-lin" because of its Tung-lin antecedents.[45] It is perhaps scarcely surprising then that the efforts of the Ch'u party at the Yung-li court appear to have been a continuation of the same struggle which the Tung-lin had waged earlier in Peking. Both attempted to reassert the power of the "outer court" against the "inner court" and a eunuch-dominated emperor, and both stood for public morality and the national interest. Thus Fu-chih's praise of the Tung-lin was more than an intellectual acknowledgment of the validity of its philosophy. It was also a salute from one who had fought—and failed—in the same cause.

The imperial verdict on Fu-chih when he submitted a memorial impeaching a Wu supporter in 1650 was that he was "partisan and headstrong," [46] and he may well have had this in mind when, defending the Tung-lin from the same criticism, he wrote:

Recently the gentlemen of the Tung-lin conducted a vigorous campaign against the Prince of Fu because they had no alternative. Those who, in discussing this, criticize them for being too headstrong fail to realize that evil heresies were already rife and that officials who had tried to present their counsels in a restrained and dignified manner had had no success whatever. To set about rescuing one's ruler from a blaze or from drowning while walking quietly and talking pleasantly is simply impossible unless one is not really concerned about what happens to him.[47]

Fu-chih thus justifies the members of the Tung-lin on the grounds that they were forced to take action in defense of the dynasty by the gravity of the ideological situation and its serious repercussions on the political life of the country. The particular issue to which Fu-chih refers was the long-drawn-out struggle over the establishment of an heir-apparent to succeed the Wan-li emperor. The struggle began in 1593, even before the Tung-lin as such had begun its activities, when the emperor tried to reduce his rightful successor to the status of an ordinary prince but was forced by the criticism of Ku Hsien-ch'eng [as] [48] and the "honest advocates" (*ch'ing-i*) [at] to reverse his decision, and continued up to and beyond the death of the Wan-li emperor in 1620. Elsewhere Fu-chih makes pointed reference to those who monopolized the emperor in order to put down the "honest advocates." [49]

The Tung-lin movement was essentially a two-pronged one which strove for moral renaissance and political reform. Indeed, such was the emphasis on ethics and the responsibilities of the scholar-official as a member of society that the two were inevitably related. As Huang Tsung-hsi observed, "Men assembled in hundreds from far and near in the conviction that to govern the world properly depended on a clear understanding of right and wrong." [50] Some critics have considered the Tung-lin movement as primarily philosophical and only secondarily, almost accidentally, political. Such a view does not take into account the Tung-lin belief in the fundamental interdependence of the moral and the political which characterized Confucian thought from the earliest times. Distressed at the social and political upheaval which they witnessed and also at the diminution of the traditional role of the bureaucracy, the Tung-lin leaders' diagnosis was that the root of the sickness lay in the heretical and amoral ideologies which prevailed among the scholar-officials who administered the country. It was therefore in theory logical to proceed to militate for a revival of ethical values and to try to replace bad officials with good ones.[51] The source of the malady was ideological, the symptoms political. Consequently, while they elaborated a comprehensive philosophical remedy to attack the source, their method of dealing with the symptoms remained basically simple—oppose and replace the bad—and so appears to be undeveloped. The political activity of the Tung-lin—like that of the "honest advocates"—was not related to any clearly formulated program of measures but was based on moral assessments of particular situations and persons. The following passage, describing Ku Hsien-ch'eng's younger brother, Yün-ch'eng,[au] [52] is typical of the attitude which lay behind such assessments:

What he abhorred throughout his life was the sanctimoniously orthodox Confucianist. "It is," he said, "when people like this occupy advantageous positions in the world that the seeds of parricide and regicide are sown secretly in the hearts of men. In learning, one should be impetuous and uncompromising when taking one's first steps, and then one will subsequently be able to attain the middle course and rest there. Nowadays, however, those who would attain the middle course fall all too often into the rut of the sanctimoniously orthodox: no sooner have they taken their first steps than they wish to rest there. . . . False honor is temperamental. True honor is based on principles of morality. The former is inadmissible, the latter indispensable. The honor which is based on principles of morality cannot be checked by arrogant bullying nor can it be repressed by starvation. But if one misrepresents principles of morality as temperament, then the all-embracing force is stifled. This is the basis of the strategy which sanctimoniously orthodox Confucianists have recently adopted in order to discredit our integrity." [53]

The division which Ku Yün-ch'eng makes here between the "sanctimoniously orthodox" (hsiang-yüan) [av] and the "impetuous and uncompromising" (k'uang-chüan) [aw] occurs frequently in Tung-lin writings and is one which stems from Confucius, who labeled the former "thieves of virtue," while he classified his disciples under the latter category, which was second only to the ideal—"those who attained the middle course." [54] Mencius further expounded the terms, describing the sanctimoniously orthodox as "eunuch-like, flattering their generation. . . . They agree with the current customs. They consent with an impure age. Their principles have a semblance of right-heartedness and truth. Their conduct has a semblance of disinterestedness, and purity. . . . A semblance which is not a reality," whereas the gentleman "seeks simply to bring back the unchanging standard, and, that being rectified, the masses are roused to virtue. When they are so aroused, forthwith perversities and glossed wickedness disappear." [55]

Wang Fu-chih endorsed the Tung-lin analysis of the contemporary philosophical climate, and when, in his commentary on the *Ssu-shu ta-ch'üan*, [ax] he came to deal with the passage from Mencius quoted above he had this to say about the *"hsiang-yüan"*:

Master Chu put Feng Tao [ay] in the category of the sanctimoniously orthodox on the basis of Five Dynasties' accounts which say he took care to adapt his conduct to varying situations in order to escape death, while his appearance and speech were those of a respectful and sincere person. Those who pursue the pleasures of barbarians and brigands have always said, "Born in this age . . . to be good is all that is needed." Thus they are eunuch-like and flattering. But Feng Tao occupied the position of chief minister and served one ruler in the morning and another by nightfall like a loose woman who takes five husbands in the space of twenty years. Everybody despised him so one can hardly consider him among the sanctimoniously orthodox of whom it was said, "If you would blame them you find nothing to allege. If you would criticize them, you have nothing to criticize." Although he followed the shifting currents in order to preserve his life, wealth, and position, he never presumed to "think himself right," so how could he "be confused with the truly virtuous"? In order to merit such descriptions one must have the semblance of a moral theory and one's own coherent course of action. If one looks for examples in the Sung dynasty then both the Su and Chekiang schools were sanctimoniously orthodox. Consider how Su Tzu-chan [az] criticized and mocked the two Ch'engs, and how Ch'en T'ung-fu [ba] replied to Master Chu's letter—in each case they reiterate the sanctimoniously orthodox scholars' criticism of the impetuous and uncompromising, saying, "Born in this age we should be of this age, to be good is all that is needed." [56] Those who "think themselves right" and win popular approval have always followed exactly the same course both in the past and the present. Luckily Ch'en T'ung-fu lived in an upright age and when his theory assailed the world there were few who respected it. Mr. Su's school flourished in the north for about two hundred years, and his literary style was plausible and perfected, eunuch-like and flattering later generations, so that it caused men to approve without realizing that the Way of Yao and Shun was no longer preserved in the present. This man was really an example of the sanctimoniously orthodox and the thief of virtue. The origins of this cancer may be traced back to Han T'ui-chih [bb] but it has become most grave in the persons of Chiao Hung [bc] and Li Chih. [bd] [57]

Chiao Hung and Li Chih were of course among those extremists of the T'ai-chou school against whom the Tung-lin directed their fiercest philosophical tirades, but such was the notoriety of the "wild Ch'anist" Li Chih among Confucianists that it seems at first as surprising for Wang to put him in the category of the *hsiang-yüan* as for Chu Hsi so to describe Feng Tao. [58] It is, however, understandable when one remembers that Wang, like the Tung-lin scholars, saw the struggle against such heresies as a rearguard action fought by the truly orthodox who were in the minority and in danger of being overwhelmed by such fashionable writers as Li Chih, who "thought themselves right," maintained that, "Born in this age we should be of this age, to be good is all that is needed," and "won popular approval." Li Chih enjoyed considerable popular support, and is elsewhere accused by Wang of "leading the whole empire into wicked excesses, and bringing disaster to the gentry of China." [59]

Wang does more than attack the same philosophical targets as the Tung-lin in the same terms: he also accords its leader Ku Hsien-ch'eng the highest praise as a philosopher,

During the present dynasty, apart from Hsüeh Wen-ch'ing,[be] [60] the only scholar among the Neo-Confucianists of the Rationalistic school who clearly understood the Way, clung resolutely to virtue, and stood out from the common herd untainted by either Buddhism or Taoism, was Ku Ching-yang.[bf] The discussions of the Hsi-shan Academy are, if one consults the records of the Academy, as clear as daylight for anyone with eyes to see. As for the Tung-lin, people only know that it was the champion of the heir-apparent. They do not realize that, confronted with a period when new doctrines and heresies were rampant, it stemmed the raging flood and thus became a heroic defender of the Way.[61]

The line Wang takes in such passages is very much the same as that which Huang Tsung-hsi took in the *Ming-ju hsüeh-an* [bg] (which he completed in 1676, a year before Wang finished his *Li-chi chang-chü,* [bh] from which the first of these passages defending the Tung-lin is taken). They even use the same metaphor to describe the Tung-lin's stand against prevailing heresies.

The Tung-lin men saw themselves in the role of the impetuous and uncompromising scholars, striving like Mencius' ideal gentleman as defenders of true philosophical orthodoxy to achieve the moral regeneration of the whole of society. Huang Tsung-hsi, in his account of the Tung-lin leader Ku Hsien-ch'eng, underlines this social commitment:

Master Ku made concern for society the basis of his discussions about learning, and used to say, "An official in the capital whose thoughts are not of his ruler, an official in the provinces whose thoughts are not of the people, an official in retirement who discusses in small groups the meaning of life and cultivates the moral virtues but whose thoughts are not of what is right for society as a whole—a gentleman will not consider such men his equal whatever other good qualities they may have.[62]

In this concern which Ku exemplifies, one may discern an advanced stage in the development of one trend in a gradual change—in the sphere of philosophical interest—which occurred during Ming times, a change in which the intellectual was in certain ways progressively subordinated to the moral, and the moral focus itself was increasingly adjusted on the individual in society.[63] Thus, when Kao P'an-lung writes, "Our investigation of things is an investigation of the highest good; goodness not knowledge is our principle consideration," [64] this is a position foreshadowed by Hsüeh Hsüan's [bi] modification of Chu Hsi's interpretation, and although there are real differences in thought between Ku and Kao and within the whole group of Tung-lin scholars, the evidence of this overall change in philosophical outlook is invariably present. On the one hand, this change may be seen as a reaction against that preoccupation with the moral development of the individual's nature which was a feature of both the Ch'eng-Chu school of the early Ming and the school of Wang Yang-ming. On the other hand, one may see it as an extension of that preoccupation, one which springs naturally from Wang Yang-ming's doctrine of the unity of knowledge and action and his vision of the ever-widening sphere within which the Confucianist sought to realize the moral mind.[65]

In this respect, the Tung-lin criticism of the *hsiang-yüan* for not going far enough in their moral cultivation would seem to be a reaction not against the moral cultivation of the individual but only against limiting it within too narrow a definition. Seen in this light, the *k'uang-chüan* of the Tung-lin, borne on their "all-embracing force," [66] and proclaiming the need for "effort" (*kung-fu*) [bj] and "practical application" (*shih-hsing*),[bk] [67] were closer to Wang Yang-ming than most of their number cared to think. Ku Hsien-ch'eng, however, although he criticized other aspects of Wang Yang-ming's thought, always defended the validity of his method of moral cultivation.[68] That the majority of Tung-lin scholars either failed to acknowledge any indebtedness to Wang or were genuinely unaware of any such debt was probably due, as Huang Tsung-hsi was among the first to suggest,[69] to their hostility to Wang's doctrines as developed by such disciples as Wang Chi.[bl] This was the Confucianism which had, in Wang Fu-chih's phrase, allowed itself to be "tainted by Buddhism and Taoism," and which encouraged scholars to retreat into that state of subjective idealism and amoral lack of concern for society which made Ku Yün-ch'eng sigh that "they would not care even if the heavens collapsed and the earth crumbled." [70] The Tung-lin view was that responsibility for this state of affairs rested with the Chekiang group of disciples of the school of Wang Yang-ming, and to some extent with Wang Yang-ming himself. The Chekiang group was led by Wang Chi, who defended the view that Confucianism, Buddhism, and Taoism were fundamentally the same, and expounded an interpretation of the "doctrine in four axioms" by Wang Yang-ming which became the focal point of Tung-lin attacks. [71]

Wang Yang-ming had originally stated: "In the original substance of the mind there is neither good nor evil. When the will becomes active there is good and evil. The function of innate knowledge is to recognize good and evil. The investigation of things is to do good and reject evil." [72] Wang Chi, however, developed this into a theory of spontaneous intuition in which good and evil are transcended and which is similar, as he himself remarked, to the sudden enlightenment of the Buddhists. [73] "If we say that in the original substance there is neither good nor evil," he maintained, "then neither can such a distinction be found in the will, in knowledge, or in things." [74]

This theory of subjective moral spontaneity was anathema to Tung-lin scholars, who emphasized the need for *kung-fu* in moral cultivation. Ku Hsien-ch'eng's reaction was typical:

To say that there is neither good nor evil is a most dangerous and insidious statement. The gentleman who strives and struggles all his life to choose the good and cleave to it is, according to this statement, wasting his time in trying to be a gentleman. The base fellow who spends his whole life in wanton licentiousness, indulging his whims and behaving recklessly is, according to this statement, happy to be a base fellow. [75]

For his part Wang Fu-chih, like Huang Tsung-hsi, saw all this as nothing more than Buddhism in another guise. "The business of Wang Lung-hsi and Ch'ien Hsü-shan [bm] receiving the doctrine of the way (from Wang Yang-ming) at T'ien-ch'üan," [bn] he wrote, "was an imitation of what Hui-neng and Shen-hsiu [bo] did, while the four statements about the absence of good and evil are simply another form of the four statements about one's own person being the tree of enlightenment." [76]

The differences which divided the Tung-lin scholars and their philosophical opponents all stemmed from this basic difference of opinion over the nature and validity of morality. The position of Wang Chi and his followers led to an emphasis on the individual as paramount, and a doctrine which was potentially antisocial and subversive—a potentiality largely realized in the case of Li Chih. For the Tung-lin, on the other hand, men were social creatures with moral duties to their fellows, upon the fulfillment of which the proper functioning of society depended. In this respect the Tung-lin scholars were reiterating the traditional orthodoxy, but their conception of man, of his nature and mind, and their philosophical justification of "orthodoxy," are steeped in the influence of Ming developments—not least the influence of Wang Yang-ming.[77] They were "revisionists" in fact, able to formulate their ideas in the light of the confrontation between the Ch'eng-Chu school and that of Wang Yang-ming, with the result that one finds them trying, as Ku-Hsien-ch'eng did, to achieve a synthesis of the best of both.[78] There was never complete philosophical unanimity among their leaders, but their common dissatisfaction with the way Wang Chi and his followers had developed Wang Yang-ming's doctrines led them to call in question the whole development of Neo-Confucianism since the Sung. Their investigations led them back to Wang Yang-ming and beyond, and the positions they adopted varied from that of the Chiang-yu school to alignments closer to the Sung philosophers.

In addition to Chu Hsi and the Ch'eng brothers, they turned with fresh interest to the works of Chou Tun-i and Chang Tsai. Thus Ku Hsien-ch'eng, who especially admired Chou, incorporated his method of "devotion to quiescence" (*chu-ching*) [bp] [79] in his own teaching, while Kao P'an-lung, who proclaimed his philosophical allegiance to Chu Hsi, was in one respect closer to Chang Tsai. Whereas the dualism of principle (*li*) and ether (*ch'i*) [bq] is fundamental to the philosophical system of Chu Hsi, Kao followed Chang in adopting a monistic view of the universe, declaring that: "Within the universe there is nothing but one mass of ether. This is what Master Chang meant when he said 'The void is ether.' This ether is perfectly empty and perfectly spiritual, but possessed of order and principles. Being perfectly empty and perfectly spiritual, in man it becomes mind. Being possessed of order and principles, in man it becomes nature." [80]

Wang Fu-chih expresses his admiration for both Ku and Kao on several occasions, but although he always gives precedence to Ku, philosophically he has more in common with Kao. Like Kao, he roundly condemns the "Ch'anism" of Wang Yang-ming, whom he accuses of making use of Confucian Classics in order to delude the world "with doctrines acquired from Buddhism and Taoism" (whereas Ku had considered him only unwittingly responsible), and adopts a form of monism close to that of Chang Tsai, on whose *Cheng-meng* br both he and Kao wrote commentaries.[81] Ku Hsien-ch'eng's reputation among his contemporaries and immediate successors undoubtedly rested to a large extent on his practical achievements and influence in both the philosophical and political spheres as leader of the Tung-lin,[82] and it was these which commended him so highly to Wang Fu-chih.

In his self-composed epitaph, Wang describes himself as one who "sought after the true doctrines of Chang Heng-ch'ü," and in a "Prefatory Argument" to his *Chang Tzu Cheng-meng chu* he declares: "Master Chang's doctrine inherited the purpose of Confucius and Mencius on the one hand, and retrieves the errors of the future on the other. Like a bright sun shining in the heavens, there is no darkness which it does not illumine. Were another sage to appear, there would be nothing for him to change in it." [83]

In this "Prefatory Argument," Wang gives a synopsis of his own view of the various stages in the history of the Confucian philosophy. He maintains that the task of the philosopher from Confucius onward had over and over again been to "bring scholars back to the middle of the brilliant Way" from which they constantly strayed, and to eliminate the excesses which were produced when correction of a tendency toward one extreme became overcorrection and resulted in a tendency toward the other extreme:

It was because, by the Eastern Chou period, evil doctrines had arisen that Confucius collated the *Book of Changes* and revealed the "Way above forms" in order to "manifest it in benevolence" and "implement it in function." Mencius emphasized the basic unity of principle between all living things in order to fathom the origins of the human feelings of "commiseration, shame and dislike, modesty and complaisance, and approving and disapproving." [84]

Both Confucius and Mencius underlined the importance of exercising the will (*chih*) bs in striving after the Way, he continues, but:

In Mencius' time, although the followers of Yang and Mo thronged the world, Confucianists had not yet stooped to distorting our Way in order to justify such heresies. . . . But from Han and Wei times onward Confucianists indulged in every kind of excess. . . . In the Sung dynasty with the appearance of Master Chou (Tun-i) began the discovery that the means of pursuing the Way of the sages was the unity which emerges from the processes of the Supreme Ultimate, the *yin* and the *yang*, the Way of man, growth, and evolution (*hua*).[bt] The two Masters Ch'eng drew on this and developed it, and gave it concrete expression in the achievement of the unity of quiescence and integrity and composure. But the followers of [their disciples] Yu (Tso) [bu] and Hsieh (Liang-tso) [bv] strayed off into the byways of Buddhism.[85]

Consequently Master Chu brought scholars back to the middle of the brilliant Way by making the exhaustion of principles (*ch'iung-li*) [bw] through the investigation of things the beginning of his teaching, yet after his doctrines had been transmitted once or twice they fell under the influence of such Confucianists as Shuang-feng [i.e., Jao Lu] and Wu-hsüan [i.e., Hsiung Ho] [bx] and were rapidly submerged in textual exegesis.[86] This was why Pai-sha [i.e., Ch'en Hsien-chang] arose and cast it aside, but in so doing paved the way for Mr. Wang of Yao-chiang, a Buddhist disguised as a Confucianist, whose heresy wronged the sages, until eventually the criminals among the people and the iniquitous eunuch factions vied with one another in their adherence to it. By applying their reckless and pernicious theory that there is neither good nor evil and confusing principles and affairs (*shih*),[by] by inciting one another and collaborating with one another, they prevented the Middle Way from being established and paved the way for further excesses of overcorrection.[87]

Wang compares the task of Chang Tsai to that of Yü the Great, whose labors in irrigation overcame the floods and saved the people from their depredations. Chang's aim was to "channel all the streams back into the course of the main river" (i.e., bring separatist sects back into orthodoxy) and "enable the people to forsake the quagmire and tread the level Way of security." But unfortunately

Master Chang taught in Kuan-chung and his disciples were not very numerous. As he was a man of ordinary status living in retirement he had no means of gaining the support of the great men and venerable scholars of his day like Fu (Pi), Wen (Yen-po), and Ssu-ma (Kuang).[bz] This is why his doctrine was never practiced to anything like the same extent as the numerology of Shao K'ang-chieh.[ca] As he had few followers in the world, the integrity of the Way was not made clear, and the pure and the heretic struggled against one another with each gaining partial victories. Thus it was that in less than one hundred years the heterodox theory of Lu Tzu-ching arose, and in another two hundred years Wang Po-an's heresy spread like wildfire. In the ensuing struggle between this and Master Chu's doctrines of investigating things and following the path of constant inquiry and study, the pure triumphed as water triumphs over fire, now succeeding now failing, but never achieving absolute victory. If the doctrines of Master Chang had shone forth in their full brilliance, correcting the will of young scholars at the start, then the Buddha's reckless confusion of life and death would have been completely destroyed. How then could the pettiness of such as Lu Tzu-ching and Wang Po-an ever have prevailed over gentlemen by reason of their esoteric knowledge, and made them the accomplices of the Buddhists in "leading animals to eat people"? [88]

Both Chang Tsai and the Tung-lin were, then, according to Wang, defenders of the true Way, rallying scholars to the traditional orthodoxy and attacking the heresies of Buddhism, Taoism, and "Buddhism disguised as Confucianism." In so doing they were preserving not only the philosophical integrity of Confucianism, but also the political health and security of the country. On a passage in which Chang Tsai criticized the influence of Buddhism on Confucianists who adopt the attitude that "we can become sages without cultivating [our moral virtue]. We can understand the great Way without studying," Wang Fu-chih comments:

In recent times Mr. Wang's theory of intuitive knowledge has been just like this. It is identical with Buddhism in that it would sever verbal communication and stop the processes of the mind, reject the physical organs and the senses and refuse to believe in knowing or seeing. In the first stage of its transmission the Wang school produced Wang Chi, and in the second stage Li Chih. When reckless doctrines prevail, all shame and modesty disappear, and thieves and brigands arise, it is all because people have in their quest for slothful attainment become lax about maintaining clear distinctions in their social relationships (*ming lun*) [cb] and investigating things. The result is that they have no regard for their ruler and do not care whether or not terms correspond to reality. The fall of the Sung dynasty upon the emergence of Lu Tzu-ching is an example of this same cancer. [89]

Here, as he does frequently elsewhere, Wang underlines the social and political consequences of the adoption of heretical philosophies, and accuses their adherents of undermining the foundations of society and orderly government and bringing about the downfall of the Sung and—the implication of his reference to Li Chih and "thieves and brigands" (i.e., peasant rebels) is clear—the Ming. If one bears in mind that the scholars whose philosophical allegiance was in question were not a limited group of academic philosophers but were the whole class of scholar-officials responsible for the administration of the country, it becomes apparent that it was by no means unreasonable for Wang to speak in such terms. That he does speak in such terms also suggests that the political factor was an important one in determining his own philosophical allegiance. In other words, he was attracted to the Tung-lin scholars and to Chang Tsai because their doctrines provided an alternative to the political chaos and disaster he encountered in his own lifetime, and also proposed a view of the universe which he intellectually accepted in a more detached way as "the true doctrines." Although no Tung-lin activist, Chang Tsai had been very much concerned with the state of the world around him, and he considered philosophy and politics to be vitally interdependent. In a letter quoted in the *Chin-ssu lu*, ^{cc} Chang wrote as follows:

Courts hold that philosophy and the art of government are two separate activities. This is precisely what, since ancient times, has been so lamentable. Would you say that Confucius and Mencius, if they could return to life, would bring forth what they had studied and apply it to the world, or constrain themselves to apply something of which they had no experience? The majority of rulers and ministers consider the way of a true king to consist of being father and mother to the world. When rulers cannot apply the feelings of a father and mother to the people, can one say this is the way of a true king? What is meant by "the feelings of a father and mother" is not just a figure of speech. One must regard all the people within the four seas as one's own children. Supposing all within the four seas were one's own children, then the study of the art of government would certainly not be so lacking in benevolence as it was under the Ch'in and Han, nor so hypocritical as it was under the five earls. You should say to the court, "It is not enough to remonstrate with a sovereign on account of the malemployment of ministers, nor to blame errors of government." If our ruler can be persuaded to love the people of the world like his own children, then the virtue of his government will be renewed every day, those given promotion will be good scholars, the way of true emperors and true kings will be perfected without any deviation from its course, and philosophy and politics grasped by the minds which do not make any distinction between them.[90]

Chang expressed similar sentiments in the *Yu-ssu* ^{cd} section of his *Cheng-meng,* and Wang endorses them in his commentary.[91] Wang was to go much further than either Chang Tsai or the Tung-lin scholars in the development of both a political theory and a program for reform, but he would certainly have had their support in declaring: "The rule of Confucianist scholars and the rule of monarchs are carried on side by side in the empire and their fortunes are interdependent. When they are in harmony the empire enjoys good government due to the Way [being practiced] and the Way is made to shine forth by the Son of Heaven." [92]

As Wang Fu-chih himself declared, his principal philosophical debt was to Chang Tsai, and I have suggested that a common political concern was a factor which attracted him to the Sung philosopher. This political concern should, however, be seen as part of a broader philosophical concern with reality as a whole, which would seem to be a logical if not inevitable consequence of a system whose very basis was an affirmation of the fundamental importance of ether (*ch'i*). ce

According to Chang, the ether is the basic stuff of the universe, within which there is in fact nothing but ether. There is no vacuum, no non-being, even what is apparently empty being full of ether in its dispersed state. The unity of this universe is a dynamic one in which all is constantly evolving as the relationships between its poles of activity shift and tensions are created and resolved. Thus, while the Supreme Ultimate (*t'ai-chi*) cf—a term which in the more speculative passages of contemporary philosophy tended to supersede the term Way, with which it was broadly synonymous as indicating both the origin and law of the universe—was interpreted by Chu Hsi as equivalent to principle (*li*),cg Chang Tsai made the following statements:

One thing with dual embodiment—is this not a description of the Supreme Ultimate?

One thing with dual embodiment is the ether (*ch'i*).93

Chang, however, generally preferred to use the terms Supreme Void (*t'ai-hsü*) ch and Supreme Harmony (*t'ai-ho*),ci each of which describes one aspect of the Supreme Ultimate. The Supreme Void describes the state in which the ether is diffuse and scattered (*san*) cj and may be mistaken for non-being (*wu*),ck while the Supreme Harmony describes the agglomeration (*chü*) cl of ether in the harmony of the *yin* and the *yang*. cm

If one accepts the implications of such basic philosophical premises— and I shall try to show below what these were in the case of Wang Fu-chih—it becomes significant that a number of Tung-lin scholars held similar views with regard to *ch'i*, ce and in this respect Chang Tsai's influence on late Ming thought has perhaps been underestimated. Kao P'an-lung, we have already seen, subscribed to Chang Tsai's teachings on *ch'i*, but so too did another Tung-lin philosopher, Liu Tsung-chou,cn 94 and his disciple, Huang Tsung-hsi. Not that where one finds a concern with contemporary political and social realities one need see only the influence of Chang. Among late Ming thinkers, the general interest in a more comprehensive philosophy, one in which the mind of man would comprehend all reality, was characteristic of a climate largely created by the

School of Wang Yang-ming. Huang Tsung-hsi's thought provides an example of how the ideas of Chang and Wang Yang-ming became fused. On the one hand, Huang maintained along with Chang Tsai that "within the universe there is only ether," and continued in the same vein to declare that "there is no principle in addition to this." [95] On the other hand, he held that "all that fills the universe is mind," [96] which recalls such statements as the following by Wang Yang-ming:

We know, then, in all that fills Heaven-and-earth there is but this clear intelligence. It is only because of their physical forms and bodies that men are separated. My clear intelligence is the master of Heaven-and-earth and spiritual beings. . . . Separated from my clear intelligence, there will be no Heaven-and-earth, spiritual beings, or myriad things, and separated from these, there will not be my intelligence. Thus they are all permeated with one material force (*ch'i*). [97]

Thus, whatever their other differences, there was important common ground between those who are generally thought of as "idealists" and those described as "materialists" in their attempts to establish the unity of mind and ether.

It was an ether-based monistic conception of the universe which provided the foundation on which Wang Fu-chih constructed his whole philosophical system, and which gave it its coherent structure. The problem of deciding at what stage in Wang's development he first came under the influence of Chang Tsai is discussed below, but a comparison of some of the ideas which Chang set out in his *Cheng-meng* with Wang's commentary reveals the relationship which existed between them by the time Wang's philosophy had fully matured. [98]

At the beginning of the first chapter, which he entitled "The Supreme Harmony," Chang wrote:

The Supreme Harmony is called the Way because it contains the essence of all processes of mutual influence, of floating and sinking, of rising and falling, of movement and quiescence, and is the origin of the processes of fusion and interaction, of conquering and being conquered, of contraction and expansion. At first it is tenuous and subtle, simple and terse, but in the end it becomes broad and great, firm and solid. Is it not [the hexagram] *ch'ien* [co] which brings knowledge from simplicity? Is it not [the hexagram] *k'un* [cp] which takes example from terseness? That which disperses, separates, and can take the form of images is the ether. That which is clear and penetrating and cannot take the form of images is the spirit (*shen*). [cq] If these were not fused together like ethereal emanations (*yeh ma*) [cr] one could not use the description Supreme Harmony. [99]

On this Wang, after noting that this chapter is a development of Chou Tun-i's *T'ai-chi t'u shuo*,[cs] makes the following comments:

The Supreme Harmony is the ultimate harmony. The Way is the pervading principle underlying the whole universe, both men and things, and is what is known as the Supreme Ultimate. The *yin* and the *yang* differ in their creative operations but in their fusion in the Supreme Void are joined in agreement without opposition or injury, and their confused mingling leaves no chink between them. This is the ultimate harmony. Before the existence of forms *(hsing)*[ct] and concrete things *(ch'i)*[cu] all is originally harmonious, and when forms and concrete things come into existence this harmony is not lost. Therefore one calls it the Supreme Harmony. . . . Fusion is the original state in which the Supreme Harmony is undivided. Interaction is the inevitable effect of principles and conditions *(shih)*. . . . In the Supreme Harmony there is the ether and the spirit. The spirit is nothing other than the clear and penetrating principle of the two ethers [i.e., the *yin* and the *yang*]. It cannot take the form of images but is in fact in the images. The *yin* and the *yang* are in harmony, the ether and the spirit are in harmony—this is what is called the Supreme Harmony.[100]

Thus far Wang is simply endorsing Chang Tsai's views, though he has already introduced a phrase which had special significance in his own philosophy—"the inevitable effect of principles and conditions"—and he is quick to assert that the link between spirit and ether is the same as that between principle and ether, that both are inextricably bound together in existing phenomena, and that "spirit is the spirit of the ether. There is no such thing as a spirit outside the ether."

Pursuing his description of the ether, Chang writes: "Although the ether of the universe agglomerates and disperses, opposing and accepting in a hundred different ways, its principle is always unwaveringly in accordance."[101] And Wang appends the following explanation:

When the ether agglomerates its existence is visible, but when it is dispersed one may suspect that it is nonexistent. Once it has agglomerated and assumed forms and images, then as regards talents *(ts'ai)*,[cv] matter *(chih)*,[cw] nature *(hsing)*,[cx] and passions *(ch'ing)*,[cy] all accord with their own categories *(lei)*.[cz] They accept what is similar and oppose what is different, and thus all things flourish in profusion and form their various categories. Each of these categories has its own organization *(t'iao-li)*.[da] So it is that dew, thunder, frost, and snow all occur at their proper times, and animals, plants, birds, and fish all keep to their own species. There can be no frost or snow during the long summer evenings, nor can there be dew or thunder in the depths of winter. Nor can there be between man and beast, plant and tree, any indiscriminate confusion of their respective principles.[102]

Here Wang has introduced another idea which, as he developed it, had significant political implications—namely the concept of order based on clear distinctions of, and in accordance with, natural categories. This idea, which he applied not only to "man and beast," but also to the constituent groups of human society in China and in the world as he knew it, finds frequent expression in such works as *Huang shu* [db] and *Tu T'ung-chien lun.* [dc] [103]

In this same chapter Chang declares: "The Supreme Void is formless and is the original substance of the ether. Its agglomeration and dispersion are but the temporary forms (*k'o hsing*) [dd] of change and evolution." [104] He elaborates on this as follows:

The ether is a thing which, when it disperses and withdraws into formlessness, maintains its original substance, and when it agglomerates and assumes the form of images does not lose its eternal nature. The Supreme Void cannot but consist of ether. The ether cannot but agglomerate to form the ten thousand things, and these in their turn cannot but disperse and revert to the Supreme Void. In following this sequence of emergence and withdrawal all have no alternative but to do so. This being the case, the sage follows out the Way within this, identifying himself [with this sequence] without being encumbered by it, and thus achieves the ultimate in preserving the spirit. [105]

Although Chang Tsai then went on to criticize the Buddhist idea of extinction in *nirvāna*, Chu Hsi attacked him for adopting another Buddhist concept, that of *samsāra*, [de] in his doctrine of the agglomerating and dispersing ether. Wang, however, in his commentary, reaffirms Chang's ideas, stating that "in the Supreme Void all is being, but it has not yet taken form. The ether is self-sufficient: through agglomeration and dispersion, change and evolution, its basic substance is neither diminished nor increased." [106] He explains the process of the agglomerating and dispersing ether in terms of the "natural effect of principles and conditions" to which one must make the correct adjustment in order to pursue the Way. He then proceeds to attack Chu Hsi. Resuming Chang's argument, he writes:

When the ether disperses, it returns to the Supreme Void, and reverts to the original substance of its state of fusion. There is no destruction. When it agglomerates and brings life to various things this arises from the eternal nature of its state of fusion. Nothing new is born or reared. . . . The agglomeration and dispersion of the ether constitute the life and death of things. When it emerges they come, and when it withdraws they go. All this is the natural effect of principles and conditions (*li shih chih tzu-jan*).[df] It cannot be stopped. One cannot by according with it become eternal. One cannot by direction accelerate the process of dispersion. One cannot by intervention delay it. This is why the gentleman is unconcerned about life and death. . . .

This passage embodies the essential meaning of the whole chapter. To achieve the correct norm (*chen*) in life and death in following out the Way of man is the outstanding doctrine of Master Chang, who developed the heritage of earlier sages in order to refute the Buddhists and Taoists and rectify the minds of men. Because he spoke of agglomeration and dispersion, and of dispersion followed by a further agglomeration, Chu Hsi criticized this as *samsāra*. My own humble opinion is that it is on the contrary Master Chu's theory which is closer to what the Buddha said about *nirodha*,[dg] and at variance with the words of the sage. Confucius said, "While you do not know life, how can you know about death?" [107] Thus it is clear that life in dispersion becomes death, and that death may through a further agglomeration become life, while the principle involved in each case follows the same lines. *The Book of Changes* says, "The essence and the ether form things, while the wandering soul produces change." [108] The phrase "wandering soul" means that the soul is dispersed and wandering in the Void. The phrase "produces change" clearly means that it returns in order to produce change and transformation.

Again it is said (in the *Book of Changes*), "It is through the influence which contraction and expansion exert on one another that advantage is produced." [109] When expansion is influenced and contracts, life becomes death. If contraction is influenced and expands, does this not mean that contraction may through the influence [of its counterpart] be brought to a further expansion? [The *Book of Changes*] also says, "Above forms it is called the Way. Below forms it is called the concrete thing." [110] By the former is meant "that which is clear and penetrating and cannot take the form of images." So concrete things are formed and destroyed, while that which cannot take the form of images is lodged within the concrete thing as its function. As it is never formed so it is never destroyed. The concrete thing wears out, but its Way never ends. Speaking in terms of things and images in the context of the processes of nature, then in spring and summer there is life, a coming, and an expansion, while in autumn and winter there is death, a going, and a contraction. But in autumn and winter the ether of life is stored in the earth, and though the branches and leaves of trees are withered their roots are firm and flourishing.

So it is not the case that in autumn and winter they are destroyed once and for all with nothing remaining. If a fire is made of a cartload of firewood, it is consumed in one blaze, and becomes flame, smoke, and ashes. But wood reverts to wood, water to water, and earth to earth: it is simply that they become so minute and subtle that man cannot see them. When one boils a pot of rice the steaming ether bubbles and boils away. It must go somewhere. If one covers the pot tightly with a lid, then it is trapped and does not disperse. When mercury comes into contact with fire it flies away, and one does not know where it has gone, but in the end it returns to earth. Given that this is true of what has form, how much more is it so of the fusion which cannot take the form of images! Clearly it has never happened that what one has amassed by painstaking effort over a period of months and years has one morning all been transformed into nothingness. This is why one speaks of coming and going, contraction and expansion, agglomeration and dispersion, obscurity and clarity, but does not speak of production and destruction, or *utpādanirodha,*[dh] which is one of the Buddha's wretched theories.[111]

When the entity, as man recognizes it in the phenomena around him, dissolves, all—body and spirit, the concrete thing and its Way—revert to ether in its original state, the Supreme Void. Nothing is lost or destroyed. Thus all is ether and all exists always either in agglomeration or dispersion. This is what scholars have referred to as Wang's theory of the indestructibility of matter.[112] He pursues the subject further in the commentary which he appends to Chang's next statement that: "Both in agglomeration and dispersion one's substance [body] is still the same substance [body]. When a man has realized that death is not destruction, he may take part in discussions about the nature."[113] Wang then writes:

In agglomeration it becomes form, and in dispersion it returns to the Supreme Void, but it is still the same ether. It is not separate from the ether but combined with it in the same substance [body], so it is still the same spirit. It is simply that what has agglomerated is visible and what has dispersed is invisible. How could their substance possibly either fail to accord or go astray! Thus the spirit of Yao and Shun and the ether of Chieh and Chou are all preserved in the state of fusion. Even now they have not changed. Now the cause of Chieh and Chou's tyranny was their ether. By nourishing it one can make it honest, by restraining it one can make it correct, and by cleansing it one can make it pure. It is something which one obtains from Heaven in the first place, and if the intuitive ability (*liang neng*)[di] of the qualities of firmness and submission is not impaired it is preserved in one's person.[114]

This prompts one, first, to remark that it is not simply matter which is indestructible according to this view but also the spirit which informs the ether, and, second, to clarify what Wang means when he says that "the cause of Chieh and Chou's tyranny was their ether," which of course raises the question of Wang's conception of the way in which human nature fits into his ether-based cosmology.

Chang had originally proposed a theory which explained human nature as having two aspects, one of which he called the universal nature (*t'ien-ti chih hsing*),[dj] or nature of heaven (*t'ien chih hsing*),[dk] and the other the physical nature (ch'i chih chih hsing).[dl] In the Ch'eng-ming [dm] chapter of the Cheng-meng he described these as follows:

The nature of Heaven in man is like the nature of water in ice. Although there is a difference between its frozen and melted states it is but one thing. . . . Nature in man is invariably good. The only problem is whether or not he is good at returning to it. . . . Once he has a form [i.e., his body] then he has a physical nature. If he is good at returning to the universal nature then it is preserved. This is why there is in the physical nature that which the gentleman refuses to call his nature. Whether a man is hard or soft, easygoing or hasty, talented or lacking in talent, depends on the bias of his ether (ch'i chih p'ien).[dn] Heaven is originally a trinity of harmony and without bias. If one cultivates one's ether and returns to this original unbiased state, then one has perfected one's nature and regained harmony with Heaven.[115]

As Wang points out in his comments on this passage, the nature of Heaven refers to the principle which, prior to man's birth, is the substance of Heaven in the Supreme Void, that is, in the dispersed ether. Once a man is born this principle exists as his nature within the ether which has agglomerated to form his body. Thus human nature is part of the nature of Heaven, part of the principle of Heaven, and there is in man the same relationship between principle and ether as that which exists in the universe as a whole.[116]

Chu Hsi was especially attracted by Chang's concept of the physical nature, as he considered that it provided an explanation of the existence of evil, which was otherwise difficult to account for within the framework of the formula that human nature was good. Chang Tsai's theory enabled him to keep faith with the Mencian tenet that human nature was good by explaining that the presence of evil in man was something which resulted from a bias or imbalance in the ether as it had agglomerated to form his person. The universal ether in the Supreme Void was of course in perfect harmony and thus "good," but as Chang was aware that "good" and "evil" were relative and interdependent terms, he suggested that one should discard the term "good" as regards human nature and speak instead as the Book of Changes does of "the nature which completes (the Way)".[117] "Evil" was that which obstructed this natural pursuit of the Way, and was the result of the loss of Harmony as ether took the form of man, which allowed his natural desires to exceed their natural norm. The task of self-cultivation was to restrain this tendency to excess and restore the balance to the ether of which one was formed.[118]

Wang Fu-chih shared Chang Tsai's conception of human nature as outlined above, but where Chu Hsi, like Ch'eng I, had interpreted it as a duality in conformity with his own theory of the basic duality of principle and ether,[119] Wang was at pains to show that the apparent duality was really only two aspects of the same thing. In his commentary he specifically dismissed Ch'eng I's views and the "old theory" of physical nature (as opposed to true nature) as being responsible for the individual man's peculiar qualities, in favor of Chang's explanation of these qualities as arising from the "talents" (*ts'ai*),[cv] the individual's capacity which varies because it "is formed from the fluctuating ether of an instant."[120] Elsewhere he wrote:

When one speaks of the physical nature this is like saying that the nature lies within the matter of the ether (*ch'i chih*). This matter (*chih*) is man's material form (*jen chih hsing chih*),[do] within the confines of which the principles of life (*sheng chih li*)[dp] are manifest. Since they (the principles of life) lie within this matter the ether permeates them, and as what fills the universe both inside and outside the human body is nothing but ether, so too it is nothing but principle. Principle operates within the ether where it controls and apportions the ether. Thus the matter [of individual things] envelops the ether, and the ether envelops principle. It is because this matter envelops the ether that a given individual possesses life, and it is because the ether envelops principle that this same individual possesses a nature. For this reason, before his envelopment has taken place there can be only the principles and ether of the universe but not the individual man. Once, however, there is the matter incorporating ether, this ether inevitably possesses principle. As far as man is concerned . . . this nature as found in the matter of the ether [i.e., the physical nature] is still the original nature.[121]

Believing as he did that man was possessed of one nature only, Wang Fu-chih, like Chang, also accepted what he argued to be the logical corollary that human desires, far from being something which one should eschew as the Buddhists—and Chu Hsi—advocated, were part of this nature and in accord with the "principles of the universe." In his commentary on Chang's passage concerning the physical nature, Wang writes:

Thus the ethers of the ears, eyes, mouth, and nose make their choices among sounds, colors, smells, and flavors, and this too is natural (*tzu-jan*)[dq] and should not be rejected. . . . Now the physical nature of which [Master Chang] speaks here is no more than what Mencius described as the relationship of the ears, eyes, mouth, and nose to sounds, colors, smells, and flavors. [He described it as the nature]. Now this nature is one of the principles of life. All men share it, and it is no different from all the other principles of life. Consequently the principles of benevolence, righteousness, propriety, and wisdom cannot be destroyed by the inferior and simple, nor can the desires for sounds, colors, smells, and flavors be dismissed by the superior and wise. All may be called the nature . . . principles and desires are all natural (tzu-jan) and not of man's making.[122]

Wang discusses the relationship between human desires and the principles of Heaven further in a passage in the Tu Ssu-shu ta-ch'üan shuo, where he deals with the advice Mencius gave to King Hsüan of Ch'i about his desires for wealth and beautiful women:

. . . the external manifestations of the principles of heaven are revealed in movement. . . . Although propriety is purely the external manifestation of the principles of Heaven it must be incorporated in human desire for there to be any manifestation. Even when dwelling in quiescence it is a principle (tse)[dr] of response to stimulus and of communication. Thus it is through change and combination that it reveals its function. This, then, is the reason there can never be a Heaven (nature) separate from man, or principles separate from desires. Only the Buddha has tried to create principles as something separate from desires. . . . Wu-feng was right when he said, "The principles of Heaven and human desires operate together in the various passions." [123] Surely this phrase combines the philosophy of Yen Yüan and Mencius in one source! Now as for the desires for wealth and sex, they are the means whereby "Heaven secretly controls all creatures," [124] and man promotes the great virtue of the universe, and are in both cases functions of conservation. This is why the Changes says, "The great virtue of the universe is life. The sage's most valuable possession is his position. The means whereby he preserves his position is benevolence. The means whereby he gathers men about him is wealth." [125] Hence in sounds, colors, smells, and flavors there is a genuine manifestation of the common desires (kung yü)[ds] of all creatures, and also of their common principles (kung li)[dt]

In this same passage Wang explains that by "combining the philosophies of Yen Yüan and Mencius" he means that one should on the one hand proceed, as Confucius advised Yen Yüan, to "subdue one's self and return to propriety" [126] by refusing to look at, listen to, or speak of anything contrary to propriety or to make any movement contrary to propriety. On the other hand, one should at the same time recognize, as Mencius did, that the desires are common to all men, and, instead of repressing one's desires, accept the sharing of them with others. Wang argued that, as principles were "lodged in" [du] the desires, if one tried to "subdue one's self" by eliminating the desires one would be left with no vehicle for principles. As he wrote elsewhere:

I am afraid that those who are contemptuous of the desires will be contemptuous of principles too, and that those who despise the idea of receiving the world will also despise the idea of serving the world . . . this is why all products of the universe have their functions. Eating, drinking, and sex all have their correct norms (*chen*).[dv] The gentleman respects the products of the universe and arranges them in categories. He gives proper emphasis to the difference between the sexes and to eating and drinking, and brings them into harmony. If he is eating fish, then it is the bream which he regards as delicious—so why should he reject it? If he is marrying a wife, then it is a woman like Chiang of Ch'i whom he considers a proper spouse—so why should he reject her? [127]

Thus the proper course of action was one in which one's responses to external stimuli were imbued with a spirit of community and impartiality and the correct norm maintained.

In explaining the existence of evil, Wang developed Chou Tun-i's theory of the *chi* [dw] which had been inspired by the statement in the *Book of Changes* that "it is through the Changes that the sage plumbs the depths, and investigates the *chi*." [128] Chou had defined his own use of the term as "movement as yet without form, in between being and nonbeing," and declared that "integrity (*ch'eng*) [dx] lies in the state of nonactivity; with the *chi* come (both) goodness and evil." [129] Wang writes as follows:

How does it come about that there is that which is not good in the nature of man in its latter-day state (*hou-t'ien chih hsing*)? [dy] This is what is meant by the statement [in the *Book of History*] that "[This is real unrighteousness and is] becoming by practice a (second) nature." [130] The nature in its original state (*hsien t'ien chih hsing*) [dz] is formed by Heaven. The nature in its latter-day state is formed by practice. Now what makes it possible for practices to form that which is not good are things (*wu*).[ea] But how can there be things which are not good? One selects things and is subsequently subject to their encroachments. This is why Master Ch'eng blamed the individual's endowment of ether. Nevertheless, how can there be that which is not good in the endowment of ether? Yet the spontaneous arrival of what is not good must start spontaneously somewhere.

It is when the endowment of ether has intercourse with things. The endowment of ether may go [toward things] and its going may be perfectly good. Things may come [toward the endowment of ether] and their coming may be perfectly good. But between their coming and going [i.e., at their meeting point] the factors of time and place [are brought into play]. As evolution (*hua*) [eb] has its part in their encounters, they cannot always be proper (*tang*) [ec] for the time and place and so there are things which are not proper. When things which are not proper are encountered, the relationship [between the endowment of ether and things] is not successful and so what is not good is produced. . . .

This is not the fault of one's physical nature. Nor is it the fault of the physical nature of the things. The fault lies in the *chi* of their encounter. There is no thing in the universe which is not good, but things do have *chi* which are not good. Things do not have *chi* which are inevitably not good. In the *chi* of my movements there are those which are not good in relationship to things, but none which is of itself not good. But when the *chi* of things coming (toward me) and the *chi* of my going (toward them) are not correct in their correspondence, *chi* which are not good are formed.[131]

In Wang's use of the term *chi* there would seem to be a sort of natural impulse which operates rather like magnetism or electricity (for whose negative and positive the Chinese use the terms *yin* and *yang*). These impulses led to actions which were evil and became, through habitual practice, a second nature which could, as he says in the *Li-chi chang-chü*, overwhelm the original nature.[132] It is significant that throughout the above passage Wang prefers to speak of what is "not good" rather than of "evil," for his concept of evil is that it is negative, not positive, simply the negation of what is good, which is itself what is in accord with the correct norm and what is proper from the point of view of "completing the Way." Moreover, as Wang's concept of the universe was that it was a constantly evolving entity, he emphasized the factors of time and place in determining what was morally proper at any given juncture in its evolution. Even the original nature of which he speaks was not, he asserts, simply something which one received once and for all at birth. He makes this quite clear in the *Ssu-wen lu* [ed] where he writes that "the nature consists of principles of life, and until one's death all is living (growing) and every day the decree (*ming*) [ee] descends and the nature is received. . . . Is man (created once and for all) like a pot as the fortune-tellers who speak of a destiny fixed at birth would make out?!" [133] And again in the *Shang-shu yin-i* [ef] he writes, "Now the nature consists of the principles of life. It is produced every day and completed every day. And as for the decree of Heaven, how could it possibly be fixed only at the moment when one is first born?!" [134]

In the first chapter of the *Chang Tzu Cheng-meng-chu*, Wang, after a statement of his monistic view of the universe, explains its dynamic character by reference to the same sort of initial spontaneous impulses whose function he discussed in the preceding passage. But whereas he explained the possibility of the emergence of what was not good in terms of the impulses of men and things, he explains the inherent dynamism of the universe in terms of the impulses of the *yin* and the *yang*:

The void is but the volume of the ether. When the ether is still a limitless flux, yet fine, subtle, and formless, men see the void but not the ether. But the void is all ether, which, when it agglomerates and is manifested, men call being, and when it disperses and is hidden, men call non-being. The spirit and the evolution are the unfathomable wonder of the ether's agglomeration and dispersion whose traces are yet visible. The nature and the decree are the eternal principles of the ether's firmness and submission which control the spirit and the evolution and are yet lodged within them without any visible sign of their existence.

In reality principle lies within the ether, and all ether is principle: the ether lies within the void and all the void is ether. All is one. There is no duality. It agglomerates and emerges in the forms of men and things: it disperses and withdraws into the Supreme Void and is there formless. There must be some cause behind this—surely it is that the *yin* and the *yang* are the dual embodiment of the ether, that [their] movement and quiescence are the dual impulses of the ether. Their (the *yin* and the *yang*) substances are the same but their functions differ, and so from their influence on one another comes movement. In movement images are formed and then comes quiescence. The initial impulses of movement and quiescence are the source of agglomeration and dispersion, emergence and withdrawal, form and formlessness. The Way which the *Changes* provides is simply a matter of *ch'ien* and *k'un*. . . . And the *yin* and the *yang* are one in the real substance of the Supreme Ultimate. It is just because they fill the void so abundantly that the change and evolution are renewed every day, and the great work of the omens of the sixty-four hexagrams is produced. The waxing and waning of the *yin* and the *yang*, their visibility and invisibility, are mysterious, but the secrets of the universe, of men and things, of contraction and expansion, of coming and going all lie therein. He who understands this exhausts the secrets of the *Changes*.[135]

In a subsequent passage Fu-chih further links this explanation of the spontaneously dynamic processes of the universe with his earlier theory of the importance of the factors of time and place in determining what was morally proper in a constantly changing universe:

By *ch'i hua* [eg] is meant the evolution of the ether. The *yin* and the *yang* are both present in the state of fusion of the Supreme Void. They alternate, now in movement, now in quiescence, and influence one another, taking advantage of time and place to display their abilities. The five elements, the ten thousand things in their combinations and processes, the birds, fish, animals, and plants, all have their own order and principles and do not deviate from them. Thus things have the Way of things, and the spirits have the Way of the spirits. He who realizes this is bound to be enlightened. He who takes his stand in this is bound to be proper (*tang*). All follow this as the proper law (*tang jan chih tse*) [eh] in which sense it is called the Way.[136]

Thus for Wang the life of man ought ideally to accord with its own moral Way, which was itself a vitally important part of the Way of the universe which comprehended all the Ways of everything within it. For, according to Wang, "to know one's nature is to know that the Way of Heaven is completed by one's nature," and, this being the case, "the nature and the Way of Heaven achieve ultimate unity." This is why the operations and manifestations of the ether "are all my concern, and their cultivation my proper role." [137] As he puts it when writing in terms of "fully exploiting the nature" (chin hsing),[ei] "everything in the world is of the same origin as myself, and depends on me for response and completion." [138]

The concept of a unity which consists of a dynamic harmony is one which pervades all his thinking, so that one finds him making similar statements about the ether and principle, substance and function, the Way and concrete things, and movement and quiescence. He is constantly thinking in terms of balance and harmony achieved through the resolution of contraries, and images of balance and harmony occur over and over again in his writings. In the preface to E-meng, for example, Wang uses one of his favorite images, that of the Chinese steelyard whose equilibrium depends on the adjustment of the weight (ch'üan) [ej] on the beam (heng): [ek] it must be shifted to the one position in which it exactly counterbalances the object weighed. The same weight shifted too much or too little will not achieve the desired equilibrium. [139] To be proper, too, we have seen, consisted in achieving the correct position in relationship to the two factors of time and place, and was the secret to be attained through study of the Book of Changes.

As will be apparent from the above quotations, Wang's commentary on Chang's Cheng-meng draws so heavily on the Book of Changes that it is almost as much a commentary on the Book of Changes itself. His "Prefatory Argument" makes it clear that this was not accidental. "Master Chang's doctrines," he declares, "are all [based on] the Book of Changes . . . Master Chang's pronouncements are all [based on] the Book of Changes." [140] (This, as Chi Wen-fu has remarked, was a case of fu-tzu tzu tao.) [el] [141] Wang wrote the Chang Tzu Cheng-meng chu when he was in his sixties, but his interest in the Book of Changes dated back to 1646, and as early as 1655 he had incorporated his ideas about it in his first philosophical work, the Chou-i wai-chuan. [142]

In this book he already presents a similar monistic view of the universe in which principle is immanent in ether and the Way is immanent in concrete things. [143] It is a universe constantly growing and in movement,[144] in which the coming and going, the life and death of men and things, are correlated processes which alternate endlessly in the Supreme Void, which is itself movement,[145] and the Supreme Harmony.[146] It is a universe of being and evolution,[147] in which the nature and the decree of Heaven are constantly renewed [148] and matter is indestructible.[149]

There are differences between the views expressed in this book and those of the *Chang Tzu Cheng-meng chu,* though they are largely differences of emphasis, which is not surprising considering the two works are separated by a quarter of a century. The most important difference is that, although Wang adopts the same monistic position as Chang Tsai with regard to the ether and principle, he does not express this in the same way as he does in the *Chang Tzu Cheng-meng chu* where, following Chang, he builds his whole system on the basis of the Supreme Void, which is all ether and in which the *yin* and the *yang* provide the dynamic impulse behind the evolution of the universe. In the *Chou-i wai-chuan,* as in the *Chang Tzu Cheng-meng chu,* the *yin* and *yang* are said to embody the Way and the Supreme Harmony (which is said to "achieve its embodiment through the *yin* and *yang,* in whose alternating flow comes transformation"), and to be responsible for producing the combination of ether and form which results in the life of man and things.[150] They are, however, described as subordinate to the Supreme Ultimate in a way which Wang was later to criticize in his *Chang Tzu Cheng-meng chu.* Whereas in the *Chou-i wai-chuan* he adopts the position that "The Supreme Ultimate moves and produces the *yang,* is quiescent and produces the *yin,*" [151] in the *Chang Tzu Cheng-meng chu* he declares:

Those who give a wrong explanation of the *Diagram of the Supreme Ultimate* say that in the Supreme Ultimate there was originally no *yin* or *yang,* that *yang* was first produced by its movement, and *yin* from its quiescence . . . but movement and quiescence are the movement and quiescence of the *yin* and *yang* . . . it is not the case that there is first movement and afterward the *yang,* first quiescence and afterward the *yin.*[152]

Moreover, whereas in the *Chang Tzu Cheng-meng chu* the emphasis is on the *yin* and *yang* as the dual embodiment of the ether, in the *Chou-i wai-chuan* it is on the *yin* and *yang* as the dual embodiment of the Way. Though it is true that Wang speaks of the ether and principle as permeating one another and insists on their interdependence, the ether as such is not given the same importance as in the *Chang Tzu Cheng-meng chu.* In the *Chou-i wai-chuan* it is the agglomerated ether in the form of concrete things whose relationship to the Way is stressed:

The world consists of nothing but concrete things. The Way is the Way (or Ways) of concrete things, but concrete things cannot be described as the concrete things of the Way. "When the Way is nonexistent, so is the concrete thing," is something anyone is capable of saying. But if the concrete thing exists, why worry about its Way not existing? The sage knows what the gentleman does not, and yet ordinary men and women can do what the sage cannot. It may be that people are not clear about the Way of some concrete thing, and so the concrete thing is not perfected, but the fact that it is not perfected does not mean it does not exist. "When the concrete thing is nonexistent, so is its Way," is something few people are capable of saying, but this is really and truly so.[153]

More surprising than such differences, however, is the fact that, despite the similarity between the ideas expressed in the *Chou-i wai-chuan* and the *Chang Tzu Cheng-meng chu*, there is in the former no mention of Chang Tsai, even where one would expect it, when Wang deals with the Supreme Harmony or the Supreme Void. Although it is impossible to date the *Chang Tzu Cheng-meng chu* exactly, all scholars agree that it must have been completed sometime after 1679.[154] Whether in 1655 Wang's position was already that of Chang's disciple, as he was by this time describing himself,[155] or whether the coincidence of views between himself and Chang was at that stage more indirect or fortuitous is, however, not clear. What is clear is that Chang's cosmology as expounded in the *Cheng-meng* provided the perfect basis for the philosophical system which Wang was already working out in the *Chou-i wai-chuan*. There is unfortunately no record of when Wang first came into contact with Chang's doctrines. We do not know when he first read the *Cheng-meng*, or even Chu Hsi's *Chin-ssu lu*, which contains extracts from the *Cheng-meng* (including Chang's theory of the Supreme Void) and other writings by Chang.[156] It is of course possible that Kao Shih-t'ai, in passing on his uncle's ideas to the young Wang Fu-chih, awakened in him an interest in this Sung philosopher who had so influenced P'an-lung. In any case, when Wang wrote the *Chou-i wai-chuan*, he would seem to have been aware, even if only indirectly, of Chang's theory of the Supreme Void— judging from his use of this term which Chang had pioneered—though he did not as yet fully incorporate it into his own philosophical system.

Liu Mao-hua [em] [157] has argued that Wang's philosophical evolution was one which led him from being a disciple of the Ch'eng-Chu school to becoming a convert to Chang's doctrines sometime after the death of his brother Chieh-chih, in 1686. According to Liu, both Wang's *Tu Ssu-shu ta-ch'üan shuo* (1665) and *Li-chi chang-chü* (1677) "honor the Ch'eng-Chu school, whereas in the *Chang Tzu Cheng-meng chu* there is not a single word in their praise. . . . In addition, his theory of the indestructibility of matter is first set forth in this book [i.e., *Chang Tzu Cheng-meng chu*]." Liu also believes that another characteristic of his later work is his rejection of Chu Hsi's interpretation of the Mencian phrase "He who has fully exploited his mind knows his nature" in favor of Chang's interpretation.

In fact, while it is true that Wang proclaimed himself a disciple of Chang only late in life, his evolution was a natural development of ideas which (like that of the indestructibility of matter) were, as we have seen, already present in the *Chou-i wai-chuan*. His respect for the Ch'engs and Chu lasted throughout his life. He was still praising them [158] in the *Chang Tzu Cheng-meng chu*—in which he occasionally criticized Chang [159]—and he was already praising Chang at their expense in the *Tu Ssu-shu ta-ch'üan shuo*, written in 1665:

Master Ch'eng grouped the mind, the nature, and Heaven together as one and the same principle in order to refute the heresy which recklessly held that the impulses (*chi*) in man constituted his mind and nature, and that Heaven was non-being (*wei shih yu*),[en] and he was right to do so. But when it comes to thinking about the subtleties and grasping the realities involved, exploring the profound and investigating impulses, and clarifying all, then Heng-ch'ü's [i.e., Chang Tsai's] theories are brilliant. Now in talking about the mind, the nature, Heaven, and principle one should really make the ether the basis of all one's discussions, because if there were no ether none of these would exist. . . . Now when [Chang] says, "From the Supreme Void is derived the term 'Heaven,' " [160] he is saying that the ether does not depend on the evolution. The ether does not depend on evolution [for its existence]: originally there was nothing but the ether. Thus Heaven is referred to in terms of the ether, and the Way in terms of Heaven's evolution. One certainly cannot speak of Heaven as something distinct from the ether. . . . Master Ch'eng said, "Heaven is principle," [161] and since he spoke of Heaven in terms of principle he also regarded Heaven as principle. But even though one regard Heaven as principle, Heaven definitely cannot be termed something distinct from the ether. It is only insofar as principle is the principle of the ether that one can go on to think of Heaven as meaning principle. Otherwise, if one sets aside all consideration of the ether and speaks only of principle, one cannot succeed in equating Heaven and principle. Why is this?

Heaven is certainly a mass of ether. Now if one speaks of Heaven in terms of principle, one proceeds to the fundamentals of principle to describe it, and so one says, "Heaven is that from which principle emerges. All principles are of Heaven." This is definitely true. But if one says, "Heaven is only principle" [as Ch'eng did], then the statement is faulty.[162]

Even in the *Chou-i wai-chuan* Wang had taken, as he takes in the above passage, a stand with regard to the immanence of principle in ether, and the Way in concrete things which was at variance with Chu Hsi's doctrine.[163] But as far as he was concerned Ch'eng I and Chu Hsi, whatever their shortcomings, were not philosophical opponents of Chang Tsai. They were, as he makes clear in his "Prefatory Argument" to the *Chang Tzu Cheng-meng chu*, outstanding Confucianists even if the place of honor was ultimately accorded to Chang. The real enemies were Wang Yang-ming and his school, and all those whose Confucianism was corrupted by Buddhistic influence. His attitude to the differences between Chang and the Ch'eng-Chu school is well illustrated by his comment on their varying interpretations of the phrase from Mencius to which Liu Mao-hua draws attention. In the *Cheng-meng* Chang had written:

By expanding one's mind one is able to embody the things of the whole world. If there are things which are not thus embodied, then there will be something that remains external to the mind. The minds of ordinary men are confined within the limits of hearing and seeing, whereas the sage by fully exploiting his nature does not allow his mind to be shackled to what he sees and hears. As he views the world there is in it not a single thing which is not his own self. This is what Mencius means when he says that through fully exploiting one's mind one can come to know one's nature and Heaven.[164]

Wang is content simply to observe:

Master Chu says that through knowing one's nature one can fully exploit one's mind, but Master Chang considers that fully exploiting one's mind is part of the task of knowing one's nature. There is a slight difference between their theories. Now if when the nature is in repose, before patterns and images have formed, one does not fully exploit one's mind in order to embody a knowledge of it in oneself, then when one proceeds to the haphazard encounters of hearing and seeing one will adopt them as the reality of one's own nature. This is how (as Mencius puts it) those in the world who discuss the nature come to arbitrary conclusions.[165]

Chang's notion of exploiting the mind until it embraced all was linked to the mystical feeling of union with the universe and the sense of moral involvement expressed in his *Western Inscription*. Although Wang shared Chang's moral concern and preferred his interpretation of the Mencian phrase to that of Chu, he himself endowed it with a pragmatism foreign to his Sung predecessor, and envisaged an altogether more objective and active process as he explains in the *Ssu-wen lu*:

What the eyes do not see is not without color.
What the ears do not hear is not without sound.
What words do not express is not without meaning.
Therefore [Confucius] said, "When you know a thing, to hold that you know it; and when you do not know a thing, to allow that you do not know it; [this is knowledge]." [166] If one knows that there exists that which one does not know, then one knows that it is there. If one proceeds with one's inquiries in this way, then when one has exhausted what one can see, the colors of what one cannot see are clear. When one has exhausted what one can hear, the sounds one cannot hear are plain. When one has exhausted what one can say, the unexpressed meaning is established. Though one knows that there is that which one does not know, one must proceed in this way in order to extend one's knowledge, and not confine oneself to seeking it within the limits of what one does not know [i.e., by speculation unrelated to what one knows by experience]. That there should be colors unseen by the eyes, sounds unheard by the ears, and meanings unattained by speech, is due to the limitations of these inferior organs. There is, however, nothing the mind cannot attain. That there should be principles which one's thought has not reached is simply due to one's not yet having thought of them. Thus [Mencius] said, "He who has fully exploited his mind knows his nature." The mind is thus the complete embodiment of Heaven. [167]

For Wang, as for Chang, man is part of the universe, so "there can never be a Heaven separate from man." [168] Again like Chang, Wang holds that man is more than just a part of the universe. He is a vitally important part of it, with a vitally important role to play. As Wang puts it in the *Chou-i wai-chuan*, "Man's relationship to the universe is that of its great completer," [169] while in the *Shang-shu yin-i* he writes that "achievement is man's part in the transformation of the universe: he certainly does not just leave it to Heaven." [170]

The catastrophic events to which he had been a witness from his earliest youth had convinced him of the folly of "leaving it to Heaven," and in his efforts to come to grips with the actual universe and play his proper role in its transformation Wang goes much further than Chang toward uniting considerations of morality and reality. The cornerstone of Chang's philosophy is the unity of all being in real and moral terms, but Wang investigates and elucidates the implications of this belief in an entirely original way.

As we have seen, in Wang's system the fundamental unity was that of the ether and principle in a universe where all existed materially. Closely related to this were the forms of unity which existed between substance and function, and between concrete things and their various Ways. Moreover, since the universe was a dynamic mass of constantly evolving matter, the order which existed in the matter as principles was not itself static, and this led to an emphasis on what was appropriate or proper at any juncture in time and space and a preoccupation with these factors of changing circumstance. Wang consequently applied himself to two spheres in which he believed the processes of the universe could be studied and the underlying thread discerned. The first was the *Book of Changes*, and the second was the history of China. In studying these he proceeded from his conception of universal change to elaborate his own philosophy of history, hoping the fruits of his studies could be applied to the contemporary situation, or, failing that, could at least serve future generations.[171]

He turned to the *Book of Changes* because he believed it codified the patterns of universal change and was thus a "revelation of the Way of Heaven"[172] which provided the answer. Of the four virtues which the *Book of Changes* attributed to the ideal gentleman, the ability to "manage affairs" is described as "being correct" (*chen*)[dv][173] and Wang adopted this term to describe the appropriate adjustment which takes the various circumstances into consideration and enables one, by achieving a norm within change, to be in accord with the Way in one's undertakings.

In the *Book of Changes*, the factors of time and position, he believed, were represented by the sixty-four hexagrams and the lines which make up the hexagrams, respectively. Change in the *Book of Changes* consisted fundamentally of the interaction of the *yin* (divided) and *yang* (undivided) lines, just as universal change consisted of the interaction of the *yin* and *yang* in the ether.[174] One should, he maintained, both consult the *Book of Changes* as an instrument of divination and study it as a text containing the lessons of the sages. The aim of both study and divination, which were, he argued, essentially complementary, was to establish not what was auspicious in the sense of lucky (*chi*),[eo] but what was morally right (*i*)[ep] in a situation where there was doubt.[175]

Whereas in his investigations into the *Book of Changes* Wang speaks of taking into consideration the factors of time and place in order to "achieve the correct norm," elsewhere he includes these factors under the term "conditions" (*shih*),[c] whose use in the *Chang Tzu Cheng-meng chu* has already been noted.

Although his historical writings are full of analyses and examples of *shih*[c] in action, it is in a passage in the *Tu Ssu-shu ta-ch'üan shuo* that Wang gives what is perhaps the clearest account of his theory of "conditions."[176]

Basically Wang believed that *shih*[c] were the product of all the factors of change which, as the universe evolved, exerted their influence on events, and he saw the Way of man as the ceaseless series of adjustments necessary to achieve order and equilibrium within the conditions of the shifting equation in which he, too, like time and place, was a factor. Moreover, since *shih* were the product of natural forces, he rejected the notion that they were necessarily incompatible with the Way. For Wang the moral task of man was inseparably bound up with a correct appreciation of the trends objectively observed in the world about him. The relationship between *shih* and *li* was another aspect of the fundamental relationship between *ch'i* and *li*. Thus in the above-mentioned passage from *Tu Ssu-shu ta-ch'üan shuo*, Wang insists on the integral unity of *shih* and *li* which makes it impossible for one to function without the other. He also distinguishes in the text between the principles (*li*) which are always present in conditions (*shih*), and the "one definite principle" which is the Way, and which, since man must shape it from the conditions, may be lost.

The informed use of *shih* must always in some respect be in accord with the Way. For example, even the Ch'in emperor, despite his immoral motives, was, insofar as he cooperated with the universal processes, unconsciously furthering the cause of the Way when he inaugurated the prefectural system.[177] He could not, in Wang's view, be held guilty of destroying the feudal system. In fact, the latter had outlived its purpose, and in recognizing the change which conditions dictated he was unconsciously acting in the "universal interest" (Wang actually uses the phrase *'T'ien chia ch'i ssu i hsing ch'i ta kung'*).[eq] But just as one whose goals are immoral is incapable of full cooperation with *shih* in a universe which is ultimately moral, so the morally well-intentioned man who does not understand *shih* is condemned by his lack of realism to moral failure in his actions. The ideal, of course, brings *shih* and the Way into perfect harmony, and he compared those who tried to practice the Way without regard to *shih* to a sailor who tried to sail a boat without paying attention to the wind.[178]

By Wang's time the term *shih* had become associated with Realist politics of power, and the emphasis he placed on it distinguishes him radically from his Neo-Confucian predecessors. He shared their belief that the ultimate order of the universe was a moral one, but he regarded the study of the actual processes of the universe as essential because true morality existed only in realistically informed action. His efforts to redress the balance between what many had come to regard as antithetical elements led him toward a position approaching a synthesis of what was morally right and practically expedient and of what one might describe as the factors of *i* and *li*.[er] [179]

In its simplest form this position would be that, the universe being morally organized, to accord with the observable pattern of events in the universe is morally right. This is the converse of the more traditional view that, the universe being morally organized, by acting according to the canons of morality one would automatically be in accord with the universal processes. In his insistence on the need to accord with *shih*, with the real conditions and processes of the universe, Wang is following in a tradition whose intellectual antecedents may be traced back to the pre-Ch'in Taoists and Realists.[180] Nevertheless, mysterious though the operation of the *shih* and the Way might be, Wang advocates no fatalistic acceptance or compliance with universal change. Change is inevitable, but within change there is the correct adjustment to be made, which, by taking into account the forces at work and acting accordingly, allows man a measure of control over the conditions with which he is confronted.[181]

In Wang's conception of universal and historical change, the mystery to which man must apply his mind arises from the complex interaction of the factors to be taken into account. In the first place there are the universal processes of change which are as inevitable as those of man's progress from birth to death and the rise and fall of dynasties.[182] These processes are relatively simple and comprehensible when seen in terms of an individual person or phenomenon, but Wang's universe is essentially a composite one in which all the components are changing together, influencing and being influenced by one another. One can only appreciate how a trend in *shih* works by a thorough analysis of the various factors which constitute it. In this way the overall historical trend may be discerned.[183] Such a trend, however, is not necessarily irreversible; only change itself is inevitable. With the constant evolution of the universe, conditions are constantly changing, too, but the manner of their change is neither predetermined nor absolutely inevitable. Man must do what he can to influence it.

The ideal is to be master of the time factor. The next best thing is to anticipate it, and the next best thing after that to accord with it. The worst thing to do is to go against it. To go against the times is fatal. When one is master of the times, the vagaries of time fluctuate in correspondence to oneself as one controls and adjusts the times. When one anticipates the times, the cardinal principle is, when one sees what is going to happen, to guide and control its realization. When one accords with the times one complies with that which the times make inevitable in order to save oneself, and so escapes from disaster.[184]

The overall tendency of change is from one pole to another. It is, however, only when a certain point of excess is reached that man loses the power to exert any control over conditions.[185] Thus Wang explains that "by the time of the last years of the reign of Hui-tsung, the conditions which made the ruin of the Sung inevitable (*pi wang chih shih*)[es] could no longer be checked, because once conditions reach the extreme point at which they can no longer be checked, it is only after a great reversal that there can be any stability." [186] One can nonetheless remain in control of change if one takes the proper measures in good time and prevents conditions from running to excess. This, according to Wang, was what Emperor Wu of the Han had done, beginning his reign with policies of great severity, but later making gradual modifications which enabled him to bring about a détente while remaining master of the situation.[187] This was what was meant by the gentleman "complying with principles, and being good at acting in accord with Heaven," and it was because they understood this that the founders of the Shang and Chou dynasties "examined into the extremes of the people's distress, assessed when this distress was due to decline, then made a correct adjustment (*chen*) and waited, achieving the completion of their designs by proceeding gradually at first, and in accordance with the will of the masses." [188] The parallel between the role of man as exemplified by the sage ruler and that of the scholar given in the description of the development of Neo-Confucianism in the *Chang Tzu Cheng-meng chu* is an obvious one.

Throughout Wang's philosophical argumentation there is, as I hope is by now clear, a strong element not only of pragmatism but of utilitarianism. Pragmatism lies of course at the heart of his whole theory of the *li-ch'i* relationship (not least in its *tao-ch'i* aspect), and the real benefit either of all mankind or of the whole Chinese people, depending on the context, is the touchstone by which one recognizes the true course of the Way. It is in this sense that Wang's references to *ta kung* [et] must be understood.

Wang's chief concern was always with practical solutions to immediate problems. As a historian his preoccupation was with the lessons the past offered for the present and the future. "Material for government (*tzu chih*)," [eu] he wrote in his major historical work, [189]

does not mean just recognizing orderly government and chaos: it means the provision of the material necessary to act vigorously in the pursuit of orderly government. . . . The material which orderly government relies on is the realization of examples in practice, but what may be good in one situation is not necessarily good in another. . . . One must discover the reasons for success and failure. In the case of success one must ponder whether one could achieve the same success in adopting a different course, and in the case of failure one must consider whether one could prevent failure in following the same direction.

Nor, although this paper has dealt at length with the philosophical basis of Wang's position, was he a mere theoretical defender of a pragmatic and utilitarian approach. In the desperate political situation of his day, Wang held the prime need to be for concrete political measures and effective action. "One must act forcefully in support of one's own people in order that the latent forces of China may be realized," he declared, [190] and went on to ask what is, in the context of his life and thought, a highly significant rhetorical question. "At present, when our people cannot preserve their own stability, what is the point of prattling about benevolence and righteousness?"

In addition to his active political involvement, Wang set out his own analysis of the contemporary situation, together with detailed proposals for retrieving it, in such works as *E-meng* and *Huang shu* (although these fall outside the scope of this paper). He hoped thereby "to remedy the situation as it exists in the context of these extremely degenerate times, without pretending to absolute perfection. Just as one shifts the weight on a steelyard because the scale is too low, and is at the same time concerned lest it should rise too high, here too there is an adjustment which brings equilibrium." [191] It was in this way that Wang gave practical expression to his belief that it was the role of man "to control events" as "the mind of the universe."

NOTES

Additional Abbreviations Used in this Chapter:

TPY   *T'ai-p'ing yang shu-tien* edition of the *Ch'uan-shan i-shu*, 1933. Adjacent numbers indicate the *ts'e* of this edition.

HY   *Harvard Yenching Institute Sinological Index Series*

1. *Ch'uan-shan*, the best known of Wang's literary names, was taken from this mountain where he lived in his old age.
2. For a discussion of this period see, for example, E. Balazs, *Political Theory and Administrative Reality in Traditional China* (New Haven, 1965).
3. This section is based on the biography which I originally compiled as part of a study entitled "Wang Fu-chih and his Political Thought," presented as a doctoral thesis at Oxford, in 1968, and which I am at present preparing for publication.
4. Especially those in TPY, 69 *Chiang-chai wen-chi*, 2/1a–10b, and 10/a–10b. A full bibliography of biographical source material on which the subsequent pages are based is given in the work mentioned in note 3 above, pp. 42–46.
5. Tsou Te-p'u was the grandson of Tsou Shou-i. Both are described by Huang Tsung-hsi as belonging to the Kiangsi branch of Wan Shou-jen's school (cf. *MJHA*, 16/1a, 4a).
6. *Hunan t'ung-chih* (1885 edition), 167/3322, and Liu Hsien-t'ing *Kuang-yang tsa-chi* (1957), 2/56.
7. Cf. for example *Chu Tzu ch'üan-shu* (Ch'eng-tu shu-chü edition, 1867), 7/5b ff.
8. Cf. *Ch'uan-hsi lu* (SPTK edition), *shang*, 9b–10a.
9. Cf. de Bary, *Self and Society*, pp. 24–50.
10. Cf. de Bary's paper "Neo-Confucian Cultivation and the Seventeenth-Century 'Enlightenment,' " this volume.
11. Cf. TPY, 69 *Chiang-chai wen-chi*, 2/1a–3b.
12. Cf., for example, TPY, 72/I-te, 2a.
13. Cf. *Ibid.*, 1b. This may have been a chapter of Wu Ying-chi's *K'uang-she*, but there is no evidence of any connection. It was perhaps because of the merging of Wu's *K'uang-she* with the *Fu-she* that Balazs (*Political Theory and Administrative Reality*, p. 14) wrote that Wang belonged to the latter.
14. Cf. H. Busch, "The Tung-lin Academy and its Political and Philosophical Significance," in *Monumenta Serica*, XIV, 142. (Hereafter referred to as Busch, "The Tung-lin Academy.")
15. Cf. TPY, 69 *Chiang-chai wen-chi*, 10/5b.
16. Cf. TPY, 72/I-te, 5b.
17. Cf. also TPY, 64 *Lung-yüan yeh-hua*, 3b.

18. Cf. TPY, 28 *Ch'un-ch'iu chia-shuo hsü*, 1a.
19. Cf. *ibid.*, 1/12a and 2/9a.
20. Cf. TPY, 69 *Chiang-chai wen-chi*, 8/2a.
21. Cf. TPY, 71 *Chiang-chai shih fen-t'i kao*, 1/1b.
22. Cf. TPY, 60 *Lien-feng chih*, 2/1b.
23. Cf. TPY, 1 *Chiang-chai kung hsing-shu*, 1b.
24. Wang and his companions in the *K'uang-she* had obtained their *chü-jen* degrees together in the Hukuang examinations of 1642, while Chang had been one of their examiners and Kao had taught in a local academy. Both Chang and Kao were *chin-shih* of 1637.
25. Cf. TPY, 59 *Yung-li shih-lu*, 7/1a–5a.
26. Cf. TPY, 1 *Chiang-chai kung hsing-shu*, 1b.
27. Cf. TPY, 72 *I-te*, 10a.
28. Cf. TPY, 69 *Chiang-chai wen-chi*, 8/2a.
29. Cf. TPY, 64 *Lung-yüan yeh-hua*, 1a–1b.
30. Cf. TPY, 71 *Chiang-chai shih fen-t'i kao*, 1/4b.
31. Cf. TPY, 59 *Yung-li shih-lu*, 1/5a and 5/2a–3a.
32. Cf. TPY, 69 *Chiang-chai wen-chi*, 8/2a.
33. Cf. TPY, 1 *Chiang-chai kung hsing-shu*, 2a.
34. Cf. TPY, 59 *Yung-li shih-lu*, 1/4b, and 7/6b–7a.
35. Cf. *ibid.*, 21/1a–2b.
36. Cf. TPY, 59 *Yung-li shih-lu*, 25/3b.
37. The Ch'u party did not, of course, consist entirely of what Ku Hsien-ch'eng would have called the "good elements": Li Ch'eng-tung, for example, had, as a collaborator, crushed pro-Ming resistance with notorious cruelty, but the moral integrity of such men as Chin Pao and Ch'ü Shih-ssu had no counterpart among their opponents, while the upright Yen Ch'i-heng threw himself behind the Ch'u party in its hour of need.
38. Cf. TPY, 59 *Yung-li shih-lu*, 2/7a; TPY, 1 *Chiang-chai kung hsing-shu*, 2a–2b.
39. Cf. TPY, 70 *Wu-shih tzu-ting kao*, 22a.
40. Cf. TPY, 73 *Nan-ch'uang man-chi*, 5a.
41. Cf. Liu Yü-sung, *Wang Ch'uan-shan hsien-sheng nien-p'u* (Nanking, 1886), *chüan* 13.
42. Liu, a loyal servant of the Chin dynasty, famous for his campaigns against the barbarians, was slandered, disgraced, and killed in prison in A.D. 317.
43. TPY, 69 *Chiang-chai wen-chi pu-i*, 2/10b–11a.
44. TPY, 64 *Lung-yüan yeh-hua*, 3a.
45. Cf. Hsieh Kuo-chen, *Ming-Ch'ing chih chi tang-she yün-tung k'ao* (1934), pp. 99–104.
46. Cf. TPY, 64 *Lung-yüan yeh-hua*, 3a.
47. TPY, 17 *Li-chi chang-chü*, 3/23b–24a.
48. Cf. *MJHA*, 58/1a–6a.
49. TPY, 52 *Tu T'ung-chien lun*, 10/1b.

50. *MJHA*, 58/28b.

51. Cf. also C. Hucker, "The Tung-lin Movement of the late Ming Period," in J. Fairbank, *Chinese Thought and Institutions*, pp. 132–62.

52. Cf. *MJHA*, 60/1a–3b.

53. *Ibid.*, 2a.

54. *Lun-yü*, 13/21 (HY supplement, pp. 16, 40).

55. *Meng Tzu*, 7b/37 (HY supplement, pp. 17, 58–59).

56. Cf. *ibid.*, p. 58.

57. TPY, 49 *Ssu-shu ta-ch'üan shuo*, 10/52b–53a.

58. Cf. Chi Wen-fu, *Wang Ch'uan-shan hsüeh-shu lun-ts'ung* (Peking, 1962), p. 70.

59. Cf. TPY, 56 *Tu T'ung-chien lun, chüan-mo*, 3b, and Chi Wen-fu, *Wang Ch'uan-shan*, p. 68.

60. That is, Hsüeh Hsüan. Wang's praise of this scholar is intriguing in the light of what Professor Chan has to say about Hsüeh's deviation from Chu Hsi's doctrine and his debt to Chang Tsai; see Chan, in de Bary, *Self and Society*, pp. 33–37.

61. TPY, 64 *Sao-shou wen*, 1b–2a.

62. *MJHA*, 58/3a.

63. Cf. also *MJHA*, 60/7b–10a.

64. *MJHA*, 58/54b–55a.

65. Cf. *Ch'uan-hsi lu, chung*, 8b–10a and 12b–15a.

66. Cf. *MJHA*, 60/2a.

67. Cf., for example, Kao's emphasis of these aspects in *MJHA*, 58/55a and 71a.

68. Cf. *Ku Tuan-wen kung i-shu* (1877 edition), "Hsiao-hsin chai cha-chi," 4/3a–3b, and Busch, "The Tung-lin Academy," pp. 113–14.

69. Cf. *MJHA*, 32/1a, and *ibid.*, 58/5a–6a.

70. *MJHA*, 60/2a.

71. Cf. *ibid.*, 12/1a–42a.

72. *Ibid.*, 1b–2a. Cf. also *Ch'uan-hsi lu, hsia* 45b–48a.

73. Cf. *MJHA*, 12/11b–12a, and Fung Yu-lan, *Chung-kuo che-hsüeh shih*, p. 970.

74. Cf. also Professors T'ang and Okada in de Bary, *Self and Society*, pp. 110–16, 126–31.

75. Cf. *Ku Tuan-wen kung i-shu* "Huan-ching lu," 24b.

76. TPY, 63 *Ssu-chieh*, 8a.

77. Even Wang Fu-chih was, despite his condemnations of Wang Yang-ming, and as Chi Wen-fu has suggested, certainly influenced by him if only in taking Yang-ming's criticism into account in what Chi calls Fu-chih's "revision" of Ch'eng-Chu theory. Cf. Chi Wen-fu, *Wang Ch'uan-shan*, pp. 118–21.

78. Cf. Busch, "The Tung-lin Academy," pp. 97 ff., and MJHA, 58/6b–7a.

79. Cf. *MJHA*, 58/6a.

80. *Ibid.*, 67b.

81. TPY, 25 *Li-chi chang-chü*, 31/1b and 7a, and TPY, 63/*Ssu-chieh*, 6a.
82. Cf. Hucker, "The Tung-lin Movement," and Busch, "The Tung-lin Academy."
83. TPY, 61 *Chang Tzu Cheng-meng chu hsü-lun*, 2b.
84. *Ibid.*, 1a–1b.
85. Cf. Chan (trans.), *Reflections on Things at Hand* (1967), pp. 52, 79.
86. Both authors of commentaries on the classics.
87. TPY, 61 *Chang Tzu Cheng-meng chu hsü-lun*, 1a–1b.
88. *Ibid.*
89. TPY, 62 *Chang Tzu Cheng-meng chu*, 9/11b–12a.
90. Chu Hsi, *Chin-ssu lu chi-chu* (SPPY edition), 8/6a–6b.
91. Cf. TPY, 62 *Chang Tzu Cheng-meng chu*, 7/1a–2b.
92. TPY, 53 *Tu T'ung-chien lun*, 15/12a.
93. TPY, 61 *Chang Tzu Cheng-meng chu*, 1/17b.
94. Cf. *MJHA*, 62/8b–9a.
95. *MJHA*, 50/2a.
96. "Nan-lei wen ting ssu chi," 1/1a, in *Li-chou i-chu hui-k'an* (1915).
97. Cf. *Ch'uan-hsi lu, hsia*, 57b ff.
98. Cf., for example, Chang Hsi-t'ang, *Wang Ch'uan-shan hsüeh-p'u* (1938), pp. 186–87, and Liu Yü-sung, *Nien p'u, hsia* 33b.
99. TPY, 61 *Chang Tzu Cheng-meng chu*, 1/1a.
100. *Ibid.*, 1/1a–1b.
101. *Ibid.*, 1/3a.
102. *Ibid.*
103. Cf. TPY, 64 *Huang shu*, 1a–1b, and ch. V of the thesis referred to in note 3 above.
104. TPY, 61 *Chang Tzu Cheng-meng chu*, 1/2a–2b.
105. *Ibid.*, 1/3b–4a.
106. *Ibid.*, 1/2b.
107. *Lun-yü*, 11/11, HY supplement, pp. 16, 20.
108. *Chou I, Hsi-tz'u, shang*/4, HY supplement, pp. 10, 40.
109. *Ibid., hsia*, 3, HY supplement, pp. 10, 46.
110. *Ibid., shang*/12, HY supplement, pp. 10, 44.
111. TPY, 61 *Chang Tzu Cheng-meng chu*, 1/3b–4b.
112. Cf. Chang Hsi-t'ang, *Hsüeh-p'u*, pp. 44–5.
113. TPY, 61 *Chang Tzu Cheng-meng chu*, 1/5a.
114. *Ibid.*, 5a–5b.
115. *Ibid.*, 3/10a–15b.
116. *Ibid.*
117. *Ibid.*, 3/16a, and see note 108 above.
118. *Ibid.*, 3/19a–19b.
119. Cf. *Chu Tzu yü-lei* (1872 edition), 1/1a.
120. Cf. TPY, 61 *Chang Tzu Cheng-meng chu*, 3/14a–14b.
121. TPY, 48 *Tu Ssu-shu ta-ch'üan shuo*, 7/9a–9b.
122. TPY, 61 *Chang Tzu Cheng-meng chu*, 3/14a.

123. A statement by the twelfth-century Confucianist, Hu Hung, quoted by Chu Hsi in his commentary on Mencius.

124. Ku Chieh-kang, *Shang-shu t'ung-chien* (1936), p. 6.

125. *Chou I, Hsi-tz'u, hsia*/1, HY supplement, pp. 10, 45.

126. *Lun-yü*, 12/1, HY supplement, pp. 16, 22.

127. TPY, 15 *Shih kuang-chuan*, 2/10b–11a.

128. *Chou I, Hsi-tz'u, shang*/9, HY supplement, pp. 10, 43.

129. Chou Tun-i, *Chou-tzu t'ung-shu* (SPPY edition), 1b.

130. Cf. Ku Chieh-kang, *Shang-shu*, p. 11.

131. TPY, 48 *Tu Ssu-shu ta ch'üan shuo*, 8/37b–38a. Wang's use of the term *hsien-t'ien* is not to be confused with that of Shao Yung. For Wang *hsien-t'ien chih hsing* refers to nature in its primordial state (where the ether is dispersed) and *hou-t'ien chih hsing* to its realization in phenomena (when the ether has agglomerated). In the case of man this comes to mean his potential and actual nature respectively.

132. Cf. TPY, 25 *Li-chi chang-chü*, 30/1a.

133. TPY, 63 *Ssu-wen lu nei-p'ien*, 8b.

134. TPY, 11 *Shang-shu yin-i*, 3/6a–6b.

135. TPY, 61 *Chang Tzu Cheng-meng chu*, 1/15b–6a.

136. *Ibid.*, 1/10b.

137. *Ibid.*, 3/10a.

138. *Ibid.*, 4/1a.

139. TPY, 63 *E-meng hsü*, 1a.

140. TPY, 61 *Chang Tzu Cheng-meng chu hsü-lun*, 2b–3a.

141. Cf. Chi Wen-fu, *Wang Ch'uan-shan*, p. 75.

142. TPY, 6 *Chou I nei-chuan fa-li*, 19b.

143. TPY, 7 *Chou I wai-chuan*, 4/3b, and TPY, 8 *Chou I wai-chuan*, 5/25a–26a.

144. TPY, 8 *Chou I wai-chuan*, 6/7a.

145. *Ibid.*, 6/7a–8b.

146. *Ibid.*, 6/10b.

147. TPY, 7 *Chou I wai-chuan*, 2/1b–2b. Throughout, I translate *hua* [eb] by evolution, despite its Darwinian associations, because of its connotations of continuous, effortless change.

148. TPY, 8 *Chou I wai-chuan*, 7/4a.

149. *Ibid.*, 6/7b.

150. TPY, 7 *Chou I wai-chuan*, 2/14b, and *ibid.*, 3/17a.

151. *Ibid.*, 1/6a.

152. TPY, 61 *Chang Tzu Cheng-meng chu*, 1/6a.

153. TPY, 8 *Chou I wai-chuan*, 5/25a.

154. See note 98 above.

155. TPY, 61 *Chang Tzu Cheng-meng chu hsü lun*, 2b–3a, and TPY, 69 *Chiang-chai wen-chi pu-i*, 2/10b–11a.

156. Chu Hsi, *Chin-ssu lu chi-chu* (SPPY edition), *yüan-hsü*, 1a and 1/16a.

157. Liu Mao-hua in *Hsin-ya hsüeh-pao*, vol. 1 (1960), p. 410. He is in part following Chang Hsi-t'ang.

158. TPY, 61 *Chang Tzu Cheng-meng chu hsü-lun*, 1b, and *ibid.*, 3/6a.
159. *Ibid.*, 1/17a and 19b.
160. TPY, 61 *Chang Tzu Cheng-meng chu*, 1/10b.
161. Chu Hsi, *Ssu-shu chang-chü chi-chu*, *Meng-tzu chi-chu*, p. 188.
162. TPY, 49 *Tu Ssu-shu ta-ch'üan shuo*, 10/32a–32b.
163. TPY, 7 *Chou I wai-chuan*, 4/3b–4a, and TPY, 8 *Chou I wai-chuan*, 5/25a.
164. TPY, 61 *Chang Tzu Cheng-meng chu*, 4/1a–1b.
165. *Ibid.*, 1b.
166. *Lun-Yü*, 2/17, HY supplement, pp. 16, 3.
167. TPY, 63 *Ssu-wen lu nei-p'ien*, 1a.
168. TPY, 48 *Tu Ssu-shu ta ch'üan shuo*, 8/10b–11a.
169. TPY, 7 *Chou I wai-chuan*, 3/1a.
170. TPY, 12 *Shang-shu yin-i*, 4/15b.
171. Cf. TPY, 64 *Huang-shu hou-hsü*, 1b, and TPY, 56 *Tu T'ung-chien lun*, 28/5b.
172. TPY, 61 *Chang Tzu Cheng-meng chu hsü-lun*, 2b.
173. *Chou I*, *shang-ching*, 1/1, HY supplement, pp. 10, 1.
174. Cf. TPY, 61 *Chang Tzu Cheng-meng chu*, 1/13b.
175. *Ibid.*, 13a–14b. This is in fact what he did himself when summoned by Sun K'o-wang. Cf. TPY, 69 *Chiang-chai wen-chi*, 8/1a.
176. TPY, 48 *Tu T'ung-chien lun*, 9/4a–5b.
177. Cf. TPY, 51 *Tu T'ung-chien lun*, 1/1a–1b.
178. Cf. TPY, 12 *Shang-shu yin-i*, 5/19b.
179. Wang retains the orthodox Confucianist's abhorrence of personal profit, but, as I indicate below, goes on to reconcile profit (which becomes the general, communal benefit, cf. pp. 454–58 this volume) on the basis of the notion, which he states as a commentary to the passage in the *Book of Changes* (*Chou I*, 1/1, HY supplement, pp. 10, 1) which says of the gentleman "benefiting all creatures he is able to be in accord with what is right." Wang adds (cf. TPY, 11 *Shang-shu yin-i*, 2/1a) "What is right being practicable, the benefit is in accord with it."
180. For a full discussion of the origins of the use of *shih*, see ch. 4 of the thesis mentioned in note 3 above.
181. Cf. TPY, 58 *Sung Lun*, 7/1a.
182. Cf. TPY, 54 *Tu T'ung-chien lun*, 20/31a.
183. Cf., for example, TPY, 56 *Tu T'ung-chien lun*, 28/16a–17a.
184. TPY, 30 *Ch'un-ch'iu shih lun*, 5/7b.
185. This Taoistic notion found, for example, in *Tao-te ching* (cf. SPPY edition, *hsia* 4a) was by no means exclusive to the Taoists.
186. TPY, 58 *Sung Lun*, 8/7b–8a.
187. Cf. *ibid.*, 7/1a–1b.
188. *Ibid.*
189. TPY, 56 *Tu T'ung-chien lun*, *chüan-mo*, 5a.
190. TPY, 64 *Huang-shu hou-hsü*, 1a.
191. TPY, 63 *E-meng hsü*, 1a.

GLOSSARY

a	石船山	ak	金聲桓	bu	游酢
b	實學	al	楚	bv	謝良佐
c	勢	am	吳	bw	窮理
d	朝聘	an	高必正	bx	熊禾
e	武夷	ao	劉越石	by	事
f	宗濂洛正傳	ap	張橫渠	bz	富弼
g	良知	aq	浙中泰州		文彥博
h	江右	ar	錢謙益		司馬光
i	鄒德溥	as	顧憲成	ca	邵康節
j	東廓	at	清議	cb	明倫
k	鄒守益	au	允成	cc	近思錄
l	眞知	av	鄉愿	cd	有司
m	實踐	aw	狂狷	ce	氣
n	誠意	ax	四書大全	cf	太極
o	伍定相	ay	馮道	cg	理
p	格物	az	蘇子瞻	ch	太虛
q	率性	ba	陳同甫	ci	太和
r	介之	bb	韓退之	cj	散
s	匡社	bc	焦竑	ck	無
t	高世泰	bd	李贄	cl	聚
u	高攀龍	be	薛文清	cm	陰陽
v	乾時	bf	顧涇陽	cn	劉宗周
w	章曠	bg	明儒學案	co	乾
x	堵胤錫	bh	禮記章句	cp	坤
y	何騰蛟	bi	薛瑄	cq	神
z	夏汝弼	bj	工夫	cr	野馬
aa	武岡	bk	實行	cs	太極圖說
ab	管嗣裘	bl	王畿	ct	形
ac	肇慶	bm	錢緒山	cu	器
ad	桂林	bn	天泉	cv	才
ae	瞿式耜	bo	慧能神秀	cw	質
af	方以智	bp	主靜	cx	性
ag	平樂	bq	理氣	cy	情
ah	嚴光	br	正蒙	cz	類
ai	魏野	bs	志	da	條理
aj	李成棟	bt	化	db	黃書

dc	讀通鑑論	ds	公欲	ei	盡性
dd	客形	dt	公理	ej	權
de	大輪廻	du	寓	ek	衡
df	理勢之自然	dv	貞	el	夫子自道
dg	滅盡	dw	幾	em	劉茂華
dh	生滅	dx	誠	en	未始有
di	良能	dy	後天之性	eo	吉
dj	天地之性	dz	先天之性	ep	義
dk	天之性	ea	物	eq	天假其私以行其大
dl	氣質之性	eb	化		公
dm	誠明	ec	當	er	利
dn	氣之偏	ed	思問錄	es	必亡之勢
do	人之形質	ee	命	et	大公
dp	生之理	ef	尚書引義	eu	資治
dq	自然	eg	氣化		
dr	則	eh	當然之則		

CHUNG-YING CHENG *Reason, Substance, and Human*

Desires in Seventeenth-Century Neo-Confucianism

Two basic facts about Neo-Confucianism are generally recognized by
scholars of Chinese philosophy. First, Neo-Confucianism is founded on
the classical Confucian texts of Confucius, Mencius, and other Confucian writings, as Neo-Confucianists understand them; second, Neo-
Confucianism arose as a result of meeting the challenge of Chinese Buddhism which had been developing since the sixth century. How to make
a precise interpretation of these two facts constitutes a problem open to
further study. It can be asserted, however, in the light of these two facts,
that Neo-Confucianism has been influenced by Chinese Buddhism and
yet is essentially Confucian. The influence of Chinese Buddhism on
Confucianism, it might be suggested, comes in two forms: (1) by way of
stimulating interest in theoretical constructions and metaphysical speculation, and (2) by way of taking substantial hints from Buddhistic views.

In Chinese Buddhism there are two major tendencies which clearly affected Neo-Confucian philosophy. The first tendency is toward an irreconcilable dualism between existence and nonexistence or nothingness.
This dualism is reflected in various forms of contrast between law *(fa)* [a]
and fact *(shih)*, [b] form *(se)* [c] and void *(k'ung)*, [d] polluted *(jan)* [e] and pure
(ching), [f] in the Buddhist vocabulary. [1] The second tendency is toward an
idealistic interpretation of reality in terms of mind. This tendency is dominant in the school of Mere Ideation *(Wei-shih)* [g] and receives an implicit
reinforcement from the development of Ch'an. [h] The first tendency is
reflected in the dualistic thinking of Ch'eng I [i] and Chu Hsi, who represent reason or principle *(li)* [j] and indeterminate substance or ether *(ch'i)* [k]
as different forms of reality: *li* is the ultimate substance of all things, it is
well structured and preserved in a static equilibrium. It is, furthermore,
the standard for judging and regulating individual instances of existence.
It is identified finally with the authority of reason and indeed with an authority which can claim reason as its ground. Thus reason is a principle
of rationality which perceives the world in a fixed order. Indeterminate

substance, on the other hand, is treated as a principle of imperfection which gives rise to a variety of concrete things and causes change, mutation, and transformation of things. Indeterminate substance is not a principle of rationality, but one of dynamic creativity. This principle of dynamic creativity, however, being essentially a manifestation of the imperfect, was not taken seriously but was instead considered merely as the basis of life, not the ideal.

The disparity between reason and indeterminate substance is furthermore reinforced in a contrast between the morality of reason and the immorality of indeterminate substance in terms of desires. Reason as the principle of rationality preserves order in society as well as in an individual. But indeterminate substance as the principle of vital existence causes passivity, desire (yü),[1] disorder, and therefore a tendency toward evil. Reason is contrasted with needs and desires, and desires are explained on the basis of "indeterminate substance." In desire there is no reason. The ontological principle of indeterminate substance thus gives rise to the demoralizing principle of desires. As values, li are paradigms of good, for good is identified with order, equilibrium, stability, status quo, and rationality. On the other hand, ch'i is treated as the antipode of reason, lacking order, rationality, stability, universality, and equilibrium. Since moral badness is experienced as disorder, instability, particularity, and acts of corruption and destruction, it is naturally identified with indeterminate substance or a variation of it. Hence we see that the ontological incompatibility of reason and indeterminate substance is concomitant with the moral opposition between reason and desires. As the ontological incompatibility between reason and indeterminate substance is derived from a generalization concerning substantial existence and the possibility of change and transformation—the world of stability (nirvāna) and the world of fluidity (anitya)—the contrast between reason and indeterminate substance, and the derivative contrast between reason and desires, can be theoretically attributed to Buddhist influence.

The other tendency toward interpreting reality in terms of mind as exhibited in the Wei-shih (Mere Ideation, Yogācāra) school of Buddhism influences Neo-Confucianism in regard to the position Neo-Confucians generally accord to mind. Not everything in the Ch'eng-Chu [m] school is idealistic, but Ch'eng-Chu considers mind (hsin) [n] as fundamental and important. Thus the statement "mind unifies nature and sentiment" (*hsin t'ung hsing-ch'ing*),[o] expressed by the Ch'eng-Chu school, indicates a consciousness of mind as a dominating concept. There is little doubt that in the Lu-Wang [p] school mind plays a role fundamental to the existence of everything, for the significance of everything depends on mind. The ontological principle of reason is identified with mind in the statement *hsin-chi-li* [q] (mind is reason). I pointed out in an earlier paper that the concept of reason in the Neo-Confucianism of Lu and Wang exhibits the subjectivity of reason in mind whereas the concept of reason in the Neo-Confucianism of Ch'eng and Chu exhibits the opposition of a duality between reason and indeterminate substance.[2]

Given the influences of Buddhism on Neo-Confucianism, it is only fair to point out that Neo-Confucians in general are opposed to Buddhism and are explicitly critical of Buddhistic philosophy. Furthermore, they are theoretically committed to constructing Neo-Confucianism in defiance of Buddhistic ideology. Perhaps with the exception of only Wang Yang-ming, Sung-Ming [r] Neo-Confucians have shown little true understanding of Buddhism, particularly the Mahāyāna Buddhism as well cultivated by the great masters of the T'ang Dynasty. This fact is not incompatible with that of the influence of Buddhism on Neo-Confucianism and the fact that Neo-Confucianism is opposed to Buddhism. What is important to note is rather that Neo-Confucians, though professing a Confucian conviction, are not necessarily thoroughly Confucian in a classical sense. They could become more Confucian or more purely Confucian by ridding themselves of the Buddhist influences we have mentioned. There is no reason why this *might* not happen *when* in a more detached perspective their Buddhist elements could be seen more clearly. A true Confucian could therefore choose to reject these elements and restore Neo-Confucianism to a state of greater coherence and more strengthened structure.

Throughout the seventeenth century there was a widespread movement toward critique, reevaluation, and reformulation of Neo-Confucianism as presented by the Sung-Ming masters. Though there were many cultural and even political factors which occasioned this movement among Confucian scholars, the phenomenon can nevertheless be regarded as an internal dialectical development of Neo-Confucianism. By this I mean that the essentially Confucian mentality has arrived at a state of consistency and perfection and has therefore come to see the weakness of Neo-Confucianism under the conceptual influence of Buddhism. From this point of view we may regard the seventeenth-century Confucian critique of Neo-Confucianism as a deeper awakening of the Confucian consciousness, which is both a continuation of the great tradition of Neo-Confucianism and an improvement upon it. In fact, even when Neo-Confucianism was at its height, there was already a trend toward antidualistic Confucian thought—with a note of pragmatism to combat the dualistic, idealistic, and basically unpragmatic thinking of the orthodox. Thus we have Ch'en Liang[s] (1143–94) and Yeh Shih[t] (1150–1223) in Sung times, who criticized the unpragmatic speculation of the Ch'eng-Chu school. We also have Wang T'ing-hsiang[u] (1474–1544) and Huang Wan[v] (1480–1554) in Ming times who criticized Wang Yang-ming[w] with regard to his phenomenalistic-spiritualistic doctrines of chih-liang-chih[x] (fulfilling innate knowledge of goodness) and chih-hsing-ho-yi[y] (unity of knowledge and action).[3] Even in the mainstream of Sung Neo-Confucianism, Chang Tsai[z] had already proved an outstanding figure in developing a philosophy with implicit, if not explicit, undertones of pragmatism, naturalism, and monism, which to a great degree comprehend the spirit of classical Confucian metaphysics of the *Book of Changes*, as seen from the seventeenth-century point of view. All these thinkers can be regarded as predecessors of the enlightenment philosophers of Confucianism in the seventeenth century.

It is the purpose of this article to accentuate the critical and constructive thinking of seventeenth-century Confucian philosophers and to make clear our view that the seventeenth century is indeed a highly significant period, traditionally neglected in the study of the development of Confucianism as well as in the study of the development of Chinese philosophy as a whole. We shall particularly focus on the basic reason and indeterminate substance (*li-ch'i*) and the reason and desires (*li-yü*) relationships as focal points for criticism of Neo-Confucianism and for new interpretations of it in the classical spirit. We shall see that these two types of relationships represent cores of Confucian thinking—the metaphysical and moral dimensions of the Confucian system. Our discussion will therefore provide a new perspective for the synthesis of the metaphysical and ethical insights of Confucian thinking. Historically, we hope that this effort will illustrate the true nature of Confucianism in the seventeenth century and will shed light on the development of Confucian thinking in the eighteenth century, a major representative of which is Tai Chen.[aa][4]

We shall start with an examination of the "reason-substance" and "reason-desires" relationships in Wang Fu-Chih,[ab] as Wang was unquestionably the most outspoken, most productive, and most original thinker in the seventeenth century. We shall then discuss Yen Yüan,[ac] Li Kung,[ad] Huang Tsung-hsi,[ae] Ch'en Ch'ueh,[af] Li Erh-ch'ü (Li Yung),[ag] and Fang I-chih,[ah] whose interpretation of reason and indeterminate substance reflects the influence of Western physical science.

INDETERMINATE SUBSTANCE AND THE "REASON-SUBSTANCE" RELATIONSHIP IN WANG FU-CHIH(1619–92)

Even though most seventeenth-century philosophers inherit the Neo-Confucian vocabulary in philosophy, the meanings of many terms are then redefined in the context of new relationships among the terms. Thus the terms "reason," "indeterminate substance," and "desires" are old terms, yet they receive new meanings in the writings of Wang Fu-chih because new relationships developed between them. Let us now concentrate on the "reason-substance" relationship in Wang Fu-chih, which gives rise to a new cosmology and a new metaphysics.

Indeterminate substance is considered the most fundamental substance in reality by Wang Fu-chih. It is the prime material from which everything is composed. It is not identified with anything definite but is considered the source from which definite things (which we call *ch'i*, in the sense of utensils and things) are derived. Following Chang Tsai, Wang Fu-chih takes indeterminate substance as something pervading imperceptible space and capable of every kind of transformation. The basic principles of transformation of indeterminate substance are concentration (*chü*)[ai] and dispersion (*san*).[aj] Concentration is the process of coming into being and assuming a form, whereas dispersion is the process of the coming out of being and disintegrating of a form, or simply coming to assume no form. Thus, by concentration, indeterminate substance becomes being (*yu*), and by dispersion indeterminate substance becomes non-being (*wu*).[ak] Thus Wang says, in commenting on Chang Tsai: "The empty is the measure of indeterminate substance. Indeterminate substance pervades the infinite and does not manifest itself in form. Thus man sees only emptiness, but no indeterminate substance. All emptiness is indeterminate substance. By concentration it manifests itself. When it disperses, it is called non-existence or non-being." [5] It is through these two processes of change that species become abundant and things fall into order and classes. We shall explain later that indeterminate substance as such involves both the momentum of change and transformation as well as a tendency of necessity toward order, regularity, and reason.

Because indeterminate substance is basically formless, even though by concentration it gives rise to form, it can be identified with Chang Tsai's "ultimate void," [al] a term designating the indeterminate matrix of reality in Chang Tsai's natural philosophy. As the ultimate void always involves change and transformation, the movements of concentration and dispersion mentioned above are inherent in the very substance of indeterminate substance and thus form its dynamic potential in giving rise to a world of things. In other words, indeterminate substance as the foundation of things is the constant and incessant source of change because of its potentiality. In this sense it is not separated from a process of inherent change which manifests itself in all forms and is called by Wang Fu-chih *yin-yün*, [am] which describes its activity of change by way of concentration and dispersion. Wang says: "*Yin-yün* is the original state of undividedness of the original harmony." "*Yin-yün* is ultimate harmony. It coincides with indeterminate substance and the substance of *yin* and *yang* are all found in it." "The ultimate voidness is discerned in the original substance of *yin-yün*." [6] *Yin-yün* is called also *ch'i-hua*, [an] or transformation of indeterminate substance, by Wang Fu-chih.

The activity of change in indeterminate substance comprehends the process of interchange of *yin* [ao] and *yang* [ap] agencies as described by the *Book of Changes*. In the tradition of the *Book of Changes*, *yin* and *yang* form two phenomenological aspects in the total reality which are opposite to each other, yet are continuous with each other and complement each other. They are the two observable and yet a priori determinable aspects of things considered as a whole. The reality which makes this whole possible is called *tao*. [aq] The dynamic process which exhibits the interchange of rise and decline is *tao* in action. Thus *yin* and *yang* are in fact not separable from *tao*, just as the substance of reality and its function are not separable. These two aspects of *tao* can be said to be the foundation for concentration in being and dispersion in non-being, for movement and rest in the transformation of "indeterminate substance." It is the very essence of change that continually and eventually gives rise to everything. Wang says:

Yin and *yang* are possessed in the ultimate void of the *yin-yün*. The interchange of *yin* and *yang* and the alternation between motion and rest in *yin-yün* generate a mutual grinding and stirring between the two and manifest their function and capacities at the right time. The fusion and flow of the five elements and ten thousand things, the formation of life in sky and water and on earth, displays a pattern of order and is not at random. Thus things have the way of things, spirits and ghosts have the way of spirits and ghosts. We can clearly know about this as a principle. In this fashion we call the process of *yin* and *yang* the Way. [7]

The activity of change is for Wang Fu-chih a process of creativity, for it gives rise to every thing and every life. Therefore it is a movement of generation and production. It is significant that Wang stresses the notion of creative production (*sheng-sheng*) [ar] and its product (*sheng*) in explaining the cosmological and ontological nature of indeterminate substance, for he considers life production, or life generation, as the manifest function of transformation of indeterminate substance. The *yin-yang* interchange and their complementarity as well as their polarization are to be considered a totality of life. One may even suggest that, for Wang, the creative production of life is the very end of the transformation of "indeterminate substance."

That change is given the purpose of the production of life is likened to the fact that every man has a nature. Thus Wang says:

That which makes it comprehend things is its nature; that which generates things is its function. What is light surfaces up, what is deep sinks down; what is close to the above lifts up, what is close to the below falls down. What moves and tends to continue is movement; what moves and tends to stop is rest. All are indeterminate substance due to the combination and mixture of *yin* and *yang*. [All have] the beginnings of necessary change in being and form a natural state of things. This is like the case of man having a nature [by the transformation of indeterminate substance]. [8]

The creative activity of indeterminate substance is continuous as well as purposive. It is purposive in that it preserves and continues life by making the creative activity of life the constant activity of reality. In a sense even death is a natural process of change which makes new life possible. Wang says: "The dispersion of life entails death; the reconcentration of indeterminate substance after death entails life. It is clear that the principle of change involved is consistent." [9]

It is on this ground that Wang is opposed to the Buddhist doctrine of generation and annihilation, according to which annihilation means no return to life and total annihilation means complete cessation of life (nir-vāna without residue). Wang insists that it is far better to describe reality as coming and going, expansion and contraction, concentration and dispersion, lightening and darkening, rather than as generation and annihilation. Wang suggests that by realizing the transformation of indeterminate substance and understanding the nature of ultimate voidness man can be made to fulfill his nature in a perennial sense and not be bothered by the phenomenon of death in particularity.[10] He says: "What pervades Heaven-and-earth and flows between them is the process of life generation. Thus it is said: 'The great virtue of Heaven-and-earth is life generation.' From the void to the real is the process of coming, from the real to the void is the process of going. . . . The yang takes life generation as its indeterminate substance and yin takes life generation as its form." [11]

The importance of life generation (sheng) [as] lies in the fact that the process of change is not merely a circular interchange of yin and yang in repetition, but one of interchange without repetition. It is a creative process of realizing the infinitely rich potentiality of the Way or reality of indeterminate substance. For, in the first place, the Way is infinitely rich. One can say that the interchange of yin and yang is a process of realizing the potentiality of life inherent in the Way. In the second place, the very process of interchange between yin and yang is a creative one in that it always brings novel things into being.

These views may not be original with Wang, as they can easily be derived from the Book of Changes and Chang Tsai. But Wang is original on a more perspicacious point: namely, the process of change is directed toward a display of a complete variety of things. In other words, the process of change is capable of evolving into a state of the full realization of all things in differentiation. He says: "The Way is born from being and will become complete when a great variety of things is present." [12] In fact he even suggests that the nature of things is daily generation and daily completion (jih-sheng jih-ch'eng): [at] [13] He also says that he knows that the

Way is rich because it generates new things every day.[14] There is a passage in his commentary on Chang Tsai (*T'ai-ho* [au] chapter) where he describes how the harmonious indeterminate substance, combined with the refined five agencies, forms man's nature and thus explains the nature of man. Even man's nature is not permanently fixed. For the nature of man can give rise to new perceptions and new feelings under new circumstances. This nature which we know through mind comprehends mind in unity, for mind itself should emerge from nature.[15]

Finally, indeterminate substance as the ultimate reality is, according to Wang, progress in a state of balance and harmony. To designate this characteristic, he adopts the term "ultimate harmony" (*t'ai-ho*), again from Chang Tsai. This ultimate harmony resides in the potentiality of indeterminate substance for realizing and maintaining an infinite order of forms in reality. It is in fact the hierarchy of forms in its potential state. It is only by considering indeterminate substance as an ultimate harmony that indeterminate substance can be identified with *tao* and the great ultimate (*t'ai-chi*).[av] Wang says:

T'ai-ho is ultimate harmony. *Tao* is the comprehensive reason of Heaven, earth, man, and things. It is what is called the great ultimate *t'ai-chi*. *Yin-yang* are different, but when interacting in the great voidness, they do not violate each other but instead mutually complement each other. This is the ultimate harmony. Before there are any concrete things, there is no lack of harmony. After there are concrete things, the original harmony is not lacking. Thus it is called the ultimate harmony.[16]

By identifying indeterminate substance as both the ultimate harmony (*t'ai-ho*) and the ultimate void (*t'ai-hsü*), Wang has achieved a monistic interpretation of reality. For, according to Wang, in the ultimate harmony there are all the possibilities of change and transformation and thus the ultimate harmony becomes the source of creation just as the ultimate void is. Similarly, in the ultimate voidness there is the infinite potentiality for relation and actualization of concrete things in proper order and thus the ultimate voidness becomes the basis of organization just as the ultimate harmony is. The ultimate voidness represents the creative agency of indeterminate substance, whereas the ultimate harmony represents its organizational agency. Thus, Wang says, "Within the ultimate harmony, there is indeterminate substance and there is spirit or the ordering power (*shen*).[aw] The spirit is nothing other than the reason and principles (*li*) of the two indeterminate substances—*yin* and *yang*—in mixture and penetration." [17]

Following Chang Tsai, Wang takes indeterminate substance as something which can be represented in concrete phenomena (*hsiang*),[ax] and spirit (*shen*) as something inherent in phenomena. This is not to say that spirit is over and above phenomena; it simply means that it is the total potentiality for order and organization which cannot be captured in single phenomena.

To summarize, indeterminate substance is the total reality. It is the reality of change between *yin* and *yang*. It is, furthermore, the creative process of life, full of novelty. It is infinite and indeterminate in its potentiality and yet contains all possibilities of formation, transformation, and organization. The most important thing to bear in mind is that indeterminate substance is both a creative agent and an ordering and organizing agent. One may therefore say that indeterminate substance contains order and organizational principles, but this can only mean that it is the potential order and harmony of things, for it is equally creative and dynamic. The dynamic and creative agency of indeterminate substance is one of ordering and concretization. The order, harmony, and organization of relations are dispositions in indeterminate substance and form what indeterminate substance is. They cannot be considered apart from a context of change and transformation.

At this point we may bring in the consideration of reason, order, and principles in Wang's metaphysical philosophy. We shall see that, for Wang as a critic of Sung-Ming Neo-Confucianism, the ultimate proposition in metaphysics is not "nature (*hsing*) [ay] is reason (*li*)," as with Ch'eng-Chu, or the proposition "nature is mind (*hsin*)," as with Wang Yang-ming, but rather the more fundamental proposition that "indeterminate substance is reason and reason is indeterminate substance." We shall explain this in the following paragraphs and, on the basis of the explanation, pave the way for an understanding and appreciation of Wang's antidualistic, naturalistic metaphysics and its significance as a foundation for his antidualistic, naturalistic ethics which incorporates the unity of reason and desires.

For Wang Fu-chih, indeterminate substance is fundamental and reason is derivative in the following senses:

(1) In the potential sense, generalized reason is nothing but ways in

which *yin* and *yang* interact, preserve harmony, and actualize the world. It can be said that before the world is actualized, there is the potential harmony of the activities of *yin* and *yang*. So in a potential and general sense reason is to be understood as the internal harmony-preserving activities of indeterminate substance. This should be clear from our earlier account of indeterminate substance as ultimate harmony. In other words, reason is the tendency toward actualization of the world and the ordering of things and presentation of life.

(2) Reason as the inner tendency toward order and harmony has to be brought out as the creative activity of indeterminate substance. In this regard, reason depends upon indeterminate substance for its realization. In fact, without a process of realization we cannot speak of reason in an actual sense—it is merely a state or mode or quality of indeterminate substance. When indeterminate substance moves and develops, reason as a mode becomes actuality, for reason is merely a mode of actualization or realization of indeterminate substance. Hence it can be considered the patterning of order and organization as revealed in the activity of indeterminate substance.

Different activities of indeterminate substance give rise to different reasons. Different degrees of intensity of activity of reason give rise to different degrees of actualization of indeterminate substance in a world of related events. Thus Wang says: "Indeterminate substance is that which reason leans upon. If indeterminate substance flourishes, then reason reaches its end. The Heaven has assembled the strong indeterminate substance; therefore it exhibits the patterning of order in things, and the changes are subtle and ever new." [18] Here the so-called Heaven (*t'ien*) [az] is the actual movement of indeterminate substance as seen in everything. The strong indeterminate substance is at its height of activity. Reason in this context clearly has no independence but is a matter of the inner manifestation of indeterminate substance. It can be said that reason is the functioning of indeterminate substance. "That which makes reason to materialize, on considering their sources, are all fine transformations of subtleties of Heaven-and-earth. The subtleties of Heaven-and-earth in their movement and interaction do not lose their function of original goodness." [19] The so-called subtleties of Heaven-and-earth are nothing other than indeterminate substance in the process of self-transformation. The ontological state of reason is undifferentiated from that of indeterminate substance. When reason and indeterminate substance are in this undifferentiated state of being, Wang speaks of the latter as the great ultimate (*t'ai-chi*), representing it as a perfect circle and referring to it as reason-substance (*li-ch'i*).[ba] He says, "Even though the great ultimate is void, reason-substance is full. There is no difference between inner and outer, void and fullness. . . . This reason-substance will become square when meeting square; become circle when meeting circle. It is either large or small. It changes and transforms and self-interacts and has no fixed substance." [20] From this view reason apparently is indeterminate substance and indeterminate substance is reason. The different aspects of this totality of reality give rise to what we have analytically termed reason and indeterminate substance. Wang says: "Throughout Heaven-and-earth there is the interacting change and transformation of reality. It is all my *original* face. Its incipient state (*ch'i*) is indeterminate substance. Its ability of realization (*shen*, spirit) is reason." [21] He sometimes refers to this totality of reality as *heaven* (*t'ien*). It is the same as the ultimate harmony and the ultimate void in Chang Tsai, and the indeterminate substance in the primary sense. That reason is derived from this ultimate harmony and ultimate void of indeterminate substance is explicitly held by Wang. "The original color of Heaven is unity and wholeness. Colorless, quantityless, objectless, numberless, it is purity. Void, one, and spacious, it is that wherefrom reason comes." [22] The dynamic identity of reason and indeterminate substance is similar to the dynamic identity of *yin* and *yang* in indeterminate substance.

(3) We have indicated that reason is ontologically undifferentiated from indeterminate substance and yet cosmologically it is a mode of actuality of indeterminate substance which consists in being the tendency of indeterminate-substance-activities toward order and organization. Now we shall advance to that aspect of reason in terms of the explicit order and organization which indeterminate-substance-activities achieve and the resulting world which displays order and organization. Wang asserts that "reason is the order conspicuously exhibited by Heaven." [23] He says again that

Reason is not something which cannot change and cannot be seen. The pattern and order of indeterminate substance are what can be seen in reason. Therefore in the beginning there is reason, and this means that one can see reason in indeterminate substance. As reason obtains, it forms a natural tendency [in indeterminate substance] and one can see reason in the necessity of the natural tendency [in indeterminate substance].[24]

When reason is actually presented in indeterminate substance, it is to be conceived in concrete terms. It is the tendency toward order and organization and also the very order and organization displayed in things. The concrete patterns and orders of concrete things are based on the general types of order and organization of reality. Although Wang did not give much attention to the general types of order and organization of things, he nevertheless indicated that the general types of order and organization are principles of change in terms of similarity, difference, contraction, expansion, and so forth. His general view is that, as indeterminate substance has different degrees of actualization and types of activity, the realization of reason also correlates with indeterminate-substance-activities on different levels and in different degrees. As indeterminate substance will reach a full realization of nature, so reason as an inherent aspect of indeterminate substance will reach a full realization of order and organization on different levels and in different forms.

Now if we concentrate on the relation between the Way (*tao*) and utensils or things (*ch'i*) in Wang's discussion, we shall be able to see a close relation between the generalized reason in general indeterminate-substance-activity and the particularized reason in indeterminate-substance-activity. The actualized world of indeterminate substance is the world of utensils (*ch'i*).[bb] Utensils or things (*ch'i*) have been used in contrast to *tao* in Sung interpretations of the *Book of Changes*. But in Wang's use, *tao* and indeterminate substance are related in the following ways. *Tao*, according to him, is the *tao* of indeterminate substance, but the indeterminate substance is not that of *tao*.[25] This position stresses the fundamental importance of indeterminate substance, not *tao*. *Tao* is merely the tendency toward order and stability in indeterminate substance and indeterminate substance in its primordial sense is the basis of *tao*. Thus he asks, "If we have the indeterminate substance, should we worry about *tao*?" Then he asserts that "if there is no indeterminate substance, there will be no *tao*." [26] The implications are not merely that, if there is such a *tao*, there is such an indeterminate substance, but also that, given any indeterminate substance, its *tao* will ensue as a consequence. He holds that there is no case in which you have arrow and bow but do not have archery, or where you have carriage and horse but not charioteering, or where there is son but no *tao* of father, or where there is younger brother but no *tao* of the elder brother. It is possible that some *tao* might have the possibility of existing, and yet not actually exist, simply because there is no corresponding indeterminate substance. To say that *tao* may possibly exist means simply that the potentiality of achieving reason is always inherent in indeterminate-substance-activity.

By making *tao* dependent on indeterminate substance, Wang has shown that reason (whose total presentation is *tao*) is dependent on indeterminate substance, and must realize itself in concrete objects (*ch'i*). Reason will not be reason in the actual sense until it has full concretization in the world of objects. One may say that utensils or things are the result of indeterminate-substance-activity with its tendency toward order and organization. Thus Wang concludes that the Way of the superior man is to fulfill the potentialities of indeterminate substance. He speaks of this to urge people to develop indeterminate substance in order to develop *tao* or to fulfill the potentiality of indeterminate substance (ether, indeterminate reality) in order to understand reason. Reason is a post-indeterminate substance production and cannot be grasped in the absence of, or before the understanding of, concrete things.[27] In other words, Wang holds that one cannot understand reason apart from indeterminate substance, or *tao* apart from utensils.

(4) A final important aspect of the *li-ch'i* relationship is related to the nature and mind of man. The formation of the mind of man results from the highest degree of activity of indeterminate substance. It is the realization of the subtle potentiality of the ultimate reality. The existence of man therefore exhibits the most valuable potential of reality and yet is related to everything else in the process of change and transformation. This is a Confucian position which all Confucian philosophers, including Neo-Confucians of the Sung and Ming, hold in common. For Wang, what is significant is that the nature and mind which distinguish man as man are not alienated from the primordial reality of indeterminate substance. Neither nature nor mind possesses independent reality over and above indeterminate substance. On this basis Wang is skeptical about Ch'eng I's claim that "mind, nature, and Heaven are just one reason." [28] This latter statement, in the light of the centrality of reason in the Ch'eng-Chu philosophy, has been understood as indicating the fundamental nature of reason. But for Wang, the mind and nature of man

share with Heaven and reason the fundamental basis of indeterminate substance, for they are regarded as deriving from indeterminate substance. He says, "To speak of mind, nature, Heaven, and reason, we must speak of them on the basis of indeterminate substance. If there is no indeterminate substance, there is none of them." [29]

Furthermore, the human mind is considered an embodiment of reason, since mind is made possible by the transformation of indeterminate substance. Wang even seems to define reason as that which is realized in human mind, just as that which is realized in Heaven is defined as phenomena (*hsiang*), and that which is realized in things is defined as numbers (*shu*) [bc] and patterns. [30] On this basis, reason is the recognition of the patterns and orders of things by mind. This is further evidenced by the statement:

The ten thousand things all have fixed functions and ten thousand affairs all have natural regularities. The so-called reasons are the reasons of these natural regularities. They are what man can necessarily know and can necessarily practice. There are no other reasons which man cannot know and cannot practice. Possessing this reason, man's knowledge is not obscured and man's action will not be dubious. This is the so-called mind. Reason is the substance of human mind, and mind is where reason is deposited and stored. [31]

In the light of this, reason can now be considered a conscious understanding of the order and regularities of nature and mind. It is a matter of knowledge and a principle of reality. In fact, it is in regard to mind that reason can now be identified with reason in the proper sense. Reason thus receives a subjective specification apart from its objective characterization in terms of order. On this level, Wang would agree with Wang Yang-ming in saying that mind is reason. But he would not take the word "is" (*chi*) [bd] to imply identity since mind is reason but many other things are reason as well. He would further qualify this by saying that many other things are reason because reason is fundamentally indeterminate substance, namely the activity or the result of the activity of indeterminate substance. For Wang explicitly holds that "what the human mind obtains before experience, from the sage to the common people, are the good capacities [of mind] due to the activity of indeterminate substance." [32]

With regard to the view that nature is reason, Wang also seems not to disagree, so long as it is understood that the nature of man and other things reveals an order which man can understand and yet is not the exclusive area where reason is to be found or the exclusive level on which reason is to be identified. At the same time reason is again understood as derived from indeterminate substance. The fallacy of "mind is reason," or "nature is reason," is twofold from this point of view: (1) reason is identified with a narrow area identified with mind or nature; (2) the fundamental nature of reason is taken for granted. Given the interpretation of reason and mind and nature in terms of indeterminate substance, Wang can accept the proposition that "mind is reason" and the proposition that "nature is reason" without committing the fallacy which Wang Yang-ming and Ch'eng-Chu, respectively, committed.

Apart from the fact that reason and nature are commonly derived from indeterminate substance, reason and nature are related furthermore as specified by the proposition that nature is the reason of living and of life-activity (*sheng*). Nature is what is endowed in a man. But it is also the order of living proper to a living individual. It defines the concrete process of living and its characteristics. Now to say that nature is the reason of living is to say that: (1) reason is derived from nature just as the pattern of order of a concrete object is derived from the object; (2) reason is recognized by mind and mind is derived from nature. Wang says: "Reason is generated from nature, and desires develop from material forms." [33] "Nature generates knowledgeability and knowledgeability knows nature and converges in the center of the void, and is unified in the oneness of mind. From this we have nature as mind." [34] "What is natural in the reason of Heaven, being the comprehensive capacity of the indeterminate substance of the ultimate harmony, is nature, fixed in man and enfolded in form. The function of form which gives rise to knowing capacity is mind." [35] Thus we can use mind to exhaust nature and use nature to correlate with *tao* and use *tao* to sense Heaven.

Finally, we note that nature for Wang is continually in the process of growth and generation. It is not something which is absolutely determined, but involves the possibility of change and transformation. This is so because nature is made from indeterminate substance with its inner dynamics of change. Wang says: "Nature is the reason of living. Before death an individual is always living, there is always time for the individual to obey necessity and receive nature. When first born, the individual realizes a quantity of nature, and daily he receives the reality of nature." [36] "Nature is the reason of living. It grows every day and accomplishes every day." [37] In the light of this dynamic growth of nature, reason can also be said to grow and change. The unchangeability of reason in Sung-Ming Neo-Confucianism is thus rejected. Again the explanation is readily apparent: reason is ultimately an aspect of indeterminate substance and indeterminate substance has change in its nature.

REASON-DESIRES RELATIONSHIP AS BASED ON REASON-SUBSTANCE RELATIONSHIP IN WANG FU-CHIH

As reason and indeterminate substance are opposed to each other in Sung-Ming Neo-Confucianism, reason and desires are naturally opposed to each other. Or, to put it differently, the dualism between reason and desires was asserted first, and then an ontological dualism between reason and indeterminate substance was developed to provide a basis for the separation between reason and desires. Now as Wang Fu-chih has developed a doctrine of cosmological and ontological unity between reason and indeterminate substance, it is natural to expect that the relationship between reason and desires in his moral philosophy would be one of unity and complementarity as well. In fact, I believe that it is by recognizing the fundamental unity between reason and indeterminate substance in metaphysics that one can have a correct understanding of the reason-desires relationship in the philosophy under discussion. In the light of the above, it is clear that reason, when applied to man, should have at least two senses: (1) Reason is the order and pattern naturally realized in the nature of man. It is the natural reason of man. (2) Reason should be the recognition and understanding of order and organization of things in the objective world. Both these senses are found in Wang. The reference to the generalization of nature and mind and the knowing capacity in mind amply testifies to these points.

There are two more senses in which reason can be applied to the existence of man. They are directly related to the ontology of indeterminate substance and bear as well on the existence of desires. They are not made explicit by Wang, but they are important for explaining why there are desires and why desires should be conceived in unity with reason. (1) Reason in the nature of man is essentially a manifestation of indeterminate substance in activity—it is the most refined indeterminate substance. In this sense reason is an active principle similar to desire, as desire is no less a creation of indeterminate substance. Reason and desire are therefore mutually transformable on the level of the activity of indeterminate substance in metaphysics. (2) Reason is the general potential which is directed toward the perfection of nature. It is a principle which should relate one individual to others and to the total reality for the full development of the individual. In this sense reason can be understood as a result of the creation of conditions for such attainment of perfection. It is in fact the practice of virtue which will satisfy the individual.

Now we can say that the above four senses of reason as applied to man correspond to the four metaphysical senses of reason mentioned in the last section. In understanding reason in these four senses, we can then clearly see that reason is in no way opposed to desire, when desire is properly understood, but instead can be understood as the embodiment of desire just as desire in a proper sense can be understood as an embodiment of reason.

Let us therefore concentrate on Wang's understanding of desire. In the first place, Wang considers desire as a natural part of life. Insofar as desire is natural it forms a pattern and an order and constitutes the existence of reason. In fact by the concretizing function of utensils (ch'i), the existence of desire should already be a display of reason. Desires such as those for food and sex are nothing undesirable in themselves. They are matters of the natural realization of life. One cannot talk of reason apart from desires. For given any reason, it must be embodied in the actual actions of life. As desire is the activity of life, desire must be presupposed for the very understanding of reason. Hence, Wang holds that "reason and desire are both natural." [38] "Reason and desire mutually transform each other. If there is desire, there must be reason. Reason and desire go together even though they are different in quality. But reason is endowed in desire." [39]

The question here is how reason and desire go together and mutually transform each other and yet can differ in quality. One answer is very simple. For Wang, reason in all senses can be desire, but desire can be reason only in the first and the third senses of reason. For desire is itself a natural manifestation of life but not a reflection of mind on life as reason can be considered. As such, desire differs from the reason of mind or the knowing capacity. But desire can also be different from reason in another sense—reason can be formed as a desire tending toward the realization of an individual in the whole reality, while desire is simply desire without such a tendency. In other words, reason is desire universalized or universalizable in regard to all men, but desire is more or less localized in a person without universalization.

In insisting that for every desire there is one reason, Wang does not ignore the phenomenological difference between reason and desire. His stress on the identity of desire and reason is to be understood in the fundamental sense of metaphysics as well as in the sense that reason and desire can be made to realize each other. What is significant about him is that he believes that such mutual realization is not only possible but necessary for life. He says that "the sage has desires, which are the reason of Heaven. Heaven has no desires. Its reason is the desires of man. A learning man has both reason and desires. To exhaust reason, one will conform to the desires of man. To extend desires, one will conform to the reason of Heaven." [40] This passage clearly indicates that the reason of ontology is precisely the natural desires of anthropology, and that thorough understanding of reason will lead to affirmation of the importance of desires.

This last point can be developed further, for it indicates how desires and reason can be mutually transformed. They are mutually transformable because to universalize desires would be to achieve reason and to seek reason to the utmost will lead to the affirming of desires. There is, therefore, an implicit criticism of Sung-Ming Neo-Confucianism. Sung-Ming Neo-Confucianism has advanced the opposition between reason and desires simply because it does not see reason in totality and does not face desire in actuality. In Wang's view, however, the only way to realize the reason of the whole world is to fulfill the desires of each individual. This is not to say that desires should be fulfilled as such; they should rather be fulfilled in the total network of desire—fulfillment in others and in everyone. This is the way to achieve political order, social harmony, familial stability, and individual well-being. Thus, Wang says:

On this basis, we see that man's desires respectively obtain fulfillment, and this is the great unity of Heaven's reason. The great unity of Heaven's reason is not different from the individual desires being respectively fulfilled. To govern people there is a Way, and this is the Way. To obey the superior there is a Way, and this is the Way. To deal with a friend there is a Way, and this is the Way. To be filially pious to parents there is a Way, and this is the Way. To realize one's person there is a Way, and this is the Way.[41]

It is on this basis that Wang argues for the unity of principle, or the Way in Confucius. The unity in other words is achieved by universalizing desires and thus by transforming desire into reason and vice versa in reality.

It is puzzling that, while denouncing the Buddhists for abandoning worldly duty and destroying life, the Sung-Ming Neo-Confucianists themselves should look down on the desires of life. Perhaps what they denounced are selfish desires or desires which are not or cannot be universalized. But in denouncing these desires because of their background of indeterminate substance, they tend to denounce all desires. Wang does not denounce them because he sees them as a manifestation of nature and their satisfaction as a perfection of nature. The very ordering of life in terms of rites (li)[be] depends on the realization and fulfillment of desires; thus he says:

Even though rites are purely patterns of order in heavenly reason, they must be embodied in human desires in order to be seen. Even though we remain at rest and do not have a regularity of feeling or commitment, we have to manifest the function of life through desires on occasions of change. Then, there cannot be Heaven apart from man and cannot be reason apart from desires.[42]

Desire embodies reason just as indeterminate substance embodies *tao*. The metaphysical principle that we have to create things in order to fulfill *tao* may even be extended to the case of desires: we have to create desire in order to fulfill reason. We can also say that reason is the reason of desires, and desire is not the desire of reason, as Wang has said that *tao* is the *tao* of indeterminate substance, but that indeterminate substance is not the indeterminate substance of *tao*. Desire is the subject, reason is a characteristic of the subject. There could be no characteristic of a subject in separation from the subject. Wang thinks that Buddhism is mistaken simply because it believes that there is such a subjectless characteristic called reason. This criticism applies to some Neo-Confucians as well.

To say that reason is not separable from desire is not to imply that every kind of desire has a reason which is conducive to the good of life. In discussing the reason-desire relationship in Wang, it is important to understand that the ultimate reason of life (which is nature) is that man should search for a full development of the potential in other men, which constitutes a basis for and a justification of one's own development of the potential in the self. Thus the universalization principle is the basis for fulfilling one's desires, as well as a principle for fulfilling one's reason.

We may now suggest a distinction between desirable desires and undesirable desires. The desirable desires are those which we naturally experience, and which apply to every man, whereas the undesirable desires are those which we do not naturally have, but are instead caused by external circumstances, and which therefore do not apply to every situation or person. Wang has implicitly made this distinction. In his doctrine of "Where there is a desire, there is reason," he holds as a theoretical consequence from his metaphysics of reason-substance that any desire has its reason. But he would not hold that therefore any desire should be fulfilled in the name of its reason. Rather he would hold that if there is a desire which has its reason and which can be universalized it should be fulfilled. We have suggested that the universalizable desires are those which every man can naturally experience. "Thus in [desires of] sound, color, smell, and taste, one will openly see the common desires of ten thousand things and see them in the reason of ten thousand things." [43] In other parts of his commentaries on the Four Books, Wang always stresses this point, namely, that to fulfill natural desires is to reach the public reason of Heaven and that there is no incompatibility between private natural desires and the public reason.[44] He also says: "Availing my heart of self-love, I can reach the reason of loving others. For I and others share the same feelings and thus share the same *tao*. The universality of human desires is the ultimate righteousness of the reason of Heaven." [45]

We may summarize our discussion of the reason-desire relationship in Wang Fu-chih in the following theses:

1. In every desire there is a reason.
2. In the universalizable desire there is the heavenly reason of life.
3. To denounce desire is ultimately to denounce life (*sheng*).
4. To fulfill a reason, one has to fulfill the corresponding desire.
5. A well-cultivated man should be able to see desire everywhere in life and see reason everywhere in life.

We have already discussed and made clear (1), (2), and (4). We should say something about (3) and (5) as final characteristics of the reason-desire relationship in Wang. As already noted, Wang is opposed to the Buddhist doctrine of the extinction of life, since life for him is nothing but the movement of the world (*t'ien-hsia-chih-tung*)[bf] which, in the human case, constitutes the reality of desire. He says that "desires develop because there are forms."[46] But forms must exist and the inherent goal of the activity of indeterminate substance is to fulfill forms, preserve them, and develop them. Thus desire has great significance in actually exhibiting the forms of life, not just in reflecting life [as in mind]. Desire is thus the foundation of the reality of man. To denounce desires is to denounce the living reality of man and to lapse into the view of the Buddhists and Taoists. Wang says: "Thus to look down upon the forms [of life] is to look down upon the natural feelings (*ch'ing*)[bg] [of life]. To do so is to look down upon life. . . . To part from life must involve saying that emptiness is real, and life is illusory, thus promoting the doctrines of the Buddhists and Taoists."[47]

Finally, the nature of man is realized in his activities of mind, which constitute reason in a certain sense, as well as in the natural activity of needs and desires. There is a unity between desire and reason as there is an ontological unity in the nature (*hsing*). The unity may be understood as one in which desire is consciously identified with reason in experience as well as in knowledge. One needs cultivation to do this, for it is a metaphysical fact which requires comprehension and concentration of mind. Wang believes that by understanding reality as such, one will be able to come to see desire as reason and reason as desire everywhere in life. He holds that this is true of Confucius and Mencius. He says, "Mencius inherits his teaching from Confucius. He sees desire everywhere in life and this is to see reason everywhere in life."[48] The point of this passage, we may nevertheless note, is that we must be creative in making reason an achievement of desire and desire an achievement of reason, both ontologically acceptable and justifiable in the activity of the indeterminate substance of life.

REASON-SUBSTANCE AND REASON-DESIRE
RELATIONSHIPS IN YEN YÜAN(1635–1704)
AND LI KUNG (1659–1733)

Wang Fu-chih's philosophy constitutes a stronghold of seventeenth-century antidualistic naturalism in both Confucian metaphysics and Confucian morality. It forms the basis both for a critique of Sung-Ming Neo-Confucianism and a foundation for a reconstruction of Confucian doctrines. This tendency is reinforced by Yen Yüan and is powerfully expressed in the eighteenth-century writings of philosophers such as Tai Chen and Chiao Hsün. To make clear the major trends of thought in seventeenth-century Confucianism, we shall take Wang as a model in that he provides a paradigm of reason-substance and reason-desire relationships which is later developed or reasserted, but not essentially modified. Our detailed statement and analysis of his position on reason-substance and reason-desire is made in the light of this general reflection of seventeenth-century Confucian rethinking.

In general, Yen Yüan subscribes to the same antidualistic naturalism in moral and metaphysical philosophy as Wang Fu-chih. On the one hand, he is not as metaphysically inclined as Wang Fu-chih or as interested in formulating a metaphysics of reason-substance and reason-desire with such refined sophistication. But on the other hand he is more explicitly critical of Sung-Ming Neo-Confucianism and Buddhism than Wang. Furthermore, he is distinguished by his great stress on pragmatic action and the living practice of Confucian arts as a way of cultivating the Confucian life. We shall see that this pragmatic element provides a more realistic and clearer basis for achieving the unity of reason and desire in life than we find in other seventeenth-century philosophers, including Wang Fu-chih.

We shall first focus on the reason-substance relationship in Yen Yüan. Yen is opposed to Sung-Ming Neo-Confucianism, for he regards it as a pseudo and artificial conformity to Confucianist form, without Confucian substance. He regards both the Ch'eng-Chu and Lu-Wang schools as deviating from the authentic practice of Confucianism in the pre-Ch'in period, and as a faint mirroring of Buddhistic quietism and Ch'an artificiality. For according to him, the Sung-Ming Neo-Confucianists share with the Taoists and the Buddhists the same belief that the natural endowments of man (*ch'i-pin*) [bh] are evil and that non-being is better than being. He fears that the prevalence of this belief will lead people down blind alleys and destroy the true life and true character of man. Because of this fear, he wrote essays entitled "Preserving Learning" and "Preserving Nature." The former is intended to explain that *tao* consists neither in empty speculation nor in pedantic accumulation of scholarship, but in the actual exercise of virtue and the practice of arts and rites useful for life. The latter is intended to clarify the position that reason and indeterminate substance are both the way of Heaven, nature and form are both mandates of Heaven, and that the nature and destiny of man, though differing in different temperaments, are both good. "Temperaments and natural endowments are functions of the nature and destiny of man and cannot be called evil." [49] From this angle, it is clear that the primary aim in Yen's thought on reason-substance relationship is that he wants to justify the goodness of the natural endowments (*ch'i-chih*) [bi] of man so that man can develop them to their fullest in action.

Though Yen considers reason and substance to be equal to the way of Heaven (*t'ien-tao*),[bj] he holds indeterminate substance to be more fundamental than reason. Like Wang Fu-chih, he accepts a cosmology of indeterminate substance and on this basis explains all kinds of things and changes in the world in terms of the activity of indeterminate substance. He speaks of indeterminate substance as "the true indeterminate substance of the cosmos (*yü-chou chen-ch'i*)" [bk] and as "the living indeterminate substance of the cosmos (*yü-chou sheng-ch'i*)." [bl] [50] Indeterminate substance is not separate from life-activity, for the very characteristic of indeterminate substance is that it is the basis for life generation. Though it is not so clear as in Wang that indeterminate substance has the life-generating creativity, overall Yen takes the phenomenon of life-generating life (*sheng-sheng*) as a basic reality and one in which indeterminate substance is involved. He says:

Heaven and earth interact and interchange and generate the ten thousand things. The number of classes of living things in sky and land and water are beyond counting. The subtlety of the combination of forms is infinite. All are natural manifestations of the heavenly reason. All that gives life is called male. All that accomplishes [life] is called female. Male and female conjoin and coalesce and there is incessant life generation. Life generation [depends] on indeterminate substance which is the indeterminate substance of Heaven, and on form which is the form of earth. In life generation the indeterminate substance of Heaven is assimilated and the form of earth absorbed. Heaven and earth are therefore the great parents of the myriad things. Parents are those who transmit the change and transformation of Heaven and earth. Man is the only existing thing which receives the complete ingredients of Heaven and earth, and thus is the most refined among the myriad things.[51]

In this passage, what is clear is that Yen has identified indeterminate substance and form (*hsing*) [bm] with Heaven and earth. Thus, as Heaven and earth are parents of all things, indeterminate substance and form should be considered the originators of all things.

Given indeterminate substance as the fundamental basis of all things, reason has no independent ontological nature apart from being the pattern of order in things generated by indeterminate substance. In his *Commentary on the Four Books (Ssu-shu cheng-wu)* [bn] he explicitly points out that "reason is the pattern of organization in wood and in wood there are originally patterns of organization." [52] Conceived in this fashion, reason is not separate from indeterminate substance and is only to be realized in objects produced by indeterminate substance. They are characteristics, such as the length or shortness of objects. In particular, the reason of man is precisely what is revealed in the organization of man as a natural product of Heaven-and-earth. Thus he says, "The true reason of the human mind is the life-generating reason of the human mind." [53] Furthermore, the reason of man is the natural disposition of man which he calls the nature *(hsing)* of man, and which is developed from indeterminate substance and the powers of Heaven-and-earth. He says, "The two indeterminate substances [*yin* and *yang*] and four powers [metal, wood, water, earth] are man not yet coalesced." [54] Since the reason of man is nature and nature is made of primordial, indeterminate substance, human nature can give rise to feelings which are the basis of the virtues.

At this point we may mention Yen's criticism of an inconsistency in Ch'eng-Chu thinking. To show this inconsistency he quotes Ch'eng I's statements that "in talking of nature *(li)* and indeterminate substance, to make two of them is not right," and that "some are good from childhood; some are bad from childhood. This is so because of natural endowments." He also quotes Chu Hsi's statements that "the moment there is the order of Heaven *(t'ien-ming)*,[bo] there are natural endowments *(ch'i-chih)*—they cannot be separated"; and that "there is reason. How can there be evil? The so-called evil is only indeterminate substance."

These statements appear incoherent and inconsistent. For it is clear that "if one says that indeterminate substance is evil, then reason is evil; and [if one says that] reason is good, then indeterminate substance is good. For indeterminate substance is the indeterminate substance of reason, and reason is the reason of indeterminate substance. How can one say that reason is purely good and natural endowment is exclusively evil?" [55] Yen even cites some examples of the ontological inseparability of reason from indeterminate substance.[56] In the case of eyes, eyeballs are natural endowments, while the brightness of seeing is nature [or reason]. For eyes to see, there must be both. Both eyeballs and brightness of seeing are heavenly ordained (*t'ien-ming*) and there is no need for separating the nature of heavenly ordainment and the nature of natural endowment. Yen then infers that

we can only properly say that Heaven has determined the nature of eyes, that the bright seeing of eyes is the goodness of the nature of eyes and that what actually sees is due to the goodness of the feelings of nature. As to how far or how close, how clearly or how dimly one can see, that is a matter of one's ability. There is no evil in it.[57]

Of course Yen admits that eyes can see wrong colors, but it is not a fault of the natural endowment of the eyes alone; it has to do with the nature of the eye. If one attributes the wrong to the natural endowment of the eyes, we will have to do away with the eyes. This, concludes Yen, is a doctrine of Buddhism. The total effect of Yen's criticism, however, is a result of his antidualistic naturalism of indeterminate substance. As he, from the very beginning, rejects any bifurcation of indeterminate substance and reason, he cannot see how Ch'eng-Chu could make the bifurcation of indeterminate substance and reason an ontological principle.

We now come to the reason-desire relationship in Yen Yüan. Like Wang Fu-chih, Yen regards desire as a form of nature and a form of reason and thus as a natural way of realizing value and reason. But further, Yen emphasizes the continuity of all virtues and the need to satisfy the basic needs (*yü*) of men. In his essay on "Preserving Man," he questions whether one can speak of man as by nature having benevolence (*jen*) [bp] and yet in real life not loving his parents and not wishing to continue life. He strongly criticizes the Buddhists for their attempt to abolish ethical relations and life's efforts to continue life. He thinks that it is impossible to do this and yet at the same time speak of benevolence and justice as the original nature of man.

Reason for him is something which consistently exhibits itself in all natural feelings and desires. As there are natural desires such as sex, one has to face them and satisfy them in order to develop one's nature and fulfill one's potential. This is a way to fulfill the reason of life. This argument is clearly presented in writings of Yen such as his essay on "Preserving Man." In that essay Yen calls on Buddhist and Taoist monks to return to secular and practical life. He also calls on meditators, foreign monks, philosophers who merely speculate on nature and fate (*ming*), and men of other deviant beliefs to do the same. He says: "Man is the finest among the myriad things; how can he alone have no feelings? Thus the attraction between the sexes is the great desire of man, and is thus the true feeling and ultimate nature [of man]." Then he asks the monks: "How could you not be moved by these [natural feelings and desires]? I believe that your wish to return to the ethical life is a natural inclination." [58]

It is clear that because there are desires and needs in man, the ethical life is possible, as is the concrete, pragmatic world of actions. And for Yen, nothing is more directly related to the fulfillment of reason than leading an ethical life and participating in the world of action. He says summarily: "If there is no natural endowment [the basis for desire], there is no nature; and if there is no natural endowment, nature cannot be seen." [59] Furthermore, in light of the relationship between nature [or reason] and the use of nature in talents (*ts'ai*),[bq] as indicated above, Yen holds in general that

the six actions are the faculty of my nature; the six arts are the capacities of my nature. Since appearances are discoveries of my nature, the nine virtues are achievements of my nature. To formulate rites and create music, to harmonize *yin* and *yang*, and to realize an actual universe, are an expansion of my nature. That the myriad things are like themselves, earth becomes peaceful, Heaven becomes complete, and the cosmos is full of ultimate harmony, is the function of my nature.[60]

Yen naturally asserts that "to realize one's nature to the utmost, one has only to reflect on one's self. To reflect on one's self is to concentrate on the movement and action to be seen in the myriad things." [61] He further points out that if the self has a body, it is a function of my nature; that if one body is defective, then one function of nature will be missing. From this it is clear that, for Yen, desire and affairs (*shih*) are parts of reason and nature which are exhibited in the functioning of desire and affairs. Thus reason and desire are ultimately related in the relationship of a substance to its functions. The distinguishing mark of Yen's doctrine is that the functions of the substance [reason and nature] have to be discharged in the form of the pragmatic cultivation of one's virtues. The metaphysical justification of the functional relationship between reason and indeterminate substance is, however, as already made clear, the same for Yen as for Wang.

Li Kung, Yen Yüan's close disciple, follows Yen in promoting the thesis that there is no reason apart from indeterminate substance and that indeterminate substance comes before reason. In his commentary on the *Lun yü* he stresses the fact that there are no reason and *tao* beyond the activity of *yin* and *yang* and the ethical relationships and actual affairs of man (*Lun-yü ch'uan-chu wen*).[br] He holds strongly to the principle that reason is an a-posteriori characteristic of affairs, for it is only when there are affairs of Heaven, man, and things, that there are reasons for these. He says: "These affairs have patterns of order and these are reasons which are in the affairs." [62]

REASON-SUBSTANCE AND REASON-DESIRE RELATION-SHIPS IN HUANG TSUNG-HSI (1610–95), CH'EN CH'UEH (1604–77), LI ERH-CH'Ü (1627–1705), AND FANG I-CHIH (1611–71)

Huang Tsung-hsi, as an intellectual historian and a thinker with a deep concern for his times, contributed to the formation of philosophical opinions in the seventeenth century through his activities and writings which include his great work, the *Ming-ju hsüeh-an* (Philosophical Records of Ming Confucianists). Even though Huang's lineage is from the Lu-Wang School of Mind (*hsin hsüeh*),[bs] he makes objective criticisms of the disasters of the School of Mind in the Ming era. In the first place, he suspects that the idealistic doctrine of pure perceptive mind as the basis of reality is very close to the Buddhistic view. He says: "[When the School of Mind] comes to (Wang) Lung-hsi,[bt] the innate faculty of moral goodness (*liang-chih*) [bu] is regarded as the Buddha nature. One hopes for enlightenment out of thin air, and ends up just playing games." [63]

In general, Huang Tsung-hsi is sympathetic with Wang Yang-ming's philosophy of mind, yet he is opposed to conceiving ultimate reality in an absolutely void mind independent of one's experience of self. He stresses the effort of self-cultivation for the attainment of truth. He furthermore attempts to reinterpret Wang Yang-ming's statement that the ultimate reality of mind is without good and evil as meaning that when the ultimate reality of mind has no good or evil intentions, it is neither good nor evil.[64] The point of this reinterpretation is profound. It consists in making a distinction between the ultimate reality of mind and mind, a distinction which Wang Yang-ming fails to make. The ultimate reality of mind is not necessarily the same as mind, for unlike mind, it may have no good or evil intentions. Yet it is not independent of good or evil. If we take good and evil as a relation and as an activity, then this implies that in Huang Tsung-hsi the ultimate reality of mind bears upon the relationship and activity of life which can be judged as good or evil.

At this point one may ask what this ultimate reality of mind is and how it bears upon the relationship of reason-substance in our discussion. Even though we have no explicit or systematic answer to this question, we have good reason to believe that Huang could take this ultimate reality of mind as fundamentally indeterminate substance and derivatively reason. In the first place, Huang praises the doctrine of his master teacher, Liu Tsung-chou—that there is no reason apart from indeterminate substance—as at last resolving a ten-thousand-year-old doubt.[65] Of course the "ten-thousand-year-old doubt" of which he speaks, is how reason and indeterminate substance are related and whether reason comes before indeterminate substance.[66]

According to this view, the ultimate reality of mind is apparently nothing but indeterminate substance. Huang concludes that apart from indeterminate substance there is no so-called reason, and apart from mind (the flow of indeterminate substance) there is no nature.[67] In his preface to Liu's collected works, Huang further says: "For throughout Heaven and earth, there is merely the nature of natural endowments, and no nature of righteousness and reason (*yi-li*).[bv] If one holds that there is the nature of righteousness and reason without grounding it in the nature of natural endowments, he simply makes no sense." [68] Furthermore, Huang is sympathetic with Lo Ch'in-shun and stresses the fact that Lo has stated that throughout Heaven and earth and throughout ancient and present times there has been and is nothing but indeterminate substance.[69] In his record of the Wang Yang-ming school in Che-chung,[bw] he criticizes Chi Pen [bx] for his contrasting reason, as the way of *yang*, with indeterminate substance, as the way of *yin*. In his view the great transformation (*ta-hua*)[by] is only one indeterminate substance, the ascending tendency of which is *yang*, and the descending tendency of which is *yin*. Thus he concludes that *yin* and *yang* are merely indeterminate substance and the only reason is the reason of the unity of *yang* and *yin*, which naturally cannot be separated from the activity of indeterminate substance itself.[70]

In the second place, Huang holds that there is no reason apart from indeterminate substance in the sense that when indeterminate substance changes, reason should not remain unchanged. For him reason changes in relation to indeterminate substance. And reason is merely a characteristic of concrete things. It is from this point of view that he criticizes Hsieh Hsüan, who, though holding that there is no reason without indeterminate substance, says that indeterminate substance can accumulate and disperse, whereas reason cannot. Hsieh advances the following example to explain this point: Reason is like sunlight while indeterminate substance is like flying birds. The birds can fly everywhere, but sunlight stays the same.[71] Huang retorts: Given this analogy, one can say that there could be sunlight but no flying birds and there could be flying birds but no sunlight. Thus the analogy to show the relation of reason to indeterminate substance is not a good one. Huang explicitly comments:

Speaking from the point of view of the unity of the great virtue, as indeterminate substance has no limitation, so reason has no limitation. Thus, not only has reason no concentration and dispersion, indeterminate substance also has no concentration and dispersion. From the point of view of the diversity of small virtues, [indeterminate substance and reason] renew themselves every day; [we cannot take] the bygone indeterminate substance as the indeterminate substance just coming, [nor can we] take the bygone reason as the reason just coming. [Thus], it is not only indeterminate substance that has concentration and dispersion, reason also has concentration and dispersion.[72]

It is clear from this that Huang would regard reason and indeterminate substance not only as coextensive in scope, but also as qualitatively the same in terms of change. What is significant is that in this context, reason, for Huang as for Wang Fu-chih, has no initial claim to unchangeability or independence of concrete things. There could not be any reason for this other than the ontological conviction that reason is only a characteristic of indeterminate substance.

In the light of his naturalistic view of the unity of reason and substance, it is to be expected that Huang would hold the unity of reason and desire in human self-realization. This is generally true in Huang.

But this aspect of the reason-desire relationship is perhaps better represented in Ch'en Ch'ueh (1604–77), who was Huang's fellow student under Liu Tsung-chou. Like Huang, Ch'en is highly critical of the Ch'eng-Chu school to the extent that he even argues that the *Great Learning (Ta hsüeh)* [bz] is not a classic of the Confucian tradition as the Ch'eng-Chu school holds. Ch'en is opposed to the *Great Learning* doctrine of resting in supreme goodness to which the Ch'eng-Chu school subscribes. Ch'en is further opposed to the multiple separation of nature, indeterminate substance, capabilities *(ts'ai)*, and feelings *(ch'ing)*. He holds, like Yen Yüan, that "the heavenly reason is just to be seen in human desires; where the desires exactly fit is where the reason of Heaven is." [73] It can be noted that in a way Ch'en's view on reason and desires reflects Liu Tsung-chou's, just as Huang's view on the reason-substance relationship reflects Liu Tsung-chou's.

Among all of the seventeenth-century thinkers, Li Erh-ch'ü (1627–1705) is perhaps the most conservative, at least in his attempt to preserve the idealistic philosophy of Wang Yang-ming by way of assimilating the doctrine of investigating things *(ko-wu)* [ca] and reaching and extending knowledge *(chih-chih)* [cb] of the Ch'eng-Chu school. Nevertheless, he exhibits the seventeenth-century spirit of pragmatism in advocating the importance of social action and the practice of virtue. He further stresses the inseparability of natural endowments and nature. This, of course, implies the unity of reason and indeterminate substance. In general he takes indeterminate substance in specific cases as a means of realizing the goodness of the nature or reason.[74] In this regard, he is not so emphatic and explicit in spelling out the relationship of unity between indeterminate substance and reason. He likewise neglects the ethical application of this principle to the unity of reason and desire. But it is significant that, although he is under the strong influence of Sung-Ming Neo-Confucianism, he does not try to follow its teaching on the duality of reason and indeterminate substance and the need to eliminate desire.

Finally, we wish to mention Fang I-chih (1611–71), whose views on investigating things have already been discussed by Willard J. Peterson. Fang is important for having advanced some novel ideas in regard to the understanding of reason and its relationship to indeterminate substance. He was influenced by the scientific knowledge brought to China by the Jesuits in his time. Indeed, we may say that the most remarkable contribution to the seventeenth-century rationalism and naturalism of the reason-substance relationship was achieved by Fang through his efforts explicitly to relate reason to scientific study as shown in his unique book *Small Insights into Principles of Things (Wu-li hsiao-shih)*.[cc]

Fang holds without ambiguity that Heaven and earth are filled with physical things *(wu)*,[cd] which include mind, nature, and necessity.[75] He says: "Heaven and earth are one *thing*. Mind is one thing. Only mind can understand heaven and earth and the ten thousand things. To know the source of heaven and earth and the ten thousand things is to fulfill one's nature to the utmost." [76] To say that mind is one thing is to say that it is not essentially different from all of the things in the world, even though mind does have its own qualities such as the capability of understanding.[77] Then comes the question of what reason is and how reason is related to indeterminate substance. There are three things which can be said in answer to this.

First, Fang affirms that there is no reason apart from things. Reason presents the physical characteristics of concrete things. It is also what mind knows when mind seeks to know external things. As things in general, including mind, are transformations of indeterminate substance, reason must be a resulting transformation of indeterminate substance. It is the regularity of things. He says:

All are made from indeterminate substance. The void is filled by indeterminate substance. Things have regularities. The void also has its regularity. From what is manifest we know the hidden and there is not a trace of anything amiss, because there is regularity. Reason is capable of being identified in experience. That is how knowledge of mind is possible.[78]

Second, to confirm our view that for Fang reason is a physical characteristic of things, we must identify things with physical objects. This is precisely what Fang does in *Small Insights into Principles of Things*. For him everything comes from indeterminate substance and indeterminate substance is explicitly described as a physical entity. In his discussion, he points to the vapor which one can see in the sunlight or in winter as an instance of indeterminate substance. He also points to the vibration from the sounding of a drum as another instance of the substantiality of indeterminate substance. In this case indeterminate substance is identified with air. Perhaps under the influence of Western science from the Jesuits, he makes a special point of discussing light and water,[79] and treats them as the result of the transformation of indeterminate substance. He says: "Indeterminate substance condenses into shape and then gives rise to light and sound." [80] "When indeterminate substance warms up and moves and meets the *yin* [wet], then there is water. Rain comes the same way." [81] In general he develops the traditional doctrine of five powers to the point that he considers all physical powers as being due to the working of indeterminate substance or ether (*ch'i*).

Besides affirming the principle that vapor condenses in shapes, accumulates to give light, and vibrates to give sound, he holds that there is much vapor which is not yet condensed, nor released or provoked in any form.[82] Thus if we identify his vapor with matter-energy in modern physics, his view will present a very close resemblance to modern physical theory. There is no question of straining to make such an identification, particularly in light of his general discussion of the relationship of philosophy to scientific studies.

Fang conceives human learning in terms of three fields of study. There is first the study called "comprehending the fundamental beginnings" (*t'ung-chi*),[ce] which consists in tracing the origins of the complicated principles of things at rest and in motion. In this sense *t'ung-chi* is philosophy in general and metaphysics in particular. Then there is the study called "inquiry into the natural characters of things" (*chih-ts'e*),[cf] which consists in investigating qualities and tendencies of concrete things and in forecasting the regularity of their changes on the basis of empirical evidence. Thus *chih-ts'e* corresponds to modern theoretical and practical sciences, and covers, as Fang himself recognizes, acoustics, optics, medicines, mathematics, and astronomy. Finally, there is the study called "inquiry into principles of government" (*tsai-li*),[cg] which consists in understanding principles of government, education, ethics, and social ethics and can be said to correspond to modern social sciences in both their theoretical and practical dimensions. According to Fang, *t'ung-chi* is contained in *chih-ts'e*.[83] This means that philosophy and metaphysics are contained in the study of science. The relevance of this point to reason-substance relationships is that there could not be independent metaphysical study of reason apart from actual study of concrete principles in concrete things. Thus the study of reason must begin with the study of concrete cases of indeterminate substance. This is the third point in answer to the above-mentioned question regarding the nature of reason and the relationship of reason-substance.

Not only is indeterminate substance more fundamental than reason, but there is no study of indeterminate substance apart from concrete nature as studied in the sciences. Fang is perceptive in suggesting in his own time that study of the natural characters of things (*chih-ts'e*) in the West is not yet complete and that one can make further advances in it. He believes that the Confucians are in general experts in the principles of government (*tsai-li*), but are weak in the study of the natural character of things. In focusing on the importance of the study of the natural character of things, Fang has performed the task of criticizing the reason-substance dualism and the empty speculation on reason and indeterminate substance in Sung-Ming Neo-Confucianism. He has also opened up in the study of the natural characters of things a road for the study of reason and indeterminate substance. Though Fang does not touch on the reason-desire relationship, it is clear that he would be in general sympathy with the main trend of seventeenth-century thinking on this problem: that is, the view that reason and desire should not be separated in ethics and should be considered a unity, so that to realize desire is the only way to save and achieve reason in life.

CONCLUSION

We have discussed reason-substance and reason-desire relationships in Wang Fu-chih, Yen Yüan, Li Kung, Huang Tsung-hsi, Ch'en Ch'üeh, Li Erh-ch'ü, and Fang I-chih. All have addressed themselves to the problem of the reason-substance relationship, and most have addressed themselves to the reason-desire relationship. In our analysis, all these philosophers have demonstrated, with degrees of variation, opposition to Sung-Ming Neo-Confucianism in a framework of antidualistic naturalism in both metaphysics and moral philosophy. The antidualistic naturalism in metaphysics consists in upholding the ontological primacy of indeterminate substance and the inherence of reason in the development of indeterminate substance. In morality it consists in asserting that the fulfillment of reason is inseparable from the fulfillment of desire and of the intrinsic right and goodness of natural desire. We have presented Wang Fu-chih as a model of this seventeenth-century Confucian antidualistic naturalism, since he has evidenced every aspect of such a philosophy in both metaphysics and morality. Next we have compared others with this model in an attempt to define similarities and differences between Wang and others. These other philosophers appear to be significant in developing or improving upon Wang's nondualistic, naturalistic model of reality and man. In particular, Yen Yüan adds a pragmatic note to the doctrine and Fang I-chih gives the reason-substance relationship a scientific outlook.

We have not covered every significant thinker in the seventeenth-century enlightenment atmosphere. Notably, we have ignored Ku Yen-wu [ch] (1613–82), Chu Chih-yü [ci] (1600–82), T'ang Chen [cj] (1630–1704), Lu Shih-i [ck] (1611–72), Fu Shan [cl] (1607–84), P'an P'ing-ko [cm] (dates unknown). All were critical of Sung-Ming Neo-Confucianism in regard to its bifurcation of reason and indeterminate substance and in regard to its idealistic tendencies. All emphasized the primacy of indeterminate substance, or utensils or things or affairs or events, over reason and *tao*, and stressed the interconnectedness of the former in a process of development. Some of them, such as T'ang Chen, further stressed a pragmatism of action over speculation.

Elsewhere in this volume Professor T'ang Chun-i discusses Liu Tsung-chou (1578–1645) as a philosopher of the early seventeenth century whose thinking draws upon Chu Hsi and Wang Yang-ming in the Sung and Ming. Liu contributed to the naturalistic and antidualistic tendencies of this period and his influence in regard to problems of reason-substance and reason-desire relationships, as we have noted, was manifested in his disciples, Huang Tsung-hsi and Ch'en Ch'üeh. We have not traced back this seventeenth-century antidualistic naturalism to earlier ages, nor discussed its impact on later times. But we should not fail to observe that it was mainly through the efforts of Wang Fu-chih, Yen Yüan, and others like them in the seventeenth century that there was the evolution in the eighteenth century of more systematic doctrines of reason-substance and reason-desire in Tai Chen (1724–77) and Chiao Hsün [cn] (1763–1820), whose contributions brought new life to Confucian thought.

NOTES

1. One may say that in the Mādhyamika School, because of the recognition of the irreconcilable opposition between "is" and "is not," one must transcend both continually.

2. See my paper "The Neo-Confucian Li: Its Conceptual Background and Ontological Types," presented at the Columbia University Seminar on Oriental Thought and Religion, May 9, 1969.

3. See Huang Wan's work *Ming-tao p'ien* co (Essay on Illuminating Tao) (Peking: Chung Hua Book Co., 1959); and Wang T'ing-hsiang's work *Shen-yen* cp (Deliberate Words) and *Ya-shu* cq (Elegant Statements), both in *Wang-shih chia-ts'ang chi* cr (Collected Works in the Family of Wang), Ming Chia-ching (12th edition). See also *Wang T'ing-hsiang hsüan-chi* cs (Selections from Wang T'ing-hsiang, edited by Hou Wai-lu, *et al.* (Peking: Chung Hua Book Co., 1965).

4. In the light of this article, we may regard the seventeenth-century philosophers here under discussion as spiritual tutors and forefathers of the anti-dualistic and naturalistic philosophy of Tai Chen. Furthermore, we hope that this discussion will exhibit the basic issues involved in Confucian thinking and will open roads for contemporary reconstruction of Confucian philosophy.

5. See Wang Fu-chih's *Chang Tzu Cheng-meng chu* ct (Commentary on Chang Tsai's essay "Rectifying Obscurities"), *T'ai-ho* chapter, edited by Chang Hsi-shen (Peking: Ku Chi Publishing Co., 1956), 1/1.

6. *Ibid.*

7. *Ibid.*

8. *Ibid.*, 1/2.

9. *Ibid.*, 1/6.

10. *Ibid.*, 1/6 ff.

11. See Wang Fu-chih's *Chou-i wai-chuan* cu (Outer Commentary on *Book of Changes*), chapter on Hsi-tz'u cv section 6, edited by Wang Hsiao-yü (Peking: Chung Hua Book Co., 1962), 5/15.

12. *Ibid.*, section 7, 5/16.

13. *Ibid.*, section 5, 5/12 ff.

14. *Ibid.*, section 6, 5/15 ff.

15. From Wang Fu-chih's *Chang Tzu Cheng-meng chu*, cited in note 5, *T'ai-ho* chapter, 1/11 ff.

16. *Ibid.*, 1/1.

17. *Ibid.*

18. From Wang Fu-chih's *Ssu-wen lu* cw (Records of Thinking and Queries), inner chapters (Peking: Ku Chi Publishing Co., 1956), p. 5.

19. *Ibid.*, p. 5.

20. *Ibid.*, p. 6.

21. *Ibid.*, pp. 3–4.

22. *Ibid.*, p. 2.

23. Wang Fu-chih, *Chang Tzu Cheng-meng chu*, cited in note 5, *Ch'eng-ming* ᶜˣ chapter 3/21.

24. Wang Fu-chih, *Tu Ssu-shu ta-ch'üan-shuo* ᶜʸ (Discourses on Reading the Complete Works of the Four Books), in *Ch'uan-shan i-shu* ᶜᶻ (The Extant Works of Wang Ch'uan-shan) (Shanghai: Tai-ping-yang Book Co., 1935), vol. 45–49, 10/24.

25. Wang Fu-chih, *Chou-i wai-chuan*, chapter on *Hsi-tz'u*, section 12, 5/24.

26. *Ibid.*, 5/25.

27. Here Wang Fu-chih is strongly opposed to the Taoist principle that one can forget concrete things if one obtains truth in language, and one can forget truth in language if one obtains what is meant by truth in language. See *ibid.*, section 5.

28. This statement is quoted from Ch'eng I ᵈᵃ in Chu Hsi's ᵈᵇ work *Meng Tzu chi-chu* ᵈᶜ (Assembled Commentaries on Mencius), in *Wu-ch'iu-pei chai Meng Tzu shih-shu* ᵈᵈ (Ten Books of Mencius in Wu-ch'iu-pei chai), no. 5, edited by Yeng Ling-feng (Taipei, 1969), p. 38.

29. Wang Fu-chih, *Tu Ssu-shu ta-ch'üan shuo*, 10/28.

30. *Ibid.*, pp. 8 ff.

31. Wang Fu-chih, *Ssu-shu hsün-i* ᵈᵉ (Explanation of Meanings in the Four Books), in *Ch'üan-shan i-shu*, vol. 32–44, 15/46.

32. Wang Fu-chih, *Ssu-wen lu*, inner chapters, p. 5.

33. Wang Fu-chih, *Chou-i wai-chuan*, chapter on *t'un*,ᵈᶠ 1/8.

34. Wang Fu-chih, *Chang Tzu Cheng-meng chu*, *T'ai-ho* chapter, 1/10–11.

35. *Ibid.*, *Ch'eng-ming* chapter, 3/12–13.

36. Wang Fu-chih, *Ssu-wen lu*, inner chapters, p. 4.

37. Wang Fu-chih, *Shang-shu yin-i* ᵈᵍ (Extending Meanings in the Book of Documents), edited by Wang Hsiao-yü (Peking: Chung Hua Book Co., 1962), chapter on *T'ai-chia*,ᵈʰ section 3, 1/4.

38. Wang Fu-chih, *Chang Tzu Cheng-meng chu*, cited in note 5, *Ch'eng-ming* chapter 3/12.

39. *Ibid.*, 3/12.

40. Wang Fu-chih, *Tu Ssu-shu ta-ch'üan shuo*, 4/7–8.

41. *Ibid.*, 4/19.

42. *Ibid.*, 8/21.

43. *Ibid.*, 8/22.

44. Wang Fu-chih says: "In the private desires of man resides the *li* of heaven." (*ibid.*, 26/4.) He also says: "The expansion of heavenly *li* is not opposed to the desires of man." (*ibid.*, 6/12–13.)

45. Wang Fu-chih, *Tu Ssu-shu ta-ch'üan shuo*, 3/5.

46. Wang Fu-chih, *Chou-i wai-chuan*, chapter on *t'un*, 1/15. We note of course that *yü* and *ch'ing* for Wang Fu-chih have the same basis in the nature of

man, for *yü* are the natural feelings of man and the natural feelings (*ch'ing*) of man are the concrete facts of the needs and desires (*yü*) of man.

47. *Ibid.*, chapter on *ta-yu*,^{di} 12/1–2.

48. Wang Fu-chih, *Tu Ssu-shu ta-ch'üan shuo*, 8/13.

49. From Yen Yüan's *Ts'un-hsüeh pien* ^{dj} (Essay on Preserving Learning), in *Yen Li ts'ung-shu* ^{dk} (Collected Works of Yen Yüan and Li Kung), edited by Ch'i Chen-lin (Peking Ssu-ts'un Learning Society, 1923), 1/4–5. Cf. also Yen Yüan's *Ssu-ts'un pien* ^{dl} (Essays on Four Preservations) (Peking: Ku Chi Publishing Co., 1957).

50. From *Hsi-chai chi-yü*,^{dm} (Shanghai: Commercial Press, 1936), 1/1–2.

51. Yen Yüan, *Ts'un-jen pien* ^{dn} (Essay on Preserving Man), in *Yen-Li ts'ung-shu*, and *Ssu-ts'un pien*, 1/4–5.

52. Yen Yüan, *Ssu-shu cheng-wu* (Rectifications of Misinterpretations of the Four Books), in *Yen Li ts'ung-shu*, 2/40.

53. Yen Yüan, *Hsi-chai chi-yü*, 1/38.

54. Yen Yüan, *Ts'un-hsing pien* ^{do} (Essay on Preserving Nature), in *Yen Li ts'ung-shu* and *Ssu-ts'un pien*, 2/28–29.

55. *Ibid.*, 1/28.

56. *Ibid.*, 1/38 ff.

57. *Ibid.*, 1/38.

58. Yen Yüan, *Ts'un-jen pien*, 1/4.

59. Yen Yüan, *Ts'un-hsing pien*, 2/29.

60. *Ibid.*, 2/30.

61. Yen Yüan, *Ts'un-jen pien*, p. 3.

62. Li Kung, *Lun-yü ch'uan-chu wen* (Queries into Commentaries on the Analects), in *Wu-ch'iu-pei chai Lun-yü chi-ch'eng* ^{dp} (Collected Works on the Analects in *Wu-ch'iu-pei chai*), edited by Yen Ling-feng (Taipei, 1966), *Tzu-chang* sections 19, 38.

63. Huang Tsung-hsi, *Ming-ju hsüeh-an* ^{dq} (Philosophical Records of Ming Confucianists) (Taipei: Commercial Press, 1965), *Shih shuo*, I, 1/7.

64. *Ibid.*, *Yao-chiang* (Wang Yang-ming) *hsüeh-an*,^{dr} II, 10/53 ff.

65. *Ibid.*, *Chi-shan* (Liu Tsung-chou) *hsüeh-an*,^{ds} II 62/31 ff.

66. *Ibid.*, 62/42 ff. Liu Tsung-chou believes that "all that exists between heaven and earth is *ch'i*," and that "what is in the human mind is the flow of one *ch'i*."

67. *Ibid.*, 62/31–40.

68. Huang Tsung-hsi, *Nan-lei wen-ting* ^{dt} (Writings by Huang Tsung-hsi) (Shanghai: Chung Hua Book Co., 1933), "Preface to the collection of essays of my former teacher Chi-shan *hsien-sheng*," p. 48.

69. Huang Tsung-hsi, *Ming-ju hsüeh-an*, IX, 47/34 ff.

70. *Ibid.*, III, 13/19 ff. *Che-chung Wang-men hsüeh-an*.^{du}

71. *Ibid.*, II, 7/1 ff. *Ho-tung hsüeh-an*.^{dv}

72. *Ibid.*, 7/4.

73. From Ch'en Ch'üeh's essay entitled "Ku-yen wu-yü tso-sheng p'ien" ^{dw}

(Statements on Becoming a Sage through Desirelessness), cited in Huang Tsung-hsi's epitaph on Ch'en Ch'ueh in *Nan-lei wen-ting*, second collection (*hou-chi*), 3/42.

74. Li Erh-ch'ü, *Ching-chiang yü yao* dx (Important Statements from Ching-Chiang), in *Erh-ch'ü chi* dy (Collected Works on Erh-ch'ü), edited by Wang Hsin-ching *et al.*, Ch'ing Kuang-hsü 3, 4/15 ff.

75. Fang I-chih, *Wu-li hsiao-shih* (Small Insights into Principles of Things), reprinted by Ning-ching Tang, Ch'ing Kuang-hsü 10, "Self-preface," 12/2.

76. *Ibid.*, "General Discussion," p. 4.

77. According to Fang I-chih, man was born the finest thing in the world. He holds that the life of man resides in the body and the body of man resides in the world. See *Wu-li hsiao-shih*, "Self-preface," 1–2.

78. *Ibid.*, "Discussion of *ch'i*," 7.

79. *Ibid.*, "Discussion of light and water," 14.

80. *Ibid.*, "Discussion of light and water," 14.

81. *Ibid.*, "Discussion of light and water," 14.

82. *Ibid.*, "Discussion of four powers and five powers," 12.

83. *Ibid.*, "Self-preface," 1–2.

GLOSSARY

a	法	ak	無	bu	良知
b	事	al	太虛	bv	義理
c	色	am	絪縕	bw	浙中
d	空	an	氣化	bx	季本
e	染	ao	陰	by	大化
f	淨	ap	陽	bz	大學
g	唯識	aq	道	ca	格物
h	禪	ar	生生	cb	致知
i	程頤	as	生	cc	物理小識
j	理	at	日生日成	cd	物
k	氣	au	太和	ce	通幾
l	欲	av	太極	cf	質測
m	程朱	aw	神	cg	宰理
n	心	ax	相	ch	顧炎武
o	心統性情	ay	性	ci	朱之瑜
p	陸王	az	天	cj	唐甄
q	心即理	ba	理氣	ck	陸世儀
r	宋明	bb	器	cl	傅山
s	陳亮	bc	數	cm	潘平格
t	葉適	bd	即	cn	焦循
u	王廷相	be	禮	co	明道篇
v	黃綰	bf	天下之動	cp	愼言
w	王陽明	bg	情	cq	雅書
x	致良知	bh	氣稟	cr	王氏家藏集
y	知行合一	bi	氣質	cs	王廷相選集
z	張載	bj	天道	ct	張子正蒙注
aa	戴震	bk	宇宙眞氣	cu	周易外傳
ab	王夫之	bl	宇宙生氣	cv	繫辭
ac	顏元	bm	形	cw	思問錄
ad	李塨	bn	四書正誤	cx	誠明
ae	黃宗羲	bo	天命	cy	讀四書大全說
af	陳確	bp	仁	cz	船山遺書
ag	李二曲（李顒）	bq	才	da	程頤
ah	方以智	br	論語傳註問	db	朱熹
ai	聚	bs	心學	dc	孟子集註
aj	散	bt	王龍溪	dd	無求備齋孟子十書

de	四書訓義	dl	四存編	ds	蕺山(劉宗周)學案
df	屯	dm	習齋記餘	dt	南雷文定
dg	尚書引義	dn	存人篇	du	浙中王門學案
dh	太甲	do	存性篇	dv	河東學案
di	大有	dp	無求備齋論語集成	dw	瞽言無欲作聖篇
dj	存學編	dq	明儒學案	dx	靖江語要
dk	顏李叢書	dr	姚江(王陽明)學案	dy	二曲集

Yen Yüan: From Inner Experience to

Lived Concreteness

As the study of Chinese thought becomes more sophisticated, some of Joseph Levenson's dichotomous interpretations of the cultural transformation of modern China may have to be substantially revised. In the meantime, however, his insight into the dilemma of the modern Chinese literatus who tries to justify his emotional attachment to traditional ideas by an apologetic appeal to a system of values imported from the West is useful. Levenson has pointed out that in so doing, the Chinese literatus both sacrifices the organismic integrity of the traditional ideas and fails to grasp the contextual variations of the imported values. As a result, neither the ideas that were historically significant in shaping the lives of the great personalities in traditional China, nor the values that are currently instrumental in orienting the thoughts of the great minds of the modern West can take root in the Chinese scholarly soil.[1]

One of the saddest consequences of this maladjustment is the conscious and unconscious distortions of more than eight centuries of Chinese thought, commonly known as the Neo-Confucian era. Scholars since Liang Ch'i-ch'ao [a] have been impelled by a sense of cultural urgency to look for Western-like values in the body of traditional ideas.[2] Their search was concentrated mostly in the ancient period. The technological ingenuity in Mo Ti,[b] the art of logic in Kung-sun Lung,[c] the spirit of science in Hsün Tzu [d] and Wang Ch'ung, [e] all these and others supported their image of what the new China should be. By comparison, Sui [f]-T'ang [g] Buddhism and Sung [h]-Ming [i] Confucianism, with the possible exception of the abortive attempt to see Chu Hsi's [j] ko-wu [k] as scientifically respectable, seemed to have no relevance. Only very near the end of the Ming dynasty did scholars find something comparable to scientism and pragmatism.[3] Their enthusiasm was later continued by the Marxian historians' attempt to characterize this period as the culmination of the early Chinese enlightenment, from a materialist point of view.[4]

An effort to study and interpret the Neo-Confucian tradition in general and seventeenth-century Chinese thought in particular is therefore confronted with the double difficulty of insufficient objective knowledge and inflated subjective judgments.

Yen Yüan (Hsi-chai, 1635–1704) [1] one of the most original thinkers of this period, is a case in point and the difficulty is further compounded by his reluctance to commit his own ideas to writing and by the modern scholars' willingness to manipulate the limited data on him for various ideological purposes. It thus seems advisable first to examine some of the "established" views on Yen Yüan.

Ironically, Yen Yüan, who was relatively unknown in his own time because he lived far from the centers of influence, gained in reputation in the early 1920s among a group of prominent intellectual activists precisely because of a well-organized campaign by those in power. The leader of the campaign was none other than the president of the Republic of China, Hsü Shih-ch'ang.[m] Under his leadership a scholastic society in honor of Yen Yüan, with the suggestive name Ssu-ts'un [n] (Four Preservations),[5] was organized in 1920. According to the records of the society, within three years the membership rose to a surprising eight hundred. In 1923 a complete and punctuated edition of the collected works of Yen Yüan and of his best disciple, Li Kung (Shu-ku,[o] 1659–1733), was published and widely circulated as an official undertaking of the society. In 1925 a high school bearing the name of the society was opened in Peking. In addition, a monthly journal dedicated to the study and promulgation of Yen Yüan's thought began publication.[6]

To go into the reasons behind Hsü's efforts would lead to all sorts of ramifications. Suffice it to say here that regional power—specifically, the Chih-li [p] faction—was primarily responsible for the movement. Hsü's attempt to revitalize the Pei-hsüeh [q] (northern learning) was definitely influenced by the demand of his Hopei [r] intellectuals to formulate a new ideology to lead the nation.[7] Of course, it was not unusual that the rise of a regional power in China should lead to the search for a justification beyond the sheer force of politics. Similar cases can be found in Wang Yang-ming's [s] appeal to the Chekiang [t] group and to a lesser degree in Ch'en Po-sha's [u] appeal to the Cantonese. Even Wang Fu-chih's [v] recent rise to prominence in the genealogy of the great materialists, whatever the articulated rationale of the party ideologue, owed much to his Hunanese origin.[8]

To be sure, if Yen Yüan had had no relevant message for modern China, he would not have been chosen simply because of his regional affiliation. The intellectual occasion for the sudden popularity of Yen Yüan, again with a touch of irony, lies in the timely visit of John Dewey from May 1919 to July 1921. The American philosopher, whose thought, unlike that of William James and Josiah Royce, was very much an indigenous response to a particular situation in the United States, was greatly honored in China as the patron saint of science, the very source of wealth and power. The rediscovery of Yen Yüan as the result of Dewey's intrusion into China is best revealed in the words of Liang Ch'i-ch'ao:

Since Dewey's lecture tour in China, pragmatism has become a fashionable teaching in our educational circles. This cannot but be said to be a welcome phenomenon. Three hundred years ago in our country there were a Mr. Yen Hsi-chai [w] and his disciple, Mr. Li Shu-ku. They established a school, commonly known as the Yen-Li [x] School. Their ideas were similar to those of Dewey and his colleagues. And in certain ways their ideas were more penetrating than those of Dewey and his colleagues.[9]

One of the most important events in the promotion of Yen Yüan's ideas was Liang's lecture on Ch'ing thought in 1923.[10] Liang characterized Yen's thought as "practical utilitarianism" (*shih-chien shih-yung chu-i*) [y] and dramatically announced that Yen and Li, in essence, had launched an "extremely violent but sincere great revolutionary movement" [11] against all the previous modes of thinking in the last two thousand years of Chinese thought. Liang was especially impressed with Yen's action-philosophy, which in his judgment was precisely what the Chinese youth needed. Liang was equally impressed by Yen Yüan's concern for practicality, which he interpreted as the spirit of experimental science. He declared further that if Yen had been born in the twentieth century, he would certainly have become a great scientist and have advocated the "omnicompetence of science" [12] (*k'o-hsüeh wan-neng*).[z]

Liang's enthusiasm aroused the interest of many other scholars, including the nationalist, Chang Ping-lin,[aa] the moderate essayist, Chou Tso-jen,[ab] and the liberal, Hu Shih.[ac] [13] Their views, however, were not so much scholarly inquiries into the thought of an original thinker as educated speculations on the relevance of Yen's approach to the solutions of many serious problems confronting China at the time. Mansfield Freeman, following in the footsteps of both Hsü Shih-ch'ang and Liang

Ch'i-ch'ao, contributed an article on "Yen Hsi-chai, a 17th Century Philosopher" to the *Journal of the North China Branch of Royal Asiatic Society* as early as 1926. After citing laudatory remarks about Yen Yüan from Hsü's introduction to his work on Yen-Li philosophy and Liang's *History of Chinese Thought of the Last Three Hundred Years*, Freeman confidently stated that the seventeenth-century "Chinese pragmatist" held a high place in the thought of contemporary Chinese scholars, and his philosophy of education had real significance for modern China.[14]

It was in the 1930s, however, with the publication of Fung Yu-lan's [ad] *History of Chinese Philosophy*, Ch'ien Mu's [ae] *History of Chinese Thought of the Last Three Hundred Years*, and Ch'en Teng-yuan's [af] *Survey of the Philosophical Thought of Yen Hsi-chai*, that Yen Yüan's ideas took root in the scholarly world. It seems remarkable that, owing to Fung's new realism, in his highly selective study of Chinese philosophy, Yen Yüan occupies a conspicuous position, whereas Ch'en Po-sha, Chan Kan-ch'üan,[ag] Liu Tsung-chou,[ah] and Huang Tsung-hsi [ai] merit only passing reference.[15] Ch'ien Mu further suggests that Yen Yüan's unprecedented act of "smashing" the whole Neo-Confucian tradition surpassed southern scholars such as Huang Tsung-hsi, Wang Fu-chih, and Ku Yen-wu [aj] in courage and decisiveness.[16] To support his point, Ch'ien even quotes Wang K'un-shen's [ak] tribute to Yen Yüan in the form of a couplet: "He opened his mouth to utter the words that for two thousand years none was able to speak, and he put down on paper the thoughts that for two thousand years none dared to write." [17]

The rise of Marxism-Leninism in China again put Yen Yüan in a new light. A systematic effort was made by the Chinese Communist historians to "restore" the true image of Yen Yüan in the development of dialectical materialism in China. Hou Wai-lu,[al] in his comprehensive study of Chinese thought, denounces the bourgeois fallacy of equating "classical utilitarianism" with "capitalistic pragmatism." [18] He calls for an overall reevaluation of the seventeenth-century Chinese philosophy and arrives at the conclusion that Yen Yüan's major contribution lies in his new world view.[19] After a rather ingenuous and somewhat distorted textual analysis, Hou implicitly labels Yen's thought as a kind of materialist realism. Although Hou also criticizes Yen's residual antiquarianism, he praises him as a progressive fighter for the truth of materialism.[20]

What, then, is the authentic image of Yen Yüan? Was he a great revolutionary, an embodiment of the spirit of science, a man of action, a confirmed pragmatist, and a progressive realist? Paradoxically, there is some truth in all of the above designations, but it seems ill-advised to accept any of them as a serious attempt to understand Yen Yüan the man. To expose, at least in part, the motivation behind these "established" views is not to brush them aside as inconsequential, but to use them as possible channels toward a more objective study of the *problematik* of Yen Yüan.

My present concern, therefore, is not to grasp the historical Yen Yüan as such nor to understand his times in terms of what actually happened. Neither the life history of Yen Yüan nor the sociocultural milieu in which he lives is our main concern. Instead, the focus will be on the intellectual mode of Yen Yüan's response to one of the major issues of his times, an issue that had not only *historical* significance, but one that continued to beset Confucian thinkers for many generations to come. Hopefully a study of this kind will throw some light on the internal development of Confucianism in the seventeenth century, especially in reference to the perennial problem of *hsiu-shen* [am] (self-cultivation) in the Confucian tradition as a whole.

When Yen Yüan was born in 1635 (the eighth year of the reign of the last Ming emperor, Ch'ung-chen),[an] the first generation of Neo-Confucian thinkers in the seventeenth century was already well on its way to national prominence: Huang Tsung-hsi (1610–95), Chang Lü-hsiang [ao] (1611–74), Ku Yen-wu (1613–82), and Lu Lung-ch'i [ap] (1630–93).[21] Yen Yüan's reputation, on the other hand, was not to go beyond a small circle of scholars during his lifetime. His native village was halfway between Peking and Tientsin, which had never before excelled as an intellectual center. His poverty-stricken father had been adopted by a Chu [aq] family in another district. When Yen Yüan was only three years old his father disappeared, allegedly captured by the Manchus during their invasion of the capital in 1638. As a result, he was raised by the Chu family and given the surname Chu.[22]

At the age of seven, Yen Yüan began his formal education with a private tutor. His mother remarried when he was eleven. A marriage was arranged for him when he was only fourteen, but under the pretext of practicing the art of Taoist self-cultivation, he managed to keep his wife at a distance. It seems obvious that Yen Yüan's education and marriage were imposed on him for utilitarian reasons by his "grandfather," the man who had adopted his father. At fifteen, when his grandfather resorted to bribery to obtain for him the first-degree status, Yen Yüan was said to have burst into tears and refused to take any food, saying, "I would rather be an authentic illiterate than a fake literatus." [23]

At eighteen (1653), he passed the first-degree examination. Two years later he decided against any further attempts to enter government service, although he was still going through the motions of practicing literary writing and taking examinations simply to please his grandparents. His attention then focused on reading Ssu-ma Kuang's [ar] *Tzu-chih t'ung-chien* [as] (Comprehensive Mirror for the Aid of Government). His involvement in the study of history and statecraft prompted him to dip into a variety of military books. He also practiced swordsmanship and self-defense. His deviation from the main course of social advancement reached a high point when he seriously engaged himself in the study of medicine with a view to making a living from it. [24]

However, in 1658, at the age of twenty-three Yen Yüan began a career as a teacher. He named his study "*Ssu-ku* (Remembering the Ancients) *chai*" [at] and himself "*Ssu-ku jen.*" [au] He wrote a treatise entitled "The Kingly Way" (*Wang-tao lun*), [av] which was based on his rather romantic ideas about the golden age of the "three sagely dynasties." Speculating on issues such as the adaptation of the well-field system, the strength of the feudal order, the contents of education in ancient times, the possible revitalization of the procedures of recommendation and election of the Han dynasty, the urgency of suppressing heterodox teachings, and reforms in land taxation, what he did was no more than an intellectual exercise in the realm of state affairs. [25] To be sure, even in this brief work he demonstrated a high level of sophistication and originality, but it was still indicative of the concerns of an idealistic young man. Unfortunately this work has been studied and analyzed by some modern scholars as a record of Yen Yüan's subtle proposal for revolutionary social reforms. One of the reasons is probably that the work was later given a new title, *Ts'un-chih pien* [aw] (The Preservation of Statecraft), and printed together with three of Yen Yüan's mature works. [26]

In 1659, after almost a decade of married life, his wife gave birth to a son whom he named Fu-k'ao [ax] (literally, "en route to examination"). Again under heavy pressures from his grandfather, he decided to take the annual examination in Peking. But his trip to the capital was unfruitful. He failed not only to pass the examination but to avail himself of the literary talent in Peking. The Manchu court severely prohibited any form of gathering by the candidates.[27] Yen Yüan's abortive attempts to enter government service and the literary societies reinforced his reluctance to commit himself to sociopolitical activities. By then he had assumed the main responsibility for supporting his family. He spent most of his time tilling the land; occasionally he also practiced medicine. It was during this period that he encountered the writings of the Neo-Confucian philosophers, especially those of the Ch'eng-Chu [ay] school. His serious, careful study of the *Hsing-li ta-ch'üan* [az] (An Anthology of Works on Human Nature and the Universal Principle) had a profound impact on both his intellectual outlook and his way of life.[28]

In 1661, Yen Yüan established an altar to the *Tao-t'ung* [ba] (the "genealogy of the way," or "orthodox succession"). His sacred line began with the legendary cultural hero, Fu-hsi,[bb] and was handed down from the Duke of Chou [bc] to Confucius. After Confucius, he singled out Yen Hui,[bd] Tseng Tzu,[be] Tzu-ssu,[bf] Mencius, Chou Tun-i,[bg] Ch'eng Hao,[bh] Ch'eng I,[bi] Chang Tsai,[bj] Shao Yung,[bk] and Chu Hsi for daily worship. In addition, he put his own preference, two legendary physicians, on the same altar. His existential—we may even say religious—commitment to Neo-Confucian teachings shaped his spiritual direction for at least the next seven years.[29] To discipline himself, he daily practiced quiet-sitting, worked in the fields, and studied the Classics and history until midnight. He also organized a literary club mainly for the purpose of mutual exhortation on moral conduct. He made scholarly tours to nearby villages to visit well-known teachers. Through a series of dialogues with these learned men, he tried to broaden and deepen his understanding of the basic Neo-Confucian ideas. Further, with the help of an intimate friend, Wang Fa-ch'ien,[bl] as his "mirror," he kept a diary to record his own self-criticism.

Viewed objectively and detachedly, Yen Yüan's method seems somewhat mechanical. He reflected on the state of his mind—his critical self-awareness—several times a day. If his mind was "purely present" (absolutely attentive) for a given period he would mark a circle in the space designated for that period. If his mind was completely absent he would mark a cross. If its presence exceeded its absence he would leave the main part of the circle in white; otherwise he left the main part of the circle in black. In 1669, three years after he had initiated the method, he added additional symbols to represent control of his speech and temper. If he made one superfluous remark he would add a line to the circle ⊖. If his superfluous remarks surpassed five he would cross off the circle ⊗. If he lost his temper once he would add a T to the circle Ȯ. If he lost his temper more than five times he would cancel the circle with three lines ⊗.[30]

This was a rather rigid application of Mencius' instruction that true learning consists of nothing but the search for the lost mind. The concentration of energy and the focus of attention in such a practice, however, required the total devotion of the practitioner. When Yen Yüan applied this rigorous self-control to his daily affairs, his mode of living became highly ritualized. Indeed, he was so ritualistic about the way he dressed, ate, walked, and talked that every transgression was faithfully recorded as a warning for future action. He even insisted on putting down his evil thoughts before they materialized. He contended that if every mistake was recorded in ink as a reminder, although the diary would be filled with black marks, there would eventually be a day for reform; if nothing was recorded, a hundred mistakes might be let off and the chances for repentance thereby diminished.[31]

Only in the light of his ritualization can we understand how the simple act of mourning the death of his "grandmother" at the age of thirty-three could inflict so much damage on his health that he never fully recovered from it. This dramatic event occurred in 1668. On the death of his grandmother he decided to assume the responsibility of the principal mourner in place of his father. Without yet knowing that his father had been adopted by the Chu family, he went into mourning with the dual role of an unfilial son (due to his father's absence) and of a gratifying grandson. The mourning period started on the fourteenth day of the second month. For the first three days, he ate nothing, and yielded to sobbing and shedding tears at least three times a day. He resisted the convention of hiring musicians, nor did he invite a monk or Taoist priest to help with the ritual. On the fourth day he ate porridge, but only once in the morning and once in the evening. He refused to bury the body until the twenty-fourth day of the second month. During the burial ceremony he cried in such an uncontrollable manner that he bumped his head on the coffin and lost consciousness.

On the sixth day of the fourth month, he built himself a small hut near the tomb. By then he had been wearing a rough hemp-cloth garment day and night for about two months, which resulted in his arms and legs swelling with lumps. He did not change into a plain nightgown in the evenings until the third day of the sixth month. By the tenth month he was critically ill. Had he not been told the story of his father's adoption by a sympathetic old man of the Chu family, which was later verified by his remarried mother, Yen might have continued with his ritualized self-torture for three years.[32]

Although Yen Yüan physically survived the traumatic experience, his spiritual orientation was profoundly altered by it. He became dissatisfied with Chu Hsi's *Chia-li*,[bm] a treatise on family rituals which he followed in minute detail during the period of mourning. He also questioned the whole Neo-Confucian emphasis on quiet-sitting and book reading.[33] In 1669, two months after his bitter experience, he completed a treatise on human nature entitled *Ts'un-hsing pien* [bn] (On the Preservation of Human Nature).[34] His arguments against Chu Hsi's dualistic interpretation of human nature and in favor of returning to Mencius' insistence on the original goodness of man anticipated Tai Chen's [bo] philosophical inquiry into the concept of the good. As a symbolic act, he changed the name of his study from *Ssu-ku chai* to *Hsi chai* [bp] (The Studio of Practice).[35] Toward the end of the same year, he completed another important treatise entitled *Ts'un-hsüeh pien* [bq] (On the Preservation of Learning), in which he severely criticized the teachings of Ch'eng I and Chu Hsi and advocated a return to the educational programs of the Duke of Chou and Confucius.[36]

Yen Yüan's attack on Ch'eng I and Chu Hsi marked a fundamental change in his spiritual orientation. Quiet-sitting and book reading were relegated to secondary importance. Activism in the form of moral practice became his central concern. The word *hsi*, which he used to rename his study, best symbolized this new direction. Etymologically *hsi* depicts a bird learning to fly. In the first line of the *Analects*, it is used to indicate the process through which one's learning becomes fully interiorized. To focus on *hsi* rather than on quiet-sitting or book reading is to emphasize the realm of concrete activities. It should be noted, however, that Yen Yüan's departure from the Ch'eng-Chu school did not constitute a rejection of its ritualism. On the contrary, after his painful experience in 1668 he became even more convinced that the most authentic approach to self-cultivation was through the practice of rituals [37] (hsi-li).[br]

In 1670 he learned that his father came from the Yen family of Po-yeh,[bs] and he made a special visit to his ancestral home in Hopei. To his happy surprise, his own grandmother, née Chang, was still alive in her eighties. When he returned home he mixed some of his blood with ink and wrote a tablet in honor of his father. He performed salutory bows in front of the tablet day and night as if his father were still present. In 1673, when his "grandfather" died, he formally reverted to the surname Yen. In 1679 he lost the sight of his left eye as the result of an infection. But this did not prevent him from completing another important treatise, originally entitled Huan mi-t'u [bt] (Calling for Those Who Have Lost the Way), but later changed to Ts'un-jen pien [bu] (On the Preservation of Humanity). Nor did the blindness in his left eye stop him from making an extensive journey to Manchuria in search of his father's whereabouts. When he arrived in Feng-t'ien fu,[bv] he kneeled down by the side of the road and distributed pamphlets describing his father. After about a year his sincere efforts produced some result: his half-sister, whom he had never met before, came to him from Manchuria with the sad news that their father had died. Thus ended Yen's long struggle to determine for himself his true origins.

In 1689 he formally accepted Li Kung as his disciple. Two years later he made his only journey to the central part of China. The entire trip lasted about six and a half months. Thereafter, except for his short-lived mastership of Chang-nan [bw] Academy, which was destroyed by flood in 1696, Yen spent the rest of his life studying, teaching, and occasionally writing. In 1701, when Li Kung was about to leave for the capital, Yen bade farewell to him by saying that to preserve the Tao on a thousand rolls (chüan) [bx] of paper is less meaningful than to entrust it to a few men of some understanding; the first order of concern in Li's trip to the north should be to rouse the students to an experiential grasp of the Confucian truth.

Yen Yüan died in 1704 at the age of sixty-nine. His last words to his beloved student were: "The world is still improvable. You should cultivate your learning and prepare yourselves for some useful task." [38]

Yen Yüan's life presents us with a number of puzzling questions. How can he be characterized as an activist when for the most part he lived like a recluse in a small village? Is there any justification for propagandizing his revolutionary spirit, as some modern scholars do, when he constantly ritualized his way of life into a conventional mode? How could he reconcile his emphasis on practical involvement in sociopolitical affairs with his own role as a teacher in an isolated environment? Indeed, how could he criticize Chu Hsi's family rituals as being too demanding when his own self-discipline was even more difficult to follow?

To answer these questions we must go beyond Yen Yüan's life and study his intellectual commitments. This cannot be done, however, without a proper understanding of the kinds of problems he confronted. The fall of the Ming dynasty had a profound impact on virtually all mid-seventeenth-century Chinese thinkers. The Confucian response to the decline and final collapse of the great Chinese empire was certainly one of the most important dimensions of seventeenth-century Chinese thought. Wang Fu-chih's advocacy of ethnoculturalism, Huang Tsung-hsi's critique of despotism, and Ku Yen-wu's advocacy of the decentralization of authority and the strengthening of provincial powers should all be understood against the background of this important event. Yen Yüan's "The Kingly Way," a treatise on statecraft, thus reflected a common concern of his generation.

However, as I have already point out, Yen Yüan's work of 1658, written in his early twenties, was not indicative of his mature views. A brief survey of his life reveals that, unlike Wang Fu-chih, Huang Tsung-hsi, and Ku Yen-wu, he did not have a broad perspective of dynastic and institutional history; unlike Huang he did not have an intimate knowledge of contemporary politics, and unlike Ku, he did not have a comprehensive understanding of local conditions. Since Yen was intellectually isolated from the major issues of his time and politically detached from the centers of power and influence, one could hardly expect his contribution to be made in what is called political thought. Yet his failure to develop a profound historical consciousness, to come to grips with the political realities of the court, or to delve deeply into the socioeconomic conditions of the provinces did not deprive him of an essential position in seventeenth-century Chinese thought. Where was his strength, then?

In response to the fall of the Ming dynasty, Yen Yüan made an often-quoted criticism of the Confucian literati: "In times of leisure they discussed with folded hands the lofty ideas of mind and human nature; when they were confronted with a crucial situation they could repay their prince only by committing suicide." [39] This may well serve as a key to Yen Yüan's *problematik*. Yet if one takes the quotation seriously, one cannot but wonder why those who actually sacrificed their lives should be singled out as targets of attack. The very decision to commit suicide required tremendous resolution; the willingness to fulfill a deep commitment by sacrificing one's own life was far from a trifling matter. Also, Yen Yüan was himself very much concerned with the issues of mind and human nature; he could not have objected to any serious discussion of these ideas. Why, then, was he so unsparing in his evaluation of the late Ming Confucian literati?

One way of answering the question is to stress Yen's "pragmatism." He did not criticize the act of committing suicide itself, nor did he attack philosophical discussion per se. He was dissatisfied with the absence of pragmatic values in both cases. It is easy to cite examples in Yen Yüan's teachings to illustrate his pragmatic concerns. His attacks on the Neo-Confucianists after his traumatic experience in 1668 is one example. Yen maintained that extensive reading or writing was damaging to one's health and ridiculed those Confucian scholars who spent most of their times on books as "shamefully acquiring the appearance of women." [40] He even found an analogy between those widowed women who wasted their lives in mourning the dead and the Neo-Confucianists who buried themselves in books. Two vivid accounts of those effete scholars are found in Yen Yüan's *Ts'un-hsüeh*. One derives from his personal observation:

My friend Chang Shih-ch'ing [by] was well versed in books. He said that he had almost completed reading the histories of the last two thousand years from the Ch'in-Han [bz] period onward. He explained the meanings of those books to his students. When his strength was exhausted he rested on the bed, panting. After a long while, he would get up and lecture again. When his strength was exhausted he would again lie down. This was indeed unusual exertion; it not only ruined his health but also failed to produce any talent. Under that kind of condition how could any of his students study the "six arts?" [41]

The other had to do with his own teacher, a scholar in Ch'i-yang: [ca]

Tiao Meng-chi [cb] of Ch'i-yang expended his strength in the learning of quiet-sitting and book reading. He read by day, contemplated by night, and wrote down his ideas in one hundred *chüan*. But every day he was run down in health, spitting and coughing. Three months before his death he even lost his voice.[42]

After a survey of such cases Yen Yüan concluded that those who sat motionlessly for hours and spent most of their time reading books were invariably weak and useless; they became the laughing stock of soldiers and farmers.[43] He thus advocated a new form of learning called *shih-hsüeh* [cc] (literally, "real learning"). It should be pointed out, however, that the concept of *shih* [cd] had long been used by Confucian scholars to describe their approaches to learning. Since the main concern of Confucianism was self-realization through moral cultivation, experiential knowledge was always considered superior to speculative theory. It is in this sense that teaching by words, in the eyes of the Confucianists, is far less effective than teaching by example. The early Ming Confucian master, Hsüeh Hsüan (Wen-ch'ing,[ce] 1389–1464), also called his approach to learning "real" (*shih-hsüeh*) because it was not an accumulation of empirical facts but a process of self-fulfillment through a series of experiential encounters with the ideas presented in the books.[44] The existential dimension of learning was so crucial to Confucianism that none of the Sung-Ming masters ever separated book reading from the actual practice of self-cultivation. What, then, was "new" in Yen Yüan's *shih-hsüeh?*

In the accounts of Yen Yüan's life it seems evident that he had never questioned the prominence of self-cultivation in the Confucian hierarchy of values. Even after he had become disillusioned with the Ch'eng-Chu school, he still followed a rigorous plan of self-discipline. Ironically, his ritualized life style could have been praised by the Ch'eng-Chu Confucianists as an excellent example of self-control. It is true that Yen Yüan severely reprehended the Sung-Yüan Confucian emphasis on tranquillity and passivity, but he faithfully adhered to its methods of "internal self-transformation." In one important sense, though, Yen Yüan substantially departed from the Ch'eng-Chu school, a departure that has been characterized by a few modern scholars as a "philosophy of dynamism." Essentially it differs little from Wang Yang-ming's advocacy of "constant practice in the midst of concrete affairs." [45] This is probably one of the reasons why Yang P'ei-chih [cf] and others maintain that Yen Yüan was deeply influenced by this great mid-Ming thinker. To illustrate this point there is a rather elaborate example of learning to play the lute given us by Yen Yüan:

The *Book of Poetry* and the *Book of History* are like an instruction book for the lute. Thoroughly mastering the instruction book and being able to explain it in detail—can this be called the actual study of the lute? This is why I said that to search for the efficacy of the Tao by way of discussing and reading is to be a thousand *li* from the truth. It is worse still if an absurd person points to the instruction book and says, "This is the lute." . . . Only when one has learned to sing the score, to master the fingering, to tune the string, to follow the rhythm, and to play in harmony, can one be said to have studied the lute.[46]

He continued to describe the state of being "versed" (*hsi*) in the lute and the state of being "competent" (*neng*) [cg] in it.

Through this analogy Yen's message seems apparent. One can never learn to play the lute by reading the instruction book, no matter how diligently and conscientiously he reads it. The art of playing the lute cannot be mastered through a mental process of internalization; it can be learned only by practice.

Yen Yüan's emphasis on practice again reminds us of Wang Yang-ming's "unity of knowledge and action." [47] Knowledge is merely empty talk if it cannot be put to use. Genuine knowledge is simultaneously a form of acting that must make a practical difference in the world, for practicality is an essential criterion of true knowledge. To *know* how to play the lute and yet not be able actually to play it is an example of misusing the word *know* to describe a state of being ignorant. It is inconceivable that one can say that one knows how to play the lute when he has merely intellectually comprehended the instruction book. But the compatibility of Yen and Wang must not be overstressed. After all, Yang-ming's activism presupposes that the ultimate basis for man's moral self-realization is a completely self-sufficient process of internal transformation, whereas Yen Yüan's dynamism insists that self-cultivation has to be carried out in the concrete world amid its practical affairs.[48]

Yen Yüan's insight into the complexity of actual practice requires further explanation. To him the real challenge of self-cultivation is not only to make a qualitative "leap" from knowing to acting, but also to continue the process of practice in a constant or even routine way. To have mastered the basic techniques of the lute is merely the beginning. Only through years of practice can one become proficient in the art. Even if one has learned all the skills of playing the music by heart, one is still far from being a virtuoso. To arrive at a state where "one's heart forgets about one's hands and one's hands no longer feel the strings," [49] one must practice diligently and unceasingly.

Similarly, ritual practice involves an incessant commitment to self-perfection. It is a daily, indeed hourly, affair, and by necessity it has to assume a concrete form. Of course there is little excitement in such trifling acts as rising early, dressing properly, eating moderately, refraining from superfluous talking, walking at an unhurried pace, sitting straight, and keeping a diary consistently. But like the training of a lute virtuoso, to integrate all these seemingly fragmentary acts into a holistic expression of the ritualized personality requires a lifelong commitment.

The act of a specific ritual practice is not only a record but also a self-revealing gesture. It in a sense offers a solution to the perennial Confucian problem of "inner and outer" (*nei-wai*),[ch] for it bridges the gap between an inner effort of self-cultivation and its outer manifestation in the family, the state, and, indeed, the entire universe. A ritualized act, in the true sense of the word, always involves both inner and outer dimensions. It is neither an unexternalizable experience nor a contentless form. On one hand, it records the attained level of self-cultivation; on the other it reveals the spiritual strength in the sociopolitical realm. Yen Yüan was especially sensitive to the symbolic meanings of ritualized acts; he insisted on the perfect execution of virtually every one of them. For example he never left his room without being properly dressed, even late in the evening when he simply got up from the bed to go to the toilet. He contended that the act of leaving the room provided an important opportunity for practicing moral self-cultivation.[50]

After all, to study the lute is to acquire a skill, but to engage in ritual practice is to master oneself. The art one must learn in mastering oneself is that of self-cultivation. Unlike the study of the lute, one cannot for a minute lay down one's instrument and rest. The moment one forsakes ritual practice, one has already deviated from the course of self-cultivation. Constant practice does not guarantee a competent performance. Yen Yüan was thus frequently in a state of "fear and trembling." He was frightened, to be sure, neither by the presence of a transcendent reality nor by the thought of retribution. Like Confucius's disciple, Tseng Tzu, he felt he was always "standing on the edge of a chasm or walking on thin ice" for fear of failing the task of self-cultivation. And this brings us to the *problematik* of Yen Yüan.

It is true that Yen Yüan never questioned the centrality of self-cultivation in the value system of Confucianism. He nevertheless challenged the workability of the Ch'eng-Chu version of it. He established the criterion of practicality to differentiate what he called the authentic Confucian self-cultivation from other non-Confucian methods of spiritual self-discipline. To him, quiet-sitting never produced truly practical values. The mysterious experiences of the Ch'an masters were merely flowers in the mirror or the moon in the water:

One can only in time of idleness amuse oneself with these delusions. If one attempts to use the light or to carry the beauty, one is bound to fail. . . . The flower and the moon are gone when the mirror and the water are taken away. When the effort of quiet-sitting continues without cessation throughout one's whole lifetime, the delusions may become more wonderful and the void may become more profound. However, that is just like the man who day after day sits for a lifetime in front of the mirror or the water, amusing himself with the flowers or the moon. He only deceives himself through his whole lifetime.[51]

Yen Yüan maintained that true self-cultivation is designed "to change the world" (chuan-shih).[ci] The aim is to strengthen one's internal self-identity so that one can change the world instead of "being changed by the world" (shih-chuan).[cj] [52] To have a tangible impact on the concrete realities of one's environment becomes an inseparable dimension of one's self-cultivation. If the new experience resulting from one's self-cultivation cannot be converted into some form of energy for the improvement of the world, it is both useless and worthless. Yen Yüan confidently stated that no matter how profound the Sung masters were philosophically, their conviction that the cult of quietude would yield the fruit of enlightenment was a fiction.[53] He was certain that values could be created only by a dynamic encounter with the realities of life. It is thus understandable why Yen Yüan went out of his way to defend the Confucian statesman, Wang An-shih [ck] (1021–86). Wang was courageous enough to confront the "brute facts" of his times, and it is also in this sense that Yen Yüan praised the activism of other Sung scholar officials.[54]

Yen Yüan's central concern thus became how to translate the spiritual strength of self-cultivation into sociopolitical forces so as to shape the world according to the Confucian ideal. To him, usefulness was the key to Confucian truth. Being useful in a modest sense means that the aim of one's private effort is not merely to attain a state of internal peace but to make a tangible contribution to one's immediate environment and to set a living example for one's folks at home. To dwell in spiritual quietude as an end in itself is a luxury no true Confucianist can afford. In fact, all

Confucian sages in history were men of action. According to Yen Yüan, it is inconceivable that a Confucianist, as differentiated from a Taoist or a Ch'an Buddhist, could live up to his true image by cultivating his spiritual self in complete isolation. The level of self-realization, in the Confucian context, is measured by the degree of its usefulness. As the sage extends his practical value to the universe in general, so the ordinary Confucianist exerts his moral influence at home. The true follower of Confucian teachings never fails to share his "inner light" with the people around him.[55]

To return to my earlier point, Yen Yüan did not object to the discussion of such fundamental issues as mind and human nature. As I shall explain later, he was himself devoted to their study. Nor did he show any disrespect for those who sacrificed their lives to symbolize their deep commitments. He remarked once: "In reading *Chia-shen hsün-nan lu* [cl] (A Record on the Loyalist Deaths of 1644), whenever I encountered the saying, 'Shamefully I am at a loss to find any means to meet the critical situation; all I have left is to repay my debt of gratitude to the emperor by dying,' I was always mournfully moved to tears." [56] Yen Yüan was well aware that it was not the intrinsic weakness of discussing the lofty ideas of mind and human nature that led to the downfall of the Ming dynasty. The fundamental issue was the inability of the best Confucianists to translate their efforts at internal self-cultivation into useful energy to meet the crisis of the state. He was so impressed with the heroic sacrifices of those Confucian loyalists, yet so disheartened by their powerlessness, that he felt it necessary to conclude that, judging by the criterion of practicality, they all died a meaningless death.

Instead of abandoning the practice of self-cultivation and concentrating on the instrumental values of statecraft exclusively, which would seem to many of us to be the natural alternative, Yen Yüan made a series of inquiries into the "roots" of man's self-realization. Contrary to the common belief that Yen Yüan was a pragmatist, his *problematik* compelled him to examine some of the most fundamental philosophical concepts in Neo-Confucianism, rather than pursue the course of "scientific empiricism." His originality actually lies in the critique of the Ch'eng-Chu concept of human nature and the formulation of a new Confucian concept of man. We shall therefore proceed to an examination of Yen Yüan's inquiry into human nature.

One of the essential concerns of Confucianism is the uniqueness of man. Since the time of Mencius, when the problem of differentiating human beings from other animals became philosophically significant, Confucian thinkers have always been involved in reflection on man's self-image. With the beginning of the Confucian revival in the Sung dynasty, they again centered on the issue of how to establish the "ultimate of man" (li jen-chi).[cm] It may be said that human reality is the point of departure for virtually all serious works by Confucian scholars and that human nature is the recurring theme in the Confucian tradition as a whole. Yen Yüan's inquiry into the nature of man therefore placed him contextually in the mainstream of Confucian thinking.

Methodologically, Yen Yüan presented his views on human nature in a series of critical comments on the sayings of Chu Hsi.[57] His main purpose was not so much to expose the weakness of the great Sung philosopher as to put his own ideas in proper perspective. It seems appropriate, therefore, to characterize his "critical comments" as sincere attempts to enter into a "dialogue" with Chu Hsi, that is, to think sympathetically with the Neo-Confucian master so as to come to grips with his real difficulties.

Yen Yüan was aware that Chu Hsi's approach to human nature had been deeply influenced by Chang Tsai's notion of ch'i [cn] (material force or vital breath), especially the more restrictive concept of ch'i-chih chih hsing [co] (physical nature). While Chu Hsi believed that Chang, by adding the "physical" dimension to the Mencian idea of man, had made a tremendous contribution to the formulation of a more balanced and more comprehensive view of human nature in the Confucian tradition, Yen Yüan felt that Chang had actually confused the issue. The thrust of his critique of Chu Hsi in this connection thus centered around Chu Hsi's attempt to incorporate Chang's concept of physical nature into the Mencian idea of man. He argued that such an attempt led to some unnecessary ramifications, and that Chu Hsi had failed to come to grips with Mencius' insight that man is intrinsically perfectible despite his weakness.

Yen Yüan agreed with Chu Hsi that, as a general principle, in the discussion of man, merely talking about physical nature without reference to moral nature is to commit the fallacy of obscurity, and merely talking about moral nature without reference to physical nature is to commit the fallacy of incompleteness.[58] He could not, however, agree with Chu Hsi that Mencius' views on man considered as a whole were still "incomplete." He felt that Chu Hsi had actually misinterpreted Mencius in his attempt to develop a more satisfactory concept of human nature. By forcing Chang Tsai's idea upon Mencius, Chu Hsi had to accept the position that "evil must also be understood as part of human nature," [59] which was indeed a major departure from Mencius' insistence upon man's inner goodness.

It should be mentioned in passing that Yen Yüan found an affinity between his role as a critic and that of Mencius: neither of them had any strong liking for argument, but both were impelled by moral indignation to take issue with the established view of their times.[60] Mencius insisted that human nature is good, so as to provide an ultimate basis for man's perfectibility through self-cultivation. He contended that the beginnings, or rather the "budding potentials" (*tuan*),[cp] of the four cardinal virtues (human-heartedness, righteousness, propriety, and wisdom) are inherent in the mind. Moral self-cultivation centers on the reflective and introspective functions of the mind. It is because of the unique ability of the human mind to transform itself into a higher order of perfection for the sake of self-realization that human nature is defined as good. It is this particular nature of man that creates moral values and distinguishes man from the rest of the animals—indeed, from any other kind of being.[61]

To say that human nature is good is thus to characterize man by his unique endowment. This is basically consistent with Confucius' teaching that the attainment of moral perfection is dependent on an inner decision: "Is humanity something remote? If I want to be humane, behold, humanity has arrived." [62] To be sure, Mencius' emphasis on the goodness of man does not overlook the physical side of man's nature, such as the instinctual demands of sex and appetite. On the contrary, he regarded these demands as a legitimate part of man. Yen Yüan was especially delighted to learn that both feeling (*ch'ing*) [cq] and ability (*ts'ai*),[cr] two important aspects of the physical nature, were designated by Mencius as good.[63] How did Mencius reconcile the apparent incongruity between the unique attributes of man and those which he shares with other animals, if he tried to label both as good? This leads us to the theory of "great body" (*ta-t'i*) [cs] and "small body" (*hsiao-t'i*).[ct]

For the sake of convenience, it may be useful to discuss Mencius' theory in terms of the depth-structure and surface-structure of human nature. The "great body" refers to the ultimate basis of man's being—his uniqueness. It is the depth-structure of human nature. The "small body" refers to the physical existence of man, or his corporeality. It is the surface-structure of human nature. Paradoxically, the depth-structure, which is described by Mencius as "great," is that tiny "bud" special to man; whereas the surface-structure, which is described by Mencius as "small," is that large "stuff" common to all animals. Self-cultivation, however, is not to develop the inherent "buds" of virtue at the expense of man's physical nature. Rather, it is to cultivate the depth-structure so that the surface-structure can also be properly "nourished." As the saying goes, "Virtue can foster the body" (te jun shen).[cu] [64] Yen Yüan pointed out that Mencius emphasized chien-hsing [cv] (realizing the bodily design) as the authentic way of self-cultivation. Only when the depth-structure is fully manifested can the physical nature be truly developed. If merely the surface-structure is manifest, it will never reveal the unique nature of man. It may even bring about its own destruction and thus ruin the corporeality as well.[65] Therefore the important message is to cultivate the depth-structure so that the surface-structure is also cultivated.

Underlying this approach to human nature is a respect for the complete man. To use the above terminology, the depth- and surface-structures are both respected, and self-cultivation is to see to it that both are fully integrated into a holistic structure. Chu Hsi's attempt to assign all human values to the depth-structure and all human evils to the surface-structure is therefore to create an unnecessary tension in the holistic structure of man. In so doing, he destroyed the unity between man's great and small bodies. If the development of the great body inevitably leads to the suppression of the small body, how can anyone "realize the bodily design" by way of self-cultivation? If the surface-structure has to be relinquished before man can become what he ought to be, how can a full manifestation of the depth-structure help the physical nature to develop itself? By formulating the concept of ch'i-chih chih hsing as the main source of evil, Chu Hsi substituted Mencius' complete man with his own version—a partial man who sacrifices his physical nature for an unreal self-fulfillment.

Yen Yüan further maintained that since self-cultivation has to be carried out in a concrete disciplinary process, the physical nature is actually the "instrumentality" for the realization of the true self. To deny the importance of human corporeality is to detach man from the very context of his existence. Chu Hsi criticized *ch'ing* (feelings) as dangerous because strong passion frequently inflicts damage upon the true nature of man. Yen Yüan contended that strong passion itself is not to be blamed. In fact, filial sons and loyal ministers are all passionate human beings. Chu Hsi followed Ch'eng I in condemning *ts'ai* (powers, drives). Yen Yüan contended that since *ts'ai*, as a constituent element of the physical nature, is one of the concrete bases of man's goodness, it is certainly not to be belittled.[66]

In addition, Yen Yüan argued that *ch'ing* is the manifestation of the inherent moral propensity of man; *ts'ai* is the means by which such a propensity reveals itself in concrete affairs. Without *ch'ing* and *ts'ai* the true nature of man cannot present itself; without the physical nature there is no point of talking about *ch'ing* and *ts'ai*. Without either, the true nature of man is also absent. Therefore *ch'ing* is none other than the manifestation (*hsien*) [cw] of true human nature, and *ts'ai* is none other than the ability (*neng*) [cx] of true human nature. The so-called *ch'i-chih* [cy] (literally, the stuff of material force, referring to that which constitutes the physical nature) is, after all, that of *ch'ing*, of *ts'ai*, and of man's true nature.[67]

Yen Yüan might have used Mencius to strengthen his case, but the message he wanted to deliver seems quite convincing. The central question can be stated as follows: whether the ideal man is a denial of his actual existence or the actual man is the very basis of his ideal manifestation. From Chu Hsi's viewpoint, what a man ought to be is attainable only when the moral agent, through a long process of self-purification, has succeeded in changing the directions of what he actually is. For example, his instinctive need for sex and food has to be sublimated or suppressed. Yen Yüan, on the other hand, suggested that what a man ought to be is rooted in the very structure of what he actually is. To attain self-realization one must be truthful to both the depth- and surface-structures of human nature. For example, to him it is basically immoral to practice celibacy as a means to attain a higher level of spirituality.

It should be mentioned in this connection that Yen Yüan's principal critique of Buddhism was its practice of celibacy. Yen Yüan declared that the relationship between husband and wife is not only the most primordial but also the most fundamental of all human relations. He stated, "Only after there have been husband and wife are there father and son; only after there have been father and son are there elder and younger brothers; only after there have been elder and younger brothers are there friends; and only after there have been friends are there lord and minister." [68] Since the sagely way begins with husband and wife, to deny the value of sexuality is to nip in the bud the basic Confucian relationships. Chu Hsi's failure to understand that the physical nature is also morally good was indicative of Buddhist influence, [69] Yen argues.

As we have already pointed out, Yen Yüan maintained that the physical nature is really the instrumentality of self-realization. Without it, man is merely an abstract concept. Only by the instrumentality of the physical nature can man become a concrete reality. To become a spiritual being completely outside the bodily form is at most a figment of the imagination. [70] It is true that his physical nature restricts man's freedom, but it is also through his physical nature that man's true potential is understood and expressed. [71] If a human being is a concrete manifestation rather than an abstract approximation, then man's physical nature is not only a work of art that demands appreciation but also a creative agent which constantly gives birth to new human realities.

In the light of the above, it seems less puzzling that Yen Yüan should have launched an attack on Chu Hsi's concept of reverence (ching),[cz] while his own life-style seems to have borne witness to its applicability. He remarked that there is nothing wrong with the concept itself. But when it is abstracted from the daily affairs of the concrete world and converted into a state of mind, its original dynamism of "carefully attending to a variety of details" is lost. Yen Yüan said:

The ancients taught men to do housework, and while doing housework to practice reverence. They taught the proper ways of dealing with people, and in these to practice reverence. They taught rituals, music, archery, riding, reading, and mathematics, but in arranging the order of the rituals, in the laws of the notes, in steadying the bow, in control of the horse, in punctuation, and in calculation, there was nothing without the practice of reverence. Therefore it is said, "Be reverent in handling public affairs," "Be reverent in your daily affairs," and "Be truly reverent in your action." All these emphasize the constant practice of reverence by the complete devotion of both the body and mind. If the traditional methods of the ancients are being laid aside and the practice of reverence is sought in quiet-sitting, meditative self-control, slow-walking, and soft-talking, it is like using the empty form of a Confucian term to do the real work of Buddhism. [72]

The fundamental issue, then, is the choice between a dynamic and active process of self-cultivation which will eventually lead to the realization of a complete and concrete man, and a static and passive course of self-control which at best leads merely to the fulfillment of a partial and abstract man. Yen Yüan contended that the most authentic method of self-cultivation is to *do* rather than to *be*. Man becomes what he should be by engaging in daily affairs. To confront the realities of the world at the moment of internal self-cultivation is, to use Mencius' words, always doing something (*pi-yu-shih yen*).[da]

To do something is to make an impact on the existing order of things. No matter how small the impact is, it makes a useful difference. Every man can exert an influence on the world by "doing something," by being active in the affairs of the world. When such deeds have accumulated sufficiently, the direction of the world is bound to change. The true value of man lies in his ability to change the world toward the good. If the Confucianists refuse to do things and insist on simply being themselves, they can never change the world; nor can they escape the fate of being passively changed, or rather destroyed, by the world under the control of others.

Yen Yüan realized that for generations many of the great personalities in the Confucian tradition had devoted themselves to the cultivation of a kind of "inner experience." They might have gained some profound insight into themselves, but they had no useful role to play in the sociopolitical realm. The very fact that they were powerless to perform a useful function in a crucial situation was an indication of the impotence of their existence. Like the helpless screams of widowed women, their sound and fury signified nothing in a world of hard reality. Even when they were determined to change the world by sacrificing their own lives, they still had no practical experience to guide them. Consequently many Confucianists died a meaningless death.

A fundamental change in the direction of self-cultivation was called for. Yen Yüan pleaded that quiet-sitting, meditation, and book reading be replaced by active participations in the world of daily affairs, or to use my earlier description, by a concrete process of ritualization. For man becomes what he ought to be by doing, practicing, and acting. Human beings never really develop themselves by sitting in meditation. The Confucianist must accordingly transform himself from the abstract state of being a partial, passive, and useless man of words to the concrete reality of being a complete, active, and useful man of deeds. If the Confucianist wants to restore his sense of mission, and indeed his right to survive, he must labor strenuously in what may be called "lived concreteness."

Finally, it must be pointed out that although Yen Yüan's central concern was not self-cultivation so much as the search for inner truth, his serious attempt to redefine the spiritual tradition of Confucianism and to reformulate what he considered essential to Confucian intentionality can be better appreciated in the light of his bitter struggle to discipline himself by an active participation in Confucian rituals. To be sure, his ideal of a complete and concrete man, which is predicated on the Mencian view of human nature, stands in tension with his almost compulsive emphasis on ritualism. He might have also failed to develop a philosophy of "human community as holy rite," to borrow the title of Herbert Fingarette's study on Confucian ritualism.[73] But his insistence on an ethicoreligious commitment as a condition prior to any form of sociopolitical activism symbolizes a defining characteristic of the humanistic world view propounded by virtually all great Neo-Confucian thinkers.

At the beginning of this discussion, I raised the question of Yen Yüan's authentic image. I am still far from providing a satisfactory answer. However, I may tentatively suggest that Yen Yüan was a "revolutionary" only in the sense that he attacked the influential Ch'eng-Chu tradition so that he could revitalize the true Confucian approach to self-cultivation. He was an "embodiment of the spirit of science" only in the sense that he detached himself from the fallacy of speculation and returned to the world of concrete objects so as to discipline himself morally. He was a "man of action" only in the sense that he denounced passivity and advocated a kind of participatory ritualism. He was a "confirmed pragmatist" only in the sense that he emphasized practicality and demanded that all human actions be useful. Finally he was a "realist" only in the sense that he upheld the view that the physical nature of man is an indispensable instrumentality for self-realization.

Unless we are willing to confine our terms to the specific designations stated above, we must conclude that Yen Yüan was not a revolutionary, for he remained faithful to virtually all the basic spiritual values in the Confucian tradition. He was not a scientist, for he never wanted to investigate or study natural phenomena, nor indeed any other phenomena, so as to obtain a purely intellectual understanding of the external world. He was not an activist either, for his ritualized acts were not ends in themselves but means to a higher goal of self-realization. He was neither a pragmatist nor a realist, for his moral concern was idealistic in orientation and his sense of mission was religious in character.

Yen Yüan's authentic image would have disappointed his modern admirers. His ideas might have also seemed remote from the urgent problems of contemporary China. Nevertheless, he was not only an original thinker of the seventeenth century, but one of the great Confucian intellectuals of all time. The *problematik* with which he struggled throughout his life comes down to the bedrock of Confucian thinking, and the inquiry to which he devoted his entire intellectual effort penetrates into one of the most profound dimensions of human reality. To study Yen Yüan's *problematik* and follow his inquiry is not to see his relevance to us, but to appreciate the intrinsic value of his thought so as to cultivate our own sense of relevance.

The best edition of Yen Yüan's collected works is the *Yen-Li ts'ung-shu,* [db] edited by *Ssu-ts'un hsüeh-hui.* [dc] The work, which was prefaced in 1923, includes more items (those listed below) than the collected works of Yen Yüan in the *Chi-fu ts'ung-shu.* [dd] (Page numbers refer to the photographic reprint by the Kuang-wen [dm] Book Co. of Taiwan.)

> *Yen Hsi-chai hsien-sheng nien-p'u,* [de] pp. 4–46.
>
> *Ssu-shu cheng-wu,* [df] pp. 47–87.
>
> *Yen Hsi-chai hsien-sheng yen-hsing lu,* [dg] pp. 90–117.
>
> *Yen Hsi-chai hsien-sheng p'i–i lu,* [dh] pp. 119–24.
>
> *Ts'un-hsüeh pien,* pp. 127–55.
>
> *Ts'un-hsing pien,* pp. 156–71.
>
> *Ts'un-chih pien,* [di] pp. 173–80.
>
> *Ts'un-jen pien,* pp. 181–97.
>
> *Chu Tzu yü-lei p'ing,* [dj] pp. 199–225.
>
> *Li-wen shou-ch'ao,* [dk] pp. 227–53.
>
> *Hsi-chai chi-yü,* [dl] pp. 255–46.

1. Joseph R. Levenson's three-volume study, *Confucian China and Its Modern Fate* (University of California Press, 1968), vol. 1, pp. xxvii-xxxiii.

2. Levenson's pioneering study on Liang Ch'i-ch'ao in the context of the predicament of modern Chinese intellectuals can be found in his *Liang Ch'i-ch'ao and the Mind of Modern China* (Harvard University Press, 1953).

3. Liang Ch'i-ch'ao, *Chung-kuo chin san-pai nien hsüeh-shu shih* [dn] (Shanghai, 1935; hereafter referred to as Liang, *Hsüeh-shu shih*), pp. 1–10, 104–49.

4. Hou Wai-lu, *Chung-kuo tsao-ch'i ch'i-meng ssu-hsiang shih* [do] (Peking, 1956; hereafter referred to as Hou, *Ssu-hsiang shih*), pp. 3–36.

5. Four of Yen Yüan's most prominent works were: *Ts'un-chih pien* (On the Preservation of Statecraft), *Ts'un-hsüeh pien* (On the Preservation of Learning), *Ts'un-jen pien* (On the Preservation of Humanity), and *Ts'un-hsing pien* (On the Preservation of Human Nature). All include the word *ts'un. Ssu-ts'un* is therefore used here to refer to Yen Yüan's teaching in general.

6. The story of the revival of interest in Yen Yüan in the 1920s can be reconstructed only from fragmentary information. See Chin Hsü-ju, [dp] *Yen Yüan yü Li Kung* [dq] (Shanghai, 1935), pp. 1–3; and Ch'en Teng-yuan, *Yen Hsi-chai che-hsüeh ssu-hsiang shu* [dr] (Nanking, prefaced in 1934), vol. 2.

7. See Chao Heng's [ds] preface to *Yen-Li ts'ung-shu,* edition of *Ssu-ts'un hsüeh-hui* (Peking, 1923).

8. It may be farfetched to correlate intellectual attachment to great personalities in the past with the politics of regionalism, but the emotional subtlety in regional pride is so important a factor in modern China that any serious study of the formulation of modern Chinese political ideologies must take into consideration the territorial origins of the leaders. Of course, in most

cases intellectual ideas were used merely to justify political aims. Frequently the very use of a specific kind of justification, however, shaped the directions of the political aims themselves.

9. Liang Ch'i-ch'ao, *"Yen-Li hsüeh-p'ai yü hsien-tai chiao-yü ssu-ch'ao"* [dt] (The Yen-Li School and the Modern Stream of Educational Thought), included in the appendix of Ch'en Teng-yuan's *Yen Hsi-chai*, vol. 2, p. 331.

10. Liang gave a series of lectures on Ch'ing thought to the students of Tsing-hua University in 1923. His *Hsüeh-shu shih* was originally written as a series of "instruction notes" (*chiang-i*).[du]

11. Liang, *Hsüeh-shu shih*, p. 105.

12. *Ibid.*, p. 123.

13. For Chang Ping-lin's article see *"Cheng Yen"* [dv] (The Rectification of Yen Yüan), in his *Chien-lun*,[dw] 4/19–22 (*Chang-shih ts'ung-shu* [dx] edition). It should be pointed out that Chang's approach to Yen is basically critical. Yet, through a critical appraisal of Yen's thought, he tried to show that Yen's relevance to modern China by far surpassed the Han Learning of Chi Yün [dy] and the Sung Learning of Weng Fang-kang. [dz] Chou Tso-jen's article appeared in the literary supplement to the *Ta-kung pao* [ea] on October 25, 1933. The article was a reflection on Tai Wang's [eb] *Yen-shih hsüeh-chi*. [ec] It was the fourth installment of his *K'u-ch'a sui-pi*. [ed] Chou's article is sarcastic. It is especially revealing to see his criticism of those who attempted to use Yen Yüan for political purposes. Both Chang's and Chou's articles are included in the appendix of Ch'en's *Yen Hsi-chai*, vol. 2, pp. 358–67.

14. Mansfield Freeman, "Yen Hsi-chai, a 17th Century Philosopher," in *Journal of the North China Branch of the Royal Asiatic Society*, vol. 57 (1926), pp. 70–91.

15. Fung Yu-lan, *Chung-kuo che-hsüeh shih* [ee] (Shanghai, 1931), vol. 2, pp. 946–48, 974–90. The reason Fung resorted to such an apparent "imbalance" seems to lie in his own commitment to philosophical realism at that time. See Fung Yu-lan, *A History of Chinese Philosophy* translated by Derk Bodde (Princeton, 1952–53), Vol. II.

16. Ch'ien Mu, *Chung-kuo chin san-pai nien hsüeh-shu shih* [ef] (Taipei: reprint, preface, 1937), p. 159.

17. *Ibid.*, p. 179.

18. Hou, *Ssu-hsiang shih*, p. 33.

19. *Ibid.*, pp. 324–49.

20. *Ibid.*, pp. 349–75.

21. Ch'en, *Yen Hsi-chai*, vol. 1, p. 45.

22. *Yen Hsi-chai hsien-sheng nien p'u*, compiled by Li Kung and edited by Wang Yüan [eg] (hereafter referred to as NP), 1/1.

23. *Ibid.*, 1/3.

24. *Ibid.*, 1/3b–5.

25. Yen Yüan's *Wang-tao-lun* was later changed to *Ts'un-chih pien* and included in his collected works as one of the *ssu-ts'un* presentations. See note 5 above.

26. Cf. Yen Yüan, *Ssu-ts'un pien*, punctuated by Wang Hsing-hsien ᵉʰ (Peking, 1957), pp. 1–3.
27. NP, 1/5b–6. Cf. Kuo Ai-ch'un, ᵉⁱ *Yen Hsi-chai hsüeh-p'u* ᵉʲ (Shanghai, 1957), p. 4.
28. NP, 1/6.
29. *Ibid.*, 1/6b–7.
30. *Ibid.*, 1/14b–15b.
31. *Ibid.*, 1/24a–b.
32. *Ibid.*, 1/16–17b.
33. Yen Yüan, *Ts'un-hsing pien*, 2/2a–b. The controversy over whether the *Chia-li* was written by Chu Hsi or not should not concern us here.
34. NP, 1/17a.
35. *Ibid.*
36. Yen Yüan, *Ts'un-hsüeh pien*, 1/8. According to his observation, the main program of the ancient Confucian sages involved the *Liu-hsing* ᵉᵏ (Six Conducts) and *Liu-i* ᵉˡ (Six Arts). The former consisted of *hsiao* ᵉᵐ (filial piety), *yu* ᵉⁿ (friendship), *mu* ᵉᵒ (kindness), *yin* ᵉᵖ (compatibility), *jen* ᵉ𐞥 (forbearance), and *hsü* ᵉʳ (charity); the latter consisted of *li* ᵉˢ (rituals), *yüeh* ᵉᵗ (music), *she* ᵉᵘ (archery), *yü* ᵉᵛ (charioteering), *shu* ᵉʷ (writing), and *shu* ᵉˣ (mathematics).
37. NP, 1/18b–21b.
38. *Ibid.*, 2/35.
39. *Ts'un-hsüeh pien*, 1/11.
40. *Ibid.*
41. *Ibid.*, 3/1b.
42. *Ibid.*
43. *Ibid.*, 3/2.
44. See Hsüeh Hsüan's *Tu-shu lu* ᵉʸ (Records on Reading, 1751 edition), 10/11b. In Chu Hsi's commentary on *Chung-yung* ᵉᶻ (The Doctrine of the Mean), Confucianism itself is characterized as *shih-hsüeh*; See his *Ssu-shu chi-chu* ᶠᵃ (Collected Commentaries on the *Four Books*), preface to *Chung-yung*.
45. For a discussion of Wang Yang-ming's influence on Yen Yüan, see Yang Pei-chih, *Yen Hsi-chai yü Li Shu-ku* ᶠᵇ (Wuhan, 1956), pp. 243–58.
46. *Ts'un-hsüeh pien*, 3/6b–7.
47. Cf. Wang Yang-ming, *Ch'uan-hsi lu* ᶠᶜ in *Yang-ming ch'üan-shu*, ᶠᵈ 1/3a–b (SPPY edition).
48. Wang's theory is much more profound, but the fact that many of his disciples failed to combine an active life with practical affairs indicates that in his philosophy there is room for those with a tendency toward quietism and passivity. Cf. Hsiung Shih-li, ᶠᵉ *Shih-li yü-yao ch'u hsü* ᶠᶠ (Hong Kong, 1949), p. 3.
49. *Ts'un-hsüeh pien*, 3/7.
50. NP, 1/22a–b.

51. *Ibid.*, 2/14a–b.
52. Yen Yüan, *Hsi-chai hsien-sheng yen-hsing lu,* edited by Chung Ling, [fg] 3/4b–5.
53. *Ts'un-hsüeh pien,* 2/14b.
54. NP, 2/22–23b. At the age of sixty-one, Yen Yüan wrote a general critique of Sung history. He defended Wang An-shih and Han T'o-chou [fh] for their activism. His appreciation of Ch'en Liang [fi] should also be understood in the light of his defense of these two men.
55. For a discussion of Yen Yüan's emphasis on usefulness, see Ch'en, *Yen Hsi-chai,* vol. i, p. 124.
56. *Ts'un-hsüeh pien,* 2/7.
57. Yen Yüan attacked Ch'eng I, Chang Tsai, Li Yen-p'ing,[fj] and many other thinkers, but his attention was concentrated mainly on Chu Hsi. See *Ts'un-hsing pien,* 1/2a–b.
58. *Ibid.*, 1/13b.
59. *Chu Tzu ch'üan-shu,*[fk] 42/15a.
60. *Ts'un-hsing pien,* 1/1b.
61. *Mencius,* 4A/28; 6A/8.
62. *Analects,* 7/29.
63. *Ts'un-hsing pien,* 1/12b–13b.
64. *Ta-hsüeh* (The Great Learning), ch. 6.
65. For a discussion of *ta-t'i* and *hsiao-t'i,* See *Mencius,* 6A/14–15.
66. *Ts'un-hsing pien,* 2/1b.
67. *Ibid.*, 2/8b–9.
68. *Ts'un-jen pien,* 1/7.
69. For Yen Yüan's criticism of Chu Hsi's concept of evil, see *Ts'un-hsing pien,* 1/7–10.
70. *Ibid.*, 1/11a–b.
71. *Ibid.*, 1/10; 2/14.
72. *Ts'un-hsüeh pien,* 4/3b–4.
73. Herbert Fingarette, "Human Community as Holy Rite," *Harvard Theological Review* (January, 1966).

GLOSSARY

a	梁啓超	ak	王崑繩	bu	存人編
b	墨翟	al	侯外盧	bv	奉天府
c	公孫龍	am	修身	bw	漳南
d	荀子	an	崇禎	bx	卷
e	王充	ao	張履祥	by	張石卿
f	隋	ap	陸隴其	bz	秦漢
g	唐	aq	朱	ca	祁陽
h	宋	ar	司馬光	cb	刁蒙吉
i	明	as	資治通鑑	cc	實學
j	朱熹	at	思古齋	cd	實
k	格物	au	思古人	ce	薛瑄(文清)
l	顏元(習齋)	av	王道論	cf	楊培之
m	徐世昌	aw	存治編	cg	能
n	四存	ax	赴考	ch	內外
o	李塨(恕谷)	ay	程朱	ci	轉世
p	直隸	az	性理大全	cj	世轉
q	北學	ba	道統	ck	王安石
r	河北	bb	伏羲	cl	甲申殉難錄
s	王陽明	bc	周	cm	立人極
t	浙江	bd	顏回	cn	氣
u	陳白沙	be	曾子	co	氣質之性
v	王夫之	bf	子思	cp	端
w	顏習齋	bg	周敦頤	cq	情
x	顏李	bh	程顥	cr	才
y	實踐實用主義	bi	程頤	cs	大體
z	科學萬能	bj	張載	ct	小體
aa	章炳麟	bk	邵雍	cu	德潤身
ab	周作人	bl	王法乾	cv	踐形
ac	胡適	bm	家禮	cw	見
ad	馮友蘭	bn	存性編	cx	能
ae	錢穆	bo	戴震	cy	氣質
af	陳登原	bp	習齋	cz	敬
ag	湛甘泉	bq	存學編	da	必有事焉
ah	劉宗周	br	習禮	db	顏李叢書
ai	黃宗羲	bs	博野	dc	四存學會
aj	顧炎武	bt	喚迷途	dd	畿輔叢書

de	顏習齋先生年譜	dw	檢論	eq	任
df	四書正誤	dx	章氏叢書	er	恤
dg	顏習齋先生言行錄	dy	紀昀	es	禮
dh	顏習齋先生闢異錄	dz	翁方綱	et	樂
di	存治編	ea	大公報	eu	射
dj	朱子語類評	eb	戴望	ev	御
dk	禮文手鈔	ec	顏氏學記	ew	書
dl	習齋記餘	ed	苦茶隨筆	ex	數
dm	廣文	ee	中國哲學史	ey	讀書錄
dn	中國近三百年學術史	ef	中國近三百年學術史	ez	中庸
do	中國早期啓蒙思想史	eg	王源	fa	四書集註
dp	金絜如	eh	王星賢	fb	顏習齋與李恕谷
dq	顏元與李塨	ei	郭靄春	fc	傳習錄
dr	顏習齋哲學思想述	ej	習齋學譜	fd	陽明全書
ds	趙衡	ek	六行	fe	熊十力
dt	顏李學派與現代教育思潮	el	六藝	ff	十力語要初續
du	講義	em	孝	fg	鍾錂
dv	正顏	en	友	fh	韓佗冑
		eo	睦	fi	陳亮
		ep	嫺	fj	李延平
				fk	朱子全書

WING-TSIT CHAN [a] *The* Hsing-li ching-i [b] *and the*

Ch'eng-Chu [c] *School of the Seventeenth Century*

The general impression of the School of Principle of Ch'eng I [d] (1033–1107) and Chu Hsi [e] (1130–1200) in the seventeenth century is that it was basically a reaction against the Wang Yang-ming [f] (1472–1529) School of Mind, that its existence was maintained by imperial authority, and that, having made no constructive contribution, it was finally demolished by a countercurrent, Simple, Concrete Learning (*p'u-hsüeh*).[g] [1] A closer examination, however, reveals that it flourished on its own strength, underwent certain transformations, and itself had something to contribute to the development of Simple, Concrete Learning.

One of the best ways to examine the situation is to analyze the *Hsing-li ching-i* (Essential Ideas of [the Ch'eng-Chu school of] Nature and Principle), for it throws considerable light on the Ch'eng-Chu School in the seventeenth century. The *Hsing-li ching-i* was compiled by Li Kuang-ti [h] (1642–1718) by order of the K'ang-hsi [i] emperor (r. 1662–1722) in 1715. As the title indicates, the book is largely an abridgement of the *Hsing-li ta-ch'üan* [j] (Philosophy of Nature and Principle in Its Completeness), an anthology of Ch'eng-Chu Neo-Confucianism compiled by Hu Kuang [k] (1370–1418) and others, in 1415, by imperial command. It is not merely a selection from the *Hsing-li ta-ch'üan*, because some new materials are added, but, basically speaking, it represents the quintessence of the earlier compilation. In the preface ascribed to him, the K'ang-hsi emperor says that because the *Hsing-li ta-ch'üan* included too much material and was split up into too many sections, he had ordered Li to select the most essential parts.

As was to be expected, the contents and arrangements of the new work follow closely those of the *Hsing-li ta-ch'üan*. Chapter 1 contains Chou Tun-i's [1] (1017–73) *T'ai-chi-t'u shuo* [m] (An Explanation of the Diagram of the Great Ultimate) and *T'ung-shu* [n] (Penetrating the *Book of Changes*); chapter 2 contains excerpts of Chang Tsai's [o] (1020–77) *Hsi-ming* [p] (Western Inscription) and *Cheng-meng* [q] (Correcting Youthful Ignorance); chapter 3 includes selections from Shao Yung's [r] (1011–77) *Huang-chi ching-shih* [s] (Supreme Principles Governing the World); chapter 4 includes selections from Chu Hsi's *I-hsüeh ch'i-meng* [t] (Introduction to the Study of the *Book of Changes*); chapter 5 consists of selections from his *Chia-li* [u] (Family Ceremonies); chapter 6 contains selections from Ts'ai Yüan-ting's [v] (1135–98) *Lü-lü hsin-shu* [w] (New Book on Pitch-pipes); chapters 7 and 8 include selections of Neo-Confucian sayings on ways of learning; chapter 9 consists of sayings on nature and destiny; chapter 10 contains selections on principle and material force (*ch'i*) [x]; and chapters 11 and 12 describe the ways to govern. About one-eighth as long as the earlier anthology, the book would seem to be no more than a reproduction of that collection in a shorter and more refined form.

But it would be a great mistake to dismiss it as a mere shortcut to the Ch'eng-Chu School of Principle. Actually, it possesses significant aspects which offer us an excellent opportunity to reexamine seventeenth-century Ch'eng-Chu philosophy from a new perspective. Let us first of all consider the fact of compilation itself. Why was it compiled? The simplest answer is that it was but one of a long series of compilations. Official compilation of huge works is an old story, but the pace under the K'ang-hsi emperor was unusually rapid. Before the *Hsing-li ching-i* there had been the *Ta-Ch'ing hui-tien* [y] (Collected Statutes of the Great Ch'ing Dynasty [1644–1912]) of 180 chapters in 1690, the *P'ei-wen yün-fu* [z] (Collection of Literary Gems Classified by Rhyme) of 443 chapters in 1704, the *Yüan-chien lei-han* [aa] (Sea of Encyclopedias) of 450 chapters in 1713, and the *Chu Tzu ch'üan-shu* [ab] (Complete Works of Master Chu) of 66 chapters in 1713, to mention only the most famous ones. Additional compilations, like the *K'ang-hsi tzu-tien* [ac] (Dictionary Compiled in the K'ang-hsi era) in 240 chapters, and the *P'ien-tzu lei-pien* [ad] (Classified Compilation of Two-word Expressions) in 140 chapters, were to follow. The *Hsing-li ching-i* was but one of the thirty-odd works and would seem to be nothing unique.

However, it differs from other compilations in several important respects. First, it came fairly late in the K'ang-hsi reign, some twenty-five years after the *Ta-Ch'ing hui-tien*. Second, it and the *Chu Tzu ch'üan-shu* a year earlier were the first anthologies sponsored by K'ang-hsi on Neo-Confucian philosophy, the others being on history and literature.

And third, while other compilations involved many compilers, in the case of the *Hsing-li ching-i*, Li Kuang-ti alone is given as the compiler. These facts put the *Hsing-li ching-i* in a class by itself.

In view of repeated Manchu efforts to subdue Chinese intellectuals, it is natural to assume that the *Hsing-li ching-i* was motivated by a desire to achieve thought control. At least one of the reasons for the large-scale compilation program from the early years of the K'ang-hsi reign to the *Ssu-k'u ch'üan-shu* [ae] (Complete Works of the Four Libraries) in 1773–82 in the Ch'ien-lung [af] era was to keep Chinese intellectuals busily occupied. The *Hsing-li ta-ch'üan* had been the official basis for civil service examinations for several hundred years and as such had functioned as an instrument of conformity and control. The *Hsing-li ching-i* could take over this function. Besides, many anti-Manchu martyrs were followers of the Wang Yang-ming School of Mind. In spite of their unorthodox morality and unconventional behavior, late Ming (1368–1644) followers of Wang often stood for freedom and defiance of authority. Since the Ch'eng-Chu School of Principle and the Wang School of Mind had been intellectual opponents for over a hundred years, it would be most strategic to bolster the Ch'eng-Chu school against Wang. Anyway, because the Ch'eng-Chu system had been closely identified with scholar-officials and served as state orthodoxy, it was advantageous for the Manchu rulers to perpetuate it. The compilation of the *Hsing-li ching-i* could serve all these purposes. The chief difficulty with these explanations is that the work was compiled in 1715—not earlier. If thought control had been the consideration, one would expect it to have come ahead of the literary and historical compilations. By 1715, the resistance of Chinese intellectuals was no longer a problem. Those who were willing to serve the Manchus had answered the summons to retired scholars in 1673. Others were attracted to the examination for Great Scholars of Extensive Learning in 1678. Those not tempted, and they were the best scholars, had gone into isolation to study and write. There was no more need for a special effort to control them at this late date. There must have been some other reason for the compilation than political control.

A possible reason is the K'ang-hsi emperor himself. He started to study the Confucian Classics as a young boy and continued throughout his life. For more than forty years during his reign, he appointed the most prominent Confucianists to lecture before him on Confucian Classics. Often the lecture would precede the imperial audience. At first, there was a lecture every other day; later, there was one every day, even during the hot summer or when rebellion broke out in the southwest. In 1671 he appointed the descendants of Ch'eng I and his brother, Ch'eng Hao [ag] (1032–85) to the highly honored doctoral chairs of the Five Classics [2] and in 1685 the descendants of Chou Tun-i to similar positions. There is no question that he had a personal interest in Neo-Confucianism. He said that in 1696, after he had personally directed the military campaign against Galdan (1644–97) in Ninghsia and won in less than a hundred days, he questioned whether it was worthwhile for him to go down in history as a military leader like the First Emperor (r. 246–210 B.C.) of Ch'in and Wu-ti [ah] (r. 140–87 B.C.) of Han. He turned to the Confucian Classics, he said, and after several decades of study had found that the Sung (960–1279) Neo-Confucianists were far superior to those before them.[3] In 1713 he asked Ch'eng-Chu scholars to submit to him reports of their knowledge of Neo-Confucianism.[4] All these indicate that although he had been reading Confucian Classics for a long time, his conversion to Neo-Confucianism was a recent one. This explains why the compilation of the *Hsing-li ching-i* came so late in his reign. Perhaps we should not take his words at face value, but in view of his long interest in the Neo-Confucian tradition, it is not unreasonable to believe that his motive for promulgating the Ch'eng-Chu doctrine was relatively pure. Surely his personal interest was a key factor in the compilation.

Another factor was Li Kuang-ti. Li obtained the *chin-shih* [ai] degree in 1670, was selected a bachelor of the Hanlin [aj] Academy, and two years later was made a compiler at the capital. When he was home in 1674, he refused to join the rebel Keng Ching-chung [ak] (d. 1682). In 1675 he secretly submitted a memorial giving intelligence about rebels in his own province. For his loyalty he was rewarded in 1677 with a readership in the Hanlin Academy. In the following year he sent relatives to guide the Manchu armies to pacify his native region. As an additional reward, he was called to the capital in 1680 and appointed a subchancellor of the Grand Secretariat. From then on, he was greatly favored by the emperor. On his recommendation, Taiwan was retaken in 1681. In 1686, as a scholar under the director of the Hanlin Academy, he lectured daily on the Confucian Classics before the emperor and also served as official recorder of the emperor's daily life. In 1703, he was promoted to minister of civil personnel. From 1705 on he saw the emperor almost daily.[5] The relationship between the two was so close that the emperor later said that "I knew Li the best and none knew me better than he." [6] It was inevitable that Li exerted a profound influence on the emperor. As has been said, "Two men influenced the K'ang-hsi emperor greatly, namely, Hsiung Tz'u-li [al] (1635–1709) and Li Kuang-ti, and Li rendered more assistance." [7]

Both Hsiung and Li were ardent followers of the Ch'eng-Chu school. When Li returned to the capital in 1680, the emperor asked him to report on his writing. In reply, he said that his study was patterned after that of the emperor and he never contradicted Ch'eng I or Chu Hsi or opposed Confucius (551–479 B.C.) or Mencius (372–289? B.C.).[8] More will be said about Li later. Suffice it to say here that he must have been an important factor in the compilation of the *Hsing-li ching-i*. If we believe in the memorial presenting the work, he took orders from the emperor in detail about selections and arrangements. But the same memorial says that they held daily consultations. It is most unlikely that these were only monologues. In preparing the *Chu Tzu ch'üan-shu*, although he submitted the draft of each chapter to the emperor for final approval, he expressed many opinions about selections and arrangements.[9] Presumably he did the same with the *Hsing-li ching-i*. It is true that politically he was subservient. As has been said, "He always agreed with the emperor." [10] Liang Ch'i-ch'ao [am] (1873–1929) describes him as pleasing the emperor for the sake of personal success.[11] In fact, Liang had little use either for the emperor or for Li as a student of Neo-Confucianism. According to him, the Manchus, lacking a refined cultural heritage, were deeply impressed with Chinese culture. But their contacts were chiefly with Confucianists whose knowledge did not go beyond the texts required for civil service examinations. Confucian scholars like Hsiung were but goody-goodies, he said, but Li was worse. He betrayed a friend, stayed in the capital instead of going home to mourn his mother's death, and kept a mistress whose son later claimed his inheritance.[12]

We shall not defend Li's political or private life. Liang's criticisms are not groundless but they are certainly one-sided, for Li also helped many people. He was a prominent intellectual leader of his time and aided many in their intellectual accomplishments. "Of all the men of prominence in the K'ang-hsi era," it has been said, "Li was the one who developed others' talents the most." [13] As to his understanding of the Ch'eng Chu philosophy, we shall see that in his treatment of Chu Hsi he had a critical approach and an independent spirit, with a knowledge ranging far beyond the examination texts.

But neither the emperor nor Li Kuang-ti operated in a vacuum. They could not have been uninfluenced by the intellectual milieu of their time. For this milieu we must turn to the Ch'eng-Chu school itself.

Most intellectual historians have not attached much importance to this school save as an official ideology. Ch'ien Mu [an] ignored it completely in his account of Chinese learning in the last three hundred years.[14] So has Fung Yu-lan [ao] in his *History of Chinese Philosophy*.[15] Their works are largely accounts of individual thinkers and therefore may be justified in omitting the school. One cannot get away from the impression, however, that in their eyes the Ch'eng-Chu movement in the seventeenth century was of no consequence. In his general account of learning in the Ch'ing dynasty, Liang Ch'i-ch'ao hardly mentions the school. He merely gives a few names, praises their moral character, but points out that their learning did not flourish.[16] There is a chapter on the school in Morimoto Chikujō's [ap] *Shinchō jugaku shi gaisetsu* [aq] (Introduction to Confucianism in the Ch'ing Dynasty), but his emphasis is on its decline and ultimate disappearance.[17] In his *Chung-kuo chin-san-pai-nien hsüeh-shu shih* [ar] (History of Chinese Learning in the Last Three Hundred Years), Liang pays more attention to the school, for here he devotes a chapter to it. He saw nothing new, however, in the Ch'eng-Chu philosophers and said their ability was quite ordinary.[18] Besides, he takes them up only after the Wang Yang-ming school. Likewise, Carsun Chang [as] has allotted a chapter to the school, but, as with Liang, the movement engaged his attention only after he had finished with all other seventeenth-century thinkers. As he saw it, the school was chiefly interested in strengthening the line of apostolic succession from Confucius and Mencius, "and so it did not stand for freedom and spontaneity of thought but rather for conformity." [19]

Chiang Wei-ch'iao [at] (1874–[?]) has a higher regard for the school, for he begins his *Chung-kuo chin-san pai-nien che-hsüeh shih* [au] (History of Chinese Philosophy in the Last Three Hundred Years) with the chapter on it, but he, too, looks upon the movement as one of decline, ultimately to be overthrown by Simple, Concrete Learning.[20] None of these writers has seen anything positive or constructive in the Ch'eng-Chu movement. This is a serious oversight and distorts not only the true picture of the Ch'eng-Chu school itself but of seventeenth-century Chinese thought in general.

The Ch'eng-Chu school at this time may be said to be represented by Lu Shih-i [av] (1611–72), Chang Lü-hsiang [aw] (1611–74), and Lu Lung-ch'i [ax] (1630–93). In his *Ch'ing hsüeh-an hsiao-shih*, [ay] (Brief Accounts of Scholars of the Ch'ing Dynasty) T'ang Chien [az] (1778–1861) considers these three and Chang Po-hsing [ba] (1652–1725) as the four "transmitters of the Way." [21] Thus these four thinkers have been considered the legitimate successors of the Ch'eng-Chu tradition. But since Chang Po-hsing flourished in the eighteenth century rather than the seventeenth, we may leave him out of our discussion and be content with brief accounts of the other three.

As a young man Lu Shih-i was attracted by Liu Tsung-chou's [bb] (1578–1645) lectures at the Chi-shan [bc] Academy [22] and always regretted that he never made the trip there. Before the total collapse of Ming, he made recommendations to the government on bandit suppression, but was ignored. He was urged to serve in the government, but he refused. After the fall of Ming, he built a pavilion on his farm to which he had retired and called it Fu-t'ing [bd] (pavilion of a sailing boat), alluding to Confucius' desire to sail abroad because he had no opportunity to put his Way into practice.[23] Hence, Lu's courtesy name, Fu-t'ing. He devoted his years to writing and intellectual discussions with friends. He lectured at the Tung-lin [be] Academy [24] and other places. He discouraged all efforts to recommend him for service under the Manchus.[25]

Lu Shih-i was not well known in his time, but Chang Po-hsing regarded him as a stronghold of the Ch'eng-Chu school. Chang said, "Some have considered Master Lu as the number one person since Master Chu. That I do not know. But for a long time he thought and sifted the way of sageliness within and kingliness without, the Six Classics,[26] the Four Books,[27] and the works of Chou Tun-i, the Ch'eng brothers, Chang Tsai, and Chu Hsi, and must be considered a stronghold of the Correct Learning." [28]

Liang Ch'i-ch'ao thinks that Lu had no particular reverence for the Ch'eng-Chu philosophy, that he was merely anti-Wang Yang-ming, and that Chang Po-hsing had edited Lu's *Ssu-pien lu* bf (Records of Thinking and Sifting) to make Lu appear as enthusiastic for the Ch'eng-Chu philosophy as possible.[29] This is not the case, for Lu's philosophy is centered on "dwelling in seriousness and investigating principle to the utmost" (*chü-ching ch'iung-li*),bg which is the Ch'eng-Chu philosophy in a nutshell. As students of Neo-Confucianism will agree, the whole Ch'eng-Chu doctrine may be summed up in Ch'eng I's saying, "Self-cultivation requires seriousness; the pursuit of learning depends on the extension of knowledge."[30] According to Chu Hsi's biography in the *Sung shih* bh (History of the Sung Dynasty), "Generally speaking, Chu Hsi's doctrine consists in investigating principle to the utmost in order to extend knowledge and returning to one's self for concrete practice, with seriousness as the foundation."[31] When someone asked Lu if the four words *chü-ching ch'iung-li* represented his basic principle, he said, "I dared not consider these four words to be my basic principle. However, in all my activities, I feel that these four words penetrate and cover all. They provide the foundation and make progress possible. The teachings of the ten thousand sages and ten thousand worthies do not go beyond them."[32] He also said, "The four words *chü-ching ch'iung-li* should be the student's first effort to learn to be a sage. From the top to the bottom, and from the beginning to the end, there is nothing but these four words."[33] To him, "dwelling in seriousness is the controlling factor while investigating principle to the utmost is the way to advance."[34] Lu Lung-ch'i was not mistaken in saying that although Lu Shih-i did not attack the Wang Yang-ming school strongly, his discernment of truth and falsehood follows the standard of Ch'eng and Chu.[35]

Chang Lü-hsiang was born in the same year as Lu Shih-i but lived for two years longer. As a young man, he studied the philosophy of the Wang Yang-ming school. At twenty-five, he began to study Chu Hsi's works. At thirty-four, he became a pupil of Liu Tsung-chou. Feeling that Liu's doctrine of being watchful over oneself while alone is nothing more than Wang's doctrine of sincerity of the will, at thirty-nine he returned to the fold of Ch'eng-Chu. In his *Pei-wang lu* bi (Memorandum) he complained that people read books of the Wang school but neglected the works of Ch'eng I and Chu Hsi and, as a result, truth was distorted.[36] He did not like Wang's *Ch'uan-hsi lu* bj (Instructions for Practical Living) at all. Going as far as to blame all China's troubles on it,[37] he published

Liu Tsung-chou's critical comments on Wang Yang-ming and called the collection *Liu Tzu ts'ui-yen* bk (Master Liu's Pure Words). Maintaining that factional disputes in the southeast and bandit uprisings in the northwest were the cause of all of China's troubles,[38] he refused to join any political club.

After the overthrow of the Ming, he led a quiet life of poverty and isolation and spent his life teaching in elementary schools, and farming.[39] Like that of Lu Shih-i, his philosophy is summed up as "dwelling in seriousness and investigating principle to the utmost." He said:

"In Lien-hsi bl [Chou Tun-i] the words are, "Regard tranquillity as fundamental." [40] In Kuan-chung bm [Chang Tsai] the words are, "Know the rules of propriety and fulfill one's nature." [41] In the Ch'eng school the words are, "Support seriousness and righteousness with each other," [42] "Preserve the mind and extend knowledge," [43] and "Principle is one but its differentiations are many." [44] In Master Chu the words are, *"chü-ching ch'iung-li."* [45] Essentially speaking, are they different? To dwell in seriousness is to preserve the mind, and to investigate principle to the utmost is to extend knowledge. Only in dwelling in seriousness can one straighten one's internal life and only in investigating principle to the utmost can one square one's external life.[46] Only when the internal life is straightened can the "great foundation of the world" be established and only when the external life is squared can one walk "the universal path of the world." [47] Dwelling in seriousness and investigating principle to the utmost are not two sharply different kinds of effort.[48]

Lu Lung-ch'i came from a poor family, but he managed to obtain the *chin-shih* degree in 1670. He became a magistrate in 1675 and won the affection of the people, but was dismissed a year later for failure to report a case of robbery although the robber had been punished. For the following two years he taught in a Hsi bn family. He became a magistrate again in 1683 and was promoted to censor in 1690 but because he submitted a memorial which denounced the selling of offices to raise funds for the campaign against Galdan, he was sentenced to banishment but pardoned. In 1691 he was dismissed. Three years later, when the K'ang-hsi emperor wanted to appoint him to a position, he had passed away. In 1724 he was honored with sacrifice in the Confucian Temple, the only Ch'ing Confucianist so honored.[49]

Like Lu Shih-i and Chang Lü-Hsiang, Lu Lung-ch'i was an ardent follower of the Ch'eng-Chu school. Like them, too, he adhered closely to the Ch'eng-Chu doctrine of dwelling in seriousness and investigating principle to the utmost. As has been said, "The basis of his learning consists in dwelling in seriousness and investigating principle to the utmost." [50] To him, "Dwelling in seriousness is to establish the foundation, and investigating principle to the utmost is to extend knowledge." [51] "To investigate principle to the utmost without dwelling in seriousness is to trifle with things, lose one's purpose, and err in a concern with isolated details, and to dwell in seriousness without investigating principle to the utmost is to wipe out what one sees and hears and nullify the difference between good and evil." [52] Because of his loyalty to the Ch'eng-Chu school, he bitterly attacked Wang Yang-ming. Characterizing Wang's doctrines as "incorrect teachings" [53] and "defective from its very source," [54] he even declared that "the fall of the Ming was not due to bandit uprisings or factionalism but to Wang's teachings." [55] He not only attacked the Wang school but also scholars whose views stood between those of the Ch'eng-Chu and Wang schools. At his time, Huang Tsung-hsi's [bo] (1610–95) philosophy prevailed in the south, Sun Ch'i-feng's [bp] (1585–1675) in the north, and Li Yung's [bq] (1627–1705) in the west. He criticized them all.[56] His advocacy of the Ch'eng-Chu philosophy would allow no room for any deviation. His Hsüeh-shu pien [br] (Critical Discussion on Learning) was devoted to this end [57] and his K'un-mien lu [bs] (Records of Distress and Effort) to defending Chu Hsi's commentaries on the Four Books against criticisms leveled at them.[58] Later scholars have considered him as representing the orthodox Confucian teaching. No wonder, in compiling the Ch'ing hsüeh-an hsiao-shih, T'ang Chien put him ahead of all other Confucianists.

The most striking thing about the three philosophers is that all of them based their philosophy on the Ch'eng-Chu doctrine of dwelling in seriousness and investigating principle to the utmost. This may be going back to the past, conformist, noncreative, and so forth, but surely not an effort to support an official orthodoxy or government indoctrination. The teaching of the investigation of things to the utmost means initiative and critical inquiry and would be a poor instrument for thought control. Two of the philosophers refused to serve the government. Although Lu Lung-ch'i did intend to take the Examination for Great Scholars of Extensive Learning in 1678, his criticism of government policy put him in disfavor with the rulers. He did, indeed, go out of his way to attack the Wang school, but the other two did not. Our point here is that the Ch'eng-Chu school prevailed on its own merits. If there was political manipulation of it, and if it was, in fact, used as a weapon against the Wang Yang-ming school, this was incidental and secondary.

Actually, the Ch'eng-Chu philosophy was widely embraced by scholars at this time. Many people have the wrong impression that Ku Yen-wu [bt] (1613–82), founder of Ch'ing scholarship, in declaring that "the study of classics is the same as the study of principle," [59] meant to ignore the Ch'eng-Chu school if not to attack it directly. In point of fact, what he advocated was the study of practical affairs discussed in the classics instead of idle speculation. He could not understand, he said, why people talked about "refinement" and "singleness of mind" [60] and not about "difficulties and poverty of the world." [61] Ku's philosophy is *ching-shih chih-yung*, [bu] that is, knowledge to put the world in order and for practical application. There is nothing in this to contradict the Ch'eng-Chu philosophy. In fact, Ku held Chu Hsi in high esteem, as can be seen in his defense of him against Wang Yang-ming [62] and his favorable comments on Chu Hsi's *Chou-i pen-i* [bv] (Original Meanings of the *Book of Changes*).[63] According to Chiang Fan [bw] (1761–1831), Ku's learning is based on Chu Hsi.[64] Yen Yüan [bx] (1635–1704) vigorously attacked the Ch'eng-Chu school, it is true. He sharply distinguished the teachings of Confucius and Mencius on one hand, and those of Ch'eng I and Chu Hsi on the other. Emphatically he said that "only when a bit of the Ch'eng-Chu philosophy is destroyed can we enter into a bit of the teachings of Confucius and Mencius." [65] To him, the principle of nature and destiny cannot be talked about, the Ch'eng-Chu theory of human nature is untenable, and their ways of learning greatly deviated from those of the ancient sages.[66] What he wanted was not book learning but actual experience. For him, true learning is that of practical arts like music, ceremony, agriculture, and military techniques. In these ways he was a merciless critic of Ch'eng-Chu metaphysical speculation, but, as we have seen, he should have had no quarrel with the practical side of the Ch'eng-Chu philosophy.

At any rate, in Yen's own time he was not influential. Wang Fu-chih's [by] (1619–92) philosophy is based on the concept of material force and was derived from Chang Tsai, but he accepted a substantial part of Chu Hsi's philosophy. For example, in his *Chung-yung yen* [bz] (The *Doctrine of the Mean*, Elaborated) and *Ta-hsüeh yen* [ca] (The *Great Learning*,

Elaborated), he followed Chu Hsi's interpretations. He also annotated Chu Hsi's anthology of Sung Neo-Confucianism, the *Chin-ssu lu* cb 67 (Reflections on Things at Hand). Even followers of the Wang Yang-ming school sought a compromise by embracing certain Ch'eng-Chu tenets, as in the cases of Sun Ch'i-feng and Li Yung. A large number of scholars were exclusively loyal to the Ch'eng-Chu school, including Wei I-chieh cc (1616–86),68 Wei Hsiang-shu cd (1617–87),69 T'ang Pin ce (1627–87),70 Hsiung Tz'u-li,71 Li Kuang-ti and Chang Po-hsing.72 We have not gone into them because they were too close to the government. Significantly, as Confucian thinkers they were far inferior to the three we have discussed. Since the Ch'eng-Chu school stood on its own feet and prevailed on its own merit, the publication of the *Hsing-li ching-i* must be taken as a reflection of this situation. In other words, it is an accounting, a restatement, a record, and a reaffirmation of the Ch'eng-Chu philosophy.

But it is more than all of these. If we go into the contents of the work, we shall find that there were certain new developments in the philosophy. First is the increased eminence of Chu Hsi. In following the Ch'eng-Chu philosophy, the Ch'ing Neo-Confucianists actually followed Chu Hsi alone. Lu Lung-ch'i put it most strongly when he said, "Master Chu was the one who continued Confucius and clarified the Six Classics. That which is not the Way of Confucius should be destroyed. Therefore, that which is not the Way of Master Chu should be destroyed." 73 He also said, "To study Confucius and Mencius without following Master Chu is like trying to enter a room without going through the door." 74

But the increased reverence for Chu Hsi can be seen in the *Hsing-li ching-i* itself. Here he emerged as the central figure of the whole Neo-Confucian tradition. In the *Hsing-li ta-ch'üan* his position is already preeminent, for selections of his sayings far outnumber those of others. Here in the *Hsing-li ching-i* it is even more the case because his sayings exceed others to an even higher degree. This can be seen in the topical chapters on the ways of learning, nature and destiny, principle and material force, and the way to govern.75 As in the *Hsing-li ta-ch'üan*, the material in most cases consists of selected sayings from Ch'eng I to Hsü Heng cf (1209–81), and in several cases to Wu Ch'eng cg (1249–1333). But in comparison with the *Hsing-li ta ch'üan*, Chu Hsi's position here is more conspicuous. To amplify the works of Chou Tun-i and Chang Tsai, selected sayings by many Neo-Confucians are used in the *Hsing-li ta-ch'üan*. Here, however, with several exceptions,[76] only Chu Hsi's sayings are selected, and the exceptions are used chiefly to explain his remarks. For Chang Tsai's *Western Inscription* in chapter 2, it is true that several sayings by Ch'eng I precede the one by Chu Hsi,[77] but in chapters 14 and 26 of Chou Tun-i's *T'ung-shu*, Ch'eng I's sayings quoted in the *Hsing-li ta-ch'üan* are no longer retained, leaving Chu Hsi as the only commentator. In addition, in the *Hsing-li ta-ch'üan*, two works by Chu Hsi's pupils are included—the *Lü lü hsin-shu* by Ts'ai Yüan-ting and the *Hung-fan huang-chi nei-p'ien* [ch] (Inner Chapter of the Supreme Principles of the *Grand Norm*) by Ts'ai Ch'en [ci] (1167–1230). In the present compilation, the former is retained but the latter is omitted. The justification is that the former represented Chu Hsi's own views but the latter does not because it was prepared after Chu Hsi's death. Here is a clear indication that Chu Hsi was considered the central focus in the *Hsing-li ching-i*.

These indications, though perhaps small, are nonetheless significant. They reflect the long tendency to assert Chu Hsi's supremacy among the Neo-Confucians. As the one who synthesized and completed Neo-Confucianism, it is only natural that he was put in the central position. In addition, for centuries there had been bitter controversies in the Neo-Confucian movement in which Chu Hsi was a principal figure. One involved the debates between Lu Hsiang-shan [cj] (1139–93) and Chu Hsi, the former "honoring the moral nature" and the latter "following the path of inquiry and study." [78] The other controversy concerned what Wang Yang-ming claimed to be Chu Hsi's "final conclusions arrived at late in life" which, Wang said, came to be the views Wang himself had adopted.[79] The whole Wang Yang-ming movement, from the fifteenth to the early seventeenth century, directed its attack on Chu Hsi. The counterattack on the Wang school brought a reaction in favor of Chu Hsi. This was the main reason for Chu Hsi's rise as the towering figure in seventeenth-century Neo-Confucianism.

There were also personal reasons, so far as the *Hsing-li ching-i* is concerned, namely, the emperor's and Li Kuang-ti's admiration for Chu Hsi. The emperor's adoration for Chu Hsi was unreserved. He said that in fifty years of study he had only learned what Chu Hsi did in his life.[80] In

1712 he conferred on Chu Hsi the high honor of placing his tablet in the main hall of the Confucian Temple among the ten Confucian disciples. No other Neo-Confucianist enjoyed such a supreme honor. Overlooking the attacks on Chu Hsi from the Wang school, Li declared that for five hundred years no one dared criticize Chu Hsi, and also that in promulgating the Way, Chu Hsi's contribution was the greatest since Confucius' and Mencius'.[81] Of all the commentaries on the Confucian Classics, the emperor regarded those by Chu Hsi as the best. He ordered Li Kuang-ti to select Chu Hsi's sayings and writings to comprise the *Chu Tzu ch'üan-shu* in sixty-six chapters, which was printed in 1714. This is an anthology drawn from the *Chu Tzu yü-lei* [ck] (Classified Conversations of Master Chu) in 140 chapters, and the *Chu Tzu wen-chi* [cl] (Collection of Literary Works by Master Chu) in 100 chapters. The anthology is called "complete works" because, according to the compiler, all of Chu Hsi's essential ideas are found here. In a sense, the *Hsing-li ching-i* is a followup to this.

The question has already been raised as to whether the emperor's idealization of Chu Hsi may not have served the purposes also of thought control. It is not only the element of lateness in time, which stands in the way of this interpretation, but also Chu Hsi's life and ideas. In his preface to the *Chu Tzu ch'üan-shu*, the emperor said that the reason for compiling the anthology was to make available Chu Hsi's own words and to prevent people from propagating their own ideas in the name of Chu Hsi. In other words, he wanted to let people study Chu Hsi himself rather than a superimposed view of him. Besides, Chu Hsi was a persistent critic of the government and many times refused to serve. His opposition to the rulers was such that he was dismissed from office and persecuted. His teachings were banned as "false learning." And an official candidate in his time even petitioned for Chu Hsi's execution.[82] The emperor would have been quite mistaken to urge people to follow the example of Chu Hsi if submission to government was his goal. In all fairness, we must allow that his primary motive was a sincere admiration for Chu Hsi, and not a desire for ideological conformity.

Similarly Li Kuang-ti was a Chu Hsi devotee. He said that for fifty years he had studied a work by Chu Hsi.[83] As the *Ch'ing-ju hsüeh-an* [cm] (Critical Accounts and Anthology of Ch'ing Scholars) says, "extensive and refined, Li's learning relies on and ends up with Chu Hsi." [84] In his

Tsun Chu yao-chih ^{cn} (Fundamental Ideas of Venerating Chu Hsi), he follows Chu Hsi chiefly on the basic concepts of principle, material force, knowledge and conduct, and seriousness. To him, Chu Hsi was the Confucius of his time.[85] As T'ang Chien has observed, Li "thought the thoughts of Chu Hsi and studied the studies of Chu Hsi," and "in his discourses on the Classics and discussions of learning, he followed Chu Hsi completely." [86]

Actually Li did not follow Chu Hsi as much as T'ang Chien made him appear to. He did not accept Chu Hsi's rearrangement of the text of the *Great Learning* or the *Doctrine of the Mean*. For the former, he preferred the ancient version and for the latter, he made his own rearrangement. In his *Chou i kuan-hsiang* ^{co} (Understanding the Symbols of the *Book of Changes*), he chose to use Wang Pi's ^{cp} (226–49) and Han K'ang-po's ^{cq} (332–87) annotations and K'ung Ying-ta's ^{cr} (574–648) commentary on the Thirteen Classics which differ from Chu Hsi's interpretations.[87] In his discussion of the *Great Learning,* he considered nothing to be missing from the text and thought Chu Hsi's addition of an "amending chapter of commentary" was superfluous.[88] What is more interesting is that, contrary to followers of Chu Hsi who exaggerated his differences with Lu Hsiang-shan, Li argued that the two philosophers agreed in their fundamentals and differed only in details,[89] and that the learning of Lu is "the same as our learning." [90] In spite of all these, he remained completely loyal to Chu Hsi. Since he was the most outstanding Neo-Confucianist when the *Chu Tzu ch'üan-shu* and the *Hsing-li ching-i* were compiled, he naturally lent weight to Chu Hsi's prestige.

Turning to Chu Hsi's doctrines, we find that a great advance is made in the *Hsing-li ching-i*. This is the recognition of one of his most important contributions to Neo-Confucianism, namely, his methodology. The *Chu Tzu yü-lei*, which begins with chapters on the Great Ultimate, principle, material force, and nature, gives the impression that with Chu Hsi these are matters of first importance. This impression is strengthened by the fact that the subsequent development of the Ch'eng-Chu school emphasized nature and principle, earning for itself the name of *Hsing-li-hsüeh*, ^{cs} or Learning of Nature and Principle. Actually there was more to Chu Hsi than metaphysics. He never forgot that Confucius "studied things on the lower level [mundane affairs] and then reached to the higher level [matters such as Heaven, nature, and destiny]." [91]

When Chu Hsi compiled the *Chin-ssu lu*, he was reluctant to include the chapter on the substance of the Way *(Tao)*,[ct] much less to make it the first chapter. According to Huang Kan [cu] (1152–1221), his son-in-law and outstanding pupil, Chu Hsi hesitated to include it, undoubtedly because its abstract character might lead to empty speculation on metaphysics, but finally he did so because otherwise the following chapters would have had no theoretical foundation.[92] There must have been objections from his pupils, too, for Huang Kan himself complained that now the book had become "Reflections on Things Far Away." Perhaps the inclusion of the first chapter was at the insistence of his collaborator, Lü Tsu-ch'ien [cv] (1137–81). Chu talked the matter over with him and asked him to write a few words about it, which Lü did in a preface justifying the inclusion. Chu Hsi said that if one read this chapter alone, the principles contained therein would be isolated, that is, unrelated to daily life, and it would be much better to read the *Analects* and the *Book of Mencius*, which are simple and straightforward.[93] All this was in 1175.

In 1190 Chu grouped the *Great Learning*, the *Analects*, the *Book of Mencius*, and the *Doctrine of the Mean* together as the Four Masters *(ssu-tzu)*,[cw] and published them. Better known as the Four Books, these became the basic texts in civil service examinations and in school education from 1414 to 1905. The grouping and publication of them together may not seem to have involved a major effort on Chu Hsi's part, but actually this was the result of long and serious thinking. Chu Hsi had studied the Four Books for several decades and commented on them. Publishing them together signified their being substituted for the Five Classics as the embodiment of Confucian doctrines. It also meant going back directly to the words of Confucius and Mencius.[94] This was significant enough. What was more so was Chu Hsi's new sense of priority of values, a new procedure of action, and a fresh method of study. "In learning," he said, "one must begin with the *Great Learning* and then successively the *Analects*, the *Book of Mencius*, and the *Doctrine of the Mean*." [95] In explanation, he said:

I want people first to read the *Great Learning* to determine a pattern, then the *Analects* to establish a foundation, then the *Book of Mencius* to see the development [of Confucian doctrines], and finally the *Doctrine of the Mean* to find out the subtleties and mysteries of the ancients. The *Great Learning* in one chapter offers definite steps and an order all in one place. It is easy to understand and should be read first. The *Analects* is solid but its sayings are scattered and it is difficult when one first reads it. There are passages in the *Book of Mencius* which inspire and arouse people. The *Doctrine of the Mean* is difficult to read and should be read after the other books.[96]

He further said that:

The *Analects*, the *Book of Mencius*, and the *Doctrine of the Mean* should be read only after the *Great Learning* has been thoroughly understood and no further reading seems necessary. The reason why the learning of the Way is not clear is basically not because the efforts on the higher level [such as abstract principles and metaphysical problems discussed in the other three books] are deficient but because efforts on the lower level [taught in the *Great Learning*] have no firm standing.[97]

He compared the *Great Learning* to a blueprint, an itinerary, and a framework.[98] He put the *Doctrine of the Mean* last because it deals with such topics as spiritual beings and forming a trinity with Heaven and Earth, and is too much on the higher level.[99]

What is the new methodology? It is based on the premise that "one must know what is first and what is last," as stated in the text of the *Great Learning*. According to this procedure, one starts with the investigation of things and then goes on step by step to the achievement of knowledge, making the will sincere, rectifying the mind, cultivating the personal life, regulating the family, ordering the state, and bringing peace to the world. As Hu Shih [cx] (1891–1962) has observed, "Only after the Sung Neo-Confucianists put forth this 1750-word *Great Learning* did the Chinese discover the new philosophical method of recent times." [100] He was thinking of the method of investigation of things. We may add that Chu Hsi was the first to offer the procedure given in the *Great Learning* as a methodology for study and living. To know what is first and what is last represents the Confucian formula for studying matters on the lower level and then matters on the higher level. Hence, the order of the Four Books. However, in the ensuing years, the first item of the eight steps, namely, investigation of things, engaged the major attention of Neo-Confucianists. The key controversy between the Ch'eng-Chu and the Wang Yang-ming schools was over this matter. Investigation of things came to mean investigation of things on the higher level.

As a result, the compiler of the *Hsing-li ta-ch'üan* put the chapters (26–37) on matters on the higher level ahead of those (43–52) on matters on the lower level. This shows that its compilers did not appreciate Chu Hsi's new methodology. In the *Chu Tzu ch'üan-shu*, the order is radically changed. The *Explanatory Statement (fan-li)*,^{cy} attributed to the emperor, says:

In chapter arrangements the *Chu Tzu yü-lei, Hsing-li ta-ch'üan*, and other works usually begin with the Great Ultimate, *yin yang* ^{cz} (weak and strong cosmic forces, respectively), principle, material force, *kuei-shen* ^{da} (spiritual forces or spiritual beings), and so forth. The order of studying things on the lower level and then understanding things on the higher level is to some extent thereby lost. Tzu-kung ^{db} (c. 520–450 B.C.) said, "We cannot hear our Master's views on human nature and the Way of Heaven." ¹⁰¹ When Tzu-lu ^{dc} (542–480 B.C.) asked about serving spiritual beings, Confucius said, "If we are not yet able to serve man, how can we serve spiritual beings?" ¹⁰² This is the order of the Learning of the Sage. If you see that in Master Chu's collected commentaries on the Four Books, the *Great Learning* comes first, then the *Analects* and the *Book of Mencius*, and finally the *Doctrine of the Mean*, you will see what his intention was. . . . In the present chapter arrangement, the first is a discussion of learning, then the Four Books, then the Six Classics, and these are succeeded by doctrines on nature, destiny, moral virtues, heaven and earth, *yin yang*, and *kuei-shen*.

The same spirit governs the arrangement of the *Hsing-li ching-i*. Its *Explanatory Statement*, written in the name of the emperor but actually prepared by Li Kuang-ti,¹⁰³ says:

In the student's studying of things on the lower level in order to understand things on the higher level, there is fundamentally an order. Therefore, Confucius "often talked about poetry, history, and the performance of the rules of propriety," ¹⁰⁴ but did not include the *Book of Changes*. Master Ch'eng taught people [Chang Tsai's] *Western Inscription* ¹⁰⁵ but kept [Chou Tun-i's] *Explanation of the Diagram of the Great Ultimate* a secret. And Master Chu, in the order of the Four Books, put the *Great Learning* first and then the *Analects*, the *Book of Mencius*, and finally the *Doctrine of the Mean*. They all had this idea of order. Following their idea, I have decreed the compilation of the *Chu Tzu ch'üan-shu*. It begins with elementary learning and the great learning and then proceeds to doctrines of the Way of Heaven, nature, and destiny. The same idea is followed in the divisions and order of this book.

Five hundred years after Chu Hsi's death, his method of procedure was formally recognized for the first time in the *Hsing-li ching-i*.

However, we must not give the emperor too much credit. Neither he nor Li Kuang-ti had made a sudden discovery. The priority of things on the lower level over those on the higher level had been urged by Neo-

Confucianists long before. In the cases of Lu Shih-i, Chang Lü-hsiang, and Lu Lung-ch'i, the investigation of principle to the utmost no longer meant the pursuit of abstract knowledge but the study of things near at hand. In taking notes from his reading, Lu Shih-i followed the order of the eight steps prescribed in the *Great Learning*. He said:

I believe that the method of investigation of things must proceed from the near to the far away and from the coarse to the refined, from one's own body and mind to the family, the state, and the world, and from ordinary matters such as eating and drinking to Heaven and earth and the ten thousand things, advancing gradually until one achieves a wide understanding. Only then can "one thread" run through Heaven and man, things and the self, the inner and the outer, the hidden and the manifest, life and death, spiritual beings, and day and night.[106]

For Chang Lü-hsiang, "In regard to daily matters one should examine and investigate everything one comes into contact with." [107] In the case of Lu Lung-ch'i, "In his conduct and concrete practice, he adhered to the principle of studying things on the lower level and then understanding things on the higher level." [108] Ku Yen-wu struck the same note, as we have already observed.

It is clear that Neo-Confucianism in the seventeenth century had already put matters of practical concern ahead of matters of abstract interest. Not only was there a change of order; there was also the deliberate effort to avoid empty speculation. This can be seen in the treatment of the Great Ultimate in the *Hsing-li ching-i*. Before Chu Hsi's time, the concept of the Great Ultimate was not important. He made it the starting point of the whole Neo-Confucian metaphysics. He had to do so because it was necessary to account for its basic doctrine of principle, the relationship between universal principle and particular principles, the relationship between principle and material force, and the possibility of production and reproduction. He, therefore, shifted the *Explanation of the Diagram of the Great Ultimate* from the end of Chou Tun-i's *T'ung-shu* to its beginning and thus gave it the eminence it enjoyed in the entire Neo-Confucian tradition. Chu Hsi did this against great odds. He had to argue that the diagram was Chou's own work and not that of a Taoist priest,[109] that the Ultimate of Non-being which gives rise to the Great Ultimate was not a Taoist concept,[110] that Chou transmitted the diagram to the Ch'eng brothers, and that they did not pass it on to their pupils because none was ready to inherit it.[111] Chu Hsi was desperate, but he had to depend on the concept of the Great Ultimate for his reconstruction of the Neo-Confucian philosophy.[112] In his anthology of Sung Neo-Confucianists, the *Chin-ssu lu*, the *Explanation of the Diagram of the Great Ultimate* comes first of all. It was also because of the supreme importance of the concept of the Great Ultimate that the *Chu Tzu yü-lei* begins with his conversations on it. Following this lead, the *Hsing-li ta-ch'üan* begins with the *Explanation*. This arrangement is repeated in the *Hsing-li ching-i*. Given the undisputed continuation of the general metaphysics and cosmology of the Ch'eng-Chu school, this was unavoidable. The *Explanatory Statement* says that the diagram is the father of Neo-Confucianism.

But from the very early days, questions about the authenticity of the diagram were raised and Chi Hsi's explanations of it were challenged. Chu Hsi himself mentioned some who questioned whether Chou Tun-i invented it,[113] and Lu Hsiang-shan debated with him at great length about the concept of the Ultimate of Non-being.[114] Subsequent debates were vigorous and unceasing. Within the Neo-Confucian tradition itself, important changes were taking place with regard to the concept of the Great Ultimate. Lu Shih-i, while remaining faithful to Chu Hsi in general, departed from him with regard to the diagram. He contended that the diagram is a logical product of the "Appended Remarks" of the *Book of Changes* where it is said that the Great Ultimate produces *yin* and *yang*, and so on.[115] Since the "Appended Remarks" comes at the end of the *Book of Changes*, he argues, so should the explanation of the diagram come at the end of the *T'ung-shu*. He rejected the theory that the diagram came from a Taoist priest, but he also said that Chu Hsi was wrong in saying that it could not be known where Chou Tun-i inherited his doctrines.[116] Chang Lü-hsiang's interest lay primarily in dwelling in seriousness and investigating principle to the utmost, and he showed little interest in the matter of the Great Ultimate. When he referred to it, he only quoted the sentence from Chou's *Explanation* about the ultimate standard for man.[117] Lu Lung-ch'i wrote a special treatise on the Great Ultimate, the "T'ai-chi lun" [dd] (Treatise on the Great Ultimate), but its central thesis is that "A discussion of the Great Ultimate should not aim at clarifying what the Great Ultimate is but at what it is in one's person. . . . When through seriousness one becomes vacuous [unobstructed] in tranquillity and straight in activity, the Great Ultimate is then in the person himself." [118] It is interesting to note that in his *Ssu-pien lu*, subjects like the Great Ultimate are found not in the main collection but in the supplementary collection.

From the foregoing we can see that the subject of the Great Ultimate had lost its abstract appeal. As early as the beginning of Ming, this was already the case. Early Ming followers of Ch'eng-Chu paid very little attention to it. To be sure, Ts'ao Tuan [de] (1376–1434) wrote a short essay on the *Explanation of the Diagram of the Great Ultimate* but, outside of this, he had almost nothing to say on the subject. Hsüeh Hsüan [df] (1389–1464) commented on it systematically, but his comments are reading notes only. In his own works no discussion of the subject is to be found. [119] The difference between the early Ming and Ch'ing Neo-Confucianists is that the earlier philosophers turned away from the Great Ultimate to internal cultivation, whereas the Ch'ing Neo-Confucianists turned away from the Great Ultimate to everyday affairs. The interest in abstract discussion had already faded away.

And equally significant development was the historical study of the diagrams and illustrations of the *Book of Changes*. There was a long series of profound studies in this area. We need only mention Mao Ch'i-ling's [dg] (1623–1716) *Ho-t'u yüan-ch'uan p'ien* [dh] (Inquiry into the Errors of the River Charts) and *T'ai-chi-t'u shuo i-i* [di] (Remaining Discussions on the Diagram of the Great Ultimate) and Hu Wei's [dj] (1633–1714) *I-t'u ming-pien* [dk] (Clarifying Critique on the Diagrams in the *Book of Changes*). Hu Wei exerted a tremendous influence. He showed that the diagrams came from Taoist sources and basically had nothing to do with Neo-Confucian philosophy and that the illustrations and charts of the *Book of Changes* did not originally belong to it. Regardless of the merits of his arguments, the effect was to shift the study of the Great Ultimate from the realm of speculation to that of objective inquiry. As Liang Ch'i-ch'ao has stated, this was a fatal blow to the speculative philosophy of Neo-Confucianism. [120]

All these developments could not have been ignored by the compiler of the *Hsing-li ching-i*. In his *Tsun Chu yao-chih*, Li Kuang-ti goes into the ideas of principle and material force but mentions the Great Ultimate only in passing. As in the *Hsing-li ta-ch'üan*, the *Explanation of the Diagram of the Great Ultimate* heads the *Hsing-li ching-i*, as we have noted. This seems to contradict the lines of thought expressed in the *Ex-*

planatory Statement of the present anthology. We shall give an explanation of this later. In later chapters the topic of the Great Ultimate has virtually disappeared. In the chapter on principle and material force in the *Hsing-li ta-ch'üan* (ch. 26), there is a special section on the Great Ultimate. Here that section is omitted. In the section on principle and material force there are two selections on the Great Ultimate, it is true, one from Chu Hsi himself and one from his pupil,[121] but in both cases they are there to explain principle. In the *Hsing-li ta-ch'üan*, selections on the Great Ultimate, principle, and material force cover eighteen pages, and on Heaven, earth, sun, and moon, twenty-four pages, or a proportion of four to three. In the *Hsing-li ching-i*, however, selections on principle and material force cover three and a half pages, while those on Heaven-and-earth, and sun-and-moon, cover ten pages, a proportion of three to one. The shift from abstract matters to the concrete is eminently clear.

This concern with practical and concrete matters was influenced by historical events, of course. Empty speculation in earlier Neo-Confucianism did not prevent social and moral decay. The national crisis in the mid-seventeenth century demanded a solution of practical problems. These were the reasons for the rise of the movement for "putting the world in order and practical application." The Ch'eng-Chu school in the seventeenth century could not escape these historical forces, and so it also turned to practical concerns. Lu Shih-i felt that "the Six Classics are not the only things people of today should study. They must study astronomy, geography, river works and irrigation, military craft, etc., which are all of practical use. Vulgar scholars who talk about nature and destiny with an air of superiority are of no help to the world." [122] As has been pointed out, Lu Shih-i "would not discuss sincerity and seriousness in a vacuum. He emphasized practical application and did not engage in the empty effort at the study of the mind and nature." [123] To Chang Lü-hsiang, "Outside of ordinary words and ordinary deeds, there are no principles of nature and destiny." [124] And Lu Lung-ch'i "would not talk about sincerity and seriousness in the abstract." [125] The spirit of practical application was in the air.

At the same time, Western science was having a great effect on the Chinese intellectual world. Ever since Father Matteo Ricci (1552–1610) and other Catholic missionaries introduced Western science into China, Chinese scholars were attracted to scientific subjects. Their main interest still lay in moral and social problems, but they made excursions into mathematics, astronomy, and the like. Huang Tsung-hsi, for example, wrote books on these subjects. Lu Shih-i also wrote on them as well as on astronomy, hydraulics, and military techniques. In his *Ssu-pien lu* he made extensive notes on astronomy, geography, river works, irrigation, and so on. Lu Lung-ch'i also had an interest in scientific subjects. He visited Ferdinand Verbiest (1623–88) several times, who showed him Western clocks and a celestial sphere. Li Kuang-ti was quite accomplished in the subjects of pitch-pipes and mathematics.

The most important figure in this new development was Mei Wen-ting [dl] (1633–1721) whom Liang Ch'i-ch'ao called the pioneering founder of modern science in China.[126] He wrote more than sixty-two works on astronomy and twenty-six on mathematics. Li Kuang-ti, whom Mei had befriended, published nine of them. In 1701 when Li was governor of Chili, he presented one of Mei's books on the calendar to the emperor, which four years later, earned him a three-day audience.[127] The emperor himself was quite enthusiastic about science. He took up the study of astronomy, physiology, physics, the calendar, and mathematics seriously and became proficient enough in mathematics to discuss the subject with Mei for three days. He granted Verbiest and other missionaries a residence nearby and summoned them to the palace to lecture on such subjects as surveying, mathematics, and physics. With their help, maps were made of the empire and the famous observatory was built. The emperor himself wrote several books on mathematics and astronomy. By that time, the study of geography by Ku Yen-wu and Yen Jo-ch'ü [dm] (1636–1704) had become well known.

There is no doubt that the new scientific spirit enhanced the rational spirit inherent in the Ch'eng-Chu philosophy. This spirit is shown in the *Hsing-li ching-i's* treatment of spiritual beings and strange phenomena. The *Explanatory Statement* says:

The Master seldom talked about spiritual beings.[128] There are few references to them in the Four Books or Six Classics. They are not important things for the student. Therefore, it was said, "If we are not yet able to serve man, how can we serve spiritual beings?" [129] and "Devote yourself earnestly to the duties due men, and respect spiritual beings but keep them at a distance." [130] This is the purpose of the Sage's instructions. . . . Let the subject of spiritual beings be omitted.

The decision was, of course, true to the original spirit of Confucian teaching. Chu Hsi discussed *kuei-shen* on many occasions. There is a special chapter (ch. 3) in the *Chu Tzu yü-lei* on the subject. But there,

kuei-shen are chiefly discussed in the sense of negative and positive cosmic forces of the universe. As explained by Chang Tsai, "The negative
and positive spiritual forces are the spontaneous activity of the two material forces [*yin* and *yang*]." [131] Chu Hsi was reluctant to discuss *kuei-shen*
in the sense of spiritual beings. He avoided the subject in the *Chin-ssu lu*
where the only saying on *kuei-shen* is Chang's saying just quoted.[132] In
the *Hsing-li ta-ch'üan* (ch. 20), however, a whole chapter is devoted to it,
with sections on spiritual beings, *hun-p'o* [dn] (heavenly and earthly components of the soul), sacrifices to ancestral spirits, and life and death. The
idea of *kuei-shen* as cosmic forces is well represented, of course, but the
main focus is on spiritual beings, especially their strange appearances, activities, and influence on man. This emphasis was clearly contrary to the
rationalistic spirit of Neo-Confucianism, not to say of Confucius himself.
The omission of the subject in the *Hsing-li ching-i* means a return to the
true character of Ch'eng-Chu rationalism. Its significance goes beyond
reflecting the rationalistic temper of the age.

The same rationalistic tendency characterizes the handling of the subject of strange phenomena. In the *Hsing-li ta-ch'üan*, the section on
"Auspicious and Strange Phenomena" precedes those on the army and
punishment (ch. 69), but in the *Hsing-li ching-i* it follows them (ch. 12).
In both cases the stress is on the moral meaning of strange phenomena as
signs of warning. The message to the ruler is that good action will result
in beneficial responses from nature while evil action will result in disasters. However, there are sayings in the *Hsing-li ta-ch'üan* about the effects
of omens, but these are deleted in the *Hsing-li ching-i*. In the *Hsing-li ta-
ch'üan*, Ch'eng I's sayings emphasize omens [133] but here his sayings
emphasize man's virtue to the effect that calamities are caused by man's
moral failures rather than by the wrath of Heaven. In the *Hsing-li ta-
ch'üan*, there is a saying by Chu Hsi on the efficacy of omens.[134] That
saying has been deleted from the *Hsing-li ching-i*. However, Lu Hsiang-
shan's saying has been retained because it stresses principle rather than
symbols. Hsü Heng's saying on fulfillment of omens is replaced by another one expressing the idea that strange, heavenly phenomena depend
on principle.[135] Furthermore, between the sections on the army and
punishment and the section on auspicious and strange phenomena in the
Hsing-li ching-i, there is another section on admonition and remonstration. It is difficult to say to what extent the arrangement is intentional

and what it actually means. The *Explanatory Statement* says nothing
about it. There seems to be an implication, however, that in the *Hsing-li
ta-ch'üan* the rewards and punishments are regarded as more important
than military operations or criminal laws, but in the *Hsing-li ching-i* they
are of least importance. It is perhaps not meaningless to have a section on
admonition and remonstration before the section on strange phenomena.
It may be meant to say that natural phenomena are secondary to the
moral efforts of man.

All the foregoing changes in the *Hsing-li ching-i* must be regarded as
improvements over the *Hsing-li ta-ch'üan* and as a reflection of the constructive developments within the Ch'eng-Chu system. In one respect,
however, the old tradition is rigidly maintained and that is the *tao-
t'ung* [do] (tradition of the Way). In this matter, the *Hsing-li ching-i* seems
to be self-contradictory. The opening section of the *Explanatory Statement* says:

The learning of nature and principle became brilliant in the Sung period. From
the time the Ch'eng brothers received it from Chou Tun-i, it was pure learning
derived from the sources of Confucius and Mencius. The Ch'engs' contemporaries, like Chang Tsai and Shao Yung, sang the same tune and amplified it.
Their pupils, like Lü Ta-lin [dp] (1044–90), Yang Shih [dq] (1053–1135), Hsieh
Liang-tso [dr] (1050–1103), and Yin T'un [ds] (1071–1142), together perpetuated it
and made it manifest. Chu Hsi was born later. He continued the heritage from
Chou and the Ch'engs, consulted and selected from Chang Tsai and Shao Yung,
and considered the agreements and disagreements, as well as what was right and
what was wrong, in his own pupils. Consequently, the teachings of Confucius
and Mencius became abundantly clear and learning finally became correct.
Scholars of Sung and Yüan (1271–1368) were all side-currents of this mainstream. Among them Chen Te-hsiu [dt] (1178–1235) of Sung and Hsü Heng of
Yüan were the purest.

This is a clear statement of the *tao-t'ung* in the preceding seven hundred
years. But later in the *Explanatory Statement* it is also said that to present
the topic of *tao-t'ung* will create controversy, and therefore that section in
the *Hsing-li ta-ch'üan* should be omitted here. This is puzzling.

The *tao-t'ung* was conceived by Chu Hsi. He contended that Chou
Tun-i received the Confucian doctrine directly from Mencius, thus by-
passing other early Sung Neo-Confucianists as well as Han and T'ang
Confucianists. He also put the Ch'eng brothers ahead of Chang Tsai and
Shao Yung even though the latter were their seniors. He ignored other

Neo-Confucianists.[136] Chu therefore fixed the *tao-t'ung* as from Confucius and Mencius to Chou Tun-i and the Ch'eng brothers with Chang Tsai and Shao Yung on the side. He took it upon himself to perpetuate the tradition. So far as Neo-Confucianism is concerned, the *tao-t'ung* has been from Chou through the Ch'eng brothers and Chu Hsi down to Hsü Heng very much as the opening section of the *Explanatory Statement* has it. But with the rise of the Wang Yang-ming school to challenge the Ch'eng-Chu philosophy, this tradition was badly shaken. In reaction to the Wang school, Ch'eng-Chu followers naturally upheld the tradition. Lu Lung-ch'i, for example, wrote the "Tao-t'ung lun" [du] (Treatise on the Tradition of the Way) in which he maintains that Chu Hsi represented the most legitimate tradition and was the most authoritative, and that what is opposed to him should be prohibited and not be allowed to spread.[137] At the same time, the new régime needed a new intellectual authority. Thus the *tao-t'ung* suited the purpose of both the Ch'eng-Chu Confucianists and the rulers. Therefore, the arrangement of the *Hsing-li ching-i* follows the line of *tao-t'ung* closely, with Chou Tun-i's *Explanation of the Diagram of the Great Ultimate* at the head in spite of the loss of interest in the Great Ultimate.

The order of selection of sayings themselves follow strictly the order of the *tao-t'ung*, here as in the *Hsing-li ta-ch'üan*, that is, from the Ch'engs to Chang Tsai, Shao Yung, pupils of the Ch'engs, Chu Hsi, his contemporaries, his pupils, and so on down to Hsü Heng. We may say that the order is adhered to more strictly here. Ssu-ma Kuang [dv] (1019–86) comes after Chang Tsai, for instance, because Ssu-ma Kuang is not in the direct line of transmission. Ou-yang Hsiu [dw] (1007–72) comes after Ch'eng I, and Chang Tsai and Chang Chiu-ch'eng [dx] (1092–1159) after Chu Hsi, even though they were chronologically earlier.[138] Curiously enough, outside of the list of Neo-Confucianists in the *Hsing-li ta-ch'üan*, only Ou-yang Hsiu is new. And none of the prominent Ming Neo-Confucianists, Wu Yü-pi [dy] (1392–1469), Hu Chü-jen [dz] (1434–84), Ts'ao Tuan, or Hsüeh Hsüan is included. One is inclined to say that not only was the *tao-t'ung* reaffirmed, but it was reaffirmed without even such modifications as would bring it up to date.

In years to come the *tao-t'ung* was to assume greater and greater importance. Chang Po-hsing devoted a whole book to it, and Fang Pao [ea] (1668–1749), founder of the T'ung-ch'eng [eb] school of literature, looked upon himself as a bearer of the torch of the tradition in his opposition to the Han Learning of Hui Tung [ec] (1697–1758) and Tai Chen [ed] (1724–77). The climax of the *tao-t'ung* was reached in T'ang Chien. His *Ch'ing hsüeh-an hsiao-shih* was specifically compiled to defend it, or in his own words, "to return to the right track of Ch'eng-Chu . . . and the true face of Confucius." [139] The book begins with Lu Lung-ch'i, Chang Lü-hsiang, Lu Shih-i, and Chang Po-hsing as "transmitters of the Way," then nineteen others, including Ku Yen-wu and Li Yung, as those "who rendered aid to the Way," and forty-four as those who "firmly adhered to the Way."

If the *tao-t'ung* loomed so large in the *Hsing-li ching-i*, why was the section on it omitted? The *Explanatory Statement* is quite explicit on this point, namely, to avoid controversy. We have repeatedly, directly or indirectly, referred to factional controversy. Scholars were tired of partisanship. This was why Ku Yen-wu, Wang Fu-chih, Yen Yüan, and others developed in their own directions. On the part of the government, consensus was desired. What was wanted in the *Hsing-li ching-i* was the established tradition without discussion.

This leads us to the effects of the *Hsing-li ching-i*. It was published for use in all schools in the country. In 1850 it was done once more, this time with the *Sheng-yü kuang-hsün* [ee] (Sacred Instructions Amplified), a set of moral axioms laid down by the K'ang-hsi emperor and later elaborated by someone unknown to us, which had been compulsory reading on public occasions. The emperor and Li Kuang-ti probably never expected that the *Hsing-li ching-i* would thus become a set of formal instructions. However, there were two constructive side-effects of this. One was the study of the *Chin-ssu lu*.

The *Chin-ssu lu* is a collection of 622 short treatises and sayings by Chou Tun-i, the Ch'eng brothers, and Chang Tsai, in 14 chapters. It is the first anthology of its kind and not merely an assemblage. Chu Hsi's selections were based on his concept of the *tao-t'ung*. [140] By treating the material as he did, he set the pattern for Neo-Confucian philosophy and reconstructed it. The anthology begins with the chapter on the substance of Tao with the *Explanation of the Diagram of the Great Ultimate* at the very start. It is followed by chapters on learning and investigation of things, and then those on personal cultivation, management of the family, the state, and the world. Essentially speaking, the *Hsing-li ta-ch'üan* had followed this pattern and subsequently so had the *Hsing-li ching-i*. As the *Ssu-k'u ch'üan-shu tsung-mu t'i-yao* ᵉᶠ (Essentials of the Title Descriptions of the Four Libraries) has said, the *Hsing-li ta-ch'üan* is an enlargement of the *Chin-ssu lu*. [141]

After its publication in 1175, it was read extensively by Chu Hsi's friends and pupils. Many times he and his pupils talked about it. [142] In the centuries to follow, it became a basic text for Neo-Confucianists. When Chang Lü-hsiang's pupils came to him, for instance, he always gave them the *Chin-ssu lu* as the first assignment. [143] We do not see any direct relation between the *Chin-ssu lu* and the *Hsing-li ching-i* except in the basic concept of *tao-t'ung* and the general pattern of arrangement, but it is significant to note that in the seventeenth and early eighteenth centuries there was a long series of anthologies inspired by the *Chin-ssu lu*. Specifically, these were: Kao P'an-lung's ᵉᵍ (1562–1626) *Chu Tzu chieh-yao* ᵉʰ (Essentials of Master Chu's Teachings); Chiang Ch'i-p'eng's ᵉⁱ (fl. 1604) *Chin-ssu pu-lu* ᵉʲ (The *Reflections on Things at Hand*, Supplemented), an anthology of Sung and Ming Neo-Confucianists including Chu Hsi; Sun Ch'eng-tse's ᵉᵏ (1593–1675) *Hsüeh-yüeh hsü-pien* ᵉˡ (Supplement to the *Essentials of Learning*), an anthology of four Ming Neo-Confucianists; Liu Yüan-lu's ᵉᵐ (1619–1700) *Chin-ssu hsü-lu* ᵉⁿ (Supplement to the *Reflections on Things at Hand*); Chu Hsien-tsu's ᵉᵒ (fl. 1684) *Chu Tzu chin-ssu lu* ᵉᵖ (Master Chu's Reflections on Things at Hand), an anthology of Chu Hsi's sayings; Wang Yu's ᵉ۹ (fl. 1685) *Wu-tzu chin-ssu lu* ᵉʳ (Reflections on Things at Hand of the Five Philosophers), which adds Chu Hsi's sayings to Chu Hsi's anthology; Chang Po-hsing's *Hsü chin-ssu lu* ᵉˢ (Supplement to the *Reflections on Things at Hand* [with sayings of Chu Hsi]); his *Kuang chin-ssu lu* ᵉᵗ (Further Records of Reflections on Things at Hand) containing sayings of Lü Tsu-ch'ien, Huang Kan, and later Neo-Confucianists; Cheng Kuang-hsi's ᵉᵘ (fl. 1700) *Hsü chin-ssu lu* ᵉᵛ (Supplements to the *Reflections on Things at Hand*), a collection of sayings by Ming thinkers including Wang Yang-ming; Chu Ch'üan's ᵉʷ (1702–59) *Hsia-hsüeh pien* ᵉˣ (Anthology on Studying Things on the Lower Level) containing Chu Hsi's sayings; and Chu's *Shu-ai lu* ᵉʸ (Records of Self-cultivation and Self-discipline), a selection of sayings from his teacher Chang Lü-hsiang's *Pi-wang lu*.

They are all patterned after the *Chin-ssu lu* in its fourteen-chapter arrangement. They totaled ten anthologies against only three before, namely, Liu Ch'ing-chih's [ez] (1139–95) *Chin-ssu hsü-lu* [fa] (Supplement to the *Reflections on Things at Hand*), sayings of Ch'engs' pupils; Ts'ai Mu's [fb] (fl. 1220) *Chin-ssu hsü-lu* [fc] (Supplement to the *Reflections on Things at Hand*), a collection of Chu Hsi's sayings and Ts'ai's *Chin-ssu pieh-lu* [fd] (Separate Records of Reflections on Things at Hand), a collection of sayings by Lü Tsu-ch'ien and Chu Hsi's friend, Chang Shih [fe] (1133–80). The intensive effort from the sixteenth century onward to make collections of Neo-Confucian sayings, particularly those of Chu Hsi, may not have contributed directly to the undertaking of the *Hsing-li ching-i*, but it surely created a conducive atmosphere. The anthologies patterned after the *Chin-ssu lu* mean that the pattern of Neo-Confucian philosophy shaped by Chu Hsi prevailed throughout the period. In this sense, the *Hsing-li ching-i* merely repeated the pattern.

Since the *Hsing-li ching-i* gave fresh attention to the collections of Neo-Confucian sayings, it inevitably gave impetus to a movement to annotate and comment on the *Chin-ssu lu*. There had been commentaries on it from the thirteenth to the fifteenth century,[144] but none after that until the seventeenth and the first half of the eighteenth. There were seven in this period, almost as many as in the four preceding centuries. These are: Wang Fu-chih, *Chin-ssu lu chieh* [ff] (the *Reflections on Things at Hand*, Explained); Chang Po-hsing, *Chin-ssu lu chi-chieh* [fg] (Collected Explanations of the *Reflections on Things at Hand*); Li Wen-chao [fh] (1672–1735), *Chin-ssu lu chi-chieh* [fi] (Collected Explanations of the *Reflections on Things at Hand*); Mao Hsing-lai [fj] (1678–1748), *Chin-ssu lu chi-chu* [fk] (Collected Commentaries on the *Reflections on Things at Hand*); Chiang Yung [fl] (1681–1762), *Chin-ssu lu chi-chu* [fm] (Collected Commentaries on the *Reflections on Things at Hand*), Shih Huang [fn] (fl. 1705), *Wu-tzu chin-ssu lu fa-ming* [fo] (Exposition of [Wang Yu's] *Wu-tzu chin-ssu lu*); Ch'en Hang [fp] (1785–1826), *Chin-ssu lu pu-chu* [fq] (Supplementary Commentaries on the *Reflections on Things at Hand*); and Wang Fu [fr] (1692–1759), *Tu Chin-ssu lu* [fs] (Notes from Reading the *Reflections on Things at Hand*). It is to be noted that only Wang Fu-chih's commentary antedated the *Hsing-li ching-i*. It is significant that it was Chang Po-hsing, Li Kuang-ti's junior and good friend, who started the annotations of the *Chin-ssu lu* in the eighteenth century. The essential spirit of these annotations and commentaries is to stress daily practical affairs.

This emphasis also contributed to the development of Simple, Con-

crete Learning. When Yen Yüan and later Tai Chen attacked idle speculation on nature and destiny, they directed their attacks at the Sung Neo-
Confucianists. They ignored the seventeenth-century Neo-Confucianists
who were traveling in the same direction as they did. It is too much to
claim that the seventeenth-century Ch'eng-Chu school created the empirical atmosphere, but certainly it shared in and contributed to it. In this
way, it restored the true spirit of the Ch'eng-Chu philosophy and contributed, if indirectly, to later Confucian developments.

NOTES

1. Also called Han-hsüeh,[ft] an intellectual movement stressing concrete subjects, supporting evidence, textual fidelity, and simple statements, all characteristic of the scholarship of the Han-period study of the classics. For this reason, sometimes the name Classical Studies is used.
2. The *Book of History*, the *Book of Odes*, the *Book of Changes*, the *Book of Rites*, and the *Spring and Autumn Annals*.
3. Preface to the *Chu Tzu ch'üan-shu*.
4. *Ta-Ch'ing Sheng-tsu Jen-huang-ti shih-lu* [fu] (Veritable Records of the K'ang-hsi Emperor of the Great Ch'ing Dynasty), 53rd year, 8th month.
5. Chao Erh-sun [fv] (1844–1929?), *Ch'ing shih kao* [fw] (Draft History of the Ch'ing Dynasty), ch. 2, biography 49; Chang Ch'i-yün [fx] (ed.), *Ch'ing shih* [fy] (History of the Ch'ing Dynasty), ch. 263, biography 49; Hsü Shih-ch'ang,[fz] *Ch'ing-ju hsüeh-an*, chs. 40–41; and Arthur Hummel (ed.), *Eminent Chinese of the Ch'ing Period* (Washington, D.C.: U.S. Government Printing Office, 1943), pp. 473–75.
6. *Ch'ing shih kao*, ch. 2, biography 49.
7. *Ch'ing-ju hsüeh-an* (Anthology and Critical Accounts of Neo-Confucianists of the Ch'ing Dynasty) (Taipei: Shih-chieh [ga] Book Co., 1962), 40/1.
8. *Yung-ts'un ch'üan-chi* [gb] (Complete Literary Works of Li Kuang-ti), 10/2b.
9. *Ibid.*, 28/1b–2a, 4a, 6a–7a, 12b, 13b–14a; 29/9a–10a; 32/12b–15a.
10. Appraising comment at the end of biography 49 in *Ch'ing shih*.
11. *Ch'ing-tai hsüeh-shu kai-lun* [gc] (Introduction to Ch'ing Dynasty Learning) (Shanghai: Commercial Press, 1932 [1921] p. 110. See translation by Immanuel C. Y. Hsü,[gd] *Intellectual Trends in the Ch'ing Period* (Harvard University Press, 1959), p. 76.
12. *Chung-kuo chin-san pai-nien hsüeh-shu shih* (Shanghai: Chung-hua [ge] Book Co., 1936), pp. 103–4.
13. *Ch'ing-ju hsüeh-an*, 41/23a.
14. *Chung-kuo chin-san-pai-nien hsüeh-shu shih* (Chinese Learning in the Last Three Hundred Years) (Shanghai: Commercial Press, 1937).
15. *A History of Chinese Philosophy*, translated by Derk Bodde, 2 vols. (Princeton University Press, 1952–53).
16. *Chung-kuo chin-san-pai-nien hsüeh-shu shih*, p. 110.
17. Tokyo, Bunshodō [gf] (1931), ch. 5.
18. Pp. 96, 98.
19. *The Development of Neo-Confucian Thought* (New York: Bookman Associates), II (1962), 317.
20. (Shanghai: Chung-hua Book Co., 1932), p. 1.
21. Chs. 1–2. The book was originally entitled *Kuo-ch'ao hsüeh-an hsiao-shih* [gg] (Brief Accounts of Scholars and Their Works of the Reigning Dynasty).

22. In Shao-hsing [gh] County, Chekiang Province.
23. *Analects*, 5/6.
24. In Wu-hsi,[gi] Kiangsu Province.
25. For Lu Shih-i, see *Ch'ing shih kao*, ch. 2, biography 295; *Ch'ing shih*, ch. 479, biography 267; *Ch'ing-ju hsüeh-an*, chs. 3–4; Hummel, *Eminent Chinese*, pp. 548–49. See also below, note 49.
26. The Five Classics and the *Classic of Music*. The latter was lost before the third century B.C. Sung Confucianists substituted the *Chou li* [gj] (Rites of Chou) for it.
27. The *Analects*, the *Great Learning*, the *Doctrine of the Mean*, and the *Book of Mencius*.
28. Preface to the *Ssu-pien lu chi-yao*.
29. *Chung-kuo chin-san pai-nien hsüeh-shu shih*, p. 99.
30. *I-shu* [gk] (Surviving Works), in *Erh-Ch'eng ch'üan-shu* [gl] (Complete Works of the Two Ch'engs) *Ssu-pu pei-yao* [gm] [Essentials of the Four Libraries] edition), 18/5b.
31. *Po-na pen* [gn] (Choice Works Edition), 429/19a.
32. *Ssu-pien lu* (*Cheng-i t'ang ch'üan shu* [go] [Complete Library of the Hall of Rectifying the Way] edition), 2/15b.
33. *Ibid.*, 2/13a.
34. *Ibid.*, 2/13b.
35. *San-yü-t'ang wen-chi* [gp] (Collection of Literary Works of the Hall Dedicated to Three Fish) (1701 edition), 9/11a–b.
36. *Ch'ing-ju hsüeh-an*, 5/4b.
37. *Ch'ing hsüeh-an hsiao-shih* (*Kuo-hsüeh chi-pen ts'ung shu* [gq] [Basic Sinological Series] edition), p. 21. For an English translation of the *Ch'uan-hsi lu*, see Wing-tsit Chan (trans.), *Instructions for Practical Living and Other Neo-Confucian Writings of Wang Yang ming* (Columbia University Press, 1963).
38. *Ch'ing hsüeh-an hsiao-shih*, pp. 20–21.
39. For Chang Lü-hsiang, see *Ch'ing shih kao*, ch. 2, biography 295; *Ch'ing shih*, ch. 479, biography 267, and Hummel, *Eminent Chinese*, pp. 45–46. See also below, note 49.
40. *Explanation of the Diagram of the Great Ultimate*, in *Chou Tzu ch'üan-shu* [gr] (Complete Works of Master Chou) (Wan-yu wen-k'u [gs] [Universal Library] edition), 1/1.
41. *Cheng-meng*, ch. 9, in *Chang Tzu ch'üan-shu*,[gt] (Complete Works of Master Chang) (*Cheng-i-t'ang ch'üan-shu* edition), 3/3b.
42. *I-shu*, 5/2b.
43. *Ibid.*, 18/4b–5a.
44. *Ts'ui-yen* [gu] (Pure Words), in *Erh-Ch'eng ch'üan-shu* (*Ssu-pu pei-yao* edition), 1/23b.
45. *Chu Tzu yü-lei* (1880 edition), 9/3a.
46. Straightening the internal life and squaring the external life refer to the *Book of Changes*, commentary on hexagram no. 2, *k'un* [gv] (earth; female).
47. The single quotations are from the *Doctrine of the Mean*, ch. 1.

48. *Ch'ing-ju hsüeh-an*, 5/9a–b.
49. For Lu Lung-ch'i, see *Ch'ing shih kao*, ch. 2, biography 52; *Ch'ing shih*, ch. 66, biography 52; and Hummel, *Eminent Chinese*, pp. 547–48. For additional material on him, Lu Shih-i, and Chang Lü-hsiang, see Carsun Chang, *The Development of Neo-Confucian Thought*, Vol. II, pp. 319–26, 332–35; Hellmut Wilhelm, "Chinese Confucianism on the Eve of the Great Encounter," in Marius Jansen (ed.), *Changing Japanese Attitudes toward Modernization* (Princeton University Press, 1964), pp. 283–99; and Alfred Forke, *Geschicte der neueren chinesischen Philosophie* (Hamburg: Friederichsen, de Gruyter and Co., 1938), pp. 498–92, 510–22.
50. *Ch'ing hsüeh-an hsiao-shih*, p. 6.
51. *San-yü-t'ang wen-chi*, 1868 edition, preface, p. 16.
52. *Ch'ing-ju hsüeh-an*, 10/1a.
53. *Lu Chia-shu wen-chi* [gw] (Collection of Literary Works of Lu Lung-ch'i), (*Cheng-i-t'ang ch'üan-shu* edition), 1/18a.
54. *Ibid.*, 1/15a.
55. *Ibid.*, 1/14b.
56. *Ssu-k'u ch'üan-shu tsung-mu t'i-yao*, p. 749.
57. *San-yü-t'ang wen-chi*, 2/1a–8a.
58. *Ssu-k'u ch'üan-shu tsung-mu t'i-yao*, p. 749.
59. Ch'üan Tsu-wang [gx] (1705–55), *Chi-ch'i-t'ing chi* [gy] (Collection of the Oysters and Irregular Edges Pavilion), 1872 edition, 12/2a.
60. Referring to the *Book of History*, "Counsels of Great Yü." [gz]
61. *Ibid.*
62. *Jih-chih lu* [ha] (Records of Daily Acquisition of Knowledge) (*Kuo-hsüeh chi-pen ts'ung-shu* edition), 6/119.
63. *Ibid.*, 1/4.
64. *Han-hsüeh shih-ch'eng chi* [hb] (Story of the Transmission of the Learning of the Han Dynasty) (*Kuo-hsüeh chi-pen ts'ung-shu* edition), p. 135.
65. Li Kung [hc] (1659–1733), *Yen Hsi-chai Hsien-sheng nien-p'u* [hd] (Chronological Biography of Master Yen Yüan), pt. 2, p. 25b, in the *Yen-Li i-shu* [he] (Surviving Works of Yen Yüan and Li Kung) (1920 edition).
66. *Ts'un-hsüeh pien* [hf] (On the Preservation of Learning), 1/3a; *Ts'un-hsing pien* [hg] (On the Preservation of Human Nature), 1/16a; and *Ts'un-hsüeh pien*, 1/1b, respectively. In *Yen-Li i-shu*.
67. For English translation of the *Chin-ssu lu*, see Chu Hsi and Lü Tsu-ch'ien, *Reflections on Things at Hand*, translated by Wing-tsit Chan (Columbia University Press, 1967).
68. For him, see *Ch'ing-ju hsüeh-an*, ch. 19.
69. *Ibid.*, ch. 20.
70. *Ibid.*, ch. 9.
71. *Ibid.*, ch. 38.
72. *Ibid.*, ch. 12.
73. *San-yü-t'ang wen-chi*, 8/7b.
74. *Ibid.*, 5/2b.

75. Chs. 7–12.
76. 1/4b, 7a, 8b.
77. 2/1a.
78. *Hsiang-shan ch'üan-chi* hh (Complete Works of Lu Hsiang-shan) (*Ssu-pu pei-yao* edition), 34/24a–b. The quotations are from the *Doctrine of the Mean*, ch. 20. See also below, note 114.
79. For Wang's contentions, see his *Instructions for Practical Living*, pp. 263–67.
80. Preface to *Chu Tzu ch'üan-shu*.
81. *Ta-Ch'ing Sheng-tzu Jen-huang-ti shih-lu*, 51st year, 1st month.
82. *Sung shih*, 429/18a–b. He declined offices in 1163, 1169, 1176, 1181, 1182, 1188, 1189, 1191, and 1192. Once he declined a position seven times in several years.
83. *Yung-ts'un ch'üan-chi*, 10/12b.
84. *Ch'ing-ju hsüeh-an*, 40/1a.
85. *Yung-ts'un ch'üan-chi*, 10/3a.
86. *Ch'ing-hsüeh-an hsiao-shih*, pp. 168, 172. Li's veneration of Chu Hsi is reflected in the *Yung-ts'un yü-lu* hi (Recorded Sayings of Li Kuang-ti), chs. 18–19, and *Yung-ts'un yü-lu hsü-lu* hj (Supplement to the *Recorded Sayings of Li Kuang-ti*), ch. 5, where Chu Hsi and the Five Masters of Sung (Chou Tun-i, Ch'eng Hao, Ch'eng I, Chang Tsai, and Shao Yung) are called the Six Masters of Sung.
87. *Ssu-k'u ch'üan-shu tsung-mu t'i-yao*, p. 93.
88. *Yung-ts'un ch'üan-chi*, 10/11a.
89. *Ibid.*, 17/21a.
90. *Ibid.*, 17/23a.
91. *Analects*, 14/37.
92. *Huang Mien-chai chi* hk (Collected Works of Huang Kan) (*Cheng-i-t'ang ch'üan-shu* edition), 2/2a.
93. *Chu Tzu yü-lei*, 105/5a.
94. I have discussed these matters in my "Chu Hsi's Completion of Neo-Confucianism," in Françoise Aubin (ed.), *Études Song—Sung Studies, In Memoriam Étienne Balazs*, Series II, no. 1 (1973), pp. 81–87.
95. *Chu Tzu yü-lei*, 14/1a.
96. *Ibid.*, 14/12b.
97. *Ibid.*, 14/1b.
98. *Ibid.*, 14/2a, 2b, respectively.
99. *Ibid.*, 62/1a, referring to the *Doctrine of the Mean*, chs. 16, 22, and so on.
100. *Hu Shih wen-ts'un* hl (Preserved Essays of Hu Shih) (Taipei: Yüan-tung hm Book Co., 1953 edition), first series, vol. 2, p. 539.
101. *Analects*, 5/12.
102. *Ibid.*, 11/11.
103. *Yung-ts'un ch'üan-chi*, 39/7a–8a.
104. *Analects*, 7/17.
105. *I-shu*, 2a/7b, 18b, 20a, etc.
106. *Ssu-pien lu*, 3/3a.

107. *Ch'ing-ju hsüeh-an*, 5/13b.
108. *Ibid.*, 10/22b.
109. *Chu Tzu wen-chi* (*Ssu-pu ts-ung-k'an* hn [Four Libraries Series] edition entitled *Chu Tzu ta-ch'üan* ho [Complete Literary Works of Master Chu]), 75/19a.
110. *Ibid.*, 36/8a–9b.
111. *Chu Tzu yü-lei*, 94/21b.
112. See my detailed discussion in "Chu Hsi's Completion of Neo-Confucianism," referred to in note 94, pp. 67–72.
113. *Chu Tzu wen-chi*, 75/19a.
114. *Hsiang-shan ch'üan-chi*, 2/6a–b, 9a–b.
115. *Ch'ing-ju hsüeh-an*, 4/1b.
116. *Ibid.*, 4/1a.
117. *Ch'ing-ju hsüeh-an*, 5/9a.
118. *San-yü-t'ang wen-chi*, 1/1a-2b.
119. See my discussion in Wm. Theodore de Bary, *Self and Society*, p. 33.
120. *Ch'ing-tai hsüeh-shu kai-lun*, p. 26; Hsü (trans.), *Intellectual Trends in the Ch'ing Period*, p. 35.
121. 10/1b, 2a.
122. *Ssu-pien lu chi-yao*, 1/16b.
123. *Ssu-k'u ch'üan-shu tsung-mu t'i-yao*, p. 1943.
124. *Ch'ing-ju hsüeh-an*, 5/3b.
125. *Ssu-k'u ch'üan-shu tsung-mu t'i-yao*, p. 1945.
126. *Ch'ing-tai hsüeh-shu kai-lun*, p. 39; Hsü, p. 42.
127. *Ch'ing-ju hsüeh-an*, 37/4a.
128. *Analects*, 7/20.
129. *Ibid.*, 11/11.
130. *Ibid.*, 6/20.
131. *Cheng-meng*, ch. 1, in *Chang Tzu ch'üan-shu*, 2/4a.
132. Chu Hsi, *Reflections on Things at Hand*, p. 32.
133. 69/16a–18b.
134. 69/18a.
135. *Hsing-li ching-i*, 12/21b.
136. This is dealt with at length in my essay, "Chu Hsi's Completion of Neo-Confucianism," referred to in note 94, pp. 73–81. For Chu Hsi's *tao-t'ung*, see the preface to his *Chung-yung chang-chü* hp (Chapter and sentence divisions of the *Doctrine of the Mean*) and *Chu Tzu wen-chi*, 86/12a.
137. *San-yü-t'ang wen-chi*, 4/8a.
138. *Hsing-li ching-i*, 8/7a, 12/11a, 7/26b respectively.
139. See his preface.
140. As I have pointed out in *Reflections on Things at Hand*, p. xxxiii.
141. *Ssu-k'u ch'üan-shu tsung-mu t'i-yao*, p. 918.
142. *Chu Tzu yü-lei*, 114/10a, 115/8b, 116/8a, 119/10a, etc.
143. *Ch'ing-ju hsüeh-an*, 5/1b.
144. See *Reflections on Things at Hand*, pp. 340–41.

GLOSSARY

a 陳榮捷　　ak 耿精忠　　bs 困勉錄
b 性理精義　　al 熊賜履　　bt 顧炎武
c 程朱　　am 梁啓超　　bu 經世致用
d 程頤　　an 錢穆　　bv 周易本義
e 朱熹　　ao 馮友蘭　　bw 江藩
f 王陽明　　ap 森本竹城　　bx 顏元
g 樸學　　aq 清朝儒教史概說　　by 王夫之
h 李光地　　ar 中國近三百年學術　　bz 中庸衍
i 康熙　　　　史　　ca 大學衍
j 性理大全　　as 張君勱　　cb 近思錄
k 胡廣　　at 蔣維喬　　cc 魏裔介
l 周敦頤　　au 中國近三百年哲學　　cd 魏象樞
m 太極圖說　　　　史　　ce 湯斌
n 通書　　av 陸世儀　　cf 許衡
o 張載　　aw 張履祥　　cg 吳澄
p 西銘　　ax 陸隴其　　ch 洪範皇極內篇
q 正蒙　　ay 清學案小識　　ci 蔡沉
r 邵雍　　az 唐鑑　　cj 陸象山
s 皇極經世　　ba 張伯行　　ck 朱子語類
t 易學啓蒙　　bb 劉宗周　　cl 朱子文集
u 家禮　　bc 蕺山　　cm 清儒學案
v 蔡元定　　bd 梓亭　　cn 尊朱要旨
w 律呂新書　　be 東林　　co 周易觀象
x 氣　　bf 思辨錄　　cp 王弼
y 大清會典　　bg 居敬窮理　　cq 韓康伯
z 佩文韻府　　bh 宋史　　cr 孔穎達
aa 淵鑑類函　　bi 備忘錄　　cs 性理學
ab 朱子全書　　bj 傳習錄　　ct 道
ac 康熙字典　　bk 劉子萃言　　cu 黃榦
ad 駢字類編　　bl 濂溪　　cv 呂祖謙
ae 四庫全書　　bm 關中　　cw 四子
af 乾隆　　bn 席　　cx 胡適
ag 程顥　　bo 黃宗羲　　cy 凡例
ah 武帝　　bp 孫奇逢　　cz 陰陽
ai 進士　　bq 李顒　　da 鬼神
aj 翰林　　br 學術辨　　db 子貢

dc	子路	eq	汪佑	gd	徐中約
dd	太極論	er	五子近思錄	ge	中華
de	曹端	es	續近思錄	gf	文書堂
df	薛瑄	et	廣近思錄	gg	國朝學案小識
dg	毛奇齡	eu	鄭光羲	gh	紹興
dh	河圖原舛篇	ev	續近思錄	gi	無錫
di	太極圖說遺議	ew	祝洤	gj	周禮
dj	胡渭	ex	下學編	gk	遺書
dk	易圖明辨	ey	淑艾錄	gl	二程全書
dl	梅文鼎	ez	劉清之	gm	四部備要
dm	閻若璩	fa	近思續錄	gn	百納本
dn	魂魄	fb	蔡模	go	正誼堂全書
do	道統	fc	近思續錄	gp	三魚堂文集
dp	呂大臨	fd	近思別錄	gq	國學基本叢書
dq	楊時	fe	張栻	gr	周子全書
dr	謝良佐	ff	近思錄解	gs	萬有文庫
ds	尹焞	fg	近思錄集解	gt	張子全書
dt	眞德秀	fh	李文炤	gu	粹言
du	道統論	fi	近思錄集解	gv	坤
dv	司馬光	fj	毛星來	gw	陸稼書文集
dw	歐陽修	fk	近思錄集註	gx	全祖望
dx	張九成	fl	江永	gy	鮚埼亭集
dy	吳與弼	fm	近思錄集註	gz	禹
dz	胡居仁	fn	施璜	ha	日知錄
ea	方苞	fo	五子近思錄發明	hb	漢學師承記
eb	桐城	fp	陳沆	hc	李塨
ec	惠棟	fq	近思錄補註	hd	顏習齋先生年譜
ed	戴震	fr	汪紱	he	顏李遺書
ee	聖諭廣訓	fs	讀近思錄	hf	存學編
ef	四庫全書總目提要	ft	漢學	hg	存性編
eg	高攀龍	fu	大清聖祖仁皇帝實	hh	象山全集
eh	朱子節要		錄	hi	榕村語錄
ei	江起鵬	fv	趙爾巽	hj	榕村語錄續錄
ej	近思補錄	fw	清史稿	hk	黃勉齋集
ek	孫承澤	fx	張其昀	hl	胡適文存
el	學約續編	fy	清史	hm	遠東
em	劉源淥	fz	徐世昌	hn	四部叢刊
en	近思續錄	ga	世界	ho	朱子大全
eo	朱顯祖	gb	榕村全集	hp	中庸章句
ep	朱子近思錄	gc	清代學術概論		

INDEX

Abe Yoshio, cited, 205

Abiding in reverence (*chu, ching*), 181; Liu Tsung-chou on, 319-21; Chu Hsi on, 320-21

Aesthetic enlightenment, *see* Enlightenment

Aleni, cited, 396-97

Analects (Confucius), 164, 177, 185, 191, 290, 333, 380, 519, 558

Animals: nonkilling and release of, 100-2; Chu-hung on, 95-97, 104-7, 111-13, 123, 128, 131; Chu-hung and Matteo Ricci controversy, 113-16

Ariès, Philippe, 72

Astronomy: Fang I-chih on, 386-92

Autobiography, 67-68, 81-84, 88

Balazs, Étienne, quoted, 345-46

Bellah, Robert, cited and quoted, 148-50, 151, 153

Blacker, Carmen, cited and quoted, 146-48

Book of Changes, see *I Ching*

Book of Odes, 292, 295

Buddhism: and Confucianism, 6, 8, 24, 43-46, 47, 51-61, 67, 80, 132, 429, 430, 434; and Neo-Confucianism, 8, 12, 24-25, 30, 94, 161-62, 287, 429, 430, 432, 469-72, 491, 511; in late Ming, 39-66 passim, 93-140 passim; lay, and Chu-hung, 93-140 passim; precepts, 95-100; in post-T'ang, 102-4; and the New Enlightenment, 188-90; in post-Han, 333-34; *see also* Ch'an Buddhism; Pure Land Buddhism

Bureaucracy and bureaucrats, 3, 15, 59, 422

Busch, Heinrich, cited, 180-83

Cahill, James, quoted, 258, 260; cited, 263

Chan, Wing-tsit, cited and quoted, 167, 175, 185-86, 208, 228, 417

Chan Kan-ch'üan, 514

Ch'an (Zen) Buddhism, 24, 161-62, 171, 176, 190; School of Mind, 40, 41, 42, 43, 82, 153; Chu Hsi's attack on, 41; schools of,

in T'ang and Sung periods, 52, 53-54, 108, 161; and Pure Land Buddhism, 57-58, 67, 76, 101, 161; reliance on authority and discipline, 82, 184; criticisms of, 108-9, 196, 287; and enlightenment, 142, 183; and orthodoxy, 152, 242, 254, 287; influence on Neo-Confucianism, 219

Chang, Carsun, cited, 33, 548

Chang Chiu-ch'eng (Heng-p'u), 176, 568

Chang Chü-cheng, 348

Chang Heng-ch'ü, *see* Chang Tsai

Chang K'uang, 421

Chang La-ta, 28

Chang Lü-hsiang, 515, 549, 550-51, 561, 562, 570, 574, 575; quoted, 564

Chang Ping-lin, 286, 513, 537

Chang Po-hsing, 549-50, 554, 568, 570, 571

Chang P'u, 342, 355-56; and Ying She, 339-41, 361; and Fu She, 342, 344-47, 350, 351-52, 357; writings of, 347, 348, 363

Chang San-feng, 28

Chang Shih, 571

Chang Tsai, 159, 162, 192, 305, 339, 431, 432, 474, 568; quoted, 155-56, 566; influence of, on Wang Fu-chih, 435-54; *Western Inscription*, 543, 555

Chang Ts'ai, 348, 351

Chang Tzu Cheng-meng chu (Wang Fu-chih), 432, 433-34, 435, 437-41, 442, 446-47, 448, 449-53, 458

Chang Wei, 84

Chao Chen-chi, 72-73, 91

Chao Meng-fu, 75

Ch'ao-p'in (Master Wu-i), 414-20, 421

Chen chih (true knowledge), 416

Chen-k'o, 67, 80-81, 85, 86; *see also* Tzu-po Ta-kuan (Chen-k'o)

Ch'en Chen-hui, 356

Ch'en Ch'üeh, 499

Ch'en Hang, 571

Ch'en Hsien-chang (Po-sha), 17, 18, 28-29, 30, 43, 179, 514

Translations From The Oriental Classics

Cold Mountain: 100 Poems by the T'ang Poet Han-shan, tr. Burton Watson. Also in paperback ed.   1970

Twenty Plays of the Nō Theatre, ed. Donald Keene. Also in paperback ed.   1970

Chūshingura: The Treasury of Loyal Retainers, tr. Donald Keene   1971

The Zen Master Hakuin: Selected Writings, tr. Philip B. Yampolsky   1971

Chinese Rhyme-Prose, tr. Burton Watson   1971

Kūkai: Major Works, tr. Yoshito S. Hakeda   1972

The Old Man Who Does as He Pleases: Selections from the Poetry and Prose of Lu Yu, tr. Burton Watson   1973

The Lion's Roar of Queen Śrīmālā, tr. Alex & Hideko Wayman   1974

Courtier and Commoner in Ancient China: Selections from the History of The Former Han by Pan Ku, tr. Burton Watson   1974

Studies In Oriental Culture

Companions To Asian Studies

Introduction To Oriental Civilizations

Wm. Theodore de Bary, *Editor*